223821

93/94

W

D1348741

LIBRARY
... TECHNICAL COLLEGE

WILLIAM COWPER

POET OF PARADISE

William Cowper

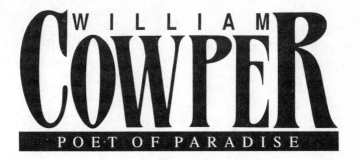

WILLIAM COWPER

POET OF PARADISE

George Melvyn Ella

 EVANGELICAL PRESS

EVANGELICAL PRESS
12 Wooler Street, Darlington, Co. Durham, DL1 1RQ, England

© Evangelical Press 1993
First published 1993

British Library cataloguing in Publication Data available

ISBN 0 85234 306 X

Cover picture reproduced by courtesy of the National Portrait Gallery, London.

Printed and bound in Great Britain by
BPCC Hazell Books Ltd
Member of BPCC Ltd

This book is dedicated
to Miss Mary Keating of Bradford, Yorkshire,
who first taught me the ways of the Lord
when I was three years old.

Acknowledgement

My heartfelt thanks are due to the staff of the Duisburg University Library for their hard work in finding most of the books listed in the bibliography for me. Without their help this book would never have been written. I would also like to thank Mrs Beverley Sanders, a busy pastor's wife, of Shepshed, Leicestershire and Mr Joseph Pollard of Zoar Books, Ossett, West Yorkshire, for their kind help in looking through my manuscript and making many helpful suggestions.

Contents

List of illustrations

Biographical table

1731 15 November (old style) 26 November (new style)	William Cowper born at Berkhamsted rectory, Hertfordshire: son of the Rev. Dr John Cowper and Ann, née Donne, of Ludham Hall, Norfolk.
1737 November	Death of his mother.
c. 1738 to c. 1740	Boarder at 'The Old Vicarage' (Dr Pittman's), Markyate Street, Herts. First strong experience of God's presence.
c. 1740 to c. 1742	Boarder in the house of Mr and Mrs Disney, eminent oculists, in London.
1742 April	Enters Westminster School.
1748 April	Admitted to the Middle Temple. Writes comic verse and 'rhyming letters'.
1749 May	Leaves Westminster School. Spends nine months with his father at Berkhamsted.
1750 to 1753	Articled to a London solicitor and attorney, Mr Chapman. Fellow clerk with Edward

Thurlow, the future Lord Chancellor. Both spend much time at Southampton Row, Hampstead, in the company of William's cousins Theadora (remained unmarried), Elizabeth (later Lady Croft) and Harriot (later Lady Hesketh), daughters of Ashley Cowper. C. writes poetry, ballads and essays for several different magazines.

1751-1754   Courtship with Theadora Cowper. C. writes his numerous 'Delia' poems.

1753 November   Moves to the Middle Temple.

1754 June   Called to the Bar.

1756 July   His father dies and depression sets in as he also loses his best friend Sir William Russell by drowning and parts from Theadora.

1757   Admitted to the Inner Temple. Writes 'Doom'd as I am in solitude to waste'.

1763   Offered a choice of three offices in the House of Lords under the patronage of Ashley Cowper. C. eventually chooses the post of Clerkship of the Journals. Under the stress of a forthcoming public examination and soul-trouble C. attempts suicide. Writes 'Hatred and Vengeance, my Eternal Portion'.

Late 1763-1764   Resigns his clerkship and is put under care at Dr Nathaniel Cotton's *Collegium Insanorum,* St Albans.

1764 July   Recovery and conversion due to reading Romans 3:25. Composes 'Song of Mercy and Judgment' and 'The Happy Change'. His hymn 'Retirement' (as opposed to his long poem of that name) was probably written at this time.

1765 June	Leaves St Albans and goes to live in Huntingdon so that he can be near his brother. Meets William Unwin and eventually becomes a boarder at his house.
1767 July	The Rev. Morley Unwin, C's landlord, dies. C. becomes acquainted with the Rev. Richard Conyers and the Rev. John Newton.
1767 October	The Unwins and C. move in with the Newtons to temporary lodgings whilst the Vicarage at Olney is being extended and renovated. Mrs Unwin becomes seriously ill and C. writes 'Walking with God'.
1768 February	The Unwins and C. move into Orchard side, Olney.
1769	William Unwin becomes rector of Stock in Essex.
1770	C's brother John is converted shortly before his death.
1771-1772	At Newton's invitation C. joins him in writing a number of hymns for use in the midweek meetings.
1773	Pressure put on Cowper to marry his 'adopted mother', Mary Unwin, by leading Evangelicals who misjudged Mrs Unwin's relationship to C. Writes 'Light Shining out of Darkness' and 'The Welcome Cross'. Becomes seriously depressed and has terrible nightmares in which he is constantly told that God has finally rejected him. Is taken care of at the Vicarage by the Newtons.

	Writes 'The Shrubbery: Written in a time of Affliction' and 'Ode to Peace'.
1774	C. is physically restored but continues to have terrible, damning nightmares for the rest of his life. Returns to Orchard Side. The Rev. Matthew Powley of Dewsbury, Yorkshire, marries Susanna Unwin and C. is now alone with his housekeeper and their servants. C. begins to write poetry drawing spiritual parallels from nature.
1779	The *Olney Hymns* published. Newton moves in December to St Mary Woolnoth, London where he is inducted as vicar. C's verse becomes more and more evangelical and he writes such poetry as 'Human Frailty' and 'A Tale Founded on a Fact'. Supports John Newton in his theological strife with Martin Madan (C's cousin) of the Countess of Huntingdon Connexion. C. makes it his aim to relieve the Olney poor and canvasses rich Evangelicals and prominent politicians for support.
1780	C. writes a number of poems against bigamous theories propagated by Martin Madan and his followers. Composes his first major poem for publication 'Anti-Thelyphthora: A Tale in Verse'.
Winter 1780-1781	C. writes 'The Progress of Error', 'Truth' and several other long poems and begins to collect his shorter poems written in previous years to his various friends. His friendship with Lady Austen commences.
1782 March	*Poems by William Cowper of the Inner Temple* published. 'John Gilpin' written and distributed anonymously.

1783	C. starts work on the *Task,* his most well-known poem.
1784	C. makes friends with Throckmortons, local gentry, writes a treatise on Christian education and begins work on his translation of Homer.
1785	The *Task* is published and C. is praised throughout the country. He takes up correspondence with his family again, especially with Lady Hesketh. Receives numerous presents from 'Anonymous', now known to be Theadora Cowper.
1786	Lady Hesketh stays at the Vicarage throughout the summer and autumn and becomes increasingly dominant in Mrs Unwin's household and in her attitude to C.
November	C. moves to 'The Lodge' in Weston Underwood. William Unwin dies.
1787	C. becomes friends with Samuel Rose. Is very ill for six months. Starts to write his 'Bill of Mortality' poems.
1788	C. writes his anti-slavery verse and 'On the Receipt of my Mother's Picture'. Begins to translate the *Odyssey.* Becomes acquainted with James Hurdis, with whom he forms a firm friendship.
1789	C. begins a series of literary criticisms for *The Analytical Review.*
1790	C's friendship with his kinsman John Johnson begins. Writes a number of epigrams and epigraphs for deceased friends.

1791	C's Homer published. Starts work on the *Milton Gallery*, 'The Four Ages of Man' and 'Yardley Oak'. Is wrongly accused of being for the slave trade. Mrs Unwin suffers a paralytic stroke.
1792	C. continues to write in favour of abolishing the slave trade and defends Wilberforce in verse. He befriends William Hayley and soon afterwards Mrs Unwin has another serious stroke. C., Mrs Unwin and Johnson visit Hayley for several months at Eartham, Sussex.
1793	Mrs Unwin's health worsens and Lady Hesketh takes over C's household. C. writes 'To Mary'. The poet's health also deteriorates as plans are made for his removal from Mrs Unwin and eventually from Weston. C. writes 'The Tale', a parable against separating friends. C. feels himself at the mercy of wrong-minded relatives but is too deep in despair to offer much resistance. The poet receives a royal pension of £300 a year through the efforts of William Hayley but owing to the negligence of the trustees he scarcely benefits from it.
1795	Cowper and Mrs Unwin are forcefully removed from Weston by Lady Hesketh and John Johnson. They live in various lodgings with Johnson before finding a home with him in East Dereham. Lady Hesketh never visits C. again.
1796	Death of Mrs Unwin.
1797	C. revises his Homer translation. Hayley moves prominent people to write cheering letters to C.

1799	C. writes 'The Ice Islands' and 'The Castaway' in English and Latin and completes his new edition of Homer. Lady Hesketh tries to have C. put in Dr Willis' asylum, Lincolnshire, a place notorious for its harsh 'strait-jacket' treatment of patients. C's health worsens.
1800 25 April	C. dies of 'worn-out constitution'. Is buried in East Dereham Parish Church.

Introduction

At least forty-five detailed biographies professing to depict Cowper's life have appeared in print since his death in 1800. Why, then, is it thought necessary to produce yet another 'Life' of Cowper? The reason lies in the uniqueness of Cowper's contribution to literature and to the spread of the gospel and in the failure of most biographers to express these facts. Cowper was not merely the leading poet of his day, but one of the most successful agents of God in spreading the good news throughout the English-speaking world during the eighteenth and nineteenth centuries. Authors who have been proclaimed as literary geniuses by the secular world and yet have been recognized as great men of God by the church of Christ have been very few in number. Perhaps there have only been three British authors to enjoy this fame since biblical times. These three are John Bunyan, John Milton and William Cowper. John Bunyan's fame has outlasted that of Milton and Cowper, but in the early nineteenth century Cowper's fame outshone them all.

Cowper's faith

Though both secular and Christian historians have praised Cowper's contribution to the revival of religion in the eighteenth century, the great bulk of his biographers, though gifted men of letters, have shown little understanding of Cowper's faith and, indeed, in most cases have shown a total ignorance of what it means to be an evangelical Christian.

Cowper's first biographer, William Hayley, was greatly handicapped in writing his 'Life' of Cowper as the poet's executor, Lady Hesketh, refused to allow him access to documents which showed his Calvinistic or 'enthusiastic' beliefs. Hayley was also forbidden to use a great deal of material referring to people who were still alive at the time or who had been prominent members of the Cowper-Madan family, as Lady Hesketh did not wish to have their private lives revealed publicly. Furthermore, Lady Hesketh, who was very intimate with the royal family, gave Hayley strict orders not to disclose anything about Cowper that might be taken as a criticism of the king or smack of democracy. In fact, when Hayley had finished writing his biography of Cowper, he complained that he had been forced to leave out more than he had put in.

Once Lady Hesketh's influence on Cowper's biographers had ceased, a few Christian biographers, such as the Rev. T. S. Grimshawe, did include much of Cowper's Christian thought, but the biographical material was still heavily censured for reasons of decorum and policy. The Calvinist-Arminian controversy was raging at the time and Grimshawe, for instance, dedicated his work to a Roman Catholic, in order to establish his neutrality and to ensure a wider readership, and toned down Cowper's staunch Calvinism, not wishing to pour oil on the very troubled waters of the debate going on amongst Evangelicals and Dissenters alike. Once biographers found themselves free to use the full material available on Cowper, it seems that there were no Christians of the poet's persuasion available to take up the task of writing his biography.

Many secular biographers have, indeed, identified Cowper's strong evangelical testimony with sheer madness and thus intentionally helped to spread the rumour that Cowper was a mad poet. Others show an amazing ignorance as to what a true Christian is. Lord David Cecil, author of the best-selling *The Stricken Deer*,[1] perhaps the most well-known of Cowper's biographers, has this to say about Evangelicals: 'The Evangelical movement stands out in violent contrast to the prevailing thought of its time — a black, melodramatic silhouette against the precise, freshly-hued colour print of eighteenth-century England.' Evangelicals, Cecil tells us, speak 'in the blood-stained imagery originally used by some half-naked prophet to an Oriental tribe among the precipitous cliffs of a

Syrian desert'. As Cecil was forced to confess that Cowper did not fit into this pattern, he wrongly concluded that the poet was not an Evangelical when he wrote his Christian verse.

We find the same kind of misconceptions concerning Evangelicals in Norman Nicholson's biography of Cowper. Writing on the Evangelical Revival he says, 'As the Revival developed in size and impetus, if not in intensity, it was to absorb into itself much of the fanaticism, the fierceness, the intolerance and vindictiveness of the old Puritans.' He describes the children of the first revivalists as being 'whipped from childhood to manhood along the road towards Salvation'. This was not a mere single reference or 'slip of the pen'. Elsewhere, writing of the same children, he says, 'Fathers and teachers were prepared to break the bodies of their children in order to save their souls — to flog them into heaven, if this was necessary.'[2] It was amongst these same second-generation evangelicals that the worldwide missionary movement developed, education began to be provided for the poor and Cowper was most read — yet, seen through the eyes of ignorant critics, these were primitive, cruel times.

When we turn to another major biographer, Hugh I'Anson Fausset, we shudder at the ungrounded, scathing criticism which Cowper earns for presenting his faith in Christ. His hymns, Fausset tells us, are 'too much choked by the conventional idiom of crude salvationism to have any poetic or individual significance'. Fausset makes his task as a commentator easy; he rejects all that is deeply Christian in Cowper's poetry and concentrates on snippets which he feels are true poetry and therefore without true religion. Such hymns as 'There is a fountain filled with blood,' Fausset finds 'barbarous' and says that they show that Cowper is blending 'hysteria with a sectarian idiom'. 'All such writing', he tells us, 'has, of course, no poetic value.'[3] The 'of course' here shows how, to use Cowper's words, 'Blind unbelief is sure to err.' It is, however, a wonder that Fausset still recognizes Cowper as an important poet and has taken the trouble to write several works about him!

Though these writers are to be blamed for not taking the trouble to delve into works such as those of the historians Lecky, Overton and Balleine, which show what a triumphant, reforming, enlightened movement the eighteenth-century revival was, there are other, more understandable, reasons for their warped view of Cowper. Up to recent years there has been no 'official' widely

accepted version of Cowper's poetry and prose, and only recently
have his works been published *en bloc* and according to modern
methods of textual criticism. Previous writers have thus had more or
less corrupt versions of Cowper's writings to work on, owing to the
methods of editing prevalent in former years and the fact that there
were no stringent copyright laws on the use of hymns and poetry.
Even Thomas Wright's well-researched work on Cowper,
published at the end of the last century, provides the reader with
mere snippets of some letters although the editor was not working
under restrictions imposed by relatives or out of respect for people
still living. By 1936 Luise Lanham could thus refer, in her excellent
thesis *The Poetry of William Cowper in its Relation to the English
Evangelical Movement,* to the many myths that had already
developed concerning Cowper's life and works. It seems that where
the sources were not available, fallen human imagination had
supplied the rest. Since the recent publication of King and
Ryskamp's mammoth and almost complete edition of Cowper's
works,[4] any biographer now has direct access to Cowper's works
more or less 'as written'.[5]

Cowper's mental illness

Cowper often maintained that the worst enemies of Christ's church
on earth were those within the fold rather than without. Thus much
contention against Cowper's testimony has been through the
mouths and pens of his fellow-Evangelicals. The poet was mentally
ill during two or three periods of his life[6] and was quite insane, or 'in
total darkness' as he himself expresses it, only once, and that was
before his conversion. Cowper's last years were spent in great
sadness, but sadness is not madness. The poet suffered from a family
illness and braved it better than several of his relations. This
tendency to melancholy was aggravated in his old age by well-
meaning but misguided relatives who tore the poet away from the
home and occupations that he loved. But the relatively short period
out of a lifetime of seventy years that Cowper was mentally ill has
not only coloured the secular critics' interpretation of Cowper, but
that of Christian writers also. In some cases, it must be said with
regret, Cowper has come under even harsher criticism from
evangelicals than from unbelievers. The poet had very good friends

amongst Anglicans, Independents, Baptists and Dissenters of all kinds. Each of these groups tended to stress that 'side' of Cowper which was nearest their own and that led other parties to protest that Cowper was quite different. Furthermore, Cowper's sporadic depressions were an embarrassment to his Evangelical and Dissenting friends. They were just unable to come to terms with his malady. Other Evangelicals and believing Dissenters, such as Mrs Mary Newton and William Bull, suffered from bouts of melancholy at the time but in Cowper's case the depression took the form of a conviction of being totally cut off from the God he loved with all his heart.

Before we judge Cowper's contemporary brethren for lack of spiritual discernment, let us reflect on the fact that we are hardly better off today. One loses count of the number of well-educated believing evangelists who tell their readers that they cannot possibly have a heart attack and be born-again Christians. There are still 'pastors' who tell their flocks to throw away their spectacles. Mental and physical illness is still largely not understood today by Christians and non-Christians alike. How often do we still hear from the pulpit that depression is due to lack of faith? George Barrell Cheever, famous amongst believers for his works on Bunyan, actually wrote a large work on Cowper[7] propounding the theory that if Cowper had exercised more faith and worked harder for God, he would not have been so melancholy. Apart from the fact that Cowper was a very hard worker in God's vineyard, Cheever seems to assume that faith is a human attribute which can be exercised — or not — at will. This is hardly sound Christian theology.

Both the Anglican John Newton and the Dissenter Samuel Greatheed disclosed their inability to come to terms with Cowper's melancholy by giving in their funeral sermons the most intimate details of his illness, with their own quite faulty interpretation of it — although they were supposed to be paying tribute to the poet and his Master. Newton committed a further act of indiscretion by preparing for publication[8] a very private account of Cowper's first major illness, before his conversion, which he had begged from his friend in strict confidence. During this illness, when Cowper was weighed down with his own sin and in a frantic bout of 'nervous fever', he tried to commit suicide. This was the first time that such information had been made public and Britain was aghast. The author of the sanest and most popular literary work of the day, the

Task, mad? These gruesome descriptions which Newton so
unwisely published are still quoted by mistaken Christian writers as
an example of the way a Christian can be moved to take his own life.[9]
This is a shocking misuse of biographical data. In the years
following Cowper's death, however, the cry went up that Calvinism
had made Cowper mad and instead of studying the poet's works
together as brethren in Christ, Christian was fighting Christian using
Cowper's melancholy as an argument either for or against certain
doctrines. The poet who had written so much against sectarian strife
had seemingly written in vain.

It was all this squabbling which forced Lady Hesketh to hold
back many of Cowper's letters and poems from publication through
fear that they would be used as grounds for quarrelling by the
opposing factions. Thus William Cowper, who after his conversion
did not write a single poem that was not the sanest of works, is
branded by both Christian and non-Christian alike today as a mad
poet. He is depicted as a shy, nervous, weak, rather effeminate,
doubting man who fled the world and all its unsolvable problems to
write his verse in solitude. This view of Cowper is a theatrical farce
and could not be further from the truth. This biography will show
that Cowper was a strong, manly figure who practised a number of
sports all his life. He was thoroughly Reformed in doctrine, loved
company and believed he had a solution to all the world's problems.
Cowper's feelings, however, were always of a most extreme kind.
When he was happy, he jumped for joy. When he was down in the
dumps he felt that the whole world — including God — had turned
against him.

Cowper's relationship with Newton

Any biography of William Cowper must also be, to a large extent,
a biography of his close friend John Newton. Yet there have been
perhaps more myths told about Newton than about Cowper himself.
This is perhaps because Newton's biographers of all persuasions
have invariably been very narrow in their choice of sources. The
writings of both William Bull and William Cowper add many
necessary details to a full picture of Newton's character and work
but biographers rarely turn to either of them. Newton is thus

invariably portrayed as a strong-willed stubborn slave-driver who left off whipping negroes only to find a new victim in Cowper.

That great man of letters Walter Bagehot, for instance, wrote to the *National Review* in July 1855 to tell its readers that Newton 'was in truth one of those men who seem intended to make excellence disagreeable. He was a converting engine. The whole of his enormous vigour of body — the whole steady intensity of a pushing, impelling, compelling, unoriginal mind, all the mental or corporeal exertion he could exact from the weak or elicit from the strong, were devoted to one sole purpose — the effectual impact of the Calvinistic tenets on the parishioners of Olney.' After misquoting words of Newton to the extent of saying that he 'preached people mad', Bagehot goes on to write, 'No more dangerous adviser, if this world had been searched over, could have been found for Cowper.' It would have surprised Bagehot to know that very many of the Olney parishioners felt that Newton was not Calvinist enough; in fact he had a very hard time combatting extreme Hyper-Calvinism and Antinomianism in the parish. Furthermore, Newton and Cowper were the closest friends at Olney, but Newton considered himself Cowper's admirer and imitator rather than his adviser, and Cowper found Newton the perfect pastor though at times too taxing. The poet would have laughed out loud if anyone had told him that he had a 'dangerous' friend. Not finding the above statements sufficient condemnation, however, Bagehot goes on to say how Newton loved to take hold of weaker brethren (thinking in particular of Cowper) and make sure that every iota of happiness was knocked out of their lives. But Bagehot is still not finished. He describes Cowper as 'a shrinking, a wounded and a tremulous mind,' who was helpless against Newton's 'bold dogmatism', 'hard volition' and 'animal nerve'.

Lord David Cecil, who talks so disparagingly of Cowper, is even more critical of Newton.[10] He finds the humble clergyman 'crude, absurd, naive, narrow, uncouth, clumsy, careless, insensitive, tactless, profane, indecent and ridiculous'. Looking around to find something good to say about Newton, Cecil adds condescendingly, 'Yet he was not at all stupid' — then goes on to say how boring, arrogant and fanatical Newton was! Cecil sums Newton's teaching up by proclaiming sarcastically, 'There was only one God, and John Newton was His prophet.'

If we ransack the archives of our respectable newspapers and

magazines over past years, in hope of finding objective articles on
Newton and Cowper, we find description after description of a
slave-driving Newton and a cringing slave, Cowper. Robert Lynd,
for instance, writing in the *London Mercury*,[11] tells us how Newton,
'who seems to have wielded the Gospel as fiercely as a slaver's
whip', was largely responsible for Cowper's terrors. He describes
Newton as a man of 'savage piety' who became 'Cowper's tyrant',
suggesting that the poet could only begin to 'breathe freely' when
Newton finally left Olney for London some twelve years after their
first meeting. Turning to that century-old magazine *Blackwoods*,[12]
one finds a similar tale. The author of one article describes 'grim
Newton' as 'a kind of Admiral Guinea'. He refers to 'the callousness
of Newton's temper' towards Cowper, adding that Olney was
'infested' during Newton's stay in Olney 'by pietists of every
complexion and every sect'.

There is little difference in tone when we turn to many a
Christian biographer. On examining the Rev. Wm Benham's
biography of Cowper we find this Christian leader testifying to the
power of God to heal and cast out devils and writing about the
infinite love of God. Yet he goes on to say, 'It became as clear to me
as any demonstration could make it, that the Calvinistic doctrine and
religious excitements threw an already trembling mind off its
balance, and aggravated a malady which but for them might
probably have been cured.' He then goes on to lay the blame for
Cowper's 'malady' firmly and squarely at Newton's feet, telling his
readers that Newton turned Cowper into a monster and when
Cowper became mad he sorrowed because he could no longer
control his Frankenstein-creation. He finds Newton immoral and
accuses him of selfishly manipulating Cowper for his own ends.
Benham somehow seems to link Calvinism with insanity. As
Cowper learned his Calvinism from Newton, Benham argues, the
poet was made insane by Newton. Again we are dealing with a
biographer who has not taken notice of the sources. Benham quotes
works which, had he read them with any care, would have shown
him clearly that Cowper was a Calvinist before he met Newton.

Indeed Cowper was a far stauncher Calvinist than his friend and
even cautioned Newton at times as, for instance, when Newton
recommended to him the arch-Arminian, John Fletcher. The
difference between the two friends was that Cowper was very
rigorous on matters of doctrine but very open on politics. Newton,

though an orthodox Christian and personally a Calvinist, was very open on doctrine in relation to others if he felt that they truly loved the Lord. On the other hand, he developed exceedingly narrow political views in the 1780s which caused him to break with Cowper for a while. However, in spite of the facts that stare every biographer who seriously consults the sources in the face, there seems to be an overwhelming agreement amongst them that 'The evil influence exercised by Newton's religion of terror has never been in dispute.'[13] This biography will certainly dispute such a groundless statement!

Newton was a great burden to Cowper at times, but not in the sense that most biographers have believed. Usually evangelical writers of a Reformed persuasion, who have a more healthy view of Newton, nevertheless still portray him as a man of rock and iron. Newton was indeed a champion of the faith but far from robust in constitution. From his childhood on he was a most sensitive person and was often in poor health.[14] He was capable of great extremes of feeling and could go into childlike and lasting tantrums. Once he had a thought in his head, however wrong, his very closest and best friends could not talk him out of it. Such stubbornness was a rarity, but it occasionally cropped up in Newton's attitude to Dissenters and to Cowper. One of his major weaknesses was that he tended to love his friends with such a passion that he was truly guilty of idolatry. He was very conscious of this failing and was continually bringing it before the Lord. It was, however, an ineradicable part of his humble nature to magnify the good points of others. Newton's wooing and eventual winning of Mary Catlett to be his wife, through many years of waiting and though a thousand other temptations came Newton's way in his slave-driving years, shows how God used this passion to a good end to keep Newton faithful to his calling.

When Newton first met Cowper, he was so struck by the man that he truly believed that he had the privilege of meeting a second Paul, a man who was going to transform the age. When Cowper became ill in 1773 and professed in his illness that God had erased his name from the Lamb's Book of Life, Newton's disappointment knew no bounds and his life was so shaken that he never really recovered from the shock. He had set up an idol and only the shattered pieces remained. This disappointment turned into envy and jealousy whenever Cowper made new friends. He felt, quite wrongly, that they were drawing the poet away from his true friend and from his true calling. He wanted Cowper — as he eventually told him after protests from the poet at his jealousy and suspicion—to think of him at all times and allow none other to take his place. This was an impossible task for Cowper as he was often surrounded by friends who adored him and Newton was extremely touchy and hard to get on with at times. In the mid-1780s Cowper was compelled to tell Newton that he could no longer look upon him as the friend of former years and as his pastor. After Cowper's third major illness in 1787, however, Newton spent five weeks with Cowper at the poet's new home in Weston where the two friends made up their differences. Cowper then reassured Newton that their relationship was almost as it had been when both were the best of friends in Newton's Olney days. Newton, however, remained extremely jealous of Cowper's other friends who, it must be added in all fairness, were usually very jealous of Newton!

Newton's most negative effect on Cowper is the harm he did to the poet's reputation after his death. Newton was continually indiscreet about the information he passed on to his friends concerning the whys and wherefores of Cowper's spiritual state, much of which threw more light on Newton's own mentality than Cowper's. He was even more lacking in tact about what he published. Once Cowper had written to Newton on how wrong it was to publish intimate accounts of the brethren that had been given in the strictest confidence. Yet Newton preached and published information about Cowper's most private life, supported by his own interpretation of it, that should have been left to die with the poet. It is sadly true to say that almost all the exaggerated accounts of Cowper's mental state that will be refuted in this biography can be traced back in one way or another to this 'information' spread by Newton.

It would be wrong, however, to leave off commenting on Newton on this note. Whatever his failings were, if it had not been for his friendship, Cowper would never have become the 'Bard of Christianity', as his first biographer William Hayley called him. Newton, already an experienced writer, 'discovered' Cowper's talents in their first months of friendship in 1767. After that date he never ceased to guide and encourage Cowper to write and opened all possible doors for him to this end. It was Newton who encouraged Cowper to write his Olney Hymns, as also his first two major poetical works, and to do a good deal of translation work. In fact for many years Cowper never had anything published without first sending it to Newton to be looked over and edited. Not only did Cowper obtain skilled instruction as to writing and publishing from Newton, but the themes of many of his poems were obviously developed during his daily discussions with his pastor. It is true to say that there is hardly a topic taken up by Cowper which was not first developed either in a hymn or sermon by Newton.

Furthermore, Cowper never forgot the kind self-offering friendship of John Newton when he took his friend under his own roof during the poet's fateful illness of 1773 and looked after him for a year and a half as a father would a son. This was done under great criticism from Newton's other friends and at the risk of Newton's own health and happiness. It is also true that Cowper had never been in contact with poor people until he met Newton and through his friend's guidance he began to visit and care for them — a service which he performed for the rest of his life.

Cowper's verse and its message

It was not until the late seventies that Cowper fully realized what God's calling for him was. He did not have the vocation and abilities to become a minister, but he came to see that God had fitted him out to become a mentor to people chiefly outside of the Christian fold, to show them through poetry how they could find their way to God. Thus when he turned his pen to this end he felt he was giving back to language its true purpose as a medium of communication between God and man. His poetic efforts were aimed at universal man, with his never-changing problems, rather than the narrow ones which beset his own times alone. There is, therefore, something timeless about his message and something which is always contemporary. It is amazing to note how Cowper's poetry applies to life towards the end of the twentieth century. It is as if Cowper had looked forward into time and written specially for our generation. So in dealing with Cowper's poetry we are not dealing with antique literary data, but rather with the problems of this age which only God can solve through such servants as Cowper.

Much of Cowper's verse is directed against the Church of England, whose archbishop was a man who had left the ways of the Lord and whose ministers to a large extent were 'cassocked huntsmen' and 'fiddling priests' who preached a life of sport, music,

theatre-going and entertainment. If they dabbled in theology at all
it was only to say that God would save everybody in the end —
including the devil. It must all sound very familiar to church-goers
of today. It was due to such eighteenth-century stalwarts as William
Cowper that the Church of England experienced a great revival and
left the Dissenting churches far behind in its ardour for the Lord.
Today's Anglican Church, though it still has a remnant of
Evangelicals, could surely be helped by learning what Cowper has
to say about what a true church is and what ministers ought to be
preaching and teaching. Cowper knew what kind of men could
reform the church from within and held up in his poems men of God
who patterned their lives on Paul, such as Whitefield, Newton and
Conyers.

Allied to this, Cowper looked askance in much of his poetry at
the warfare going on amongst believers of all denominations.
Though himself a convinced Anglican who could not accept free-
church tenets, he nevertheless could accept free-church believers
with open arms and increasingly became their friend and adviser.
Several poems came from his pen outlining how foolish it was for
brother to war against brother. What Cowper hated was to enter into
a conversation with a fellow-Christian that turned into a mere
wrangle about being dipped or sprinkled. To him it was a touch of
Paradise Regained to see Presbyterians, Anglicans and Baptists
living in harmony.

One of the reasons why Cowper tended to seek fellowship with
Dissenters rather than Anglicans was the latter's preoccupation with
organs, choirs, concerts and jiggish tunes. The church was listening
to the crowds calling, 'Tickle and entertain us or we die,' rather than
giving them the preached Word of the Bread of Life. Thus it is no
surprise to find Cowper coming down very heavily on church
services that had become mere musical theatricals. This, to the poet,
would be sacrilege if it were not so ludicrous. What would Cowper
think of our present-day church in which Anglicans and free
churchmen alike believe that transforming the pulpit into a
sounding-board for musical activities will bring the people from the
streets and prepare them for heaven?

Nowadays many Christians are dissatisfied with the state school
systems, and private schools sponsored and run by Christian
organizations are once again coming into vogue. This would have
thrilled Cowper's heart as he was an educational reformer of note.

He looked upon the pagan schools of his day as nothing but menageries for parking children and teaching them more about the world of the heathen than about the real world as described in the Bible. To him contemporary education had no foundation for its theories and no aims and was thus a senseless undertaking. He put forward ideas whereby education should be based on God's divine plan for man as his representative and steward on earth and he developed curricula to this end. Education should be twofold: to prepare the human child for becoming the child of God and to equip the child with the wherewithal to prepare the world in a spiritual and physical sense for the restitution of all things before the triumphant and final advent of Christ. Cowper was foursquare in line with modern ideas of a 'green' world, but went even further and believed that the conservation, preservation and cultivation of nature was one of the major global duties of man which should go hand in hand with the evangelization of the world.

The eighteenth century followed closely after the so-called Restoration period brought into being by that playboy king, Charles II. As a result of this movement all culture had been brought down to the level of the gutter and both the theatre and literature had become to a great extent debauched. The public taste had grown so used to the dirty drivellings of promiscuous heroes that when Samuel Richardson (1689-1761) started writing books with God-fearing men and women as their main characters, there was a public outcry. George Colman, the playwright and one of Cowper's best friends, is remembered by posterity for his summing up of the situation. 'A man might as well turn his daughter loose in Covent Garden,' he said, 'as trust the cultivation of her mind to a circulating library.' One of Cowper's very first poems was a defence of the Christian hero in literature, and time and time again he campaigned for a clean-up. The low level of sexual morality in literature and the arts had created such a laxity of conduct in Cowper's day that powdered, painted and perfumed effeminate men militantly flaunted their lack of manliness and forced themselves under the public's noses in arrogant defiance of all propriety. It became a fashion to be perverse. Cowper called these shameful beings a 'raree show' and wrote many a line against their misuse of their bodies. There is nothing new under the sun and once again after the cleaning-up of the eighteenth and nineteenth centuries, because morals in literature and show-business are again so low, the

shocking fashion of transvestite men has come into vogue. The plea
of the churches to respect these people as they are also God's
creatures would have brought from Cowper a bevy of poetry
teaching these ecclesiastical institutions the difference between a
man wallowing with pleasure and lust in his fallen nature and one
transformed by God from being a mere creature to becoming a child
of God. Nor does Cowper spare 'the fairer sex' with the sting of his
poetry. Women who beget children only to leave them in the hands
of others whilst they live a life in society away from home either at
work or play, 'developing their personality and freedom,' find no
favour with Cowper. Many of his letters and several of his poems are
taken up with the subject of make-up or 'face-painting', as he more
accurately called it. Such deceptions have no part in a natural new-
born society of Christians according to Cowper.

Perhaps the greatest contribution Cowper could make to our
present society is his insistence on the fact that the Christian ought
to be a happy man, full of the thrill and joy of living for God. Though
the poet knew many a melancholy hour, he was in his heart of hearts
a very happy man who could jump for joy at the sound of a bird, at
a well-spoken word or even at the ringing of a church bell. To him
preaching the Word in sermons or poetry was a spreading of rich
delight and long-faced Christians were a contradiction in terms.
Naturally when confronted with his own sins or the problems of the
world, a Christian must needs be depressed, but on turning to the
Maker and Creator of all things new he cannot but be joyful. Thus
it will be found that William Cowper, described by so many as a
'mad' poet, wrote much of the happiest, most joyful poetry ever
written.

There is another, sadder, aspect of Cowper's life that may point
a warning finger to our generation. It is becoming increasingly
common for younger people to disregard the interests of the elderly
and feel that society does her best duty to them when they are
removed from their familiar surroundings and are 'taken into care'
and put into special 'homes' where they have a great deal of
organized attention but are compelled to surrender their own wills
and interests. Cowper was thus wrenched from his own home,
though only sixty-three years of age, by younger relatives who
should have known better, and forced to live a life that robbed him
of his intellectual and physical independence and caused great
turmoil in his walk with God. From a life of extreme activity, in

which he was striving to perfect his poetry to God's glory, he was suddenly transported into a world of lethargy and boredom so that, though surrounded by caring people, he yet felt himself lost and alone.

All this would be reason enough for an author to take up his pen to help present a truer picture of William Cowper, the Christian poet, and give a more substantial account of his Christian teaching. There is a further reason. Cowper's last great task was to write a commentary on Milton's *Paradise Lost* and *Paradise Regained*. He informed Newton in a letter written 20 February 1792 why he had decided on this undertaking. 'His two principal poems', Cowper told his friend, 'are of a kind that call for an Editor who believes the Gospel and is well grounded in all Evangelical doctrine. Such an Editor they have never had yet, though only such a one can be qualified for the office.' Cowper therefore believed firmly that he had a God-given duty to attempt the task. Cowper himself has suffered through the ages in the same way as Milton. Though almost two hundred years have gone by since Cowper's death in 1800, there is still a need for an editor or biographer who believes the gospel and is well grounded in all evangelical doctrine to present to the public the life of William Cowper as it was really lived, thus taking note of his outstanding Christian testimony rather than mere literary status. The present author confesses that he believes himself called to this task and would pray with Cowper:

> Who seeks to praise Thee, and to make Thee known
> To other hearts, must have Thee in his own.
> Come, prompt me with benevolent desires,
> Teach me to kindle at Thy gentle fires,
> And though disgrac'd and slighted, to redeem
> A poet's name, by making Thee the theme.[15]

1.
The early years

Ann Cowper wiped a tear of joy from her cheek and joined her husband John in a prayer of thanks to their Maker. It was 13 December 1731 and the occasion of their son's baptism and Ann especially had every good reason to thank God. The last five years had brought her sorrow upon sorrow.

At twenty-three she had become very fond of a prosperous merchant, Samuel Hudson, who had left her in 1726 to attend to his property in Italy, taking with him a lock of her hair and her picture. Hudson never returned, dying in Tuscany soon after his arrival there. A year later Ann met the Rev. John Cowper D.D., a fellow of Merton College, Oxford, chaplain to the king, Commissioner of Bankrupts and rector of Berkhamsted. John, a gifted poet and earnest Christian, eventually won Ann's heart and the two were married in 1728. John, though sturdy physically, was of a very sensitive nature and suffered from serious bouts of depression. Ann was very delicately built and also of a highly sensitive constitution and was far from robust in health. A son, Simon, was born to her in 1729 but the frail child died after only five weeks. Nine months later twins, John and Ann, were born, but again they were very weak and died within two days of their birth. On 15 November 1731 a son was born, whom Ann and John named William after several distinguished ancestors. This child appeared to be of robust health and showed every sign of being able to survive to a ripe old age. It was William's baptism that the Cowpers were now celebrating.

Cowper's family

Americans often boast at the birth of a son that they have produced
a future President of the United States. It seems that the British are
no different. When John Cowper realized that William was going to
survive, he boasted that his son was certain to become Lord
Chancellor. In this particular case, John's was not, humanly
speaking, an idle boast. There had been Lord Chancellors in both
John's and Ann's families in the not too distant past, and the
Cowpers still enjoyed immense political influence. William used to
stress the folly of too ambitious parents by jestingly saying that his
father had hoped for a Lord Chancellor but had only given birth to
a poet.

Yet William was really born with a silver spoon in his mouth. His
mother's maiden name was Donne and she could look back on a long
noble line of ancestors, including the Boleyns, the Careys, the
Howards, the Mowbrays and Sir Thomas More. She was directly
related to Henry III through four different lines. Ann was also a
descendent of John Donne, the famous Dean of St Paul's and author
of much spiritual verse. William Cowper greatly treasured this
connection with the famous poet who had died in 1631, exactly a
hundred years before his birth. He always felt more drawn to the
Donne side of his family than to the Cowper side.

William's father could also boast of being of noble descent. The
family often joked that they were descendants of a poor Scotsman
who had left Fifeshire to seek his fortune in England carrying all his
worldly belongings on his back, but this must have been many
hundreds of years before William's time. The Cowpers played an
important role in England during the Wars of the Roses, one lineal
ancestor was Sheriff of London in 1551, and there were at least
baronets (and poets) in the family by the commencement of the
seventeenth century.[1] One namesake of Cowper's, Sir William
Cowper,[2] was created a Nova Scotia baronet by James I and later an
English baronet by Charles I. At the beginning of the eighteenth
century two Cowpers held seats in the House of Peers. One was
Chief Justice Spencer Cowper,[3] John Cowper's father; the other,
Lord High Chancellor Sir William Cowper, Spencer's elder brother,
was mentioned in Pope's *Dunciad* as 'Great Cowper' and extolled
in the *Tatler* and the *Spectator* and the works of numerous writers
as a great patron of literature.[4]

All this goes to explain why Cowper was always looked upon by the common people as 'the squire' and was expected by politicians and church leaders alike to exercise some form of leadership.[5] It is impossible to understand poems of Cowper's such as 'Retirement' and 'Tirocinium' without bearing in mind that Cowper was a member of the gentry.

We never find Cowper boasting of his ancestry, however, or striving to gain any privilege by it. The poet rejected sinecure posts and always maintained that learning the gospel from one's parents was the greatest inheritance anyone could have. In God's providence Cowper was privileged to be born into a keenly Evangelical family. Thus we find the poet, many years later, looking back on his childhood and writing of his deceased mother and father:

But oh the thought, that thou art safe, and he!
That thought is joy, arrive what may to me.
My boast is not, that I deduce my birth
From loins enthron'd and rulers of the earth,
But higher far my proud pretentions rise—
The son of parents pass'd into the skies.[6]

Not only were Cowper's parents true Christians but so were many of his aunts, uncles and cousins. There were also several Bible-believing clergymen in his family and at least one Evangelical bishop. Martin Madan, the poet's cousin on his father's side, became one of the earliest preachers in the Evangelical Revival and was a good friend of both Whitefield and Wesley. Madan, supported by the Countess of Huntingdon, founded a work amongst vagrant women in London which was carried on by Thomas Scott, the Evangelical commentator. Madan was also a hymn-writer, a poet and musician and the co-author and compiler of one of the earliest hymn books, *Psalms and Hymns,* which went through a record number of editions. Madan composed well over thirty hymn-tunes of which 'Helmsley' and 'Huddersfield' are perhaps the best known today. Most members of Cowper's family were hymn-writers and poets of various degrees of proficiency and used poetry to express the Christian way of life.

It is also obvious that William received a very sound schooling in the Scriptures at home as a young child. When he visited other families or boarded at school, the child was quick to notice where

such teaching was missing.[7] Though this grounding in the Word of
God remained relatively latent for many years as an adult, when
Cowper was eventually converted in 1764 he at once showed an
amazing knowledge of the Bible and a full grasp of Reformed
doctrine. Throughout his later life Cowper was to campaign for
Scripture as a 'must' in education without which no child — or adult
— could ever hope to attain to a true knowledge of the natural world
and God's purpose for it.[8]

During the first six years of his life, Cowper must have been quite
the happiest boy alive. His parents were so devoted to him and left
such a deep impression upon him that in middle age he could still lift
his hands in praise to his Maker and thank him for such recollections
of sweet happiness. He remembered his mother's visits to his
nursery at bedtime when she sang him a lullaby or said a prayer. He
remembered how she used to spoil him with a biscuit or candied
plum before he was taken to school by Robin the gardener. He
remembered helping his mother when dressmaking to prick out the
patterns with a pin. Above all, he remembered the look of sheer joy
on his mother's face when she talked softly to him and stroked his
head, obviously thankful to God for giving her such a child who had
survived. Everyone who knew Ann Cowper could only say of her
that she was like an angel and the sweetest person on earth. And this
is how her son, too, remembered her.

Death of his mother

William's happiness, however, was to come to a swift and abrupt
end. Ann had given birth to another child, Theadora Judith, a year
after William, but the little girl died at two years of age. In 1734 a
son, Thomas, was born, but he died after a short life of only two weeks.
Finally, much weakened, Ann Cowper gave birth to another boy, John,
on 7 November 1737. The baby survived but Anne was so frail that she
was unable to recover from the birth and died six days later. She was
only thirty-four. Later on, looking back on this sad day, her elder son,
now the foremost poet in the kingdom, was to write:

> My mother! when I learned that thou wast dead,
> Say, wast thou conscious of the tears I shed?
> Hovered thy spirit o'er thy sorrowing son,

Ann Cowper, the poet's mother

Wretch even then, life's journey just begun?
Perhaps thou gav'st me, though unfelt, a kiss:
Perhaps a tear, if souls can weep in bliss—
Ah, that maternal smile! it answers— Yes.[9]

Ann's foolish but well-intentioned maids tried to keep the news
from William and told the poor boy that his mother had gone on a
journey and would soon be back. William, however, had understood
more than the maids realized. Looking back on those unhappy days
Cowper wrote,

I heard the bell tolled on thy burial day,
I saw the hearse that bore thee slow away,
And turning from my nursery window, drew
A long, long sigh, and wept a last adieu.[10]

The maids, however, persisted in telling William tales of his
mother's impending return, so that the child began to believe that he
had misunderstood death and to hope against hope that he would see
his mother again in this life. When he was finally forced to accept
reality and see that the maids had been talking foolish nonsense, his
grief was all the greater.

William's father was now left with a newborn child and a boy of
six, and the records show that he had a far from easy time caring for
them. Dr John Cowper has been heavily criticized by biographers
for neglecting his duties where William and John were concerned.
Few of these inexperienced critics have seen the difficulties a single
parent is faced with when bringing up small children. They also fail
to take into account that Dr John Cowper's health was not at its best.
He suffered from an inherited illness that was difficult to diagnose
and impossible to cure. It was also an illness that struck most
members of his family from time to time and especially his two
surviving sons, William and John. This illness was what William
was to call 'gloomy thoughts, led on by spleen' and, after his wife's
untimely death, John Cowper was often beset by such thoughts,
even to the point of contemplating the efficacy of suicide.

Whatever one might say in hindsight about John Cowper as a
parent, however, William was ever thankful that his father had
provided him with good books throughout his childhood, which,
Cowper tells us, taught him to 'learn with wonder how this world
began, Who made, who marr'd, and who has ransom'd man'. First

amongst childhood memories of good books well read for Cowper was Bunyan's *Pilgrim's Progress*. Of Bunyan Cowper wrote,

Oh, thou, whom, borne on fancy's eager wing
Back to the season of life's happy spring,
I pleas'd remember, and, while mem'ry yet
Holds fast her office here, can ne'er forget;
Ingenious dreamer, in whose well-told tale
Sweet fiction and sweet truth alike prevail;
Whose hum'rous vein, strong sense, and simple style,
May teach the gayest, make the gravest smile;
Witty, and well employ'd, and, like thy Lord,
Speaking in parables his slighted word.[11]

The 'Old Vicarage'

William was sent to a local school shortly before his mother died, but this proved to be an absolute failure. This was not William's fault as he was a most able pupil. The school had fallen on bad days and came increasingly under criticism for totally neglecting the education of the boys put under its care. This led to court cases between enraged parents and the school staff. Thus John Cowper had to look further afield for his son's education and was faced with having to board him out at the tender age of six.

The school Dr Cowper chose was the 'Old Vicarage' at Markyate Street, a village on the Bedfordshire and Hertfordshire border. It was one of the foremost prep-schools of the day and run by William Pittman, a clergyman and noted Cambridge scholar. The fact that Pittman was an old friend of Dr Cowper's and famed for his skill in teaching young boys must have made the choice easier. Pittman was an able classicist and published several textbooks for school use in this field. Apart from the classics, little else was taught in the school and William complained that the pupils never had a chance to 'frisk and skip about'. William's brother John, who went to the same school some years later, complained that he had been sent there because he was 'the son of a gentleman', but the school had taught him Greek and nothing else. The poverty of education for gentlemen's sons at that time moved both brothers to work out better forms of education in later life.

It was at the 'Old Vicarage' that William was to go through one of his deepest pre-conversion experiences of God's protecting hand. As in most schools, there was a school bully at the 'Old Vicarage'. He was a fifteen-year-old lout who lived according to the motto 'Strong in arm and weak in head'. His sole delight seemed to be in tormenting and even torturing small boys. When he met gentle, refined six-year-old William, with his quick wit and obviously superior intelligence, the bully knew he had found a fitting victim. Thus day after day, week after week he tormented Cowper so cruelly that the poor boy dared not look him in the face, so great was his dread. Later the poet was to write, 'I well remember being afraid to lift my eyes upon him higher than his knees, and that I knew him by his shoe buckles better than by any other part of his dress.'[12] It is typical of Cowper that he goes on to write, 'May the Lord pardon him and may we meet in glory!'

Cowper had, however, been taught many a passage of Scripture at home and had learnt to pray. This was to be God's way of delivering the small boy from the big menace. God is always prepared to assist the Davids of this world against Goliaths! Cowper relates how it happened:

> One day I was sitting alone upon a bench in the school, melancholy and almost ready to weep at the recollection of what I had already suffered at his hands and at the apprehension of what was yet to come, expecting at the same time my tormentor every moment, these words of the Psalmist came into my mind, "I will not fear what man can do unto me." I applied them to my own use with a degree of trust and confidence in God that would have been in no disgrace to a much more experienced Christian. — Instantly, I perceived in myself a briskness of spirits and a cheerfulness which I had never felt before, and took several paces up and down the school with a joyful alacrity, his gift in whom I trusted.[13]

What started as an ordeal for Cowper ended in a triumph of grace and an exhilarating experience the poet never forgot. There was no more bullying. Shortly after this incident Cowper's antagonist was found out and expelled. Cowper related this years later, after his conversion, to show how the hand of God was on him even as a child. The poet often complained that his eyes had often been turned to

God in childhood when in need, but his heavenly Father was forgotten when things went smoothly. All of us, with shame, know what he meant.

Life was not all Greek and no play for William. During the holidays he would visit his numerous cousins, many of whom were his own age and shared his interests, and have lots of fun. He had a particularly good friend in John Duncombe, whom he especially liked as he was so good at bringing a smile to his father's face when in a sad mood. Most of all he liked to go to the home of his mother's brother at Catfield in Norfolk. Roger Donne was a rector, like William's own father, and William had a special liking for his Norfolk cousins, who were unaffected, good-tempered and always cheerful. Looking back on his early childhood when sixty-four years of age, Cowper wrote that he had passed some of the happiest days of his life in Norfolk in company with those whom he loved and by whom he was loved.[14]

William was often, however, dogged by illness and suffered greatly with his eyes. When eight years of age, his eyesight was so adversely affected that it was thought that he would become blind in at least one eye. It is difficult to know just what was wrong with his eyes as he merely refers to 'specks' on them. It seems that there was some sort of film caused by inflammation which threatened to cover his eyes. Because of this Dr Cowper withdrew William from the 'Old Vicarage' and sent him to live with a married couple by the name of Disney who were both eminent oculists. Cowper stayed two years with the Disneys but he claimed that it was 'to no good purpose'. Apparently young William did not get on with the family and resented their worldliness. He longed to have the Scriptures read and to be able to enter into prayer with others. The Disneys, however, were not believers. Nor were they able to cure William's 'specks'. We do not know whether Cowper went to school during this time or was taught by the Disneys. We do know that his brother was sent to the 'Old Vicarage' for a few years and then put into the hands of a private tutor. This was probably William's lot also.

Westminster School

In April 1742 John Cowper decided to send William to Westminster School to continue his education. John had strong reasons for doing so. First the Cowpers had attended Westminster for generations. They were Whigs to a man and Westminster fostered Whiggish traditions as opposed to those of its Tory rival Eton. Westminster was considered at that time to be the foremost school in England and Dr Cowper wanted nothing but the best for his son. It was also famed for laying a foundation suitable for the study of law and Dr Cowper made no secret of the fact that he wished his son to become a great lawyer before becoming Lord Chancellor.

So when William started at Westminster he joined several of his near relations, as well as at least sixty future peers of the realm, ten future bishops, a future prime minister, a good number of future Cabinet ministers and several colonial governors to-be. Surprisingly enough, as there was little religious education at Westminster, the school produced quite a number of Evangelicals, Wesleyan Methodists and Dissenting believers during the eighteenth century. These included Charles Wesley, the hymn-writer, Martin Madan of the Countess of Huntingdon Connexion, Lord Dartmouth, whom Cowper described as 'one who wears a coronet and prays', Sir Richard Hill, who defended Calvinism so ably against Wesleyan attacks and Lewis Bagot, who became successively Bishop of Bristol, Norwich and St Asaph.

Although Westminster enjoyed a reputation as *the* school for nobility, not all the 354 pupils who attended in 1742 were rich. Nor were they all boarded under similar circumstances. Some forty boys lived in at the college, several of whom had rooms to themselves and were attended by their own personal servants, whereas most of the boys boarded out, paying between £25-£30 a year, depending on whether they went home for the holidays or not. Very often the boys had to live under very poor, overcrowded conditions with little supervision. The 'dames' who ran most of the boarding houses were very often elderly widows who relied on Westminster boys to provide them with their only means of income. Mrs Anne Playford, who became William's 'dame', was able to offer him a far better kind of accommodation than that occupied by many of his schoolmates. Mrs Playford's husband had been a very successful publisher of music and when he died he left his wife a substantial amount of property, including a four-storeyed house in Little Dean's Yard, close to the school and it was here that William was to live. Mrs Playford died at the end of Cowper's first year at Westminster but she was succeeded by younger relations who had a son at the school.

Modern teachers complain heartily when there are more than twenty-five pupils to a class. Westminster in the 1740s could only boast two masters and six ushers for all the 350-odd boys. Classes of over fifty pupils were quite common. Cowper, however, developed a great liking for at least three of his teachers and was ever to be thankful for the kindness he experienced at their hands. He was especially fond of Dr Pierson Lloyd, called 'Tappy' by the boys because rumour had it that he was the son of a public-house tapster. Dr Lloyd enthused Cowper with a keen interest in prosody and impressed him because of his kindness, strong sense of humour and gentle nature. At his death Cowper transposed the Latin thoughts expressed at a Westminster ceremony in honour of Lloyd into English verse:

Th' old man, our amiable old man is gone—
Second in harmless pleasantry to none.
Ye, once his pupils, who with rev'rence just
View'd him, as all that were his pupils must,
Whether, his health yet firm, he gently strove
To rear and form you with a parent's love,
Or worn with Age, and pleas'd to be at large,
He came still mindfull of his former charge,
To smile on this glad circle ev'ry year,
And charm you with his humor, drop a tear.

Cowper's favourite teacher was undoubtedly Vincent Bourne, or 'Vinney' as he was known amongst the pupils. Bourne was a great classicist and lover of nature and had made a name for himself as being the last great Latin poet in England. Cowper has left us a fine pen-portrait of his former teacher in a letter to William Unwin written in May 1781, when Cowper was undertaking a translation of Bourne's Latin poems. The poet writes,

I love the Memory of Vinny Bourne. I think him a better Latin poet than Tibullus, Propertius, Ausonius, or any of the Writers in his way, except Ovid, and not at all inferior to Him. I love him too with a Love of Partiality, because he was Usher of the 5th form at Westminster when I pass'd through it. He was so good natur'd and so indolent, that I lost more than I got by him, for he made me as idle as himself. He was such a Sloven, as if he had trusted to his Genius as a cloak for every

thing that could disgust you in his person; and indeed in his
Writings he has almost made amends for all. His humor is
entirely original, he can speak of a Magpie or a Cat in terms
so exquisitely appropriated to the Character he draws, that
one would suppose him animated by the Spirit of the
Creatures he describes. And with all this drollery there is a
mixture of rational and even religious Reflection at times, and
always an air of pleasantry, good nature and Humanity, that
makes him in my Mind one of the most Amiable Writers in
the World. It is not common to meet with an Author who can
make you smile, and yet at nobody's Expense, who is always
entertaining, and yet always harmless, and who though
elegant and classical to a degree not always found even in the
Classics themselves, charms more by the Simplicity &
playfullness of his Ideas, than by the neatness & purity of his
Verse. Yet such was poor Vinney.[15]

Cowper got on well at Westminster and eventually became
house captain, a leading prefect and one of the brightest lights of the
sixth form. He found the freedom given the boys under Dr Nicoll,
the headmaster, quite to his liking. Nicoll was a reform educator
who did not believe in the old system of 'knocking sense' into boys.
He encouraged pupils to develop their own talents and preferred to
hand out praise rather than criticism. Cowper was able to work well
under such circumstances and studied hard in the many free periods
he had. He was rewarded by having his work passed from class to
class by his teachers so that everyone could admire it. It was not
unusual for Cowper to receive silver coins from his masters as a
token of their appreciation of his work.[16] At sport, too, he showed
great talent and excelled in football and cricket. In later years
Cowper was to lay great stress on sport in education and he always
kept himself physically fit by long walks in all weathers, playing
quoits, swimming in the Ouse and playing battledore and
shuttlecock when confined indoors. His favourite sport, however,
was always archery. The first painting ever made of Cowper as a
child depicts him with a bow and arrows, and over fifty years later
the poet was painted by Abbott wearing the green coat and buff
waistcoat of the Olney Archers.[17] He was a member of an archery
club until his dying day. Unlike most of his class, Cowper did not

like horse-riding and was a vowed opponent of the fashionable 'sport' of fox-hunting.

At times supervision at Westminster was certainly too lax. Cowper found out very early that it was easy to play truant and would go for long walks in school time along the banks of the Thames. This had a positive influence on him, however, as it strengthened his awareness of nature and made him a keen observer of flora and fauna. Feeling very close to nature moved him to breed mice in secret in a drawer at school. He was overjoyed when a female mouse had young but gave up the experiment in disgust when he found that the mouse had eaten up all its offspring.

Some of the boys' escapades at Westminster during Cowper's time there would have gained a place of honour in any boy's book of British school life. Neither Richmal Crompton's William nor Frank Richards' Billy Bunter could have thought out anything as hilarious as did Cowper's schoolmate Lord Higham-Ferrers. One day the school was thrown into great activity through the sudden announcement that a high-ranking lady was to come on a tour of inspection. Everything was speedily tidied up and made shipshape in time for the august arrival. At the time appointed a stately carriage rolled up[18] accompanied by footmen in full livery. The headmaster put on his best gown and went out to greet the lady. This noble personage gave the headmaster her hand and descended from the carriage. The headmaster led the lady to the main doors of the school flanked by the pupils who had been turned out for parade. Suddenly Dr Nicoll was horrified to hear certain boys giggling loudly. Soon there were roars of laughter all around as one boy after the other could not keep a stiff face. The head was shocked and apologized profusely to the lady, who reacted scandalously by removing her wig. The whole scene had been organized by the boys and the 'lady' was no less than young Lord Higham-Ferrers, always ready for a joke. The prank does not seem to have harmed Lord Higham-Ferrers' career in any way as twenty years later he became Prime Minister of England. Other jokes, however, were of a more serious nature and overstepped the boundaries of good humour. The Duke of Richmond found Vinney Bourne's long greasy locks too much of a temptation. When the usher was looking the other way, Richmond set fire to his hair and, after waiting a few minutes, beat him mercilessly about the head in order to put out the flames.

On the whole there was a lack of moral guidance in the school and Cowper was later to complain that he had been taught more at school about pagan religions than Christianity and the Bible. Lying was especially rampant amongst the boys. To his shame, Cowper confessed in later years that he became very proficient at telling untruths even where his own family was concerned. Once Cowper's father gave him a beautiful pair of silver shoe buckles. He could ill afford them as he was going through difficult times financially, but, as Cowper frequently informs us, he was very generous where his sons were concerned. Without thinking of his father's sacrifice, William sold the buckles to gain a bit of extra pocket money. At the end of term he returned home and his father, noticing that he was not wearing the buckles, asked where they were. Cowper replied that he had taken the buckles off to save them from the kicks when playing football. He had then put them in his waistcoat pocket and hung his clothes on a post. A 'blackguard boy' had been hanging around at the time, so he must have taken them.

Cowper became so skilled in telling untruths that he could write, 'I became such an adept in the infernal art of lying, that I was seldom guilty of a fault for which I could not invent an apology capable of deceiving the wisest.'[19] Most of Cowper's major biographers have thought the poet's self-criticism in the matter of lying to be mere morbid self-examination. He was guilty of, at worst, mere schoolboy pranks, they tell us. As a converted Christian, Cowper was of quite another opinion and, foreseeing criticism, wrote, 'These, I know, are called schoolboy's tricks; but a total depravity of principle, and the work of the father of lies, are universally at the bottom of them.'[20]

A biographer always searches for evidence to see how the various experiences in his subject's life serve to influence his further development. It is thus legitimate to ask at this stage how life at Westminster fitted Cowper out to become not only the most famous poet of his age, but one who pointed out the way to God through Christ to succeeding generations. Cowper could not have had a better grounding in poetry than that which he received at school. He studied verse forms and metre closely under Lloyd and, under Nicoll's guidance, worked through Homer with his friend Dick Sutton. It was at Westminster that Cowper adopted Tully's motto *'Nulla dies sine linea'* and never let a day go by without translating at least a few lines of classical poetry and writing Latin and Greek verse himself. So it was that Cowper became proficient at writing pastorals, dirges and elegies. He became equally at home with heroic couplets as with blank verse and could put his alexandrines, iambics, trochees and spondees to expressive, natural-sounding use.

Cowper was one of the few poets who could really scan verse correctly and learned to pay particular attention to the length of vowels and diction. Poetry became a natural form of oral expression and communication to him. Criticizing Dr Johnson's attitude to poetry years later, he stressed that Johnson had not learnt to treat poetry as a mode of natural expression and indeed did not know how to read poetry aloud. At least as far as the mechanics of poetry were concerned, Cowper became a master of all measures at Westminster. In 'Table Talk', Cowper's essay in verse on Christian poetry, he writes,

> At Westminster, where little poets strive
> To set a distich upon six and five,
> Where discipline helps op'ning buds of sense,
> And makes his pupils proud with silver-pence,
> I was a poet too—[21]

In spite of the lack of true religion taught at Westminster, Cowper had several experiences that brought him nearer to God. At fourteen years of age he discovered Milton's *Paradise Lost* and *Paradise Regained*. He was to recollect the experience of exhilaration in his poem *The Task*:

> Then Milton had indeed a poet's charms:
> New to my taste, his Paradise surpass'd
> The struggling efforts of my boyish tongue
> To speak its excellence. I danced for joy.
> I marvell'd much that, at so ripe an age
> As twice sev'n years, his beauties had then first
> Engag'd my wonder, and, admiring still
> And still admiring, with regret suppos'd
> The joy half lost because not sooner found.[22]

After his conversion Cowper resolved to do for the eighteenth century what Milton had done in poetry for the seventeenth and make his major poetic theme the fall of man and his ascension in Christ.

Late one evening Cowper was crossing through St Margaret's

Churchyard when a glimmer of light some distance away excited his
curiosity and the young boy went up to investigate what was going
on. A gravedigger was at work by the light of a lantern, preparing a
new grave. Just as Cowper approached the grave, the digger threw
out a skull, which struck Cowper on the leg. At once the boy's
conscience was touched and he began to think of death and the perils
of going unrepentant to the grave. Experiences like this were not
infrequent but Cowper tells us that no sooner did they happen than
he forgot their spiritual relevance.

One part of Cowper's education had a strong and lasting effect
on the boy's soul. However negligent the masters were in the matter
of religion, Dr Nicoll insisted that the boys should be prepared well
for confirmation and in the case of Cowper's class, he took upon
himself the task of tutor. Remembering this occasion in later years,
the poet wrote, 'The old man acquitted himself of this duty like one
who had a deep sense of its importance, and I believe most of us were
struck by his manner, and affected by his exhortation.' Dr Nicoll's
sincerity so impressed Cowper that the boy started to pray in secret.
Perhaps Cowper should have discussed the problems of prayer with
his tutor. As it was, Cowper found it very difficult to keep up a
regular prayer life and gradually stopped praying. Cowper
commented later, 'I relapsed into a total forgetfulness of God with
the usual disadvantage of being more hardened for having been
softened to no purpose.'

At eighteen Cowper left Westminster, well qualified in school
subjects but, to use his own words, as ignorant in all points of
religion as the satchel on his back.

2.
Apprentice to the law

Dr Cowper had already taken the next step towards making his son Lord Chancellor a year before William left Westminster in 1749. He had obtained admittance for William to the Society of the Middle Temple so that he might be trained in law. But first, after leaving school, William was invited by his father to spend some months at home before starting out on a career. Dr Cowper had remarried and young William now had time to get to know his father and stepmother better and also to explore the beautiful countryside around Berkhamsted.

Stay in Berkhamsted

The nine months he spent at home proved to be a time of deep happiness for Cowper and provided a further training ground in preparing him for his future task as a poet of nature and nature's God. Dr Cowper kept the very best of intellectual and spiritual company and there were often guests at his home who were prepared to discuss the merits and demerits of both classical and modern poetry.

Two of these guests, William Duncombe and his son John, were particular favourites of Cowper's and were able to render him much assistance as a poet throughout the coming years. William Duncombe had retired from the Navy Office at the early age of thirty-five to look after his estate at Stocks and spend a life devoted to literature. John Duncombe was two years older than Cowper and

had been educated at Felsted School, where the poet's younger
brother, John Cowper, later attended. He was elected school captain
and made a name for himself as a classicist even before leaving
school. Young John Cowper, now twelve years of age, was already
considered a promising scholar and entered into the many literary
discussions between his father, brother and the Duncombes.

Later the Duncombes, assisted by William Cowper, were to
translate and publish a number of Horatian odes. John Duncombe
became a minister of the gospel and also chief reviewer for the
Gentleman's Magazine. It was most likely Duncombe who gave
William such a good write-up when he published his first volume of
poems. When Dr John Cowper died in 1757 William wrote to John
Duncombe saying that he wished him to have his father's gold
sleeve-buttons as a keepsake and said, 'You & I have spent many
merry hours together in the Parsonage, my poor Father has often
been the better for your Drollery, for you had the Knack, or the
Natural Gift of making him Laugh, when no Creature else could
have done it.'[1]

Berkhamsted in Cowper's time was a tiny market town of less
than two thousand inhabitants. The town was closely connected to
the Crown, which was in possession of the ruined castle and manor
house, and had once boasted Geoffrey Chaucer as its Clerk of the
Works. Berkhamsted's days of fame were gone, however, by 1749
and the only people of note there, as Cowper tells us afterwards,
were the Cowpers themselves. During his days of leisure Cowper
went for long walks in the surrounding countryside, drinking in its
beauties and feeling on top of the world. He felt so much part of the
woods and fields around him that he was later to write, 'There was
neither tree, nor gate, nor stile, in all that country, to which I did not
feel a relation.'[2]

It was not until his father's death, and the surprising news (for
him) that his father did not own the house in which he was brought
up, that Cowper realized just how much he loved Berkhamsted and
how much he would miss the beautiful countryside. Indeed, the
Hertfordshire fields became a symbol to him of the pre-conversion
grace of God which had afforded him great happiness even when he
cared less about spiritual matters. Writing to his Evangelical aunt,
Mrs Madan, after revisiting Berkhamsted with John Newton in
1767, Cowper says,

LIBRARY
TECHNICAL COLLEGE

Berkhamsted Rectory — Cowper's birthplace and the home of Dr John Cowper

The sight of them [the hills around Berkhamsted] affected me much, and awakened in me a lively Recollection of the Goodness of the Lord in caring for and Protecting me in those dark and dangerous days of Ignorance and Enmity against him, and his own Blessed Word teaches me to draw an Inference from these Premises of more Worth than Millions of Gold and Silver; If while I was an Enemy he loved Me, much more reason have I to rest assured of his Love, being reconciled by the Blood of his Son.[3]

Cowper had every reason to write in this way. After leaving Westminster, he was in grave danger of becoming a snob, despising those who had not enjoyed the same education. Also when penning the above words to his aunt, he had a bad conscience for not having been more patient and loving with his father.

Apprenticeship in London

Some time at the beginning of 1750 Cowper was apprenticed to a London attorney, a Mr Chapman who was also a solicitor and had chambers very near the Temple. He was to remain three years with Mr Chapman and receive a thorough grounding in the law before going on to the Middle Temple. That, at least, is what Dr John Cowper planned.

William's fellow-apprentice was Edward Thurlow, who was to obtain great legal and political fame. Thurlow and Cowper became good friends at once. They had the same intense interest in poetry and the classics and were both bent on experiencing to the full what London society could offer them. Both men were capable of intensive study when necessary but both apparently spent as much time out of their chambers as in them. This was mostly Cowper's fault as he had several pretty cousins living nearby with whom William and Edward spent several hours a day 'giggling and making giggle'.[4]

Though they had much in common the two young men differed greatly in character. Cowper was gentle and refined and, though his interest in spiritual things had waned considerably, he considered himself a Christian. Thurlow was more of a rough diamond and had been expelled from Cambridge for repeated acts of impudence and for refusing to keep up the necessary attendance at chapel. In those days there was an Act of Parliament which compelled all lawyers and government officials to demonstrate their allegiance to church and Crown by receiving Holy Communion in the Church of England before taking up a post. Such was Thurlow's antagonism to religion that when he was called to the Bar, he merely popped into the church to take communion and, with his hat still on his head, took the bread and wine and popped out again without taking part in the rest of the service.

Thurlow was, however, a very kind-hearted person and was ever ready to help the poor and needy. Cowper marvelled at his energy, his talents and his kind nature and felt that he was the very man who could one day earn the title that Dr John Cowper coveted so much for his son. Once, when Thurlow was joking with Cowper and his cousins, Cowper exclaimed, full of admiration for his friend, 'Thurlow, I am nobody, and shall be always nobody, and you will be Chancellor. You shall provide for me when you are.' Thurlow smiled and replied, 'I surely will.' Cowper stressed that he meant every word and added, 'These ladies are witnesses.' Thurlow replied, 'Let them be so, for I will certainly do it.' Part of Cowper's premonition came true. Thurlow did become Lord Chancellor — but just when Cowper needed the help Thurlow had promised him, no help came. Thurlow dropped Cowper after his first major breakdown and only took up correspondence with his old friend again when his political power was waning and Cowper had become famous. In 1783 the poet wrote of Thurlow in 'The Valediction':

> Your senatorial dignity of face,
> Sound sense, intrepid spirit, manly grace,
> Have rais'd you high as talents can ascend,
> Made you a peer, but spoilt you for a friend.

Cowper goes on to outline his opinion of true friendship, closing with the words:

> 'Tis grace, 'tis bounty, and it calls for praise,
> If God give health, that sunshine of our days—
> And if he add, a blessing shar'd by few,
> Content of heart, more praises still are due—
> But if he grant a friend, that boon possess'd

Indeed is treasure, and crowns all the rest;
And giving one whose heart is in the skies,
Born from above and made divinely wise,
He gives what bankrupt Nature never can,
Whose noblest coin is light and brittle man,
Gold purer far than Ophir ever knew,
A soul an image of Himself, and therefore true.

In God's providence Cowper was never short of such good
twice-born friends, although, as he would have said himself, one
cannot have too many of them.

Ashley Cowper and his family

The three young ladies whose company Cowper and Thurlow
enjoyed so much during their days at Chapman's were Harriot,
Theadora and Elizabeth Cowper, daughters of Ashley Cowper, Dr
John Cowper's elder brother. Ashley Cowper was a very small,
plump man who was usually to be seen under a very wide-brimmed
white hat with a yellow lining. This led William, who was very fond
of his uncle, to remark that if one were not careful one would pick
up Ashley mistaking him for a mushroom!

Ashley had studied law at the Middle Temple and had reached an
eminent position, chiefly through the influence of his father, Chief
Justice Spencer Cowper, who had purchased the office of Clerk of
the Parliaments. Ashley thus held the patronage of several lucrative
posts, one of which, that of Clerk of the Journals, he was to offer
William. Although Ashley was virtually responsible for the entire
clerical staff of the House of Lords, rumour had it that he had never
appeared there in person and considered his position, which brought
him several thousand pounds a year, merely as a sinecure. Be this as
it may, Ashley Cowper certainly had a great deal of time to busy
himself with poetry, writing much himself and collecting and
publishing the poems of his very many poetic relations.

Critics tend to stress the fact that though Ashley professed to be
a God-fearing man and often folded his hands in prayer, his poetry
was at times harsh and even vulgar. He is thus branded as a
hypocrite. Ashley had, however, more than a large share of the
family illness. He could be in the highest spirits one day and then

spend months in a depressive state, shutting himself in his room and speaking to nobody. Like his nephew William, he was able to write in whatever mood he happened to be, describing his feelings. This kind of writing does not always make for good reading. Before becoming too harsh ourselves in judging Ashley Cowper we must also remember what a general low moral state the English language was in during the first half of the eighteenth century.

The state of English literature

Ashley's generation were shaking off the enormous filth in literature which had accrued through the so-called Restoration period. Ever since the enthronement of Charles II it had been thought 'clever' to write long boring stories about adultery and prostitution with the 'hero' inevitably either promiscuous or a drunkard. The language of the gutter and the whore-house had become that of the fashionable theatre and God's name was blasphemed in a bevy of popular curses. One has only to read the letters of the famous Fourth Earl of Chesterfield to his son to realize how perverted the manners of the educated classes had become. Here we have a man of the most noble blood, writing to his young son in order to lead him into a life of vice rather than a life of virtue. It is no wonder that Cowper wrote of Chesterfield, 'All the muses weep for thee.'

Cowper's reference to the press of his day as 'Thou ever bubbling spring of endless lies,' will go down in history, yet it was the novelists of his day who gained the most censure from him for perverting both language and morals. In 'The Progress of Error' Cowper reprimands these 'doers of no good' by writing,

Ye writers of what none with safety reads,
Footing it in the dance that fancy leads.
Ye novelists who mar what ye would mend,
Sniv'ling and driv'ling folly without end.[5]

When Samuel Richardson tried to put a stop to this by writing novels featuring heroes who behaved in a Christian way there was a flood of protest in the press arguing that Christians have not the stuff that heroes and gentlemen are made of. They dubbed

Richardson 'Mr Serious' and 'Mr Gravity' and thought he was a menace to cultured society. Augustine Birrel in his *Res Judicatæ* summed up the situation in a nutshell by writing, 'The real truth I believe to be is this: we are annoyed by Richardson because he violates a tradition. The proper place for an eighteenth-century novelist was either the pot or the sponging-house. He ought to be either disguised in liquor or confined for debt. Richardson was neither the one nor the other.'

Fittingly enough Cowper, during his law days, long before his conversion, entered into the fray and defended Richardson's stance in his 'Ode on Reading Mr. Richardson's History of Sir Charles Grandison' in 1754. The following sample verse illustrates the gist of his poem, which is that if anyone wants to read about heroic deeds of glory, then he must turn to the Christian way of life:

> Would you the race of Glory run,
> Know the Devout, and They alone,
> Are equal to the Task,
> The Labours of th'Illustrious Course
> Far other than th'unaided force
> Of Human Vigour ask.

Richardson treasured his personal copy of the poem, in William Cowper's own hand, until his dying day and most of his novels, like Cowper's poems, became best sellers, showing that the reading public as a whole preferred cleanliness to dirt.

Cowper made it his life's ambition to clean up the language of literature and make it as near as possible to what he called the language of Eden. It was Christian writers such as William Cowper, William Romaine, James Hervey, Edward Young, John Newton, Henry Venn and John Wesley that transformed the English written language, making it available to all classes and purifying it in its subject matter. When modern secular critics condemn the language of the Restoration period, they do so rightly. They tend to forget, however, that it is the Christian writers of the post-Restoration period who gave them the cleaner language they themselves use.

Here again we can compare our own age with that of Cowper in the 1750s. The stage is once more debauched and the primitive, debased language of the television soap-opera is undermining our language. The majestic language of the Psalms is being substituted

in our churches by silly little kindergarten choruses with as much
theological content as an empty shoe-box. Reading the works of
language reformers such as Cowper, Hervey and Young could help
us put our language back in order today.

Cowper's view of Christianity at this time

Whatever Ashley Cowper's true state of religion was, he set
William an example by attending church regularly with his whole
family and taking his nephew with him. Years later Cowper looked
back on these church visits with gratitude saying, 'Here [at
Chapman's] I might have lived and died without hearing or seeing
anything that might remind me of a single christian duty.'[6] At this
time Cowper was very eager to be considered a Christian and there
is much in his writings that could be interpreted as a strong Christian
testimony. Writing to his friend Chase Price in 1750 on the death of
a mutual friend, Cowper, ever prone to express his deepest thoughts
in poetry rather than prose, wrote in the manner of Cowley:

> If I my friend should drop before you
> Think the Joyful Prize is mine,
> A whole Eternity of Glory
> While poor Mortality is thine,
> Then if one silent Tear should fall
> One Sigh escape let that be all,
> Lest bitter Envy claim a part
> In thy Friendly faithfull Heart.
> Death's the best Blessing Heaven can give;
> We live to Dye but dye to Live.

However, Cowper had as yet a faulty understanding of
Christianity. Shocked by the, at times, disgusting ways of his fellow
clerks, he began to lay great stress on personal conduct and
decorum. 'I began to think myself somebody,' he said. But it was all
self-effort and made him more than a little self-righteous. He was to
pursue for several years to come what he would later call a 'legal
course'. Cowper meant by this term that he was relying on fulfilling
the letter of the law of God rather than trusting in Christ's
righteousness. This attitude bought with it three burdens that

Cowper found difficult to bear. The first was that he knew in his heart that he could never, of himself, find acceptance with God. This caused his sensitive conscience to trouble him constantly. The second burden was that most of Cowper's relations, whether Christians or not, held it as an axiom that he was a Christian of the noblest kind. This again upset him because he knew his own soul. The third great burden brought on by Cowper's 'legal course' was that when he was finally converted, he had great difficulty in persuading his relations that his old self had been a mere sham. After conversion Cowper was to describe his situation at this period in his hymn, 'The Heart Healed and Changed by Mercy':

> Friends and ministers said much
> The gospel to enforce;
> But my blindness still was such,
> I chose a legal course:
>
> Much I fasted, watch'd and strove,
> Scarce would shew my face abroad,
> Fear'd, almost, to speak or move,
> A stranger still to God.[7]

Cowper's fault was that he was trying to eliminate sin by sheer personal effort and thus running away from two realities: the reality of the world at large, which he, like the Pharisees of old, strove to avoid, and the reality of his own inability. He knew nothing then of the need for personal forgiveness. Thus he ended the hymn quoted above with the words:

> Thus afraid to trust his grace,
> Long time did I rebel;
> Till, despairing of my case,
> Down at his feet I fell:
>
> Then my stubborn heart he broke,
> And subdu'd me to his sway;
> By a simple word he spoke,
> 'Thy sins are done away.'

At the Temple

After gaining enough practical experience at Chapman's, Cowper took chambers at the Middle Temple in November 1753, later moving to the Inner Temple. He was now twenty-two years of age and, though it could not be said that his heart was in the law, he was determined to succeed in it because of the good money involved.[8] Cowper was in an excellent position to become a successful lawyer: he had a natural talent for reading and doing research, he was very able to express himself elegantly both in speech and writing, he had an intensively analytical mind and he had a great number of relations and friends who could offer him the best of legal advice and provide him with the right kind of literature. We know, for instance, that Ashley Cowper, Martin Madan, Edward Thurlow and William de Grey (later Lord Walsingham and Attorney-General), the husband of the poet's cousin Mary Cowper, all assisted him to a great degree, and there may have been others. He had also built up quite an impressive legal library himself by this time.

Cowper, however, very foolishly started to burn his candle at both ends. He had a great variety of interests and tried to exercise them all at once. He was also gradually becoming something of a rake. Hunting during the day, dancing all night, reading a vast number of books and practising law whenever a spare moment popped up were gradually wearing him down. Apart from this Cowper had fallen in love with his cousin Theadora, Ashley's daughter, and he was meeting her daily.

It is no wonder then, that we find Cowper writing,

> I was struck not long after my settlement in the Temple with such a dejection of spirits as none but they who have felt the same can have the least conception of. Day and night I was upon the rack, lying down in horror and rising in despair. I presently lost all relish to those studies I had been closely attached to; the classics had no longer any charm for me; I had need of something more salutary than mere amusement, but had none to direct me where to find it.[9]

He took more and more to writing verse to ward off the depressing thoughts that constantly assailed him. We have his poem

to his Westminster friend Robert Lloyd, written in 1754, in which
Cowper says he is not writing in poetry to show any genius or wit
but,

> 'Tis not with either of these views,
> That I presume t'address the Muse:
> But to divert a fierce banditti
> (Sworn foes to ev'ry thing that's witty),
> That, with a black infernal train,
> Make cruel inroads in my brain,
> And daily threaten to drive thence
> My little garrison of sense:
> The fierce banditti which I mean,
> Are gloomy thoughts led on by Spleen.

As on so many other occasions in his life, Cowper was to find
God's smiling face behind the dark clouds. He found great comfort
in George Herbert's poems and was once again able to approach
God in prayer. Cowper's comments on the help he received from
Herbert are interesting. He found the hymns 'uncouth' and 'Gothic',
yet they spoke to his soul. Over two hundred years later Herbert's
hymns might strike us as being more 'Gothic' than ever and the
language almost too quaint for us to bother to read it. Some of
Herbert's hymns are still sung today, however, including 'King of
glory, King of peace', which is still one of the finest hymns of praise
in any hymn-book. 'Teach me, my God and King', though written
at the beginning of the seventeenth century, still speaks directly to
the soul. Herbert's hymns dealing with anxieties and prayer, which
are the ones Cowper is most likely to have read, are indeed very
uncouth in their language, reminding of the poems of John Donne,
Cowper's ancestor. They convey, however, if one takes care to get
behind the symbolism in them, a very personal and comforting
message. Here is Herbert talking in the name of God to the sad heart:

The Dawning

> Awake sad heart, whom sorrow ever drowns;
> Take up thine eyes, which feed on earth;
> Unfold thy forehead gather'd into frowns:
> Thy Saviour comes, and with him mirth:

> Awake, awake;
> And with a thankfull heart his comforts take.
> But thou dost still lament, and pine, and crie;
> And feel his death, but not his victorie.
>
> Arise sad heart; if thou doe not withstand,
> Christ's resurrection thine may be:
> Do not by hanging down break from the hand,
> Which as it riseth, raiseth thee:
> Arise, arise;
> And with his buriall-linen drie thine eyes:
> Christ left his grave-clothes, that we might, when grief
> Draws tears, or bloud, not want a handkerchief.

In his poem 'The Method', Herbert explains how God's ear is open even to his foes, thus creating hope for everyone who wishes to pray but is frightened and faint to do so. As this is so true, says Herbert:

> Then once more pray.
> Down with thy knees, up with thy voice.
> Seek pardon first, and God will say,
> 'Glad heart rejoice.'

Shortly after discovering Herbert, Cowper went to stay for a few months in Southampton with some good friends. It was there that he had a marvellous experience of the grace of God. It was not a conversion experience but deep enough to show him that God would not 'break the bruised reed nor quench the smoking flax'. The poet was sitting with his friends enjoying the reflection of the morning sun on the sea, flanked by the most beautiful scenery he had ever seen. We shall let the poet continue in his own words:

> Here it was that on a sudden, as if another sun had been kindled that instant in the heavens on purpose to dispel sorrow and vexation of spirit, I felt the weight of all my misery taken off. My heart became light and joyous in a moment, and had I been alone, I could have wept with transport. I must needs believe that nothing less than the Almighty Fiat could have filled me with such inexpressible

delight, not by a gradual dawning of peace, but, as it were, with one flash of His life-giving countenance.

Immediately after the experience Cowper was able to thank God for the peace that he had gained. It was not long, however, before he viewed what had happened as coming merely from a change of air. He thus strove to experience as much change and variety in his life as possible, which was the very thing that had made him depressed in the first place. Soon Cowper stopped praying again and even burnt the written prayers he had prepared. But God did not leave the poet alone and gave him many an opportunity to thank him for deliverance. Once when Cowper was out hunting, he crawled through a hedge pulling his loaded gun after him. As he took hold of the barrel and drew it towards him, he heard a sharp click and feared the worst. The barrel was pointing at his stomach. A twig had caught in the trigger and cocked the gun. It did not go off. On another occasion he was running down a street when a large brick fell from the top of a three-storeyed building, landing at the tip of his foot and covering him with dust from its impact on the ground. On discussing his experiences with non-Christian friends he agreed with them that nothing but coincidence could explain what had happened. Cowper spent the next ten years or so with a seared conscience, only now and then considering that he was living at enmity with God.

A troubled romance

Although Westminster boys went home for the holidays and could go home at weekends and even spend the evenings away from school, their time was mostly spent in a single-sex environment. This often made boys shy of the opposite sex after leaving school. Even Cowper, who had spent holiday after holiday in the company of his female cousins, felt rather shy and ill at ease with new female acquaintances. In respect of such ladies he writes in his poem 'On Himself',

> William was once a bashful youth,
> His modesty was such,
> That one might say (to say the truth),
> He rather had too much.[10]

After joining Chapman's Cowper had ample opportunity of mixing with women of his own station and even became something of a ladies' man. He took great care with his outer appearance and the clothes he wore and before very long was cutting quite a dashing figure. Furthermore Cowper was charming, witty, a good conversationalist and always very much a gentleman. His friend and biographer Hayley testified that women always found Cowper highly fascinating, even when he was no longer a young man. Much of this change was due to his cousin Theadora, Ashley's daughter, who strove to make him 'presentable' in society. Indeed after 1749 Theadora and William were seen more and more often together and by the end of 1750 they had fallen deeply in love. Thus we find Cowper not only acknowledging Theadora's transforming influence in his life but after penning the above words in 'On Himself' he went on to write,

Now that a miracle so strange
May not in vain be shown,
Let the dear maid who wrought the change
E'er claim him for her own.

Cowper and Theadora had very much in common. They were of the same class and background and shared a very large number of mutual friends, including many relations, with whom they got on well. The were both highly religious and deeply concerned to live an upright and righteous life, though they had not yet come to realize and experience the full truths of the gospel. They were both keen on languages and literature and loved to take long walks, breathing in the fragrant country air, listening to the sounds of nature (which to them was the best of music) and admiring God's creation. Theadora lived not far from Hampstead Heath in Southampton Row, a one-sided street of detached houses looking out onto the countryside. As Cowper was often a guest at Theadora's home he had ample opportunity to stroll from, say, Hampstead to Primrose Hill with his dear friend.

It is at this time we first find Cowper writing about Eden, which was to become one of his major themes. Of course, his Eden was shared by Theadora, or 'Delia', as Cowper named her. During these walks with Delia, Cowper would forget the world and imagine himself as Adam before the Fall with his still innocent Eve.

Oh! to some distant scene, a willing exile
From the wild uproar of the busy world,
Were it my fate with Delia to retire;
With her to wander through the sylvan shade
Each morn, or o'er the moss-imbrowned turf,
Where blest as the prime parents of mankind
In their own Eden, we would envy none;
But, greatly pitying whom the world calls happy,
Gently spin out the silken thread of life.[11]

Time and time again we find Cowper returning to this theme
even up to the last poetry of his old age. He wanted to find again the
lost language of innocence, in which man could once again
commune freely with his God and see God dwelling with a
ransomed and redeemed mankind where all sin was banished, all
tears removed and all joy ever present.

The old proverb tells us that the path of true love never runs
smooth and at times the path was rough indeed for Theadora and
William. Though they shared so many blessings together, they also
shared the disease that brought down so many of their family,
including Theadora's father Ashley, who could be in the best of
spirits one day and then spend months in solitary melancholia.
Theadora was extremely highly strung and this, coupled with a very
strong will and a tendency to melancholia, made her a very unstable
companion. Cowper, too, could be very stubborn when he was in the
mood and at times he was of a most sensitive nature. So we find the
romance between the two blowing now hot, now cold, fraying the
couple's nerves. At times Cowper was so much in love that he did
not know, as they say, whether he was coming or going. Of course,
he wrote about this in poetry, as he did about almost anything of
importance in his life:

Would my Delia know if I love, let her take
My last thought at night, and the first when I wake;
With my prayers and best wishes, preferr'd for her sake.

Let her guess what I muse on, when rambling alone
I stride o'er the stubble each day with my gun,
Never ready to shoot till the covey is flown.

Let her think what odd whimsies I have in my brain,
When I read one page over and over again
And discover at last that I read it in vain.[12]

As William met Theadora almost daily over a period of seven
years, one would have expected the couple to have settled down to
a mutual relationship of trust not broken by absence. In fact, the
opposite was the case. Both Theadora and William were so
frightened that their courtship would break up at any time that they
lived in perpetual terror when parted. William sums up this mutual
feeling in the words:

The heart of a lover is never at rest,
With joy overwhelm'd, or with sorrow oppress'd:
When Delia is near, all is ecstasy then,
And I even forget I must lose her again:
When absent, as wretched as happy before,
Despairing I cry, 'I shall see her no more.'[13]

Their tiffs were numerous and at times Cowper was afraid to
meet Theadora, fearful that he might not find her in the right mood.
He would beg of her:

With kindness bless the present hour,
Or oh! we meet in vain!
What can we do in absence more
Than suffer and complain?[14]

At other times, after they had made up after a quarrel, the poet
could write, wishfully thinking:

Happy! when we but seek t'endure
A little pain, then find a cure
By double joy requited;
For friendship, like a sever'd bone,
Improves and joins a stronger tone
When aptly reunited.[15]

Cowper once said that he never experienced anything in
moderation but that all his feelings were of the more intensive kind.

When he was happy, he was on top of the world; when he was sad, he was the most unhappy of men. By 1755 his nerves were beginning to fail and the extremes between his moods were only too evident. When asleep he began to have terrible threatening nightmares and when he was awake his thoughts plagued him with the most frightening visions. At other times, however, he would be transported with delight, seeing all his problems vanished, and peace would enter his soul. Perhaps such extremes of temperament are the lot of many a person fighting against bad health and a bad conscience as Cowper was. Most of us, whether rightly or wrongly, keep quiet about such moods, or at least find great difficulty in expressing what we are going through. Cowper had a unique gift of being able to describe his most intimate fears and highest joys at a time when other people are so taken up with their experiences that they are stuck for words.

Cowper's poems written at this time give the full depth and height of the poet's experience of torment and love. They also show that Cowper's mind was breaking and that he was experiencing far from normal fears. The following poem 'Written in a Fit of Illness' must be quoted in full to show what extremes of feeling Cowper was going through during his courtship with Theadora. The verses are reminiscent of Edgar Allen Poe in their expressive contents, yet Poe wrote fiction and Cowper was writing about the all too painful facts of his own existence:

Written in a Fit of Illness

In these sad hours, a prey to ceaseless pain,
While feverish pulses leap in ev'ry vein,
When each faint breath the last short effort seems
Of life just parting from my feeble limbs;
How wild so'er my wandering thoughts may be,
Still, gentle Delia! still they turn on thee!
At length if, slumbering to a short repose,
A sweet oblivion frees me from my woes,
Thy form appears, thy footsteps I pursue,
Through springy vales, and meadows wash'd in dew;
Thy arm supports me to the fountain's brink,
Where, by some secret pow'r forbid to drink,
Gasping with thirst, I view the tempting flood

That flies my touch, or thickens into mud,
Till thine own hand immersed the goblet dips,
And bears it streaming to my burning lips;
Then borne aloft on fancy's wing we fly,
Like souls embodied to their native sky;
Now ev'ry rock, each mountain, disappears;
And the round earth an even surface wears;
When lo! the force of some resistless weight
Bears me straight down from that pernicious height;
Parting, in vain our struggling arms we close;
Abhorred forms, dire phantoms interpose;
With trembling voice on thy loved name I call,
And gulphs yawn ready to receive my fall;
From these fallacious visions of distress
I wake; nor are my real sorrows less.
Thy absence, Delia! heightens every ill,
And gives e'en trivial pains the power to kill.
Oh! wert thou near me; yet that wish forbear!
'Twere vain, my love — 'twere vain to wish thee near,
Thy tender heart would heave with anguish too;
And by partaking, but increase my woe.
Alone I'll grieve, till, gloomy sorrow past,
Health, like the cheerful day-spring, comes at last—
Comes fraught with bliss to banish ev' ry pain,
Hope, joy, and peace, and Delia in her train!

After a long courtship of ups and downs William and Theadora finally had to face the fact that they could never marry. They were both, by this time, on the verge of breaking down completely and Ashley Cowper was especially opposed to the match. He knew from experience the torments and tortures of the family disease and realized that both his daughter and his nephew had inherited it in large measure. He also had grave doubts that William would have the strength and financial resources to be able to provide for his daughter. Such a state of affairs would put any father off giving his blessing to such a union. Theadora accepted her father's decision. The two parted never more to see each other again this side of eternity. William, however, still retained hope for several years to come, writing,

Absence from whom we love is worse than death,
And frustrate hope severer than despair.[16]

The years 1756-57 proved very fateful for Cowper. His father
died, leaving him without the financial support he had hitherto
received from his parent. His courtship broke up and his best friend
and old schoolmate, Sir William Russell, drowned whilst swimming in the Thames. Cowper wrote what has been hailed as one of
his major poems, full of sincerity and passion. It is, however, but the
beatings of a broken heart.

Doom'd, as I am, in solitude to waste

Doom'd, as I am, in solitude to waste
The present moments, and regret the past;
Depriv'd of every joy, I valued most,
My Friend torn from me, and my Mistress lost;
Call not this gloom, I wear, this anxious mien,
The dull effect of humour, or of spleen
Still, still, I mourn, with each returning day,
Him snatch'd by Fate, in early youth, away.
And Her — thro' tedious years of doubt and pain,
Fix'd in her choice, and faithful — but in vain!
O prone to pity, generous, and sincere,
Whose eye ne'er yet refus'd the wretch a tear;
Whose heart the real claim of friendship knows,
Nor thinks a lover's are but fancied woes;
See me — ere yet my destin'd course half done,
Cast forth a wand'rer on a wild unknown!
See me neglected on the world's rude coast,
Each dear companion of my voyage lost!
Nor ask why clouds of sorrow shade my brow!
And ready tears wait only leave to flow!
Why all, that sooths a heart, from anguish free,
All that delights the happy — palls with me!

The word 'palls' in the final line has long been taken as an
ominous pun by biographers, since 'pall' can mean both 'of no
interest' and 'a funeral shroud'. The fact is that Cowper was made

of sterner stuff than one might think and, true to his own judgement of himself, whenever he was down he was not without hope of soon finding his feet again.

The Nonsense Club and early literary productions

It was during this period that Cowper threw himself heart and soul into the affairs of the Nonsense Club. This organization was formed by former pupils of Westminster School who dined together each Thursday (thus they were often known as the Thursday Club), and debated the foibles of the society in which they lived and the state of the world in general. The club was probably founded as a less serious counterpart to the Scriblerus Club brought into life by the poet Pope. The Nonsense Club members cut quite a figure in the literary and political world of the day and Boswell, Dr Johnson's companion and biographer, called them 'the London Geniuses'. Cowper belonged to the inner circle which included Bonnell Thornton and George Colman, joint editors of the *Connoisseur,* and the poets Robert Lloyd and Charles Churchill. Robert Lloyd was the son of 'Tappy' Lloyd, Cowper's former teacher at Westminster. Joseph Hill, who became a most successful lawyer and received one of Thurlow's secretaryships, was very closely attached to the group, as was also Charles Price, alias 'Toby', who was called 'the Falstaff of his age', and William Hogarth, the famous painter and caricaturist.

The most notorious member of the Nonsense Club was certainly John Wilkes, Member of Parliament for Aylesbury, the only one in the club who had not been at Westminster. Wilkes, editor of *The North Briton*, was twice expelled from his seat in Parliament by George III and was outlawed for a time. As an inexperienced young man, George III almost made the same mistake as Charles I in his method of dealing with Parliament. He had Wilkes arrested twice and even committed to the Tower for criticizing the government though he knew that it was unlawful to cut out opposition in this way. If Wilkes had not been freed from the Tower by the interception of the courts, there could well have been a second revolution in England, as Wilkes had a tremendous following amongst the people.

The members of the club were always ready to pull the public's leg and organized concerts, plays and exhibitions in which they parodied more serious and sober representations. One of their most successful parodies was when they staged an art gallery exhibition which turned out to be an exhibition of sign and public house paintings. Hogarth, assisting under a pseudonym, helped make a success of the show. The exhibition caused loud protests from fashionable artists who felt their high calling had been besmirched and the joke had gone too far.

There was also a more seious side to the club's activities. Members worked closely with Christopher Smart in publishing his *Parables of our Lord and Saviour Jesus Christ*, which contained a dedication to Thornton's eldest son. Cowper translated at least one psalm for Smart's new translation of the Psalms of David and Smart also included works by Cowper in his *Poems on Several Occasions*. Cowper, who chaired the club for some time, was well able to combine both the sober and jocular aspects of the club's activities. He thus wrote several articles, for the *Connoisseur* and other magazines associated with the club besides the *Gentleman's Magazine*, which were very humorous but at the same time revealed a real desire to reform the society in which he lived.

One of the exciting features of research into the lives of William Cowper and his good friend John Newton is that works from their pens which have remained unknown to readers for over two hundred years are still being found. What has made tracing their works difficult is the fact that they either published anonymously, as Newton did at times, or used a great number of pen-names, such as Alethes, Giles Gingerbread, T. H. Andrew Fridze, Jeremy Sago, Madge, Indagator and Christopher Ironside, which were Cowper's favourite names for himself.

One of these articles, 'The Present State of Country Churches', published anonymously in the *Connoisseur* for August 1756, shows how, even before he became an Evangelical, Cowper was already highly critical of the hypocrisy associated with church life. He playfully poured scorn on the 'jiggish measures' used in sacred hymns and on the antics of the instrumentalists and choir singers who were beginning to become fashionable even in country churches. Part of this essay is reminiscent of the book of Haggai, where the prophet reproves the people's negligence in letting the house of the Lord remain in ruins whilst the Jews build comfortable homes for themselves. In Cowper's essay, however, it is not the people of God who are being criticized but the parson:

The ruinous condition of some of these churches gave me great offence; and I could not help wishing, that the honest vicar, instead of indulging his genius for improvements, by inclosing his gooseberry bushes with a Chinese rail, and converting half an acre of his glebe-land into a bowling-green, would have applied part of his income to the more laudable purpose of sheltering his parishioners from the weather during their attendance on divine service. It is no uncommon thing to see the parsonage-house well thatched, and in exceeding good repair, while the church perhaps has no better roof than the ivy that grows over it. The noise of owls, bats and magpies makes a principal part of the church musick in many of these ancient edifices; and the walls, like a large map, seem to be portioned out into capes, seas, and promontories by the various colours with which the damps have stained them.

An essay he had published during this period on the importance of being able to keep secrets affected him so much that he resolved never to break one.

One of Cowper's most scathing articles at this time is his essay on Billy Suckling, the Mother's darling. Cowper hated any display of effeminacy in his own sex and published many a broadside against the use of make-up and perfume by men. Whatever the poet has to say about the subject is very relevant today. It is once more common to see men dressed up in the gaudiest of attire, wearing jewellery and make-up, with their hair permed and dyed. This century is experiencing a re-enactment of the eighteenth-century beaux, rakes and coxcombs! Teaching a class of young men nowadays often reminds the nose of a lady's boudoir. Cowper writes of Billy to the *Connoisseur* for March 1756:

You have already given us several instances of those ambiguous creatures among the men, who are both male and female: permit me to add to them an account of those lady-like gentlemen, whom we may distinguish by the title of their mothers' own sons; who have in vain changed the bib and leading-strings for the breeches, and stick as close to their mammas, as a great calf to the side of an old cow. I am intimately acquainted with one of these over-grown babies; who is indeed too big to be dandled in lap, or fed with a pap-spoon, though he is no more weaned from his mother, than if he had not yet quitted the nursery.

The delicate Billy Suckling is the contempt of the men, the jest of the women, and the darling of his mamma. She doats on him to distraction; and is in perpetual admiration of his wit, and anxiety for his health. The good young gentleman, for his part, is neither undutiful nor ungrateful: she is the only woman, that he does not look on with indifference; and she is his tutoress, his physician, and his nurse. She provides his broth every evening; will not suffer him to look into a book by candle-light, lest he should hurt his eyes; and takes care to have his bed warmed: nay, I have known him sit with his mamma's white handkerchief round his neck through a whole visit, to guard him from the wind of *that ugly door*, or *that terrible chink* in the wainscot.

The most amusing account Cowper wrote for *The Connoisseur* is obviously based on his own experience as a bachelor at the home of Ashley Cowper, whose wife and three daughters loved to tease Cowper. Under the name of Christopher Ironside he writes,

A friend of mine, whom I frequently visit, has a wife and three daughters, the youngest of which has persecuted me these ten years. These ingenious young ladies have not only found out the sole end and purpose of my being themselves, but have likewise communicated their discovery to all the girls in the neighbourhood. So that if they happen at any time to be apprized of my coming (which I take all possible care to prevent) they immediately dispatch half a dozen cards to their faithful allies, to beg the favour of their company to drink coffee, and help teaze Mr. Ironside. Upon these occasions, my entry into the room is sometimes obstructed by a cord fastened across the bottom of the door-case, which as I am a little near-sighted, I seldom discover till it has brought me upon my knees before them. While I am employed in brushing the dust from my black rollers,[17] or chafing my broken shins, my wig is suddenly conveyed away, and either stuffed behind the looking-glass, or tossed from one to the other so dextrously and with such velocity, that after many a fruitless attempt to recover it, I am obliged to sit down bare-headed, to the great diversion of the spectators. The last time I found myself in these distressful circumstances, the eldest girl, a sprightly mischievous jade, stepped briskly up to me, and promised to restore my wig, if I would play her a tune on a small flute she held in her hand. I instantly applied it to my lips, and blowing lustily into it, to my inconceivable surprise, was immediately choked and blinded with a cloud of soot that issued from every hole in the instrument. The younger part of the company declared I had not executed the conditions, and refused to surrender my wig; but the father, who had a rough kind of facetiousness about him, insisted on its being delivered up, and protested that he never knew the Black joke better performed in his life.

Now we can understand why Cowper wrote of 'giggling and making giggle' at Southampton Row.

Other publications at this time were translations of a few of Horace's satires (1759) and of four books of Voltaire's *Henriade* (1762) (four being also translated by Cowper's brother, John) The complete edition was edited by Tobias Smollett and Thomas Francklin. Cowper told Newton that he had also written 'several halfpenny ballads' at this time, '2 or three of which had the honour to be popular'.[18] Cowper's early expertise at ballad writing is shown in his humorous treatment of matrimonial problems in 'The Sorrowfull Husband'. The reader of these early verses will search in vain for poems on nature topics (apart from a brief allusion to Alpine mountains) for which Cowper became most famous. As we shall see, Cowper only took up this theme in poetry after working closely with John Newton on the *Olney Hymns*.

During this period Cowper also attended the meetings of the more radical Robin Hood Society, notorious as a collecting ground for atheists, Deists and dissidents of all kinds. He loved a wrangle and it is very likely that he visited the meetings merely to exercise his debating powers and defend what he felt was orthodoxy against heresy. Deism was especially rampant in England at the time and it was becoming increasingly fashionable to refer to God as having set the universe in motion at creation and left it to spin on under its own powers. Referring to his pre-conversion days, Cowper tells us in his *Memoir*: 'When in company with Deists I have heard the Gospel blasphemed, I never failed to assert the truth of it with much

vehemence of disputation, for which I was the better qualified
having always been a dilligent inquirer into the evidences by which
it was externally supported.'[19] The poet's use of the phrase 'externally supported' would indicate that he was relying on academic
knowledge to confound his antagonists rather than inner spiritual
conviction. In his post-conversion poetry Cowper was to attack
Deism time and time again, as, for instance, in his long poem the
Task:

> Some say that in the origin of things
> When all creation started into birth
> The infant elements received a law
> From which they swerve not since. That under force
> Of that controuling ordinance they move
> And need not his immediate hand, who first
> Prescribed their course, to regulate it now
> Thus dream they, and contrive to save a God
> The incumbrance of his own concerns, and spare
> The great Artificer of all that moves
> The stress of a continual act, the pain
> Of unremitted vigilance and care
> As too laborious and severe a task.[20]

In the same poem he also argues that:

> …One spirit — His
> Who wore the platted thorns with bleeding brows—
> Rules universal nature.[21]

In 1756 Cowper was called to the Bar. In those days a gentleman
was considered to have fulfilled the conditions of a course of legal
training when certain lectures and 'moots' had been attended,
certain 'dinners' eaten, certain 'exercises' carried out and fines paid
when the other conditions were not met. Examinations, as we know
them today, were thought entirely superfluous. This lack of training
in taking examinations was to prove disastrous for Cowper, as we
shall see in the next chapter. He had now finished his apprenticeship
to the law of England but he was still labouring very much under the
yoke of the Old Testament law that was to bring him down to the
lowest step before the throne of grace.

3.
Crisis and conversion

By the end of 1757, Cowper seems to have recovered his spirits but he was leading a life as rakish as ever. He had inherited from his father the post of Commissioner of Bankrupts, which brought him an income of £60 per annum, and was also earning a little as a none too ambitious lawyer. His income was thus comparable with the wages of a country curate, and hardly enough to keep a young man of the world active and alive in the heart of London. His letters at this time show that he was feeling the pinch and money problems were a major topic of discussion.

Apart from the sinecure post of Commissioner of Bankrupts, it appears that William and John Cowper had hardly received a penny at the death of their father; in fact the allowances they had been receiving up to then had stopped. As William's nearest relations and friends had assured Theadora that the man she might have married was to inherit a substantial fortune, this seems strange. It seems that Cowper's step-mother, Rebecca Cowper, whom none of the family liked, had kept a tight hand on the family finances. Such was her manner of living and lack of business sense, however, that when she died at Bath on 31 July 1762 she was virtually penniless except for a house in London which the brothers tried to sell under great difficulties. Cowper wrote to his cousin Harriot, now Lady Hesketh, to tell her that at his step-mother's death he had become thoroughly independent, which meant he had nothing to depend on! Jokingly he tells his cousin that he and his brother are to split their step-mother's fortune, which is like splitting a hair. He adds that as his brother is a logician and he is a lawyer, they ought both to be perfectly good at this task!

Though Cowper knew what it was to be seriously depressed, he
never let money matters get him down. Even in the letter quoted
above where he speaks of inheriting a 'split hair', he tells his cousin
that 'The comforts of life lie so near the ground, that we poor folks
are sure to find them.'[1] Writing to Clotworthy Rowley, a fellow
Templar, Cowper muses on the theory that one must be dishonest to
become rich and goes on to say, 'Upon the whole my dear Rowley,
there is a degree of Poverty that has no Disgrace belonging to it, that
degree of it I mean in which a man enjoys clean Linnen and good
Company, & if I never sink below this degree of it, I care not if I
never rise above it.'[2] Cowper also tells Rowley that he is resolved
never to be melancholy as long as he has a hundred pounds in his
pocket. It is here that we see how far Cowper is deviating from his
Christian upbringing and clinging to the stiff-upper-lip morals of his
classical training at school. In the same letter to Rowley, Cowper
writes that his ideas are those of the Stoics, and adds: 'Till the Stoics
became Coxcombs they were in my Opinion a very sensible sect.'
A later letter suggests that the hundred pounds that Cowper had in
his pocket at this time were borrowed.

Troubled by conscience

Cowper knew, however, that he was fooling himself. He was also
aware that he could not fool God. Full of remorse when looking back
on this period a few years later, Cowper writes,

> I obtained, at length, so complete a victory over my
> conscience, that all remonstrances from that quarter were in
> vain, and in a manner silenced, though sometimes, indeed, a
> question would arise in my mind, whether it were safe to
> proceed any further in a course so plainly and utterly
> condemned in the Scriptures. I saw clearly that if the Gospel
> were true, such a conduct must inevitably end in my
> destruction; but I saw not by what means I could change my
> Ethiopian complexion, or overcome such an inveterate habit
> of rebelling against God.

Such troubled thoughts moved Cowper to write,

Anxious as sad Offenders are,
Whose troubled days are spent
'Twixt Hope of Pardon, and the Fear
Of Final Punishment,

Is the poor Wretch whose Vital Heat
Diseases daily chill;
Whom Hopes of Life uncertain yet,
And Fears of Death assail.

O save me Lord! dispell my Fears!
Let this O God suffice,
Confound not thus my growing Years,
With Age's Miserys.

For ah, I feel and long have felt
What grief the Sick-Man knows,
In secret sorrowing for the Guilt,
From whence those Griefs arose.

When Health supply'd each steady Nerve,
And Vigour fill'd my Frame,
The Being I forgot to serve
From whom that Vigour came.

In Health tho' I despis'd the Fear,
The Thought of future Pain,
In Sickness let me not despair
To know that Health again.

Yes I will hope, for thou hast said,
Come to me ye distressed,
All ye that Labour, and are sad;
And I will give you rest.

O then my God I will repent,
Thy Burthen is but light,
Absence from thee is Banishment
And Heav'n is in thy Sight.

So often it pleases God to shake unrepentant sinners out of their complacency by means of non-Christians rather than Christians, especially if those sinners make some pretence at being 'pious'. Cowper, too, was to experience the voice of God from a most unexpected quarter. One day, when arguing 'half-intoxicated' with a Deist, Cowper claimed that the revelation in the Bible was true. The Deist interrupted Cowper's animated discourse by telling him plainly, ' If what you say is true, then you must certainly be damned by your own scheme.' This caused Cowper to take a little more care with his life and made him realize that God was still being patient with him.

This feeling was strengthened soon afterwards by an incident that Cowper felt had been staged especially for him. It was the end of the season and, like all the gentry, Cowper would leave London for the seaside to await the coming of the winter. Sometimes Cowper would spend the summer at Southampton, sometimes at New Barns on a friend's estate, sometimes at Margate or Maidenhead and sometimes on the estates of his namesake Earl Cowper or at Hertingfordbury at the home of another namesake Major William Cowper. This time he was staying at Brighton, or Brighthelmston, as the town was then called. He was walking along the cliff-edge when he saw a strange sight. A dog was guarding the sheep at some distance from the cliff. Suddenly the dog picked up a sheep by the scruff of its neck and ran, dragging it, at full speed to the cliff-edge. Cowper thought that both animals would be dashed to pieces but the dog stopped in its tracks on the very edge of the cliff. The frightened sheep stood trembling but the dog lay down patiently and calmly with his nose almost touching that of the sheep. Cowper saw this as an obvious warning. God was showing him the abyss on the edge of which he was living. After a while, the dog let the sheep go back to the flock. Cowper thought that this could mean that God was still giving him a chance. He thought this, but tells us that he did not act on it.

A candidate for a post in the House of Lords

Now Cowper began to grasp after the privileges of his family connections. He told a friend that if the Clerk of the Journals in the House of Lords died, Ashley Cowper would see to it that he got the post. Shortly afterwards the clerk did indeed die and his post became vacant. At the same time, William de Grey, married to Cowper's cousin Mary Cowper, resigned from his more senior posts as Reading Clerk and Clerk of the Committees to climb even higher.

Ashley called on William one day and invited him to go for a walk in the garden. As they were strolling along, Ashley offered him William de Grey's old posts. Completely dazzled at the chance of such a lucrative offer and thinking that he would be a made man though only thirty-one years of age, William accepted without hesitation. When he got back to his chambers, however, he saw the matter in quite a different light. He realized that the two posts entailed public work in the House of Lords in the course of which he would have to take down the minutes of the Lords' committee work and brief them on the wording of bills, acts and other papers of interest. This threw Cowper into a cold sweat and caused him to spend a whole week regretting his decision. He knew that he could not work under pressure and that such a post demanded the highest competence. He also knew that the post of Clerk of the Journals, which he had originally hoped for, did not entail public appearances and he felt that his legal abilities were more in keeping with such an office.

He therefore wrote a letter to Ashley begging him to accept his change of mind and suggesting that Matthew Arnot, a good friend of the family, should be given the other positions. Ashley agreed and informed the House that William was to become Clerk of the Journals and Arnot Reading Clerk and Clerk of Committees. William felt a great feeling of relief now that all was settled. His troubles, however, were just about to begin.

Ashley Cowper had not given the post of Clerk of Journals to the previous incumbent, Francis Macklay, out of the goodness of his heart, or because Macklay was especially gifted for the job. He had made a business deal and had sold Macklay the post in 1736 for £300, a tidy sum in those days. So, when Macklay died, his son, William Macklay, claimed the position as his own on the grounds that it was his father's property and he had inherited it.

Now the Cowpers belonged to the old Puritan and revolutionary party, the Whigs, and their star was somewhat waning in Parliament. What they took to be Ashley's high-handed manner gave the Conservatives a chance to get even with the Whigs for many an old score and they protested strongly at the sinecure privileges placed in the hands of the Cowper family. The clerkships themselves demanded that only those people should get the posts who were capable and that patenteeships should be abandoned. Thus William, who had wanted the easiest way out, found himself at the centre of great controversy. The matter was debated in the Lords and it was agreed that Cowper should be given the opportunity to appear before the Bar of the House and be examined publicly as to his abilities for the post. His dismay at this news is best expressed in his own words. 'A thunderbolt', he tells us, 'would have been as welcome to me as this intelligence.'

Cowper was now in real difficulties. The very idea of his appearing before the peers and being examined like a schoolboy scared him. He suspected the whole idea had been thought out to give the Lords a legal reason for doing away with the Cowper family's sinecures. They only needed to fail Ashley's candidates and non-Whigs could take their place. Cowper's first thought was to withdraw but then he thought of the honour of his family which was at stake. If he withdrew or failed the examination, the Cowpers would be done for as a political power. Furthermore the whole family urged him to take up the family banner and prepare himself for the task.

As the examination called for a specialized knowledge of the House's Journals Cowper got to work months before the examination to study them. The staff of the Journals Office, however, refused point blank to cooperate and offered him no assistance whatsoever. Every time Cowper entered the office he was greeted by cold, blank stares. 'The feelings of a man when he arrives at the place of execution,' Cowper tells us, 'are probably much like what I experienced every time I set my foot in the office, which was almost every day, near half a day together.'[3] The trouble was that Cowper had been given no idea at all about the contents of the examination and did not know just what he ought to study in particular.

A letter written to Lady Hesketh at this time tells us that Cowper spent his days reading about the journals and his nights dreaming about them. Though he strives to be light-hearted his fear breaks through. It is obvious that he is again turning his gaze on God and feeling what a disappointment he is. He tells his cousin, 'Certainly I am not an absolute fool; but I have more weaknesses than the greatest of all fools I can recollect at present. In short, if I was as fit for the next world, as I am unfit for this, and God forbid I should speak in vanity, I would not change conditions with any Saint in Christendom.'[4]

It was now the end of yet another season and Cowper set off for Margate to forget his woes for a month or two. The next time we hear from him personally is in a letter written to Joseph Hill on 24 June 1765, almost two years later. During this time Cowper had gone through the biggest crisis of his life and had been converted.

At Margate Cowper was at first plagued with frightening thoughts concerning his future but gradually, through 'cheerful company and a new scene', he began to recover his spirits and managed to drive all thoughts of the examination from his mind. In October, however, he returned to London for the final 'push', as he called it. By now he was fully aware that he was not fitted for the task before him but he dare not tell Ashley Cowper this for fear of bringing the family into ill-repute. Again his thoughts returned to God but only in a complaining way. One minute he would believe himself responsible for his own distress and the next minute he would cry out to God saying, 'What sins have I committed to deserve this misery?' He realized that only God could deliver him, but he did not believe that God would do so and therefore he did not ask. Instead Cowper turned to doctor after doctor to find a remedy. In his heart he felt that this was wrong and that he should go direct to God, comparing his own situation with that of Saul when he visited the witch at Endor instead of relying on the Lord.

He tried once more to pray and turned to the standard popular theological work of the day, *The Whole Duty of Man,* for prayer models. This work, called by Bishop Ryle, 'that mischievous and defective volume',[5] was to be found chained to the pews in many a parish church and was considered a fair exposition of the teaching of the Anglican Church of the day.[6] In reality the book was a reaction against Puritan doctrines and there is little basic Christianity regarding sin and salvation in it. There is, however, a strong stoic emphasis on ethics without personal holiness. George Whitefield said the author knew no more about Christianity than Mohammed, and when Henry Venn read it he was prompted to write his *The Complete Duty of Man,* which not only had an enormous influence on Evangelicals but became a best seller amongst the general reading public. Needless to say, *The Whole Duty of Man* failed to lead Cowper to Christ.

Attempts at suicide

Cowper now ceased to be rational and gave himself over to his hysterical fantasies. 'The only way out is madness,' he thought, and therefore longed to become insane. He became convinced that he was rapidly losing his senses but instead of fighting this, he craved for insanity with all his heart as a means of escape. He still felt that he was in complete control of his senses, which made him more desperate than ever to become insane.

Next he thought of suicide. His father had discussed the subject with him and Cowper now convinced himself that his father would have approved of it. He was thinking in Greek and Latin terms, whereby suicide was an honourable exit from the problems of this world. He was using Cato and Brutus as examples, instead of being guided by Scripture. He considered his life to be his own property, to be dispensed with as he, the owner, thought fit. Instead of seeking out his Christian friends and relations, Cowper went round the taverns and chop-houses seeking solace there. It seems that everyone he spoke to assured him that suicide was an honourable way out. It only dawned on Cowper a few years later that these false friends, who were so much in favour of self-murder, had not practised what they preached on themselves!

One evening in November, as soon as it was dark, Cowper, pretending to be in the best of spirits, went into a chemist's shop and asked for half an ounce of laudanum. It was just a week before the examination and he believed he knew how he was to die if nothing happened to spare him. The chemist looked suspiciously at Cowper, or so the candidate for suicide thought, but gave him a small phial of the drug.

During the following week, no relief came to Cowper. It was now the day before the examination and Cowper was breakfasting at a coffee-house in Fleet Street. Seeking diversion, he picked up a newspaper and began to read. It was then that his brain really began to snap. He had the idea that the author of the article had written it in the full knowledge that he would pick up the newspaper in that very coffee-house and read it. What Cowper read, or thought he read, was a mocking satire on his own life with the author urging him, daring him personally, to go and terminate it. Cowper rushed out of the coffee-house in a fit of passion saying to himself, 'Your cruelty shall be gratified; you shall have your revenge.' He wandered half a mile looking for a place where he could end his life.

Then suddenly he grew calmer and had the crazy idea of selling the little he had, travelling to France, becoming a Roman Catholic and finding a 'comfortable asylum' in a monastery. He went home to pack. Whilst packing, Cowper changed his mind again. How about drowning? His best friend had died that way. Cowper took a coach to the Tower Wharf, prepared to throw himself off the Custom House quay. When he reached the Thames, the tide was out and he gazed on yards of oozing mud. Besides there were porters sitting around as if placed especially there to stop Cowper's insane act — or so he told himself. He had himself driven back to the Temple. On the way Cowper pulled the shutters up and took out his phial of laudanum from his pocket. 'That should do the trick,' he thought. He put the phial to his lips, but he was paralysed with fear and hardly able to move. He managed to get a few drops onto his lips but was surprised to find that he was physically unable to pour the fluid down his throat.

He arrived home still alive and rushed to his rooms prepared to be successful at the cost of his life. He poured the laudanum into a basin, undressed and wrapped himself in the blankets staring at the basin and shaking with fear. He called himself a coward for not drinking the poison and, at the same time, seemed to be telling himself, 'Think what you are doing; consider and live.' Before Cowper could do anything further, he heard the key turn in the outer door of his rooms and a servant came in to see to some chores. Cowper got up, hid the basin and dressed himself. The servant left and Cowper began to realize what he had almost done. In disgust, he poured the poison into a bucket of dirty water and threw the phial out of the window.

He then spent several hours rethinking his situation but obtaining no peace. In the evening a friend called, congratulating him on the prospects of the following day. Apparently Cowper was able to talk to him with some semblance of cheerfulness. As soon as the friend left, Cowper went to bed and actually slept until three o'clock on the morning of his examination day. Then he got up, took his penknife, pointed it at his heart and forced it into his chest. The tip of the knife, however, was broken off and Cowper could not get the blade to penetrate.

Next he thought of his garters. He put a garter round his neck, and fixed it to the top of his iron bed-post. He lifted up his legs in order to swing freely and felt the noose tighten. The bed-post bent and the garter slipped off. Then Cowper thought of the doorway. The door

was a very high one so he climbed onto a chair, fixed the garter onto
the top of the door-case, put his head in the loop and kicked the chair
away. This was almost the end. He swung for a time and became
unconscious, but the garter could not stand the strain and broke —
just in time — and Cowper tumbled to the floor. He came to himself
lying face downwards. He had a dark crimson ring around his neck,
his eyes were swollen and bloodshot and one side of his face was
heavily bruised. The laundress had heard the noise and came in to
investigate. Cowper explained what had happened and sent her for
help.

Eventually Ashley was found sitting in a coffee-house and he
rushed to Cowper's chambers. As soon as he heard what had
happened, he exclaimed, 'My dear Mr Cowper, you terrify me to
death. To be sure you cannot hold the office at this rate.' Cowper
then tells us laconically in his *Memoir*, 'And thus ended all my
connection with the Parliament Office.'

Madness strikes

Cowper had longed for insanity and insanity had come, but in a form
that was not at all congenial to his plans. He had wanted a swift bout
of insanity that would serve him as an alibi for not taking the
examination before the Lords. Then he wanted to return to normal.
The idea was madness in itself. When insanity came to Cowper, in
God's providence, it came to stay for many months. Just as Saul had
to suffer the consequences of calling up the witch at Endor, so
Cowper now had to face the consequences of wishing madness
would overtake him. With the problem of the examination over,
Cowper had supposed he would gain peace once more. He was to be
severely disappointed.

For the first time in his life he experienced a deep conviction of
sin and an equally deep conviction that he needed salvation. He now
became full of self-reproach and despised himself utterly for the
meanness of his behaviour and for tempting God in such a way.
God's wrath became a frightening reality to him, coupled with an
overwhelming sense of being unable to flee from it, do what he
might.

The amazing thing about Cowper is that even when suffering
under the severest trials, he was able to express his thoughts in

words. He thus put his awful sense of doom into poetry. The ensuing verses have moved most critics to regard them as Cowper's first really great poem. This seems an ironic mockery as they portray the poet in the very depths of despair:

Hatred and Vengeance

Hatred and vengeance, my eternal portion,
Scarce can endure delay of execution—
Wait, with impatient readiness, to seize my
Soul in a moment.

Damn'd below Judas; more abhorr'd than he was,
Who, for a few pence, sold his holy master.
Twice betray'd, Jesus me, the last delinquent,
Deems the profanest.

Man disavows, and Deity disowns me.
Hell might afford my miseries a shelter;
Therefore hell keeps her ever hungry mouths all
Bolted against me.

Hard lot! Encompass'd with a thousand dangers,
Weary, faint, trembling with a thousand terrors,
Fall'n, and if vanquish'd, to receive a sentence
Worse than Abiram's:

Him, the vindictive rod of angry justice
Sent, quick and howling, to the centre headlong;
I, fed with judgments, in a fleshly tomb, am
Buried above ground.

By now Cowper was not just mentally but also physically very ill. Apart from his spiritual terrors, and his wild and haunting thoughts, he experienced constant flame-like flashings in front of his eyes and great hammering pains in his head.

Even in these days of torment, Cowper was not without good friends. One particular friend, most likely William Alston, cared for him faithfully throughout all his ravings. Even Cowper's London relations, who had suffered so much through his conduct, did not withdraw from him completely and invited him to their homes. He felt too ashamed, however, to confide in them too much though now he wanted with all his heart to talk to someone about his soul.

Then Cowper thought of his brother John at Cambridge who had already reached fame there. In his happier days, William and John had corresponded closely, writing all the time in rhyming verse. So William now wrote to John outlining all that had happened to him over the last months. Whilst waiting for a reply Cowper could not help meditating on the barren fig-tree and firmly believed that when Jesus put a curse on it, he had William Cowper especially in mind.

Once again Cowper turned to the wrong places for comfort. He read through 'all Archbishop Tillotson's sermons' and discussed them with John when he arrived. Tillotson's works[7] are similar in their spirituality to the contents of *The Whole Duty of Man*, which had previously failed to comfort him. Furthermore, unlike other members of the Cowper family who were real out-and-out Evangelicals or Methodists, such as Judith Cowper and the Madans, John could, at the most, be merely classified as 'God-fearing'. William was in fact to lead John to Christ some years later. Thus William received no comfort from Tillotson and none from his brother and could only moan, 'O Lord Thou didst vex me with all Thy storms, all thy billows went over me. In the day time thou didst run upon me like a giant; and in the night season Thou didst scare me with visions.'[8]

Cowper's state grew gradually worse. He began to lose his sense of balance and could only stagger around. He was frightened to show himself in public because he thought everybody was talking about him. If he heard a hawker, for instance, singing the ballads he was selling, Cowper believed that he was the topic of the songs. Wherever he went he was conscious that he was a sinner being closely watched by God but 'as yet', he tells us, 'I saw not a glimpse of the mercy of God in Jesus.'

By degrees, Cowper began to believe that he had committed the unpardonable sin against the Holy Spirit. He remembered the beautiful experience he had enjoyed at Southampton, where the Lord had filled his heart with peace and happiness. He remembered, also, that he had put the experience down to a mere change of air. Was this the sin against the Holy Spirit? Cowper was convinced it was.

John was amazed at what was going on in his brother's mind and decided to stay with him some time to help him. Whatever he said to comfort William proved in vain. Whatever William did to comfort himself proved equally futile. He tried to say the Creed, but forgot the words and took this to mean that God would not let him abuse the Creed by saying it. He began to howl in horror, shaking in all his parts and screaming at John, 'Oh brother, I am damned — damned. Think of eternity, and then think what it is to be damned.' Not yet knowing, as Cowper said later, that 'Christ was exalted to give repentance,' he despaired of ever attaining it.

At last William thought of Martin Madan and sent his brother to fetch him. 'I had been used to think of him an enthusiast,' Cowper explains in his *Memoir*, 'but now it seemed that if there was any "balm in Gilead" for me his hand must administer it.'

Now things went better for a time. Martin was found, after John had spent many hours searching for him, and rushed to his cousin's side. He saw at once what was wrong. For all his background, William was more than ignorant of the basic facts of salvation. He had a wrong view of sin and wrong views of righteousness and of grace. Martin began at the beginning. He spoke of how sin came into the world and how mankind fell. William began to listen intently. He had always regarded himself as quite different from every other man and now he realized that he was one of a whole fallen race. This gave him hope. If he were no different from the rest, and the rest could be saved, then he too could experience God's grace. Then Martin, using the Scriptures, pressed home to William the all-atoning efficacy of the blood of Jesus and his infinitely perfect righteousness for our justification. William began to weep, seeing clearly the remedy he needed. Now Martin urged the necessity of a lively personal faith in Jesus, who alone could work out God's plan of salvation in our lives. William could only cry out, 'I wish he would; I wish he would.'

Seeing that at last he was on the verge of finding the answer to all his problems, William begged Martin to arrange that he should live in his neighbourhood, so Martin hired lodgings for his cousin in a house next door to his own. There William was able to discuss the way of salvation further with his cousin and his assistant, Thomas Haweis. Cowper began to feel that salvation was near.

The move to St Albans

The next few days, however, found Cowper worse than ever. The pains in his head grew more and more severe, as did also his nightmares and visions. He became wild and incoherent and lost control over his mind completely. The only thoughts that came to him for several days were a sense of sin and a feeling of doom. Otherwise he could feel only darkness and pain as if his brain were being perpetually beaten.

John, Martin and Thomas consulted one another and decided that William must be put into an asylum. They chose Dr Nathaniel Cotton's *Collegium Insanorum* at St Albans and they could not have made a better choice. Nathaniel Cotton (1705-88) had been educated chiefly in Holland at Leyden and by this time was well known for his compassionate and often successful treatment of the mentally ill. So often in those days, mentally ill people were merely shut away from the world in establishments like Bedlam where they hardly received any medical, spiritual or humanitarian care at all. Cotton, a friend of Edward Young and the Countess of Huntingdon, believed in providing a Christian home for his patients in which they could find peace and rest. He thus kept the number of those in his care to between five and twenty, so that the feeling of being in a family might remain. His 'college' was a spacious Elizabethan building and stood in pleasant grounds. Though he did not force the Christian gospel on his patients, Cotton made sure that Bibles were available in most rooms and that his patients had ample opportunity to have spiritual conversations with him. Apart from being a first-class doctor, Cotton had made quite a name for himself as a poet and prose writer.

When John and Martin told William that they had decided to send him to Dr Cotton's, he refused point blank to go. 'Do you think I am mad?', he said. 'What business have I with Dr Cotton, or he with me?' He then asked John if he thought it would do him good and when John replied most emphatically in the affirmative, he relented.

A few minutes later he was suddenly overcome by joy and found himself thanking God on his knees. The coach trip to St Albans was a strange one indeed. William and John sat together. William, who was ill, was quite composed and full of joy. John, who was well, was nervous and terrified because of the change in his brother and what might lie ahead. It was as well that both brothers were already slightly known to Dr Cotton, otherwise at their arrival he would have thought that John was the patient and William his escort.

Once again William's mood was to change in a twinkling. On their arrival at the hospital, it was thought best to put the patient into solitary confinement. Now whether ill or healthy, Cowper always dreaded being in a locked room and his relations and friends were well aware of this. He could work for hours in the tiniest of rooms, as he did later when composing his poetry—if he knew the door was only on the latch. If he were in a palace hall and knew the door was locked, he experienced claustrophobia. It took three or four strong men to get Cowper into the cell and for some time afterwards it took as many to get him out again.

Cowper felt as if he were a condemned criminal in prison awaiting execution and resolved once more to take his life. Although his warders kept an eagle eye on him, they failed to prevent his discovery of a long knitting needle in the ashes of his fire. Cowper managed to stick it behind the wallpaper and awaited his chance. That night he took the needle and plunged it into his heart. As a bone got in the way he plunged it in time and time again until the needle broke on his ribs. When the deed was discovered Cowper was watched day and night but he remained more or less out of his mind for eight months.[9]

Deliverance at last

The pendulum of Cowper's temperament slowly began to swing back towards normal. He realized this through his hallucinations. At first they were all evil and threatening, but gradually the pictures he saw in his delirium took on a more positive shape. One evening when he was pacing backwards and forwards in his room he had a vision of such exquisite heavenly beauty that he could only cry out, 'Bless me; I see a glory all around me.'

Gradually Cowper was allowed to go out of doors on his own and he found that the talks with Dr Cotton were doing him good. This news was sent to John Cowper in June 1764 so John immediately visited his brother. William noticed the look of disappointment on his face when they met. John had expected to see his brother fit and well. On asking William how he was, John received the answer, 'As much better as despair can make me.' John could not hold back his feelings and protested strongly at his brother's attitude, telling him that it was all a delusion. This touched William greatly who said, 'If it be a delusion then am I the happiest of beings.' After that William became more cheerful, constantly occupying his thoughts with the words: 'Still there is mercy.'

That night Cowper slept well and had the loveliest of dreams. He awoke more refreshed than he had been for many months. Before breakfast he went for a walk in the garden and found a Bible on a bench. He started to read and found he was reading the story of the raising of Lazarus from the dead. 'I saw so much benevolence and mercy,' he later wrote, 'so much goodness and sympathy with miserable mankind in our Saviour's conduct as melted my heart.' Then he adds, 'Little did I know that it was an exact type of the mercy which Jesus was upon the point of extending towards myself. I sighed and said, "Oh that I had not rejected so good a Redeemer! that I had not forfeited all His favour!"'

Cowper went to breakfast and felt a change coming over him. He felt lighter and was almost happy. After breakfast he continued to muse on the change he was experiencing yet he was frightened to hope too much as he knew that he was capable of extremes of feeling. The dark clouds were, however, departing and soon Cowper would see the sunshine of God's smiling face.

What happened next is best told in Cowper's own words:

> The happy period that was to strike off my fetters and to afford me a clear opening into the free mercy of the Blessed God in Jesus was now arrived. I flung myself into a chair near the window seat and, seeing a Bible there, ventured once more to apply to it for comfort and instruction. The first verse I saw was the twenty-fifth of the third chapter to the Romans where Jesus is set forth as the propitiation for our sins. Immediately I received strength to believe it. Immediately the full beams of the sun of righteousness shone upon me. I saw the sufficiency of the atonement He had made, my pardon sealed in His blood, and all the fullness and completeness of my justification. In a moment I believed and received the Gospel. Whatsoever my friend Madan had said to me so long before recurred to me with the clearest evidence of its truth, 'with demonstration of the Spirit and with power'.

Unless the Almighty Arm had been under me I think I should have died with gratitude and joy. My eyes filled with tears and my voice was choked with transport. I could only look up to Heaven in silence, overwhelmed with love and wonder! But the work of the Holy Ghost is best described in His own words. It was 'joy unspeakable and full of glory'. Thus was my Heavenly Father in Christ Jesus pleased to give me the full assurance of faith at once, and out of a stony and unbelieving heart to raise up a child unto Abraham.

After this great experience Cowper spent many weeks in praise and prayer, his heart overflowing. Dr Cotton did not know what to believe, at first, and examined him intensively concerning what had happened. Soon, however, he became convinced that a great work of God had occurred in his patient's life and that Cowper was not only now converted but also cured of his insanity.

Such was the friendship of the two men that neither wanted to become separated from the other so Cowper stayed on at St Albans another year. During this time Cowper studied the Scriptures diligently, read a large number of biblical studies by men such as Walter Marshall and poured out his praise to God in verse. The following hymn is Cowper's very first testimony of the change that the Lord had wrought in him.

Behold I Make All Things New

How blest thy creature is, O God!
When with a single Eye,
He views the lustre of thy Word,
The day spring from on high.

Thro' all the storms that vail the skies
And frown on earthly things;
The Sun of Righteousness he Eyes
With healing on his wings.

Struck by that light, the Human heart,
A barren soil no more,
Sends the sweet smell of Grace abroad,
Where Serpents lurk'd before.

The soul a dreary province once,
Of Satan's dark domain;
Feels a new empire form'd within,
And owns an heav'nly reign.

The glorious orb whose golden beams,
The fruitful year controul
Since first obedient to thy word,
He started from the Goal;

Has chear'd the nations with the joys
His orient rays impart,
But Jesus, 'tis thy light alone,
Can shine upon the heart.

Now that Cowper was cured and converted he began to think about where he should live and how he should occupy his time. He was still Commissioner of Bankrupts and this post alone would have sufficed to provide him with a livelihood. The commissioner did not merely receive the £60 remuneration per annum, but was also able to obtain a percentage of goods confiscated when their owners could not pay their debts. But now Cowper was a Christian he felt that sinecure posts, and especially posts that made the owner rich at the expense of impoverishing others, were sinful. He thus decided to give up the office, believing that he would rather starve than deliberately offend his Saviour. The words of Isaiah were a great comfort to him: 'He that walketh righteously ... he shall dwell on high: his place of defence shall be the munitions of rocks: bread shall be given him; his waters shall be sure.'[10]

Feeling that there was no purpose in returning to London, Cowper asked his brother to find lodgings for him near Cambridge. Rooms were found for him at Huntingdon, sixteen miles from Cambridge and in June 1765, eighteen months after arriving at St Albans, Cowper left to face the future as a child of God.

4.
New and lasting friendships

Jim Styles, in his *The Story of Squire Cowper,* suggests that the nicest epitaph for Cowper would be the words: 'In all his troubles he never lacked a friend.' This was the kind of man Cowper was. Not only in his troubles, but also in the many seasons of joy he experienced, he found people who loved, respected and admired him to a high degree.

Of course, Cowper did his best to cultivate such friendships. He was very choosy with his friends, but once they were established as such, they could depend on him to be an exceedingly faithful companion. Friendship for Cowper should always be a 'do-as-you-would-be-done-by' relationship. He thought that those who do not strive to make a friendship work themselves cannot expect their so-called friends to make an effort. Thus Cowper ends his long essay in poetry on the subject with the self-admonishing words:

Oh Friendship! if my soul forego
Thy dear delights while here below;
To mortify and grieve me,
May I myself at last appear
Unworthy, base and insincere,
Or may my friend deceive me!

For Cowper, true friendship was true bliss and this could only be obtained where the would-be friends were brothers in Christ. He expresses his feelings on this subject in his long poem 'Conversation':

True bliss, if man may reach it, is compos'd
Of hearts in union mutually disclos'd;
And, farewell else all hope of pure delight,
Those hearts should be reclaim'd, renew'd, upright.
Bad men, profaning friendship's hallow'd name,
Form, in its stead, a covenant of shame,
A dark confed'racy against the laws
Of virtue, and religion's glorious cause...
But souls that carry on a blest exchange
Of joys they meet with in their heav'nly range,
And with a fearless confidence make known
The sorrows sympathy esteems its own,
Daily derive increasing light and force
From such communion in their pleasant course,
Feel less the journey's roughness and its length,
Meet their opposers with united strength,
And, one in heart, in int'rest and design,
Gird up each other to the race divine.[1]

Even non-Christians were moved to be their very best in Cowper's presence. One man, who loved and admired Cowper with all his heart was William Hayley, the poet's first biographer. Hayley loved Cowper's company partly because he always found himself on his best behaviour when he was with the poet. Writing of 'those tender and temperate passions in their purest state' that were awakened in people who were with Cowper, he says, 'It may be questioned, if any mortal could be more sincerely beloved and revered, than Cowper was by those, who were best acquainted with his private hours.' Such testimonies are numerous.

It was during the springtime of his new faith at Huntingdon that Cowper was to gain friends who would remain such all their lives. Some would disappoint him at times and he would disappoint them, but good friends they remained. At least five of the friends Cowper made at Huntingdon became closer to him than a brother and offered him a selfless devotion that has rarely been equalled.

Joseph Hill

Now that Cowper was a changed man in different circumstances, he felt little drawn to the company of his former Nonsense Club friends.

It is also equally true to say that Cowper's former acquaintances felt little drawn to him. There was one great exception — Joseph Hill (1733-1811).

Hill had studied law and had got off to a good start as a clerk in Chancery Lane. He quickly climbed up the careers ladder, becoming a solicitor, then an attorney, then a sworn clerk in Chancery and finally Secretary to the Lord Chancellor and, ironically enough, Secretary of Lunatics. He managed to build up a clientele of very rich business people who made him rich in return. Hill was to become Cowper's financial manager and always found money for the poet when the latter was in need. More than a little of this money obviously came from Hill's own pocket.

After twenty-five years of unbroken friendship, Cowper wrote his 'An Epistle to Joseph Hill Esq', in which he tells the story of an Eastern emperor who punishes friendship-breakers by forcing them to go about bare-chested in all weathers so that everybody would know that 'All was naught within, and all found out.' Thinking of those friends who had deserted him and of Hill who had remained faithful, Cowper goes on to write,

> Oh, happy Britain! we have not to fear
> Such hard and arbitrary measure here;
> Else, could a law like that which I relate
> Once have the sanction of our triple state,
> Some few that I have known in days of old,
> Would run most dreadful risk of catching cold;
> While you, my friend, whatever wind should blow,
> Might traverse England safely to and fro,
> An honest man, close-button'd to the chin,
> Broad-cloth without, and a warm heart within.

Hill had looked after Cowper's affairs during his illness and rescued what he could of Cowper's property, including his cat. This had been a difficult task as when Cowper was taken to St Albans a complete stranger had occupied his chambers at the Temple without permission and had taken the liberty of doing what he wished with Cowper's belongings. Much of Cowper's legal literature and poetic writings, including all his rhyming correspondence with his brother, disappeared at this time never more to be found. It was thus fitting that Joseph Hill was one of the very first old friends to whom Cowper wrote after leaving St Albans.

His letter also shows how he treasured friendship and someone near him whom he could trust. Whilst at St Albans, Cowper had been given a servant, Samuel Roberts, who had begged the poet to make him his personal servant after leaving the hospital. Cowper explains in his letter why he granted Roberts his wish:

Dear Joe,
The only Recompense I can make you for your friendly Attention to my Affairs, during my Illness, is to tell you that by the Mercy of God I am restored to perfect Health both of Mind and Body. This I believe will give you Pleasure, and I would gladly do any thing from which you may receive it.

I left St. Albans on the 17th., arrived that day at Cambridge, spent some time there with my Brother, and came hither on the 22d. I have a Lodging that puts me continually in mind of our Summer Excursions; we have had many worse, and except the Size of it which however is sufficient for a single Man, but few better. I am not quite alone, having brought a Servant with me from St. Albans, who is the very Mirrour of Fidelity and Affection for his Master. And whereas the Turkish Spy[2] says he kept no Servant because he would not have an Enemy in his House, I hired mine because I would have a Friend. Men do not usually bestow these Encomiums upon their Lacqueys, nor do they usually deserve them, but I have had Experience of mine both in Sickness and Health and never saw his Fellow.[3]

Samuel Roberts was not the only person Cowper took with him to Huntingdon. At St Albans he had rescued a six-year-old boy from being totally neglected by his drunkard father. Cowper adopted the boy and arranged for him to be educated. Joseph Hill' wrote to Cowper asking for more details about the boy and the poet replied:

I drew yesterday for Mr. Unwin's Money; and when I have drawn about 6£ more for the Young Gentleman's Maintenance whose Birth and Parentage you inquire after, I shall have drawn my last for the present.

He is the Son of a drunken Cob[b]ler at St. Albans, who would probably have starved him to death by this time or have poisoned him with Gin, if Providence had not thrown it in my way to rescue him. I was glad of an Opportunity to shew some Mercy in a place where I had received so much, and hope God will give a Blessing to my Endeavours to preserve him. He is a fine Boy, of a good Temper and Understanding, and if the Notice that is taken of him by the Neighbours here don't spoil him, will probably turn out well. His Name is Richard Colman; for further particulars enquire of Dr. Cotton.

At present I have thoughts of dealing with him much after the same Manner when he is a Year or two Older, as I do with my present Servant. He will be about Nine Years of Age when my Man leaves me, at which time I think of taking him into my Service, for he will be old enough to do all the Business for which I shall want him, and of a right Age to be taught the Trade and Mystery of a Breeches' Maker. This though not so cheap a way as keeping no Servant, will yet be a considerable Saving to me, for I shall have but one to maintain instead of two, and in the mean time an Advantage will result from it not to be overlooked, the Securing him I mean from ill Example and bad Company, which if I turn him quite loose into another Family, cannot be so easily done. But after all, my Measures in this Instance and in all others, are precarious things, because my Income is so, but God will order All for the best.[4]

Cowper's optimism concerning the boy proved vain. Richard Coleman grew up to be an 'utterly good-for-nothing' and proved a great burden on Cowper's heart and pocket. On becoming an adult Coleman thought he had no other obligations towards Cowper than to allow himself, his wife and child to be housed, fed and clothed at the poet's expense.

Such acts of benevolence were to become commonplace in Cowper's life and, wherever he lived, one could be sure that there would also be a number of children rejected by their parents, manservants who brought all their family with them and friends visiting, accompanied by their servants. Lady Hesketh was to write on this subject to another member of the family in 1793 saying, 'I shall be glad if you will write to me as soon as you can, by return of post if possible, and let me know as much as you can of the present state of the family? … I have this Summer given him [Cowper] hints of the many *idle people* his unbounded liberality helped to make such, and of ye *swarms* who lived in his kitchen, but he took no

notice of this.'⁵ As Lady Hesketh was helping to pay for the needs
of these 'swarms', we can perhaps understand her anxiety.

Up to this time Cowper had been used to living in comparative
luxury, taking his meals in inns and coffee-houses and being
dressed, groomed and cared for by skilled servants. When he wished
to have anything special to eat, or, for instance, received presents of
game from his brother, he would send the food to a local inn and have
it cooked for him. Now he had very little income and had to learn to
look after his own housekeeping. As Roberts had no idea how to
cook, this task was left to Cowper, who informed Hill in his second
letter how he was coping — or rather, not coping.

Dear Joe,
    Whatever you may think of the Matter it is no such easy
thing to keep House for two People. A Man cannot always
live upon Sheeps' Heads and Liver & Lights like the Lions in
the Tower, and a Joint of Meat in so small a Family is an
endless Incumbrance. My Butcher's Bill for last Week
amounted to four Shillings & Ten pence — I set off with a Leg
of Lamb, & was forced to give part of it away to my Washer
woman; then I made an Experiment upon a Sheep's Heart,
and that was too little; next, I put three pounds of Beef into a
Pye, and This had like to have been too much, for it lasted
three days tho' my Landlord was admitted to a Share in it.
Then as to Small Beer, I am puzzled to pieces about it. I have
bought as much for a Shilling as will serve us at least a Month,
and it is grown sower [sour] already. In short I never knew
how to pity poor Housekeepers before, but now I cease to
wonder at that Politic Cast which their Occupation usually
gives to their Countenance, for it is really a Matter full of
Perplexity.⁶

The Madans

Now that Cowper was converted, he got in touch with the members
of his family whom he had neglected for years.

Amongst the first to whom Cowper turned was his aunt, Judith
Madan, neé Cowper, who was a close friend of the Countess of
Huntingdon and looked to John Wesley as her spiritual father. Her

daughter Maria Cowper, neé Madan, became another correspondent of Cowper's. Maria gave up a promising career as an actress to turn to Christ and put her brilliant linguistic skills (she had acted in Racine's *Athalie* in French) to use for the spread of the gospel.

Of course, Cowper did not neglect to keep in touch with Martin Madan, his cousin, to whom he could now write as a brother in Christ. He wrote to Madan immediately on settling down in Huntingdon. His letter is a happy confession of thanks to his cousin for all his assistance in paving the way for his conversion and is a sure statement of his new-found faith. Cowper writes,

My Dear Martin,

I have long had a desire to write to you, indeed ever since it pleased God to restore to me the perfect health both of my mind and body; and have with difficulty prevailed upon myself to defer it 'till I had left St. Albans. I have suppressed my impatience to do it hitherto in the full persuasion that a letter from me in a state of *enlargement* would be more acceptable to you, than anything I could send from that *suspected* quarter. Blessed be God! I am indeed *enlarged*, and you, who know so well the Spiritual as well as ordinary import of *that* word, will easily apprehend how much I mean to crowd into it. Martin, I have never forgot, nor ever shall forget, the instruction you gave me at our Interview in my chambers. It was the first lesson of the kind I had ever heard with attention, perhaps I may say, the first I ever had heard at all — And notwithstanding the terrible disorder of mind I fell into soon after, not all the thousand deliriums that afflicted me have been able to efface it. My heavenly Father intended it should be to me an earnest of His love, which is the reason I have not lost it, but by His blessing upon it, it has been a key to me, together with the assistance of His grace, to right understanding of the Scriptures ever since. I bless His holy name for every sigh, and every groan, and every tear I have shed in my illness. He woundeth and His hands make whole — they heal the wounds which He Himself hath made for our chastizement, and those deeper wounds which by our sins we have inflicted upon ourselves.

You remember the poor wretch[7] whose illness so much

resembled mine, and you remember too how he was seen
'Clothed, and in his right mind, and sitting at the feet of Jesus'
— I thank God I resemble him in my recovery, and in the
blessed effects of it, as well as in my distemper. Pray for me,
Martin, that I ever may, and believe me that I suppress much
lest I should alarm even you by the warmth of my
expressions; but you might read it in my eyes.

Give my love to all your family, and to your mother.

Yours Martin very thankfully and very affectionately

W. C.[8]

One notable feature of this letter is that Cowper looks at all that
has happened to him as coming from the hand of God. He saw God
at work, remoulding him, even in his illness. This is a sobering
thought for today's believers. We so often hear so-called
evangelicals claiming that there is no divine healing purpose in
illness and that sickness is merely due to lack of faith. Cowper
gained faith through sickness. The poet was to stress this time and
time again when referring to his conversion. In later life he was
always conscious of the hand of God at work, no matter whether he
was going through a high mountain experience or suffering in the
deep valley.

At this time Cowper describes his conversion experience in
verse. His words have not the poetic beauty of later testimonies to
his conversion but in simple, stark language he leaves no facts
uncovered:

A Song of Mercy and Judgment

Lord, I love the Habitation
Where the Saviour's Honour dwells;
At the Sound of thy Salvation
With Delight my Bosom swells.
Grace Divine, how sweet the Sound,
Sweet the grace which I have found.

Me thro' Waves of deep Affliction,
Dearest Saviour! thou hast brought,

Fiery Deeps of sharp Conviction
Hard to bear and passing Thought.
Sweet the Sound of Grace Divine,
Sweet the grace which makes me thine.

From the cheerful Beams of Morning
Sad I turn'd mine Eyes away:
And the Shades of Night returning
Fill'd my Soul with new Dismay.
Grace Divine, how sweet the Sound
Sweet the grace which I have found.

Food I loath'd nor ever tasted
But by Violence constrain'd.
Strength decay'd and Body wasted,
Spoke the Terrors I sustain'd.
Sweet the Sound of Grace Divine,
Sweet the grace which made me thine.

Bound and watch'd, Lest life abhorring
I should my own Death procure,
For to me the Pit of Roaring
Seem'd more easy to endure.
Grace Divine, how sweet the Sound,
Sweet the grace which I have found.

Fear of Thee, with gloomy Sadness,
Overwhelm'd thy guilty Worm,
'Till reduced to moping Madness
Reason sank beneath the Storm.
Sweet the sound of Grace Divine,
Sweet the grace which made thee mine.

Then what Soul-distressing Noises
Seem'd to reach me from below,
Visionary Scenes and Voices,
Flames of Hell and Screams of woe.
Grace Divine, how sweet the Sound,
Sweet the grace which I have found.

But at length a Word of Healing
Sweeter than an Angel's Note,
From the Saviour's Lips distilling
Chas'd Despair and chang'd my Lot.
Sweet the sound of Grace Divine,
Sweet the grace which made me thine.

'Twas a Word well tim'd and suited
To the Need of such an Hour,
Sweet to One like me polluted,
Spoke in Love and seal'd with Pow'r.
Grace Divine, how sweet the Sound,
Sweet the grace which I have found.

'I,' He said, 'have seen thee grieving,
Lov'd thee as I pass'd thee by;
Be not faithless, but Believing,
Look, and Live, and never Die.'
Sweet the Sound of Grace Divine,
Sweet the grace which makes me thine.

'Take the Bloody Seal I give thee,
Deep impress'd upon thy Soul,
God, thy God, will now receive thee,
Faith hath sav'd thee, thou art Whole.'
Grace Divine, how sweet the Sound,
Sweet the grace which I have found.

All at once my Chains were broken,
From my Feet my Fetters fell,
And that Word in Pity spoken,
Snatch'd me from the gates of Hell.
Grace Divine, how sweet the Sound,
Sweet the grace which I have found.

Since that Hour, in Hope of Glory,
With thy Foll'wers I am found,
And relate the wond'rous Story
To thy list'ning saints around.
Sweet the sound of Grace Divine
Sweet the grace which makes me thine.

From now on Cowper's ambition was to be 'useful', as he put it, in relating the wondrous story. How he was to accomplish this, he still did not know.

Harriot Hesketh

Another friend who was to show Cowper lasting affection and loyalty was his cousin Harriot Hesketh. Harriot was Ashley Cowper's daughter and sister to Theadora. She had always been very fond of Cowper and her letters show that she had been very near to falling in love with him. She was warm, affectionate and kind but extremely fussy and she tended to be rather hysterical.

It is difficult to judge the depth of Lady Hesketh's faith in Christ though she knew her Bible extremely well. She was a sturdy defender of the Church of England and had a constant suspicion of anything that might be critical of the church and the monarchy. It has been repeatedly emphasized that she had an aversion to any labels such as 'Enthusiast', 'Methodist', or even 'Calvinist' and strove to argue that Cowper was none of all three. She did this, however, at a time when both Calvinists and Arminians in all denominations were claiming Cowper as their own and arguing amongst themselves. She felt this was doing great harm to the poet's memory and message. Lady Hesketh's allegiance to the Church of England, however, did not stop her from criticizing its clergy, and especially the bishops, for teaching mere 'ethics' rather than preaching the full gospel. Writing to John Johnson, a relation very dear to Cowper, who had recently been ordained to the Anglican ministry, Lady Hesketh says,

> My dear Johnny
>   allow me pray to recommend if you won't think me Impertinent, Sermons by that best of men the late Bishop of Sodar and Man, Dr. Wilson, they are not Eloquent nor at all fine writing, but they seem to me to be just what all sermons ought to be, level to all Capacitys and containing exactly in plain, good sound language the Important Truths of the Gospel, which you I trust dear Johnny will always preach — you know I am no Methodist — neither was Dr. Wilson, but I am always sorry when the Clergy indulge themselves in *mere moral* Essays which are always to be found in better

language in Addison's 'Spectator', and can never certainly be called *Sermons*; the great Duty of the Clergy is to explain and insist on the great truths of Christianity, and to rest simply on the beauty of Virtue, and moral Rectitude will never do in the Pulpit — That Christ dy'd for our sins and that we are to accept Him as a Saviour, is the great Truth on which every thing turns and where this is neglected we make Him *Dye in Vain*.

Excuse me my good friend having got so much out of my line and out of my Depth and consider what I have said as arising principally from the mention of these Books as well as of the Sincere regard I have for you and my earnest wish to see you useful in your profession which will be always a real pleasure.[9]

Cowper's letters to Lady Hesketh contain some of the finest testimonies to the poet's faith that he ever wrote. Although John Newton was to become Cowper's closest correspondent in matters of theology, the poet always looked to Newton as a monitor in the faith and his own spiritual counsellor. There was thus often a stiffness, brought about by an honest respect for Newton, in Cowper's letters to him. It was to Newton, more than any other correspondent, that Cowper poured out his heart when troubles assailed him. With Lady Hesketh the relationship was quite different. With her Cowper was always gallant, at ease and his everyday, natural self. He never knew just where she stood in matters of faith and the Christian advice and teaching he gave her was always gently and succinctly put and very much to the point. It was usually, however, presented in such a homely, even humorous way, that it was impossible for Lady Hesketh to feel that her cousin was 'preaching' at her.

Cowper's conversion was obviously the theme of his first letters to his cousin from Huntingdon. This was always coupled with thanks to God for the Christian friends he had found. To Lady Hesketh he writes, for instance:

How happy it is to believe with a steadfast assurance, that our petitions are heard even while we are making them — and how delightful to meet with a proof of it in the effectual and actual grant of them! Surely it is a gracious finishing given to those means, which the Almighty has been pleased to make use of for my conversion — after having been deservedly rendered unfit for any society, to be again qualified for it, and admitted at once into the fellowship of those, whom God regards as the excellent of the earth, and whom, in the emphatical language of Scripture, he preserves as the apple of his eye, is a blessing, which carries with it the stamp and visible superscription of divine bounty — a grace unlimited as undeserved; and, like its glorious Author, free in its course, and blessed in its operation!

My dear Cousin! Health and happiness, and above all, the favour of our great and gracious Lord attend you! While we seek it in spirit and in truth, we are infinitely more secure of it than of the next breath we expect to draw. Heaven and earth have their destined periods, ten thousand worlds will vanish at the consummation of all things, but the word of God standeth fast, and they who trust in him shall never be confounded.

My love to all who enquire after me.

Yours affectionately,

W.C.[10]

Cowper had two problems to contend with in Lady Hesketh. On the one hand, her high regard and admiration for her cousin had led her to feel that he was a true Christian before his illness. On the other hand, she felt that the suffering Cowper had gone through stood in no logical relationship to a conversion according to the Scriptures. Thus Cowper had to convince his cousin that he had been a worse character than she believed and that God must often chastise stubborn hearts until they repent. Dealing with Lady Hesketh's first problem, Cowper wrote,

You think I always believed, and I thought so too, but you were deceived, and so was I. I called myself indeed a Christian, but he who knows my heart knows that I never did a right thing, nor abstained from a wrong one, because I was so. But if I did either, it was under the influence of some other motive. And it is such seeming Christians, such pretending believers, that do most mischief to the cause, and furnish the strongest arguments to support the infidelity of its enemies:

unless profession and conduct go together, the man's life is
a lie, and the validity of what he professes itself is called in
question. The difference between a Christian and an
Unbeliever would be so striking, if the treacherous allies of
the Church would go over at once to the other side, that I am
satisfied religion would be no loser by the bargain.[11]

Cowper was to write time and time again about such 'treacherous
allies' within the church, who were confessors of the Word but not
doers of it. These 'insiders' were far more dangerous to the Christian
cause, the poet always argued, than 'outsiders', who would only
mock the church because of the Judases within it.

Explaining the part his illness had played in his conversion was
a more difficult matter. Striving to make this plain, the poet tells his
cousin shortly after leaving St Albans:

Since the visit you were so kind as to pay me in the Temple
(the only time I ever saw you without pleasure), what have I
not suffered? And since it has pleased God to restore me to the
use of my reason, what have I not enjoyed? You know by
experience, how pleasant it is to feel the first approaches of
health after a fever; but, Oh the fever of the brain! To feel the
quenching of that fire is indeed a blessing which I think it
impossible to receive without the most consummate
gratitude. Terrible as this chastizement is, I acknowledge in
it the hand of an infinite justice; nor is it at all more difficult
for me to perceive in it the hand of an infinite mercy likewise,
when I consider the effect it has had upon me. I am
exceedingly thankful for it, and, without hypocrisy, esteem it
the greatest blessing, next to life itself, I ever received from
the divine bounty. I pray God that I may ever retain this sense
of it, and then I am sure I shall continue to be as I am at present,
really happy.

I write thus to you that you may not think me a forlorn and
wretched creature; which you might be apt to do, considering
my very distant removal from every friend I have in the world
— a circumstance which, before this event befel[l] me, would
undoubtedly have made me so; but my affliction has taught
me a road to happiness which without it I should never have
found; and I know, and have experience of it every day, that

the mercy of God, to him who believes himself the object of it, is more than sufficient to compensate for the loss of every other blessing.

You may now inform all those whom you think really interested in my welfare, that they have no need to be apprehensive on the score of my happiness at present. And you yourself will believe that my happiness is no dream, because I have told you the foundation on which it is built. What I have written would appear like enthusiasm to many, for we are apt to give that name to every warm affection of the mind in others, which we have not experienced in ourselves; but to you, who have so much to be thankful for, and a temper inclined to gratitude, it will not appear so.[12]

Cowper had one more burden on his mind that he felt he must share with his cousin. He wanted so much to be useful as a witness to Christ's saving grace, but felt constantly that he was by nature ill-equipped for the task. He was rather shaken, for instance, by the thought that people might be suspicious of the witness of a former inmate of an asylum. He thus wrote to Lady Hesketh,

It gives me some concern, though at the same time it increases my gratitude, to reflect that a convert made in Bedlam is more likely to be a stumbling-block to others, than to advance their faith. But if it has that effect upon any, it is owing to their reasoning amiss, and drawing their conclusions from false premises. He who can ascribe an amendment of life and manners, and a reformation of the heart itself, to madness, is guilty of an absurdity that in any other case would fasten the imputation of madness upon himself; for by so doing, he ascribes a reasonable effect to an unreasonable cause, and a positive effect to a negative.[13]

Lady Hesketh's correspondence with her cousin became sporadic for several years as she accompanied her husband on his travels abroad in pursuit of better health. The couple eventually settled down in Italy for a few years but Sir Thomas Hesketh became increasingly ill. When Sir Thomas, who had been a good friend of Cowper's during his Temple days, died in 1778, he left the poet a legacy of £100. After making her home in England again, Lady

Hesketh became a favourite of the royal family and spent a great deal of time in court and literary circles. She reopened regular contact with Cowper, now become famous, in 1785.

Mrs Thrale, friend of Dr Samuel Johnson, described Lady Hesketh as having 'more Beauty than almost any body, as much Wit as many a body; and six times the quantity of polite Literature'. She added, however, 'I can never find out what that woman does to keep the people from adoring her.'[14] In a better mood and in another connection, Mrs Thrale wrote, 'A friend may often be found and lost but an *old friend* never can be found, and nature has provided that he cannot easily be lost.'[15] Such was Lady Hesketh's friendship for Cowper. It could not be easily lost, and the poet often had reason to thank God after she returned into his life during the eighties.

Lady Hesketh had one weakness, however. She was extremely stubborn and believed she knew best what was good for other people, including Cowper, who told her from experience, 'I know well, my cousin, how formidable a creature you are when you become once outrageous. No sprat in a storm is half so terrible.'[16] In his youth Cowper had playfully 'snapped his fingers' at Lady Hesketh's tantrums but as a sixty-five-year-old he had neither the strength nor the ability to prevail against her iron will. As a result Lady Hesketh, who insisted on making all Cowper's plans for him from 1793 until his death in 1800, made the poet as unhappy then as she had made him happy in their youth.

The Unwins

After living for two months in Huntingdon, Cowper was to find two friends who became like old friends to him almost from the moment of meeting them. A young theological student by the name of William Unwin had observed Cowper at church on several occasions and was very impressed by his conduct. He approached Cowper one Sunday after the morning service and opened conversation with him. The poet, immediately struck by the young man's honest character, invited him to tea. The two found they shared the same faith and agreed to meet again.

Cowper recorded this meeting in glowing words in his *Memoir*, writing,

To my inexpressible joy I found him one whose notions of religion were spiritual and lively, one whom the Lord had trained from his infancy for the service of the temple. We opened our hearts to each other at the first interview, and when we parted I immediately retired to my chamber and prayed the Lord who had been the Author to be the Guardian of our friendship, to grant to it fervency and perpetuity even unto death, and I doubt not but my gracious Father has heard this prayer also.[17]

Cowper's heavenly Father did hear this prayer and graciously answered it. The two Williams were to remain lifelong friends.

Cowper was invited to have dinner with the Unwins on the following Sunday. William, aged twenty-one, was present, along with his father, Morley Unwin, a Church of England minister who was around sixty years of age, his mother, Mary Unwin, who was about forty-one, and his sister, Susanna, who was nineteen. Cowper was now almost thirty-four. He felt at home with the Unwins at once.

Writing to his various relations and friends, Cowper describes his first impressions of the family. Morley Unwin, he finds, is 'a Man of Learning and good Sense, and as simple as Parson Adams'. Mary Unwin 'has a very uncommon Understanding, has read much to excellent purpose, and is more polite than a Dutchess'. William Unwin, Cowper finds, is 'one of the most unreserved and amiable young men I ever conversed with. He is not yet arrived at that time of life, when suspicion recommends itself to us in the form of wisdom, and sets every thing but our own dear selves at an immeasurable distance from our esteem and confidence. Consequently he is known almost as soon as seen, and having nothing in his heart that makes it necessary for him to keep it barred and bolted, opens it to the perusal even of a stranger.' Cowper says less about the character of Susanna Unwin, although Lady Hesketh pressed him to give her a full description of the young lady. In his reply Cowper writes that Susanna 'resembles her Mother in her great piety, who is one of the most remarkable instances of it I have ever seen'. In other words, Susanna had not captured Cowper's gaze as much as Lady Hesketh had supposed. It was Mrs Unwin who had impressed Cowper the most. There was a good reason for this. Mary Unwin was a well-read, well-spoken, well-educated motherly woman who had obviously recently gone through a deep Christian experience.

To cut a long story short, Cowper found in Mary Unwin all the characteristics that he remembered in his own mother and had so missed in his stepmother. In fact, describing Mrs Unwin's faith and character to his cousin Maria Madan, now Mrs Cowper, the poet says, 'I could almost fancy my own Mother restored to Life again.' We thus find him writing shortly after meeting Mrs Unwin, 'That woman is a blessing to me, and I never see her without being the better for her company.' He adds, underlining the fact that he had found a home from home, 'I am treated in the family as if I was a near relation, and have been repeatedly invited to call upon them at all times. You know what a shy fellow I am; I cannot prevail with myself to make so much use of this privilege as I am sure they intend I should, but perhaps this aukwardness will wear off hereafter.'[18]

This 'aukwardness' did wear off. Cowper was becoming dissatisfied with his cramped quarters and having to manage all the housekeeping himself. On counting up all his assets he had £300 to call his own, plus the rent from his Temple quarters. Joseph Hill had taken to task the man who had occupied Cowper's rooms, and slowly a few pounds were coming in from that quarter. This was, however, very little for a man who had a servant, a boy to educate, no occupation and very little coming in through allowances from his family. Besides, the five Huntingdon families, including the Unwins, with whom Cowper was on the best of terms, caused the poet to long for a more stable family life. He began to pray about this very much and soon saw what might be an answer.

The Rev. Morley Unwin had been a master at the Grammar School in Huntingdon that had once seen Oliver Cromwell as its pupil. He was now in the ministry but still took in students, as a means of extra income, in order to prepare them for Cambridge. The last boarder-student had just left and Cowper began to dream about how wonderful it would be to take such a lodger's place and live permanently with the Unwins.

For three days Cowper was plagued with uncertainty concerning his wishes. Was it the Lord's will to take such a step or not? Should he not be content with his lot as it was? Was it mere selfishness that moved him to entertain such a hope? Whatever question Cowper asked himself he received the conviction that 'The Lord God of truth will do this.' He broached the subject with Morley Unwin and was overjoyed to hear that the Unwins were prepared to take him on, not only as a boarder but as a friend and member of the family.

Morley must have been very lenient as to what he charged, as

Cowper wrote to Hill on 5 November 1765, just six days before moving to the Unwins, claiming that he would now save £50-£60 per annum by being a boarder. Cowper agreed always to pay Unwin six months in advance for his board.

Cowper now severed his last connections with his former life as a lawyer. As a member of the Inner Temple he was required to deliver lectures to the students and to attend various ceremonies there. He therefore wrote to Hill, who had obviously reminded him of his responsibilities, asking him to find a substitute for him. This was unfair of Cowper as the lecturer had the responsibility of providing a 'treat' for the students out of his own pocket. Thus anybody taking Cowper's place would have quite a large caterer's bill to pay. Cowper later apologized to Hill for this but added that he felt it wrong to be thus scrounged upon by the Temple. Cowper also asked Hill at this time to give his library of legal works to his cousin Major Cowper. It seems that the poet made a short trip to London in order to trace these books and met Hill there.

At this time, too, Cowper became very conscious of a number of debts he had accrued just before and during his illness and realized it was his duty to pay back these sums. His main concern was Dr Cotton, to whom he still owed over £50. Apparently the poet corresponded regularly with Dr Cotton, whom he regarded as a spiritual father. (None of these letters has been discovered.) Cowper explained in a letter to Lady Hesketh how he felt he was cured as soon as he was converted but he was conscious that he needed much teaching in the Christian way of life. This convinced him that he ought to stay on at Dr Cotton's until he had grown a little in grace.

Dr Cotton was not Cowper's only creditor. He still owed his old Nonsense Club friend Bensley seven of the hundred pounds he had borrowed. As Bensley had died, Cowper arranged for them to be sent to his brother. Thurlow had lent Cowper five guineas which also had to be paid back. These sums were nothing compared to the money Cowper owed several fashionable tailors. He was to spend at least three years tracing them so he could pay them for their former services.

Life with the Unwins

On 11 November 1765 Cowper moved in with the Unwins. It was one major move that he was never to regret. He entered into deep spiritual talks with the family, read a great deal of Puritan,

Evangelical and Dissenting literature, went swimming three times
a week in the Ouse and started to play battledore and shuttlecock in
the Unwins' paddock. Mrs Unwin was a dab hand at this game and
they played with two shuttlecocks in the air at once. Cowper wrote
to Lady Hesketh saying that his life now 'anticipated in some
measure, the joys of that heavenly society, which the soul shall
actually possess hereafter'.

Once outside the Unwins' home, however, there were increasing
signs that their upper-class neigbours did not see eye to eye with the
way the Unwins and Cowper lived. These neighbours were people
who had a great deal of time on their hands which they strove to 'kill'
by organizing card games in one another's houses and going from
party to party. Judging by Mrs Unwin's letters written before her
conversion, this was the life she too had formerly lived but she had
given it up on finding a far better way of redeeming the time. It
seemed strange to many that the bright-eyed belle of many a ball
should now spend her time knitting stockings, gardening, reading
the Bible and singing hymns. This ignorant criticism became very
vocal and was one of the reasons why Mary Unwin later decided to
leave snobbish, foolish Huntingdon and settle down in the more
sensible working-class Olney, where more attention was given to
Christian virtue.

Cowper wrote to his cousin Mrs Cowper, telling her of the life on
which they had gladly turned their backs and the kind of life they
chose to live:

> I am obliged to you for the Interest you take in my Welfare,
> and for your enquiring so particularly after the manner in
> which my time passes here. As to Amusements, I mean what
> the World calls such, we have none: the Place indeed swarms
> with them, and Cards and Dancing are the professed Business
> of almost all the Gentle Inhabitants of Huntingdon. We refuse
> to take part in them, or to be Accessories to this way of
> Murthering our Time, and by so doing have acquired the
> Name of Methodists. Having told you how we do not spend
> our time, I will next say how we do. We Breakfast commonly
> between 8 and 9, 'till 11, we read either the Scripture, or the
> Sermons of some faithfull Preacher of those holy Mysteries:
> at 11 we attend divine Service which is performed here twice
> every day, and from 12 to 3 we separate and amuse ourselves

as we please. During that Interval I either Read in my own Apartment, or Walk or Ride, or work in the Garden. We seldom sit an hour after Dinner, but if the Weather permits adjourn to the Garden, where with Mrs. Unwin and her Son I have generally the Pleasure of Religious Conversation 'till Tea time; if it Rains or is too windy for Walking, we either Converse within Doors, or sing some Hymns of Martin's Collection,[19] and by the Help of Mrs. Unwin's Harpsichord make up a tolerable Concert, in which however our Hearts I hope are the best and most musical Performers. After Tea we sally forth to walk in good earnest. Mrs. Unwin is a good Walker, and we have generally travel'd about 4 Miles before we see Home again. When the Days are short we make this Excursion in the former part of the Day, between Church time and Dinner. At Night we read and Converse as before 'till Supper, and commonly finish the Evening either with Hymns or a Sermon, and last of all the Family are called in to Prayers. — I need not tell you that such a Life as this is consistent with the utmost cheerfullness, accordingly we are all happy, and dwell together in Unity as Brethren. Mrs. Unwin has almost a maternal Affection for me, and I have something very like a filial one for her, and her Son and I are Brothers. Blessed be the God of my Salvation for such Companions, and for such a Life above all, for an Heart to like it.[20]

Such a life, of course, is an ideal life of spiritual luxury which few Christians can afford, and to which few are called. Cowper realized this and knew that he could not always live in such pre-heavenly bliss. He thus started looking out for an occupation that would suit him better than being a lawyer. He thought most seriously of entering the ministry, but, as he told his cousin, Mrs Cowper, their were strong reasons against this:

I have had many anxious Thoughts about taking Orders: and I believe every new Convert is apt to think himself called upon for that purpose; but it has pleased God, by means which there is no need to particularize, to give me full Satisfaction as to the Propriety of declining it. Indeed, they who have the least Idea of what I have suffered from the Dread of public Exhibitions, will readily excuse my never attempting them

hereafter. In the mean time, if it please the Almighty, I may
be an Instrument of turning many to the Truth, in a private
way, & hope that my Endeavours in this Way have not been
entirely unsuccessfull. Had I the Zeal of Moses, I should want
an Aaron to be my Spokesman.

Rather than finding an Aaron to be a spokesman for his zeal,
Cowper soon found that he himself was to be cast in the role of an
Aaron assisting a Moses in the shape of John Newton. The poet was
to spend many years catering for the needs of the poor at Olney,
Buckinghamshire, continuing to do so long after Newton had left the
town. Meanwhile Cowper wrote a forty-five-page account of his
own life and conversion which was initially prepared for the Unwins
as a testimony to God's saving grace and so that his new family
might know what he had gone through. Later Newton begged a copy
from the poet and apparently let all and sundry copy it in spite of its
very intimate contents. Appended to these memoirs were six verses
of praise which poetically anticipate the language of the Romantic
age and theologically express the wonders of the new birth:

Far from the world, O Lord, I flee,
From strife and tumult far,
From scenes, where Satan wages still
His most successful war.

The calm retreat, the silent shade,
With prayer and praise agree;
And seem by Thy sweet bounty made,
For those who follow Thee.

There, if Thy Spirit touch the Soul,
And grace her mean abode;
O with what peace, and joy, and love,
She communes with her God!

There, like the nightingale she pours
Her solitary lays;
Nor asks a witness of her song,
Nor thirsts for human praise.

Author, and Guardian of my life,
Sweet fount of light divine!
And all endearing names in one,
My Saviour — I am Thine!

What thanks I owe Thee, and what love,
A boundless, endless store;
Shall echo thro' the realms above,
When time shall be no more.

Cowper's friendship with his brother John increased during his time at Huntingdon and as Morley Unwin often drove his carriage to Cambridge, the poet would accompany him. As William Unwin was also at Cambridge such a journey was a twofold delight for Cowper.

The trips to Cambridge with Morley had given Cowper the chance to sound out his friend concerning his faith. Cowper had noticed that Unwin could not enter into fellowship in the same manner that his wife and children did. Cowper soon found out why. Unwin believed in following the moral law rather than biblical revelation. This caused him to reject the divinity of Christ and also not to believe in the merits of Christ's sufferings. He was a very religious man but he relied on his own good works to win favour with God. Cowper now saw that he had work to do for the Lord in his new family.

Now that he had more time on his hands, Cowper sent a detailed account of his conversion to his relatives. Perhaps the most ardent Evangelical in the family was Maria Cowper, Martin Madan's sister. Cowper knew that he could open up his heart completely to her and did so, showing how biblical and eloquent his style of writing was becoming in his eagerness to write about the Lord. In his letter, already quoted from in connection with Mrs Unwin, William tells Maria,

The deceitfullness of the natural Heart, the Mystery of Iniquity that works there, is inconceivable. I know well that I passed upon my Friends for a person at least religiously inclined, if not actually religious, and what is more wonderfull, I even thought Myself a Christian. Thought myself a Christian when I had no Faith in Christ, when I saw no Beauty in him that I should desire him, in short when I had neither Faith, nor Love nor any Christian Grace whatever, but a thousand Seeds of Rebellion instead, evermore springing up in Enmity against him. Thus qualified for the Christian Life, and by the additional Help of a little Hypocritical Attendance upon Ordinances, I thought myself as well off in point of Security as most, and though my Iniquities had set me on fire round about, I knew it not, and though they burned me, yet I laid it not to heart. But Blessed be God, even the God who is become my Salvation! The hail of Affliction and Rebuke for Sin, has swept away the Refuge of Lies. It pleased the Almighty in great Mercy to me, to set all my Misdeeds before me, and to thunder into my very Heart with the Curses of his broken Law in such manner that for near a Twelvemonth I believed myself Sealed up under eternal Wrath and the Sentence of unquenchable Vengeance. Then all my Christian Seeming, all my fair & specious Professions which had been my Support and Confidence before, became the Objects of my Horror and Detestation. At length the Storm being past, and having answered all the gracious purposes of Him who sent it forth to convince me of Sin, of Righteousness, and of Judgment, a quiet and peacefull Serenity of Soul succeeded, such as ever attends the Gift of a lively Faith in the all-sufficient Attonement, and the sweet Sense of Mercy and Pardon purchased by the Blood of Christ. Thus did he break me and bind me up, thus did he wound me and his Hands made whole.

Cowper spent over a year and a half of intense happiness at the Unwins, deepening his faith in fellowship with Mary and William Unwin and through reading good Christian books. He made sure that the Unwins became well known to his own relations and introduced William in particular to influential members of his family such as Ashley Cowper and Martin Madan. Cowper was never shy of using his connections to advance the prospects of a good friend.

Always interested in nature, the poet discovered he had green fingers and spent a good deal of time assisting the family budget by gardening. Thus he was, perhaps unknowingly, gathering material for his later eschatological poetry on the subject of the Christian as God's under-gardener in an Eden restored.[21]

Meanwhile, Morley Unwin attended to the needs of the two churches in Huntingdon where he was lecturer. Unwin had become very fond of Cowper and one day he told his wife that if anything happened to him, she should not hesitate to keep Cowper on as a boarder and family friend. That 'anything' was soon to happen.

One Sunday night in June 1767, Unwin was returning from his pastoral duties when his horse took fright about a mile from home and bolted. Unwin was thrown off and fractured his skull. He was put to bed in a poor man's cottage and the doctor called for. The doctor said that his case was hopeless and he would die within a few hours. He actually hung on, however, for another three days. Unwin was too ill to be moved so his family and Cowper gathered around him during his dying hours in which he was in great pain. To the great joy of all his loved ones, when Unwin became conscious at intervals he professed a need of salvation and a sturdy faith in Christ, emphasizing the fact that 'Jesus Christ is God, and therefore he can save me.'

The search for a new home

Cowper's sojourn in Huntingdon was about to come to an end. It seems that the Evangelical witness in the town had grown weaker and that it had only been Morley Unwin's duties that had kept the Unwins in Huntingdon. The situation for Cowper was even more difficult. He had originally come to live in Huntingdon to be near his brother but had become so used to viewing Mrs Unwin as his housekeeper and friend that he did not want to find himself alone again.

Cowper therefore contacted his Evangelical relations and friends for help and advice and William Unwin asked around at Cambridge to see if there were any houses to be had near to a biblical ministry. Cowper thought particularly of Martin Madan's assistant, Thomas Haweis, who now had a church at Aldwinkle in Northamptonshire and William Unwin got in touch with Richard Conyers, a leading Evangelical who had recently taken his L.L.D. at Cambridge and was now vicar of Helmsley in Yorkshire.

Conyers had a good friend by the name of John Newton who had recently become a curate in Olney, where Moses Browne, one of the earliest leaders of the Evangelical Revival, was vicar. On hearing that Mrs Unwin needed help, Conyers went to visit her, taking John

Newton with him. By this time Cowper felt he ought to stay with Mrs Unwin, whatever happened. He outlined his reasons in a letter to his aunt, Mrs Madan, saying,

> Pray for us, my dear Aunt, that it may please the Good Shepherd, to lead us by the Footsteps of the Flock, and to feed us in his own Pastures for my Soul within me is Sick of the Spiritless unedifying Ministry at Huntingdon. It is a Matter of the utmost Indifference to us where we settle, provided it be within the Sound of the Glad Tidings of Salvation. I shall be much obliged to you, if you will beg my Friend Martin to assist us, whose extensive Knowledge of those Places where the Gospel is ministered, may perhaps enable him under God, to direct us.
>
> I am a sort of adopted Son in this Family, where Mrs. Unwin has always treated me with Parental Tenderness: Therefore by the Lord's leave, I shall still continue a Member of it. Our Aim and End are the same, the Means of Grace & the Hopes of Glory; so that there seems to be no Reason why we should be parted.[22]

To Maria Cowper he wrote,

> The Effect of [Unwin's death] upon my Circumstances will only be a Change of the Place of my abode, for I shall still, by God's leave, continue with Mrs. Unwin, whose Behaviour to me has always been that of a Mother to a Son. By this afflictive Providence, it has pleased God, who always drops Comfort into the bitterest Cup, to open a Door for us out of an unevangelical Pasture, such as this is, into some better Ministry where we may hear the glad Tidings of Salvation, and be nourished by the Sincere Milk of the Word. We know not yet where we shall settle, but we trust that the Lord whom we seek, will go before us, and prepare a Rest for us.[23]

Richard Conyers was to remain a close friend of William Unwin's and would always look upon him as a worthy guest-preacher and lecturer at his church. His connection with Cowper never deepened although the poet thought highly of Conyers and felt that he was a great apologist for the Christian faith. Referring to the difficulty that rich people have to enter heaven through the straight and narrow gate, Cowper wrote in 'Truth',

> 'Tis open, and ye cannot enter — why?
> Because ye will not, Conyers would reply—
> And he says much that many may dispute
> And cavil at with ease, but none refute.[24]

Conyers quickly saw the value of Cowper's poems relating to his earliest Christian experiences and published them in 1772 in his *A Collection of Psalms and Hymns from various Authors for the use of Serious and Devout Christians of all Denominations*.

When Cowper met Newton the two men 'hit it off', as the saying goes, at once. It was the start of a long and deep friendship which brought both men a great deal in spiritual and literary gain. For the next twelve years the two friends were to grow in grace together, never being separated for more than twelve hours at a time.

After getting to know the Unwins and Cowper at Huntingdon, Newton invited them to take up residence in Olney. Cowper was thrilled with the prospect as he longed to come under the sound of the gospel, and opposition to the way of life lived at the Unwins was growing amongst their Huntingdon neighbours. Moving to Olney, however, was no simple task. Newton was still without a permanent home and was living in cramped quarters a mile or so from the town. There was a vicarage at Olney but it was being repaired and enlarged through the kindness of Lord Dartmouth. Cowper went to Olney with his Huntingdon friends in August 1767 to reconnoitre and was so impressed by the work Newton was doing that he decided to move to Olney the following month. The Newtons had kindly asked Cowper and the Unwins to stay with them in their hired rooms until the Vicarage was finished.

Mrs Newton expressed a great interest in having Mrs Unwin at Olney as she realized what an enormous help and support the latter would be to her in her work as a pastor's wife. Shortly after settling down in Olney, however, Mrs Unwin became seriously ill. After several weeks of great pain, it seemed certain that the Lord was about to call her home. Cowper wrote to his aunt, Mrs Madan, and poured out his soul to her. The letter must be quoted here in full to show not only how near Cowper had grown to the Lord but also how much he was in need of the fellowship he had enjoyed with Mrs

Unwin. It also shows how Cowper was prepared to lose all for Christ's sake. This letter also gives us deep insight into how Cowper's creative mind worked and how he produced one of the earliest and sweetest of his hymns.

Dear Aunt,

I should not have suffered your last kind Letter to have laid by me so long unanswer'd, had it not been for many Hindrances and especially One, which has engaged much of my Attention. My dear Friend Mrs. Unwin, whom the Lord gave me to be a Comfort to me in that Wilderness from which he has just delivered me, has been for many Weeks past in so declining a way, and has suffered so many Attacks of the most excruciating Pain, that I have hardly been able to keep alive the faintest Hope of her Recovery. I know that our God heareth Prayer, and I know that he hath opened mine and many Hearts amongst this People to pray for her. Here lies my chief Support, without which I should look upon myself as already deprived of her. Again when I consider the great Meetness to which the Lord has wrought her for the Inheritance in Light, her most exemplary Patience under the sharpest Sufferings, her truly Christian Humility and Resignation, I am more than ever inclined to believe that her Hour is come. Let me engage your Prayers for Her, and for Me. You know what I have most need of upon an Occasion like this: Pray that I may receive it at His Hands from whom every good and perfect Gift proceeds. She is the chief Blessing I have met with in my Journey since the Lord was pleased to call me, and I hope the Influence of her edifying and Excellent Example will never leave me. Her Illness has been a sharp Trial to me — Oh that it may have a sanctified Effect, that I may rejoice to Surrender up to the Lord my dearest Comforts the Moment he shall require them. Oh! for no Will but the Will of my Heavenly Father! Doctor Cotton for whose advice we went together to St. Albans about a Month since, seemed to have so little Expectation that Medicine could help her, that he might be said to give her over. He prescribed however, but she has hardly been able to take his Medicines. Her Disorder is a Nervous Atrophy attended with violent Spasms of the Chest and Throat, and

This is a bad Day with her; worse than common. I return you many Thanks for the Verses you favor'd me with, which speak sweetly the Language of a Christian Soul. I wish I could pay you in kind, but must be contented to pay you in the best kind I can. I began to compose them Yesterday Morning before Daybreak, but fell asleep at the End of the two first Lines, when I awaked again the third and fourth were whisper'd to my Heart in a way which I have often experienced.

Oh for a closer Walk with God,
A calm & heav'nly Frame,
A Light to shine upon the Road
That leads me to the Lamb!

Where is the Blessedness I knew
When first I saw the Lord?
Where is the Soul-refreshing View
Of Jesus in his Word?

What peacefull Hours I then enjoy'd,
How sweet their Mem'ry still!
But they have left an Aching Void
The World can never fill.

Return, O Holy Dove, Return,
Sweet Messenger of Rest,
I hate the Sins that made thee mourn
And drove thee from my Breast.

The dearest Idol I have known,
Whate'er that Idol be,
Help me to tear it from Thy Throne,
And worship Only Thee.

Then shall my Walk be close with God,
Calm and serene my Frame,
Then purer Light shall mark the Road
That leads me to the Lamb.

Yours my dear Aunt in the Bands of that Love which
cannot be quenched

Olney. Dece. 10. 67.

Wm Cowper.

Mrs Unwin gradually recovered but remained weak for several
months. Her complaint seems to have been brought on by the heavy
strains she had suffered through the loss of her husband, the wicked
talk of the neighbours and moving from a home she had loved
dearly.

After several weeks of living in very cramped circumstances, the
Newtons finally moved into their modernized vicarage. Meanwhile,
Mrs Newton had found a house for Cowper close by which had
recently been left empty. It was, however, in a bad state of repair so
she again invited the Unwins and Cowper to stay with them at the
Vicarage until they could move into their new home. This house,
called Orchard Side, was more or less ready for habitation by
February 1768 when Cowper, accompanied by the Unwins, took
possession of it. Cowper was now quite settled in his mind that he
would stay in Olney, the town that has become permanently
attached to his name.

5.
The mariner's tale

The life of John Newton[1] is, from now on, so closely connected and interwoven with that of Cowper that it is necessary to take a closer look at this remarkable person. Only then can one understand the friendship the two men enjoyed.

There is a saying that truth is stranger than fiction. Nowhere is this better illustrated than in the case of John Newton, whose life must be one of the most interesting ever recorded.

Newton's childhood

John Newton was born in 1725, the son of a Jesuit-trained sea-captain and a Dissenting mother. Such a parental combination is a wonder in itself! Unlike Cowper's father, who showed his sons true comradeship and even indulgence, Newton's father was extremely strict and unbending. As a child, John was frightened of his father, who tried repeatedly to break the boy's spirit. In his autobiography Newton, striving to be fair to his father, writes, 'I am persuaded that my father loved me,' but adds, 'though he seemed not willing that I should know it.'

Again, unlike Cowper, who had loved to play marbles and other pavement games and was a good cricketer and football-player, Newton as a child detested such 'noisy' games and preferred the company of his mother.

Cowper had the privilege of the best education England could offer, but Newton spent only two years at school. It is difficult to believe that a prosperous family should neglect the education of their son in this way. Little blame, however, can be attached to Mrs Newton. John's mother was a faithful believer who taught her son to read the Scriptures at a very early age. John also learnt a number of Watts' poems and hymns at his mother's knee. As in the case of Cowper, John Newton loved his mother and felt security and ease when he was in her presence. Sadly he was to experience the same kind of sorrow as Cowper. Mrs Newton died when John was only six years of age.

Life at sea

John Newton was only eleven years old when Captain Newton took him to sea to be trained as a midshipman. After some four years at sea, Captain Newton tried to settle his son in some occupation in Spain which proved abortive because of John's rebellious spirit. The captain therefore decided to send his son, now seventeen years of age, to Jamaica to learn to be a merchant.

Before going out to Jamaica, however, John was invited to visit some of his mother's relations, named Catlett, who lived in Kent, so, as the ship bound for Jamaica was not yet ready to sail, he visited them. There Newton found his future wife. The daughter of the house was called Mary, a girl of only thirteen years of age. John fell for her at once and years later could say, 'I was impressed with an affection for her which never abated or lost its influence over me. None of the scenes of misery and wickedness I afterwards experienced ever banished her for an hour from my waking thoughts for the seven following years.'

Newton's ship was to sail for Jamaica in three days. He stayed three weeks at the Catletts' and the ship left without him. Captain Newton then tried to settle his son in Venice, where John kept evil company and disobeyed his father's wishes.

A year later Newton was back in Kent to see his beloved Mary — once more in opposition to his father's wishes. It was here that Newton was press-ganged and forced into joining the crew of the *Harwich*, a man-of-war. Lovesick Newton made himself thoroughly unpopular on board by secretly stealing off to visit Mary. One day Newton was sent to bring back a party of deserters and decided to use the opportunity to desert himself. He was brought back to the ship by soldiers, flogged, degraded and cast into irons. Like Cowper in other circumstances, Newton's despair, rage and disappointment were so great that he contemplated committing suicide and planned to drown himself. Cowper, when he had reached this stage of despair, had lost his Theadora and not yet found God. Newton's life was a godless one but the thought of Mary Catlett saved him.

When a ship bound for Africa (Newton's own ship was bound for India) asked the man-of-war to provide them with two seamen, the captain of the *Harwich* discharged Newton that he might leave the vessel. This may have been because of his kind heart, or because he wanted to get rid of a trouble-maker. Once on the new ship, Newton found himself a free man and also soon discovered that his new captain was a friend of his father's. Newton's behaviour on board his new ship was worse than ever and when the ship reached Africa, before sailing for the West Indies, Newton was more or less compelled to go on land without being paid a penny in wages. He then entered the services of a slave-trader.

Servant to a slave-trader

Instead of an improvement in Newton's situation, his plight grew even worse. The slave-trader had a negro wife who took exception to Newton at once. Shortly after the trader went away on business, Newton became very ill but had no one to look after him. The trader's wife showed him the greatest contempt and refused to give him food apart from a few scraps from the leftovers on her own plate. He had to go out into the fields and pull up roots and vegetables and eat them raw in secret to survive. Newton's situation was so bad that even the slaves in chains felt sorry for him and gave him something of their very meagre fare. Any man, no matter how strong in constitution, would have died under the treatment Newton received, yet God had other plans for him and kept him strong.

It is amazing how Newton was preserved from going mad. He had just one possession, apart from a few articles of clothing. It was a copy of Barrow's *Euclid*. He used to ponder over this book for hours, drawing the geometrical figures in the sand. He soon mastered the first six books of *Euclid* and became something of an expert at geometry. Some fifty years later the poet William

Wordsworth started to write a long poem, 'The Prelude', which is seen as the very best of his work. In the sixth book of this long poem, the poet pens the words:

> 'Tis told by one whom stormy waters threw,
> With fellow-sufferers by the shipwreck spared,
> Upon a desert coast, that having brought
> To land a single volume, saved by chance
> A treatise of Geometry he wont
> Although of food and clothing destitute
> And beyond common wretchedness depressed,
> To part from company and take this book
> (Then first a self-taught pupil in its truths)
> To spots remote, and draw his diagrams
> With a long staff upon the sand, and thus
> Did oft beguile his sorrow, and almost
> Forget his feeling.

Anyone familiar with Newton's *Authentic Narrative* will recognize that Wordsworth has lifted these lines, with little change, directly out of Newton's account. Thus Newton kept himself sane fifteen long months by writing in the sand with nothing else to beguile his sorrows or to alleviate his misery.

Newton had been able to dispatch a letter to his father, who had asked a trader friend to rescue his son. The trader did not go out of his way to find Newton, but by the grace of God, he did sail near to where Newton was, and being told by another trader that Captain Newton's son was near at hand, he went to fetch him. Meanwhile Newton's lot had improved as he had found a new master. Nevertheless he went on board the ship which set sail for England via Newfoundland. It was now January 1748 and Newton was twenty-three.

A storm at sea

By March the ship had reached North America and Newton was becoming of a more serious turn of mind and reading Thomas à Kempis. The weather turned, however, and a terrible storm blew up, sweeping men overboard and whipping the masts off the vessel as if they had been matchsticks. The boat began to fill with water but, as if by a miracle, it did not sink. The light cargo of beeswax and wood kept it afloat.

Newton prayed for God's mercy for the first time in many years. A night spent working at the pumps sobered him up even more to the facts of the gospel. He began to pray and think of Christ whom he had long derided. When he was relieved at his work for a short time, he began to read his New Testament and found great consolation there. Newton was experiencing what Cowper had experienced when he wrote, 'How naturally does affliction make us Christians! and how impossible is it when all human help is vain, and the whole earth too poor and trifling to furnish us with one moment's peace, how impossible is it then to avoid looking at the Gospel!'[2]

For two weeks the boat was blown along, in the wrong direction, a floating wreck. The water had to be pumped out continually and the food and drinking water began to run out. The cry of the crew was taken up by Samuel Taylor Coleridge in his poem 'The Rime of the Ancyent Marinere':

> Water, water, everywhere
> And all the boards did shrink;
> Water, water everywhere,
> Nor any drop to drink

The captain pinned his fury on Newton and blamed him for being a Jonah, saying that only if he were thrown overboard would they be saved. Then the wind turned and the boat was blown for two weeks towards Ireland where it gently landed. The cook had the very last of the food in the pot. Newton wrote, 'I began to know that there is a God who hears and answers prayer.' The work of grace had begun.

When Wordsworth was writing the 'Prelude', he was visited by Coleridge who was writing the 'Ancyent Marinere'. There is a strong case supporting the theory that Newton was Coleridge's prototype for his poem.

A new life begins

Newton made no delay in contacting his Mary, who had waited patiently for him. He confessed that he would perhaps never be able to offer her his hand because of his lack of a qualified profession but learned the good news that once he had established himself in a more stable way of life, he could trust that Mary would wait.

Newton was offered the captaincy of a ship bound for Africa, but decided to sail as a mate first in order to gain more experience. He had not forgotten the way God had answered prayer and thought much about spiritual things. During the voyage Newton had a great deal of leisure and decided to work hard at Latin, though he had only a Horace reader. Later he was able to correspond in Latin with some of the most learned Dutch divines. On his arrival in Africa Newton spent as much time as he could in the woods and the fields pouring out his heart to God.

When Newton returned from Africa, his dream of seven years before came true. He married Mary Catlett on 12 February 1750, after hearing that he had been awarded a captain's ticket.

In August Newton sailed again for Africa in his own 150-ton ship and with a crew of thirty men. His letters to his wife during this time show how he was growing in grace. During the voyage he continued his studies of Latin and read the best classical authors. When in Africa, Newton decided he would like to see the negro woman who had made him her slave. He sent a longboat out for her and when she came aboard the crew gave her a full royal salute. She was then heaped with presents and Newton told her that the difficulties he had gone through at her cruel hand had made him turn to God. The natives stared at Newton and said, 'Look, there is Newton in stockings and shoes!' They had only seen him in rags and destitute before.

Fifteen months later Newton was in England again, determined to be filled with the Spirit. He thus drew up a long list of Christian exercises which he hoped to perform regularly. In July 1752, he sailed once more for Africa, spending much of his spare time studying and praying. He set apart special days for fasting and praying for the crew.

Newton was, however, lonely. He longed for Christian fellowship, for the communion of the saints. Years later William Cowper was to write of the loneliness of Alexander Selkirk in his island paradise. His words are very similar to Newton's own at this time:

Religion! what treasure untold
Resides in the heavenly word!

More precious than silver and gold,
Or all that this earth can afford.
But the sound of the church-going bell
These vallies and rocks never heard,
Ne'er sigh'd at the sound of a knell,
Or smil'd when a sabbath appear'd.

Newton longed to meet with like-minded believers; he was lonely, but he was at peace. Sometimes sleepless nights heightened his predicament and made loneliness seem all the greater. Yet he was given strength to sum up his state in words of expressive beauty and faithfulness:

In desert woods, with thee my God,
Where human footsteps never trod,
How happy could I be!
Thou my repose from care, my light
Amidst the darkness of the night,
In solitude my company.[3]

Cowper expresses similar thoughts through the medium of shipwrecked Alexander Selkirk, who felt loneliness the most at night-time but received comfort from God:

But the sea-fowl is gone to her nest,
The beast is laid down in his lair,
Ev'n here is a season of rest,
And I to my cabin repair.
There is mercy in every place;
And mercy, encouraging thought!
Gives even affliction a grace,
And reconciles man to his lot.

At this time Newton's crew threatened to mutiny and the slaves were discovered plotting a break-out. He had a vivid dream about being stung by a scorpion and receiving an antidote from an unknown person. This he interpreted as a warning that he was to go through a difficult time but he would be saved from harm.

Soon after the dream a business acquaintance began to spread tales that Newton was an adulterer. This was especially obnoxious to Newton as he was so much in love with his dear Mary. The public scandal that ensued soon died down when it became obvious that the scandalmonger was lying. Newton was to suffer a great deal from persons whom he put together under the title 'Miss Report'. These mis-reports often made him very angry, or, to use his own words 'take fire too readily', so that he was often driven to God in prayer in order to gain strength over his temper. Newton was able to overcome all these difficulties by looking to God for guidance and gaining confidence that God would protect him and cause him to grow in grace.

Newton and the slave-trade

There have been many 'mis-reports' about Newton in the hundreds of articles written about him concerning his dealings with the slave-trade, even when he was obviously a true Christian. It is difficult for us evangelicals today to believe that Newton, who was now so close to God, could spend his time buying and selling human beings. During his voyages to Africa, however, Newton was not aware that there was anything wrong with his trade. When writing in 1763 he says,

> The reader may perhaps wonder, as I now do myself, that … I did not at the time start with horror at my own employment as an agent in promoting it. Custom, example, and interest, had blinded my eyes. I did it ignorantly, for I am sure had I thought of the slave trade then as I have thought of it since, no considerations would have induced me to continue in it. Though my religious views were not very clear, my conscience was very tender, and I durst not have displeased God by acting against the light of my mind. Indeed a slave ship, while on the coast, is exposed to such innumerable and continual dangers, that I was often then, and still am, astonished that any one, much more that so many, should leave the coast in safety. I was then favoured with an uncommon degree of dependence upon the providence of God, which supported me; but this confidence must have failed in a moment, and I should have been overwhelmed with distress and terror, if I had known, or even suspected,

that I was acting wrongly. I felt greatly the disagreeableness of the business. The office of a gaoler, and the restraints under which I was obliged to keep my prisoners, were not suitable to my feelings; but I considered it as the line of life which God in His providence had allotted me, and as a cross which I ought to bear with patience and thankfulness till he should be pleased to deliver me from it. Till then I only thought myself bound to treat the slaves under my care with gentleness, and to consult their ease and convenience so far as was consistent with the safety of the whole family of whites and blacks on board my ship.

Later Newton was to write his *Thoughts upon the African Slave Trade,* which, together with the work of the so-called Clapham Sect, assisted by the anti-slavery songs of William Cowper, was to help gain a majority in Parliament against the evil trafficking in human beings.

Now in 1753, not yet realizing the human misery he was causing, Newton sailed again for England with a cargo of Negroes. On his way he read Dr Doddridge's *Life of Col. James Gardiner.* This book influenced him greatly and on reading it he says, 'I burst two or three times into tears, which I hope proceeded from sincere repentance and shame, and was from thence brought upon my knees (as I trust) by the impression of the Holy Spirit, to humble myself for my unworthiness before the Lord with an earnestness and warmth that has in some measure continued hitherto.'

After only six weeks in England, Newton left again for Africa on his third and last voyage as a slave-trader. During the voyage, his thoughts turned to other occupations which would be more fitting for him as a Christian. He strove to sort out his financial difficulties and make provisions for the poor. On 12 February 1754, his wedding anniversary, he thought especially of the time when he had felt like committing suicide and thanked God that it was the thought of Mary Catlett that had kept him from death. He prayed fervently that God would bless their marriage.

Newton's diary reveals that this journey was a time of great testing for him. The sea-captain began to realize more than ever what sin, repentance and salvation meant and earnestly sought the face of the Lord in forgiveness. His own sin in the past weighed particularly on him; he caught a fever which almost killed him and he became very depressed. A fanciful notion possessed him that God would overlook him amongst the thousands who were to obtain salvation. After a time of deep perplexity the words, 'The Lord knoweth them that are his,' came to Newton and brought him assurance. Years later, when William Cowper was haunted by the selfsame fears, Newton was able to tell him of the comfort he had received at God's hand.

When Newton arrived at St Kitts in May 1754, instead of the spiritual loneliness which he had experienced there on former voyages, he met a fellow-believer, Captain Clunie, who was able to lead him into deeper and surer fellowship with the Lord. Clunie taught Newton the Bible truths of the covenant of grace and that he should expect to be preserved by the power and promises of God and not his own holiness. Newton's new friend expounded not only the gospel to him but gave him a good picture of the state of the church and the errors that were being spread at the time. He gave Newton addresses of sound believers in London and by the time Newton left St Kitts he felt he had learned enough to occupy his thoughts and prayers for the remaining seven weeks of his voyage.

Immediately on arriving in England, Newton started to prepare for his next voyage. But God had quite a different course in view for him.

Forced to give up the sea

One day Newton was sitting at the tea table with his wife when he was suddenly struck by a fit which rendered him for a while unable to speak, move or know what was going on around him. When he came round, signs of the seizure remained with him and his doctors, advisers and employers were compelled to see that Newton was in no shape to take on another voyage. This was a hard blow to the shipping company who had bought and rigged out a special ship just for Newton. Mr Manesty, however, the owner of the ship, had become Newton's close friend and would not hear of him taking on anything that might prove too much for his health. Mrs Newton, a very sensitive creature at the best of times, was so shaken by what had happened to her husband that she was ill for many months. Thus Newton had to face the fact that his sea-going days had come to an end.

Newton wasted no time in getting in touch with the believers Captain Clunie had recommended and was introduced by them to George Whitefield, John Wesley and William Romaine. Now Newton was in the very best of Christian company. He continued his practice of going out into the fields to draw near to God and also began to read Christian authors such as Wesley, Mathew Henry and James Hervey. He spent hours going over Christian doctrine with his new friends and was particularly impressed by the doctrine of imputed righteousness.

Tide-surveyor in Liverpool

As another sea voyage seemed out of the question, Mr Manesty, Newton's employer, got him a job as a tide-surveyor at Liverpool. Newton took this as a sign that he should give up the African trade for good. Mrs Newton had, however, become very ill by this time and John was obliged to travel to Liverpool alone.

Newton's new post was a very lucrative one indeed. This was not so much because of the basic wages he received but because of the many extra 'perks' that were associated with the post. Newton's main job was to serve as a kind of customs officer, examining the cargoes of incoming ships and dealing with the protection of wrecked vessels. It was customary for the tide-surveyors to accept gratuities from the captains of these vessels and even claim a percentage of the goods saved after a wreckage. Though Newton had taken an oath not to accept bribes, he found himself eagerly accepting the financial perks that came his way. This caused him a great deal of heart-searching and troubled his conscience for many months. At last a book by Wesley on keeping oaths helped Newton to take a firm stand.

Newton was one of the few believers in imputed righteousness who was able to keep up an unbroken correspondence with John Wesley. The fact that he always wrote to Wesley as a pupil ever willing to learn enabled him to put over views which Wesley would have rejected in anger from any other Evangelical. Once Newton heard Wesley preaching in Liverpool on the doctrine of perfection. After expressing his disagreement with Wesley, he commented: 'I would rather pray for and press to nearer advances towards it [perfection] than fight and dispute against it. I am sure that to keep the commandments, to redeem time, to abstain from all appearances of evil, is the best way to maintain light and joy and communion with the Lord; yet after all I expect to be saved as a sinner, and not as a saint!' Rarely has such a great truth been put more succinctly!

At Liverpool Newton found good fellowship with the Baptists, began to visit people in need, especially the illiterate and drunkards, and to write articles for magazines and private distribution, as well as his autobiography. He also spent much time on Latin, Hebrew and Greek studies. Very soon Newton could read the historical books of the Old Testament and the Psalms in the original 'with tolerable ease'. He became proficient in reading and writing French and could read Latin authors with no difficulty. This is an amazing feat when we consider that Newton had started school at eight years of age and finished when he was only ten.

After several months Mrs Newton, much recovered, joined her husband and the two settled down to nine years of happiness at Liverpool.

Call to the ministry

From October 1757 Newton began to feel a calling to the ministry, though, at first, only on a lay basis. His centre of service was to be Yorkshire, where he had made many friends, including William Grimshaw of Haworth and Henry Venn of Huddersfield.

Motivated by the example, but not the advice, of men of God such as Whitefield, Newton decided to preach his first sermon in Leeds extemporary. He got off to a good start, soon lost his thread and had to end confused after a few minutes. His comment afterwards can well be appreciated by the thousands of ministers who have had a similar experience: 'It is not easy or possible to describe the storm of temptation and distress I went through the next day.' From then onwards, Newton decided to use notes, although this handicapped his delivery greatly owing to his being very short-sighted.

Soon after this Newton was invited to take over a curacy in the Church of England by an Evangelical minister, Mr Crooke, with whom Newton was on very friendly terms. The ex-slave-trader had now, however, gained such a reputation as a Methodist that he had great difficulty finding the sponsorship and testimonials needed.

John Newton

First the Bishop of Chester, then the Archbishop of Canterbury, then the Archbishop of York all refused Newton ordination. Dr Edward Young of Welwyn was applied to for help, but although he felt Newton should be ordained his influence was not great enough to persuade any of his friends in church authority to consider Newton's application. Despairing of getting help from the bishops, Mr Crooke turned to Henry Venn and asked him to use his influence on Lord Dartmouth, who was in charge of several livings.

At this time several Independent churches called Newton to their pastorates, making his situation very difficult. William Romaine was so convinced that Newton had a calling to the ministry that he advised him to take up an Independent church. Meanwhile, apart from carrying out his duties at the docks, Newton was preaching and publishing sermons — even those that he had never preached!

Now Lady Huntingdon joined Newton's friends in seeking to find a church for him and Newton was beginning to think his future service must be in Yorkshire. At this time he wrote of that county as if it were a foretaste of heaven. He told Captain Clunie,

> I have lately been a journey into Yorkshire. That is a flourishing country indeed, like Eden, the garden of the Lord, watered on every side by the streams of the gospel. There the voice of the turtle is heard in all quarters, and multitudes rejoice in the light. I have a pretty large acquaintance there among various denominations, who, though they differ in some lesser things, are all agreed to exalt Jesus and His salvation. I do not mean that the truth is preached in every church and meeting through the county, but in many — perhaps in more, proportionably, than in any other part of the land, and with greater effect, both as to numbers and as to the depth of the work in particular persons. It is very refreshing to go from place to place and find the same fruits of faith, love, joy, and peace.'

In 1764 God called John Newton to the full-time ministry in a totally different area of England. Newton had been corresponding with Thomas Haweis, Martin Madan's assistant, and Haweis had been offered the curacy of Olney in Buckinghamshire. The vicar there was Moses Browne, a former curate of James Hervey and one of the pioneers of the Evangelical Revival.

Browne had been appointed vicar by Lord Dartmouth, who was in charge of the living. Though Browne was a keen Evangelical, he was influenced by the established views of the day whereby a minister could have several livings in order to be provided with a good income, having no responsibility to shepherd his flocks. Thus Browne was vicar of several churches in the Olney area but lived in Blackheath, where he served Morden College in the capacity of chaplain. In this way he 'earned' well over an extra £100 a year which helped him care for his extremely large family. Second-generation Evangelicals, including Newton, fought against this misuse of a shepherd's duties and of money.

When Haweis received the invitation to Olney, he immediately thought of John Newton and asked Lord Dartmouth to consider appointing Newton rather than himself to the office. So it was that on 1 March 1764 Newton received two letters, one from Haweis telling him to pack his bags and travel to London for ordination, and the other from Lord Dartmouth offering him the curacy of Olney and £60 a year. With Lord Dartmouth's full backing, Newton soon found a bishop — the Bishop of Lincoln — who agreed to ordain him. The neighbouring Anglican clergy, however, rebelled at the thought of having a 'Methodist' at hand and refused to give Newton the testimonials he needed. The Independent and Baptist churches in the district, on the other hand, rejoiced to have Newton with them.

Eventually all obstacles were removed and Newton first preached at Olney on 27 May 1764. His diary entry for that day shows that he knew his curacy would not be a bed of roses: 'I find a cordial reception amongst those who know the truth, but many are far otherwise minded. I desire to be faithful and honest, and patiently to pursue the path of duty through both good and ill report.'

God blessed Newton's ministry from the start. People of all denominations flocked to hear him preach, so that he was obliged to increase the seating capacity of the church and erect a gallery to make room for the newcomers. He preached in the surrounding villages and soon found a group of ministers from various denominations who were keen to work with him. The greatest Evangelical stalwarts of the day, such as Whitefield, Romaine, Venn, Hill, Bull and Berridge, offered him their prayers and support and promised him they would be prepared to assist him in the Olney pulpit whenever he thought it necessary.

Olney Parish Church

What Newton and Cowper had in common

We have once more reached the time of Cowper's first contact with Newton in Huntingdon. The differences in background between these two men are now obvious. The two friends, however, had very much in common regarding their characters and experiences.

Both friends spent their earliest years in a secure Christian environment but lost their mothers before the age of seven. Neither friend experienced a normal family life during his childhood from that time on.

Both men experienced times of wantonness and rebellion against God which made them go to very grave extremes. Both went through times of great depression. Both were guilty of contemplating murder, though Cowper to a lesser extent than Newton. Both seriously contemplated suicide on at least one occasion. Newton often reminded himself that it was his love for Mary Catlett that had saved him from going as far as Cowper did. Both men's depressions increased with growing age. Newton, however, was far more able to cope with his than Cowper. He would merely tell himself that he was getting old and weak, so what could you expect? Cowper could never rationalize in this way and looked upon his depressions as the chastising hand of God. Whatever happened to both men, however, they accepted it as the just and righteous will of God.

Neither of the two friends enjoyed good physical health and both experienced major bouts of illness from time to time. Newton used to say that his health was as his wealth — strictly mediocre!

Both men had extraordinary dreams at times and were prepared to be led by them. Cowper always insisted, however, that what God deemed unnecessary to reveal in Scripture, he would not reveal in any other way. Newton, especially in his earlier years as a minister, looked upon dreams as a legitimate method of revelation parallel to the Scriptures.

Reading through the lives of these two men reveals how both stressed time and time again that they were living wonders and stood in a completely different relationship to God from any other men. The words, 'There was never a case like mine,' or similar expressions, occur like a refrain in their writings. This belief always made Newton praise God the more, whereas the same conviction caused Cowper much anxious thought.

Both men were very fond of Milton and Herbert. Both men were gentle in their nature, though they could both be very stubborn. Newton, like Cowper, was very demanding of his friends and this led to disappointments and jealousies at times. Both were convinced Calvinists and loyal to the Church of England but neither held back their criticisms of their church and both had good fellowship with Baptists, Presbyterians and Independents on a personal level. Both friends campaigned for full political and social freedom for Roman Catholics, reformed as they were!

The two men had very similar experiences in obtaining new appointments. Cowper had coveted the position of Clerk of the Journals whilst it was still occupied. Newton's employer had striven to obtain the post of tide-surveyor for him whilst it was still occupied, too. Both occupants suddenly died leaving the positions free. In both cases there was a strong political opposition. Newton gained the post but Cowper lost his.

When Cowper was to take up a senior post under Ashley Cowper's patronage, the matter was debated in the House of Lords. As a result, Ashley Cowper's privileges were modified and Cowper had to take that fateful examination. When Newton was given the living of St Mary Woolnoth, London, under the patronage of the Thorntons, many parishioners protested strongly as they believed a church should be free to call its own pastor. This matter, too, was debated in the House of Lords with the result that the Thorntons' right to fill the living was confirmed.

Newton's position as a tide-surveyor was very similar to Cowper's work as a Commisioner for Bankrupts. There were also sinecures involved which troubled both friends in the same way.

Both Newton and Cowper had to endure wagging tongues, even from their closest associates, for many years. Newton was accused of being unchaste as a Christian slave-trader and Cowper was looked upon by some in the same light for remaining under Mrs Unwin's care. Both men were completely innocent of such evil charges.

Both friends had the same love for the countryside. Indeed, when we compare their expressions of joy in viewing God's nature, it is as if they spoke in one voice. This similarity of language both in their verse and prose is very evident. The two friends even shared the same kind of humour so that when their jokes and teasings are seen in print, it is impossible to say which of them was the author.

Scholars are still puzzling their heads about a lengthier work which most are convinced is Cowper's, yet a few others are just as convinced that it is Newton's.[4]

All this helps us to understand Newton's constant reference to himself and Cowper as sharing one heart.

A doting friend

Newton's attachment to Cowper was so strong that it was only surpassed by his love for his wife, Mary. Looking back on those early years at Olney together, Newton wrote that he was full of admiration for Cowper and that he strove to imitate him. What impressed him the most was Cowper's command of God's Word and his ability, with God's help, to live by it.

Whereas Cowper constantly mourned his lack of holiness, Newton said of his friend in later years, 'The wisdom which is from above, which is pure and peaceable, gentle and easy to be entreated, full of mercy and good works, without partiality and without hypocrisy, possessed and filled his heart. The wonders and riches of redeeming love, as manifested by the glorious gospel of the blessed God, were the food of his soul, the source of his joys, the habitual subject of his study, and suggested the leading topics of his conversation. Like the apostle, he was determined to know nothing comparatively but Jesus Christ and Him crucified.'

Whereas Cowper felt he could hardly ever pray aright, if at all, Newton says that when Cowper prayed, 'He seemed to speak, though with self-abasement and humiliation of spirit, yet with that freedom and fervency, as if he saw the Lord whom he addressed face to face.'

Cowper tended to be very critical towards himself in his writings, stressing his failures. One might thus even gain the impression at times that he was a lazy, self-indulgent, good-for-nothing who had deserved all the bolts that God could throw at him. It is only when reading the evaluations of his friends and his works that we see what a man of God Cowper really was.

Newton's admiration of Cowper,was, however, a source of embarrassment to the poet at times, because he felt that his friend never really knew him. He just could not identify himself with the picture Newton had of him. The plain fact was that Newton was extremely sensitive and unduly doting in his friendship. He certainly put Cowper on too high a pedestal and was all the more disappointed when his friend did not live up to his expectations. These particulars help to explain the nature of Cowper's letters to Newton, which are invariably more self-critical and self-searching than his letters to other friends and reveal his most intimate thoughts and fears, which he did not reveal to others.

Newton sometimes went through greatly exaggerated anxieties because of his over-protective interest in Cowper. He became very worried, for instance, when Cowper made new friends, frightened all the time that they might not be the right ones. In some instances his behaviour towards William Unwin, John Cowper, Lady Hesketh and William Hayley can only be understood by realizing that Newton was jealous of them. There is no other rational explanation.

Shortly after Cowper's death, though himself now very feeble, extremely deaf and almost blind, Newton penned the following tribute in verse to his friend:

> I had a friend beloved; and well we knew
> Union of heart, confiding, fond, and true.
> We dwelt together, and I watched him still
> An untired pilgrim toward the heavenly hill—
> A soldier, 'mid a troop of hostile foes—
> A Christian, finding 'neath the cross repose.
> I watched him, and admired, when lowly bent
> He owned the cup of grief in mercy sent
> For he had watched earth's treasures fade away,
> And sought in God his refuge and his stay.
> I heard him, and admired, for he could bring
> From his soft harp such strains as angels sing—
> Could tell of free salvation, grace, and love
> Till angels listened from their home above.
> I woke my lyre to join his rapturous strain—
> We sang together of the Lamb once slain.

It is obvious from this loving tribute to Cowper that Newton was encouraged to write hymns by Cowper's Christian testimony in verse. We shall see in subsequent chapters how Cowper, in his turn, received a major impetus to become a professional Christian poet through his fellowship with John Newton. Not only do the *Olney*

Hymns show the marks of a close co-operation and calling between these two friends, but so does much of the literature that issued from their pens during the many productive years that followed. They became partners both in prose and poetry. Cowper's productions are, on the whole, of a higher literary standard but he produced far less in writing than his friend Newton. Newton's works contain much that is doggerel and bathos but at times he reaches heights of beauty and pathos that equal the best of Cowper.

6.
Life at Olney

The Unwins' house in Huntingdon had been a very pleasantly situated building in a rural area. The neighbours were all comparatively well off and there was little poverty to be seen in the town. When the Unwins first saw their new home at Silver End, Olney, it presented a completely different picture and they were very disappointed. 'It looks like a prison,' was William Unwin's first comment as he surveyed the sober-looking brick-faced building with mock battlements around its rooftop.

Had Cowper been the solace-seeker and hermit depicted in the many myths which have grown up around his name, Orchard Side, as the building was called, would probably have been the last place on earth he would have chosen for a home. The north-facing building stood directly on the causeway of the main road without so much as a strip of garden to protect it from the noise of the London-bound traffic. Immediately opposite stood the market-place and fair grounds and Orchard Side seemed to be surrounded by inns and public houses, so that Cowper was scarcely exaggerating when he said that in Olney you could not walk twenty paces without passing one. This was because the town had been an important tolling station and was still a much-used resting-place for coach parties passing between London and the north and for pedlars and merchants journeying to the Bedford markets.

Cowper's new home was flanked on both sides by some of the poorest cottages in the town, in which their inhabitants slept on straw and were constantly near starvation in spite of their great industry in lacemaking. No one could be more proud of Olney than

Orchard Side, home of Cowper and Mrs Unwin at Olney
(now the Cowper and Newton museum)

Thomas Wright, the Olney schoolteacher and Cowper's biographer. When referring to Orchard Side, however, he drops into laconic understatement by saying, 'It was not the most agreeably situated house in the town, truly,' and goes on to call Silver End 'the Alsatia of Olney.'[1]

Once inside the house, what the friends saw did not serve to give them a better opinion of their new premises. One half of the house adjacent to the poorer dwellings had become ramshackle and was infested with rats. There were signs of damp in the floors and walls. For years afterwards this part of the house (the larger part) was merely boarded up and left to rot undisturbed. Mrs Unwin, still weak from her illness, must have had a fright when she saw the cooking facilities. They were primitive, even by mid-eighteenth century standards. When they rose on the morning of the first day, impressions of the house did not improve. Orchard Side was so close to the River Ouse that clouds of mist, later nicknamed 'marsh miasma', by Cowper, enveloped the lower storey of the house and smells similar to rotting vegetables greeted their newly awakened noses.

The back of the house was, however, far more pleasant. Behind a useful-looking outhouse there was a large, though narrow, vegetable garden with a pretty little garden-house in it. Further on in the direction of Newton's new home there was an orchard (hence the name 'Orchard Side') which belonged to a Mrs Aspray. Cowper and Newton called this the 'Guinea Field' as they paid a guinea a year to use it as a shortcut between the Vicarage and Orchard Side. When Cowper first saw Newton's newly enlarged and renovated vicarage, there was perhaps a touch of envy in his description of it. He found the house 'a smart stone building, well sashed, much too good for the living'. Newton had a doorway cut into his garden wall facing the Guinea Field so he could quickly walk over to Orchard Side. Soon the two friends were spending so much time in each other's houses that they seemed to live permanently in both.

The town

Olney in Cowper's day was 'a large and necessitous parish', as Newton's biographer, Richard Cecil, called it, and an important centre of the lacemaking industry. At least 1,500 of the inhabitants

Olney market-place

were connected with that trade. Cowper wrote that 1,200 of the lacemakers were living on the verge of starvation because prices had dropped with the declining demand owing to foreign competition and the new tastes of the day.

The town boasted a town hall, a prison, a school, a flour mill and a host of maltsters and breweries to supply the fifty-six or so public houses. The off-door breweries also served the inhabitants directly, as tea-drinking was still a luxury amongst working-class people and the customary drink was beer. There was a fairly large general store in the town, as well as a baker's, a draper's, an ironmonger's, a barber's, a butcher's, a carpenter's, a wagoner's and a blacksmith's. The Olney inhabitants were avid newspaper readers so a 'newsmonger's'[2] also graced the town. There was also a regular daily post service to and from Olney.

There may have been some affluence in the town as there were a number of watchmakers in business there who did not seem to be of the poorest sort. Perhaps they looked to the officers of the drummer corps stationed at Olney for their custom. There were no gentry resident in the town although there were several rows of very large stone houses, dating from the seventeenth century, which had been built by more prosperous citizens. By Cowper's day, however, a number of them had been turned into lodging-houses or were inhabited by several families. Indeed, overcrowding was rampant in the town as there was a shortage of housing and of money to pay rents. The various large manor houses at Olney testified to the fact that the town had grown out of several smaller communities which had attracted nobility in better times. One of these manor houses, the Great House, owned by Cowper's Westminster friend, Lord Dartmouth, was used by Newton as a community hall and as a place of prayer during the week.

Evangelical activity

What Olney lacked in worldly splendour, it made up for in evangelical activity. The town had long been a centre of good preaching and since Moses Browne had become the minister most of the British Evangelical and Dissenting leaders had preached there. Thus the people of Olney became used to hearing Hill, Venn, Berridge, Romaine and even Whitefield, besides Newton, Thomas

Scott, Andrew Fuller, William Bull and the Rylands. Apart from the large cathedral-like Anglican church, Olney had several Independent meeting-houses, a Baptist church and a Quaker meeting-place. Ministerial convocations were often held there, weather permitting, in the field between Newton's and Cowper's houses.

The Baptists in Olney were particularly strong and it was through the auspices of John Sutcliff, the Baptist minister, that Jonathan Edwards' books were introduced into England. A famous member of Sutcliff's church was William Carey, who became one of Britain's first missionaries in the modern sense of the word.

One of the most interesting characters in Olney was William Wilson, the town's barber. Wilson was an ardent member of Newton's church but became a Baptist after Newton left Olney.[3] He caused visiting wealthy ladies a great deal of discomfort because of his Christian witness. It was the fashion for the ladies to have their hair piled up as much as a foot and more high on Sunday mornings so that they would look fine for the church service. Wilson, however, respected the Sabbath and would not set the ladies' hair on that day. Thus the poor women who put beauty before comfort had to have their hair done on a Saturday and stay up all night sitting in a straight-backed chair so as not to spoil their lovely locks.

One of Cowper's earliest letters from Olney shows how the various denominations in the town could live peacefully together sharing a great oneness in Christ. Cowper, writing to Mrs Madan, says,

We have had a Holiday Week at Olney. The Association of Baptist Ministers met here on Wednesday. We had three Sermons from them that day, and One on Thursday, besides Mr. Newton's in the Evening. One of the Preachers was Mr. Booth,[4] who has lately published an excellent Work called the Reign of Grace. He was bred a Weaver, and has been forced to work with his Hands hitherto for the Maintenance of himself and a large Family. But the Lord who has given him excellent Endowments, has now called him from the small Congregation he minister'd to in Nottinghamshire, to supply Mr. Burford's Place in London.[5] It was a comfortable Sight to see thirteen Gospel Ministers together. Most of them either Preach'd or Pray'd and All that did so approved themselves sound in the Word and Doctrine, whence a good Presumption arises in favour of the rest. I should be glad if the Partition Wall between Christians of different Denominations would every where fall down flat as it has done at Olney. The Dissenters here, most of them at least who are serious, forget that our Meeting House has a Steeple to it, and we that theirs has none. This shall be the Case universally, may the Lord hasten it in his time!

I am my dear Aunt your very affectionate Nephew

Wm Cowper.[6]

It was this spiritual side of Olney that had drawn Cowper to the town and not a longing to live in luxury and ease. Thus the poet settled down to life at Olney far better than the Unwin children, who did not stay there long. Mrs Unwin, devoted as she was to serving Cowper, would have stayed with him wherever he went.

Rumours and gossip

Strangely enough, Cowper was hardly settled in Olney when tongues began to wag that he was to be married to Mrs Unwin. Mrs Cowper, William's cousin, was even told that he had already married. The very idea was preposterous. How these stories got about, Cowper did not know, but it is obvious that some of his closest friends, including Newton, were to be blamed. Newton, who was so very happily married himself, did not yet know of the terrible experiences Cowper had had with Theadora, nor did he yet understand the relationship between Mrs Unwin and his new friend. Christian friends who were supporting Newton saw that Mrs Unwin was obviously a deeply spiritual person, well read and well mannered and devoted to Cowper. They also noticed that she was a most handsome woman and somehow deduced from this 'evidence' that she must be romantically attracted to the poet. Gossip like this hurt both Mrs Unwin and Cowper deeply and was obviously one of the reasons which led to Cowper's second serious depression in 1773.

Newton first let himself be persuaded that marriage would be the best plan for Cowper and Mrs Unwin, but gradually came to see that it was folly to suppose that there was any romance between his two friends. Later Newton was to back Cowper up when tongues wagged, as wag they did for a further five years or so.

Both Cowper's and Mrs Unwin's letters testify to a deep friendship and an unusually strong mother-son relationship between the two. There is, however, no trace of anything tending towards romantic love in their letters to each other. Although Cowper did call Mrs Unwin by her first name, this was according to his station and the decorum of the age. Mrs Unwin always called him 'Mr Cowper' and referred to him as such even to her most intimate friends.

Co-operation with Newton

The next five or six years were the busiest in Cowper's whole life. He spent most of the day with Newton, assisting him in his work and literary studies. Newton was so taken up with Cowper that he thought the poet was the very man who could, as he put it, transform the age.

Wherever he went on visiting or preaching tours, he would ask Cowper to go with him, very often accompanied by Mrs Unwin. Apparently Mrs Unwin played a prominent role in assisting Newton in his work, as often when ministers who had been to Olney wrote to Newton, they sent greetings especially to her. It seems that Mrs Unwin accompanied Newton to lead the singing, as even on the occasions when Cowper could not accompany his friend, she tramped across the fields with Newton, or rode on horseback with him from hamlet to hamlet.

Time and time again we find records of Cowper leading the prayer and mid-week meetings and visiting the poor. Andrew Fuller,[7] later a frequent visitor to Olney, writes, 'I know a person who heard him pray frequently at these meetings, and have heard him say, "Of all the men that I have ever heard pray, no one equalled Mr. Cowper."'

The poet was also kept busy writing verse for the various anniversaries and new ventures of the Olney Church. Newton hardly ever made a significant move without recording the most minute particulars of how it came about. Then, for years afterwards, he would celebrate its anniversary. One of his favourite anniversary celebrations was Cowper's arrival at Olney. Not a year passed

whilst Newton remained at Olney, without him calling on Cowper
on 15 February and sharing in a time of praise and prayer with him.
Another favourite anniversary for Newton was to celebrate the
opening of the Great House for the mid-week prayer meetings.
Cowper contributed to these occasions by writing hymns such as
'Jesus, where'er Thy people meet':

> Jesus, where'er thy people meet,
> There they behold thy mercy-seat;
> Where'er they seek thee thou art found,
> And ev'ry place is hallow'd ground.
>
> For thou, within no walls confin'd,
> Inhabitest the humble mind;
> Such ever bring thee, where they come,
> And going, take thee to their home.
>
> Dear Shepherd of thy chosen few!
> Thy former mercies here renew;
> Here, to our waiting hearts, proclaim
> The sweetness of thy saving name.
>
> Here may we prove the pow'r of pray'r,
> To strengthen faith, and sweeten care;
> To teach our faint desires to rise,
> And bring all heav'n before our eyes.
>
> Behold! at thy commanding word,
> We stretch the curtain and the cord;
> Come thou, and fill this wider space,
> And bless us with a large increase.
>
> Lord, we are few, but thou art near;
> Nor short thine arm, nor deaf thine ear;
> Oh rend the heav'ns, come quickly down,
> And make a thousand hearts thine own!

What a hallowed place the platform must have been in the Great
House! Newton and Cowper shared it now and then with Martin
Madan, at times with Berridge or with Venn, sometimes with

Rowland Hill, and on occasions with either William Bull, William Romaine or Lord Dartmouth. Even Samson Occum, the Mohegan Indian pastor, preached at Olney on his tour of England under the auspices of Lady Huntingdon. How blessed the people of Olney must have been to have sat under such ministries of preaching and prayer! Cowper knew Lord Dartmouth far better than Newton, as the two had been to school together, but he would never have met the other great men of the Evangelical Revival if it had not been for Newton.

The following letter to Mrs Madan illustrates how happy Cowper was in his new surroundings and how eagerly he sought to be close to God. It also pays high tribute to the kind of spiritual life that Newton was fostering in Olney.

My dear Aunt,

It is fit I should acknowledge the Goodness of the Lord in bringing me to this Place, abounding with Palm Trees and Wells of living Water. The Lord put into my Heart to desire to partake of his Ordinances and to dwell with his People, and has graciously given me my Heart's Desire: Nothing can exceed the Kindness and Hospitality with which we are received here by his dear Servant Newton: and to be brought under the Ministry of so Wise and faithfull a Steward of his Holy Mysteries is a Blessing for which I can never be sufficiently thankfull. May our heavenly Father grant that our Souls may thrive and flourish in some Proportion to the Abundant Means of Grace we enjoy: for the whole Day is but one continued Opportunity either of seeking him, or conversing about the things of his Kingdom. I find it a difficult matter when surrounded with the Blessings of Providence, to remember that I seek a Country, and that this is not the Place of my Rest. God glorifies himself by bringing Good out of Evil, but it is the Reproach of Man that he is able and always inclined to produce Evil out of the greatest Blessings. The Lord has dealt graciously with me since I came, and I trust I have in two Instances had much delightfull Communion with him: Yet this Liberty of Access was indulged to me in such a way, as to teach me at the same time his great Care that I might not turn it to my Prejudice. I expected that in some Sermon or Exposition I should find him, and that the Lips of this excellent Minister would be the Instrument by which the Lord would work upon & soften my obdurate Heart. But he saw my proneness to idolize the Means, and to praise the Creature more than the Creator, & therefore though he gave me the thing I hoped for, yet he conveyed it to me in a way which I did not look to. On the last Sabbath Morning at a Prayer Meeting before Service, while the poor Folks were singing a Hymn and my Vile Thoughts were rambling to the Ends of the Earth, a single Sentence (And is there no Pity in Jesus's Breast?) seized my attention at once, and my Heart within me seemed to return Answer, Yes, or I had never been here. The Sweetness of this Visit lasted almost thro' the Day, and I was once more enabled to weep under a Sense of the Mercies of a God in Jesus. — On Thursday Morning I attended a Meeting of Children, and found that Passage 'Out of the Mouth of Babes & Sucklings thou hast ordained Praise' Verified in a Sense I little thought of. For at almost every Word they spoke in answer to the several Questions proposed to them, my Heart burned within me, and melted into Tears of Gratitude and Love.

I thought the Singularity of this Dispensation worth your Notice, and having communicated it, am in a manner obliged to break off rather abruptly. Mr. Newton has just brought me one of Martin's Pamphlets, which makes it impossible for me to write any longer. Pray tell him he is a bit of a Traytor for not sending my Narratives at the same time with his own, for I want much to shew it to Mr. and Mrs. Newton.

Yours my dear Aunt affectionately

Wm Cowper.[8]

Cowper witnesses to friends

At Olney Cowper increased his efforts to lead those dear to him to Christ. Soon his manservant, Samuel Roberts, confessed Christ as his Saviour and Mrs Unwin's maid followed suit. The maid's testimony was, however, merely one of convenience and she soon left off pretending to be a Christian, turned into quite the opposite and had to be dismissed. Roberts, however, served the Lord faithfully from then on until his death as a very old man in 1832.

Cowper's attention now turned to Joseph Hill, a difficult task as Hill had known Cowper in his worldly, rakish days and still did not know how to interpret his change of lifestyle. Cowper was also anxious not to lose a very close friend by being too bombastic in his approach. Hill became very ill during the winter of 1768-69 and on his recovery Cowper felt he should use the opportunity to witness in a more definite way to his friend. He therefore sent him the following letter which is clear, concise and very much to the gospel point.

Dear Joe,

I rejoice with you in your Recovery, and that you have escaped from the Hands of One from whose Hands you will not always escape. Death is either the most formidable or the most comfortable thing we have in Prospect on this Side of Eternity. To be brought near to him and to discern neither of these Features in his Face, would argue a Degree of Insensibility of which I will not suspect my Friend whom I know to be a thinking Man. You have been brought down to the Sides of the Grave, and you have been raised again by Him who has the Keys of the invisible World, who opens and none can shut, who shuts and none can open. I do not forget to return Thanks to him on your behalf, and to pray that your Life which he has spared may be devoted to his Service. Behold! I stand at the Door and knock, is the Word of Him on whom both our Mortal and immortal Life depend, and blessed be his Name, it is the Word of One who wounds only that he may heal, and who waits to be Gracious. The Language of every such Dispensation is, Prepare to Meet Thy God. It speaks with the Voice of Mercy and Goodness, for without such Notices whatever Preparation we might make for other Events, we should make none for This. My dear Friend, I desire and pray that when this last Enemy shall come to execute an Unlimited Commission upon us, we may be found ready, being established and rooted in a well grounded Faith in his Name, who conquer'd and triumph'd over him upon his Cross.

Yours ever

Wm Cowper.[9]

Cowper half expected his friend to reply in anger and was overjoyed to receive a letter from Hill which indicated that his friend was far from antagonistic to his Christian views. It would seem that Hill had complimented Cowper on his faith, so the poet wrote back post-haste to assure him that death can only be overcome by grace and not conquered by any inherent virtues.

My dear Joe,

I have drawn upon you by this Post for the Sum of Ten pound Seven Shillings payable to Mr. Alexander Clunie or Order.

I have just a Moment to spare 'till the Tea Kettle boils to tell you that your Letter is just come to hand, and to thank you for it. I do assure you, the Gentleness and Candour of your manner, engages my Affections to you very much. You answer with Mildness to an Admonition which would have provoked many to Anger. I have not time to add more, except just to hint that if I am ever enabled to look forward to Death with Comfort, which I thank God, is some times the case with me, I do not take my View of it from the Top of my own Works & deservings, though God is Witness that the Labour of my Life is to keep a Conscience void of Offence towards him. He is always formidable to me, but when I see him disarmed of his Sting by having sheath'd it in the Body of Christ Jesus.

Yours my dear Friend

Wm Cowper.
Olney.[10]

We do not know whether Joseph Hill came to a saving knowledge of Christ or not. What we learn from Cowper's correspondence with him, however, is that he was sympathetic towards the gospel and showed Cowper an unlimited faithful friendship not surpassed by Cowper's converted friends.

Conversion and death of his brother John

Cowper's evangelistic activities regarding Hill were diverted for a time due to a rapid decline in the state of John Cowper's health. His letters to Hill during the whole of 1770 are thus taken up with news of his brother's illness, his conversion, death and the resulting problems concerning his legacy. This was not merely because Cowper's thoughts were so full of his brother's plight. Joseph Hill was also a good friend of John Cowper's and acted as his financial adviser in a similar capacity to the way he assisted William.

Ever since his own conversion Cowper had been anxious to see his brother John come to know the Lord. John was now in the ministry but had not yet come to see that sinners can only be saved by a power outside of themselves.

Since leaving Huntingdon William and John only managed to see each other two or three times a year owing to both brothers' aversion to travelling far. In order to keep up contact they decided to visit each other at least once a year and then spend as many days as possible together. John's visits to Olney had become, however, rather embarrassing for both sides. John was still unconverted and and behaved as if his brother's faith was a pollution of true Christianity. John hated controversy, so, in order to keep the peace, he decided never to comment on spiritual things whilst at Olney and above all, never to get entangled in a religious conversation.

Cowper hardly knew what to do in the circumstances, as he told his aunt:

> I think I write to you with an Aching Heart upon my poor Brother's Account. He is with us. And his Presence necessarily gives a Turn to the Conversation that we have not been much used to. So much said about nothing, and so little about Jesus, is very painfull to us, but what can be done? May the good Lord make me thankfull that he has given me, I trust, an understanding to know him that is true, and may he in his due time afford me an Occasion of thanking him for the same unspeakable Mercy bestowed upon my Brother. He is going with us this Evening to a Prayer-Meeting at the Vicarage, and we shall have two Sermons preach'd here in the course of the Week. Oh that his Ears may be unstopped, and his Eyes opened to the Things that concern his Peace.[11]

Newton was invariably at Orchard Side when John visited his brother but the two did not get on too well at all. John thought that Newton merely preached what he had 'borrowed' from writers such

as Witsius and had nothing original to offer. William's explanation
that neither Newton nor Witsius sought to preach novelties, but they
were united in a mutual belief in the same faith that the apostle Paul
also enjoyed, did not impress John. Although John visited Olney
Church on several occasions, Newton could, of course, never ask
him to take a service as he usually did when Evangelical ministers
were visiting. Nor was John allowed to take family prayers at Olney
when Newton was present. William thought this might give offence
to his brother but the latter never complained.

The truth was that John's aloofness to scriptural truths was all
outward show. He knew full well that something was lacking in his
own life. When he eventually came to know the truth, his thoughts
turned immediately in Christian love to Newton, whom he was
anxious should hear the good news. Ever since his brother's
conversion, he had suspected that he, himself, did not know the real
gospel. He had thus begun to read Evangelical and Reformed writers
and study the Scriptures diligently, often reading theological and
devotional works with an open Bible so as to check whatever was
written.

In September 1769 Cowper was summoned by John's friends to
Cambridge as his brother was dangerously ill. John had been
working hard on a translation of Apollonius Rhodius and his friends,
fearing for his health, had persuaded him to give up working for a
few weeks and go on a journey to Wales. Rather than recuperating
there, he caught a very bad cold which developed into a fever. His
condition deteriorated and he began to vomit a great deal of blood
so that his doctor feared the worst. William spent ten days with John
but was heartbroken to find that his brother professed no interest in
God and eternity and felt that he was in no danger of dying. Some
time afterwards John told William that he had indeed been thinking
of God but could not bring himself to open up to his brother. As John
grew rapidly better, William returned to Olney after ten days,
wondering why his brother had come so near to eternity yet refused
to give way to God.

Though John was soon up and about, William was called again
to his brother's bedside on 16 February of the following year. This
time there seemed to be no doubt that John was declining fast. He
was suffering badly from asthma, a complaint that affected several
other members of his family, including Martin Madan. He had also
what William calls 'an imposthume in his liver' which had led to

dropsy, a complaint from which Cowper was also to suffer. Again William was alarmed to find that John was in cheerful spirits and had apparently no idea of the seriousness of his condition both bodily and spiritually. John did, however, consent to pray with his brother. Gradually John lost his reserve and began to discuss spiritual matters with William.

On 26 February John was seized with a severe attack of asthma which lasted the whole day. He was in great pain and could hardly breathe. Cowper assured his brother of the presence of Christ and that many friends were praying for him. John began to reply in a way that showed he fully knew what a hopeless spiritual state he was in. When he was exhausted or depressed, John, like his brother, tended to feel that it was God's chastening hand upon him. When the attack had lost its severity and he could talk freely, John said sadly to his brother, 'Brother, I seem marked out for misery; you know some people are so.' William then tells us, 'That moment I felt my heart enlarged and such persuasion of the Love of God to him was wrought in my soul that I replied with confidence, and as if I had authority given me to say it, "But that is not your case, you are marked out for mercy."'[12]

Further attacks came on the next day. Cowper heard his brother crying in great pain, 'Thy rod and thy staff support and comfort me.' He spoke of himself in repentance and in acknowledgement that he was far from God. William's comment later in writing was: 'I thought I could discern in these expressions the glimpses of approaching day and have no doubt at present but that the Spirit of God was gradually preparing him in a way of true humiliation for that bright display of Gospel grace, which He was afterwards pleased to afford him.'

John continued in great suffering until 10 March, when Cowper heard him at prayer, exclaiming, 'Behold, I create new heavens and a new earth!' to which he added the words, 'Ay, and he is able to do it too.' William realized what was happening and a day later he was able to write to Mrs Unwin about the miracle that had occurred:

I am in haste to make you a partaker of my joy. Oh praise the Lord with me, and let us exalt his Name together. Yesterday, in the afternoon, my Brother suddenly burst into tears, and said with a loud cry, 'Oh! forsake me not!' I went to his bed-side, when he grasped my hand, and I presently by his eyes and countenance found that he was in prayer. Then, turning to me, he said, 'Brother, I am full of what I could say to you.' I left him for about an hour, lest he should fatigue himself by too much talking, and because I wanted to praise the Lord for what I understood to be a clear evidence of a work begun. When I returned, he said, 'Brother, if I live, you and I shall be more like one another than we have been. Whether I live or not live, all is well and will be so. I know it will, for I have felt that which I never felt before; and I am sure that God has visited me with this sickness, in order to teach me what I was too proud to learn in health. I never had satisfaction till now. The doctrines I had been used to referred me to myself for the foundation of my hope, and there I could find nothing to rest upon. The sheet anchor of the soul was wanting. I thought you wrong, yet wanted to believe as you did. I found myself unable to believe, yet always thought that I should one day be brought to do so. You suffered more than I have done, before you believed these truths, but our sufferings, though different in their kind and measure, were directed to the same end. I hope he has taught me that which he teaches none but his own. I hope so. These things were foolishness to me once, I could not understand them, but now I have a solid foundation and am satisfied.'

When I went to bid him good night, he resumed his discourse as follows — 'As empty, yet full, as having nothing, and yet possessing all things. I see the rock upon which I once split, and I see the Rock of my salvation. I have peace, myself, and if I live, I hope it will be that I may be made a messenger of the same peace to others. I have learnt that in a moment, which I could not have learnt by reading many books for many years. I have often studied these points, and studied them with great attention, but was blinded by prejudice, and unless He who alone is worthy to unloose the seals, had opened the book to me, I had been blinded still. Now they appear so plain, that though I am convinced no comment could ever have made me understand them, I wonder I did not see them before. Yet my doubts and difficulties have only served to pave the way, and now they are solved, they make it plainer. The light I have received comes late, but it is a comfort to me, that I never made the

Gospel truths a subject of ridicule. Though I was averse to the persuasion and the ways of God's people, I ever thought them respectable, and therefore not proper to be made a jest of. The evil I suffer, is the consequence of my descent from the corrupt original stock, and of my own transgressions. The good I enjoy, comes to me as the overflowing of his bounty. But the crown of all his mercies is this, that he has given me a Saviour, and not only the Saviour of mankind, but *my* Saviour.'

He said that the moment when he sent forth that cry was the moment when light was darted into his soul.

March 12. In the evening, he said, 'This bed would be a bed of misery, and it is so; but it is likewise a bed of joy, and it is a bed of discipline. Were I to die this night, I know I should be happy. This assurance, I trust, is quite consistent with the word of God. It is built upon a sense of my own utter insufficiency, and the all-sufficiency of Christ. — Brother, I have been building my glory upon a sandy foundation. I have laboured night and day to perfect myself in things of no profit. I have sacrificed my health to these pursuits, and am now suffering the consequences. But how contemptible do the writers I once so highly valued appear to me now. Yea, doubtless, and I account all things loss and dung for the excellency of the knowledge of Christ Jesus my Lord. I must now go to a new school. I have many things to learn. I succeeded in my former pursuits. I wanted to be highly applauded, and I was so. I was flattered up to the height of my wishes. Now I must learn a new lesson.'

March 13. In the morning — 'God is very good to me. I have had a charming night. I hope I shall recover. These sweats have been my cure. They are not the effect of medicine; they are the finger of God. I see it, and hope I am thankful for it. But my desire of recovery extends no further than my hope of usefulness. Unless I live to be an instrument of good to others, it were better for me to die now. What comfort I have in this bed! miserable as I seem to be. Brother! I love to look at you. I see now who was right, and who was mistaken. But it seems wonderful that almost a miracle should be necessary to [en]force that which appears so very plain. I wish myself at Olney. You have a good river there, better than all the rivers of Damascus. What a scene is passing before me! Ideas upon these subjects, crowd faster upon me than I can give them utterance. How plain do many texts appear, to which I could hardly once affix a meaning, after consulting all the commentators, and now they are as clear as the day, without any Comment at all. There is but one key to the New Testament. There is but one Interpreter. I cannot describe to you, nor shall ever be able to describe what I felt in the moment He gave it to me. I shudder to think of the danger I have just escaped. I had made up my mind on these subjects, and was determined to hazard all upon the justness of my own opinions.'

March 18. The sweats which seemed so favourable at first to my brother's recovery, have at last greatly lowered him both in strength and spirits, so that it is found necessary to check them. He is so weak, he can hardly move a limb. His difficulty of breathing is returned; yet the clearness of his views remain, even though he is delirious at times. Last night, he spoke as follows— 'There is more joy over one sinner that repenteth, than over ninety and nine just persons that need no repentance. That text has been sadly misunderstood — Where is that just person to be found? Alas! what must have become of me, if I had died this day sennight! What should I have had to plead? My own righteousness? That would have been of great service to me, to be sure. Well, whither then? Why to the mercy of God — but I had no reason to hope for that, except upon scriptural grounds. Well, whither next? Why, to the mountains, to cover us, and to the rocks to fall upon us! I am not duly thankful for the mercy I have received. Perhaps I may ascribe some part of my insensibility to my great weakness of body. I hope, at least, that if I was better in health, it would be better with me in these respects also.'

He is indeed exceedingly weak, and complains a little that his understanding fails him. His speech is like that of an infant, and it is not possible that he should be laid much lower than he is.

He said just now— 'I have been proud — I have been vain of my understanding, and of my acquirements in this place; and now God has made me little better than an idiot, as much as to say, Now be proud if you can.' And again he said, 'While I have any senses left, my thoughts will be poured out in the praise of God. I have an interest in Christ, in his blood and sufferings, and my sins are forgiven me. Have I not cause to praise him? When my understanding fails me quite, as I think it will soon, then he will consider my weakness.'

W. C.[13]

During the sweet fellowship that William now enjoyed for a few days with his brother, John's thoughts went out to Olney. He expressed a strong wish to meet with believers there but he wept at the thought, thinking himself unworthy of their company. Then he spoke of Newton and said that if he lived, he would rejoice if he could have at least an hour's conversation with that saint. When Newton heard from Cowper that his brother had become a Christian, he wrote, 'Remember me affectionately to your brother. I can truly say I esteemed him; I loved him before. My regard has been increased by the share I have taken in his concerns during his illness; but how much more is he dear to me since I knew that we were united in the love of the truth! With what pleasure shall I now receive him at Olney, now the restraints we were mutually under, for fear of giving each other pain, are removed.'[14]

John's sense of his own worthlessness was now so strong that he was more afraid of living than of dying lest he should prove useless to the Lord. On the evening of 19 March there were signs that he would live rather than die and William left him for the night with a cheerful heart. When William went into John's room the following morning, his brother seemed to be sleeping peacefully. It was the peace, however, of a dying man who was right with God. A few minutes later he was with his new-found Master. William wrote, 'But the Lord, in Whose sight the death of His saints is precious, cut short his sufferings and gave him a speedy and peaceful departure.'

Though William was overjoyed at John's conversion, his brother's death still came as a great shock. He was advised not to stay for the funeral on the grounds that it would be too much for his tender nerves. Perhaps a more valid reason was that John's university friends felt that William had done John a disservice by leading him to Christ and wanted to say farewell to their friend in their own semi-pagan way. Thus Cowper, who had to live with the accusations of these 'friends' for quite some time after his brother's death, returned to Olney after paying his last respects to his brother at his bedside.

A period of busy activity

Once back at Orchard Side, Cowper threw himself into the work
with Newton with renewed vigour, though there were signs that he
was living under great nervous strain. Of this time Newton writes,

> We were, as, I have said, very much together; for, besides
> our frequent walks and visits at home, occasional journeys
> seldom parted us. We usually travelled together. He was soon
> known in many places, and everywhere admired by
> competent judges, as a gentleman and a scholar. He was a
> great blessing to the Lord's poor and afflicted people at Olney
> in the still higher and more important character of an eminent
> and exemplary Christian. For he had drunk deeply into the
> spirit of his Lord; he loved the poor, often visited them in their
> cottages, conversed with them in the most condescending
> manner, sympathised with them, counselled and comforted
> them in their distresses, and those who were seriously
> disposed were often cheered and animated by his prayers...
> While I remained at Olney we had meetings two or three
> times in a week for prayer. These he constantly attended with
> me. For a time his natural constitutional unwillingness to be
> noticed in public kept him in silence. But it was not very long
> before, the ardency of his love to the Saviour, and his desire
> of being useful to others broke through every restraint.[15]

The long walks that Newton and Cowper took together almost
daily were used by the friends to deepen their fellowship, prepare
their witness for the following days and to discuss literature with
each other. When Newton left Olney to take up new duties in
London, he often bemoaned the fact that he could not replenish his
spirit in the woods and fields around Olney. Cowper got so used to
marching off into the countryside for several hours at a time with
Newton that when his friend left Olney Cowper continued to take
the walks by himself, notebook in hand, jotting down any spiritual
thought or poetic lines that came to mind.

Cowper's life was now so busy that his relations became
concerned that he was overdoing it. His work as Newton's unpaid
curate gave him very little time for poetic work and letter-writing.
Nevertheless after John Cowper's death, he found time to write

lengthy letters to his relations, telling them of John's last illness and conversion. These letters are bright and cheerful, full of joy in his brother's conversion and hope that he would meet him again in glory. Cowper also renewed his efforts to introduce Joseph Hill to Christ and plainly pointed out to him the one and only way. He had also a great deal of correspondence to take care of regarding his brother's debts which had to be cleared up and his assets which had to be sold. Financially speaking, William was a loser by John's death as he had formerly received a regular allowance from him. Otherwise he had no fixed income apart from endowments from his various relations and the interest and profit gained from some stock he held. Thus when Joseph Hill found out that John Cowper had £700 in the bank, he wrote to Cowper straight away to tell him the good news. Cowper discovered to his dismay, however, that £350 of the money belonged to John Cowper's college and he was left with £350 out of which he had to pay a considerable amount in settling his brother's affairs. He was, however, able to pay some long-standing tailor's bills with the remainder.

During these early Olney years Mrs Unwin had a great deal of worry with her housekeeping and servants and had to dig deep into her own savings to make ends meet. She had particular difficulty with the maids. The first maid at Olney had to be sacked because of bad conduct. The second maid, who was sent her by Cowper's aunt, had to be sacked after only a week because she was 'absolutely unqualified in every Respect both as Cook & Housemaid, and unable to do the least thing aright', as Cowper told Mrs Madan. The third maid, Molly, entered into Mrs Unwin's service in the summer of 1768 and quickly proved to be a most excellent choice, not only serving Mrs Unwin with great skill but also causing her great joy by her Christian profession.

Molly, however, became very ill with smallpox and died in early 1771 and, as the disease was highly contagious, the other inhabitants had to leave Orchard Side. As Mr and Mrs Newton were on a preaching tour at the time, there was no other roof in the town available apart from one of the many Olney inns. Thus Cowper and Mrs Unwin found themselves guests at the very noisy, bad-smelling Bull Inn.

When John Newton wrote informing Cowper of the blessings he was experiencing, he went on to say,

How is it I have written so much about myself before I
expressed my great grief to think of the inconveniences to
which Mrs. Unwin and yourself must be exposed at the Bull?
I think, had we been at Olney, we could not have suffered you
to have gone there. I long for Tuesday, that I may again think
of you as living snugly at Orchard Side. What can you both
do at the Bull, surrounded with noise and nonsense, day and
night? Well, we cannot help it now. You have had a great
cross, and I hope the Lord has sweetened it, and enabled you
to bear it. I know His presence can comfort you in the midst
of bulls and bears. That Molly should stay a day or two after
the time appointed for her departure, on purpose that she
might die in the house, was a very serious dispensation; but
it was not by chance. Some voice, some end, there certainly
was in this providence, though I am at present unable to guess
it. The Lord can easily make up to you and Mrs. Unwin the
trouble it has occasioned.[16]

Newton wasted no time in finding a new maid for Mrs Unwin. He
visited Mrs Wilberforce, aunt of the famous abolitionist William
Wilberforce, during his preaching tour and broached the subject
with her. Soon he could write to Orchard Side saying that Mrs
Wilberforce had found a new maid for his Olney friends.

Cowper's thoughts now turned more than ever to writing about
the Christian faith and during the next two-and-a-half years he wrote
well over fifty hymns. John Cowper had clearly testified to the
difference between a born-again Christian and one who was a mere
nominal believer. Cowper versified these thoughts in his hymn-
poem 'The Christian':

Honor and happiness unite
To make the christian's name a praise;
How fair the scene, how clear the light,
That fills the remnant of his days!

A kingly character he bears,
No change his priestly office knows;
Unfading is the crown he wears,
His joys can never reach a close.

Adorn'd with glory from on high,
Salvation shines upon his face;
His robe is of th'etherial dye,
His steps are dignity and grace.

Inferior honors he disdains,
Nor stoops to take applause from earth;
The King of kings himself, maintains
Th'expences of his heav'nly birth.

The noblest creature seen below,
Ordain'd to fill a throne above;
God gives him all he can bestow,
His kingdom of eternal love!

My soul is ravish'd at the thought!
Methinks from earth I see him rise;
Angels congratulate his lot,
And shout him welcome to the skies!

Cowper began to study the Word with renewed effort and started to examine the relationship between language and revelation. He saw clearly that though sin had 'marred all' that was a product of human nature, the Word of God, in his divine plan of salvation, had been spared this corruption. With these thoughts in mind, he composed 'The Light and Glory of the Word':

The Spirit breathes upon the word,
And brings the truth to sight;
Precepts and promises afford
A sanctifying light.

A glory gilds the sacred page,
Majestic like the sun;
It gives a light to ev'ry age,
It gives, but borrows none.

The hand that gave it, still supplies
The gracious light and heat;

His truths upon the nations rise,
They rise, but never set.

Let everlasting thanks be thine!
For such a bright display,
As makes a world of darkness shine
With beams of heav'nly day.

My soul rejoices to pursue
The steps of him I love;
Till glory breaks upon my view
In brighter worlds above.

Olney was not only a snug little nest of humble, Bible-believing Christians, though most of its inhabitants would have called themselves such. There were very many bigots, Hyper-Calvinists and Antinomians in the town. These 'believers' proved a thorn in John Newton's flesh and an even greater burden to Thomas Scott, who became curate in Olney some time after Newton left.

Newton, for instance, loved to have fellowship with the Baptists and received great blessings from their ministers' conferences. Bigots in the parish, however, felt that Baptists were not 'of the chosen few' and compelled their pastor to refrain from attending the Baptist meetings. Newton followed their wishes in order to keep the peace but nevertheless invited visiting Baptist ministers to dine with him whenever the occasion offered itself. At times Newton breakfasted in the Vicarage with as many as a dozen Dissenting and Baptist ministers at once.

Newton, however, refused point blank to give way to the Antinomians in the parish. He could not even accept Antinomians as born-again believers and called them 'pretending Christians'. His argument was that 'While they have laid claim to faith, [they] have renounced and blasphemed that holiness without which no man shall see the Lord.'[17] Cowper was of one mind with his friend on this subject and circulated the following poem, entitled 'Antinomians' amongst the Olney believers. It is bitingly strong in its language and shows how Cowper abhorred any attempt of the Antinomians to tempt God.

Too many Lord, abuse thy grace
In this Licentious Day,

And while they boast they see thy Face,
They turn their Own away.

Thy Book displays a gracious Light,
That can the Blind restore,
But These are dazzled by the Sight,
And Blinded still the more.

The Pardon such presume upon,
They do not Beg but Steal,
And when they plead it at thy Throne,
Oh, where's the Gospel Seal?

Was it for This, ye Lawless Tribe,
The dear Redeemer Bled?
Is This the grace the Saints imbibe
From Christ the Living Head?

Oh Lord! we know thy Chosen Few,
Are fed with heav'nly Fare,
But These — the wretched Husks they chew,
Proclaim them what they are.

The Liberty our Hearts implore,
Is, not to Live in Sin,
But still to wait at Wisdom's Door,
Till Mercy calls us in.

Cowper's idea of writing poetry at this time was to put Bible truths in verse form to make them easier to learn off by heart and keep in memory. Editors have often left these early hymns and poems out of their collections on the grounds that they are unsingable and unpoetic. Cowper neither wrote these to be sung nor strove to produce a masterpiece of poetic diction, but solely wished to put divine truths over in a simple, easily understood way. If commentators and critics were to bear this in mind, they would find a feast of good heavenly fare in Cowper's earlier Christian verse.

The poet did not, however, stop at hymn-writing. In his efforts to be useful to God he tried his hand at writing a commentary on John's Gospel. In this commentary that covers only the first chapter of John, Cowper shows he is very familiar with the fashionable heresies prevalent in his day such as Arianism, Socinianism and the so-called Enlightenment. There is also good teaching against Arminianism and the Perfectionism of the Wesleyans to be found in the commentary. A few verses will suffice to show the excellency of this work which was last published in 1868.

Ver. 9. *Christ is the Light that lighteth every man that cometh into the world.* Whether it be the light of reason or the light of grace all is from Him. Surely, then, infidels would blush at their ingratitude, if they did but know that the very reason which they employ to the subversion of the faith is His gift who also gives them the gospel, and that they are perverting one of our Saviour's blessings in order to defeat another.

Ver. 10. *...the world knew Him not.* A lamentable argument of the sad consequences of Adam's fall. Man saw his Maker in the person of Christ face to face, yet knew Him not. Thousands still see Him in the glass of the gospel, and acknowledge Him not. How few have eyes to behold the light of the knowledge of the glory of God in the face of Jesus Christ!

Ver. 11,12,13. *He came unto His own* — His own both by indisputable right of creation and of purchase; yet He was despised and rejected by them, and they said, as in the parable, We will not have this man to reign over us. They who are truly Christ's, having received Him into their hearts by faith, shall be His for ever; for He is stronger than all, and none plucketh them out of His hand. They have received the spirit of adoption, whereby they cry, Abba, Father! being regenerated by the Holy Ghost, and created in Christ Jesus unto good works. Where is the tongue or the heart that can be sufficiently thankful for such an inestimable privilege?

Ver. 14. *And the Word was made flesh.* This Divine Word, who was from all eternity in the bosom of the Father, by whom all things were created, the Light of the world; and the Life of all the elect of God, was at length incarnate, and became in fashion as a man; and the apostle alleges here His own testimony and that of the other apostles, having been eye-witnesses of His excellence, to prove that He was more than human. Such grace and truth could belong to none but a God incarnate.

Ver. 15. *John bare witness of Him.* John was six months older than Christ in the flesh yet he says that Christ was before him. A full refutation of all such heretics as deny the pre-existence of our Saviour.

Ver. 16. *Grace upon grace,* in the original *Vide* Cant.: Eat, O friends; drink, yea, drink abundantly, O beloved! And in Him dwelleth all the fulness of the Godhead bodily. Believers have all things in Christ, and in Him are treasures of inexhaustible grace. In Him we are regenerated, sanctified, justified, glorified.

John Newton had been a friend and correspondent of George Whitefield for a number of years. When news of Whitefield's death reached Olney in November 1770. Newton preached a funeral sermon for him on John 5:35, 'He was a bright and shining light.' Cowper believed Whitefield to be as pure a Christian as possible on this side of eternity. He was shocked by the abuse that Whitefield had to put up with and never ceased to wonder that such a holy man was considered a danger to society by so many. He thus wrote of Whitefield who:

Stood pilloried on infamy's high stage,
And bore the pelting scorn of half an age,
The very butt of slander, and the blot
For ev'ry dart that malice ever shot.
The man that mentioned him, at once dismiss'd
All mercy from his lips, and sneer'd and hiss'd;
His crimes were such as Sodom never knew,
And perjury stood up to swear all true;
His aim was mischief, and his zeal pretence,
His speech rebellion against common sense,
A knave when tried on honesty's plain rule,
And when by that of reason, a mere fool,
The world's best comfort was, his doom was pass'd,
Die when he might, he must be damn'd at last.
Now truth perform thine office, waft aside
The curtain drawn by prejudice and pride,
Reveal (the man is dead) to wond'ring eyes,
This more than monster in his proper guise:
He lov'd the world that hated him, the tear
That dropped upon his Bible was sincere.

Assail'd by scandal and the tongue of strife,
His only answer was a blameless life,
And he that forged and he that threw the dart,
Had each a brother's interest in his heart.
Paul's love of Christ, and steadiness unbrib'd,
Were copied close in him, and well transcrib'd;
He followed Paul, his zeal a kindred flame,
His apostolic charity the same,
Like him cross'd chearfully tempestuous seas,
Forsaking country, kindred, friends, and ease;
Like him he labour'd, and like him, content
To bear it, suffer'd shame where'er he went.
Blush calumny! and write upon his tomb,
If honest eulogy can spare thee room,
Thy deep repentance of thy thousand lies,
Which aim'd at him, have pierc'd th' offended skies,
And say, blot out my sin, confess'd, deplor'd,
Against thine image in thy saint, oh Lord![18]

The shadows of trouble to come

At the beginning of 1771 Newton spent several weeks in London
with his wife. His letters to Cowper hint that the poet is going
through unspecified difficult times. He writes, 'Pray for me that my
heart may be looking to Jesus for peace, wisdom, and strength.
Without Him all is waste and desert. And every thought in which he
has not a place or rule is treason. I trust, yea, I know, He will be with
you. He will cover your head in the day of battle, and give you many
a song of triumph before the great day of decision, when all enemies
shall be finally bruised under your feet.'

A few days later he wrote, ' I thank you for yours of the 21st. I
pity your conflicts, and I try not to envy your comforts. You are in
safe hands. All your combats and all your victories are already
marked out for you.'

In the same letter we gain deep insight into the quality of love and
fellowship shown by the Newtons to Cowper and Mrs Unwin. He
goes on to write:

I trust we live in the daily remembrance of you and dear
Mrs. Unwin, and we doubt not we are the better for your

prayers. I think we shall be both glad to see Olney again. Yet, as I am abroad, I hope to make myself tolerably easy till the time comes. Please to give our love to Miss Unwin, Mr. Foster, Mr. Palmer, &c. To Mrs. Unwin and Sir Cowper we join in more than a common salutation. We are bound to you both by the fourfold cord of Esteem, Friendship, Communion, and Obligation. Judge, then, how warmly and sincerely we can assure you that we are most affectionately yours,

John and M. Newton.[19]

Though Cowper's letters hardly indicate that there is anything amiss, Newton's diary entries and letters show that he was worried about his friend's nervous state. Writing to his wife on 9 July 1772 he says, 'Dear Sir Cowper is in the depths as much as ever. The manner of his prayer last night led me to speak from Heb. ii.18. I do not think he was much the better for it, but perhaps it might suit others.'

This letter also serves to illustrate Newton's new method of preaching. As a young preacher he had experienced embarrassing times through preaching unprepared. He thus began to write his sermons out word for word and read them to his hearers. This greatly limited their effectiveness in delivery as Newton was very short-sighted and had to hold his notes close to his nose. So, after several years in the ministry, he began to seek subjects for his sermons from the immediate problems of his parishioners and preach more or less spontaneously in an effort to assist those in need. He often found that a sermon aimed at one person did not go unattended by many other hearers. This method gave Newton more time to take more services and soon he was holding at least three mid-week services in Olney and taking other services in the surrounding villages besides his usual weekend services. Cowper was invariably his companion at all these services.

Following Cowper's example, Newton began to consider writing hymns in earnest. His reasons for doing so were similar to Cowper's but went even further. He realized how difficult it was for a poor Olney lace-worker to follow a sermon and retain it for any length of time in her memory. He felt that if he could only condense a sermon into a form which was easy to learn off by heart, then the parishioners could 'take the sermon home' and repeat it to themselves throughout their working day. He thus decided to reduce a sermon he had recently preached, or one that he intended to preach, into a few rhyming verses and expound these line for line in the less formal services held at the Great House.

On Sunday, 6 December 1772, Newton made a start with his new scheme and his diary entry for the day reads, 'Expounded my new hymn at the Great House on the subject of a burdened sinner.' Soon Newton's diaries show that he was writing and expounding two hymns a week and even expounding the hymns in the main Sunday church service. Within the next six years or so Newton was to write over three hundred hymns in this way. As writing a new hymn took him up to two days to complete, it would seem that much of the time he saved in sermon preparation was spent in hymn-writing. Another 'popular' move on Newton's part at this time was to read and comment on *Pilgrim's Progress* during the mid-week meetings.

We find Cowper faithfully witnessing to the Lord's work in his life until the end of 1772. One of his last letters of that year was written to Joseph Hill, who had invited Cowper to visit him in London. The poet, remembering his own worldly ways in London and his pre-conversion illness, confessed that he never wanted to return to the scenes of such experiences again. He thus declined the offer saying, 'Glory be to the Name of Jesus, those days are past, & I trust never to return.' Cowper's very last extant letter for 1772 was to Joseph Hill whom he told that there was nowhere else in all the kingdom where he could be as happy as in Olney.

Cowper's worldly ways were, in the providence of God, gone for ever. That same providence had, however, reserved for William Cowper another time of trial and testing which serves as a sober reminder that God's judgements are unsearchable and his ways past finding out. On the first day of January 1773 Cowper was walking over the Olney fields when he received a sudden premonition that a second time of darkness and depression was about to fall on him. With his heart turned to God, he struggled home and immediately wrote down a confession of his faith in verse form before that darkness came upon him. Those verses formed the hymn which has come to be called 'Light Shining out of Darkness'.

> God moves in a mysterious way,
> His wonders to perform,
> He plants his footsteps in the Sea,
> And rides upon the Storm.

Deep in unfathomable Mines,
Of never failing Skill,
He treasures up his bright designs,
And works his Sovereign Will.

Ye fearfull Saints fresh courage take,
The clouds ye so much dread,
Are big with Mercy, and shall break
In blessings on your head.

Judge not the Lord by feeble sense,
But trust him for his Grace,
Behind a frowning Providence
He hides a Smiling face.

His purposes will ripen fast,
Unfolding every hour,
The Bud may have a bitter taste,
But *wait*, to *Smell the flower*.

Blind unbelief is sure to err,
And scan his work in vain,
God is his own Interpreter,
And he will make it plain.

Illness strikes again

Newton was called over to Orchard Side early in the morning of the following day. A sight met him that both astonished and grieved him immeasurably. Cowper was in delirium and full of terror. Newton now continued to visit his friend daily, not so much to share fellowship with him as to comfort him. The pastor would first take family prayers in the Vicarage and then go straight over to Orchard Side to lead the family prayers there. The two friends went for their usual walks together but how great was the change! Instead of conversing animatedly about the work of the Lord and discussing literature and politics as before, Newton had to guide his friend along as if he were a walking doll. Cowper was reduced to a childlike imbecility and did not seem to notice what was going on around him.

He was obviously not fully out of his mind and could give rational answers to questions put to him. He never, however, attempted to enter into conversation himself and was plagued by attacks of panic, terror and hallucinations.

Two weeks later, we find Newton writing in his diary, 'My dear friend still walks in darkness. I can hardly conceive that any one in a state of grace and favour with God can be in greater distress; and yet no one walked more closely with Him, or was more simply devoted to Him in all things.'

On 15 February Mr and Mrs Newton went over to Orchard Side to celebrate the anniversary of Cowper's arrival there. Usually these occasions were filled with praise and mirth. This time Newton could merely enter in his diary: 'The late dispensation has brought a cloud over our former pleasure.'

Towards the end of February, Cowper's terror increased. He had a terrible nightmare in which he thought God appeared to him and pronounced the words: *'Actum est de te, periisti'* which Cowper understood to mean, 'It is all over with thee, thou hast perished.' Cowper was to experience this dream, that would shake any Christian to the core, not just this once but time and time again throughout the remainder of his life, so that at times, when he was weak and downcast, he really believed that the Lord had rejected him. The astonishing thing is that this repeated experience of doom rarely deterred Cowper from writing in glowing terms of the goodness of God.

Newton's world was also being severely shaken. Cowper had been a major support to him and a great influence on his own ministry. The poet had been the stronger personality of the two. Now the roles of the two friends were totally changed. Though Newton was baffled and amazed, and indeed never recovered from the shock he received at the sudden change in his friend, he was determined to nurse him back to health and was given great patience and strength by the Lord to do so. For the next three months Newton could be found at all hours at Orchard Side caring for and comforting his friend. His diary informs us that even when Cowper called for help in the middle of the night, Newton would rush over and spend hours talking his friend out of his terrors and hallucinations. Cowper was not seriously ill all the time but would recover now and then only to relapse again speedily. Thus Newton was plagued constantly with fears that turned into hope and hope that was dispersed by fears.

This went on until 12 April when the annual fair day was held at Olney. The noise became so intense and disagreeable to Cowper that he went over to the Vicarage, accompanied by Mrs Unwin, to escape from it. The Newtons welcomed their friends with open arms, little knowing that Cowper would be staying with them until the end of May of the following year! Once at the Vicarage, Cowper's state deteriorated. He felt that everyone hated him and even that they were trying to poison him. He would allow only Mrs Unwin to look after his food, but at times even suspected her of wanting to take his life.

Attacks on Mrs Unwin's character

To make matters worse, tongues began to wag again concerning Cowper's relationship with Mrs Unwin. William Unwin was now in the ministry at Stock in Essex and Cowper was living alone with Mrs Unwin and her daughter, both of whom were considered very eligible ladies. It would appear that, though Cowper had no qualms in looking upon Mrs Unwin as his housekeeper and good friend, influential believers found great difficulty in accepting the fact that a well-educated woman such as Mrs Unwin would 'stoop' to look after Cowper even to the point of knitting his stockings and preparing his meals. She must, they thought, have ulterior motives.

The worst gossip came from a very unexpected place. John Thornton, the wealthy merchant, had been financing Newton's work ever since he commenced his ministry at Olney. This perhaps made him think he could dictate to Newton how he should treat his friends. He began to put pressure on Newton to get rid of Cowper and Mrs Unwin on the dubious grounds that there was 'a snake in the grass' in Mrs Unwin's life. Noticing how devotedly Mrs Unwin served Cowper and ignoring how devoutly she did this, Thornton argued that she must have a romantic attachment to the poet, otherwise she would not be so interested in him. Were Mr Cowper a woman, he argued, Mrs Unwin would not have shown him such loving attention. Newton, however, knew that Mrs Unwin had shown equal devotion to a homeless, sick woman whom she found on the streets and looked after at Orchard Side. Mary Unwin was that kind of selfless, godly person.

Thornton's groundless suspicions were centred solely around Mrs Unwin and he obviously thought Cowper was above such

things. Instead of taking Mrs Unwin's side, which would have been
an easy matter for him, Newton strove to convince Thornton that
Cowper could handle the matter. In doing so he totally overstated his
case and left Thornton with the surprising impression that Cowper
was physically unable to be attracted by the opposite sex. Letters
written by Cowper both before and after this period show what
nonsense such a theory was.[20]

Oddly enough, no one seems to have considered Susanna Unwin,
now twenty-seven, a 'danger' for Cowper. All the gossip centred
around Mrs Unwin. That good woman bore the gossip bravely but
it obviously weighed Cowper down very much, for her sake.

This situation became even worse in 1774. Matthew Powley
(1740-1806), an Oxford graduate and Evangelical minister, had
been converted through the ministry of Haweis in 1760 at Magdalen
College. He became such an ardent winner of souls that alarm was
raised in the college and he was threatened with expulsion for
holding 'Methodistical tenets'. Henry Venn and the Countess of
Huntingdon defended Powley successfully and eventually found
him a church in Yorkshire. Newton met Powley and was impressed
by him from the start and invited him to preach on numerous
occasions at Olney. There Powley met Cowper, and through
Cowper Susanna Unwin, with whom he fell in love, and the two
were married in 1774. Thus Cowper and Mrs Unwin were left alone
and tongues wagged all the more.

If there had been any dubious relationship between Cowper and
Mrs Unwin, surely the first to know about it would have been
Susanna and William Unwin and Matthew Powley. Susanna's only
criticism, however, against Cowper was that she thought her mother
was not charging him enough for his keep. William Unwin and
Matthew Powley, two Evangelicals of the Evangelicals, looked on
Cowper and Mrs Unwin with the greatest love and respect and very
obviously saw no reason whatsoever for alarm.

Newton, even though faced with the scorn of the very people who
were financing his work at Olney, finally stopped taking any notice
of their gossip and slander. He had come to understand the
relationship between Cowper and Mrs Unwin and had given it his
blessing. He thus refused to order Cowper to leave his house and
reintensified his efforts to find a cure for his friend.

The Vicarage, Olney, home of John and Mary Newton,
where Cowper and Mrs Unwin stayed during the poet's illness.

Cowper's illness and its effect on Newton

Electrical treatment was seen in those days as a cure-all and Newton bought an electrical machine and treated Cowper with it. He made several visits to St Albans in order to procure the services of Dr Cotton, who prescribed various medicines for Cowper.

Many friends wrote, astonished and distressed at the change that had taken place in the life of such a saint and Newton went to great pains to explain to them how his friend was faring. These letters show how Newton just could not understand what was happening to his friend and how such a righteous man could be required at God's hand to suffer so much. In a letter to his friend Mr Brewer, Newton writes, for instance,

> Heavy indeed is the trial with which the Lord has visited him, and, to appearance, no one needed it less. I can hardly form an idea of a closer walk with God than he uniformly maintained. Communion with God and the good of His people seemed to be the only object he had in view from the beginning to the end of the year, and he was remarkably thriving and happy to the very hour when this trouble overtook him. But the Lord is wise. Mysterious as the dispensation seems, I dare not question its expediency, nor, though it continues so long, can I despond as to the event. In the meantime, it is upon many accounts a very great trial to me. But I hope I am learning (though I am a slow scholar) to silence all vain reasonings and unbelieving complaints with the consideration of the Lord's sovereignty, wisdom, and love.[21]

At times when Cowper was clear in his mind, Newton was able to talk to him about the Lord's work and question him about his assurance that God was with him. Of these times he wrote,

> In the beginning of his disorder, when he was more capable of conversing than he was sometimes afterwards, how often have I heard him adore and submit to the sovereignty of God, and declare, though in the most agonising and inconceivable distress, he was so perfectly satisfied of the wisdom and rectitude of the Lord's appointments, that if he

was sure of relieving himself only by stretching out his hand, he would not do it, unless he was equally sure it was agreeable to His will that he should do it.[22]

It was probably during these early months of his illness that Cowper composed the hymn, 'The Welcome Cross' which testifies to a stable and solid faith in face of great afflictions.

'Tis my happiness below
Not to live without the cross;
But the Saviour's pow'r to know,
Sanctifying ev'ry loss:

Trials must and will befall;
But with humble faith to see
Love inscrib'd upon them all,
This is happiness to me.

Poor tho' I am, despis'd, forgot,
Yet God, my God, forgets me not;
And he is safe and must succeed,
For whom the Lord vouchsafes to plead.

Thou art as ready to forgive,
As I am ready to repine;
Thou, therefore, all the praise receive,
Be shame, and self-abhorrence, mine.

Ah! were I buffetted all day,
Mock'd, crown'd with thorns, and spit upon;
I yet should have no right to say,
My great distress is mine alone.

Let me not angrily declare
No pain was ever sharp like mine;
Nor murmur at the cross I bear,
But rather weep rememb'ring thine.

It is obvious that Newton suffered greatly during Cowper's stay with him. His letters to friends show how evil 'reports and

misconstructions' were getting him down and how he was being
blamed on all sides, either for being too lenient with Cowper, or for
helping to drive him mad. There was now a rumour going through
Olney and the surrounding districts that Newton preached people
mad and Cowper's case was being quoted as proof of this. Newton's
spiritual life began to suffer so that he could not find ready access
to the throne of grace. It was almost impossible to find peace enough
at the Vicarage to commune with God, so Newton went daily to the
Great House for his times of personal prayer and Bible study. The
nervous strain and sleepless nights attending his friend brought on
coughing spasms, fever and deafness and Newton, too, became very
ill for a time. This serious illness, however, brought back to Newton
the feeling of God's presence with him so that he could say, 'When
I was sick, I was well.'

We can hardly blame Newton, however, when his diary records
that during Cowper's prolonged stay at the Vicarage, Newton went
on more and more preaching tours, taking his wife with him. During
one of these tours in October 1773, Mrs Unwin wrote to Mrs Newton
informing her of Cowper's progress. The letter shows Mrs Unwin
to be a most spiritual-minded practical person, eager to do the will
of the Lord and happy to be able to care for her beloved invalid.

> I hope my Dear Madam this will meet you well & safely
> returned thus far on your Journey. Though it will be a sincere
> pleasure to me to see you & Dear Mr. Newton again, yet I beg
> you will not put yourselves to the least inconvenience or
> hurry to reach home till the most fit & agreeable time. The
> Lord is very gracious to us; for though the cloud of affliction
> still hangs heavy on Mr. Cowper yet he is quite calm &
> persuadable in every respect He has been for these few days
> past more open & communicative than heretofore. It is
> amazing how subtilly the cruel adversary has worked upon
> him & and wonderfull to see how the Lord has frustrated his
> wicked machinations; for though He has not seen good to
> prevent the most violent temptations & distressing delusions,
> yet he has prevented the Mischievous effects the enemy
> designed by them. A most Marvellous story will this Dear
> Child of God have to relate when by His Almighty power he
> is set at liberty. As nothing short of omnipotence could have
> supported him through this sharp Affliction so nothing less

can set him free from it. I allow that means are in general not only lawfull but also expedient, but in the present case we must I am convinced advert to our first Sentiment, that this is a peculiar & exempt one, & that the Lord Jehovah wil be alone Exalted when the day of deliverance comes.

I must beg the favour of you to buy for me two pounds of Chocolate, half a pound or ten Ounces of white sixpenny Worsted, half a Dozen Lemons, & two Sets of Knitting Needles, Six in a Set, one the finest that can be got of Iron or Steel, the other a Size Coarser. Sally Nor Judy know of my writing else I am sure they would desire me to insert their Duty.

Pray present my Affectionate remembrance to Mr. Newton, & my Sincere Respects to Mr. & Mrs. Trinder & Miss Smith & believe me to be My Dearest Madam your truly Affectionate & highly indebted friend

M. Unwin.

Meanwhile Cowper was fighting hard trying to discern which visions of those he saw were real and which were mere figments of his vivid fantasy. He soon found out that if he worked very hard manually, he experienced fewer spasms of fear, thoughts of doom and fewer hallucinations. He therefore set to work growing vegetables for the two families, keeping hens, building hutches, replacing broken windows and even painting pictures. Whatever Cowper turned his hand to in this way prospered. He became so adept at animal husbandry that the *Gentleman's Magazine* published a lengthy account on the care of hares that he wrote some years later. One at least of his etchings was also published.

The time spent in gardening was a training-ground for Cowper's future theory of the work of a Christian as a sub-gardener under God preparing for paradise regained. It also brought him very near to nature, which was also to become a major theme in his future poetry. But whenever Cowper left off working, terror and darkness gripped his soul for many months to come. It was no wonder that Cowper was to write in 'Retirement':

Absence of occupation is not rest,
A mind quite vacant is a mind distress'd.

It was Cowper's sense of humour that the Lord used to bring the poet back to sanity. On 14 May 1774, Cowper was feeding the chickens. They looked so funny as they competed one with the other to get the best scraps of food that Cowper just had to smile. It was the first time he had smiled, Newton tells us, for sixteen months.

A few days later Cowper surprised everybody by suddenly saying that it was high time that he and Mrs Unwin were back at Orchard Side. By the end of the month Orchard Side was again inhabited after standing more or less derelict for fourteen months. Cowper was now forty-two years of age and was about to enter an entirely new phase of life.

7.
The child of God walking in darkness

After returning to Orchard Side Cowper set about putting the house and garden in order and did all in his power to shake off the gloom that had burdened him so long. Peace with God was the one perpetual plea of his heart. The nightmares continued, however, and time and time again Cowper felt that he could hear God's voice telling him that he had been rejected. Newton commented, 'His health is better; he works almost incessantly in the garden, and while employed is tolerably easy; but as soon as he leaves off he is instantly swallowed up by the most gloomy apprehensions, though in everything that does not concern his own peace he is as sensible and discovers as quick a judgment as ever.'[1]

Cowper's animals

A number of small children were the first to help Cowper back to health and sanity. They had been playing with a baby hare and found looking after it too difficult, so they asked the poet if he would like to have it. Cowper began to care for the little animal and succeeded not only in keeping it alive, but also in taming it. Soon word spread around the town that Cowper could tame wild hares and neighbour after neighbour brought him baby hares that they had caught in the fields around Olney. Soon, Cowper tells us, he had enough leverets to 'stock a paddock'.

Three of the hares, Puss, Tiney and Bess, became favourite pets of the poet and he made hutches in the hall for them to sleep in. A small doorway was made in the wall so that the hares could run through into the parlour of an evening and entertain the delighted humans. Bess needed no taming, Puss was tamed by love and affection but Tiney always kept his distance. Of Tiney Cowper said,

> I kept him for his humour's sake,
> For he would oft beguile
> My heart of thoughts that made it ache,
> And force me to a smile.[2]

Soon Cowper was looking after a menagerie of animals. He had a large number of rabbits and guinea pigs, two dogs, several cats, a squirrel, at least eight pairs of pigeons, a magpie, a jay, a starling, several linnets and robins, two canary birds and two goldfinches, besides the hens, ducks and geese which he normally kept. More animals were to follow. Cowper built a greenhouse and a number of cold frames, cutting the glass which he bought at the factory himself to save money. With the aid of heating pipes, he was soon growing summer flowers and vegetables in winter and, what with all the animals who played with one another and all the plants which came from the four corners of the world, Cowper tells us that he felt like God's under-gardener in paradise.

Around the late 1770s, when Cowper had recovered much of his Christian optimism, he began to write poetry about his gardening and nature experiences, drawing Christian morals from what he observed. It is at this time that Cowper's great interest in the animal world showed him how cruel man was to his dumb friends. Cowper was one of the first poets of the eighteenth century to argue for a display of human feelings to be shown to animals. Typical of such poems from this period is Cowper's 'On a Goldfinch Starved to Death in his Cage':

> Time was when I was free as air,
> The thistle's downy seed my fare,
> My drink the morning dew;
> I perch'd at will on ev'ry spray,
> My form genteel, my plumage gay,
> My strains for ever new.

But gaudy plumage, sprightly strain,
And form genteel, were all in vain,
And of a transient date;
For, caught and cag'd, and starv'd to death,
In dying sighs my little breath
Soon pass'd the wiry grate.

Thanks, gentle swain, for all my woes,
And thanks for this effectual close
And cure of ev'ry ill!
More cruelty could none express;
And I, if you had shown me less,
Had been your pris'ner still.

The longing for peace

Meanwhile Cowper's constant prayer was for peace of heart and
deliverance from the thoughts of being eternally rejected by God.
The poet, believing that it was wrong to ask God to go against his
own decree, at times dared not pray and poured out his sorrow in
verse instead. At other times, however, Cowper was heard pouring
his heart out to God in the middle of the night, apparently praying
in his sleep.

The poems that Cowper wrote at this time are thought by most
critics to show a new development in quality and a lyrical
proficiency showing that he was becoming a poet of note. For
Cowper, however, they were merely the lamentations of despair and
are testimonies to the fact that Cowper felt God had turned his back
on him. One such poem is 'Ode to Peace':

Come, peace of mind, delightful guest!
Return and make thy downy nest
Once more in this sad heart! ——
Nor riches I, nor pow'r, pursue,
Nor hold forbidden joys in view;
We therefore need not part.

Where wilt thou dwell if not with me,
From av'rice and ambition free,

And pleasure's fatal wiles?
For whom, alas! dost thou prepare
The sweets that I was wont to share.
The banquet of thy smiles?

The great, the gay, shall they partake
The heav'n that thou alone canst make?
And wilt thou quit the stream
That murmurs through the dewy mead,
The grove and the sequester'd shed,
To be a guest with them?

For thee I panted, thee I priz'd,
For thee I gladly sacrific'd
Whate'er I lov'd before;
And shall I see thee start away,
And, helpless, hopeless, hear thee say—
Farewell! we meet no more?

The last verse makes it clear that Cowper is not merely speaking of peace as such but of the God of peace, whom he once knew so intimately and whom he now felt he had lost. In his poems of lament of this period Cowper deals with nature for the first time as a major subject for poetry. He was beginning to see that a right relationship with God was essential to understanding and appreciating God's purposes in nature. A non-Christian cannot possibly enjoy nature as God intended it should be enjoyed. Thus throughout the years 1773-1777 we find Cowper describing nature in all its charms as a nature which has become lost to him. Typical of this attitude of dispair is 'The Shrubbery', with its sub-title 'Written in a Time of Affliction'. It was in this shrubbery that Cowper used to retire to to pray with Newton.

Oh, happy shades — to me unblest
Friendly to peace, but not to me!
How ill the scene that offers rest,
And heart that cannot rest, agree!

This glassy stream, that spreading pine,
Those alders quiv'ring to the breeze,

Might sooth a soul less hurt than mine,
And please, if any thing could please.

But fix'd unalterable care
Foregoes not what she feels within,
Shows the same sadness ev'ry where,
And slights the season and the scene.

For all that pleas'd in wood or lawn
While peace possess'd these silent bow'rs,
Her animating smile withdrawn.
Has lost its beauties and its pow'rs.

The saint or moralist should tread
This moss-grown alley, musing, slow;
They seek, like me, the secret shade,
But not, like me, to nourish woe!

Me fruitful scenes and prospects waste
Alike admonish not to roam;
These tell me of enjoyments past,
And those of sorrows yet to come.

It would be wrong to presume that this attitude of despair in Cowper was fixed and permanent. There is a manuscript in his handwriting rescued by his faithful servant Sam when the poet's home at Weston was forcedly broken up. It contains two of Cowper's darkest poems, 'Hatred and Vengeance' and *'Heu! quam remotus vescor omnibus'*; the latter being a Latin poem in which Cowper writes of his soul being lost in the black seas of hell. There is, however, a third poem on this piece of paper. It is 'To Jesus the Crown of my Hope', and is surely one of the most beautiful expositions ever penned of 1 Peter 1:8: 'Whom having not seen, ye love: in whom, though now ye see him not, yet believing, ye rejoice with joy unspeakable and full of glory.'

To Jesus, the Crown of my Hope,
My soul is in haste to be gone:
O bear me, ye Cherubims, up,
And waft me away to his throne.

My Saviour, whom absent I love,
Whom not having seen I adore;
Whose Name is exalted above
 All Glory, Dominion, and Power,

Dissolve Thou the bond that detains
My soul from her portion in Thee,
And strike off the adamant chains,
 And make me eternally free.

When that happy æra begins,
When array'd in thy beauty I shine,
Nor pierce any more by my sins
The bosom, on which I recline.

Three things become very clear as we read Cowper's letters from this time on and study his verse. First, he had by no means lost his Christian convictions and often looked back with joy to the time when he was converted. Second, he really felt at times that God was prepared to ban him eternally from his presence because of his constant sin and rebellion. Third, in spite of this, Cowper still exercised deep faith in God in terms of Job's claim: 'Though he slay me, yet will I trust him.' Writing to Newton about an intended visit from William Bull, the Dissenting pastor, Cowper says, 'He [Bull] would wonder that a man whose views of the Scripture are just like his own, who is a Calvinist from experience, & knows his election, should be furnished with a Shield of despair impenetrable to every argument by which he might attempt to comfort him. But so it is, & in the end it will be accounted for.'[3] Cowper tended to think that he must be the only person on earth to have come to a knowledge of the truth, put his trust in God and yet be rejected.

Jonathan Edwards, who studied revival in general and examined particular conversions very carefully, spoke of several cases that would appear similar to Cowper's. In his *A Narrative of Conversions,* published in England in 1737 by Drs Isaac Watts and John Guyse, Edwards writes,

> As to those in whom awakenings seem to have a saving issue, commonly the first thing that appears after their legal troubles, is a conviction of the justice of God in their

condemnation, appearing in a sense of their own exceeding sinfulness, and the vileness of all their performances. In giving an account of this they expressed themselves very variously; some, that they saw God was sovereign, and might revive others and reject them; some, that they were convinced, God might justly bestow mercy on every person in the town, in the world, and damn themselves to all eternity; some, that they see God may justly have no regard to all the pains they have taken, and all the prayers they have made; some, that if they should seek, and take the most uttermost pains all their lives, God might justly cast them into hell at last, because all their labours, prayers, and tears cannot make an atonement for the least sin, nor merit any blessing in the hands of God, that he may dispose of them just as he pleases; some, that God may glorify himself in their damnation, and they wonder that God has suffered them to live so long, and has not cast them into hell long ago.[4]

Every single one of these features is traceable in Cowper's letters. Edwards goes on to describe how he has interviewed people who have experienced, alternatively, a sense of the 'sufficiency of Christ and the richness of his divine grace', and who afterwards 'return to greater distress than ever'. Again, this is true of Cowper, especially in his later years. However, Edwards does not brand these people as insane, unchristian, or even uncalvinistic, or in any way odd at all. In fact, he admits that these symptoms arise *after* conversion. He confesses that though he has done his best to comfort these people, he is 'sensible the practice would have been safer in the hands of one of a riper judgment and greater experience'. Edwards thus turned to friends in Scotland and England for assistance. In a similar way Newton, who realized he could only help Cowper a little, introduced his friend to the Rev. William Bull, who had greater experience in these matters.

The Olney Hymns

In February 1779 John Newton published a collection of his and Cowper's hymns under the name of the *Olney Hymns*. Such collections were still something of a novelty in the eighteenth century and opinions were very strongly divided as to their use in church worship.

Earlier hymn collections

Watts' hymn-book had already become a standard work amongst Dissenters and was often used in family worship, prayer meetings and mid-week services, but it was also gaining ground in the more formal Sunday services.

The most popular Dissenting hymn-writer after Watts was certainly Joseph Hart, who composed hymns to be sung at his chapel in Jewin Street, London and published them in 1759 under the title *Hymns composed on various subjects, with the Author's experience.* Hart's hymns show a marked difference from those of Watts in that, though the quality of their language is inferior, their music is of a more developed and varied nature, being seen as a form of worship in itself. Hart was obviously influenced in this by the Moravians amongst whom he was converted.

The Church of England had been less affected by Watts' and Hart's hymn-books, as the new version of the Psalms then in vogue guaranteed that the congregation could take part in the services by singing. In those days the Psalms were not chanted but sung as hymns are sung today. The chanting of Psalms developed in the cathedral churches and was looked upon as 'papist' by many Evangelicals of the eighteenth century. Independents and Baptists, however, did not use the Anglican liturgies or Psalms and felt a need for some kind of singing in worship to supplant them.

Martin Madan, Cowper's cousin, was one of the first Anglicans to compile a hymn-book and his *Psalms and Hymns* went into very many editions well into the nineteenth century. Madan set hymns to his own tunes and introduced many of the Wesleys' hymns, which he altered at will.

Another early Anglican hymn-book was John Berridge's *Collection of Divine Songs,* which did not have the high musical and literary merit of Madan's work but nevertheless became popular in revival circles.

The Wesleys, of course, brought out a number of hymn-books, influenced, as in the case of Hart, by the German Moravians. John Wesley often used hymns as a means of conveying propaganda in his fight for Arminianism and Perfectionism against the Calvinists.

Dr Conyers, John Newton's friend, published a hymn-book in 1767 incorporating several of Cowper's earlier hymns.

The use of hymns in worship

There were still many Evangelicals in the eighteenth century, however, who not only did not approve of using artistic musical measures in worship, but saw little point in using man-made hymns at all. William Romaine (1714-1795), for instance, a man with great backing amongst Evangelicals, saw hymn-singing as a substitute for true worship and a grave departure from the scriptural norm. Wherever there was a lack of 'vital religion', he thought, people left off praying, singing the Psalms and hearing the Word and descended into singing Watts' 'flights of fancy', along with other flippant pastimes. The words of man had become more important to a backsliding church than the Word of God. Romaine thus argued that sung worship dropped to the level of entertainment when hymns were used. He was especially against church choirs who 'sing to be admired for their fine voices' and force the congregation into passivity. To counteract this trend Romaine published his own collection of biblical Psalms to be sung and provided each psalm with a short introduction and devotional application.

Cowper's and Newton's hymn compositions were an attempt to carry tne view of church worship fostered by Romaine further than Romaine was prepared to go. Rather than merely supplying their congregation with the Psalms of David with an introduction and commentary, as did Romaine, the Olney friends strove to provide their parishioners with sermon texts from all parts of the Bible in verse form. Romaine compiled his psalm-book to be used in the sung liturgy, whereas Cowper and Newton wrote their hymns for personal edification and instruction rather than for the more formal gathered church worship.

Neither author planned originally to have his hymns sung. Cowper's earlier hymns were composed as poems and Newton's diary entries over a period of years show that his hymns were written for exposition only. Singing hymns is rarely mentioned by Cowper and Newton except at their homes in small devotional circles and in cottage meetings. Indeed, even when the two friends do refer to singing, they often use the word in the old classical sense of reciting.[5]

Indeed if John Newton and William Cowper were to take part in many a late twentieth-century evangelical Sunday service, the main difference they would notice and, indeed, be shocked at, would be the vast percentage of time devoted to chorus and hymn-singing and musical interludes and the relatively short amount of time taken up by the sermon and spoken exhortations. It would be no use shaking one's head at the two friends' amazement and telling them that 'Times have changed,' for 'times', in this sense, have not changed in any way. All these Sunday worship 'trimmings' were coming into vogue in the middle of the eighteenth century amongst certain religious groups and, although both Newton and Cowper were fond of singing, and were such good hymn-writers that their hymns are still sung all over the world today, they had an entirely different view of what a hymn was and how a hymn should be sung. Newton criticized the misuse of music and singing in church services in numerous sermons and this topic was often the subject under discussion in the two friends' weekly correspondence with each other when Newton left Olney.

Cowper and Newton were particularly against singing hymns in the main Sunday services as the unconverted present could not possibly join in. They argued that only the redeemed could partake in joint worship. If people sang of Christ's redemption who had not experienced it, what futile bluff! If the congregation sang of God's wrath to unsaved sinners and did not believe in it, what folly!

Their chief criticism, however, was of the music rather than the texts. This is one reason why the *Olney Hymns* were published without any music or any instrumentalization. Up to the latter part of the seventeenth century there was no instrumental accompaniment in church services apart from in the larger cathedrals, which had been highly influenced by German court music. There was no organ in the Olney Church and Newton would not have one. When Newton left for a parish in London, some Olney citizens campaigned to have an organ installed in the parish church. They approached Cowper for assistance in their venture, thinking that a hymn-writer would be the very man to head a campaign for an organ. Cowper told them clearly and unmistakably that he would have nothing to do with such folly.

He had already playfully poured scorn on the modern jingle-jangles of church music used with the new versions of the Psalms in an essay published in *The Connoisseur*. In this article he was also probably taking a dig at his cousin Martin Madan and John Wesley, who were responsible for introducing some of these 'new-fashioned' tunes such as Winchester New into church services.

> The good old practice of psalm-singing is, indeed, wonderfully improved in many country churches since the days of Sternhold and Hopkins; and there is scarce a parish-clerk, who has so little taste as not to pick his staves out of the New Version. This has occasioned great complaints in some places, where the clerk has been forced to bawl by himself, because the rest of the congregation cannot find the psalm at the end of their prayer-books; while others are highly disgusted at the innovation, and stick as obstinately to the Old Version as to the Old Stile. The tunes themselves have also been new-set to jiggish measures; and the sober drawl, which used to accompany the two first staves of the hundredth psalm with the *gloria patri*, is now split into as many quavers as an *Italian* air. For this purpose there is in every county an itinerant band of vocal musicians, who make it their business to go round to all the churches in their turns, and, after a prelude with the pitchpipe, astonish the audience with hymns set to the new *Winchester* measure and anthems of their own composing.

It might be argued that Cowper wrote the above as an unconverted man and he would have changed his mind as a Christian taking part in communal worship. This is not the case at all. In his poem 'Table Talk', published in 1782, Cowper claims that one simple psalm of Sternhold and Hopkins is better than all the endeavours of later, wittier, more skilled and more polished versifiers.

Why the Olney Hymns were published

In spite of all these factors which might have spoken against the Olney friends bringing out a book of hymns, Newton was still moved to have over two hundred of his own productions and sixty-eight of Cowper's published. There were numerous reasons for this action.

First of all, Newton genuinely believed that the hymns would prove a source of blessing to a wider group of believers.

Secondly, John Thornton, Newton's benefactor, had stressed his interest in such a project and was prepared to go a long way in financing it.

The third reason was that Newton had been very generous in allowing friends to copy his and Cowper's hymns and quite a number had already been published as what are now called 'pirate copies'. There are several letters extant in which, for instance, Newton informs Cowper that he has read one of his poems in a magazine and Cowper writes back to tell Newton that he had not published the poem and the only copy in existence was in Newton's possession. These copyists often changed the original hymns to suit their literary and theological tastes. Newton thus felt that an 'official' version of the hymns would put a stop to this clandestine publishing.

The fourth reason was Newton's very own. He wished the collection to be 'a monument to perpetuate the remembrance of an intimate and endeared friendship', i.e. his friendship with Cowper. Newton was feeling a call to leave Olney and he thought that the Olney Hymns would serve as a fitting memorial to the many years he had spent there in fellowship with Cowper.

The style of the hymns

Taking into consideration what has been said above concerning the aims of Cowper and Newton in writing hymns, it will be no surprise to modern readers to note that the two friends did not chiefly strive to write lyrical poetry when composing the hymns. Functionality and utility were their guidelines. Newton's comment in his preface was: 'Perspicuity, simplicity and ease, should be chiefly attended to; and the imagery and colouring of poetry, if admitted at all, should be indulged very sparingly and with great judgment.'

Newton then humbly adds, 'If the Lord whom I serve, has been pleased to favour me with that mediocrity of talent which may qualify me for usefulness to the weak and the poor of his flock, without quite disgusting persons of superior discernment, I have reason to be satisfied.' Newton and Cowper maintained that in writing the hymns they had 'plain people' in mind. The fact, however, that not only 'plain people' but Christians of all educational levels still sing many of the *Olney Hymns* with deep feeling and fervour shows that the two friends were highly successful in their task. The Gospel Standard Churches in Britain, for instance, have over seventy of these glorious testimonies to God's grace in their hymn-book.

Should we, however, accept Wordsworth's definition of poetry as 'the spontaneous overflow of powerful feeling',⁶ then what could be more beautiful poetry to the Christian than Cowper's 'Hark, my soul! it is the Lord!' or Newton's 'How sweet the name of Jesus sounds!'? Wordsworth, in his definition of poetry, merely thought of the feelings engendered in the poet and not in 'lesser mortals'. His language was only a one-way communication. Cowper and Newton aimed to make their hymns a form of two-way communication between God and man whereby man's powerful feelings of praise blended with the Word of God reflected in the hymns and thus full fellowship with God was attained. This was the kind of true poetry — Christian poetry — the two friends sought to write. They saw all true Christians as true poets.

Newton mentions Watts in his preface and it is obvious that he has been influenced by Watts in the composition of the collection. Like Watts' famous *Hymns and Spiritual Songs,* the *Olney Hymns* are divided into three books.

Book I

The first book, as in Watts' collection, contains hymns on 'Select Passages of Scripture'. There is a great difference, however, between Newton's and Cowper's method of dealing with Scripture and that of Watts. The latter always strove to 'Christianize' Old Testament texts. Watts argues in his *Preface to the Psalms of David imitated in the language of the New Testament, and applied to the Christian State and Worship,* that 'It is necessary to divest David and Asaph, etc. of every other character but that of a psalmist and a saint, and to make them always speak the common sense of a christian.' Thus references to Old Testament rites and rituals were immediately translated into what he believed were their New Testament counterparts. Watts thought that it was of little use to refer to Old Testament concepts, as 'By keeping too close to David in the house of God, the veil of Moses is thrown over our hearts.' In his introductory words to his *Hymns and Spiritual Songs* Watts explains further what he means by this. He tells us that whenever mention is made of 'goats or bullocks' for the altar he translates this directly into terms of Christ's sacrifice. When David 'attends the Ark with shouting into Zion', Watts tells us, 'I sing the ascension of my Saviour into heaven, or his presence in his church on earth.'

This method of Old Testament interpretation led Watts to omit psalms such as Psalm 137 (which was the first Cowper ever translated), as they smacked too much of a bygone religion. Watts' arguments for not transcribing the whole of the original Psalms for church worship reveal a weak view of the use of Scripture and could be used as an argument against his own hymns. The Dissenter argued that it was little use singing the whole Psalms as people would be asking forgiveness for sins that they had not committed, thanking God for victories that they had not won and asking God's protection against enemies they did not have. He even went so far as to write that such irrelevant material should not be translated at all.

Such an argument would shock those who see the Psalms as the fully inspired Word of God and when it was applied to hymns, apart from the Psalms, could prove conclusive for those who believe that hymn-singing is for personal edification and the edification of the church alone and should not be used in general church services where the unconverted are present.

Newton and Cowper, although they revered Watts, were nevertheless aware of the theological and didactic weaknesses of his method. They were careful to teach the full significance of the Old Testament to the church of the Lord Jesus Christ both theologically and historically and outlined its sacrificial system in full, pointing out its typological purpose.

Their method is well illustrated by Book I, Hymn II. Here we read of Abel's presenting a more excellent sacrifice than Cain, of Cain's jealousy and fratricide. First the authors point out that Abel's base deed illustrates the outworkings of the Fall and then they go on to explain how Abel's sacrifice was a type of our Redeemer's sacrifice. Then, of course, we have the application:

> Such was the wicked murd'rer Cain
> And such by nature still are we,
> Until by grace we're born again,
> Malicious, blind and proud, as he.

Watts seems to have thought that the Old Testament themes were far too morbid for a Christian and sought to write happy hymns. In this way he pioneered much of the modern hymn-singing mentality. Newton and Cowper were made of more sober and more realistic stuff. They saw the need first to preach the law, so that grace may then abound more abundantly.

Critics throughout the ages have stressed unfairly that the *Olney Hymns* are too severe, morbid and Old Testament-centred. Norman Nicholson, one of Cowper's biographers, and himself a poet, even suggests that Cowper's 'There is a fountain fill'd with blood' makes us 'aware of rituals even older than the Old Testament'! A brief look at Book I should dispel this criticism. The hymns are based on books from Genesis to Revelation. The twenty-five Old Testament books referred to are illustrated by seventy-five hymns, whereas the thirteen New Testament books referred to are illustrated by fifty-nine hymns. This would seem a balanced selection in view of the size of the Old Testament in relation to the New, particularly when we consider that all the Old Testament hymns have New Testament applications.

The *Olney Hymns* have a very low view of man but a correspondingly high view of God. This is perhaps why they have been called 'morbid' by many a critic who seemingly expects hymns to be always 'hymns of triumph' of the man-centred type illustrated in the verse:

Rise up, ye saints of God!
The church for you doth wait,
Her strength unequal to her task,
Rise up and make her great.

Such hymns never came from Cowper's or Newton's pens! It cannot be doubted that one of the central themes of Book I is man's utter insufficiency to save himself. In this Newton and Cowper certainly have both Scripture and experience on their side.

Another theme, however, is just as scriptural and brings nothing but joy for sinful man. The two authors stress time and time again the sovereign grace of God in saving the undeserving. Cowper's 'Oh! for a closer walk with God', 'Ere God had built the mountains', and 'My God! How perfect are thy ways', can hardly be called gloomy, nor can Newton's 'How sweet the name of Jesus sounds!', 'Amazing grace!' or 'One there is, above all others, Well deserves the name of Friend'. These are all to be found in the Old Testament section. In the New we find Newton's beautiful 'The church a garden is' and Cowper's 'Hark, my soul! it is the Lord'. Here there are many allusions to seafaring dangers and rescue at sea as Newton, the ex-mariner, expounds such texts as Matthew 15:28-31 and John 6:16-21. Even Cowper uses sea imagery when expounding Philippians 4:2 on contentment:

> Fierce passions discompose the mind,
> As tempests vex the sea;
> But calm content and peace we find,
> When, Lord, we turn to thee.

Book II

Book II of the Olney Hymns deals with occasional subjects under the headings 'Seasons, Ordinances, Providences and Creation'. Newton is perhaps at his most lyrical and poetical in this book, as illustrated by the second verse of Hymn I:

> As the winged arrow flies
> Speedily the mark to find
> As the lightning from the skies
> Darts, and leaves no trace behind,
> Swiftly thus our fleeting days
> Bear us down life's rapid stream;
> Upwards, Lord, our spirits raise
> All below is but a dream.

There is much in this second book that might seem sentimental to modern readers and the hymns are perhaps the least singable in the whole collection. Both Newton and Cowper are quite clearly at their best when dealing directly with a given biblical theme and not preaching topically.

The solemn note sounded in many of the hymns for children would seem especially out of place in today's worship. What Sunday School class would sing Newton's Hymn XXIX today?

> Alas! by nature how deprav'd,
> How prone to ev'ry ill!
> Our lives, to Satan, how enslav'd
> How obstinate our will!

Yet can we in fairness ask such a question, with its negative bias, when we so often neglect to give our children strong meat nowadays and are content with teaching them choruses which are at best 'milky' and in some cases theologically unsound and untrue? The following example of a modern chorus is a case in point:

One, two, three,
The devil's after me.
Four, five, six,
He's always throwing bricks.
Seven, eight, nine,
He misses every time.
Hallelujah, hallelujah, amen.

Perhaps we need to be reminded of the fact that Newton and Cowper both got on very well with children and did good pioneer work in making the gospel available to them. Newton's Sunday School at Olney was one of the first in the land and Cowper was to work closely with Rowland Hill, a great pioneer of children's work, in bringing out a hymn-book for children. Today there are many evangelical Sunday Schools where the children are even taken out of church before the sermon and given a set of paints and told to paint a 'religious' picture. Such 'teachers' could learn much from Cowper's and Newton's writings on dealing with children.

Book II provides us with some of Newton's loveliest nature hymns and here again his lyrical skill reaches great heights, in spite of what he says in the preface concerning the lack of good poetry in the hymns. In these modern days of 'back to nature' movements it seems a pity that Newton's nature hymns, such as 'Pleasing spring again is here!' (XXXIII), and his poem 'The Garden' (XCV) are not used at all. There is a fine development in Newton's view of nature. At first he felt, along with James Hervey, the 'prose poet', that the seasons merely pointed to the fact that all earthly life must pass away. Then he began to look upon the seasons as a sign of renewal in nature, pointing to the time when God would renew all things. Cowper took up this view later in his most famous poem, the *Task*; indeed Newton introduces many themes concerning nature in the *Olney Hymns* which reappear at a later date in Cowper's poetry.

Newton also makes it quite clear in his nature verse, as Cowper in his later poetry, that only the redeemed have eyes to see the true

significance of nature and only they can share in its true blessings.
In Hymn LXXXI, 'The Book of Creation', we read,

> The book of nature open lies
> With much instruction stor'd,
> But till the Lord anoints our eyes
> We cannot read a word.

The best-known hymn by Cowper in this book is 'Jesus,
where'er thy people meet', which, as we have seen, was specially
written for the prayer meeting in the Great House. This large room
had seating for 130 and the people of Olney 'thronged exceedingly'
to the meetings, to use Newton's phrase. There is a great similarity
in the hymns of prayer written by the two friends, which is to be
expected when we consider that they prayed daily together for so
many years.

Book III

Book III is entitled 'On the Rise, Progress, Changes, and Comforts
of the Spiritual Life', and is divided into eight sections dealing with
topics such as conflicts in the lives of Christians, dedication and
surrender to God, warnings against certain ways of life, and hymns
of praise. The hymns headed 'Solemn Addresses to Sinners' are
especially forthright and evangelistic. Here Newton pleads with
sinners as, for instance, in Hymn II, which is entitled 'Alarm':

> Stop, poor sinner! stop and think
> Before you farther go,
> Will you sport upon the brink
> Of everlasting woe?

In the section entitled 'Seeking, Pleading and Hoping' we find
Cowper's hymn 'The Shining Light' (VIII), which depicts the
anguish of the repentant sinner for whom hope comes in the form of
'the still small voice':

> My former hopes are fled,
> My terror now begins;

I feel, alas! that I am dead
In trespasses and sins.

Ah, whither shall I fly?
I hear the thunder roar;
The law proclaims destruction nigh,
And vengeance at the door.

When I review my ways,
I dread impending doom;
But sure, a friendly whisper says,
'Flee from the wrath to come.'

I see, or think I see,
A glimm'ring from afar;
A beam of day that shines for me,
To save me from despair.

Forerunner of the sun,
It marks the Pilgrim's way;
I'll gaze upon it while I run,
And watch the rising day.

There are few hymns that match the sheer spiritual, Christian beauty and poetic splendour of Newton's Hymn XII in this section:

Approach, my soul, the mercy-seat
Where Jesus answers pray'r;
There humbly fall before his feet
For none can perish there.

Thy promise is my only plea,
With this I venture nigh
Thou callest burden'd souls to thee,
And such, O Lord, am I.

Bow'd down beneath a load of sin,
By Satan sorely press'd
By war without, and fears within
I come to thee for rest.

Be thou my shield and hiding-place!
That, sheltered near thy side,
I may my fierce accuser face,
And tell him, 'Thou hast died.'

Oh wond'rous love! to bleed and die,
To bear the cross and shame;
That guilty sinners such as I,
Might plead thy gracious name.

'Poor tempest-tossed soul, be still,
My promis'd grace receive;'
'Tis Jesus speaks — I must, I will,
I can, I do believe.

Here is a hymn with meat in it indeed for those who hunger and
thirst after righteousness. And yet so many critics say Newton's
hymns are crude. One suspects that such hymns are only classified
as crude because their critics have neither seen the depths of their
own sin nor experienced the heights of salvation in Christ.

In the section marked 'Comfort' we find Cowper's hymn 'How
blest thy creature is, O God!' (XLIV) and also his well-known' Joy
and Peace in Believing' (XLVIII), which begins:

Sometimes a light surprises
The Christian while he sings;
It is the Lord who rises
With healing in his wings:
When comforts are declining,
He grants the soul again
A season of clear shining
To cheer it after rain.

In holy contemplation,
We sweetly then pursue
The theme of God's salvation
And find it ever new:
Set free from present sorrow,
We cheerfully can say,
E'en let th'unknown tomorrow,
Bring with it what it may.

It can bring with it nothing
But he will bear us thro';
Who gives the lilies clothing
Will clothe his people too:
Beneath the spreading heavens,
No creature but is fed;
And he who feeds the ravens,
Will give his children bread.

Tho' vine, nor fig-tree neither,
Their wonted fruit should bear,
Tho' all the fields should wither,
Nor flocks, nor herds be there:
Yet God the same abiding,
His praise shall tune my voice;
For while in him confiding,
I cannot but rejoice.

Hardly any of Newton's hymns in this section are sung nowadays, but his beautiful hymn 'Peace Restored' (LIII) is well worth noting. It begins:

Oh, speak that gracious word again
And cheer my drooping heart!
No voice but thine can soothe my pain
Or bid my fears depart.

The final verse reads:

Dear Lord, I wonder and adore,
Thy grace is all divine;
Oh keep me, that I sin no more
Against such love as thine!

We find one of Newton's most rousing hymns (LXXXII) under the sub-heading 'Praise'. This provides an excellent example of the two friends' didactic purpose in writing the hymns and shows how a good sermon ought to be delivered. First there is the introduction, which contains all the salient points of the hymn:

> Let us love and sing and wonder,
> Let us praise the Saviour's name!

Then each of these points is expounded and exemplified, with a
verse on 'love', one on 'sing' , and so on. After each verse there is
a short application to drive the point home, and then at the end of the
hymn-cum-sermon there is a general conclusion and more specific
application.

In this section, too, we find Cowper's beautiful poem, 'I will
praise the Lord at all times' (LXXXIII). This is his only nature poem
in the whole series. The poet often used to joke that the difference
between him and other poets was that they waited until the spring to
be inspired but he felt the urge to write in the middle of winter. Thus
Cowper starts his poem on the seasons with the coldest month. Like
Newton in his nature poems, Cowper stresses that nature points to
an eternal renewal and everlasting rest in Christ.

> Winter has a joy for me,
> While the Saviour's charms I read,
> Lowly, meek, from blemish free,
> In the snowdrop's pensive head.
>
> Spring returns, and brings along
> Life-invigorating suns:
> Hark! the turtle's plaintive song,
> Seems to speak his dying grones!
>
> Summer has a thousand charms,
> All expressive of his worth;
> 'Tis his sun that lights and warms,
> His the air that cools the earth.
>
> What! has autumn left to say
> Nothing of a Saviour's grace?
> Yes, the beams of milder day
> Tell me of his smiling face.
>
> Light appears with early dawn;
> While the sun makes haste to rise,

See his bleeding beauties, drawn
On the blushes of the skies.

Ev'ning, with a silent pace,
Slowly moving in the west,
Shews an emblem of his grace,
Points to an eternal rest.

The last section of Book III is entirely the work of Newton and contains a number of short hymns and doxologies. Of these perhaps the only one which is still sung is Newton's paraphrase of 2 Corinthians 13:14:

May the grace of Christ our Saviour
And the Father's boundless love,
With the Holy Spirit's favour,
Rest upon us from above!
Thus may we abide in union
With each other and the Lord;
And possess, in sweet communion
Joys which earth cannot afford.

The doctrinal content of the hymns

Most of the criticism levelled at the *Olney Hymns* decries the lack of beauty in them. But how can one depict sin in a beautiful way? It would be ridiculous to try. These hymns were written as expressions of experience and thus portray the life of a sinner through all the stages up to being convicted, converted and enjoying a life in Christ. Thus we see both authors portraying the highest mountain-top experiences but also the despair of doubt and fears of hell. What shocks most unreformed critics is that both Cowper and Newton are so open in expressing the doubts felt by Christians and their dissatisfaction with themselves. Thus we find Newton writing in Book I, Hymn CXIX:

'Tis a point I long to know,
Oft it causes anxious thought;
Do I love the Lord or no?
Am I his, or am I not?

If I love, why am I thus?
Why this dull and lifeless frame?
Hardly, sure can they be worse,
Who have never heard his name!

In this hymn the preacher is dealing with Christ's words to Peter,
'Lovest thou me?' He is applying them to himself and to every
Christian and sees that we are not perfected in the faith in this life
as the Wesleyans taught we could be. This is why Newton ends his
hymn with the practical prayer:

Let me love thee more and more,
If I love at all, I pray;
If I have not lov'd before,
Help me to begin to day.

Another example of the humbling Christian experience of doubt
is Cowper's hymn 'Jehovah our righteousness' (Book I, Hymn
LXVII):

My God! how perfect are thy ways!
But mine polluted are;
Sin twines itself about my praise,
And slides into my pray'r.

When I would speak what thou hast done
To save me from my sin;
I cannot make thy mercies known
But self-applause creeps in.

Divine desire, that holy flame
Thy grace creates in me;
Alas! impatience is its name,
When it returns to thee.

This heart, a fountain of vile thoughts,
How does it overflow?
While self upon the surface floats
Still bubbling from below.

Let others in the gaudy dress
Of fancied merit shine;
The Lord shall be my righteousness,
The Lord for ever mine.

Here Cowper is expounding Jeremiah 23:6, where the prophet extols the New Covenant in which God's children will be saved through the Lord's righteousness alone and through none other. Cowper is witnessing to the truth of the Scriptures, which make it clear that no 'fancied merit' ever saved a man.

Theologically the *Olney Hymns* are unmistakably Calvinistic. This is particularly emphasized in the preface, as many of the hymns being published at the time were thoroughly Arminian. Newton writes here in the first person but he says nothing in which we cannot include Cowper, as we shall see:

Many gracious persons (for many such I am persuaded there are) who differ from me, more or less, in those points which are called Calvinistic, appear desirous that the Calvinists should, for their sakes, studiously avoid every expression which they cannot approve. Yet few of them, I believe, impose a like restraint upon themselves, but think the importance of what they deem to be truth, justifies them in speaking their sentiments plainly, and strongly. May I not plead for an equal liberty? The views I have received of the doctrines of grace are essential to my peace, I could not live comfortably a day or an hour without them. I likewise believe, yea, so far as my poor attainments warrant me to speak, I know them to be friendly to holiness, and to have a direct influence in producing and maintaining a gospel conversation, and therefore I must not be ashamed of them.

Cowper's hymns would make a first-class commentary on the 'Five Points' of Calvinism. Anyone writing,

I feel alas! that I am dead
In trespasses and sins,

as Cowper does in his hymn 'The Shining Light', shows that he believes in the total depravity of man.

Unconditional election is reflected in that beautiful verse from
'Hark my soul':

> I deliver'd thee when bound,
> And, when wounded, heal'd thy wound
> Sought thee wand'ring, set thee right,
> Turn'd thy darkness into light.

The poet's words in 'The Narrow Way' show how faithfully he
believed in particular atonement:

> None but the chosen tribes of God
> Will seek or choose it for their own.

God's irresistible grace is shown in 'The Lord Proclaims his
Grace Abroad,' and anyone reading 'Behold I Make All Things
New,' or 'Praise for the Fountains Opened,' will understand what
Cowper means when he writes,

> Lord, I believe thou hast prepar'd
> (Unworthy tho' I be)
> For me a blood-bought free reward,
> A golden harp for me!

> 'Tis strung, and tun'd, *for endless years*,
> And form'd by pow'r divine;
> To sound, in God the Father's ears,
> No other name but thine.

A new friend for John Newton

When Newton wrote in his preface that he wished the *Olney Hymns*
to serve as a memorial to a great friendship, he was particularly
thinking of the deep fellowship and guidance he had experienced
through spending hours a day with William Cowper. These times
were now gone. Cowper had not recovered his former joy in the
Lord and could no longer enter into the same kind of fellowship that
he had enjoyed with Newton before his second major breakdown.
   Newton had thus lost one of the major props in his life, for he had

so relied on Cowper's friendship that he had made no other close friend for over ten years. In 1775 he had started up a friendship with Thomas Scott, a self-made man who had become a curate in neighbouring Weston. Newton's dealings with Scott were, however, more on a pastoral basis as he gradually led the unconverted minister into a saving knowledge of Christ. A deep friendship with Scott never developed. Newton needed a friend he could look up to and be guided by.

Such a friend he found in nearby Newport Pagnell in the person of William Bull. This Dissenting minister was in many ways similar to Cowper. He was a man of letters who had a great sense of humour which was only revealed after his initial shyness had worn off. He was a staunch Calvinist but, like Cowper, was subject to bouts of tender melancholy. He was a born leader of men and always exercised a robust energy in doing his duty to God. He was in such demand as a preacher that even Evangelicals of the Church of England, such as Newton and Berridge, gladly opened their pulpits to him.

Newton was at first put off by Bull's exterior but we soon find him referring to Bull in the same way as he had formerly spoken of Cowper. Writing of Bull on 30 November 1775, Newton says, 'He has just called and spent an hour with me. I seem to shrink into nothing when before him, to be a poor, empty, superficial creature. I could sit silent half a day to listen to him, and am almost unwilling to speak a word for fear of preventing him.'

We now find that Newton wished to spend hours of the day in Bull's company rather than Cowper's. Thus in December we find Newton writing that he had walked over to Newport to have breakfast with Bull, after which he stayed there until three o'clock in the afternoon. Commenting on this visit, Newton writes, 'I admire Mr Bull, so humble, so spiritual, so judicious, and so savoury. He seems well pleased with me, though surely not with the same reason. However, I rejoice in what the Lord has done for him, and I think he will be my most profitable companion in these parts.' Of his many visits to Newport he wrote,

A Theosphic pipe with Brother B.
Beneath the shadow of his fav'rite tree;
And then how happy I! how cheerful he!

Mary Newton was obviously alarmed at her husband's sudden switch in friends. 'I think Mr. Bull is Your pope,' she told him.

Newton prepares to move on

Meanwhile Newton was not happy at Olney. His popularity was waning and he was making mistakes. There was a growing opposition to his dealings with Dissenters and Baptists which caused the Olney parishoners to feel they were being neglected and that their pastor was inconsistent in matters of doctrine. Newton often took large numbers of like-minded parishoners to hear Mr Bull at Newport, took part in Baptist meetings as far away as Birmingham and opened his pulpit to Christians of all persuasions. Soon one half of the parish seemed to be criticizing Newton because he was too lenient with Christians of other persuasions, and the other half that he was too strict with his own people.

Mary Newton tended to side with Newton's critics on this matter. Once, in the safety of far away London, she gained courage enough to broach the subject with her husband in a letter written after hearing Wesley preach:

> I do not care about Your going to hear the Baptists tho I am very glad You did not dine with them. I am likewise glad You do not see with their eyes. Yet I think if You was to keep Your self to Your self as they do I should like it better. You see their party spirit. meet of a Tyesday then preach in the evening. before Symonds was dipt He would not have left you to have gone among them & if there had been a meeting of dippers next day He would not have din'd with You. I know You will not scold me now I am so far off & You will forget it by the time I come Home. but I would much rather be a Methodist than a Baptist.[7]

Another cause for complaint was that Newton often visited London, the Midlands and Yorkshire and it was supposed — correctly — by his parish that their pastor was seeking a church elsewhere. Newton seemed to have a definite preference for Yorkshire. His choice of preachers who filled in for him whilst he was on preaching tours left much to be desired. Nobody could criticize Bull on matters of doctrine as he was orthodox to the core — but he was not an Anglican. Powley was a good sound man — but he came from Yorkshire, the very place that was tempting their pastor away. Scott, who stood in for Newton on occasions, was an Anglican — but he was still not fully commited to Christ.

At times Newton left it to the parishioners to find a supply for him and they chose a Mr Page from nearby Clifton. This was obviously to spite Newton, who felt Page was extremely shaky on doctrine. Page's text when once preaching at Olney was Genesis 35:8: 'But Deborah Rebekah's nurse died, and was burried beneath Bethel under an oak: and the name of it was called Allon-bachuth.' Deborah, Page told his Olney hearers, signified the law, Rebekah the church and the oak the cross of Christ. He thus concluded that the power of the law is dead and buried in its relation to believers.

Soon Newton was being criticized for matters with which he had no dealings whatsoever. Many of the Olney citizens were very critical of the government and the way it was treating the poor, and republican sympathy was growing. This feeling was perhaps at its strongest amongst the Dissenters and Baptists who had no attachments through their churches with the Crown as the Anglicans had. William Carey, for instance, was privately a convinced republican though he never allowed his politics to colour or mar his Christian testimony.

Carey's friend John Ryland did not show the same restraint. He was so opposed to the American War that he publicly proclaimed, 'If I were General Washington I would summon all my officers around me, and make them draw blood from their arms into a basin, and, dipping their swords into it, swear that they would not sheath them till America had gained her independence.'[8] A special king's messenger was sent to Ryland to warn him and for some time a rumour was spread about the land that Ryland had been arrested.

Newton's name began to be mentioned in connection with the rebels and soon we find him having to write a letter to Lord Dartmouth clearing himself of these charges and professing that he was one of the 'quiet in the land'.[9] This did not make him any the more popular in Olney and may explain why Newton was to react angrily against Dissenters a decade later, accusing them of plotting to overthrow the government.

Eventually Newton became very interested in a church at Deptford in London but he was only their second choice and his friend Dr Conyers, who was given first offer of the post, accepted it. Newton then received a call to Hull which he accepted and made preparations to move. At the last minute, however, the church switched their preferences and another clergyman was chosen. Newton was far from being his own master in these matters, as his two patrons, Dartmouth and Thorton, kept urging him to apply here and there. At one time Lord Dartmouth even expressed a wish to send Newton off to North America.

Things really came to a head in October 1777, when Newton was away for most of the month in London. During this time a huge fire broke out in the town of Olney and did a great deal of damage. Newton quickly made an appeal in London and collected £200 for the relief of those who had lost their homes and property. When he returned home, however, he as good as told his parishioners that the fire was their own fault and ordered them to dispense with the coming bonfire celebrations on 5 November. He suggested that the practice of putting lighted candles in the windows on such occasions was irresponsible and should be abolished. All this was common sense but many parishioners felt that Newton was being too one-sided and acting above his authority. When Bonfire Night came that year there were open riots in the town and citizens went to extremes in their eagerness to show Newton that he could not dictate over them.

One party became so violent that they organized a march on the Vicarage, which they had decided to attack. Windows were smashed all along the way and a crowd of angry hooligans surrounded Newton's house ready to storm it. Newton was all for going out and talking to the mob but Mrs Newton had a nervous collapse and begged her husband not to show himself. So Newton sent a servant out to speak with the captain of the mob and hand over a bribe so that they would not attack. The money and the servant's arguments prevailed and the mob withdrew. Newton confessed in letters to his friends that he was ashamed of his action, but it made him more determined than ever to seek a new calling.

It was then that Mr Thornton came to Newton's rescue by offering him the parish of St Mary Woolnoth in London which he felt he ought to accept. Before making a final decision, however, Newton went over to Orchard Side and had a long chat with Cowper and Mrs Unwin. Cowper was grieved beyond measure but he assured his friend that under the present circumstances it would seem the Lord's will that Newton should accept the offer. Then Newton wrote to Bull begging him not to blame him for leaving Olney.

There was, however, a great protest at St Mary's as many of the congregation believed that they should be asked to call a pastor and that it was an abuse of the system of patronages if the man with the money also dictated to the parish who their pastor should be. This difficulty was temporarily overcome and Newton started to pack. Now that he was actually leaving Olney, he realized how much he had grown to love the place. He told Bull, 'London is the last situation I should have chosen for myself. The throng and hurry of the busy world, and noise and party contentions of the religious world, are very disagreeable to me. I love woods and fields and streams and trees — to hear the birds sing and the sheep bleat. I thank the Lord for His goodness to me here. Here I have rejoiced to live — here I have often wished and prayed that I might die. I am sure no outward change can make me happier, but it becomes not a soldier to choose his own post.'

Newton's last days at Olney were filled with sorrow. Thomas Scott had now come to a true understanding of his own sins and had received a glorious assurance of forgiveness. He became an ardent soldier for Christ and Newton set to work to have him made curate at Olney. Moses Browne, the ever absent vicar, was in favour and so was Lord Dartmouth, who owned the living. To Newton's dismay, however, the Olney Church resented the fact that they were to have Scott thrust on them and made it quite clear that he was not wanted. One of the reasons was that Scott wished to keep the curacy of Weston and thus take services at Weston and Olney alternately. The Olney parish had had their fill of absentee clergymen, and as Moses Browne was now very aged, they felt the time had come for him to stand down and prepare the way for a resident vicar who would take care of them and them alone. Moses Browne, however, though in his mid-seventies, would not consider giving up the income obtained through Olney and Weston and clung to the title of vicar.

Seeing how great the opposition was, Scott gave up any thought of succeeding Newton and the church made the biggest mistake of their history by calling Page to the curacy. When Page arrived he quarrelled with his parishioners, with the workmen who were repairing the church, so that they left, with his benefactors and, when he himself finally left Olney in disgrace, he even quarrelled with the auctioneer who sold his goods. The worst person to suffer from Page, however, was his wife, with whom he not only quarrelled day and night but whom he also beat most soundly. The man seemed to delight in making enemies. As may be imagined, there was quite an exodus of believers from the Anglican church to the Dissenting churches in the neighbourhood and Cowper resolved firmly never to have anything to do with Mr Page.

In the midst of all this confusion, in January 1780 Newton left behind him a church in turmoil to take up a new church far away where he knew the parishioners were not unanimously pleased to have him.

Meanwhile Cowper could not really understand what was going on. He appears not to have realized how great the opposition was to Newton as it had all developed during his illness. He told his friend, 'You were beloved at Olney and if you preached to the Chicksaws and Chactaws would be equally beloved to them.' He thus wrote to Mrs Newton in early March:

> The Vicarage became a Melancholy Object, as soon as Mr. Newton had left it: When You left it, it became more melancholy: now it is actually occupied by another Family. Even I cannot look at it without being shocked. As I walked in the Garden this Evening I saw the Smoke issue from the Study Chimney, and said to myself, that used to be a Sign that Mr. Newton was there, but it is so no longer. The Walls of the House know nothing of the Change that has taken Place, the Bolt of the Chamber Door sounds just as it used to do, and when Mr. Page goes up Stairs, for aught I know or ever shall know, the Fall of his Foot could hardly perhaps be distinguished from that of Mr. Newton: But Mr. Newton's Foot will never be heard upon that Stair case again. — These Reflections, and such as these, occurred to me upon the Occasion, and though in many respects I have no more Sensibility left than there is in Brick and Mortar, yet I am not permitted to be quite unfeeling upon this Subject. If I were in a Condition to leave Olney too, I certainly would not stay in it; it is no Attachment to the Place that binds me here, but an

Unfitness for every other. I lived in it once, but now I am buried in it, and have no Business with the World on the Outside of my Sepulchre; my Appearance would Startle them, and theirs would be shocking to me.

Such are my Thoughts about the Matter — Others are more deeply affected, & by more weighty Considerations. They have been many Years the Objects of a Ministry which they had reason to account themselves happy in the Possession of. They fear they shall find themselves great Sufferers by the alteration that has taken Place they would have had reason to fear it in any Case, but Mr. Newton's Successor does not bring with him the happiest Presages, so that in the present State of things they have double Reason for their Fears. Tho' I can never be the better for Mr. Page, Mr. Page shall never be the worse for me. If his Conduct should even Justify the worst Apprehensions that have been formed of his Character, it is no personal Concern of mine; but this I can venture to say, that if he is not Spotless, his Spots will be seen, & the plainer, because he comes after Mr. Newton.[10]

New interests for Cowper

Cowper's melancholy was, in the goodness of God, rapidly disappearing and new thoughts were occupying his mind. His humour was returning and his letters begin to show that spark of wit and piety for which he has since become famous.

Newton began to miss Cowper in London as Cowper missed Newton. This led the two friends to promise to write to each other on a regular basis, setting apart Saturday evening as their time of epistolary fellowship. This new development also led Newton not to be so possessive of his friendship with Bull. The Dissenting minister had begged Newton to introduce him to Cowper on the grounds that it was extremely frustrating living very near such a man of genius and piety and not being able to visit him.[11] Up to his leaving Olney, Newton, for reasons known only to himself, had refused to do so. Now he came to see that if any man could understand and sympathize with Cowper, it must be Bull. Newton therefore wrote to Bull and told him he would like him to visit Cowper and wrote to the poet telling him to expect a visitor soon. Thus, one day shortly afterwards, Cowper opened the door to find the Rev. William Bull standing on the pavement.

The two found they were birds of a feather at once. Cowper expressed his great liking for Bull in a letter to Unwin in which he says,

> You are not acquainted with the Revd. Mr. Bull of Newport. Perhaps it is as well for you that you are not. You would regret still more than you do, that there are so many Miles interposed between us. He spends part of the day with us tomorrow. A Dissenter, but a liberal one; a man of Letters and of Genius, master of a fine imagination, or rather not master of it; an imagination, which when he finds himself in the company he loves and can confide in, runs away with him into such fields of speculation as amuse and enliven every other imagination that has the happiness to be of the party. At other times he has a tender and delicate sort of melancholy in his disposition, not less agreeable in its way. No men are better qualified for companions in such a world as this, than men of such a temperament. Every scene of life has two sides, a dark and a bright one, and the mind that has an equal mixture of melancholy and vivacity, is best of all qualified for the contemplation of either. It can be lively without levity, and pensive without dejection. Such a man is Mr. Bull. But he smokes tobacco — nothing is perfect.[12]

Cowper had become a very changed man by 1780. Before his second major breakdown he had been very evangelical but often in an overbearing, off-putting way. He had become so used to speaking in highly biblical language that many non-Christians must have had great difficulty in understanding him. This is very much the case with many of Cowper's biographers, who confess themselves baffled at many an expression in Cowper's earlier letters which are as plain as day to those who know their Bibles.

Also, from reading Cowper's letters, one could get the impression that he was the laziest man alive. The truth is that he had nearly always overestimated his strength and worked intensively hard since coming to Olney. Whatever he did, he tended to do with such a display of energy that he soon became tired out. Even when he prayed, Newton tells us, he prayed with such force that the sweat poured down his face, even in mid-winter. The poet never seemed to be really relaxed and was always thinking that if he did not do more for God he would be guilty of not doing his duty.

One very harrowing factor for Cowper had been that he did not know what God intended him to do for an occupation. He had been brought up as a gentleman, that is, to live more or less on sinecures, patronages and preferments, but his whole Christian nature now rebelled against such an idea and he wanted to earn a living in a way more fitting for a child of God. He had failed as a lawyer and felt himself incapable of becoming a minister. No other occupation had occurred to him until his breakdown in 1773.

Cowper emerged gradually from the depths of melancholy as a living paradox. He was, on the one hand, far more mature as a Christian and in his knowledge of human nature. He was far clearer in his mind concerning God's purpose for man and his plan of salvation. He began to develop a fine sense of humour and a feel for language and an ability to use these gifts so that he could make divine truths palatable to the most unlikely people.

On the other hand, Cowper's sense of his own worthlessness and the doom that he felt must be his was never very far from his thoughts. He could spend days of intense joy and high spirits, only to relapse for a time into deep melancholy where there was no presence of God to be felt. He was never again to be driven as low as he was in 1763 and 1773 but his life was to become a permanent interchange of silver linings and clouds. Newton referred to this aspect of Cowper's life in his last tribute to his friend in 1800 when he said that he was a burning bush that was never consumed.

Throughout the 1770s, however, Cowper came to realize that God was forcing him to become a teacher and a poet. Before going on to see how this came to be, it is necessary to look at one aspect of Cowper's life that has been almost neglected up till now and that needs to be dealt with in the following chapter.

8.
Cowper's library

Before going on to show how Cowper developed into a major Christian poet, it is essential to know how large a part reading played in his life. Earlier biographers have left their readers with the erroneous impression that Cowper was not a well-read man.[1] By any standards, however, William Cowper must have been very well read indeed. In August 1787, when he was given the free use of a nobleman's library, he wrote to his cousin Lady Hesketh saying that this was 'an acquisition of great value to me, who never have been able to live without books since I first Knew my letters'.

Cowper read much and very fast. He used to say that he always read as if the librarian was at his elbow urging him that it was time to return the book. This was because after Cowper lost the bulk of his library during his first major illness, he spent many years 'living' on borrowed books. In spite of this speed, Cowper could retain in his memory for years the most detailed arguments of a book he had read only once.

As a young Templar he had built up a library, 'a valuable collection, partly inherited from my father, partly from my brother, and partly made by myself'. During his convalesence and his time at Huntingdon he would sometimes, especially in the winter, read all day long. From then on, right up to the 1790s, he would read aloud at special times of the day for the sake of Mrs Unwin, his visitors and any servants who were not on duty. Over the years Cowper read through an enormous amount of books, not taking into account those he read in private study. Even in the late 1790s when he was ill and depressed and suffering from eye-trouble, his friends used to comfort, edify and entertain him by reading a great variety of works to him.

Cowper read many books on travel, science, medicine and gardening, but the greatest number of books he read were by Puritan, Evangelical and Dissenting writers as well as books by such authors as Samuel Richardson, who moved in evangelical circles. If Cowper specialized at all, it was more on the exegetical side, although he read a great deal of devotional literature and works on missionary strategy. Apart from books Cowper read a surprising number of newspapers and theological and literary magazines and sought to be always in the news concerning politics, world trade and general international affairs.

It must also be added that Cowper read original works in at least five different languages. When writing to William Unwin in November 1781 he gave him the advice, 'He that would write should read, not that he may retail the observations of other men, but that being thus refreshed and replenished, he may find himself in a condition to make and produce his own.' Cowper was reading a French book — in the original — at the time.

Lancelot Andrews and the Puritans

One of the most ancient books of devotion Cowper read was Lancelot Andrews' *Preces Privatae Quotidianae*. Andrews (1555-1626), a friend of Richard Hooker and George Herbert, was responsible for the Pentateuch and the historical books in the Authorized Version of 1611. This Anglican bishop, though sharing the Reformed faith, was unpopular with many Puritans of the day because of his political views (or rather lack of them) and the fact that he preferred episcopacy to presbyterianism. Andrews, however, was open in matters of church government and thus became unpopular on the episcopal side, too, as he would not argue that churches which had given up the episcopacy were no longer true biblical churches. This was more or less Cowper's view of the subject and he in turn reaped much criticism for refusing to come down on one particular side. This has lead to Anglicans, Presbyterians, Independents and Baptists all claiming Cowper as their own.

Cowper, like Andrews, was interested in getting at the true

meaning of a biblical text and some of his earliest poems were translations and paraphrases of Bible passages. To help him, the poet used a number of linguistic aids from the Puritan period. Thus we find him referring to John Buxtorf's *Lexicon Hebraicum* and also George Pasor's *Lexicon Graeco-Latinum in Novum Testamentum*. Cowper was more than proficient in Greek but was weak at Hebrew. His brother John, however, was so much at home in the Hebrew language that he was able to publish original verse in Hebrew. He would certainly have helped William with difficult passages.

Here is Cowper's rendering of Psalm 137, one of the so-called imprecatory psalms, in which the psalmist calls down judgement on God's enemies, set alongside the text of the Authorized (or King James) Version, to show how closely Cowper kept to the language of this translation. Later Cowper was to argue for the language of this Bible version as that most suitable for English poetry.

Psalm 137
Authorized version:

By the rivers of Babylon, there we sat down, yea, we wept, when we remembered Zion.

We hanged our harps upon the willows in the midst thereof.

For there they that carried us away captive required of us a song; and they that wasted us required of us mirth, saying, Sing us one of the songs of Zion.

How shall we sing the Lord's song in a strange land?

If I forget thee, O Jerusalem, let my right hand forget her cunning.

If I do not remember thee, let my tongue cleave to the roof of my mouth; if I prefer not Jerusalem above my chief joy.

Cowper's version:

To Babylon's proud waters brought,
In bondage where we lay,
With tears on Sion's Hill we thought,
And sigh'd our hours away;
Neglected on the willows hung
Our useless harps, while ev'ry tongue
Bewail'd the fatal day.

Then did the base insulting foe
Some joyous notes demand,
Such as in Sion used to flow
 From Judah's happy band—
Alas! what joyous notes have we
Our country spoil'd, no longer free,
And in a foreign land?

Oh! Solyma! if e'er thy praise
Be silent in my song,
Rude and unpleasing be the lays,
And artless be my tongue!
Thy name my fancy still employs;
To thee, great fountain of my joys,
My sweetest airs belong.

Remember, O Lord, the children of Edom in the day of Jerusalem; who said, Rase it, rase it, even to the foundation thereof.

Remember, Lord! that hostile sound,
When Edom's children cry'd,
Razed be her turrets to the ground,
And humbled be her pride;
Remember, Lord! and let the foe
The terror of thy vengeance know—
The vengeance they defied.

O daughter of Babylon, who art to be destroyed; happy shall he be, that rewardeth thee as thou hast served us.

Happy shall he be, that taketh and dasheth thy little ones against the stones.

Thou too, great Babylon, shall fall
A victim to our God;
Thy monstrous crimes already call
For Heaven's chastising rod.
Happy who shall thy little ones
Relentless dash against the stones,
And spread their limbs abroad.

George Herbert (1593-1633), whose works had comforted Cowper at the Inner Temple, remained a favourite with the poet. Herbert had also been educated at Westminster and Cowper confessed that he was prejudiced in favour of anyone who came from that school. He was impressed by Herbert's deep devotion.

Other Puritan works that Cowper read at this time were the works of Edward Reynolds (1599-1676), the poetry and essays of John Milton (1608-74), *The Saints' Everlasting Rest* by Richard Baxter (1615-91) and *The Nature of the Remainders of Indwelling Sin in Believers* by John Owen (1616-83). Cowper's views on indwelling sin were identical to those of Owen and were probably influenced by them. It was Cowper's feeling of sin and lack of growth in grace that used to plague him during his depressions and make him feel, at times, that in spite of his conversion, God would only be acting justly if he assigned Cowper to everlasting punishment.

The influence of John Milton

Next to John Newton, John Milton (1608-74) was the author who was to influence Cowper the most in his poetry. Cowper became fascinated with Milton as a schoolboy and learnt much of his verse off by heart. His first impressions of Milton were recorded in the *Task*:

No bard could please me but whose lyre was tun'd
To Nature's praises. Heroes and their feats
Fatigued me, never weary of the pipe
Of Tityrus, assembling, as he sang,
The rustic throng beneath his fav'rite beech.
Then Milton had indeed a poet's charms:
New to my taste, his Paradise surpass'd
The struggling efforts of my boyish tongue
To speak its excellence. I danced for joy.
I marvell'd much that, at so ripe an age
As twice sev'n years, his beauties had then first
Engag'd my wonder; and, admiring still,
And still admiring, with regret suppos'd
The Joy half lost because not sooner found.[2]

Even in middle age and when a comparatively old man, Cowper
could still quote with ease the English, Latin and Italian verse of
Milton's which he had learnt as a boy. Writing to his old Temple
friend Clotworthy Rowley in October 1791, he told him, 'Few
people have studied Milton more, or are more familiar with his
poetry than myself.' This is the reason why Joseph Johnson, who
acted as publisher for Newton and Cowper, turned to Cowper for
assistance when he republished Milton's works with a commentary
on *Paradise Lost*. Cowper's commentary is an epitome of Reformed
theology.

It is interesting to follow the correspondence of Cowper with
John Newton concerning Cowper's poetry. Newton served as
Cowper's editor, telling him what he would omit or add and why. On
the few occasions where Cowper felt that he could not follow
Newton's advice, it was when he felt Milton offered a better
alternative. Cowper loved to read Milton because he found him a
true Christian poet who had managed to work out a language which
was most capable of conveying the gospel.

Later evangelical men of letters, such as Alexander Knox, felt
that Cowper had even surpassed Milton. This is probably because
Milton's Arthurian sense of being a gentleman often got in the way
of his Christianity. A case in point is the Fall itself. Adam is hardly
portrayed as falling in the true biblical sense as, when he sees that
Eve has sinned, he tastes of the forbidden fruit because of a
gentlemanly view of 'solidarity' with his wife! In his commentary,

which will be looked at in a later chapter, Cowper is quick to point out failings in Milton's evangelical make-up.

Walter Marshall

Walter Marshall (1628-80) was one of Cowper's favourite authors. The poet read and reread Marshall's *Gospel Mystery of Sanctification*. Writing in March 1767 to an Evangelical cousin, Cowper says,

> The Book you mention lies now upon my Table. Marshall is an Old Acquaintance of mine; I have both read him and heard him read with Pleasure and Edification. The Doctrines he maintains are under the Influence of the Spirit of Christ, the very Life of my Soul, and the Soul of all my Happiness. That Jesus is a present Saviour, from the Guilt of Sin by his most precious Blood, and from the Power of it by his Spirit, that corrupt and wretched in ourselves, in Him, and in Him only we are complete, that being united to Jesus by a lively Faith, we have a solid and Eternal Interest in his Obedience & Sufferings, to Justify us before the Face of our Heavenly Father, and that All this inestimable Treasure, the Earnest of which is in Grace, and its Consummation in Glory, is Given, freely Given to us of God, without Regard to our Sins on the one hand, to hold it back, or to our imperfect Services on the other to bring it forward, in short that he hath opened the Kingdom of Heaven to all Believers, these are the Truths which by the Grace of God, shall ever be dearer to me than Life itself, shall ever be placed next my Heart as the Throne whereon the Saviour himself shall sit, to sway all its Motions, and reduce that World of Iniquity and Rebellion to a State of Filial and Affectionate Obedience to the Will of the most Holy.
>
> These, my dear Cousin, are the Truths to which by Nature we are Enemies, they abase the Sinner and exalt the Saviour to a degree which the Pride of our Hearts, 'till Almighty Grace subdue them, is determined never to allow. For the Reception of these Truths, of this only Gospel, it pleased the Lord to prepare me by many and great Afflictions, by

Temporal Distress, by a Conscience full of the Terrors of
Eternal Death, by the Fire of his Law. Thus humbled, I was
glad to receive the Lord Jesus in his own appointed way; the
Self-righteous, Self-justifying Spirit of Pride was laid low,
and was no longer a Barrier, to shut in Destruction and
Misery, and to keep out the Saviour. May the Almighty reveal
his Son in our Hearts continually more and more, and teach
us to increase in Love towards him continually for having
given us the unspeakable Riches of Christ.

My Love to my dear Friend the Major, & to all my little
Cousins. May the Lord Bless them & make them all true
Members of his Mystical Body.

Yours faithfully

Wm Cowper.

This letter gives deep insight into Cowper's firm grasp of Bible
doctrine and his awareness that Christ died to secure our salvation
rather than merely to procure it, as Cowper's Wesleyan contemporaries were teaching. Nothing in our 'imperfect services' is sufficient to secure our salvation. If Christ merely procured our salvation
and then offered it to us, should we be righteous enough, so that we
might make it secure, then there would be little hope indeed for
sinful man.

In another letter to his cousin on the subject of Marshall, Cowper
wrote,

I think Marshal one of the best Writers and the most
Spiritual Expositor of Scripture I ever read. I admire the
Strength of his Argument and the clearness of his Reasonings
upon those parts of our most Holy Religion, which are
generally least understood even by real Christians, as Master-
pieces of the kind. His Section upon the Union of the Soul
with Christ is an Instance of what I mean, in which he has
spoken of a most Mysterious Truth with admirable Perspicuity, and with great Good Sense, making it all the while
subservient to his main purpose of proving Holiness to be the
Fruit and Effect of Faith.

I subjoin thus much upon that Author, because though you
desired my Opinion of him, I remember that in my last, I
rather left you to find it out by Inference, than expressed it as

I ought to have done. I never met with a Man who understood the Plan of Salvation better, or was more happy in explaining it.[3]

Cowper spent a good deal of time reading the works of John Flavel (1630-91) including his sermons and his 'Method of Grace'.

Tillotson

John Tillotson (1630-94) is one of the very few non-Puritans or non-Evangelicals whom Cowper quotes. We have seen that Cowper turned to Tillotson when plagued with a sense of sin and in acute depression. As Cowper was battling with the idea that he had committed the unpardonable sin, he may have read Tillotson's sermon 'Of the Unpardonable Sin against the Holy Ghost'. However much Tillotson has been criticized for preaching mere morals rather than the gospel, it must be said in fairness that he reformed the language of preaching, making it less bookish and learned and more suitable for the so-called common man to understand. This was also the aim of George Whitefield and John Newton, who wished to speak to people in their own language, even the language of the market-place.

One of the most balanced writers of the eighteenth century, Dr P. Doddridge (1702-51), has much that is positive to say about Tillotson. Commenting on 'Writers of the Established Church' (Doddridge was a Dissenter) he says of Tillotson,

> *Tillotson.* — There is such an easiness in his style, and beautiful simplicity of expression, as seems easy to be imitated, yet nothing more difficult. — He had some puritanical expressions. — Sometimes pathetic. — His method admirably clear, — beyond almost any other man — Many of his sermons, contain nothing remarkable; — especially his posthumous ones; — yet there are some of them equal to any he published in his lifetime. — His best pieces are at the beginning of his first and second volumes folio. — His discourse on evil speaking is excellent — He made great use of *Barrow* and *Wilkins*;—with whom compare some of his sermons. — There is sometimes great tautology; — but in

controversy no man found such lucky arguments, — nor represented the sentiments of his adversaries artfully, and advantageously for confutation.

Doddridge often comments on Tillotson's 'easy and pure style' and speaks highly of his way of putting truths over to children. Cowper is obviously referring to Tillotson's gift of clarity of expression when he writes to Lady Hesketh in April 1786, 'It is a noble thing to be a Poet. It makes all the world so lively. I might have preached more Sermons than ever Tillotson did, and better, and the world have been still fast asleep. But a volume of Verse is a fiddle that puts the Universe in motion.' Here Cowper is obviously commenting negatively on Tillotson, indicating that in spite of his fine language, Tillotson did not convey the gospel message. Cowper had just heard that the court circles were reading his Christian poems. He is also referring to his view of poetry as being true, original, expressive language, nearer to the language of Eden than prose. This view of Cowper's will be dealt with in a subsequent chapter.

Doddridge and Watts

Cowper was also familiar with the works of Doddridge himself. In a letter dated 18 April 1766, Cowper writes to Mrs Cowper, concerning the state of the blessed in heaven and whether or not there is communication amongst them,

> But you doubt whether there is any Communication between the Blessed at all, neither do I recollect any Scripture that proves it, or that bears any Relation to the Subject. But Reason seems to require it so peremptorily, that a Society without Social Intercourse seems to be a Solecism and a Contradiction in Terms, and the Inhabitants of those Regions are called you know in Scripture an innumerable *Company* & an *Assembly*, which seem to convey the Idea of Society as clearly as the Word itself. Human Testimony weighs but little in matters of this sort, but let it have all the Weight it can. I know no greater Names in Divinity than Watts and Doddridge. They were both of this Opinion, and I send you

the very Words of the latter. 'Our *Companions in glory* may probably assist us by their wise and good Observations, when we come to make the Providence of God here upon Earth, under the Guidance and Direction of our Lord Jesus Christ, *the Subject of our mutual Converse.*'

Cowper is quoting from a sermon preached by Doddridge at the Rev. James Shepherd's funeral entitled 'Christ's Mysterious Conduct to be Unfolded Hereafter'. Cowper wisely goes on to say, 'Thus, my dear Cousin, I have spread out my Reasons before you for an Opinion which whether admitted or denied, affects not the State or interest of the Soul. may our Creator, Redeemer, and Sanctifier conduct us into his own Jerusalem where there shall be no Night neither any darkness at all, where we shall be free even from innocent Error, and perfect in the Light of the Knowledge of the Glory of God in the Face of Jesus Christ!'

In this passage Cowper refers to Isaac Watts (1674-1748) of whom he was very fond. Most readers will only be familiar with Watts as a poet and hymn-writer but the Dissenting minister left behind him a large number of writings on many different subjects. Cowper was familiar with these works.

In January 1772 Cowper's wider family were shocked by the sudden disappearance of twenty-five-year-old William Cowper, the son of Major William and Maria Cowper. It seems that he had suddenly left his post at the House of Lords and gone abroad. The newspapers, however, reported that he was missing, believed lost. Cowper wrote to comfort Maria several times. When William turned up like the prodigal son, Cowper at once wrote, 'May he come home in the best sense, home to God, and home to the Mediator of the new covenant: then, after having been tossed, as the Lord says, like a ball into a far country, he shall find in the smiles of a reconciled God and Father what Dr. Watts calls —

"A young heaven on earthly ground.
And glory in the bud."'

This letter is still extant. In the margin where Cowper wrote these thoughts, Mrs Cowper added the words: 'This came to Pass, 4 Years after!'

Cowper was shocked to find that Dr Johnson found Watts'

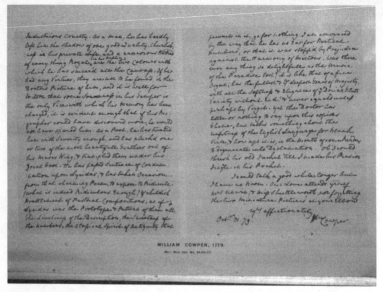

WILLIAM COWPER, 1779.

Part of a letter from Cowper in which he discusses Dr Johnson's views
on Milton

devotional poetry 'unsatisfactory'. He complained to Newton about
this, mistakenly thinking that Johnson did not respect Watts as a
person. Newton, who had friends in common with Johnson and was
about to send him a copy of Cowper's first volume of poems, wrote
back to tell Cowper that Johnson thought highly of Watts' moral
character, though he could not admire his Christian poetry. Johnson
and Cowper would never have agreed on poetry. Cowper was as sure
that religion was the true and original topic of poetry as Johnson was
that religion had nothing to do with poetry at all. Johnson was thus
not only critical of Watts but disliked Milton's poetry, too.

Addison

Joseph Addison (1672-1719), editor of the *Spectator* and author of
'The spacious firmament on high', was an author whom Cowper
respected for the simplicity of his language and for his tender

humour, which hurt no one. Addison's reputation has changed greatly over the past two hundred years but in the eighteenth century he was often quoted by Evangelicals such as James Hervey for his illuminating thoughts on Scripture and on God's person.

During his day literature was still, on the whole, lewd and perverted because of Restoration morals introduced by that playboy king, Charles II. Addison sought to cleanse the English language from all its filth and reform society by providing 'clean' literature. He also sought to create a language which could be understood by all social and occupational levels and thus criticized the use of technical jargon and 'hard words'.

Nowadays Addison is considered by evangelicals to be too deistic and high church. Modern evangelicals, however, have at their disposal the literature of a host of able theologians who wrote after Addison's time. In the first quarter of the eighteenth century good Christian works were rarely published and Evangelicals had to make do with a far less wholesome spiritual fare than that which we enjoy today.

Addison wrote extensively on Milton, Cowper's favourite poet, and did much, through his eighteen or so essays on Milton in the *Spectator*, to make Milton known to the British reading public. It was thus natural that Cowper would be interested in Addison as a Christian, author and commentator. When Cowper started his own commentary on *Paradise Lost*, he used Addison and Dr Thomas Newton as his main aids.

In one of Cowper's longer poems, 'Table Talk', he traces the ups and downs of poetry from creation through the Fall to his own day. After castigating the 'vice taught by rule' of Charles II's court, in which poetry had to be about 'rank obscenity' or it was not considered poetry at all, Cowper hails Addison as the forerunner of a better age in which,

> Sublimity and Attic taste, combin'd
> To polish, furnish, and delight the mind.

After discussing Addison, Pope and Churchill in this poem, Cowper goes on to state just what he expects from poetry and argues that poetry must once again take up its prophetic function and, like Isaiah of old, proclaim Christ to the nations.

Thomas Newton

Thomas Newton (1704-82), mentioned above, was one of the first Christian writers to be studied in earnest by Cowper. Robert Hodson, the minister of St Mary's, Huntingdon during Cowper's stay there, was a good friend of Bishop Newton and it is most probable that it was he who introduced Cowper to Newton's works. Cowper had read Newton's *Dissertation on the Prophesies*, a three-volumed work published between 1754 and 1758, and wrote to Lady Hesketh in July 1765 saying that these books were 'the most demonstrative proof of the truth of Christianity' that had ever been published. Writing again to Lady Hesketh a week later, Cowper says,

> Our mentioning Newton's Treatise on the Prophecies brings to my mind an anecdote of Dr. Young, who you know died lately at Welwyn. Dr. Cotton who was intimate with him, paid him a visit about a fortnight before he was seized with his last illness. The old man was then in perfect health. The antiquity of his person—the gravity of his utterance, and the earnestness with which he discoursed about religion, gave him, in the doctor's eye, the appearance of a prophet. They had been delivering their sentiments upon this book of Newton, when Young closed up the Conference thus:— 'My friend, there are three considerations on which my faith in Christ is built as upon a rock. The Fall of Man — The Redemption of Man — and the Resurrection of Man — these cardinal articles of our religion are such as human ingenuity could never have invented. Therefore they must be divine. The other argument is this — If the Prophecies have been fulfilled, (of which there is abundant demonstration) the Scripture must be the Word of God, and if the Scripture is the Word of God, Christianity must be true.'
> This Treatise on the Prophecies serves a double purpose. It not only proves the truth of our religion in a manner that never has been, nor ever can be controverted, but it proves likewise that the Roman Catholic is the apostate and antichristian church so frequently foretold both in the old and new Testament. Indeed so fatally connected is the refutation of popery with the truth of Christianity, when the latter is evinced by the completion of the Prophecies, that in

proportion as light is thrown upon the one, the deformities and errors of the other are more plainly exhibited. But I leave you to the book itself. There are parts of it which may possibly afford you less entertainment than the rest because you have never been a schoolboy, but in the main it is so interesting, and you are so fond of what is so, that I am sure you will like it.

Twenty years later, we find Cowper writing to John Newton about several articles by his namesake which had been recently discussed in the *Monthly Review*, a magazine to which he and John Newton subscribed. Cowper was shocked to find that though Bishop Newton was so biblical on prophecy, in the mellowness of old age he had come to reject hell as a place of eternal damnation and believed that all, including the devil himself, would eventually be saved. Cowper argued that though Dr Newton accused the Methodists of being papists, he was really a follower of Rome himself, as he believed in a kind of purgatory after death in which the sinner would be purged of his sin. Cowper adds, 'When I think of the poor Bishop I think too of some who shall say hereafter, have we not prophesied in thy name, and in thy name done many wonderous works? Then shall he say unto them, depart from me, for I never knew you.'

Laurence Sterne

A writer very much in vogue in the middle of the eighteenth Century was Prebendary Laurence Sterne (1713-68) of York Minster. Sterne became famous in two quite different fields, publishing not only best-selling novels such as *Tristram Shandy* but also collections of sermons under the title *The Sermons of Mr Yorick*. There is a legend that whenever Sterne climbed up into the pulpit at York Minster to preach, half the congregation got up and left in protest. Sterne was a brilliant orator and wit but his writings show a shocking and confusing mixture of high morals and downright indecency. In striving to give a true portrait of certain characters in all their lewdness, Sterne went too far by titivating the appetite for that kind of description. The tragedy of Sterne is that he began to delight in playing the roles of the more sordid characters he had created.

Joseph Hill wrote to Cowper in April 1766, asking him if he had read the latest works of Cowper's old friend George Colman and Laurence Sterne. Cowper replied,

> I read a great deal though I have neither read Colman nor Sterne. I agree with you entirely in your Judgment of the Works of the latter considered as Moral Performances, for the two first Volumes of his Sermons I read in London. He is a great Master of the Pathetic, and if that or any other Species of Rhetoric could renew the Human Heart and turn it from the Power of Satan unto God, I know no Writer better qualified to make Proselytes to the Cause of Virtue than Sterne. But alas! my Dear Joe the Evil of a corrupt nature is too deeply rooted in us all to be extirpated by the puny Efforts of Wit or Genius. The Way which God has appointed must be the true and the only Way to Virtue, and that is, Faith in Christ. He who has received that inestimable Blessing deep into his Heart, has received a Principle of Virtue that will never fail him. *This is the Victory that overcometh the World, even our Faith*, and there is no other. — The World by *Wisdom* knew not God, it therefore pleased Him by the *Foolishness* of Preaching to save them that believe. To save them from their Sinfull Nature here and from his Wrath hereafter, by that plain but despised and rejected Remedy, Faith in Christ. Therefore it is that though I admire Sterne as a Man of Genius, I can never admire him as a Preacher. For to say the least of him he mistakes the Weapon of his Warfare, and fights not with the Sword of the Spirit for which only he was ordained a Minister of the Gospel, but with that Wisdom which shone with as effectual a Light before our Saviour came as since, and which therefore cannot be the Wisdom which he came to Reveal to us.

Contemporary Evangelical writers

Cowper was familiar with the works of most of his contemporary Evangelicals. He possessed three volumes of Ralf Erskin's sermons, printed in 1763. He enjoyed reading Richard Pearsall's works, especially his *Reliquiae Sacra or meditations on Select Passages of Scripture* (1765) and had in his library a copy of William Romaine's *Life of Faith* which was printed in 1764.

Cowper thought highly of John Berridge of Everton, whose *Christian World Unmasked* (1773) had a special place on his bookshelves. Although Cowper had mixed feelings about Thomas Scott's abilities as a minister, he kept up a lively aquaintance with him and used to exchange books with him. Scott sought out Newton's assistance in writing his autobiography but when it was published, he was still not satisfied with the style so he gave it to Cowper for a thorough final revision.

Rowland Hill also looked to Cowper to mend the style of his children's hymn-book and sent it to the poet anonymously with a request that he should look over the work. Cowper edited the texts at times drastically and trimmed up quite a few hymns, adding two original compositions of his own into the bargain. Hill had met Cowper on several occasions in Olney and had obviously visited him at Orchard Side. Hill's biographer, his nephew Edwin Sidney, says that Hill always spoke of the kindness and attention he had received from Cowper. We have preserved a letter from Cowper dated 29 March 1790 which Cowper wrote to Hill on finding out that he was the author of the hymn-book. In it the poet writes,

My dear sir,

The moment when you ceased to be incog. I ought to have written you at least a few lines of apology for the liberties I had taken with your hymns, but being extremely busy at that time, and hoping that you would be so charitable as to pardon the omission, I desired Mr. Bull to be my proxy, charging him to make my excuses, and to assure you that I was perfectly satisfied with your making any alterations that you might see to be necessary in my text. If any thing fell from my pen that seemed to countenance the heresy of *universal redemption*, you did well to displace it, for it contradicted the Scripture, and belied me.

I am much obliged to you for the little volumes which I received safe on Saturday; and because I suppose that your end will be best answered by dispersion, if I should have occasion for half a dozen more, will order them from your bookseller without scruple.

I am, my dear sir, with much respect, and with Mrs. Unwin's compliments,

Your affectionate humble servant,

Wm. Cowper.

Should you want me on any similar occasion hereafter, I am always at your disposal.

It must have been quite a surprise to Cowper, a convinced Calvinist, to find that someone so theologically astute as Hill should think him unclear on the doctrine of redemption.

Jonathan Edwards (1703-1758) was another Christian writer of whom Cowper was very fond. The Evangelicals and Baptists at Olney had found Edwards' earlier works, such as *On the Freedom of the Will,* heavy-going and rather too philosophical. Edwards' works on eschatology, revival and missionary enterprises were, however, welcomed with great joy at Olney and obviously did much to motivate the pioneering work done in foreign missions which found its cradle in that town.

During the early nineties, when Cowper was housebound because of his literary tasks and looking after Mary Unwin, whose health was rapidly deteriorating, he distributed and read an enormous amount of literature. He seemed to have new books in his possession as soon as they came from the press. Thus in June 1791, when Cowper received a copy of Edwards' *The Salvation of all Men Strictly Examined* from his American friend James Cogswell, he could reply that he already had a copy of the book and had read it with pleasure. Edwards' book had only been published in New Haven the previous year yet Cowper had already obtained a copy.

Cowper must have been very familiar with Edwards' *Humble Attempt to Promote Explicit Agreement and Visible Union of God's People,* which was first published in America in 1748, but republished in Olney by the Baptists in 1789. Edwards' optimistic view of the fulfilment of prophecy regarding both the visible and spiritual worlds is echoed, at times almost verbatim, in Cowper's poetry. This could be because both authors held to the same interpretation of Scripture but it is highly probable that Cowper was influenced by Edwards in his treatment of many a prophetic and poetic theme.

Writing to Cogswell in the letter mentioned above, Cowper gives us some insight into the kind of books that he preferred himself. He says,

I send you in return for the Volumes with which you have favour'd me, three, on religious subjects, popular productions, that have not been long published, and that may not therefore yet have reached your country. — The Christian Officer's panoply — by a marine officer — The Importance of the Manners of the Great — and — an Estimate of the Religion of the Fashionable World. The two last are said to be written by a Lady — Miss Hannah More, and are universally read by people of that rank to which she addresses them. Your manners, I suppose, may be purer than ours, yet it is not unlikely that even among you may be found some to whom her strictures are applicable.

The first work was published with a warm recommendation by Sir Richard Hill (1732-1808), an old schoolfriend of Cowper's and elder brother of Rowland Hill. Richard Hill had been instrumental in the conversion of his more famous younger brother but also made a name for himself in defending Augustus Toplady against the wild accusations of John Wesley and also for defending in print a number of Evangelical students who were expelled from Oxford in 1768 for holding 'Methodist' views. Hill joined Newton and Cowper in battling for monogamy when certain Evangelicals close to them misguidedly advocated polygamy as a way to get prostitutes off the streets.

The two other books by Hannah More (1745-1833) thrilled Cowper, who at first thought they were written by William Wilberforce, and prompted him to write a great deal in More's praise. On hearing from Lady Hesketh, who belonged to Hannah More's 'blue-stockinged' circle, that she had written a poem against slavery, Cowper wrote, 'I shall be glad to see Hannah Moore's poem; she is a favourite writer with me, and has more nerve and energy both in her thoughts and language than half the He rhimers in the kingdom.'[4] Cowper excused himself to Lady Hesketh for believing that More's book on the reformation of manners amongst the nobility, published anonymously, had been written by Wilberforce by writing, 'If any thing could have raised Miss More to a higher rank in my opinion than she posssessed before, it could only be your information that after all, she and not Mr. Wilberforce, is the author of that volume. How comes it to pass, that she being a woman, writes so little like one? With a force and energy, and a correctness hitherto arrogated by the men, and not very frequently displayed even by the men themselves?'[5] Eventually Cowper became quite familiar with the More sisters through correspondence and through the agency of Lady Hesketh and John Newton, who was a close friend and adviser of Hannah More.

Patty More (1759?-1819), the youngest of Hannah's four sisters, asked Newton to use his influence in getting Cowper to write a poem especially for her which she could put in her autograph book. Newton promised her that he would get Cowper to write something very fine and elegant. Cowper, who was very busy at the time, complied but swiftly sent off four lines of the conventional autograph-book kind to please, as he wrote 'an old friend and a young lady'. Instead of passing the poem on, however, Newton sent it back, saying that he was greatly disappointed and Cowper should produce something better. With the same post came another request from a lady who wished Cowper to write a poem on behalf of her daughter on a theme determined by her. This may have made Cowper a little irate, as he complained in his reply to Newton that he was not allowed to write poetry as he thought fit, but as his friends thought he should. He added that he had been requested to write trifles and indeed was too busy to write more than trifles. He then repunctuated the four-lined verse to Patty, altered the syntax a little — and sent it back.[6]

Hannah More was very fond of reading Cowper's verse and told friends that she had at last found an author whom she could recommend with no reserves to her friends. So she could write, 'The best pleasure I have found for a long time, is to sit over a great fire and read Cowper's poems. I am enchanted with this poet; his images are so natural and so much his own! Such an original and philosophic thinker! such genuine Christianity! and such a divine simplicity! but rather rambling, and the order not very lucid. He seems to put down every thought as it arises, and never to retrench or alter anything.'[7] This later criticism would have been taken as a compliment by Cowper, who felt that artefacts and artificiality had no part in poetry and that true artistry was to depict the spontaneous experiences of the outward and inward eye and comment didactically on them.

One booklet of More's impressed not only Cowper but the entire Christian community in England. This was *Village Politics*, of which the Eclectic Society, founded by Newton, said that 'It had most essentially contributed, under Providence, to prevent a revolution.'[8] The book, which was sold in hundreds of thousands, was a direct criticism, from a Christian point of view, of the revolutionary theories of Tom Paine.

Cowper was closely connected with several of the Evangelical students who were expelled from Oxford in 1768, as mentioned above in connection with Sir Richard Hill. One of these was Thomas Jones, who became curate at Clifton, near Olney, in 1772. Jones was brother-in-law to Lady Austen who was to become a great friend of Cowper and Mrs Unwin's. Whatever Jones' piety was like at Oxford, Cowper felt that his neighbour dealt too deeply in politics to be a good pastor, especially considering the delicacy of the government's efforts to keep peace with France and North America. He thus wrote in February 1780 to Newton, who had helped to obtain the living for Jones, saying, 'I do not know how long Mr. Jones may continue to officiate in this place, but if you should write to him before his Ministry closes, perhaps it would be worth your while to caution him against assuming the Politician's character in the Pulpit. I suppose he is but indifferently qualified for a statesman, & his hearers on such subjects may be nearly as wise as he can make them.' Newton's assistance in the matter obviously proved successful as Jones remained at Clifton until 1792.

Another of the expelled students was Erasmus Middleton (1739-1805) who, like William Romaine, had to spend years as a lecturer at various churches as the church authorities found him too 'enthusiastic' to be made a curate or vicar. Unlike Jones, however, who seemed to be always falling out with his benefactors, Middleton gained great support from a large section of the Evangelical community amongst the gentry, the clergy and the common people and eventually became rector of Turvey and successor to Augustus Toplady as editor of the *Gospel Magazine.*

Middleton decided to write a church history dealing with all the greatest saints in Christendom from Wycliffe, Hus and Jerome of Prague to his contemporaries Toplady, Condor and Maddock. Nearly all the Evangelicals and awakened Dissenters of note, some 450 all told, helped to pay for the mammoth task by subscription. Middleton dealt with 189 of the great stalwarts of the Reformation and early Evangelical Revival on the Continent, in Britain, Ireland and North America. The work was published in four volumes from 1779 to 1786 and consisted of 2,064 pages. The biographies are very well researched and each entry is followed by a most detailed list of the writings and publications of the subjects. Reading the list of subscribers is a blessing in itself. John Berridge of Everton is there, as are also Richard Cecil, Richard Conyers, Lord Dartmouth, Moses Browne, the Fullers, the Countess of Huntingdon, Abraham Maddock (who died before the work was completed), John Newton, William Romaine, John Ryland Sr, Thomas Scott, Ambrose Searle and several members of the Cowper family and the Madans. William Cowper's edition has his coat of arms on the book-plate and his crest stamped on the spine of each volume. Any enlightened mind reading these volumes cannot help but be uplifted, edified and educated in the ways of the Lord.

John Newton

Cowper revered one author more than all others because of his clarity of style, choice of language, aptitude of expression and edifying subject matter. This was none other than John Newton, the man who was to be such a strong formative influence in Cowper's own literary career.

The fact that both secular and Christian publishing-houses still keep many of Newton's works in print goes to show what a mighty pen Newton had. Alexander Whyte echoed the thoughts of many when he said, 'For myself, I keep John Newton on my select shelf of spiritual books: by far the best kind of books in the world of books!' Wordsworth, judging by his famous 'Preface', tended to think that true poetry was his own invention, yet he acknowledged Newton as a true poet and copied his words. Overton, the church historian, speaks of Newton's letters as 'singularly plaintive and beautiful'.

Many Christians were shocked and as many more were thrilled when Newton's hymn 'Amazing Grace' became top of the Hit Parade in the 1970s. Surely this must be a tribute to the timeless language of that (then) two-hundred-year-old poem. Writing in a language which would still be understood years hence became one of the main aims of Cowper.

We have no need to turn to secular novels for tales of the high seas, of shipwrecks and skirmishes and adventure galore. It is all to be found in Newton's *Authentic Narrative*. If we wish to consult a scholarly work on the history of the early church, we could do far worse than consult Newton's *Review of Ecclesiastical History*. Of this book Cowper wrote, 'I never saw a Work that I thought more likely to serve the cause of Truth, nor History applied to so good a purpose: the facts incontestable, the grand Observation upon them all, irrefragable, and the Stile in my judgment, incomparably better than that of Robertson or Gibbon.' William Robertson (1721-93), the historian, was acclaimed as one of the leading figures of the Enlightenment and Walpole judged him to be the best modern historian. Cowper found him 'full of Pomp and Strut' and highly affected. Edward Gibbon (1737-94) was at Westminster with Cowper and was well known by Cowper's whole family. He became famous for his mammoth *The Decline and Fall of the Roman Empire*. Cowper found that he was too 'finical' [i.e. finicky] by far and thought his writing had more of a French flair about it than plain English. Cowper praised the fact that Newton said what he had to say, obviously fully immersed in the subject. Robertson and Gibbon 'sang' rather than 'said', and this merely for self-exhibition. For them the subject matter was quite secondary. Cowper's comments are not merely those of a biased friend. The poet was also an acclaimed literary critic and reviewer.

Newton could also write in a moving way which brought tears to the eyes of his readers, as in the case of his *Memoirs of Eliza Cunningham*, which Cowper found 'clear and affectionate'. Commenting on the happy death of Newton's young niece who had lived faithfully with the Lord, Cowper wrote, 'How much more beneficial to the world might such a memorial of an unknown but pious and believing child eventually prove, would the supercilious Learned condescend to read it, than the history of all the Kings and heroes that ever lived! But the world has its objects of admiration, and God has objects of his love. These make a noise and perish, and those weep silently for a short season, and live for ever. I had rather have been your niece or the writer of her story than any Caesar that ever thunder'd.'[9]

Of great political influence was Newton's *Thoughts upon the African Slave Trade,* which caused a large stir in the Houses of Parliament and linked Newton's name with that of Wilberforce as a major contender against that sub-bestial practice. Cowper praised the 'conscientious candour and moderation' of the work and told Newton that it was, 'to all prudent persons the most satisfying

publication on the subject'.[10] Writing about his friend's combination
of tact and accuracy of expression in his writings, Cowper said,
'You can draw a hair stroke where other men would make a Blot as
broad as a Sixpence.'[11] Such was Newton's literary influence on
Cowper that the poet published very little work until he was well
established as a writer without first sending it to Newton to be edited
or pronounced good. When Cowper eventually thought of
publishing his first volume of verse, he naturally turned to Newton
for a preface, expressing the hope that they would walk 'arm in arm
into the public notice' together.

Cowper remained an ardent reader of evangelical literature until
his very last days. This is shown not only by the books he kept during
this period but by the ones he continued to buy and borrow well into
the late 1790s. Even when the poet was removed from his home in
Weston to be cared for in the last few years of his life by his kinsman
Joseph Johnson at East Dereham in Norfolk, he took with him works
by Calvin, Baxter, Flavel, Edwards, Gillies, Owen, Romaine,
Hervey, Doddridge, More and Newton, to provide edification and
comfort for him during life's eventide.

9.
Walking into public notice

After the publication of the *Olney Hymns* in 1779 Cowper's health improved greatly and the poet began to look around for new themes for his pen. Most of these he gathered from the news he obtained through his correspondence with friends such as William Unwin, Joseph Hill and John Newton and from the events recorded in the newspapers. Unwin, for instance, wrote complaining of those in politics who talk about virtue, but, because they do not know Christ, cannot implement it. This topic moved Cowper to write 'Human Frailty' which uses the seafaring imagery, so often used by him to portray the Christian life, as seen in the following excerpt:

> Bound on a Voy'ge of awfull Length
> And Dangers Little known,
> A Stranger to Superior Strength
> Man vainly trusts his own:
>
> But Oars alas could ne'er prevail
> To reach the distant Coast,
> The Breath of Heav'n must Swell the Sail,
> Or all the Toil is lost.

Concern for the poor

Cowper's illness and convalescence had not put a stop to his care for the poor in any way and he used what influence he could to raise funds for bedding, food and clothing for the destitute Olney lacemakers. Up to April 1780 the Olney lace trade had enjoyed a measure of protection from competition abroad and in Ireland by means of laws restricting cheap imports. There was much talk in Parliament, however, of lifting these restrictions, which would cause the price of lace in England to sink to such a low level that even the most industrious would not have been able to earn a living.

Cowper thought of his old friend Thurlow, now Chancellor, and decided to approach him through their joint friend Joseph Hill, who held an important office on Thurlow's staff, Cowper said to Hill,

> If you ever take the Tip of the Chancellor's Ear between your Finger and Thumb, you can hardly improve the Opportunity to better Purpose, than if you should Whisper into it the Voice of Compassion & Lenity to the Lace Makers. I am an Eye Witness of their Poverty, and do know, that Hundreds in this little Town, are upon the Point of Starving, & that the most unremitting Industry is but barely sufficient to keep them from it. I know that the Bill by which they would have been so fatally affected is thrown out, but Lord Stormont threatens them with another, and if another like it should pass, they are undone. We lately sent a Petition from hence to Lord Dartmouth. I signed it, and am sure the Contents are true. — The Purport of it was to inform him that there are very near 1200 Lace Makers in this Beggarly Town, the most of whom had Reason enough while the Bill was in Agitation, to look upon every Loaf they bought as the last they should ever be able to Earn... The Measure is like a Scythe, and the poor Lacemakers are the Sickly Crop that trembles before the Edge of it. The Prospect of Peace with America is like the Streak of Dawn in their Horizon, but this Bill is like a Black Cloud behind it, that threatens their Hope of a comfortable Day with utter Extinction.

Correspondence with Unwin

Cowper always treated Unwin as a younger brother of whom he was very fond. He was always ready to impart something of life's wisdom to him and help him in the many theological and legal battles he had as a minister and as a man who was taking part more and more in public life. Unwin scarcely ever tackled a problem without first turning to his 'elder brother' for advice. Some of Cowper's answers are puzzling as he still writes from time to time as if he were utterly cut off from God. Nevertheless, his words show great spiritual insight and an understanding of human nature coupled with a real evangelical fervour.

Unwin, for instance, was troubled in 1780 about Sabbath-keeping and when a young convert approached him for advice, he turned at once to Cowper for a biblical point of view. Cowper answered:

> With respect to the Advice you are required to give to a young Lady, that she may be properly instructed in the manner of keeping the Sabbath, you are so well qualified for the Task yourself that it is impossible you should need any Assistance, at least it is hardly possible that I should afford you any, who consider myself as no longer interested in the Question. As you desire it however, & I am not willing to refuse you the little that is in my Power, I just subjoin a few Hints that have occurred to me upon the Occasion, not because I think you want them, but because it would seem unkind to withold them. The Sabbath then I think may be consider'd.
>
> 1st. As a Commandment, no less binding upon modern Christians than upon ancient Jews. Because the spiritual People amongst them, did not think it enough to abstain from manual Occupations upon that Day, but entering more deeply into the meaning of the Precept, allotted those Hours they took from the World, to the Cultivation of Holiness in their own Souls. Which ever was & ever will be a Duty incumbent upon all who ever heard of a Sabbath, & is of perpetual Obligation, both upon Jews & Christians. The Commandment therefore injoins it, the Prophets have also inforced it, & in many Instances both Scriptural & modern, the Breach of it has been punish'd with a Providential & Judicial Severity that may make By standers tremble.
>
> 2. As a Privilege, which you will know how to dilate upon better than I can tell you.
>
> 3. As a Sign of that Covenant by which Believers are entitled to a Rest that yet remaineth.
>
> 4. As the *Sine qua non* of the Christian Character & upon

this Head I should guard against being misunderstood to mean no more than two Attendances upon Public Worship, which is a Form complied with by Thousands, who never kept a Sabbath in their Lives. Consistency is necessary to give Substance & Solidity to the whole.

To Sanctify the Day at church, & to trifle it away out of church, is Profanation & vitiates all.

After all, I could ask my Catechumen one short Question, do you Love the Day, or do you not? If you Love it, you will never enquire how far you may safely deprive yourself of the Enjoyment of it. If you do not Love it, & you find yourself obliged in Conscience to acknowledge it, that is an alarming Symptom, & ought to make you tremble. If you do not Love it, then it is a Weariness to you & you wish it was over. The Ideas of Labor & Rest are not more opposite to each other, than the Idea of a Sabbath, & that Dislike and Disgust with which it fills the Soul of thousands to be obliged to keep it. It is worse than bodily Labor, more fatiguing than the Drudgery of an Ass.[1]

Unwin knew a gardener who was an Independent but chose to work on Sundays giving very 'pious' reasons for doing so. Cowper called his arguments 'paultry' and referring to the practice of Wilson the barber (now turned Baptist) he wrote, 'The Barber and Hairdresser who officiates me, would not wait upon the King himself on a Sunday, though he could easily make Apologies more plausible than any adduced by the old man you mention, were he disposed to tresspass against his duty and his Conscience.'[2] Cowper, though a keen gardener himself, did not work in the garden on Sundays and told his friends, who often ordered fowls from him, that they could not expect him to kill and prepare the birds on a Sunday.

One small incident at this time shows how keen Cowper still was to be used as a messenger of God, whatever his view of his own salvation. Unwin wrote, asking him to supply him with a few verses for a lady friend who was about to celebrate her birthday. Cowper responded with evangelical enthusiasm as he knew the person concerned and her need for the one thing that she lacked in her affluent life. Thus when the big day came, a certain Miss Stella Crewzé received the following lines:

To Miss Crewzé on her Birthday

How many between East and West,
Disgrace their Parent Earth,
Whose Deeds constrain us to detest
The Day that gave them Birth !

Not so, when Stella's natal Morn
Revolving Months restore,
We can rejoice that She was Born,
And wish her Born once more.

The call to be a poet

Cowper was beginning to see that God was calling him to be a teacher and mentor. At first he took this to mean working as a private tutor, preparing boys for the university and making sure that they received a Christian education, which was not available to them in secular schools. He encouraged Unwin, for instance, to educate his children himself and equipped him with a series of letters proposing suitable literature and teaching methods. He went on to prepare courses for his own pupils and started work on a treatise on education. Over the next few years, however, Cowper gradually realized that his scope was to be far wider than preparing children for higher education. He was to put his classical and poetic skills to his Master's use as a mentor for the whole country, calling England back to God.

Before 1780, although Cowper had composed what he termed 'a bookful' of verse, he still had no intention of publishing, believing that he had as much claim to the title of 'poet' as a maker of mousetraps had to the title of engineer. He thus sent much verse of a more trivial and playful nature to Unwin and Hill as 'thank yous' for the parcels of fish or books which they often sent him. The poet was very fond of fish, calling himself 'the most ichthyophagous of men', so the small poems that went to Joseph Hill's address accompanied by fruit, vegetables and poultry, in lieu of payment for mackerel and oysters, became quite numerous.

One of the most delightful of these small poems is the fable of 'The Pine Apple and the Bee', which Cowper sent to Hill. The poet had imported pineapple plants from Jamaica and was growing them in cold frames which he had made himself. He noticed that instead of obtaining honey from the many flowers available, the bees would buzz around the cold frames trying in vain to get at the pineapple blooms. Cowper goes on to observe how the world wastes time in vainly wishing for what they cannot have and how:

> Our dear Delights are often such,
> Exposed to View but not to Touch,
> The Sight our foolish Heart inflames,
> We Long for Pine Apples in Frames,
> With hopeless Wish One Looks & Lingers,
> One breaks the Glass & Cuts his Fingers,
> But they whom Truth & Wisdom lead,
> Can gather Honey from a Weed.

Cowper playfully described this poetic moralizing as 'fiddling for fish' and he might have remained a poet at this level if it had not been for Newton's constant request that he should write poetry of a more serious and wide-reaching nature.

Although Newton now lived far away from Olney and had made new friends, he still regarded with mistrust any friendship shown by Cowper to others. He was particularly jealous of William Unwin, who had already gained a high reputation as a preacher, scholar and social benefactor.

Cowper had written to Unwin saying, 'You are my Mahogany Box with a slit in the Lid of it, to which I Commit my Productions of the Lyrik kind, in perfect Confidence that they are safe, & will go no further.'[3] But Cowper's letters, with their poetic contents, were not as safe as he thought. Newton somehow gained access to Cowper's letters to William Unwin at the latter's home at Stock. He read them and deduced that Cowper was being more friendly towards Unwin and enclosing more poetry in letters to him than to himself. This news shocked Newton so much that he wrote a complaining letter to Cowper.

At first Cowper was quite at a loss to understand why Newton should be so interested in his letters to Unwin and at an even greater loss to understand his jealousy. He sent Newton a letter in which he emphasized that there was sense in the practice of writing different letters to different people and not sending off copies of the same letter to everyone. The letter leaves very much for Newton to read between the lines and is as fine an example of diplomacy as Cowper was ever to write.

My dear Sir—

Though I should never think of sending the same Letter to two Correspondants, yet I confess I am not sorry that your communication with Stock is cut off, at least for the present. I have indeed sometimes wish'd that it had never been opened, & for a reason obvious enough. Though I never make one Letter a Copy of another, yet I have sometimes found myself rather at a plunge, & puzzled when I have attempted to find variety for two. I know you have a sight of those I write to Mr. Unwin, which would, if possible, be still less worth your seeing, if you had before read them addressed to yourself. You may think perhaps that I deal more liberally with Him in the way of poetical export than I do with You & I believe you have reason. The truth is This — If I walked the Streets with a Fiddle under my Arm, I should never think of performing before the Window of a Privy Counsellor or a chief Justice, but should rather make free with Ears more likely to be open to such amusement. The trifles I produce in this way are indeed such trifles that I cannot think them seasonable Presents for you. Mr. Unwin himself would not be affronted if I was to tell him that there is this difference between him & Mr. Newton: That the latter is already an Apostle while He himself is only undergoing the business of Incubation, with a hope that he may be hatched in time. When my Muse comes forth arrayed in sables, at least in a robe of graver cast, I make no scruple to direct her to my friend at Hoxton.[4] This has been one reason why I have so long delayed the Riddle, but lest I should seem to set a value upon it that I do not by making it an Object of still further enquiry, here it comes.

I am just Two & Two, I am warm, I am cold
And the Parent of numbers that cannot be told
I am lawfull, unlawfull, a duty, a fault

I am often sold dear, good for nothing when bought.
An extraordinary boon, & a matter of course
And yielded with pleasure when taken by force
Alike the delight of the Poor & the Rich
Tho' the vulgar is apt to present me his breech.[5]

The fact that Cowper sent Newton this rather vulgar riddle[6] shows that he obviously wanted to make the point that Newton had not missed much by not receiving copies of the ditties Cowper had sent to other friends. When the *Gentleman's Magazine* published the riddle many years later, they censured the last two lines, thinking them too vulgar for gentlemen's eyes.

The controversy with Madan

Another reason for Newton's lack of understanding regarding Cowper's attitude towards Unwin and petty verse was that he had been urging his friend for months to take up his pen to champion the Evangelical cause against Martin Madan, who was behaving in a most unseemly way. This matter should have first priority, Newton thought. Martin Madan was, however, the very person who had helped lead Cowper to Christ and he was Cowper's first cousin. Newton must have realized the difficulties of conscience Cowper would have in combatting in public a man who was his good friend, brother in Christ and also his own cousin.

Newton's stubbornness eventually won Cowper's co-operation and it was through his anti-Madan writings that Cowper was to start on the road to success as a poet. Before turning to this matter in detail, however, it will be fitting to look closely at the life and character of Martin Madan, friend of Whitefield, Wesley, Toplady and Newton, and one of the earliest supporters of Lady Huntingdon.

Life of Madan

Madan was six years older than Cowper but had perhaps shared at least one year at Westminster with his cousin. After Westminster Madan went on to Christ Church, Oxford, where he obtained a B. A. in 1746. After Oxford, Madan studied law at the Inner Temple and was called to the Bar in 1748. Madan was considered a brilliant scholar and successful lawyer and it was to a great extent due to his help and the loan of his notes that Cowper was able to complete his own studies. Madan's legal career was, however, to end abruptly in 1750.

The lawyer was sitting in a coffee-house joking with his colleagues about an event that was taking place in the neighbourhood. John Wesley was holding a meeting and the friends decided it would add to the evening's amusement if one of them should go and watch Wesley for a few minutes and then come back and take him off. Madan, who was a gifted speaker and mimic, was thought to be the best person to be given the task, so he was dispatched to go and hear Wesley preach. The evangelist was just giving out his text as Madan came in. It was Amos 4:12: 'Prepare to meet thy God, O Israel.' At once Madan was convicted and convinced that he was not prepared to meet his God and, as he listened, he realized that, far from his being able to 'take Wesley off', Wesley could describe every detail of Madan's own sinful character. The lawyer left the meeting-house a changed man. When his friends greeted him on his return to the coffee-house with the words, 'Can you take Wesley off?' he could merely reply truthfully, 'No, but he can take me off', and left the place never to return.[7]

In the same year as his encounter with Wesley and with God, Madan became an itinerant preacher and seven years later was ordained in the Church of England. During this time he became closely acquainted with leading members of the Evangelical Revival and in 1762 was appointed by Lady Huntingdon as Chaplain of the Lock Hospital for vagrant women at Hyde Park Corner, London.

In 1765 Cowper wrote to Madan's sister expressing his great sense of the debt he owed to her brother for helping him on the way to Christ. 'Your Brother Martin', he told her, 'has been kind to me, having wrote to me twice (since my Enlargement), in a stile which though it once was irksome to me to say the least, I now know how to value. I pray God to forgive me the many light things I have said and thought of Him and his labours. Hereafter I shall consider him as a burning and a shining Light, and as one of those who have turned many to Righteousness, shall shine hereafter as the Stars for ever and ever.'

Madan's use of music in worship

Madan's light, however, was to wane considerably throughout the following years and to become, after 1780, a mere shadow of its former flame. Towards the beginning of his ministry Madan concentrated on the spoken word. He preached with power and could reach the hearts of the most hardened hearers. Madan also loved music and loved to sing. Indeed his love for music and singing gripped him more than his love for the spoken word. He wrote many hymns, edited the hymns of other Evangelicals, such as Charles Wesley, and composed music for them.

As current sacred singing did not tickle the ear enough for Madan, he put more rhythm and pep into it and encouraged his congregation to speed up their sung praise. He also introduced musical instruments into his services to 'liven them up' and added choirs for good measure to 'lead' and keep up the pace of the singing. His next experiment was to have the choir take part in sung worship without the participation of the congregation. Soon his services were offering mere 'Christian entertainment' whereby a passive congregation received their religious worship presented to them in a fully orchestrated way.

At first many Evangelicals were delighted with Madan's new way of getting street walkers 'off the streets'. John Wesley, in particular, was keen on this new method of West End evangelism. Wesley approved of the fashionable custom of singing hymns in church meetings as long as it was 'singing with the spirit and understanding also'.[8] Methodist music, he argued, should be like the music of the ancients — pure melody, which he explained as an arrangement of single notes as opposed to singing in parts, which he called harmony.[9]

After a few visits to the Lock, however, the evangelist began to doubt the sense of Madan's musical activities. In February 1764, we find Wesley entering in his diary:

> I heard 'Judith,' an Oratorio, performed at the Lock. Some parts of it were exceeding fine; but there are two things in all modern pieces of music, which I could never reconcile to common sense. One is, singing the same words ten times over; the other, singing different words by different persons, at one and the same time. And this, in the most solemn

addresses to God, whether by way of prayer or of thanksgiving. This can never be defended by all the musicians in Europe, till reason is quite out of date.

Wesley also began to condemn the use of choirs hired to do the congregation's singing for them, thus shutting them out of the worship. Writing in 1768 after taking part in a sung service, Wesley says,

> I began reading prayers at six, but was greatly disgusted at the manner of the singing. 1. Twelve or fourteen persons kept it to themselves, and quite shut out the congregation: 2. These repeated the same words, contrary to all sense and reason, six or eight times or ten times over: 3. According to the shocking custom of modern music, different persons sung different words at one and the same moment; an intolerable insult on common sense, and utterly incompatible with any devotion.[10]

Wesley quotes in support of his argument an author who writes, 'The singing different words by different persons at the very same time necessarily prevents attention to the sense, so it frequently destroys melody for the sake of harmony; meantime it destroys the very end of music, which is to affect the passions.'[11]

Cowper objected strongly to a minister taking part in such musical entertainment when there were so many churchgoers who were hungry for the Word of God. It was most likely Martin Madan and his brother Spencer that Cowper had in mind when he drew his scathing pen-portrait of the fiddling pastor who was too busy with his music to do real pastoral work:

> Occiduus[12] is a pastor of renown,
> When he has pray'd and preach'd the sabbath down,
> With wire and catgut he concludes the day,
> Quav'ring and semiquav'ring care away.
> The full concerto swells upon your ear;
> All elbows shake. Look in, and you would swear
> The Babylonian tyrant with a nod
> Had summon'd them to serve his golden god.
> So well that thought th' employment seems to suit,
> Psalt'ry and sackbut, dulcimer, and flute.

Oh fie! 'tis evangelical and pure!
Observe each face, how sober and demure!
Ecstasy sets her stamp on ev'ry mien;
Chins fall'n, and not an eye-ball to be seen.
Still I insist, though music heretofore
Has charm'd me much, (not e'en Occiduus more)
Love, joy, and peace, make harmony more meet
For sabbath ev'nings, and perhaps as sweet.
Will not the sickliest sheep of every flock
Resort to this example as a rock;
There stand, and justify the foul abuse
Of sabbath hours with plausible excuse?
If apostolic gravity be free
To play the fool on Sundays, why not we?
If he the tinkling harpsichord regards
As inoffensive, what offence in cards ?
Strike up the fiddles, let us all be gay!
Laymen have leave to dance, if parsons play.

Cowper was particularly critical of this kind of music-making as
it occurred on Sundays when the parson ought to be looking after his
flock. Indeed, he knew of ministers who were so taken up with their
Sunday musical revelries that they had no time to deal with those
who needed spiritual help and told their maids to tell Sunday callers
that they were not at home. Thus the poet goes on to write,

Oh Italy ! — thy sabbaths will be soon
Our sabbaths, clos'd with mumm'ry and buffoon.
Preaching and pranks will share the motley scene:
Our's parcell'd out, as thine have ever been
God's worship and the mountebank between.
What says the prophet? Let that day be blest
With holiness and consecrated rest.
Pastime and bus'ness both it should exclude
And bar the door the moment they intrude;
Nobly distinguish'd above all the six.
By deeds in which the world must never mix.
Hear him again. He calls it a delight,
A day of luxury, observ'd aright,
When the glad soul is made heav'n's welcome guest,

Sits banqueting, and God provides the feast.
But triflers are engag'd and cannot come;
Their answer to the call is — Not at home.[13]

Rather than learning from criticism Occiduus got worse and soon his Sunday services were mere musical presentations void of any trace of God's Word. Commenting on 'Occiduus' when writing to Newton in September 1781 Cowper sadly says, 'I am sorry to find that the censure I have passed upon Occiduus is even better founded than I supposed. Lady Austen has been at his Sabbatical concerts, which it seems are composed of song tunes and psalm tunes indiscriminately, music without words, and I suppose one may say, consequently without devotion.'

Cowper was deeply concerned for the minister's welfare and goes on to discuss what the disadvantages and advantages of music are to one's spiritual life:

He seems, together with others of our aquaintance, to have suffered considerably in his spiritual character by his attachment to Music. The lawfullness of it, when used with moderation, and in its proper place, is unquestionable; but I believe Wine itself, though a man be guilty of habitual intoxication, does not more debauch and befool the natural understanding, than Music, always Music, Music in season and out of season, weakens and destroys the spiritual discernment. If it is not used with an unfeigned reference to the worship of God, and with a design to assist the Soul in the performance of it, which cannot be the case when it is the only Occupation, it degenerates into a sensual delight, and becomes a most powerfull advocate for the admission of other pleasures, grosser perhaps in degree, but in their kind the same.

Cowper and Newton were by no means alone in these seeming strictures. We read in the *Memoirs* of Hannah More, a most cultivated lady and member of the *literati*, the following interesting account: 'I have just received a card invitation from a Countess, to a concert next *Sunday*, with a conditional postscript, "if I ever do such things on a Sunday;" and I have sent for answer, that I never do such a thing. After such a public testimony as I have given, one would have thought I should have escaped such an invitation.'[14]

Such words from the mouth of a leading Evangelical of more than two hundred years ago should give us food for thought today. We are living in times when the follies of the eighteenth century are returning and evangelical churches *en masse* seem to be jumping on the musical bandwagon and giving their church members tunes instead of sermons. Once a church departs from gospel-preaching, anything can happen in it, as the subsequent history of Martin Madan shows.

Madan advocates polygamy

Cowper's cousin was to discredit himself even further and thus separate himself from the Evangelical Movement as a whole. To be fair to Madan, it must be said that his health was very poor at this time and he had been given up for dead on at least one occasion in the seventies. His mind also seemed to have been affected by the family complaint and by an unhealthy reliance on astrology. He was not the same man mentally and physically in 1780 that he had been when he had helped lead Cowper to Christ. The events which led up to this lapse on Madan's part show how good-hearted and well-intentioned the man was but also how little respect he had for the high moral standards of a Christian.

Madan realized that many of the women who came under his care had been forced onto the streets by having affairs with men who had deceived them and then left them to their fate. He believed strongly that if a man were sexually intimate with a woman, he should be compelled to marry her and to support her. Madan soon found out, however, that a great number of the women under his care had lost their virginity through their dealings with married men. Thus Madan came up with the bizarre idea that these married men should be compelled to turn bigamists and marry the women they had wronged. He was naïve enough to think that all the prostitutes under his care were such wronged women who only needed a good home and financial support and they would mend their ways.

Both Cowper and Newton were closely attached to Madan and had followed the development of his ideas with astonishment and horror. Both saw that Madan, in his effort to better the lot of the prostitutes under his care, had failed to see how such a solution would wrong the malefactor's real, lawful wife. Cowper, always more able to express his views more spontaneously in verse than in prose, reacted to Madan's 'brainwave' with the words:

Oh rare Device! the Wife betray'd,
The Modest, chaste, Domestic Woman,
To Save a worthless, Wanton Jade,
From being, what she would be, Common.

Madan's great error was that he believed the Scriptures viewed
bigamy as a Christian norm and that such a form of matrimony was
part of the divine law. He thus started work on a multi-volumed book
to prove his point. His sub-title summed up his position exactly:
'Shewing by what *means*, and by what *degrees*, the *laws* of Jehovah
concerning *marriage*, were *opposed* and *abrogated*, and a New
System invented and established by Christian Churchmen.'[15] On
page 75 of the first volume he even argued that bigamy was
'allowed, owned, and even blessed of God' and 'in no one instance,
amongst the many recorded in Scripture, so much as disapproved'.

When Madan's circle heard that their friend was about to publish
a three-volumed book to 'prove' from Scripture that bigamy was
biblical, they bombarded him with letters of entreaty begging him
not to disgrace the gospel in this way. They knew what a brilliant
exegete Madan was and how earnestly and convincingly he was able
to put over a case. Relying on his great learning in Hebrew and
Greek, Madan proudly refused to listen to anyone who was not as
versed in these languages as he was. Tempers were lost on both
sides. The Rev. Thomas Haweis, once Madan's closest friend,
started to prepare a slanderous attack on him, calling him 'disordered' in both head and heart. To make matters worse, Haweis
threatened to make public certain confessions that Madan had made
to Haweis in strict brotherly fellowship.

As Haweis owed his livelihood to Madan, Newton felt this was
a great lack of taste and Christian responsibility and soon found his
fellow Evangelicals looking to him to write to Haweis and stop his
unwise publication. Newton wrote to Cowper asking his advice on
how he should tackle the problem, stressing that the poet's thoughts
would be invaluable to him. Cowper replied,

You do me an Honor I little deserve when you Ask my
Opinion upon any Occasion, and Speak of being determined
by it. Such as it is however it is always at your Service, and
would be if it were better worth your having. — The Dictates
of Compassion and Humanity Prompt you to Interpose your
good Offices in order to prevent the Publication with which

this unhappy Man is threat'ned by Mr. Haweis. They are Advisers you may safely Listen to, and deserve the more Attention on the present Occasion, as you are perhaps the only Man in the World to whom such a Design has been Suggested, and who would know how to manage the Execution of it with sufficient Delicacy & Discretion. The Book and the Author are distinct Subjects, and will be for ever accounted such by all reasonable Persons. The Author indeed may Suffer by the Follies of the Book, but the latter ought not to be Judged by the character of the Writer. If it were otherwise, yet in this Case there can be no Need of Mr. Haweis, the Point in Dispute being already tried, and Mr. Madan's Arguments condemn'd at the Bar of the Public. Mr. Haweis will hurt himself more by One such ungenerous Proceeding, than he can possibly Hurt Mr. Madan by divulging, if he can do it, a thousand Irregularities in his Conduct. Sensual & Lawless Gratifications are odious enough, especially in a Minister, but double Detestation attends the Man who to Gratify a present Enmity, avails himself of Secrets he could never have had Possession of, had he not once professed himself a Friend. If it should happen too that Mr. Madan's Intellects should be Swept away by such a Deluge of Obloquy & Detraction, following close upon his present Disappointment (an Event not at all improbable,) Mr. Haweis will have reason to wish that he had taken his Life rather than destroy'd his character. He thinks perhaps the Interest of the Cause demands it of him; but when was the Cause promoted by a Discovery of the Vices or Follies of its Advocates & Professors? — On the whole therefore if I must Advise, I would Advise to Write.[16]

John Newton accordingly wrote and soon found himself urging more than one fellow opponent not to go to equally dangerous extremes in presenting an opposite case. Instead of being thankful to Newton for appealing for fairness, Madan saw his old friend as his chief opponent, obviously thinking of the 'mis reports' concerning Newton's past referred to in chapter 6, and reproached him for not doing anything against prostitution and not setting an example by taking another wife alongside his beloved Mary. Newton had told Haweis, Madan's friend, of the false charges of immorality levelled against him and Haweis had obviously passed this information on to Madan, who was now misusing it. As John and Mary were well-known public figures by this time, and Madan spoke and wrote openly about his views, Cowper again responded in verse to protect his friend, publishing the following lines in the *Gentleman's Magazine*:

> If John marries Mary, and Mary alone,
> 'Tis a very good match between Mary and John.
> Should John wed a score, oh! the claws and the scratches!
> It can't be a match: — 'tis a bundle of matches.

On reading the poem Newton wrote to Cowper saying:

> Your epigram made us sharers in your laugh, but the occasion and subject summoned my muscles back to their pristine seriousness. I am afraid there will be many bundles of matches, and many families inflamed by them with the fire of contention. How can that be true in theory which if reduced to practice must be mischievous! Your dilemma (with three horns) will hold good. He that is happy with one wife will want no more, he that is not happy with one has one too many. Or, suppose we Sternholdize[17] the thought—

> What different senses of that word, A Wife!
> It means the comfort or the bain of life.
> The happiest state is to be pleased with one,
> The next degree is found in having none.[18]

Newton saw that Cowper had a great skill in presenting a case without being bellicose and indeed slanderous. He also realized that Cowper was one of the few Evangelicals who had legal and linguistic abilities comparable to those of Madan and the literary skill to combat him. Thus Newton approached Cowper to lead Evangelicals against Madan in print.

Cowper felt he ought to decline for a number of reasons. For one thing, Cowper had already brought scorn on his family in particular, and the Whigs in general by his failing to appear before the House of Peers as the Whigs' candidate for a preferment which had led to his first major breakdown. Furthermore, Martin Madan was not the first of the Cowper clan to promote bigamy. Lord Chancellor Cowper, the brother of William's and Martin's grandfather, had written a treatise in defence of bigamy which had caused a national scandal and had done much to lessen the power of the Whigs in England. Cowper did not wish to bring more scorn on his family by highlighting the fact that its members still campaigned for bigamy.

Another good reason why Cowper felt that he could not combat Madan was his cousin's linguistic abilities. When Cowper started to read Madan's book, published under the pretentious name of *Thelyphthora*, he saw at once that whereas he could easily cope with Madan's arguments from the Greek, he had not the command of Hebrew to prove a worthy combatant. He realized also that Madan's point of view was so closely argued and so skilfully put that it would be extremely difficult to defeat him on his own ground.

Madan's notorious work was eventually published on 31 May 1780. Some thirty writers, mainly of an Evangelical bent, took up their pens in reply, but most of them were no match for the would-be bigamist. Although Cowper told Newton that Madan had exposed himself to the censure of those who think and the laughter of those who do not,[19] the book sold well and Madan published a new edition, adding twenty-seven reasons from the pen of a Birmingham clergyman, why bigamy was acceptable to a Christian. The author, John Riland, challenged anyone to refute his reasoning. This moved Cowper, who found Riland's arguments unbiblical and illogical, to take up his pen and refute all twenty-seven of them in prose. His replies, however, are no longer extant but Cowper seems to have been successful as Riland recanted his views shortly afterwards.[20]

Cowper takes up the challenge

Once Cowper had committed himself he was too much of a 'Valiant for Truth' to leave things at that and gradually became convinced before God that he must answer Madan at length in verse or he would disgrace himself by not taking up the challenge. Seeing that Mrs Newton was bearing the brunt of the burden of the controversy between Madan and Newton and knowing that her nerves were possibly even more tender than his own, he sent her a personal poem as a token that he was prepared to take up the gauntlet. Once again Cowper strove to solve human problems by taking an example from the animal world. The poem was originally called 'Anti-thely-phthora', like his later major poem on the topic, but when Cowper published the poem two years later, he removed all references to Madan's book and renamed the poem 'The Doves'.

Muse, Mark the much lamented Day,
When like a Tempest fear'd
Forth issuing on the last of May,
Thelyphthora appear'd.

That fateful Eve I wander'd late,
And heard the Voice of Love;
The Turtle thus address'd her Mate,
And Sooth'd the list'ning Dove—

Our mutual Bond of Faith and Truth,
No Time shall disengage;
Those Blessings of our Early Youth
Shall cheer our latest Age:

While Innocence without Disguise,
And constancy Sincere,
Shall fill the Circles of those Eyes,
And Mine can Read them there;

Those Ills that wait on all Below
Shall ne'er be felt by Me,
Or gently felt, and Only so,
As being shar'd with Thee.

When Lightnings Flash among the Trees,
Or Kites are Hov'ring near,
I fear lest Thee alone they Seize,
And know no other Fear.

'Tis then I feel myself a Wife,
And Press thy Wedded Side,
Resolv'd an Union form'd for Life
Death never shall Divide.

But Oh! if, fickle and Unchaste
(Forgive a transient Thought)
Thou couldst become unkind at last,
And Scorn thy present Lot,

No need of Lightnings from on high,
Or Kites with cruel Beak;
Denied th' Endearments of thine Eye,
This Widow'd Heart would Break.

Thus Sang the Sweet Sequester'd Bird
 Soft as the passing Wind,
And I Recorded what I heard—
A Lesson for Mankind.[21]

This practice of teaching Christian and human conduct through
pictures from nature was to become a major feature of Cowper's
work and would link him closely with John Bunyan and the emblem
poets. On many an occasion Cowper was to mourn that man had
fallen lower than the beasts in moral duties and that whereas a pair
of doves remained true to each other, it was often thought genteel by
humans to live adulterously.

Cowper did not neglect his other friends during this time and in
the summer of 1780 he sent William Unwin, among others, a poem
entitled 'Love Abused: The Thought Suggested by "Thelyphthora":

What is there in the Vale of Life
Half so delightfull as a Wife,
When Friendship, Love, and Peace combine
To Stamp the Marriage Bond Divine?
The Stream of pure and genuine Love
Derives its Current from Above,
And Earth a Second Eden Shows
Where'er the Healing Water flows.
But Ah! if from the Dykes and Drains
Of sensual Nature's fev'rish Veins,
Lust like a lawless headstrong Flood
Impregnated with Ooze and Mud,
Descending fast on ev'ry Side,
Once Mingles with the Sacred Tide,

Farewell the Soul enliv'ning Scene!
The Banks that wore a Smiling Green
With rank Defilement overspread,
Bewail their Flow'ry Beauties dead;
The Stream polluted, dark and dull,
Diffused into a Stygian Pool,
Thro' Life's last melancholy Years
Is fed with everflowing Tears;
Complaints supply the Zephyr's Part,
And Sighs that Heave a Breaking Heart.

In this poem, too, there is a reference to a topic — the second Eden — which was to become prominent in the poet's later works.

Soon Cowper was to find a poetic theme which would enable him to strike out at Madan without being personal and without getting tied up in theological and linguistic knots. In October 1780 an article appeared in the *Monthly Review* dealing critically with Madan's book. The author, the Rev. Samuel Badcock, tackled his subject in a learned, biblical and humorous way. Cowper saw at once that he had found a prototype in Badcock for the hero of a dramatic poem in which he could put all his talents to the service of the Lord. Cowper thus determined to write an allegory in a mock-Spenserian manner in which Sir Marmadan, Knight of the Silver Moon (Badcock), fights against Sir Airy del Castro (Madan). Sir Airy is under the spell of an evil fairy named Hypothesis who has charmed him into believing:

That Wedlock is not rig'rous as suppos'd,
But Man within a wider Pale inclos'd
May Rove at Will, where Appetite shall lead,
Free as the Lordly Bull that ranges o'er the mead.
That Forms and Rites are Tricks of Human law,
As idle as the Chatt'ring of a Daw,
That lewd Incontinence and lawless Rape
Are Marriage in its true and proper shape,
That Man by Faith and Truth is made a Slave,
The Ring a Bauble, and the priest a Knave.[22]

Sir Marmadan is well protected with the Christian armour of Truth and Righteousness, but Sir Airy has a shield, inscribed with

Hebrew words, (the Old Testament) which he believes will make
him invincible. Cowper sums up the whole futile state of Madan's
defence in two couplets:

> His Shield with Hebrew lore was scribbled round,
> But snatching it impatiently from the ground,
> And slinging it revers'd upon his Arm,
> He chang'd it to a Cabbalistic charm.

In other words, the Bible misused is truth abused and no shield
at all. As Madan had called his treatise *Thelyphthora,* a word
meaning 'corruption of woman', Cowper entitled his poem 'Anti-
Thelyphthora'. Such Greek-sounding names seem out of place in
today's English but in Cowper's day it was fashionable to use them.

When Newton received the text from Cowper he was greatly
surprised. It was quite different from what he had expected. Instead
of a learned treatise, here was a swashbuckling adventure poem,
similar in style to the Wakefield and York Morality Plays which the
so-called common folk performed on the village green. It was as full
of humour as it was of sense! Newton must have thought of his own
lectures on Bunyan's works which he had delivered at Olney and
which were attended by Cowper. He had expounded Bunyan's
arguments for using literary devices and 'types, shadows and
metaphors' to put the truth over and thus viewed Cowper's long
poem with Bunyan's eyes when he wrote,

> This book is writ in such dialect
> As may the minds of listless men affect;
> It seems a novelty, and yet contains
> Nothing but sound and honest gospel strains.[23]

Newton, realizing that Cowper had taken up the cudgels for the
truth in a way the average reader would understand and appreciate,
approached his own publisher, Joseph Johnson of St Paul's Churchyard, with the poem. Johnson looked upon his business with far
more vision than that of an ordinary businessman. He was very
careful to choose works for publication that were sound and sensible
yet daring and even radical in scope. He obviously believed
Cowper's poem to be in this category and agreed to publish it as it
was. Cowper stressed, however, that the poem was to appear

anonymously, to which Newton agreed saying, 'Your secret is locked up in a strong box of which only Mrs Newton, Mr Johnson and myself have the key.' The poem was published as a twenty-paged quarto pamphlet in December 1780 and was Cowper's first independent production.

'Anti-Thelyphthora' was not, however, Cowper's last effort in this field and he wrote several shorter poems on the subject, chiefly in defence of Newton, who reviewed a later edition of Madan's book and incurred Madan's full wrath. Madan was once again critical of the Newtons' marriage and Cowper decided to write a poem void of allegory and symbolism, attacking Madan directly in person. The result was his 'On Madan's Answer to Newton's Comments on Thelyphthora':

> M. quarrels with N. — for M. wrote a book,
> And N. did not like it, which M. could not brook.
> So he call'd him a Bigot, a wrangler, a Monk,
> With as many hard names as would line a good trunk,
> And set up his back, and claw'd like a Cat,
> But N. lik'd it never the better for that.
> Now N. had a Wife, and he wanted but One,
> Which stuck in M's Stomach as cross as a bone.
> It has always been reckon'd a just cause of Strife
> For a Man to make free with another Man's Wife;
> But the Strife is the strangest that ever was known,
> If a man must be scolded for loving his own.

Peace only came to Newton when Madan swore never to have anything to do with him again. Madan had to leave the Lock, where he was eventually succeeded by Newton's friend Thomas Scott, and spent the rest of his life in academic studies and ill health.

After Cowper's death Lady Hesketh, Cowper's legatee, refused to allow biographers permission to publish 'Anti-Thelyphthora' for fear of hurting the feelings of the Madan family. It was thus not known for many years that Cowper's correspondence with John Newton had first led the poet to go into print as a Christian author. Instead of this the more 'romantic' theory developed that it was Mrs Unwin who encouraged Cowper to start publishing Christian verse — a theory which still holds sway even in more enlightened times.

Literary co-operation with Newton

Cowper was now beginning to see his way before him. He saw what an able weapon poetry was in the fight against evil and also that poetry reached people and homes where the gospel was otherwise never heard. Urged on by Newton, Cowper began his long evangelical poem 'The Progress of Error'. Newton, encouraged by Cowper's success, asked Cowper for help in producing his own works. Thus the two friends started a mutual clearing-house in which they vetted each other's works before sending them off to their publisher.

One of the ways in which Cowper helped Newton was in suggesting titles and mottos for several of the latter's works. One day, for instance, in the summer of 1780, Cowper received the following lines from Newton concerning a new literary venture: 'I shall be obliged to your ingenuity to hammer me out a title and a motto — my name is not to be prefixed. Can you compound me a nice Greek word as pretty in sound and as scholastically put together as *Thelyphthora,* and as much more favourable import as you please, to stand at the top of the title-page, and serve as a handle for an inquirer?'[24] Always willing to oblige his good friend, Cowper sent him a title page which Newton accepted gladly:

Cardiphonia
or the
Utterance of the Heart
In a Collection of Letters written in the Course of
a Real Correspondence
On a Variety of Religious Subjects
by Omicron

Haec Res et jungit, junctos et servat Amico.[25]

At the same time he wrote,

My dear Friend—
    It is difficult to find a Motto for a Book containing almost as many Subjects as Pages, and those Subjects, of the Religious kind. Horace and my Memory are the only Motto-mongers I am possessed of. The former could furnish me with nothing suitable to the Occasion, but the latter after a deal of

Persuasion & Enquiry, has at last supplied me with one that I hope will please you. I think my Greek Word as Characteristic of the Book as need be; I am sure it is a very legitimate Combination, and both my Ears inform me that it is more Musical than *Thelyphthora*. Thus having Puffed my Performance sufficiently, I leave it to your Admiration, and from yours, (if it so please you) recommend it to that of the Public.

Horace will furnish me with a Motto for the ensuing Paragraph as Pat as Heart can wish.

> ... *nec meus audet*
> *Rem tentare Pudor, quam Vires ferre recusent.*[26]

Several examples of Newton's help to Cowper can be found in their correspondence concerning 'The Progress of Error', which Cowper had originally intended as a further criticism of Madan and a castigation of Lord Chesterfield for encouraging his own son to lead an immoral life. Cowper had referred to *Thelyphthora* as 'curs'd' and had used very strong language against Chesterfield. Newton asked Cowper to mellow his language as it 'grated on the ear' and complained especially about the use of the word 'curs'd'. Cowper replied,

> As to the word you mention, I a little suspected that you would object to it. Though I really thought that a Book which cannot be supposed to have been written under a Blessing, and that has certainly carried Mischief with it into many Families, deserved an Epithet as harsh as that which I had given it. It is a bargain however that I have made with my Lady Muse, never to defend or stickle for any thing that you object to. So the Line may stand if you please, thus.

> Abhorr'd Thelyphthora, thy daring page—

> Not *tainted page* for the reason I give in the Letter which contains the Epitaph on Lord Chesterfield. — You will meet with the obnoxious word again in the Copy I send you now, but coupled with a Substantive of so filthy a Character that I persuade myself you will have no Objection to the use of it in such a Connexion. I am no friend to the Use of words taken

from what an Uncle of mine call'd the diabolical Dictionary,
but it happens sometimes that a coarse Expression is almost
necessary to do Justice to the Indignation excited by an
abominable Subject. I am obliged to you however for your
Opinion; and though Poetry is apt to betray one into a
Warmth that one is not sensible of in writing Prose, shall
always desire to be set down by it.[27]

Cowper's decision 'never to defend or stickle' anything that
Newton objected to eventually led him to drop all further attacks on
Martin Madan and erase any direct references to Lord Chesterfield.

The ten years from 1770 to 1780 had witnessed writers such as
John Wesley, Walter Sellon, Thomas Olivers and Augustus
Toplady writing articles full of abusive language in their efforts to
fight for Arminianism or Calvinism according to their various
convictions. Newton, though looked upon as a leader by both
parties, had steadfastly refused to join in these unholy slanging
matches and was very anxious that Cowper, who loved a wrangle,
should not spoil his message and his style by stooping to the level
of his contemporary Christian writers. Thus, whenever Cowper
inclined too much towards invective Newton was always there to
calm him down.

A good example of this occurred when Cowper went on to write
a poem which he called 'Expostulation', in which he denounced the
Roman Catholic Church in no uncertain terms. Newton, who always
campaigned for religious liberty, advised Cowper not to publish
such offending lines. The following excerpt from one of Cowper's
letters on the subject shows how intensely the two friends exchanged ideas about their works and how willing Cowper was to
follow Newton's advice.

Though when I wrote the passage in question, I was not at
all aware of any impropriety in it, and though I have frequently since that time both read and recollected it with the
same approbation, I lately became uneasy upon the subject,
and had no rest in my mind for three days 'till I resolved to
submitt it to a trial at your tribunal, and to dispose of it
ultimately according to your sentence. I am glad you have
condemned it, and though I do not feel as if I could presently
supply its place, shall be willing to attempt the task whatever
labour it may cost me, and rejoice that it will not be in the

power of the Critics whatever else they may charge me with, to accuse me of Bigotry, or a design to make a certain denomination of Christians odious, at the hazard of the public peace. I had rather my book were burnt than that a single line guilty of such a tendency, should escape me.

We thank you for two copies of your address to your parishioners; the first I lent to Mr. Scott, whom I have not seen since I put it into his hands. You have managed your Subject well, have applied yourself to Despisers and Absentees of every description, in terms so expressive of the interest you take in their welfare, that the most wrongheaded person cannot be offended. We both wish it may have the effect you intend, and that prejudices and groundless apprehensions being removed, the immediate objects of your ministry may make a more considerable part of your Congregation.[28]

The first volume of poems published

After 1780 Cowper became convinced that he was to be a professional poet with the task of turning the minds of his pagan and backsliding contemporaries back to God and to his purpose and plan for the world and for mankind.

Shortly before Christmas 1780 Cowper wrote to Newton saying that he would soon be receiving an even longer poem than 'Antithelyphthora' (i. e. the 'Progress of Error' already mentioned), and it would be quickly followed by another poem of still uncertain length entitled 'The Truth'. It seems that hard work had been one of the causes of Cowper's last serious illness, so to put Newton's fears at bay he wrote, 'Don't be alarmed. I ride Pegasus in a curb. He will never run away with me again. I have convinced Mrs Unwin that I can manage him, & make him stop when I please.'

By the following January we find Cowper writing to Newton rejoicing that his friend had received the poem safely and was pleased with it. More mention is made of 'Truth' and a few days later Cowper is writing to say that he had finished a long poem entitled 'Table Talk'. In other words, Cowper had written three long poems of some 2,000 lines in all in a matter of a few weeks, not counting numerous pieces of verse of various lengths which he sent to other friends.

From now on Cowper's output was enormous by any standards.

The fact was that he believed that God had a special 'niche' for every person and only those could serve a life useful to God who were given grace to recognize their 'niche' and live in it. Cowper had now found his place in God's purpose and though melancholy took over at times, whenever he was working for God as his poet he found true happiness.

Although Cowper promised Newton that he could stop when he pleased he kept on writing verse intensively well into February when he wrote to his friend,

> Notwithstanding my purpose to shake hands with the Muse & take my leave of her for the present, we have already had a tete a tete since I sent you the last production. I am as much or rather more pleas'd with my new plan than with any of the foregoing. I mean to give a short Summary of the Jewish Story, the miraculous Interpositions in behalf of that people, their great privileges, their Abuse of them & their consequent destruction, and then by way of Comparison such another Display of the favors vouchsaf'd to this Country, the similar Ingratitude with which they have requited them, and the punishment they have therefore reason to expect, unless Reformation interpose to prevent it. Expostulation is its present title. But I have not yet found in the writing it that facility & readiness without which I shall despair to finish it well or indeed to finish it at all.[29]

Although in this letter Cowper gives the impression of being at the end of his ideas, 'Expostulation' was in fact soon finished and in April the poet sent Newton a large parcel, wrapped up in brown paper, with the request that he should forward it to Johnson the publisher. Newton unpacked the completed manuscript of his long poems, 'Table Talk', 'Truth', 'Expostulation' and 'The Progress of Error', as well as several minor pieces, all neatly numbered so that Johnson would know just in what order they were to be printed. Newton wasted no time in contacting Johnson, who professed delight at the poems and promised they would be speedily printed.

In his covering letter sent with the parcel, Cowper mentions to Newton that he feels his poem 'The Truth' is so true and to the point that readers will be offended by its directness and goes on to say,

I think therefore that in Order to obviate in some measure those prejudices that will naturally erect their bristles against it, an explanatory preface, such as You, (and nobody so well as you) can furnish me with, will have ev'ry grace of propriety to recommend it. Or if you are not averse to the task, and your Avocations will allow you to undertake it, and if you think it would be still more proper, I should be glad to be indebted to you for a preface to the whole. I wish you however to consult your own Judgment upon the Occasion, and to engage in either of these works, or neither, just as your discretion guides you.

Newton was only too pleased to assist his friend and soon got down to the task.

William Unwin feels left out

Meanwhile Cowper had a most difficult problem on his hands. As soon as Newton had protested that Cowper was showing more friendship to Unwin than himself, the poet had begun to supply Newton with the bulk of his work and ask his more experienced friend for help with his manuscripts. Not willing to cause strife, Cowper had not informed Unwin that he was now sending copy at a tremendous rate to Newton and that he was hoping to publish a whole volume of poems in the near future. Unwin was living under the apprehension that the small poems Cowper kept sending him were the whole of his verse. It seems that though Newton knew what was going on at the Unwins' home at Stock, Unwin had no idea of the extent of Cowper's correspondence with Newton.

The day came, however, when Cowper felt he must tell Unwin of his literary progress. Thus on 1 May 1781, after preparing the way by writing twenty-one lines of 'small talk', Cowper broke the news to Unwin saying,

In the Press and speedily will be published in one Volume Octavo, price three Shillings, Poems by William Cowper of the Inner Temple Esqr. You may Suppose by the Size of the publication that the greatest part of them have been long kept secret, because you yourself have never seen them. But the truth is that they are most of them except what you have in your possession, the produce of the last Winter. Two thirds of the Compilation will be occupied by 4 pieces, the first of which sprung up in the Month of December, and the last of them in the Month of March; they contain I suppose in all, about 2500 lines, are known, or are to be known in due time by the names of

Table Talk	Truth
The Progress of Error	Expostulation.

Mr. Newton writes a preface, and Johnson is the printer. The principal, I may say the only reason why I never mention'd to you till now, an Affair which I am just going to make known to all the World, if *that* Mr. All the World should think it worth his knowing, has been this; that 'till within these few days I had not the honor to know it myself. This may seem strange but it is true. For not knowing where to find underwriters who would chuse to insure them, and not finding it convenient to a purse like mine to run any hazard even upon the Credit of my own Ingenuity, I was very much in doubt for some Weeks whether any Bookseller would be willing to subject himself to an Ambiguity that might prove very expensive in case of a bad Market. But Johnson has heroically set all peradventures at defiance, and takes the whole charge upon himself — so Out I come.

Yours my dear friend with your Mother's Love—

Wm Cowper.

Cowper must have written these lines in great apprehension and with a very guilty conscience, yet evidently did not wish to give Unwin the full story about Newton's former protests. The poet had known, however, for several months that he might soon be able to go to print and the fact that he had not been absolutely sure until a short time before he wrote to Unwin was neither here nor there. Good friends usually inform one another about their work. Cowper, indeed, was always talking about friends sharing everything, but in order to keep the threefold peace between Newton, Unwin and himself, he had on this occasion been too reserved by far towards Unwin who, after all, was an even older Christian friend than Newton.

Unwin was, not surprisingly, deeply hurt and his reaction shows how deep was his friendship for Cowper and how suspicious he was of the poet's friendship with others. He lost no time in telling Cowper what he thought of his secrecy and the poet was made to regret what he had done. He was at first at a loss to find words to comfort Unwin but, not wishing to offend such a good friend further, he wrote,

My dear friend—

It is Friday; I have just drank tea, and just perused your Letter; and though this Answer to it cannot set off 'till Sunday, I obey the warm impulse I feel, which will not permitt me to postpone the business 'till the regular time of writing.

I expected you would be griev'd; if you had not been so, those Sensibilities which attend you upon every other Occasion, must have left you upon this. I am sorry that I have given you pain, but not sorry that you have felt it. A concern of that sort would be absurd, because it would be to regret your friendship for me, and to be dissatisfied with the Effects of it. Allow yourself however three Minutes only for Reflection, and your penetration must necessarily dive into the motives of my Conduct. In the first place, and by way of preface, remember that I do not, whatever your partiality may incline you to do, account it of much Consequence to any friend of mine, whether he is or is not employ'd by me upon such an Occasion. But all affected renunciations of poetical merit apart, and all unaffected Expressions of the Sense I have of my own Littleness in the poetical Character too, the obvious and only reason why I resorted to Mr. Newton and not to my friend Unwin was this — that the former lived in London, the latter at Stock; the former was upon the Spot, to correct that press, to give Instructions respecting any sudden Alterations, and to settle with the publisher every thing that might possibly occurr in the course of such a business. The latter could not be applied to for these purposes without what I thought would be a manifest Incroachment upon his kindness; because it might happen, that the troublesome Office might cost him now and then a Journey, which it was absolutely imposs-ible for me to endure the thought of.

When I wrote to you for the Copies you have sent me, I told

you that I was making a Collection, but not with a design to publish. There is nothing truer than that at that time, I had not the smallest Expectation of sending a Volume of poems to the Press. I had several small pieces that might amuse, but I would not when I publish make the Amusement of the Reader my only Object. When the Winter depriv'd me of other Employments, I began to compose; and seeing 6 or 7 Months before me which would naturally afford me much leisure for such a purpose, I undertook a piece of some length; that finish'd; another; and so on, 'till I had amass'd the Number of lines I mentiond in my last... Believe of me what you please, but not that I am indifferent to you, or your friendship for me, on any Occasion.[30]

As soon as Cowper had posted off this appeasing letter his conscience pricked him again and he decided to send another letter including a poem to pacify Unwin further. As the post had already gone, Cowper sent the letter by some other unofficial route.

Unknown to Unwin, Cowper had written a poem in his honour and had forwarded it to Newton in the brown paper parcel to be included in his volume. He had wanted it to be a surprise for Unwin when he eventually received Cowper's work. Now Cowper thought he had better send Unwin the poem so that he would see for himself that Cowper always thought well of him. The poem is as follows:

To the Revd. William Unwin

Unwin, I should but ill repay
The kindness of a friend,
Whose worth deserves as warm a lay
As ever Friendship penn'd,
Thy name omitted in a page
That would reclaim a vicious age.

An Union form'd as mine with thee,
Not rashly or in sport,
May be as fervent in degree,
And faithfull in its sort,
And may as rich in comfort prove,
As that of true fraternal Love.

The Bud inserted in the rind,
The Bud of Peach or Rose,
Adorns, though diff'ring in its kind,
The Stock whereon it grows
With flow'r as sweet or fruit as fair
As if produc'd by Nature there.

Not rich, I render what I may,
I seize thy Name in haste,[31]
And place it in this first Assay,
Lest this should prove the last—
'Tis where it should be, in a plan
That holds in view the good of Man.

The poet's Lyre, to fix his fame,
Should be the poet's heart;
Affection lights a brighter flame,
Than ever blaz'd by Art.
No Muses on these lines attend,
I sink the poet in the friend.

From this time on Cowper kept Unwin minutely informed of the progress of his book. Taking advantage of this latest change on Cowper's part, Unwin pressed the poet to allow him to be his contact-man at the publisher's instead of Newton. Cowper refused point-blank and, to be freed of strife, even went so far as to tell Newton that his services were no longer needed either. Cowper soon regretted this latter move and asked Newton to continue his work and read and check the proofs as soon as they came from the printer's. Johnson, however, intervened himself and took over much of the humdrum work of proof-checking.

The news that Newton had been privy to Cowper's confidence, whereas he himself had been left in the dark, could not have come at a worse time for Unwin. He had recently become governor of Christ's Hospital, a school with a very high academic reputation. Unwin was able to submit candidates for the school and obtain bursaries for them. Not wishing to be accused of misusing his privilege, however, he had refrained from making use of his right of nomination.

When Newton heard of Unwin's appointment, he at once begged

Mrs Unwin to use all the influence she could on her son to get a
nomination for his own nephew. For over a year he bombarded Mrs
Unwin and Cowper with this request and even gave them a deadline
when he expected them to come up with the nomination. Just before
hearing Cowper's news about his literary co-operation with Newton, Unwin finally broke his practice and had Newton's nephew
admitted to Christ's Hospital. He did this at great risk to his own
reputation and expected Newton to show him real gratitude when he
personally presented him with the nomination. To his surprise,
Newton received the news without any great display of thanks and,
indeed, dealt with Unwin rather brusquely.

This caused Unwin to write to his mother and Cowper complaining bitterly of Newton's unthankful conduct and at the same time
expressing his shock at Cowper's news concerning his intended
publication. Cowper thus wrote to soothe Unwin about not taking
him into his confidence regarding Newton's editorship and, in the
same letter, Mrs Unwin tried to calm her son down concerning his
disappointment at Newton's hands. Mrs Unwin wrote,

My dear Billy,
    accept my most sincere thanks for your favour done me,
by that conferred on Mr. Newton's relation. I am sorry Mr.
Newton's manner shocked you; but am rejoiced it had no
other Effect. It was not for want of sensibility of the obligation I am certain; but I never in my life knew One that
seemed so much at a loss as he is for expressing his feelings
by word of mouth. — Last Sunday's post brought Mr.
Cowper a letter from him with the following passage. 'Yesterday Mr. Unwin came into the vestry & presented me with
a Nomination to the Hospital. He did it very Cordially &
handsomely, & I thanked him very heartily & honestly. For
though I had no right to expect such a favour from him merely
on my own account, I am very willing to consider myself
personally obliged to him for it. I know Mrs. Unwin will
believe I am duly sensible of her kindness, & I call my best
thanks to her but a pepper Corn, because they fall short of
what I mean:— I am no loser by this disbursement of thanks
to him & to her, for Mr. & Mrs. Nind have paed me in kind'—
    I am my dear Billy your obliged & affectionate Mother:
                                   M.U.

When Unwin received Cowper's first four long poems, he wasted no time in giving his comments on them. He felt 'Truth' to be far too near the truth for unsaved people and suggested that Cowper should make it less obviously evangelical. Cowper looked upon 'Truth' as his own statement of faith and wanted to lead up to it with other lighter poems so that when readers had worked their way through more enticing fare they would suddenly find themselves confronted with the image of themselves in the eyes of God. This idea did not seem to appeal to Unwin but Cowper stood firm and wrote,

> I reply therefore, not peevishly but with a Sense of the Kindness of your Intentions that I hope you may make yourself very easy on a Subject that I can perceive has occasion'd you some Sollicitude. When I wrote the Poem called Truth, by which is intended Religious Truth, it was indispensibly necessary that I should set forth that doctrine which I know to be true, and that I should pass what I understand to be a just Censure upon Opinions and persuasions that differ from, or stand in direct Opposition to it. Because though some Errors may be innocent, and even religious Errors are not always pernicious, yet in a case where the Faith and Hope of a Christian are concern'd, they must necessarily be destructive. And because neglecting This, I should have betray'd my Subject; either suppressing what in my Judgment is of the last importance, or giving Countenance by a timid Silence to the very Evils it was my design to combat. That you may understand me better, I will subjoin — that I wrote that Poem on purpose to inculcate the eleemosynary Character of the Gospel, as a dispensation of Mercy in the most absolute Sense of the word, to the Exclusion of all claims of Merit on the part of the Receiver. Consequently to set the brand of Invalidity upon the Plea of Works, and to discover upon Scriptural ground the absurdity of that Notion which includes a Solecism in the very terms of it, that Man by Repentance and good works may deserve the Mercy of his Maker. I call it a Solecism, because Mercy deserved, ceases to be Mercy, and must take the name of Justice. This is the Opinion which I said in my last the World would not acquiesce in, but except this I do not recollect that I have introduced

a syllable into any of my pieces that they can possibly object
to. And even this, I have endeavor'd to deliver from doctrinal
dryness, by as many pretty things in the way of trinket and
play thing, as I could muster upon the Subject. So that if I have
rubb'd their Gums, I have taken care to do it with a Coral, and
even that Coral embellish'd by the Ribbon to which it is tied,
and recommended by the tinkling of all the bells I could
contrive to annex to it.[32]

More poetic output

When Cowper sent his parcel of poems off to Newton for publication in April, he told his friend that he had worked so hard that he
was now going to give free range to his 'Love of fine weather, Love
of Indolence, and Love of gardening Employments'. This was the
way he usually spoke to Newton in order to belittle his enormous
appetite for work. Just two weeks later, however, he was already
working on a further poem called 'Hope', which he believed would
run into 1,000 lines.

Johnson, meanwhile, realizing that the gentry were leaving
London for the season to enjoy their leisure at places such as
Brighton, Southampton, Ramsgate and Bristol, decided not to
publish until the winter and informed Cowper that he could make his
book as thick as he liked. The poet thus continued to write 'Hope'
with a view to adding it to the volume already at the publishers.
Then, only days after writing that he would soon be in print and
enjoying his garden, he found himself producing more poetry than
ever.

Although he told Unwin that since he had begun to write long
poems, he turned up his nose at short ones, he proceeded to translate
and rewrite a number of Latin poems which his old teacher Bourne
had written. These he gave a more Christian turn and made sure that
they had a moral application. He then started to revise the poems he
had already written, omitting those sections which were of mere
topical interest and replacing them with other new compositions.

By July Cowper had not only composed several anti-Madan
poems mentioned above but also a 635-lined work entitled 'Charity'
and was halfway through a 900-lined poem called 'Conversation'.

Cowper wrote a great many letters in verse, most of which have been lost. One rhyming letter, however, which he wrote to Newton telling him about 'Charity' has been preserved. Cowper tells Newton:

> I have writ Charity, not for popularity, but as well as I could, in hopes to do good. And if the Review'r, should say to be sure, the Gentleman's Muse, wears Methodist shoes, you may know by her pace, and talk about grace, that she and her bard, have little regard, for the tastes and fashions, and ruling passions, and hoyd'ning play, of the modern day, and though She assume, a borrow'd plume, and now and then wear, a tittering air, 'tis only her plan, to catch if She can, the giddy and gay, as they go that way, by a production, on a new construction, and has baited her trap, in hopes to snap, all that may come, with a Sugar plumb, his Opinion in this, will not be amiss, 'tis what I intend, my principal End, and if it Succeed, and folks should read, 'till a few are brought, to a serious thought, I shall think I am paid, for all I have said, and all I have done, though I have run, many a time, after a rhime, as far as from hence, to the end of my Sense, and by hook or crook, write another book, if I live and am here, another year.[33]

In August we find Cowper writing to Newton,

> I have already begun and proceeded a little way in a poem call[ed] Retirement. My view in chusing that Subject is to direct to the proper use of the opportunities it affords for the cultivation of a Man's best Interests; to censure the Vices and the follies which people carry with them into their Retreats, where they make no other use of their leisure than to gratify themselves with the Indulgence of their favorite appetites, and to pay themselves by a life of pleasure for a life of Business. In conclusion I would enlarge upon the happiness of that State when discreetly enjoyed and religiously improved. But all this is at present in Embryo. I generally despair of my progress when I begin, but if like my travelling Squire, I should kindle as I go, this likewise may make a part of the Volume, for I have time enough before me.[34]

Not forgetting his promise to send Newton samples of his trivial verse, too, Cowper enclosed the following lines concerning the high price of food as a result of the political situation, together with the promise of a brace of fowls and a duck sent on via a friend.

Cocoa nut naught,
Fish too dear,
None must be bought
For us that are here.

No Lobster on Earth,
That ever I saw,
To me would be worth
Sixpence a claw.

So dear Madam wait
Till fish can be got,
At a reas'nable rate,
Whether Lobster or not

Till the French and the Dutch
Have quitted the Seas,
And then send as much
And as oft' as you please.

Newton's preface

By September 1781 Cowper had enough poems ready to fill 450 octavo pages and Johnson felt the time was coming to bring out the book. He therefore promised Cowper it would be out shortly after Christmas. Newton thus put the finishing touches to his preface and showed it to Eli Bates, a fellow Evangelical and founder member of the Eclectic Society, for approval. Bates found the preface too severe by far and warned Newton that he was supposed to motivate readers to read on rather than frighten them off. Nevertheless Newton forwarded the preface to Cowper without altering it, though he informed the poet of Bates' objections.

On reading the preface Cowper confessed that Newton had shown true friendship and only queried one sentence which he felt was not easily understandable. The rest, he believed, should remain exactly as it was. Of Bates' censures Cowper wrote,

> Mr Bates, without intending it, has passed a severer censure upon the modern world of Readers, than any that can be found in my volume. If they are so merrily disposed in the midst of a thousand calamities, that they will not deign to read a preface of three or four pages, because the purport of it is serious, they are far gone indeed, and in the last stage of a frenzy such as I suppose has prevailed in all nations that have been exemplarily punished, just before the infliction of the Sentence. But though he lives in the world he has so ill an Opinion of, and ought therefore to know it better than I who have no intercourse with it at all, I am willing to hope that he may be mistaken. [35]

The first part of Newton's preface is a very personal affirmation of his friendship for Cowper in which he says how pleasing and flattering it is for him to have his own name perpetuated on the title-page along with that of Cowper. He goes on to outline how he and the poor people of Olney have benefited from Cowper's friendship over many years.

After this, however, Newton becomes rather indiscreet and too personal. He had already referred in print to Cowper's illness in his preface to the *Olney Hymns*, though it was hardly a fitting place to mention it. Now Newton went even further in outlining Cowper's former indisposition, even suggesting that the poet was now past his spiritual best. Such information had nothing to do with the contents of the book and could hardly be considered as necessary background information for an appreciation of the poems. With hindsight it is easy to see that the remarks are in very bad taste.

The rest of the preface is a brilliant outline of the Christian gospel and would have served as a jewel in the crown of any book written by a man of God. In this section Newton says of Cowper:

> He aims to communicate his own perceptions of the truth, beauty, and influence of the religion of the Bible, — a religion, which, however discredited by the misconduct of many, who have not renounced the Christian name, proves itself, when rightly understood, and cordially embraced, to be

the grand *desideratum* which alone can relieve the mind of
man from painful and unavoidable anxieties, inspire it with
stable peace and solid hope, and furnish those motives and
prospects, which in the present state of things, are absolutely
necessary to produce a conduct worthy of a rational creature,
distinguished by a vastness of capacity, which no assemblage
of earthly good can satisfy, and by a principle and pre-
intimation of immortality.

After explaining how Cowper's poems encourage experimental
Christianity, as opposed to mere head-knowledge and lip-con-
fession, Newton ends with the stirring words: 'We are now certain,
that the gospel of Christ is the power of God unto salvation to every
one that believeth. It has reconciled us to God, and to ourselves, to
our duty, and our situation. It is the balm and cordial of the present
life, and a sovereign antidote against the fear of death.'

Although several of Newton's friends strove to persuade him to
cut out the parts least applicable to the contents of Cowper's poems
and the gospel, Newton remained adamant that the preface was to
remain unaltered. This dismayed Johnson, who thought that some of
Newton's words were hardly a good introduction to a new author's
work and the publisher, who counted Newton as one of his best
friends, finally decided that he could not publish his words as they
stood. Newton was very hurt but remained unbending and managed
to arrange with Johnson for a few copies to be produced with his
preface for private distribution.

He then turned again to Cowper asking him to have his name put
on the title-page as editor in spite of Johnson's feelings regarding the
preface. Cowper agreed to this, although at this time he had no
intention of publishing under his own name. Johnson, however,
would not hear of it and Newton's name was left out. This was very
hard on Newton who had put in a great deal of work both on
Cowper's and Johnson's behalf. He had read and transcribed
hundreds of handwritten pages, edited them, pointed out passages
which he felt should be omitted and made dozens of sensible
suggestions as to how other passages could be bettered.

Eight years later when Cowper's poems were being proclaimed
as the very best and there was no danger of their not selling well,
Johnson relented and published Cowper's complete works up to that
date with Newton's preface.

Into print at last

Now that his poems were actually being printed, Cowper, though calm on the surface, was obviously worried about what the critics might say. He wrote to Unwin declaring his stand on the matter:

> The Critics cannot deprive me of the pleasure I have in reflecting that so far as my leisure has been employed in writing for the public, it has been conscientiously employed, and with a view to their advantage. There is nothing agreeable to be sure in being chronicled for a dunce, but I believe there lives not a man upon earth who would be less affected by it than myself. With all this Indifference to Fame, which you know me too well to suppose me capable of affecting, I have taken the utmost pains to deserve it. This may appear a mystery or a paradox in practise, but it is true. I consider'd that the taste of the day is refined and delicate to excess, and that to disgust that delicacy of taste by a slovenly inattention to it, would be to forfeit at once all hope of being usefull; and for this reason, though I have written more verse this last year than perhaps any man in England, have finished and polished and touched and retouched with the utmost care. If after all I should be converted into waste paper, it may be my misfortune, but it will not be my fault, & I shall bear it with the most perfect Serenity.[36]

Cowper, however, could not stop writing and soon he had composed a lengthy poem on the subject of friendship and one entitled 'Ætna' about what happens when a country turns its back on God. Oddly enough 'Friendship' was the first and one of the very few poems of Cowper's that Johnson refused to publish. It was also one of the poems that Cowper himself was most pleased with. However, he did not insist on its publication, believing that Johnson knew best what would be acceptable.

One of the last poems to be added to the volume was 'The Love of the World Reproved; or, Hypocrisy Detected' which Newton had already published in the *Leeds Mercury* and *Gentleman's Magazine* with six lines added of his own. This is the poem dealing with the various ideas of 'sin' amongst believers and is probably the source of the common expression 'going the whole hog'.

By December Cowper had to stop sending in new poems as printing was in progress. Looking back at the way Johnson had accepted and praised his poetry Cowper told Newton that he had 'reason to be very much satisfied' with his publisher.

The first day of March 1782 saw the publication of the largest collection of Christian verse in one volume by one author to be issued since the days of John Bunyan. The volume carried the unpretentious title of *Poems by William Cowper, of the Inner Temple, Esq.*

As Cowper intended his work to be of use to the general reading public, he was particularly anxious that secular reviewers should also see the value of his work. He need not have worried. On the whole, though not jubilant in praise, the secular magazines and journals of the day gave Cowper a most positive write-up.

The reviewer in the *Gentleman's Magazine* stressed that he had known Cowper when he was 'a keen sportsman in the classic fields of Westminster' and had written essays for the *Connoisseur*. He wrote, 'We have perused, with great pleasure, both the serious and humourous pieces, the Latin and English, of which this collection consists.'

The *Monthly Review* took some time to come out with their comments but when Cowper read them, he had every reason to be pleased. They proclaimed Cowper as a good poet, quite different to all others, writing,

> *Most* poets have no character at all; being, for the chief part, only echoes of those who have sung before them. For while not only their sentiments and diction are borrowed, but their very modes of thinking, as well as versification, are copied from the said models, discrimination of character must of course be scarcely perceptible. Confining themselves, like pack-horses, to the same beaten track and uniformity of pace, and, like them too, having their bells from the same shop, they go jingling along in uninterrupted unison with each other. This, however, is not the case with Mr. Cowper; he is a poet *sui generis*, for as his notes are peculiar to himself, he classes not with any known species of bards that have preceded him: his style of composition, as well as his modes of thinking, are entirely his own. The ideas, with which his mind seems to have been either endowed by nature,

or to have been enriched by learning and reflection, as they lie in no regular order, so are they promiscuously brought forth as they accidentally present themselves.

The *London Magazine* was high in praise of Cowper's verse, saying that it was 'an entertaining collection upon a variety of subjects, temporary, moral, and satirical; composed with sound judgment, good taste, and no small share of wit and humour'.

The only criticism Cowper received in the press was from the staunchly conservative *Critical Review,* which was a vowed opponent of anything Whiggish and anything that was as critical as Cowper about the abuses of the Established Church. The reviewer liked Cowper's smaller, non-religious pieces but said he should keep his hand off religious topics as 'his genius seems but ill adapted' for such work. The magazine, so used to the pompous language of the neo-classical poets, found Cowper's simple language 'coarse and vulgar'.

Cowper had foreseen such criticism when writing of weaknesses in the up-and-coming Higher Criticism of the Bible in 'The Progress of Error', where he says,

When some hypothesis absurd and vain
Has fill'd with all its fumes a critic's brain,
The text that sorts not with his darling whim,
Though plain to others, is obscure to him.[37]

Besides, Cowper had little time to worry about what the critics had to say. He was busy working on his second volume.

10.
The *Poems*

Most of Cowper's biographers have paid little attention to his poetry when portraying his life and have gleaned their biographical data from his few prose writings and his numerous letters, rather than from his verse. His poetry is widely seen by them as merely a highly imaginative form of escapism from the supposedly humdrum, melancholy life he was living in the small, insignificant town of Olney.

There is an old maxim often quoted by literary critics that 'All poets are liars.' This seems to have influenced most commentators in their views of the subject matter of Cowper's poetry. Thus although Cowper's poems are filled with Evangelical fervour, David Cecil, for instance, in his biography *The Stricken Deer*, says that the poet was 'through with evangelicalism' long before his illness of 1773 and was bored with it over a decade before writing his first volume of poems. One gains the impression that such critics are only too eager to erase all of Cowper's Christian verse from their area of research and then pronounce Cowper not only a non-Evangelical but even a contender against Evangelical principles. Hugh I'Anson Fausset, considered by many to be an authority on Cowper, recoils with disgust at Cowper's display of faith and refuses point-blank to deal with it. He thus concentrates his criticism on snippets of Cowper's verse which he finds acceptable.

Other critics, such as Vincent Newey, go to the other extreme and recognize the depths of feeling and faith in Cowper's poems but because of the poet's optimism and sheer joy in believing they say he cannot be an Evangelical Calvinist as the God of Calvinism is 'a stern and arbitrary Deity who rules a bleak world of reprobate and justified souls'.[1] Newey thus deduces that Cowper's faith is at times a rebellion against the God of the orthodox Christian faith, at other times a mere flight of poetic fantasy, now and then an afterthought merely put in for form's sake, and, in some cases, a mere adaptation to the whims of his readers.

Cowper's own opinions on these matters are of little significance to such biographers. They rule him out of court as a reliable witness to his own beliefs. This is the reason why most biographers have portrayed Cowper as a mere shadow of what he really was.

Cowper's view of his calling

In biblical criticism the one main difference between the liberal critic and the evangelical commentator is that the former looks first for external information to guide his views on Scripture whereas the evangelical allows the text to first speak for itself. If the evangelical approach is used on Cowper's poetry, a new Cowper emerges. His poetry will then be found to be highly biographical and it will become obvious that Cowper saw himself first and foremost as a Christian mentor whose task was:

> To catch the triflers of the time,
> And tell them truths divine and clear,
> Which couch'd in prose, they will not hear.[2]

He was also under no delusions about the times in which he was living and, rather than play up to the Christian views of his readers and merely pretend to be an Evangelical, he aimed at the non-Christian reader who, he knew, would be very reluctant to be taught the things of God. Summing up the average view of the British readers of his day, Cowper said that they had but one thing in mind: 'Tickle and entertain us or we die.'[3] He thus wrote to Unwin saying, 'To aim with success at the spiritual good of mankind, and to become popular by writing on scriptural subjects, were an unreasonable ambition even for a poet to entertain in days like these.'[4]

If Cowper had pandered to public taste he would never have been remembered for his Christian verse. The urge to write about his faith was, however, so strong within him that he told Newton in May

1786, 'Thus far therefore it is plain that I have not chosen or prescribed to myself my own way, but have been providentially led to it. Perhaps I might say with equal propriety, compelled and scourged into it.' This was Cowper's way of echoing Paul's words: 'Woe be unto me if I preach not the gospel.' The poet explained his calling to his readers later in the *Task* by saying,

> But when a poet, or one like me,
> Happy to rove among poetic flow'rs,
> Though poor in skill to rear them, lights at last
> On some fair theme, some theme divinely fair,
> Such is the impulse and the spur he feels
> To give it praise proportioned to its worth,
> That not t'attempt it, arduous as he deems
> The labor, were a task more arduous still.[5]

We see Cowper again expressing a call to evangelize mankind in verse in a letter he wrote to Lady Hesketh in 1786:

> We certainly do not honour God when we bury or when we neglect to improve, as far as we may, whatsoever talent he may have bestowed on us, whether it be little or much. In natural things as well as spiritual it is a never-failing truth, that to him who *hath*, that is to him who occupies what he hath diligently and so as to increase it — more shall be given. Set me down therefore, my dear, for an industrious rhymer so long as I shall have the ability, for in this only is it possible for me, as far as I can see, either to honour God or to serve man, or even to serve myself.[6]

Poetry versus prose

Cowper makes it clear on numerous occasions that if people wish to know his hopes and aspirations, his views on life and the faith that was in him, then they should turn to his verse and not to his prose. He gives us a very clear picture of this in a letter-cum-poem to Lady Austen, in which he tells his Evangelical friend that prose

> Serves, in a plain, and homely way,
>   T' express th' occurrence of the day;

Our health, the weather, and the news;
What walks we take, what books we chuse;
And all the floating thoughts, we find
Upon the surface of the mind.

Poetry, however, for Cowper, is quite another matter and it goes far deeper.

But when a Poet takes the pen,
Far more alive than other men,
He feels a gentle tingling come
Down to his finger and his thumb,
Deriv'd from nature's noblest part,
The centre of a glowing heart![7]

After writing these words Cowper goes on to explain in verse how God has called him to be a poet of divine truths.

Cowper expressed similar views on verse in a letter to William Unwin. Writing about the American rebellion in general and 'French Corruption' in particular, he says, 'Were I to express what I feel upon such Occasions in Prose, it would be Verbose, inflated, and disgusting, I therefore have recourse to Verse, as a suitable Vehicle for the most vehement Expressions my Thoughts suggest to me.'[8]

Elsewhere on several occasions Cowper explained to his friends that whenever he thought deeply, he tended to think in verse.[9]

Prose, then, has its place for Cowper as a purveyor of descriptions concerning the superficial things of life but more serious matters must be dealt with in verse. Given this fact any biographer would be neglecting his best sources if he did not look for biographical details dealing with the deeper matters of Cowper's life in his verse rather than in his letters. It is only here that we are able to obtain a fuller, true, objective picture of what Cowper really experienced, felt and believed.

The desire to be useful

The poet was well aware, however, that neither prose nor verse of themselves could be of any use in spreading the truth if they were not accompanied by the will of God and his Spirit. This he was very careful to point out when he informed Mrs Cowper, Martin Madan's sister, of his project. Mrs Cowper had sent her cousin some of her own verse for appraisal and comment. In his answer Cowper said,

> My sole drift is to be usefull, a point which however, I knew, I should in vain aim at, unless I could be likewise entertaining. I have therefore fixed these two strings upon my Bow, and by the help of both have done my best to send my Arrow to the mark. My Readers will hardly have begun to laugh, before they will find themselves called upon to correct that levity, and peruse me with a more serious air. As to the Effect, I leave it in his hands who can alone produce it; neither prose nor Verse, can reform the manners of a dissolute age, much less can they inspire a Sense of religious obligation, unless assisted and made efficacious by the power who superintends the truth he has vouchsafed to impart.[10]

Cowper was quite clear in his mind about what directives to follow in composing his first volume. His favourite expression to describe this conviction was 'being useful'. By this he meant that his poetry was to be a statement of his faith and a medium for spreading the good news to the general public.[11] In other words, both Cowper's volumes of poems were highly doctrinal but also highly biographical.

Poetry as the language of Eden

The poet was well aware, however, that most readers of poetry would turn to a book of poems for entertainment rather than instruction, so he opened his first volume, which he called simply *Poems*, with 'Table Talk', in which he prepares the reader for what is to come by describing the calling and tasks of a Christian poet.

In this poem Cowper argues that his poetry is nothing more and nothing less than an attempt to recall the language of Eden in which man had once communed without hindrance with his Maker. Since the Fall language had degenerated and poetry's function had been perverted along with everything else to which man had turned his hand. Artistry and artificiality had taken the place of simplicity, elegance and innocence. Thus the poet could write,

In Eden ere yet innocence of heart
Had faded, poetry was not an art;
Language above all teaching, or if taught,
Only by gratitude and glowing thought,
Elegant as simplicity, and warm
As exstasy, unmanacl'd by form,
Not prompted as in our degen'rate days,
By low ambition and the thirst of praise,
Was natural as is the flowing stream,
And yet magnificent, a God the theme.[12]

Cowper realized that though sin had 'marr'd all' and language had fallen, the Word of God had remained unstained. It was the only medium known to man which had retained its Edenic purity. He thus confessed that the language he aimed at was the lost language of Eden, a language which would reunite man with God. Defending Christian optimism and the use of humour in poetry, the poet attacked those who taught that 'Mirth is sin, and we should always cry', and argued in 'Conversation':

But though life's valley be a vale of tears,
A brighter scene beyond that vale appears,
Shoots between scatter'd rocks and op'ning shades,
And while it shows the land the soul desires,
The language of the land she seeks inspires.[13]

It is obvious that Cowper is here declaring that the true language of poetry for him is the language of the Paradise Regained which has in some measure been bestowed on the born-again poet as he contemplates that blessed 'land'. He goes on to say,

Thus touch'd, the tongue receives a sacred cure,
Of all that was absurd, profane, impure;
Held within modest bounds, the tide of speech
Pursues the course that truth and nature teach.[14]

Cowper thus sought to model his poetry as nearly as possible on the language of Scripture and the believer's appreciation of God's earth. By taking the themes of Eden past and future as his subject matter and describing God's plan of salvation in Christ, Cowper believed that he could make his calling sure in his endeavours

> To trace him in his word, his works, his way
> Then spread the rich discov'ry, and invite
> Mankind to share in the divine delight.[15]

In outlining his view of the aim and scope of Christian poetry Cowper was basing his ideas on beliefs he held in common with Newton on the various means of revelation through which God spoke to man. Newton and his circle of friends called these methods 'God's library' of four books. Book One was 'the Word', God's supreme revelation in the Bible, which outlined the way of salvation. Book Two was 'Creation', called 'God's works' by Cowper, which taught unregenerate man the existence of God and made him aware of his conscience. Book Three was 'Divine Providence', termed 'God's ways' by Cowper, which showed man how God planned and ruled the world, and Book Four was 'the Heart', that is, experience and observations which taught regenerate man dependency on God through everyday contact with him.[16] Cowper referred to this last book when he spoke of 'sharing in the divine delight' of Christian experience. He also based his views on a firm belief that God would in some measure put an end to the groaning and travailing of nature because of man's sin and restore nature before the Second Advent of Christ.

The need for a renewal of true poetry

Apart from Herbert, Bunyan, Milton and Watts, Cowper saw few major poets who had ever shared his views and thus exclaimed in the opening pages of his first volume:

> Pity! Religion has so seldom found
> A skilful guide into poetic ground,
> The flow'rs would spring where'er she deign'd to stray,
> And ev'ry muse attend her in her way.
> Virtue indeed meets many a rhiming friend,
> And many a compliment politely penn'd,
> But unattir'd in that becoming vest
> Religion weaves for her, and half undress'd,

Stands in the desart shiv'ring and forlorn,
A wint'ry figure, like a wither'd thorn.[17]

The reason for this, as Cowper shows in 'Table Talk', was that poetry had degenerated since earlier times and had become a hackneyed reproduction of tales of dubious heroes and corrupt kings. One poet copied the ideas of another and 'poetic traditions' were handed down from writer to writer without any due sense of originality or calling. Cowper's comment on this was:

The shelves are full, all other themes are sped,
Hackney'd and worn to the last flimsy thread,
Satyr has long since done his best, and curst
And loathsome ribaldry has done his worst,
Fancy has sported all her pow'rs away
In tales, in trifles, and in children's play,
And 'tis the sad complaint, and almost true,
Whate'er we write, we bring forth nothing new.[18]

Cowper believed that he knew what was the one new thing necessary to revive true poetry and wrote comparing the Christian poet to the prophets of old:

'Twere new indeed, to see a bard all fire,
Touch'd with a coal from heav'n assume the Lyre,
And tell the world, still kindling as he sung,
With more than mortal music on his tongue,
That he who died below, and reigns above
Inspires the song, and that his name is love.[19]

It was Cowper's one ambition to be such a mentor to the public at large and to transform poetry back to its original function. Thus we find Cowper constantly asking God to bless him in his calling, recognizing that only a man walking with God could ever succeed as a true poet. So in 'Charity' we find him praying:

Prosper (I press thee with a pow'rful plea)
A task I venture on, impell'd by thee:
Oh never seen but in thy blest effects,
Nor felt but in the soul that heav'n selects,

Who seeks to praise thee, and to make thee known
To other hearts, must have thee in his own.
Come, prompt me with benevolent desires,
Teach me to kindle at thy gentle fires,
And though disgrac'd and slighted, to redeem
A poet's name, by making thee the theme.[20]

Lord Macaulay, writing in his *Critical Essays*, grasped what
Cowper was striving to do with language and wrote that he was the
'forerunner of the great restoration of our literature'. The essayist
claimed that Cowper found poetry 'in the lowest state of degener-
ation, feeble, artificial, and altogether nerveless', and possessed the
talents which fitted him for the task 'of raising it from that deep
abasement'. Macaulay, summing up Cowper's contribution to poetry, sees that he 'did not deal in mechanical versification and
conventional phrases' and that he was so very new as a poet because
he wrote about themes which set his 'heart on fire'. [21]

Macaulay also praises Cowper for departing from the pseudo-
learning of his contemporaries and writing verse for ordinary people
about ordinary people. He tells us, 'Instead of raving about imaginary Chloes and Sylvias, Cowper wrote of Mrs. Unwin's knitting-
needles.' [22]

Distorted views of Cowper's poetry

High as Macaulay's praise for Cowper is, even more severe is his
condemnation of Cowper's major biographer, Robert Southey, the
Poet Laureate. Southey, more than any other writer, has established
a host of myths concerning Cowper and Newton which subsequent
biographers have accepted uncritically. Of Southey Macaulay
writes, 'It is, indeed, most extraordinary, that a mind like Mr.
Southey's, a mind richly endowed in many respects by nature, and
highly cultivated by study, a mind which has exercised considerable
influence on the most enlightened generation of the most enlightened people that ever existed, should be utterly destitute of the
power of discerning truth from falsehood. Yet such is the fact.'[23]

Macaulay criticizes Southey for making cardinal virtues out of
'theological sins', such as hatred, pride and vengeance, and for
despising anything that appears 'soft or humane'. He accuses the

courtly poet of being apathetic towards the subjects of his biographies and not bringing facts forward to support his views. Yet such is the man who has paved the way for a critical 'appreciation' of Cowper's poems. It is no wonder that subsequent critics, ignorant of the Christian way of life, have become highly suspicious of Cowper's verse when seen through the glasses they have inherited from Southey!

The 'Progress of Error'

Macaulay praises Cowper for the manliness of his verse as opposed to the effeminate warblings of Pope and his contemporaries. There is certainly nothing 'soft' to be seen in Cowper's 'The Progress of Error', which follows on after 'Table Talk'. Cowper starts off with a very sombre note, pointing out that he is dealing with the facts of sin and not poetic fancies:

> Sing muse (if such a theme, so dark, so long,
> May find a muse to grace it with a song)
> By what unseen and unsuspected arts
> The serpent error twines round human hearts,
> Tell where she lurks, beneath what flow'ry shades,
> That not a glimpse of genuine light pervades,
> The pois'nous, black, insinuating worm,
> Successfully conceals her loathsome form.
> Take, if ye can, ye careless and supine!
> Counsel and caution from a voice like mine;
> Truths that the theorist could never reach,
> And observations taught me, I would teach.[24]

It is Cowper's evangelical honesty concerning the grip which sin had on himself and his readers that has caused so many of Cowper's biographers to call the poet 'morbid', and even 'mad'. Cowper, however, knew man's heart — including his own — and goes on to castigate much that was considered the normal social life of his time. Asking the question, 'What is man?' he decries the passion for entertainment and lack of sober thinking going on in his day but is especially heavy on the 'cassock'd huntsman and fiddling priest' who were going the way of the world instead of rescuing their parishes from it. These people, Cowper argues, are striving to inaugurate a 'British paradise' where the cure for man's boredom with himself was thought to be distractions, rather than a life in God's care and keeping. Cowper's list of man's surrogates for a purposeful life contains nothing that is not prevalent in our modern affluent Western society. This is in keeping with Cowper's plan, as he always aimed to write not only for his own time but for the future also.

As Cowper felt so strongly about the purpose of true language, it is no surprise to find him especially harsh in his condemnation of those who pervert language as a medium of communication. Journalists and writers of novels are given a tough time. Cowper was himself an avid reader of newspapers and magazines, but was also well aware of how the press could adapt the truth to suit its own policy. Thus he can write,

> How shall I speak thee, or thy pow'r address,
> Thou God of our idolatry, the press?
> By thee, religion, liberty and laws
> Exert their influence, and advance their cause,
> By thee, worse plagues than Pharaoh's land befell,
> Diffus'd, make earth the vestibule of hell:
> Thou fountain, at which drink the good and wise,
> Thou ever-bubbling spring of endless lies,
> Like Eden's dread probationary tree,
> Knowledge of good and evil is from thee.[25]

As he does so often, Cowper uses Eden as a measure by which he measures society. In his long poem on Christian love called 'Charity' Cowper envisages a Christian press used to transform society and says:

> Did Charity prevail, the press would prove
> A vehicle of virtue, truth and love,
> And I might spare myself the pains to show
> What few can learn, and all suppose they know.[26]

Though Cowper read a great deal, his favourite books were on theological, scientific, travel and gardening themes. He enjoyed reading the classics at all times and even read an occasional play.

What he could not stomach were the lewd novels and romances which were still being written during the eighteenth century, though the vulgar so-called 'restoration' in literature brought about under Charles II had declined greatly in public taste. As these novels were often written for women readers, Cowper, the gentleman, writes,

> Ye writers of what none with safety reads,
> Footing it in the dance that fancy leads,
> Ye novellists who marr what ye would mend,
> Sniv'ling and driv'ling folly without end,
> Whose corresponding misses fill the ream
> With sentimental frippery and dream,
> Caught in a delicate soft silken net
> By some lewd Earl, or rake-hell Baronet;
> Ye pimps, who under virtue's fair pretence,
> Steal to the closet of young innocence,
> And teach her unexperienc'd yet and green,
> To scribble as you scribble at fifteen;
> Who kindling a combustion of desire,
> With some cold moral think to quench the fire,
> Though all your engineering proves in vain,
> The dribbling stream ne'er puts it out again;
> Oh that a verse had pow'r, and could command
> Far, far away, these flesh-flies of the land,
> Who fasten without mercy on the fair,
> And suck, and leave a craving maggot there.[27]

To Cowper, who was living at a time when the veracity of Scripture was coming under fire, man's folly was to adopt the free-thinker's philosophy which decreed that the Bible was lies and blasphemy common sense. All this was self-delusion and Cowper ends 'The Progress of Error' with a stirring warning and a message of hope in the cross of the Lord Jesus Christ:

> Hear the just law, the judgment of the skies!
> He that hates truth shall be the dupe of lies.
> And he that will be cheated to the last,
> Delusions, strong as hell, shall bind him fast.
> But if the wand'rer his mistake discern,
> Judge his own ways, and sigh for a return,

Bewilder'd once, must he bewail his loss
For ever and for ever? No — the cross.
There and there only (though the deist rave,
And atheist, if earth bear so base a slave)
There and there only, is the pow'r to save.
There no delusive hope invites despair,
No mock'ry meets you, no deception there.
The spells and charms that blinded you before,
All vanish there, and fascinate no more.
I am no preacher, let this hint suffice,
The cross once seen, is death to ev'ry vice:
Else he that hung there, suffer'd all his pain,
Bled, groan'd and agoniz'd, and died in vain.[28]

It is a miracle of the grace of God that such a courageous public
testimony to God's hatred of sin and his love for the sinner was read
by thousands upon thousands of sinners all the world over, so that
the gospel as taught by Cowper entered the homes of many who
would never have considered going to hear a preacher.

True and false Christianity

Most of 'The Progress of Error' makes depressing reading because
of the seriousness of the subject and the obvious truth of its
condemnation of a mankind hell-bent in its opposition to God. In
Cowper's next poem, 'Truth', the poet points out a more positive
way and uses his gentle satire to point out the real Christian from the
Pharisee and hypocrite. Likening the Pharisee to the peacock and the
Christian to the pheasant, the poet writes,

The self-applauding bird, the peacock see—
Mark what a sumptuous Pharisee is he!
Meridian sun-beams tempt him to unfold
His radiant glories, azure, green, and gold;
He treads as if some solemn music near,
His measur'd step were govern'd by his ear,
And seems to say, ye meaner fowl, give place,
I am all splendor, dignity and grace.
Not so the pheasant on his charms presumes,

Though he too has a glory in his plumes.
He, christian like, retreats with modest mien,
To the close copse or far sequester'd green,
And shines without desiring to be seen.[29]

Cowper goes on to deal with the false hopes of nominal Christians who believe that their good works will persuade God to grant them salvation. In so doing he draws amusing, though highly critical, pen-portraits of the Roman Catholic ascetic,

... in shirt of hair and weeds of canvass dress'd,
Girt with a bell-rope that the Pope has bless'd,

and of the Protestant prude who

...half an angel in her own account,
Doubts not hereafter with the saints to mount.

It must have surprised many a reader to find himself condemned with these pseudo-Christians as being worse than an Indian Brahmin.

Joseph Johnson, Cowper's publisher, was a man of radical views who did not hesitate to publish highly reactionary and revolutionary articles. When, however, he read Cowper's original version of the passage about the Roman Catholic hermit, his stomach turned and he refused to print Cowper's words. The poet had described the hermit as 'lice infested', which was too much for the publisher's delicate breeding. Cowper, however, refused to alter the passage informing Johnson that:

No man living abhorrs a louse more than I do, but Hermits are notoriously infested with those vermin; it is even a part of their supposed meritorious mortification to encourage the breed. The fact being true becomes an important feature in the face of that folly I mean to expose, and having occasion to mention the loathsome Animal I cannot, I think, do better than call him by his loathsome name. It is a false delicacy that is offended by the mention of any thing that God has seen fit to create, where the laws of modesty are not violated, and therefore we will not mind it.[30]

For once Johnson proved more stubborn than Cowper and the offending beast was removed from the poem. Cowper, however, attacked the theory of justification by works time and time again in *Poems* and firmly declared in 'Charity':

> No works shall find acceptance in that day
> When all disguises shall be rent away,
> That square not truly with the Scripture plan,
> Nor spring from love to God, or love to man.[31]

Poet of the poor

Whatever else Cowper was, he was certainly the poet of the poor. It was becoming fashionable amongst poets of his day to idealize and romanticize the fate of such people. This reached its climax in the poetry of Wordsworth, whose 'poor' remind one more of the nymphs and dryads of Greek literature than the underprivileged and uncared-for inhabitants of British towns and villages. Cowper would have none of this and described the poverty these people experienced in no uncertain objective terms.

Always one to break a lance for such sufferers, Cowper takes up the name of the popular 'hero' of the day, Voltaire. Here was a man whose praise was on everybody's lips as being a propagator of sense and reason. He was, however, a man who loved luxury and blasphemed God. Cowper compared him with a more sober kind of heroine, the poor cottager who nevertheless loved the Lord. The poet scathingly criticizes this learned man who used the Bible as a joke-book until he happened to be ill, when he suddenly became temporally 'pious'. According to Cowper, Voltaire died 'smothered in flattery and praised to death'. On the other hand:

> Yon cottager who weaves at her own door,
> Pillow and bobbins all her little store,
> Content though mean, and chearful, if not gay,
> Shuffling her threads about the live-long day,
> Just earns a scanty pittance, and at night
> Lies down secure, her heart and pocket light;
> She for her humble sphere by nature fit,
> Has little understanding, and no wit,

Receives no praise, but (though her lot be such,
Toilsome and indigent) she renders much;
Just knows, and knows no more, her bible true,
A truth the brilliant Frenchman never knew,
And in that charter reads with sparkling eyes,
Her title to a treasure in the skies.
Oh happy peasant! Oh unhappy bard!
His the mere tinsel, her the rich reward;
He prais'd perhaps for ages yet to come,
She never heard of half a mile from home;
He lost in errors his vain heart prefers,
She safe in the simplicity of hers.[32]

Cowper is seldom one-sided and after explaining how hard it is for his own class to 'enter in at the straight gate' he says,

...the silver trumpet's heav'nly call,
Sounds for the poor, but sounds alike for all,

and points out that God has his chosen ones even 'upon the topmost bough', referring to his dear old school friend Lord Dartmouth who 'wears a coronet and prays'.

Cowper's view of trade and commerce

In *Poems* Cowper has much to say about the worldwide spread of trade and commerce which played such a prominent part in the optimistic outlook of Britain's foreign policy during Hanoverian times. On the whole Cowper shared this optimism and saw commerce as an agent to be used in preparing the world for Paradise Regained. He saw commerce as a means of worldwide sharing, in which all countries of the world, standing as equal parties in trade, could each provide the other nations with goods that they themselves could not manufacture or grow. The West could export manufactured goods to the East, fully conscious that they in turn were dependent on the East for tropical foods, plants and spices.

Again — the band of commerce was design'd
T' associate all the branches of mankind,

And if a boundless plenty be the robe,
Trade is the golden girdle of the globe;
Wise to promote whatever end he means,
God opens fruitful nature's various scenes,
Each climate needs what other climes produce,
And offers something to the gen'ral use;
No land but listens to the common call,
And in return receives supply from all;
This genial intercourse and mutual aid,
Cheers what were else an universal shade,
Calls nature from her ivy-mantled den,
And softens human rockwork into men.[33]

Cowper was extremely interested in international transport and saw the many trading vessels leaving Britain's shores as messengers of God to needy nations, taking the Word of God and Christian culture to countries in spiritual darkness. So he could write in 'Charity':

Heav'n speed the canvass gallantly unfurl'd
To furnish and accommodate a world;
To give the Pole the produce of the sun,
And knit th' unsocial climates into one.—
Soft airs and gentle heavings of the wave
Impel the fleet whose errand is to save,
To succour wasted regions, and replace
The smile of opulence in sorrow's face.—
Let nothing adverse, nothing unforeseen,
Impede the bark that plows the deep serene,
Charg'd with a freight transcending in its worth
The gems of India, nature's rarest birth,
That flies like Gabriel on his Lord's commands,
An herald of God's love, to pagan lands.[34]

It was in this way, the poet believed, that God would gradually transform the world ready for paradise regained. Such a transform-ation would only come to pass, however, when the Word of God was proclaimed worldwide. The Evangelical Awakening and the mis-sionary outreach which was engendered by it were thus very much in Cowper's mind when he wrote 'Hope'. His words here reflect his reading of Whitefield, Wesley, Jonathan Edwards and the Moravian missionaries:

> But above all, in her own light arrayed
> See mercy's grand apocalypse display'd!
> The sacred book no longer suffers wrong,
> Bound in the fetters of an unknown tongue,
> But speaks with plainness art could never mend,
> What simplest minds can soonest comprehend.
> God gives the word, the preachers throng around,
> Live from his lips, and spread the glorious sound:
> That sound bespeaks salvation on her way,
> The trumpet of a life-restoring day;
> 'Tis heard where England's eastern glory shines,
> And in the gulphs of her Cornubian mines.
> And still it spreads. See Germany send forth
> Her sons to pour it on the farthest north:
> Fir'd with a zeal peculiar, they defy
> The rage and rigor of a polar sky,
> And plant successfully sweet Sharon's rose,
> On icy plains and in eternal snows.[35]

However, Cowper's optimism and idealism are heavily tinged with realism, as he notes how traders depart from his ideal and not only use commerce for selfish ends but even go so far as to trade in human beings as if they were mere goods. He thus ends his eulogy of trade quoted above from 'Charity' with the warning words:

> But ah! what wish can prosper, or what pray'r,
> For merchants rich in cargoes of despair,
> Who drive a loathsome traffic, gage and span,
> And buy the muscles and the bones of man?[36]

It is when dealing with the obnoxious traffic in slavery that Cowper is most scathing against his fellow-countrymen. In 'Charity' he pleads with his readers:

> Canst thou, and honour'd with a Christian name,
> Buy what is woman-born, and feel no shame?

Trade in the blood of innocence, and plead
Expedience as a warrant for the deed?[37]

He goes on to argue that a Briton is inexcusable and has deserved the
wrath of God if he supports such an evil trade.

A Briton knows, or if he knows it not,
The Scripture plac'd within his reach, he ought,
That souls have no discriminating hue,
Alike important in their Maker's view,
That none are free from blemish since the fall,
And love divine has paid one price for all.
The wretch that works and weeps without relief,
Has one that notices his silent grief,
He from whose hands alone all pow'r proceeds,
Ranks its abuse among the foulest deeds...
Remember, heav'n has an avenging rod;
To smite the poor is treason against God.[38]

Cowper was passionately anti-colonial[39] and looked with dread
upon the way India was being brought to her feet by the greed of the
English. It became almost a fixed idea with him to open his daily
newspaper and swiftly glance over the headlines to see if there was
any good news from India informing readers that she had been freed
from her European yoke. On this theme, to which Cowper returns
time and time again in his poetry, he writes in 'Expostulation':

Hast thou, though suckl'd at fair freedom's breast,
Exported slav'ry to the conquer'd East,
Pull'd down the tyrants India serv'd with dread,
And rais'd thyself, a greater, in their stead,
Gone thither arm'd and hungry, returned full,
Fed from the richest veins of the Mogul,
A despot big with pow'r obtain'd by wealth,
And that obtain'd by rapine and by stealth?
With Asiatic vices stor'd thy mind,
But left their virtues and thine own behind,
And having truck'd thy soul, brought home the fee,
To tempt the poor to sell himself to thee?[40]

Cowper and the Jews

It had become a fashion in the England of Cowper's day to compare 'the sceptred isle' with paradise and the British nation with the Jews. William Blake was certainly not alone in expressing such thoughts as those contained in his famous hymn 'Jerusalem':

> I will not cease from mental fight,
> Nor shall my sword sleep in my hand,
> Till we have built Jerusalem
> In England's green and pleasant land.[41]

Blake's views of the Jews and paradise were, however, merely symbolic and ethereal. Cowper was far more down-to-earth and expressed a more biblical position in his attitude to the Jews. In fact, in 'Expostulation' Cowper starts with a resounding condemnation of the Jews' rejection of Christ in the words:

> When he that rul'd them with a shepherd's rod,
> In form a man, in dignity a God,
> Came not expected in that humble guise,
> To sift, and search them with unerring eyes,
> He found conceal'd beneath a fair outside,
> The filth of rottenness and worm of pride,
> Their piety a system of deceit,
> Scripture employ'd to sanctify the cheat,
> The pharisee the dupe of his own art,
> Self-idolized and yet a knave at heart.[42]

It is obvious that whenever Cowper writes about the Jews and hopes for their salvation, he always believes that Jews — like Gentiles — can be saved only through faith in Christ. The modern superstition among so many evangelicals that the Gentiles are saved by faith and the Jews because of their race was quite foreign to Cowper. He thus goes on in 'Expostulation' to liken the nominal church in England of his day to the base faith and hypocrisy of Jewish Phariseeism and firmly denounces both the Jew and the English. Although Cowper was a faithful member of the Church of England, he rarely spared his scorn for such Anglican clergy who gave their congregations stones instead of bread and substituted form and ceremony for true Christian experience. The poet could thus write:

> When nations are to perish in their sins,
> 'Tis in the church the leprosy begins:
> The priest whose office is, with zeal sincere
> To watch the fountain, and preserve it clear,
> Carelessly nods and sleeps upon the brink,
> While others poison what the flock must drink;
> Or waking at the call of lust alone,
> Infuses lies and errors of his own:
> His unsuspecting sheep believe it pure,
> And tainted by the very means of cure,
> Catch from each other a contagious spot,
> The foul forerunner of a general rot:
> Then truth is hush'd that heresy may preach,
> And all is trash that reason cannot reach;
> Then God's own image on the soul impress'd,
> Becomes a mock'ry and a standing jest,
> And faith, the root whence only can arise
> The graces of a life that wins the skies,
> Loses at once all value and esteem,
> Pronounc'd by gray beards a pernicious dream:
> Then ceremony leads her bigots forth,
> Prepar'd to fight for shadows of no worth,
> While truths on which eternal things depend,
> Find not, or hardly find a single friend:
> As soldiers watch the signal of command,
> They learn to bow, to kneel, to sit, to stand,
> Happy to fill religion's vacant place
> With hollow form and gesture and grimace.[43]

Abuses in British society

Cowper was also very critical of the connection between church and state and the abuses that went with it. The law of the land specified that only members of the Anglican Church could be given a public office and before taking up such an office, they should take the

Lord's Supper to prove their conformity. This was the notorious Test Act which caused, as we have seen, the future Lord Chancellor Thurlow to walk into church with his hat on, take the bread and wine, and walk out again straight away, his duty done. Cowper wrote of this abuse in 'Expostulation':

Hast thou by statute shov'd from its design
The Savior's feast, his own blest bread and wine,
And made the symbols of atoning grace
An office-key, a pick-lock to a place,
That infidels may prove their title good
By an oath dipp'd in sacramental blood?
A blot that will be still a blot, in spite
Of all that grave apologists may write,
And though a Bishop toil to cleanse the stain,
He wipes and scours the silver cup in vain.[44]

High society in Cowper's days was full of 'emancipated' ladies and dandified men who perverted their own sex in an effort to be thought modern and avant-garde. Cowper, whose ideal in society was the Christian family, thought this fashionable practice highly objectionable and said so in verse. Homosexuals with their painted faces and gaudy clothing were allowed to display themselves at fashionable parties in the name of liberalism. At Westminster a doctor was employed to look after the many cases of venereal disease amongst the pupils, several of whom kept a private whore. In all that he says about this abuse of humanity Cowper is still very much up to date and has a most definite word from God to the late twentieth century.

Hast thou within thee sin that in old time
Brought fire from heav'n, the sex-abusing crime,
Whose horrid perpetration stamps disgrace
Baboons are free from, upon human race?
Think on the fruitful and well-water'd spot
That fed the flocks and herds of wealthy Lot,
Where Paradise seem'd still vouchsaf'd on earth,
Burning and scorch'd into perpetual dearth,
Or in his words who damn'd the base desire,
Suff'ring the vengeance of eternal fire:

Then nature injur'd, scandaliz'd, defil'd,
Unveil'd her blushing cheek, look'd on and smil'd,
Beheld with joy the lovely scene defac'd,
And prais'd the wrath that lay'd her beauties waste.[45]

Lessons from history

Cowper does not merely lift a warning finger at Britain in 'Expostulation' but reminds her by reiterating her long history how gracious God has been to her. It is interesting to note that Cowper, arguing that all history is the history of salvation, stops at the Reformation, which he sees as the culmination of God's grace towards an undeserving country. He then dwells on the purpose of God in creation and the testimony of the saints in history saying:

So then — as darkness overspread the deep,
Ere nature rose from her eternal sleep,
And this delightful earth and that fair sky
Leap'd out of nothing, call'd by the Most High,
By such a change thy darkness is made light,
Thy chaos order, and thy weakness, might,
And he whose pow'r mere nullity obeys,
Who found thee nothing, form'd thee for his praise.
To praise him is to serve him, and fulfil,
Doing and suff'ring, his unquestion'd will,
'Tis to believe what men inspir'd of old,
Faithful and faithfully inform'd, unfold;
Candid and just, with no false aim in view,
To take for truth what cannot but be true,
To learn in God's own school the Christian part,
And bind the task assign'd thee to thine heart:
Happy the man there seeking and there found,
Happy the nation where such men abound.[46]

Science and philosophy

Up to the enlightening days of the Reformation the Roman church had kept learning to a minimum and banned scientific investigation on the whole as a work of the devil. The scholar who used a microscope was criticized for communicating with the 'demons' seen through its lenses and the man who discovered in his telescope worlds which the so-called church knew nothing about was deemed a heretic and committed to the flames or the executioner's axe. The freedom of thought which came with the Reformation and the British Puritans brought with it a revival of science as man became free to read the book of nature.

This thirst for knowledge was carried on into the eighteentth century and we find preachers such as Increase and Cotton Mather, Jonathan Edwards, Isaac Watts, James Hervey and William Romaine showing intense interest in scientific research. This enthusiasm was also shared by John Newton and William Cowper who were, for instance, very interested in the development of electricity as a therapeutic medium. There have been a number of articles and dissertations written on Cowper's deep concern to gain scientific knowledge and this interest is reflected in many of his poems. When writing about spiritual, intellectual and political freedom in 'Table Talk' Cowper says, for instance:

> No. Freedom has a thousand charms to show,
> That slaves, howe'er contented, never know.
> The mind attains beneath her happy reign,
> The growth that nature meant she should attain.
> The varied fields of science, ever new,
> Op'ning and wider op'ning on her view,
> She ventures onward with a prosp'rous force,
> While no base fear impedes her in her course.[47]

It is of course, typical of Cowper to stress that true scientific freedom can only be found and rightly used when not only the body is emancipated but the soul, too.

There is one branch of science that Cowper, however, cannot accept as having the least bearing on true scientific achievement. This is what he calls 'speculative science', which is an attempt to create laws describing the origin and nature of the world, including man and his language, by thinkers who do not think clearly enough and cannot see the hand of God in creation. When writing about these pseudo-scientists who make their own rules into natural laws, the poet sadly says in 'Truth':

Not many wise, rich, noble, or profound
In science, win one inch of heav'nly ground.[48]

Cowper regards this mock science as a fallen philosophy which
serves merely to make man think that he is god of all he examines.
He uses his poetry to call such misguided searchers after truth back
to God's Word and to an awareness that:

The lamp of revelation only, shows,
What human wisdom cannot but oppose,
That man in nature's richest mantle clad,
And graced with all philosophy can add,
Though fair without, and luminous within,
Is still the progeny and heir of sin.
Thus taught down falls the plumage of his pride,
He feels his need of an unerring guide,
And knows that falling he shall rise no more,
Unless the pow'r that bade him stand, restore.[49]

Only when a man comes to an understanding of his own blind-
ness can he hope to bask in the rays of true heavenly knowledge,
which is the crown of all sciences. Thus Cowper goes on to write:

This is indeed philosophy; this known,
Makes wisdom, worthy of the name, his own;
And without this, whatever he discuss,
Whether the space between the stars and us,
Whether he measure earth, compute the sea,
Weigh sunbeams, carve a fly, or spit a flea,
The solemn trifler with his boasted skill
Toils much, and is a solemn trifler still,
Blind was he born, and his misguided eyes
Grown dim in trifling studies, blind he dies.
Self-knowledge truly learn'd, of course implies
The rich possession of a nobler prize,
For self to self, and God to man reveal'd,
(Two themes to nature's eye for ever seal'd)
Are taught by rays that fly with equal pace
From the same center of enlight'ning grace.[50]

Theories of evolution were being propagated by many critics of God's Word in Cowper's day and the poet read their findings with great scepticism and not a little display of mirth. There were also 'Christian' counter-theories of evolution which were worked out to combat those who could not accept the biblical account of creation. Thus the theory found today in many a Christian apologist's book that the world was created as smooth as a billiard ball and only acquired its mountains and valleys after the flood was equally vociferously propagated in Cowper's day. The poet rejected such explanations of God's doings as these were also highly speculative, and science had to do with knowledge and not with guesswork. Thus Cowper wrote scathingly in his very first Christian long poem, 'Antithelyphthora', of the matchless Lady Hypothesis, who maintained:

That Forms Material, whatsoe'er we Dream,
Are not at all, or are not what they seem,
That Substances and Modes of ev'ry kind,
Are but Impressions on the Mind,
And He that Splits his Cranium, breaks at most,
A Fancied Head against a Fancied Post.[51]

Even today, this passage would still be a fine criticism of the 'Christian Scientists'. But the poet puts the 'smooth earth' theorists in the same boat as Mary Baker Eddy's followers as he continues:

Others, that Earth, ere Sin had drown'd it all,
Was smooth and Even as an Iv'ry Ball,
That all the Various Beauties we Survey,
Hills, Valleys, Rivers, and the boundless Sea,
Are but departures from the first Design,
Effects of Punishment and Wrath divine.[52]

'Conversation'

One of the lightest of Cowper's long poems is 'Conversation', in which the poet uses much gentle satire to show how a Christian ought to converse, discuss and reason with his fellow men. He argued that showing 'good breeding' was all very well in conversation but it was no substitute for the conversation of born-again believers. He thus told his readers to:

> Admit it true, the consequence is clear,
> Our polished manners are a mask we wear,
> And at the bottom, barb'rous still and rude,
> We are restrained indeed, but not subdued.[53]

Cowper makes it quite clear that certain kinds of talk bore him. There is the conversation, for instance, of those who are always moaning about their health. Of such hypochondriacs the poet says,

> Some men employ their health, an ugly trick,
> In making known how oft they have been sick,
> And give us in recitals of disease
> A doctor's trouble, but without the fees:
> Relate how many weeks they kept their bed,
> How an emetic or cathartic sped,
> Nothing is slightly touched, much less forgot,
> Nose, ears, and eyes seem present on the spot.
> Now the distemper spite of draught or pill
> Victorious seem'd, and now the doctor's skill;
> And now — alas for unforeseen mishaps!
> They put on a damp night-cap and relapse;
> They thought they must have died they were so bad,
> Their peevish hearers almost wish they had.[54]

Then Cowper obviously has difficulties in chatting to pipe-smoking companions. Tobacco for him was good as a weed and insect-killer but of little further use. The poet was doubly distressed with tobacco fumes as he was often the companion of pipe-smoking Newton and smoke-inhaling Bull. Cowper used to retire with his friends for quiet conversation to a very tiny garden-house situated behind Orchard Side. The men were forced to do this as Mrs Unwin would not have people smoking in her presence. When Bull and Newton visited Cowper, as they often did together, they would get the poet to sit between them on the cramped tiny bench in the shed, take their pipes out of a little trap-door in the floor and puff away, so that Cowper found himself trapped in the middle, gasping for

The Summer House behind Orchard Side, where Cowper, Newton and Bull retired for conversation.

breath. This was no doubt the kind of situation Cowper had in mind when he wrote of the hazards of talking to a smoker:

> The pipe with solemn interposing puff,
> Makes half a sentence at a time enough;
> The dozing sages drop the drowsy strain,
> Then pause, and puff — and speak, and pause again.
> Such often like the tube they so admire,
> Important trifles! have more smoke than fire.
> Pernicious weed! whose scent the fair annoys
> Unfriendly to society's chief joys,
> Thy worst effect is banishing for hours
> The sex whose presence civilizes ours:
> Thou art indeed the drug a gard'ner wants,
> To poison vermin that infest his plants,
> But are we so to wit and beauty blind,
> As to despise the glory of our kind,
> And show the softest minds and fairest forms
> As little mercy as the grubs and worms?[55]

Cowper found the sneering, flattering, creepy-crawly conversation of the perfumed and powdered beaux of his age completely obnoxious. Of these imitators of dolls and puppets he says,

> I cannot talk with civet in the room,
> A fine puss-gentleman that's all perfume;
> The sight's enough — no need to smell a beau—
> Who thrusts his nose into a raree-show?
> His odoriferous attempts to please,
> Perhaps might prosper with a swarm of bees,
> But we that make no honey though we sting,
> Poets, are sometimes apt to mawl the thing.
> 'Tis wrong to bring into a mixt resort,
> What makes some sick, and others a-la-mort,
> An argument of cogence, we may say,
> Why such an one should keep himself away.[56]

In these more unenlightened times when churches are again opening membership to men and women who adorn themselves like artificial butterflies and commit open sins that baboons would be ashamed of, it is healthy reading indeed to see what a Christian stance Cowper takes against these perverters of the image of God in human nature.

In 'Conversation' Cowper also gives the public speaker and preacher a number of tips so that the hearers will not get the 'fidgets', or their 'patience fail'. The following is just one of many:

> A tale should be judicious, clear, succinct,
> The language plain, and incidents well-link'd,
> Tell not as new what ev'ry body knows,
> And new or old, still hasten to a close,
> There centring in a focus, round and neat,
> Let all your rays of information meet.[57]

As is usual in Cowper's poetry, he starts off by saying how his topic is abused and then goes on to speak about the Christian ideal. The poet takes as his model the biblical account of the conversation of Jesus and two of his followers on the road to Emmaus. For Cowper, no conversation could have been sweeter because it had Christ as its subject. The following extract is rather lengthy but any attempt to shorten it would lessen its impact.

> It happened on a solemn even-tide
> Soon after He that was our surety died,
> Two bosom-friends each pensively inclined,
> The scene of all those sorrows left behind,
> Sought their own village, busied as they went
> In musings worthy of the great event:
> They spake of him they loved, of him whose life
> Though blameless, had incurred perpetual strife,
> Whose deeds had left, in spite of hostile arts,
> A deep memorial graven on their hearts:
> The recollection like a vein of ore,
> The farther traced enrich'd them still the more,
> They thought him, and they justly thought him one
> Sent to do more than he appear'd to have done,
> T' exalt a people, and to place them high
> Above all else, and wonder'd he should die.
> Ere yet they brought their journey to an end,
> A stranger joined them, courteous as a friend,

And asked them with a kind engaging air,
What their affliction was, and begged a share.
Informed, he gather'd up the broken thread,
And truth and wisdom gracing all he said,
Explained, illustrated and searched so well
The tender theme on which they chose to dwell,
That reaching home, the night, they said, is near,
We must not now be parted, sojourn here—
The new acquaintance soon became a guest,
And made so welcome at their simple feast,
He blessed the bread, but vanish'd at the word,
And left them both exclaiming, 'twas the Lord!
Did not our hearts feel all he deigned to say,
Did they not burn within us by the way?

Then Cowper goes on to apply his teaching:

Now theirs was converse such as it behoves
Man to maintain, and such as God approves;
Their views indeed were indistinct and dim,
But yet successful being aimed at him.
Christ and his character their only scope,
Their object and their subject and their hope,
They felt what it became them much to feel,
And wanting him to loose the sacred seal,
Found him as prompt as their desire was true,
To spread the new-born glories in their view.[58]

Nature and its role

Cowper is chiefly seen by his literary critics as a nature poet who delights in Nature for what she is and exquisitely describes her in all her various attractions. They love to quote passages such as Cowper's description of a storm, which is taken form 'Truth':

See where it smoaks along the sounding plain,
Blown all aslant, a driving dashing rain,
Peal upon peal redoubling all around,
Shakes it again and faster to the ground,

Now flashing wide, now glancing as in play,
Swift beyond thought the light'nings dart away.[59]

Another favourite of the critics is where Cowper writes, in
'Hope',

See nature gay as when she first began,
With smiles alluring her admirer, man,
She spreads the morning over eastern hills,
Earth glitters with the drops the night distils,
The sun obedient, at her call appears
To fling his glories o'er the robe she wears,
Banks cloath'd with flow'rs, groves fill'd with sprightly sounds,
The yellow tilth, green meads, rocks, rising grounds,
Streams edg'd with osiers, fatt'ning ev'ry field
Where'er they flow, now seen and now conceal'd,
From the blue rim where skies and mountains meet,
Down to the very turf beneath thy feet,
Ten thousand charms that only fools despise,
Or pride can look at with indiff'rent eyes,
All speak one language, all with one sweet voice
Cry to her universal realm, rejoice.[60]

Such passages are usually quoted completely out of context.
Cowper is in no way portraying or idealizing nature for its own sake,
but using nature didactically to make people aware of God's love for
mankind and the fact that only a truly born-again person can see
nature as she really is. Seen in its proper context Cowper's description of the rain in 'Truth', quoted above, is part of a comparison
between someone who is caught in a storm but reaches a safe haven,
and someone who is assailed by this world but finds peace with God.
After referring to the wayfarer who escapes from bad weather
Cowper goes on to teach that:

So fares it with the sinner when he feels,
A growing dread of vengeance at his heels.
His conscience like a glassy lake before,
Lash'd into foaming waves begins to roar,
The law grown clamorous, though silent long,
Arraigns him, charges him with every wrong,

> Asserts the rights of his offended Lord,
> And death or restitution is the word;
> The last impossible, he fears the first,
> And having well deserv'd, expects the worst:
> Then welcome refuge, and a peaceful home,
> Oh for a shelter from the wrath to come!
> Crush me ye rocks, ye falling mountains hide,
> Or bury me in ocean's angry tide—
> The scrutiny of those all-seeing eyes
> I dare not — and you need not, God replies;
> The remedy you want I freely give,
> The book shall teach you, read, believe and live:
> 'Tis done — the raging storm is heard no more,
> Mercy receives him on her peaceful shore,
> And justice, guardian of the dread command,
> Drops the red vengeance from his willing hand.[61]

Words such as these made historians such as Lecky, Overton and Balleine compare Cowper's evangelical outreach with that of Wesley and Whitefield, but literary critics have, on the whole, remained silent about this important aspect of Cowper's teaching.

In a similar way Cowper never refers to nature without thinking of God's purpose in it and his plan of salvation for man. Nature is God's 'handmaid' to assist her true observers to come to an awareness of God. Cowper writes in 'Hope':

> The just Creator condescends to write
> In beams of inextinguishable light,
> His names of wisdom, goodness, pow'r and love,
> On all that blooms below or shines above,
> To catch the wand'ring notice of mankind,
> And teach the world, if not perversely blind,
> His gracious attributes, and prove the share
> His offspring hold in his paternal care.
> If led from earthly things to things divine,
> His creature thwart not his august design,
> Then praise is heard instead of reas'ning pride,
> And captious cavil and complaint subside.
> Nature employ'd in her allotted place,
> Is hand-maid to the purposes of grace,

By good vouchsaf'd makes known superior good,
And bliss not seen by blessings understood.[62]

One never finds Cowper, however, teaching the heresy that a man can become one with God and enjoy saving communion with him through meditating on nature. The key to understanding nature is only to be found in Scripture. Thus Cowper writes in 'Retirement':

> The cloud-surmounting alps, the fruitful vales,
> Seas on which ev'ry nation spreads her sails,
> The sun, a world whence other worlds drink light,
> The crescent moon, the diadem of night,
> Stars countless, each in his appointed place,
> Fast-anchor'd in the deep abyss of space—
> At such a sight to catch the poet's flame,
> And with a rapture like his own exclaim,
> These are thy glorious works, thou source of good,
> How dimly seen, how faintly understood! —
> Thine, and upheld by thy paternal care,
> This universal frame, thus wond'rous fair;
> Thy pow'r divine and bounty beyond thought, —
> Ador'd and prais'd in all that thou hast wrought.
> Absorbed in that immensity I see,
> I shrink abased, and yet aspire to thee;
> Instruct me, guide me to that heav'nly day,
> Thy words, more clearly than thy works display,
> That while thy truths my grosser thoughts refine,
> I may resemble thee and call thee mine.[63]

Nor could Cowper be condemned for writing about the old creation to the detriment of the new. When the poet speaks about 'God's works' he does not isolate God's work in Christ in creation from God's work in Christ in redemption. He relates both to the new world after the dissolution. For example, in 'Hope', after dealing with the miracle of conversion in which souls are re-created for an earth-transcending eternity with God, he goes on to say,

> These are thy glorious works, eternal truth,
> The scoff of wither'd age and beardless youth,

These move the censure and illib'ral grin
Of fools that hate thee and delight in sin:
But these shall last when night has quench'd the pole,
And heav'n is all departed as a scroll:
And when, as justice has long since decreed,
This earth shall blaze, and a new world succeed,
Then these thy glorious works, and they that share
That Hope which can alone exclude despair,
Shall live exempt from weakness and decay,
The brightest wonders of an endless day.[64]

Cowper believed most strongly, however, that nature was one of man's greatest blessings on earth. Seen through redeemed eyes it was a foretaste of glory to come, a veritable Eden. In 'Retirement' Cowper tells his unsaved readers :

To thee the day-spring and the blaze of noon,
The purple evening and resplendent moon,
The stars that sprinkled o'er the vault of night,
Seem drops descending in a show'r of light,
Shine not, or undesired and hated shine,
Seen through the medium of a cloud like thine:
Yet seek him, in his favour life is found,
All bliss beside, a shadow or a sound:
Then heav'n eclipsed so long, and this dull earth
Shall seem to start into a second birth,
Nature assuming a more lovely face,
Borrowing a beauty from the works of grace,
Shall be despised and overlook'd no more,
Shall fill thee with delights unfelt before,
Impart to things inanimate a voice,
And bid her mountains and her hills rejoice,
The sound shall run along the winding vales,
And thou enjoy an Eden ere it fails.[65]

A triumphant faith

Cowper's expressions of faith in the *Poems* are certainly his own. It is also just as certain that, unlike the picture of Cowper usually presented to the public, the poet's first volume presents a faith which is triumphant in suffering and optimistic in outreach. Summing up the teaching in his poem 'Truth' and referring back to the start of the poem, where the poet stresses that he is writing about his own experience, Cowper says,

> Since that dear hour that brought me to thy foot,
> And cut up all my follies by the root,
> I never trusted in an arm but thine,
> Nor hop'd, but in thy righteousness divine:
> My pray'rs and alms, imperfect and defil'd,
> Were but the feeble efforts of a child,
> Howe'er perform'd, it was their brightest part,
> That they proceeded from a grateful heart:
> Cleans'd in thine own all-purifying blood,
> Forgive their evil and accept their good;
> I cast them at thy feet — my only plea
> Is what it was, dependence upon thee;
> While struggling in the vale of tears below,
> That never fail'd, nor shall it fail me now.[66]

However much one twists and turns this passage and however often Cowper might have tasted despair, this poem shows that, in 1782 at least, the poet knew in whom he had believed and was fully persuaded that God was able to keep him in the faith.

Shorter poems

Cowper was in his element writing longer poems in which he could develop his theme at leisure. He used to liken writing to going for a walk with a dear friend, commenting on the things that drew his attention on the way. So he tended to 'turn up his nose' at short poems.[67] Nevertheless there are some real gems to be found amongst the shorter pieces of verse in Cowper's first volume. In fact, it is these shorter poems that tend to attract the interest of the critics, rather than the so-called longer 'moral satires'. Many of these short poems have been commented on in previous chapters and they are mainly poems which were sent to friends without any thought of having them published. A number resemble fables and teach

Christian truths through the behaviour of insects, birds and animals.
Cowper had expressed a longing in 'Charity' that:

> Relenting forms would lose their pow'r and cease,
> And ev'n the dipt[68] and sprinkled, live in peace;
> Each heart would quit its prison in the breast,
> And flow in free communion with the rest.[69]

He went on in his shorter poems to tell tales of harmony (imaginary
and otherwise) found in nature, and urge his fellow-Christians to
live in similar harmony.

Typical of such fables is the story of 'The Nightingale and the
Glow-Worm', who came to the decision that 'singing' and 'glowing' were two equal gifts and consequently were prepared to
harmonize them in peace. Cowper relates this to church divisions:

> Hence jarring sectaries may learn,
> Their real int'rest to discern:
> That brother should not war with brother,
> But sing and shine by sweet consent,
> 'Till life's poor transient night is spent,
> Respecting in each other's case
> The gifts of nature and of grace.

Several of these fables in verse are translations from the Latin of
Cowper's former schoolmaster, Vincent Bourne. These are very
freely translated and adapted to contain more Christian teaching.
The way Cowper deals with classic but pagan authors is illustrated
by his rendering of *Horace,* Book 2, 10th Ode. After translating
faithfully Horace's view of a moral life which avoids extremes,
Cowper adds his own thoughts in an appendix entitled 'A Reflection
on the Foregoing Ode',where he asks,

> And is this all? Can reason do no more
> Than bid me shun the deep and dread the shore?
> Sweet moralist! afloat on life's rough sea
> The christian has an art unknown to thee;
> He holds no parley with unmanly fears,
> Where duty bids he confidently steers,
> Faces a thousand dangers at her call,
> And trusting in his God, surmounts them all.

Biographically speaking, one of the shorter poems is of special interest. This is 'Verses Supposed to be Written by Alexander Selkirk', which begins with the well-known lines:

I am monarch of all I survey,
My right there is none to dispute.

Cowper's fellow-poets have ridiculed this poem for being 'little above the level of a boy's recitation', and 'commonplace'.[70] Norman Nicholson says dogmatically, 'It is not poetry,' and Wordsworth makes laborious fun of its language.[71] Be that as it may, this poem has proved to be one of the most often read of Cowper's and it is still to be found in many anthologies of British verse.

In the poem Cowper puts himself into the shoes of the man who came to be Daniel Defoe's prototype for his shipwrecked Robinson Crusoe. Little as the critics respect the poetic feeling and message Cowper is striving to express in the poem, they nevertheless emphasize the biographical importance of the poem. They see it as a wonderful opportunity to psychoanalyse Cowper and find out about his own view of his life.

Cowper has Selkirk say,

I am out of humanity's reach,
I must finish my journey alone,
Never hear the sweet music of speech;
I start at the sound of my own.
The beasts, that roam over the plain,
My form with indifference see;
They are so unacquainted with man,
Their tameness is shocking to me.

This has commentators drawing a host of comparisons. Olney is Cowper's desert island, on which he is marooned with sock-darning Mrs Unwin as his Man Friday. He feels deserted by all his friends and God and even the animals ignore him. Thus the myth is spread with religious fervour that Cowper felt he was a recluse forsaken both by man's fellowship and God's mercy.

The poem, however, in no way reflects such a morbid picture of Cowper's mental, spiritual and physical state. Whatever else Cowper felt he lacked, it was never necessary for him to complain of a lack of friends — neither amongst humans nor animals. He was blessed with a host of loved ones who were devoted to him and he to them. Nor is there any trace of spiritual hopelessness in this poem. Critics have an uncanny knack of not quoting it in full.[72] If they did, they would find that the poem tells quite a different story and closes with these beautiful lines of trust and hope in times of loneliness:

> But the sea fowl is gone to her nest,
> The beast is laid down in his lair,
> Ev'n here is a season of rest,
> And I to my cabbin repair.
> There is mercy in ev'ry place,
> And mercy, encouraging thought!
> Gives even affliction a grace,
> And reconciles man to his lot.

There was one big difference between Alexander Selkirk and William Cowper. Selkirk's main problem on his island was not having a fellow human-being to talk to. He was out of humanity's reach. Cowper's trouble was that, at times, he felt he could not commune with God. God was out of his reach. Indeed, he felt rejected by God. Whenever the poet was in such a state of spiritual loneliness, however, he would repair to his 'cabbin'. This was a tiny shed at the back of the house which he called his 'verse factory'. There he would write of his calling to 'mend mankind'[73] and it was there that God gave him the grace to be reconciled to his lot and also, on numerous occasions, gave him a new sense of trust and assurance. This is why Cowper always argued that a soul could only grow in grace when performing the tasks that God had provided him to do. This is perhaps why Cowper decided to call the second volume he was preparing *The Task*.

11.
Second spring

The four years that separated Cowper's completion of *Poems* from his publication of the *Task* found him in far better spirits than he had been for almost a decade. He had done most of his work for his first volume in the long dark hours of the winter and it has become traditional for biographers to call the following period Cowper's Second Spring.[1] Writing to Lady Hesketh, with whom he was once again in close contact the poet wrote, 'We are all grown young again, and the days that I thought I should see no more are actually returned.'[2] Cowper was a ripe fifty-four-year-old when he wrote that.

The reasons for this new lease of life were that Cowper was now firmly convinced of his calling as a Christian poet, he had begun once again to correspond with the friends of his youth and he was making new friends who brought him great happiness.

Renewing old friendships

Cowper had now no need to worry about criticism from his own family circle for not practising a profession. Most of the Cowpers and Madans had such close ties with literary men and women that it was deemed an honour for them to have a poet of standing in the family. In fact, the more Cowper was recognized as a poet, the more his family wished to take up contact with him again. This was especially true of Lady Hesketh but also of Mrs Cowper, the poet's Evangelical cousin who was closely in touch with Newton in

London and was anxious to regain fellowship with Cowper. The poet's illness in the early seventies and his verse condemning the activities of Martin Madan (Mrs Cowper's brother and Lady Hesketh's cousin) had done much to strain family connections and Cowper was happy to resume correspondence with them.

Cowper had also often thought of the friends he had lost on becoming a Christian but, with the exception of Joseph Hill, he had not kept in touch with them. This was partly because their interests were now very different from his own, and partly because many of them had reached great heights in their various spheres and Cowper had always felt himself a nobody, as he had told Thurlow when both young men were 'giggling and making giggle' at his Uncle Ashley's home in London.

Of all his old non-Christian friends the one Cowper appeared to miss the most was Thurlow, who was now Lord Chancellor, as Cowper had foreseen. As Cowper and Thurlow had last seen each other when Cowper was contemplating suicide in his rooms at the Inner Temple, the poet was most eager to give the Lord Chancellor a more positive picture of himself and what God had done for him. He therefore forwarded Thurlow a copy of *Poems*, accompanied by a most cautious and even stiffly formal letter, signing himself, 'Your Lordship's Faithful and most obedient humble Servant'.[3]

It is obvious that Cowper longed to take up his friendship with Thurlow where they had left off but under far different circumstances. The poet wished the Lord Chancellor to read his verse speedily, see that its message held out hope for him and reply quickly affirming some form of acceptance of the Christian message. Cowper thus wrote to Joseph Hill, Thurlow's secretary, and to several other friends informing them of his high hopes of a renewed acquaintance. Although Cowper still did not know where Hill stood as far as the gospel was concerned, he made it quite clear to him that he wished to see Thurlow converted.

The weeks went by, however, bringing no reply and Cowper became very anxious. He wrote to William Unwin on 18 March 1782 saying,

> Whether I shall receive any answer from his Chancellorship or not, is at present in ambiguous, and will probably continue in the same state of ambiguity much longer. He is so busy a man, and at this time, if the papers may be credited, so

particularly busy, that I am forced to mortify myself with the thought that both my Book and my Letter may be thrown into a corner as too insignificant for a Statesman's notice, and never found 'till his Executor finds them. This affair however is neither *ad* my *libitum* nor his. I have sent him the Truth, and the Truth which I know he is ignorant of. He that put it into the heart of a certain Eastern Monarch to amuse himself one sleepless night with listening to the records of his Kingdom, is able to give birth to such another occasion in Lord Thurlow's instance, and inspire him with a curiosity to know what he has received from a friend he once loved and valued. If an answer comes however, you shall not long be a stranger to the Contents of it.

By April Cowper was giving up hope of a reply and wrote to Hill that he was very much afraid that Thurlow had read the book but could not accept its message as 'There are not two men upon Earth more opposite upon the subject of Religion than his Lordship and myself, and my volume, whatever pains I may have taken to adorn it with character or to enliven it with an air of cheerfulness, is at the bottom a religious business, a transcript of my own experience, and a summary of such Truths as I know to be the most valuable in themselves, because the most important in their consequences. But they are such as men of his Lordship's principles have ever accounted foolishness, and will to the end of time.' Cowper was most probably not merely thinking of the Christian faith here but also his own attitude to slavery, which he had written against in *Poems*. Thurlow was an energetic advocate of the slave-trade and must have reacted strongly against his old friend's arguments for abolishing it.

Cowper waited impatiently for an answer which had still not come a year later. Many references to Thurlow, however, during this year show how upset Cowper was to know that his very closest friend in his student and lawyer days did not want anything to do with him, nor with the truths he believed. Writing to Hill at the end of a year's wait Cowper referred to an etching which he had of Thurlow hanging over the parlour mantelpiece and added, 'Our friendship is dead and buried, yours is the only surviving one of all with which I was once honour'd.'[4]

Some years later, when Cowper was being hailed as the leading poet in England, Thurlow once again began to correspond with him and amongst the list of subscribers for Cowper's translation of Homer appears the title 'Lord High Chancellor'. Thurlow's letters show, however, that though he was only too pleased to write to Cowper on matters of translation techniques, his old friend's religion could not draw him in any way.

He continues to write poetry

Meanwhile, though still often beset by fears that God had struck him from the list of the elect, Cowper continued to believe firmly in the saving power of the gospel and the need to be saved from the consequences of sin. Whilst Cowper's thoughts were with a number of his old friends and his prayers for their conversion, he heard a story, probably from Matthew Powley in Dewsbury, telling of the extraordinary conversion and death of a Yorkshire miner. Cowper was so struck by the divine intervention shown by this testimony that he turned it into verse and sent it to John Wesley's *Arminian Magazine*, which published it in the June 1783 issue.

A Tale, Founded on a Fact, which Happened in January, 1779

> Where Humber pours his rich commercial Stream,
> There dwelt a Wretch, who Breath'd but to Blaspheme.
> In subterraneous Caves his Life he led,
> Black as the Mine in which he wrought for Bread.
> When on a day, Emerging from the Deep,
> A Sabbath day — such Sabbaths thousands keep—
> The Wages of his Weekly Toil he bore
> To Buy a Cock, whose Blood might win him more.
> As if the Noblest of the Feather'd Kind
> Were but for Battle and for Death design'd,
> As if the Consecrated Hours were meant
> For Sport to Minds on Cruelty intent.
> It chanced — such Chances Providence Obey—
> He met a Fellow Lab'rer on the Way,
> Whose Heart the same Desires had once inflam'd
> But now the Savage Temper was reclaim'd.
> Persuasion on his Lips had taken Place,
> (For All Plead well who Plead the Cause of Grace).

His Iron Heart with Scripture he Assail'd,
Wooed him to hear a Sermon and prevail'd.
His faithfull Bow the Mighty Preacher drew,
Swift as the Lightning Glimpse his Arrows flew:
He wept, he trembled, cast his Eyes around
To find a worse than he, but none he found,
He felt his Sins, and wonder'd he should feel,
Grace made the Wound, and only Grace could Heal.
Now farewell Oaths and Blasphemies and Lies,
He quits the Sinner's for the Martyr's Prize—
That Holy Day was wash'd with many a Tear,
Gilded with Hope, yet shaded too by Fear:
The next, his swarthy Brethren of the Mine
Learn'd from his alter'd Speech the Change Divine;
Laugh'd where they should have Wept, and Swore the Day
Was nigh, when he would Swear as fast as They.
No, said the Penitent, such Words shall Share
This Breath no more, Devoted now to Pray'r.
Oh if thou seest (thine Eye the Future sees)
That I shall yet again Blaspheme like These,
Now Strike me to the Ground on which I kneel,
Ere yet this Heart relapses into Steel.
Now take me to that Heav'n I once defy'd,
Thy Presence, thy Embrace — He spoke, and Died.
Short was the Race allotted him to Run,
Just Enter'd in the Lists he Gain'd the Crown,
His Pray'r scarce Ended, e'er his Praise begun.

Although Cowper rarely let a day go by without composing or revising some verse his attitude to his poetry was to change radically. Most of the verse included in his first volume was sent to his friends as gifts, or for comments, and he hardly took a step in writing any form of verse without informing his most intimate friends about it. Before his first volume was in print, he had told most of his friends that he was going to write a second one. Now that Cowper was established as a poet his policy was quite different. His letters rarely include allusions to his poems and anyone reading through his correspondence for 1782-1784, for instance, would hardly guess that the writer was about to produce a fairly large volume which was to make him famous. It would seem that Cowper now had a more sober conception of his work after the first flush of success, regarding it as his due service to God. He no longer needed the encouragement from his friends which was necessary when he started out as a poet.

Thus, without making too much ado about it, before Cowper's second volume of poems appeared in 1785 he had already had numerous poems of different lengths published in the *Public Adver-tiser*, the *Westminster Magazine*, the *Theological Miscellany*, the *New London Magazine*, the *Gentleman's Magazine* and the *Arminian Magazine*. Several of these poems were also published in a number of broadsheets and anthologies.

Cowper also sent a poem to the *World* which was not published. The *World* was notorious for its enmity against the Cowper family and in 1790 was brought to court for slander against the already deceased Earl Cowper.[5] The fact that the Cowpers won damages against a newspaper which had slandered a man after his death made legal history at the time.

Friendship with Samuel Teedon

One of the oddest characters to enter Cowper's life at this time was the Olney schoolmaster Samuel Teedon. This person has been ridiculed by most biographers and has been regarded as something of a 'country yokel' whom Cowper kept as a kind of court fool. So, when Cowper turned in his later years to Teedon for help and advice, this is taken by critics as a sure sign that Cowper was mentally ill.[6] This view of Teedon and Cowper is totally wrong.

Teedon came to Olney in 1775 to set up a school for the lacemakers' children at the Shiel Hall. Far from being an ignoramus, he had enjoyed a full theological education, was fluent in Greek and Latin, was well-versed in English literature and had a fair knowl-edge of the French language. Throughout the years Teedon wrote over 126 letters to Cowper and at least sixty-two to Mrs Unwin. We know of seventy-two letters Cowper wrote to Teedon and of seventeen that Mrs Unwin wrote to him.

It was difficult to take Teedon seriously because of his flowery use of the English language, which he had modelled on Hervey's style, and his deep piety, which few took to be genuine. What made Teedon obnoxious to many was the way in which he perpetually scrounged from his neighbours. In this art he had no master and managed to obtain money from the most unlikely sources, chiefly because he was so persistent. Teedon would go up to any person who had any connection with Olney whatsoever and insist that they gave him money, claiming it was their duty to support him.

We know from Teedon's extant diary that Cowper was no exception in receiving such advances, and the poet and two of his cousins made Teedon regular allowances, Cowper donating £7.10s a quarter from his own pocket. Lady Hesketh gave Teedon money on several occasions but at last sent him packing with a flea in his ear. She wrote to a relative about Teedon, in her usual rambling style,

> A man like Teedon with the full use of his eyes, his legs and wings should expect to be maintained in idleness; was he blind or a cripple the case would be very different — but no doubt there are thousands in ye world equally as great objects of charity as Teedon, who yet would never think of asking it, still less in the obstreperous and violent manner he does, pour soul! I confess I wish I knew the man's character and situation, for that I do not, this only I know (at least have heard) that Lord Dartmouth once allowed him £10 a year but withdrew it after a time — now Lord Dartmouth is so good a man, that I think he never would have withdrawn his bounty had he not had some particular reason.[7]

To be fair to Teedon, he was striving to keep a school going under extremely difficult circumstances. He wished to give his poor pupils a good education, employing, for instance, an expert in mathematics to assist him in order to do so. His income did not suffice in any way to cover his own needs and those of his family, not counting the needs of the school. Thomas Wright, Cowper's biographer and the publisher of Teedon's diary, is one of the very few writers to appreciate Teedon's circumstances. Wright ran his own school in Olney so he was able to sympathize fully with his fellow-teacher. In his private notes, kept at the Cowper and Newton Museum, Olney, Wright comments on Lady Hesketh's harsh words and says that Teedon was receiving a mere pittance for his work in the town and ten pounds was nothing to Lord Dartmouth.

Teedon was obviously very fond of Cowper and showed a

tendency, common to all Cowper's friends, to consider himself the closest of all to him. In this connection he proved himself a master of flattery. He told Cowper, without blinking an eyelid, that he had longed to live near the great and famous and now that he lived in such close proximity to the poet his life's wish had been granted.

At first Cowper did not know what to think of the Olney schoolmaster, who often entered his home, clasped his hands and immediately and without invitation prayed for 'the Squire and Madam', as he called Cowper and Mrs Unwin. At times this became rather tedious for Cowper, especially when he was feeling depressed and in no mood to pray, so he worked out a number of excuses for not entertaining Teedon when a visit from him was inconvenient. Teedon would, however, check Cowper's excuses and take the poet to task if he thought that he had not been quite honest. Once, for instance, a servant opened the door to find Teedon standing outside, requesting to see the 'Squire'. Cowper sent word that he was just going out, so he could not ask the schoolmaster in. Teedon pretended to leave but doubled back after a while and again knocked at Cowper's door. It was opened by the poet himself and Teedon told him in mock surprise that he had not expected him to be still at home.

The letters which Cowper sent to Teedon and the schoolmaster's replies are all couched in strong evangelical jargon, such as Cowper's insistence that his plight must be 'watered with prayer and tears'. Literary critics tend to turn up their noses at such language, which would hardly raise an eyebrow in evangelical circles, and find it extreme.

Cowper's friendship with Teedon had its ups and downs but it cannot be denied that the poet gained a great deal of comfort from the schoolmaster's active faith, especially in the 1790s, at a time when Cowper badly needed a believing friend.

A growing friendship with William Bull

Meanwhile Cowper's friendship with William Bull strengthened and deepened. He felt sure that Bull's melancholy was not inherited like his own but the product of Bull's studious life and odd mannerisms. Instead of going for walks in the country, as Cowper prescribed, Bull would gain his exercise by walking along the verges of his relatively small garden. Round and round he would go, working out the mileage by the aid of his watch and the length of his stride. He would then retire for hours to a tiny niche which he had cut in the hedge, allowing room for one tiny chair with barely an inch to spare all round. He had made a slit in the hedge so that he could see the outside world from his cramped quarters, puffing away at his pipe. Cowper thought it was little wonder that his friend became depressed!

Bull himself was caused much anxiety by his pipe, as he knew the habit was bad and encouraged his own son not to smoke. He was gradually able to reduce his smoking to one pipe a day but never gave it up entirely. Cowper felt rather ashamed that he had indirectly criticized his friend in his verse on smoking[8] so he stressed in his letters that Bull was always welcome to smoke a pipe at Orchard Side, an invitation the minister was glad to take up.

The works of the French Quietist Fenelon were being avidly read by Evangelicals in all denominations at the time and Bull was no exception. He then went on to read the works of Fenelon's friend and pupil, Madame de la Motte Guyon. Her Christian verse thrilled Bull, so he passed a volume on to Cowper and asked him to translate the poems into English. Cowper, who loved the French language although he was a thorough Francophobe, thought the verse to be the best French work he had ever read.

However, Madame Guyon's too familiar way of addressing the Godhead and her nihilistic view of man shocked Cowper, so he determined to 'Christianize' such features. For instance, he changed 'Amant' ('Lover') to 'Saviour'; 'mon adorable Epoux' ('my adorable Husband') to 'Christ'; and rendered her view of man as 'worm' instead of 'ne … rien' ('nothing'). In essence Cowper's translation is a re-creation and evangelicalization of Mme Guyon's theology, but much of her fervent passion and spiritual insight has been retained. The poems are a mighty testimony to the magnitude of God and his magnanimous grace, showing that:

He at whose voice heav'n trembles, even He,
Great as he is, knows how to stoop to me.[9]

William Bull waited until a year after Cowper's death before he had the verses published and stressed in his foreword that it would be as ridiculous to suggest that Cowper was a Quietist because he translated Mme de la Motte Guyon as it would be to call him a pagan because he translated Homer. Perhaps Bull felt that there was a real danger of such a misunderstanding, bearing in mind Lady Hesketh's protest that all factions were wanting to claim Cowper as their very own.

The Jones family and Lady Austen

There are many references in Cowper's letters to the Rev. Thomas Jones of nearby Clifton but the two only saw each other about once in three months. Though Clifton was so near it was almost inaccessible from Olney during the winter and rainy seasons because of the derelict state of the road and constant overflooding.[10]

Jones had started his working life as a wig-maker but was later trained by Newton with a view to studying for the ministry. At first Newton found him 'forward and conceited to an extreme', but the young man grew in grace under Newton's supervision.

When Jones was sacked from St Edmund's Hall, Oxford, the main arguments levelled against him were that he was bred to a trade, he was destitute of knowledge of the 'learned languages', an enemy to the doctrines and discipline of the Church of England and he preached in the fields. Jones in his defence admitted that he was of humble origin but claimed that the training he had received under John Newton's care fully made up for this. Jones' tutors all vouched for the fact that he was indeed a good scholar. The court, however, preferred to accept the witness of John Welling, a commoner of St Edmund's, who was of even more humble birth than Jones or any of the six expelled from Oxford at the time. Welling had been given the nickname 'the Infidel' by his friends because of his wicked life, yet his criticism of Jones' robust Christian faith won the day and Jones and his five brethren were expelled for being in essence Bible-believing scholars.[11]

One day in the summer of 1781 the Joneses were visited by Mrs Jones' sister Anna, the widow of Sir Robert Austen, Bart. Lady Austen had been living for many years in France with her husband but after his death she had decided to return to England and look for a place of residence. Lady Austen's name will always be associated romantically with that of Cowper, though this linking of their names owes more to the romantic inclinations of Cowper's biographers than to the sober facts of what actually took place.

According to William Hayley, for instance, the two sisters decided to go shopping to Olney and as they were entering a store opposite Orchard Side they were spotted by Cowper from his front window. Cowper, ever curious to know what was going on around him and impressed with the appearance of the stranger, requested Mrs Unwin to invite the two ladies to tea. The two accepted the invitation and, after their shopping was over, visited Orchard Side. Cowper took some time in coming down from his study to greet them as he was unsure whether he had done the right thing and had become quite shy. Once introductions were over, however, Lady Austen and Cowper found that they had a great deal in common and such was Cowper's interest in the lady that he accompanied the sisters back to Clifton after tea.

So much for Hayley's story. What actually happened was completely different. We know from Cowper's correspondence with Newton that Lady Austen was already known to the two men some time before her visit to Olney. Another letter from Cowper tells how, on the day mentioned above, there was a sudden knock at the door. When the door was opened, it revealed Lady Austen who, without any ceremony whatsoever, invited herself in.[12]

From now on, Cowper had in Lady Austen a friend who was as witty as she was lively and as clever as she was spiritual in her conversation. In less than no time the two were calling each other 'brother' and 'sister', at Lady Austen's request, and Cowper praised the day when he had been led to meet Anna Austen. The poet was happy, too for Mrs Unwin's sake, as she also got on very well with Lady Austen. She was in dire need of such a friend as there were few women of her abilities and talents in the whole neighbourhood. Cowper began to talk of theirs being a threefold cord which could not be broken.

Cowper was soon writing poetic epistles to his new friend in which he stressed the theme of his earlier hymns that dark clouds have silver linings and those who wait in patience on the Lord will gradually see his will developing to the good of his children.

Through Lady Austen, Cowper's acquaintance with Thomas Jones deepened and the Joneses, accompanied by Lady Austen, saw quite a lot of Cowper and Mrs Unwin. At one time, for instance, they all went on a picnic together. Lady Austen's servant helped Cowper's gardener load a large wheelbarrow with food and cutlery and the party made off at noon for the countryside on the outskirts

Mrs Unwin

Lady Austen

of Olney. Late in the afternoon they found a natural arbour lined with ivy and moss in a wood and decided to have their meal there. A board was placed over the wheelbarrow in lieu of a table and the servants, who had already dined under an elm tree some way off, soon got the kettle boiling and tea was served. After tea the party wandered off towards Weston and the grounds of the Throgmorton family. They finally reached Olney by eight o'clock, 'having spent the day together from noon till evening without one cross occurrence, or the least weariness of each other.'[13] Such experiences were the best possible medicine for Cowper as he had had to make the best of his own company for far too long after Newton had left Olney.

Lady Austen was thrilled with Olney. She had been to hear Scott preach and felt his was the very kind of ministry she needed, whilst her love for Cowper and Mrs Unwin knew no bounds. She therefore decided to rent the second half of Orchard Side, which had been derelict for years but now housed Richard Coleman, whom Cowper had adopted as a boy. Coleman was now married but he had never thrown off the influence of alcohol which had been instilled in him in his earliest years and, though still a young man, he was a thorough alcoholic and a great burden on Cowper's nerves, patience and purse.[14]

Visitors to Orchard Side nowadays will notice that several rooms on the east side are decorated with Georgian stucco and wooden fittings of a type superior to the fittings in Cowper's old part of the house. These improvements were probably made at Lady Austen's request, as she planned to occupy the east wing of Orchard Side from the summer of 1782 after first winding up her affairs in London.

As Mrs Unwin did not like writing letters Cowper took up correspondence with Lady Austen whilst she was away in the capital. This proved a difficult task as Lady Austen would weigh every word of Cowper's on a gold scale and read into his letters things that he never even thought of putting in. She also repeated Newton's mistake of putting Cowper on too high a pedestal thus greatly embarrassing the poet.

Cowper decided to write to Lady Austen to dampen her ardour. Later he told William Unwin, 'I wrote to remind her that we were mortal, to recommend it to her not to think more highly of us than the subject would warrant, and intimating that when we embellish a creature with colors taken from our own fancy, and so adorned, admire and praise it beyond its real merits, we make it an Idol, and have nothing to expect in the end but that it will deceive our hopes, and that we shall derive nothing from it but a painfull conviction of our error.'[15] Cowper went over the letter word for word with Mrs Unwin and when both were satisfied that they had been as diplomatic as possible, the letter was sent off. Lady Austen replied speedily telling Cowper that he had 'mortally offended' her. Furthermore, she expressed herself in such a tone that Cowper felt it pointless to write back.

Thinking that was the end of that, both Mrs Unwin and Cowper were sorry to have lost a good friend, although they had found her too energetic and demanding. A few weeks later, however, Mr Jones called to present Cowper with three pairs of ruffles which Lady Austen had promised to make for Cowper before their quarrel. He also learnt that a fourth pair was on its way. Feeling it only right that he should send Lady Austen some acknowledgement, the poet sent her a note with a copy of his book. He informed William Unwin, however, that he did not wish to take up correspondence with Lady Austen again as it was impossible to be real friends with someone so touchy.

Cowper had also heard that Lady Austen was doing a tour with 'a dissipated woman of fashion and a haughty beauty', females of a type he could very well do without. The very thought of Lady Austen visiting Orchard Side accompanied by such belles made him exclaim, 'We will not go into the world, and if the world would come to us, we must give it the French answer — Monsieur et Madame ne sont pas visibles.'[16]

The next lady to visit Orchard Side, however, was no worldly belle but the Evangelical Mrs Jones, who brought a letter from her sister saying that she was on her way — alone. Soon afterwards Lady Austen rushed in full of tears and apologies, giving Mrs Unwin a great hug. Cowper stood there feeling awkward and not knowing what to say or do. Eventually the three were reconciled and Lady Austen outlined her plans. She felt she could not live without the two at Orchard Side and proposed they should buy a beautiful house at the top of Clifton Hill and all live there happily together. Cowper, knowing Lady Austen's lively imagination, did not take this too seriously and decided to wait and see how things developed.

For the time being Lady Austen would stay with her sister and later with the Scotts. Cowper and Mrs Unwin did not ask her to stay at Orchard Side. Such a stay seemed to be inevitable, however, as a few weeks later there was a knock at Cowper's door and outside stood Mr Scott with a swooning Lady Austen in his arms. She had been taken ill during his Thursday evening meeting and had insisted on being taken to Mrs Unwin's. She was put into bed and the next morning got up feeling quite well. She stayed until Saturday but as evening approached again, she went into a 'hysterical fit' and had to spend two further nights at Orchard Side. She then set off for Clifton on the back of an ass as the road was flooded.

A few days later she was back at Orchard Side, accompanied by Mrs Jones and her daughter, with the news that burglars were trying to break into the Joneses' house. The three women spent the night at Orchard Side whilst armed men were sent off to Clifton but the burglars had already fled. The Joneses left the next day but Lady Austen begged Mrs Unwin to let her stay at Orchard Side until her rooms at the Vicarage were ready.

Neither Cowper nor Mrs Unwin seemed to realize that Lady Austen's actions were speaking louder than her words and that she was in love with Cowper. True, Cowper was over fifty years of age, but descriptions of him at this time depict a smart, well-dressed gentleman with light brown hair and a ruddy complexion. He was still in remarkably good physical form as a result of taking long walks in all weather, playing battledore and shuttlecock, doing exercises with dumbbells and pursuing the hobby of archery — besides working long hours in the garden. The poet must have been regarded as a good match for an Evangelical lady who herself reflected his talents and physical stamina.

For the next two years Lady Austen was the constant companion of Mrs Unwin and Cowper. The three sometimes spent their hours in Lady Austen's cramped quarters at the Vicarage; at other times they were all at Orchard Side or they went for long walks together. Lady Austen was very musical so Cowper composed some lovely pastoral (in both senses of the word) songs for her. It was also Lady Austen who encouraged Cowper to write his two most famous poems.

On one occasion, when Cowper was down in the dumps again, Lady Anna told him a true, funny story to cheer him up. It was about a gentleman by the name of John Gilpin who, to save money on his wedding anniversary, sent his wife and family off to the inn where they were to dine in a cheap carriage that had only room for them, intending to follow them on a borrowed horse. The horse bolted and

Part of the manuscript of 'The Diverting History of John Gilpin'

The sofa which, following Lady Austen's suggestion, is mentioned in the opening lines of the *Task*

so John Gilpin's hilarious (for the hearer or reader of the tale) adventure began. Always one for a good story, Cowper began to chuckle and then to laugh. Lady Austen had done the trick! The poet could not sleep for laughing and went over the story in his mind time and time again. Gradually the tale took on verse form and when morning came, the tired but merry poet produced the draft of his 'The Diverting History of John Gilpin', better known now among pupils of English as 'John Gilpin's Ride'.[17]

Cowper soon had the poem published but the demand for it became so great that pirate copies sprang up all over the country and broadsheets containing it were sold in thousands at street corners. Actors recited it on the stage for years and John Gilpin picture books and toys appeared in thousands of nurseries. Sequels to the story, written by many a pseudo-Cowper, appeared both in poetry and prose, some telling of John Gilpin's further adventures and others dealing with Mrs Gilpin. Soon all Britain and even North America were laughing with Cowper — but nobody knew that he was the author as he had published the poem anonymously.

Another time Cowper confessed that he was at a loss for a theme for a new poem. Lady Austen told him that he was so gifted that he could write about anything. Pointing to Cowper's then very modern sofa (still on view at the Cowper and Newton Museum, Orchard Side, Olney) Lady Austen said, 'Write a poem about that.' Cowper followed her advice and starting with that domestic subject, he went on to express his view of the Christian life in what was to become the most read book in the English-speaking world after the Bible and Bunyan's *Pilgrim's Progress*.

Cowper could always write best in the mornings but the two ladies made this task difficult. Mrs Unwin insisted on breakfasting at 10 a.m. whereas Lady Austen was equally insistent that Cowper should wait on her at 11 a.m. sharp and she then kept him occupied for most of the day. The poet found that he could only fit in half an hour or so in the evenings for his poetry. Cowper told Lady Hesketh in confidence that he had had great difficulty writing the *Olney Hymns* because Newton had demanded his attention almost twelve hours a day. Now he complained to her in like manner concerning Lady Austen. He was too much a gentleman, however, to offend Lady Austen by insisting that he needed more time to work.

Lady Austen must have sensed that she was presuming on Cowper too much for in May 1784 she decided to go to Bath for a change of air. Once there she realized that it would be better for all concerned if she did not return to Olney. Cowper wrote to William Unwin some time later to tell him, 'Lady A. is neither returned nor returnable.'[18] There has been much speculation among biographers as to why Lady Austen did not return and it is generally implied that she was 'banished' by Cowper and that their friendship ended in animosity. This can hardly have been the case as after Lady Austen left Olney, Cowper still spoke of her with respect and acted as a legal adviser to help her obtain some inherited property which the trustees insisted on withholding from her.

Continuing correspondence with William Unwin

Undoubtedly Cowper's main source of fellowship and even joy at this time was his correspondence with Mrs Unwin's son, William. In these letters there is seldom a note of complaint, no morbidity at all and very often a note of evangelical fervour and sheer good humour. It was not unusual for Cowper to begin his letters to Unwin with phrases such as, 'We rejoice with you', or 'Nothing has given me so much pleasure as…', or 'I thank you for your letter. It made me laugh.'

Cowper had a very close relationship with Unwin because the latter was the first new friend Cowper made on becoming a Christian and he cherished Unwin not only with the love of a Christian brother but also with that of a father to a son. Unwin, in his turn, looked to Cowper as his tutor, adviser and counsellor in almost everything he undertook to do. Thus there are constant references in the two friends' letters to problems in Unwin's parish concerning keeping the Sabbath, wearing make-up, going to law with one's fellow Christians, how to interpret the Scripture on offering the other cheek and, above all, how to train children.

Cowper, always a keen educator, convinced Unwin that it would be to his children's advantage to educate them himself and kept him supplied with information on books and teaching methods. Throughout the years 1782-1784 he worked on a thesis in verse on education which he dedicated to his friend.

Although Unwin was in demand amongst Evangelicals as a preacher, he did not hesitate to beg a sermon outline from Cowper when needed.[19]

Unwin would write to Cowper about the small things in life which give happiness, not at all ashamed that his friend might think them bagatelles. Once a picture moved him to think of Christ and when he told Cowper this the poet wrote,

> Be not sorry that your Love of Christ was excited in you by a picture. Could a dog or a cat suggest to me the thought that Christ is precious, I would not despise that thought because a dog or a cat suggested it. The meanness of the instrument cannot debase the nobleness of the principle. He that kneels before a picture of Christ is an idolater, but He in whose heart the sight of such a picture kindles a warm remembrance of the Savior's sufferings, must be a Christian. Suppose that I dream as Gardener[20] did, that Christ walks before me, that he turns and smiles upon me, and fills my soul with ineffable Love and joy — will a man tell me that I am deceived, that I ought not to Love or to rejoice in him for such a reason, because a dream is merely a picture drawn upon the imagination? I hold not with such Divinity. To love Christ is the greatest dignity of man, be that affection wrought in him how it may.[21]

Cowper would also convey to his friend every tiny delight, as, for example, when he recounts how he found a bird's nest which provided an illustration of how he regarded his poetry and his home: 'Your Mother and I walked yesterday in the Wilderness. As I enter'd the gate a glimpse of something white contained in a little hole in the gate-post caught my eye. I looked again and discover'd a bird's nest with two tiney eggs in it. By and by they will be fledged and tailed and get wing-feathers and fly. My case is somewhat similar to that of the parent bird. My nest is in a little nook, here I brood and hatch, and in due time my progeny takes wing and whistles.'[22]

Though success and a measure of affluence came Unwin's way, he remained humble and content with life as a parish priest. As he hardly ever published anything, Unwin would probably have remained unknown to the general Christian public and to history if William Cowper had not preserved so many good things about him in his letters.

Problems in the Olney Church

During the years 1781-1785 Cowper wrote to his old regular correspondents apologizing for having neglected them somewhat whilst writing *Poems*. He wrote to Newton, for instance, suggesting that they once again correspond weekly instead of fortnightly as their practice had become. Soon Cowper was complaining that he was writing three letters to Newton's one.

His letters from this period are full of guarded gossip about the state of Olney Parish Church, still pastored — but not for long — by Newton's successor, the Rev. Benjamin Page. It had become a tradition that a local carpenter, Mr Thomas Raban, should take care of all repairs to the church fabric but Mr Page took an intense dislike to him — chiefly because Raban had said he could not stand Page's preaching — and refused to pay him for work done in altering a pew. This caused two factions to develop in the church, one, including the churchwarden and a local government official, taking Mr Page's side and the other defending Mr Raban. The affair took on greater dimensions when sixteen church members died of the smallpox and Mr Page refused to give Raban an order for the coffins although he was the only man locally in a position to make them. This led to a long delay in the burial of the infected bodies.

Raban wasted no opportunity in making several journeys to London to consult Newton on the matter. The latter, perhaps unwisely, took part in the debate and sided with Raban. Although Newton thought that Raban was servile towards those above him and harsh to those he thought beneath him, he expressed a genuine affection for Raban and was concerned for his large family, who relied for their maintenance on work obtained within the parish.[23] After gaining the backing of Newton, Raban made numerous visits to Orchard Side and found a measure of support in Cowper. Thus we find the poet writing to Newton,

> The Curate and Church warden,
> And eke Exciseman too,
> Have treated poor Tom Raban
> As if he was a Jew.

> For they have sent him packing
> No more in Church to work,

Whatever may be lacking,
As if he was a Turk.

Thus carry they the Farce on,
Which is great Cause of Grief,
Untill that Page the Parson
Turn over a New Leaf.[24]

As it became obvious that Mr Page must soon leave Olney —
otherwise the church would split and a great many of the parishioners would join the Baptists and Independents — Scott renewed his
interest in taking over the curacy at Olney and was eventually
accepted by Moses Browne as the new curate. By the time he took
up this appointment, however, a number of the 'serious' who had
suported Newton had already left for the Independent Church,
where they enjoyed the ministry of a number of good men, including
Bull and his pupil Samuel Greatheed. Mr Page went to Ravenstone
but did not stay there long.

Much as Cowper disliked Page, he could not reconcile himself
to the thought of having Scott as his minister. For one thing, Cowper
thought Scott was too avaricious by far and felt that his plan to take
over the Olney Church while keeping his curacy at Weston, along
with other preaching engagements, for the financial security they
offered, was a poor display of trust in God's providence. Newton
was still keen on having Scott at Olney and wrote several letters to
Cowper soliciting his help to make it easier for Scott to gain
acceptance there. Cowper used to tease Newton with various reports
of Scott, such as the one where Scott, mixing up his words, closed
the service by admonishing the congregation to 'open their wide
mouths' (instead of opening their mouths wide) so that the Lord
could bless them.

To add to the troubles in the parish Mr Raban suddenly announced himself to be a preacher called by God and insisted that he
should be officially recognized as Scott's 'deputy'. Mr Page embarrassed Scott even further by taking over a house in Weston and
making it clear to Scott that he would take over part of the ministry
there.

Newton asked Cowper to mediate between the two and sent him
a long list of instructions as to how he should deal with both Scott
and Raban. Cowper declined to mediate at first, feeling he was not

the right man for the job and fearing that Newton's interference might escalate the strife. He gradually gave in to Newton's persuasion and promised to speak to both of them. He felt, however, that the advice Newton had given him might lead to more trouble, so he stressed to his friend that he would use his own arguments and common sense in the matter.

Cowper then had several long conversations with both Scott and Raban, showing a measure of support to the former whilst urging the latter to give up his ideas of forcing Scott to take him on as an assistant. He asked Raban to put himself in Scott's shoes and consider how he would feel if he were suddenly lumbered with an unwanted 'curate'. Raban seemed to give in and promised that he would desist from his intention to preach. Cowper was therefore very surprised when the very next day Raban went to see Scott and insisted on preaching the following Sunday evening. His argument was that the flock at Olney had been used to two services a day on Sundays but Scott could only preach once, as he had to take a Sunday service at Weston, too. Raban also thought that the church needed variety in preaching.

Scott refused to allow Raban to minister but promised to preach three times each Sunday at Olney himself. He was able to make this promise as Mr Jones of nearby Clifton had offered to take the Sunday services at Weston when needed. This promise forced Raban to give up his plan and he assured Scott that he would only preach if and when Scott requested it.

Raban seems to have regarded Cowper's interest in him as a display of friendship and he became a frequent visitor at Orchard Side, often bringing news and gifts, such as a barrel of oysters from Newton. Once in the house Raban would choose a comfortable chair, stretch out his legs to the full, cross them, fold his arms, yawn profusely, say nothing and wait to be entertained. After describing this scene in detail to Newton Cowper drily adds the words: 'This is not always pleasing.'

Questions of prophecy

Raban kept his word about not setting himself up as a rival preacher within the church but accepted a call to a small Independent work at Yardley, a few miles from Olney. William Bull attended the inaugural service and Cowper tells us he questioned Raban very closely as to his calling. The new Independent minister, however, developed a great interest in prophecy and lost many of his supporters for a while by indulging in what was little short of fortune-telling. Cowper informed Newton of this after a visit from Raban in January 1783:

He arrived brimfull of admiration at the wonderfull performances of a certain Soothsayer whom I recollect you mentioned when we saw you at Olney. I do not, I hope, offend against the Law of Charity in my judgment of this man. To say truth I account him rather an object of pity than censure; but as to the Intelligence with which he is furnished it seems to be derived merely from a Spirit of Divination. We know that in old time, persons influenced by such a Spirit were ready enough to bear testimony to the Apostles and their doctrine, but they refused the testimony and rebuked the Spirit.[25] His extraordinary remembrance and application of Scripture therefore do not seem to warrant his pretensions to any higher character than that of a Diviner. An Opinion I am the more confirmed in when I recollect that he is ambitious to be thought an intimate friend of the Angel Gabriel, and that he calls Christ his Brother and God his Father in a stile of familiarity that seems to bespeak no small share of spiritual pride & Vanity. Mr. Raban admired his Interpretation of some scriptures relating to the Day of Judgment, and gave him credit for having placed them in a new light. But in our opinion that Light was darkness, inasmuch as it was derogatory from the honour of the Judge, and contrary to the tenour of every passage that speaks of him in that office. But perhaps I have a heavier charge than any of these to alledge against Mr. Best or at least his Oracle. A Woman of most infamous character, too vile for description, had the curiosity to visit him. He examined her palm as usual, and pronounced her little less than an Angel. He was even so enamour'd of her that he was with...

The letter has been mutilated here, possibly by some relative of Cowper's unwilling that indelicate topics should see the light of publication. Some of his other letters from this period, however, show that Antinomianism was a direct product of the 'modern prophets' (as the poet called them). These preachers tended to believe that they were so close to God that they were above the Scriptures and had a freedom in personal conduct not enjoyed by others of lower spiritual rank.

The subject of prophecy is one to which Cowper returns on several occasions during this period due to its prominence in the minds of certain preachers in the neighbourhood and, indeed, in the thinking of the public at large. He remained most suspicious of claims to prophecy, believing that 'What the God of the Scriptures has seen fit to conceal, he will not, as the God of Nature, publish.' Cowper argued that such 'prophets' tended to draw more from nature as a means of revealing God's will than from Scripture and claimed for themselves a spiritual status unwarranted by God's Word. This conviction led him to teach more and more in his poetry that only a person who is enlightened by the Word of God can even begin to see God's revelation in nature.

Writing to Newton in June 1783 about his own views on the dating of the Last Things, Cowper tells his friend that:

> The day of Judgment is spoken of not only as a Surprise but a Snare, a Snare upon all the Inhabitants of the Earth. A difference indeed will obtain in favor of the Godly, which is that though a snare, a sudden, in some sense an unexpected, and in every sense an awefull Event, it will yet find Them prepared to meet it. But the Day being thus characterized, a wide field is consequently opened to conjecture. Some will look for it at one period and some at another; we shall most of us prove at last to have been mistaken, and if any should prove to have guessed aright, they will reap no advantage, the felicity of their conjecture being incapable of proof 'till the day itself shall prove it: my own Sentiments upon the Subject appear to me to be perfectly Scriptural, though I have no doubt but they differ totally from those of all that have ever thought about it. Being however so singular, and of no importance to the happiness of mankind, and being moreover difficult to swallow just in proportion as they are peculiar, I keep them to myself.

The whole Western world was greatly interested in prophetic speculations at the time, as a number of volcanic eruptions and devastating earthquakes in Italy and Greece as well as terrible storms in the West Indies had caused many to believe that the end of the world was at hand. Both national and local newspapers were full of more or less 'religious' explanations of these phenomena. Even prominent men of the church took up their pens in the debates which ensued and vied with their Independent and lay contemporaries in stretching their imaginations.

The *Northampton Mercury* told the story of a German Lutheran bishop called Ziehen who preached at the Hanoverian Court. This learned divine prophesied to members of the royal family that a great earthquake would start in the Alps, destroy St Gothard and cause the Rhine and three other rivers to disappear completely into a large gulf. Europe would then be divided by a deep canyon, running from Switzerland to Holland and engulfing the Zuider Sea and British Channel, and some 7000 cities, towns and villages would be destroyed. So sure was this church leader of his prediction that he named the very year — 1786 — when this disaster was to be accomplished and he gained a host of supporters all over the world.

Commenting on this fantastic vision of the near future a year before the event was supposed to take place, Cowper adds playfully,

> Nothing in the whole affair pleases me so much, as that he has named a short day for the completion of his prophecy. It is tedious work to hold the judgment in suspense for many years, but any body methinks may wait with patience 'till a twelvemonth shall pass away, especially when an Earthquake of such magnitude is in question. I do not say that Mr. Ziehen is deceived, but if he be not, I will say that he is the first modern prophet who has not both been a subject of deception himself, and a deceiver of others. A year will show.

Though Cowper told Newton in the letter quoted above that he would keep his own views to himself, he nevertheless decided, in the dubious light of such 'prophecies', to give his own account of prophecy and the Second Coming of the Lord in his next volume of poems.

Scott's ministry at Olney

Scott worked hard to establish himself at Olney and, using Newton
as his example, preached and visited regularly and was at all times
available for pastoral talks. It soon became clear that he was exerting
himself too much and was growing harsh, irritable and even angry
in his preaching. He also began to suffer frequently from attacks of
asthma which hindered the impact of his preaching all the more. This
caused William Bull, who was now visiting Cowper weekly, to go
over to see Scott and have a brotherly but firm word with him. He
then returned to Orchard Side and gave Cowper a full report which
the poet recorded verbatim:

> Mr. Bull began — addressing himself to the former
> [Scott] — my friend you are in trouble; you are unhappy; I
> read it in your countenance. Mr. Scott replied he had been so,
> but he was better. Come then, says Mr. Bull, I will expound
> to you the cause of all your anxiety. You are too common; you
> make yourself cheap. Visit your people less, and converse
> more with your own heart. How often do you speak to them
> in the Week? twice — Ay, there it is — your Sermons are an
> Old Ballad, your prayers are an Old ballad, and you are an Old
> ballad too. — I would wish to tread in the steps of Mr. Newton
> — you do well to follow his steps in all other instances, but
> in this instance you are wrong, and so was he. Mr. Newton
> trod a path which no man but himself could have used so long
> as he did, and he wore it out long before he went from Olney.
> Too much familiarity and condescension cost him the esti-
> mation of his people. He thought he should insure their Love
> to which he had the best possible title, and by those very
> means he lost it. Be wise my friend, take warning, make
> yourself scarce, if you wish that persons of little understand-
> ing should know how to prize you.[26]

To make matters worse for Scott the rumour was quickly spread
in the parish that he was an Arminian. This was not true at all but
Scott had protested against 'the Calvinists' in the parish on several
occasions. It is obvious, however, that Scott used the term
sarcastically to denote those who called themselves by that name but
who had become presumptuous, looking upon their adherence to

Calvinism as something which earned them merit in God's sight.[27] There were many such amongst the believers at Olney.

So great were the difficulties experienced by Thomas Scott that though he had striven for years to obtain the curacy at Olney, when he eventually obtained it he was far from happy and was only too willing to leave Olney a mere four years later to take up the chaplaincy of the Lock Hospital held initially by Martin Madan.

It was during Scott's curacy in Olney that he embarked on his famous autobiography *The Force of Truth*, in which he tells of the great help Newton had been in his conversion and calling. The manuscript of the first edition was sent to Newton to be edited but it appears that he merely made a few alterations in theological expressions. Scott was still not satisfied with the work so he asked Cowper to assist him in writing a second edition. Cowper did not alter any of the theological sentiments in the work but found it necessary to make a large number of alterations in the language and style. It is this second version that has spoken to the hearts of so many readers since its publication during Scott's years in his Olney parish.

Scott became well known in the evangelical world because of his *Commentary on the Bible*, which he commenced towards the end of 1785 whilst at the Lock Hospital.

Cowper was always very wary in his attitude towards Scott. The two men visited each other regularly, yet they never got to know each other any more closely than the average student-professor relationship. Nearly all Cowper's comments about Scott are similar to those which a teacher might make about a pupil who has many negative attributes, but who nevertheless shows great promise that something might one day come of him.

The surprising thing is that, although Cowper would pay Scott a call to discuss, for instance, his sermons for the day, he never actually heard Scott preach, as far as we know. This was partly because he found Scott too harsh for words, partly because he could accept no substitute for Newton and partly because he had a fixed idea that God did not wish him to enjoy the privileges of the elect.

When men and women in need of spiritual comfort went to Scott, they would often return disappointed and in a sad spiritual state. Cowper would then arrange for them to pay Newton a visit, to their great benefit. In this way, several who were rejected by Scott found acceptance in Christ through a visit to Newton.

Though Scott's labours at Olney were fraught with difficulties, not all of which by any means were of his own making, one notable event in his ministry claims for him a permanent place in the history of the church and especially in the history of foreign missions. It was under Scott's ministry that William Carey, the pioneer missionary to India, was converted.

Perfectionism

Cowper's letters to Newton during this period still reflect a profound interest in theology and show that in many ways he was less inclined towards leniency than his friend in judging those of other persuasions.

Newton had recommended John Fletcher (1729-1785) to Cowper but at the same time the poet had heard very negative reports of the Methodist from Matthew Powley in Yorkshire. Cowper decided to believe Powley's account of Fletcher rather than Newton's and wrote,

> Mr. Fletcher on his recovery from his late dangerous illness, has started up a Perfectionist. He preached Perfection not long since at Dewsbury where Mr. Powley and his Curate heard him. He told the people that He that Sinned was no Christian, that he himself did not Sin, Ergo had a right to the Appellation. Mr. Powley was so shock'd by his violent distortion of the scriptures by which he attempted to prove his doctrine, that he thought it necessary to preach expressly against him the ensuing Sabbath. And when he was desired to admitt the perfect man into his pulpit, of course refused it. I have heard that he is remarkably spiritual. Can this be? Is it possible that a person of that description can be left to indulge himself in such a proud conceit, is it possible he should be so defective in Self-knowledge, and so little acquainted with his own heart? If I had not heard you yourself speak favorably of him, I should little scruple to say, that having spent much of his Life and exerted all his talents in the defence of Arminian errors, he is at last left to fall into an error more pernicious than Arminius is to be charged with, or the most ignorant of his disciples. When I hear that you are engaged in the

propagation of Error, I shall believe that an humble and dependent mind is not yet secured from it, and that the Promises which annex the blessing of Instruction to a temper teachable and truely child-like, are to be received *cum grano salis,* and understood with a limitation. Mr. Wesley has also been very troublesome in the same place, and asserted in perfect harmony of sentiment with his brother Fletcher, that Mr. Whitfield disseminated more false doctrine in the nation, than he should ever be able to eradicate. Methinks they do not see through a glass darkly but for want of a glass, they see not at all.[28]

Powley went on to write a book against perfectionism and sent the manuscript to Cowper for his comments and advice on publishing. The poet in his turn appealed to Newton for his opinion. Cowper was of the opinion that such a book would have no impact on Arminians because 'Pope John' (i.e. John Wesley) would forbid his followers to read it. He also thought that any believer who was not an Arminian did not need a book to teach him what Scripture plainly teaches about man's sinful nature. Nevertheless he cautiously advised Powley to print.

Newton, however, advised against printing, arguing that it is better to 'preach the truth in love' than enter into controversy. He believed that such heresies as Fletcher's, if left alone, would be forgotten very soon, whereas Powley's book would perpetuate the error by keeping it in the public's attention.

Cowper sent his own advice to Powley but also included Newton's letter on the subject. Powley had hoped that Cowper would revise and edit the work but the poet claimed he was 'indifferently qualified' to perform the task and politely declined.[29]

Influences on Cowper's mental state

Newton always awaited Cowper's letters with trepidation, wondering what kind of a mood his friend would be in. Very often, however, Newton actually encouraged Cowper to write in a melancholy fashion by continually referring to the poet's sporadic conviction of being a castaway — even when he himself had not been thinking on those lines for some time.[30]

Though Cowper loved Newton for his kind attention and prayers, his advice sometimes exasperated the poet. One of these occasions was when Newton told Cowper the story of Simon Browne (1680-1732), believing that the case might help his friend to have a more positive attitude to his own salvation. Simon Browne was a Dissenting minister who experienced great spiritual suffering following the loss of his wife and son and — as the legend goes — after strangling a highwayman! After these terrible experiences, Browne continued to lead a normal life, writing theological works and one of the very earliest English dictionaries, but for one significant fact. He felt that he had been personally rejected by God, who had then taken away his soul and reduced him to the status of an animal. Browne wrote a book called *A Defence of the Religion of Nature,* which he dedicated to Queen Caroline, requesting her prayers for the recovery of his soul. Although Newton seems to have led Cowper to believe that Browne was eventually restored to spiritual and mental sanity, in fact the unhappy minister died in dark despair.

Now such a comparison with Cowper was ludicrous on all counts and could hardly serve to comfort a man of his spiritual convictions. There are really no parallels at all. Cowper had not suffered a similar loss to Browne's, and though he at times felt rejected by God this was far from being a permanent conviction. Cowper never supposed that he had lost his soul or that he had been reduced to the level of an animal. Also Cowper's criticism of the lack of spiritual foresight shown by the royal family was so strong at this time that he would hardly have turned to them for spiritual help! It was, however, the sheer faulty logic of Newton's conclusions that moved Cowper to comment to his friend on the comparison, saying,

> I was not unacquainted with Mr. Brown's extraordinary case, before you favour'd me with his Letter, and his intended Dedication to the Queen, though I am obliged to you for a sight of those two curiosities which I do not recollect to have ever seen 'till you sent them. I could however, were it not a subject that would make us all melancholy, point out to you some essential differences between his state of mind and my own, which would prove mine to be by far the most deplorable of the two. I suppose no man would despair, if he did not apprehend something singular in the circumstances of his

own story, something that discriminates it from that of every other man, and that induces Despair as an inevitable consequence. You may encounter his unhappy persuasion with as many instances as you please, of persons who like him having renounced all hope were yet restored, and may thence inferr that he like them shall meet with a season of restoration — but it is in vain. Every such individual accounts himself an exception to all rules, and therefore the blessed reverse that others have experienced affords no ground of comfortable expectation to Him. But you will say, it is reasonable to conclude that as all your predecessors in this vale of misery and horror have found themselves delightfully disappointed at last, so will you. I grant the reasonableness of it; it would be sinfull perhaps, because uncharitable, to reason otherwise. But an argument hypothetical in its nature however rationally conducted, may lead to a false conclusion, and in this instance, so will yours. But I forbear, for the cause abovementioned I will say no more, though it is a subject on which I could write more than the mail would carry. I must deal with you as I deal with poor Mrs. Unwin in all our disputes about it, cutting all controversy short by an appeal to the Event.[31]

Cowper's conviction that he was unlike anyone else had been strongly with him since his childhood days and has always interested his biographers greatly. This conviction grew deeper throughout his life. It need not, however, be the result of Cowper's inherited malady but owes much to the thinking of his age and is linked with the truly Christian belief that God has a special plan for each member of his creation. This factor has, on the whole, been disregarded by biographers, who have tended to view Cowper in isolation from his contemporaries. Newton, as we know from his letters, often expresed the conviction that 'Never was a case like mine,' and felt that God's dealings with him were unique.[32]

Nor does Cowper's melancholy separate him from the feelings of his fellow men. Historians and literary critics call this age 'the Age of Sensibility' or they use a German term, *Empfindsamkeit*, to describe it. The seventeenth century, they say, was an age of stoicism, whereas the eighteenth century reacted against this by expressing tender feelings of melancholy.[33] Be that as it may, there is hardly a writer of Cowper's day, including Collins, Smart, Swift,

Blair, Hervey, Young, Samuel Johnson and Boswell, who did not express himself in self-indulgent grief or melancholy, or who did not live in constant fear of becoming insane.

It was the time of 'the Graveyard School', in which Evangelicals took a leading part in encouraging people to have thoughts which were 'serious and mournfully pleasing'.[34] Cowper, like Hervey, looked upon this feeling as highly positive and praised writings such as Henry Mackenzie's *The Man of Feeling* which reflected it. Bull often compared his own melancholy with that of Cowper, and Mary Newton experienced something similar. Cowper was thus not merely explaining away his own symptoms when he told the wife of an old school friend that melancholy was the national characteristic.[35]

It cannot be denied, however, that, common as it was at this time to express strong feelings of melancholy, in Cowper's case at roughly ten-year intervals the melancholia took on the form of acute depression. There is much in his letters which might suggest another cause for this than a natural tendency to depression.

A severe epidemic raged in Olney throughout the summer of 1783. Newton was staying with Cowper at the time and became seriously ill, followed by Cowper and Scott. Newton went into a delirium and apparently lost control of his senses, not realizing what he was saying. True to the stalwart Christian character of the man, Newton's speech, even when he was void of his senses, was honouring to God and full of Christian sentiments. Cowper, whose fever reached its height after Newton had left Olney, had been sitting by his friend's bed whilst Newton was delirious and later told him that his feverish ramblings were 'a comfortable evidence of the predominant bias of your heart and mind to the best subjects'. When it was Cowper's turn to be in a high fever, he fought successfully against delirium but became terribly depressed.[36]

It is significant to note that Cowper, who was often prone to attacks of fever, always resorted to laudanum, a tincture of opium, for relief. Apparently Newton, who was also prone to fevers, did not. The poet knew that opium was a dangerous drug but thought that it helped him keep his head when attacked by fevers or severe migraine. It may well be that though opium kept Cowper from becoming delirious its effects on his psyche and conscience produced a deep melancholy which was no less irrational.

If this were the case, we would expect Cowper's conduct to be especially melancholy after taking opium and more cheerful when not under the drug's influence.[37] This is indeed the case, as witnessed by two letters from Cowper referring to the oncoming winter, one written shortly after he had taken opium and the other some time later.

In the first letter Cowper wrote to Newton saying, 'I now see a long Winter before me and am to get through it as I can. I know the ground before I tread upon it. It is hollow, it is agitated, it suffers shocks in every direction, it is like the soil of Calabria,[38] all whirlpool and undulation. But I must reel through it, at least if I be not swallowed up by the way.'[39] Though Cowper boasts in this letter that he, unlike Newton, never goes into a delirium, the language is nevertheless abnormal — even delirious.

A month later, describing his feelings concerning the same winter to Joseph Hill, Cowper is once again cheerful and positive:

> I see the Winter approaching without much concern, though a passionate lover of fine weather, and the pleasanter scenes of Summer. But the long Evenings have their comforts too, and there is hardly to be found upon the earth, I suppose, so snug a creature as an Englishman by his fire-side in the Winter. I mean however an Englishman that lives in the country, for in London it is not very easy to avoid Intrusion. I have two Ladies to read to; sometimes more, but never less. At present we are circumnavigating the globe, and I find the old story with which I amused myself some years since, through the great felicity of a memory not very retentive, almost new. I am however sadly at a loss for Cooke's second voyage, written by himself. Lord Dartmouth furnish'd me with it once, but his books are all at Sandwell, the book in question at least is there, and he I suppose by this time in town. Besides, having no correspondence with his Lordship, I cannot fairly claim a right to trouble him. Can you help me at this plunge? Have you it, can you borrow it, or can you hire it, and will you send it? I shall be glad of Forster's[40] too. These together, will make the Winter pass merrily, and you will much oblige me.

Here there is not a trace of anxiety but a clear pen-portrait of the domestic bliss which Cowper tells us he so often enjoyed — especially in the winter!

Cowper's views on political matters

Although Cowper's correspondence with Newton continued regularly, he was constantly teasing his friend for being so slow to reply. This was mainly because Newton had now become quite famous as a leader of the Evangelicals and was in great demand nationwide not only as a correspondent but also as a visitor and this left him with less time to offer his old friends.

Newton was also becoming increasingly involved with believers in the upper classes and those engaged in politics. We find that his letters to Cowper become increasingly concerned with the political state of the country and deal with a world on which the poet had irrevocably turned his back. This led to some friction between the two in the autumn of 1782. Newton was in touch with some of the leading politicians of the day, whereas Cowper protested that his only source of political knowledge was the newspaper. Newton seems to have interpreted Cowper's lack of enthusiasm to discuss political questions as a lack of patriotism and criticized his friend accordingly.

Cowper was always very considerate towards Mrs Newton and after patching up his quarrel with Newton he wrote to her in November 1782 to put her mind at ease. After writing at length about the fate of poor believers at Olney Cowper ends the letter with a reference to his disagreement with Newton:

> Mr. Newton and I are of one mind on the subject of Patriotism. Our dispute was no sooner begun than it ended. It would be well perhaps if when two Disputants began to engage, their friends would hurry each into a separate chaise, and order them to opposite points of the compass. Let one travel 20 miles East, the other as many West, then let them write their opinions by the Post. Much altercation and chafing of the Spirit would be prevented, they would sooner come to a right understanding, and running away from each other, would carry on the combat more judiciously in exact proportion to the distance.

My Love to that Gentleman if you please, and tell him that like Him, though I Love my Country I hate its follies and its Sins, and had rather see it scourged in mercy, than judiciously harden'd by prosperity.

It would appear from this letter that Newton and Cowper had disagreed when they last spoke together and their reconciliation had come about through letter-writing. Their difference of opinion had arisen because though Newton was more inclined to leniency in matters of doctrine than Cowper, when it came to politics the poet showed more forbearance than his friend could accept. Newton's position was that only true Christians ought to be given posts in Parliament, whereas Cowper maintained that the fact that a minister may have visited the gaming-table or supported the royal party does not in itself make him a traitor to his country or unfit to hold office. The plain fact was, Cowper stressed, that Christian politicians were few and far between and the business of government must go on with the best men suitable for the job at the time. Cowper, therefore, criticized Pitt[41] and his faction (whom Newton tended to support) for being harsh, obstinate and bad-tempered, but praised the spirit of 'British liberty' of those of other parties (such as Fox and Lord North) who showed 'forbearance and lenity' towards Pitt.

Although Cowper would have Newton believe that he was very much an amateur in politics, he had been brought up in the company of, and gone to school with, many of the very men who were leading the country at the time. He was also intimately acquainted with their characters. Cowper probably gained a thorough knowledge of the political ideas of the older members of the government whilst working with them in his days as a lawyer, when he was closely attached to Parliament. Thus he was fully conversant with the politics of Pitt the Elder, remembering that he had at all times sided with the poor and had had the courage to stand up to the king on a number of occasions. His son, however, especially in his days as Chancellor of the Exchequer, angered Cowper by pushing through Acts of Parliament which were directly opposed to the interests of the poor and resulted in increased poverty for the Olney lacemakers.

Typical of these laws was the severe taxation on candles. The Olney poor had to work hours at their lace-cushions, both in the mornings and evenings during the dark winter months, assisted by the light of a candle which was often their only source of warmth.

Inside the lacemakers's cottage

Pitt's reasoning shows how little he understood the plight of the poor. When told that the poor would suffer if the act was passed he denied this, saying that they were too poor to buy candles anyway. The extra half-penny tax which was put on each pound of candles did in fact put candles beyond the reach of of many poverty-stricken workers. According to Cowper, by the time the candles had moved from the manufacturers to the consumers the extra half-penny had swollen to twopence. Without light, however, the poor were unable to work, and so became even poorer. Cowper said that Pitt's reasoning was 'an argument which for its cruelty and effrontery seems worthy of a Nero'.[42]

He was even more incensed a year or so later when Pitt put a 'luxury tax' on gloves. The poor, who were already denied the warmth of a candle, would now not be able to warm their hands with gloves. Once again Pitt showed how little he knew of the circumstances of the poor when he argued that gloves were a mere luxury which could easily be dispensed with. Writing to Newton in June 1785, Cowper told his friend that he could foresee the day when a tax would be set on breeches because theoretically one could do without them and the poor would be unable to afford them anyway! Cowper's criticism of Pitt for deviating from the course set by his father in regard to the poor seems to have borne fruit as several influential followers of Pitt — friends of Newton — afterwards sent Cowper generous donations to distribute amongst the Olney lace-workers.

Although Cowper belonged to the same theological school as the Evangelicals who were backing Pitt, he did not see eye to eye with them on all social matters. The Evangelicals were pioneering inoculation amongst the poor in Britain and huge sums of money were being raised for this purpose. Cowper, who was careful to protect the rights of the poor, disagreed with the way inoculation was being practised and outlined his protest in a letter written to Lady Hesketh on 1 January 1788:

> The Small Pox has done, I believe, all that it has to do at Weston, and Hannah[43] seems now secure. Jove has commanded sometimes Eurus and sometimes Zephyrus to puff forcibly at one end of the town so as to sweep the street even to the other, and the consequence is that we are all sweet again. None have died but our Samuel's eldest boy,[44] though

old folks and even women with child have been inoculated. We talk of our freedom, and some of us are free enough, but not the poor. Dependent as they are upon Parish bounty they are sometimes obliged to submit to impositions which perhaps in France itself could hardly be parallell'd. Can man or woman be said to be free, who is commanded to take a distemper sometimes at least mortal, and in circumstances most likely to make it so? No circumstance whatever was permitted to exempt the Inhabitants of Weston. The old as well as the young, and the pregnant as well as they who had only themselves within them, have been all inoculated. Were I ask'd Who is the most arbitrary Sov'reign on earth? I should answer — neither the King of France, nor the Grand Signor, but an Overseer of the Poor in England.

Sydney Smith constantly urged the Evangelicals in Parliament, amongst them some good friends of Cowper, not to make one law for the poor and another for the rich.[45] Sadly this great politician rejected the gospel because he did not see Evangelicals living according to it. If he had read Cowper's works, he would have found a man with a heart both for the gospel and for the poor and one who constantly argued that the law of the land should treat rich and poor alike.

Cowper was always at his most political when reviewing Britain's colonial policy. He could not tolerate the arrogance of the government in sending men out to the so-called undiscovered areas of the world and claiming them as British territory. At the time he was busy reading Captain Cook's voyages, in which the famous Yorkshireman set up flag after flag in lands belonging to others, claiming them as the property of King George.[46] The poet was especially incensed at Britain's conduct in India. The East India Company, instead of remaining a trading company, claimed absolute political supremacy over millions of Indians and Cowper believed this was blatant tyranny. Writing to Newton in January 1784 concerning the new charter for the company, he says,

It constitutes them a Trading Company and gives them an exclusive right to traffic in the East Indies. But it does no more. It invests them with no Sovereignty, it does not convey to them the royal prerogative of making war and peace, which the King cannot alienate if he would. But this prerogative they have exercised, and forgetting the terms of their institution have possessed themselves of an immense territory, which they have ruled with a rod of Iron, to which it is impossible they should ever have a right, unless such an one as it is a disgrace to plead, the right of conquest. The Potentates of this Country they dash in pieces like a potter's vessel as often as they please, making the happiness of 30 millions of mankind a consideration subordinate to that of their own emolument, oppressing them as often as it may serve a lucrative purpose, and in no instance that I have ever heard, consulting their interest or advantage.

Needless to say, Cowper hoped fervently, but in vain, that the charter would not be renewed. He laid the chief blame for the irresponsible colonialism at the feet of the king, whom he criticized openly in many letters to Newton. For example, Cowper writes, 'The patronage of the East Indies will be a dangerous weapon in whatever hands. I had rather however see it lodged anywhere than with the Crown. In that event I should say adieu for ever to every hope of an uncorrupt representation, and consequently to every hope of constitutional liberty for the Subject.'

Such radical thoughts on Cowper's part gradually leaked out so that in time prominent members of the movement for independence in America approached him for help in their cause. However, the poet regarded the move for independence in the American colonies in a very different light. There it was a question of brother fighting brother, not of the oppressed natives throwing off their yoke. Indeed, Cowper believed the British in America already enjoyed, before the revolution, a freedom such as those in the mother country could only dream of and he could not therefore understand their fight for liberty.

Newton's relationships with members of other churches

Newton had now won a great measure of support from his church in London and was very happy there. 'How unlike the gaping, staring, sleepy mortals who make the bulk of our auditory at Olney',[47] he had told Cowper on settling down in his new church. He also told his friend that the congregation was 'the flower and picking of all the denominations of professors'.[48] This was literally true, as many believers from various churches left them and began to attend the services at St Mary's instead. Many of these people came from John Wesley's followers in London.

Newton still sometimes found himself the object of criticism but when it came, it was mostly from Independents and Baptists. He had always been a friend of Dissenting churches provided they were true to their Lord. William Bull, for instance, treasured Newton's advice so greatly that when he founded an Independent college he invited Newton, though he was an Anglican, to draw up its rules.[49] So little was Newton interested in denominational allegiance among all who were truly born-again Christians, that he could write to a Scots friend, 'I pray the Lord bless you and all who love his name in Scotland, whether Kirk, Circus, Relief, Burghers, Antiburghers, Independents, Methodists, or by whatever name they chose to be called. Yea, if you know a Papist, who sincerely loves Jesus, and trusts in him for salvation, give my love to him.'[50] Oddly enough, such dealings with Dissenters were resented by many in their own circles who had difficulty in accepting the Church of England as a true church. They believed that if Newton were a true Christian, he should leave the Anglican Church. They even accused him of having ulterior motives in belonging to the Church of England and insincerity in his allegiance to her.[51]

The Independents criticized Newton because of his views on church government and the Baptists naturally resented Newton's doctrine of baptism. It was becoming more and more common for Baptist churches to refrain from sharing fellowship with other believers and practise a closed communion, allowing only Baptists to take part in the Lord's Supper with them. Often they would only allow what they called 'the local church' to share communion fellowship and shut out other believers, even in their own denomination, from the Lord's Table.

The Olney Baptists, with whom Newton still had good fellowship, at first withstood pressure to become 'closed' from leaders such as Andrew Fuller (1754-1815), but gradually relented during the latter part of the eighteenth century. This caused great unrest in the many interdenominational movements which were coming into being at the time, as what such people as Fuller were really saying was that non-Baptists were at best second-class believers.

William Carey, who had become a Baptist in 1783, argued against this move and when he became a missionary in India he worked closely with Anglicans, such as the Rev. David Brown, and shared the Lord's Table with them. Fuller, who was one of three members of the Home Board, eventually persuaded Carey to toe the line even though Fuller himself canvassed widely amongst Anglicans to help finance Carey's work. Indeed it was a strong Anglican lobby in Parliament that kept India open for Carey's mission.

Both Newton and Cowper regarded any shutting out of fellow-believers because of views on church order or baptism as bigotry in the extreme. So when Wilson, Cowper's barber, decided conclusively that he would join the Baptists, Cowper felt compelled to warn him against what he thought was their narrowness.

Newton reacted in print to Dissenting criticism against him and published his *Apology* (in the form of several letters to an Independent brother) to show how he had become an Anglican and why he could continue as such with an easy conscience. Newton's *Apology* is still in print[52] and serves as an excellent statement of an Evangelical Anglican's point of view. In it he maintains that he finds that the Anglican Church reflects the New Testament church order far more than any Congregational church he knows of and he criticizes the Baptists for confusing John's baptism with Christian baptism. Newton writes full of brotherly love for his Dissenting brethren, at the same time admitting that he is well aware of the faults inherent in the Anglican Church. The whole work is a plea for tolerance.

When Cowper received the manuscript from Newton, he replied in glowing terms:

> I return you many thanks for your Apology which I have read with great pleasure. You know of old that your stile always pleases me, and having in a former letter given you the reasons for which I like it, I spare you now the pain of a repetition. The Spirit too in which you write, pleases me as much... To assert and to prove that an enlighten'd Minister of the Gospel may without any violation of his conscience and even upon the ground of prudence and propriety, continue in the Establishment — and to do this with the most absolute composure, must be very provoking to the dignity of some dissenting Doctors. And to nettle them still the more, you in a manner impose upon them the necessity of being

silent, by declaring that you will be so yourself. Upon the whole however I have no doubt that your Apology will do good. If it should irritate some who have more zeal than knowledge, and more of bigotry than of either, it may serve to enlarge the views of others and to convince them that there may be Grace, Truth and Efficacy in the Ministry of a Church, of which They are not members. I wish it success, and all that attention to which both from the nature of the subject and the manner in which you have treated it, it is so well entitled.[53]

Relationship with Newton at this period

It cannot be denied that a detailed analysis of Newton's correspondence with Cowper reveals a movement in theological and pastoral content away from the intimacy and fellowship of former years.

On comparing Scott's letters and sermons with those of Newton one finds that those of the former, though devotional, are more analytical and scholarly than personal and pastoral. They smack of the lecture hall rather than the pulpit. Newton, however, could identify himself fully with the needs of his hearers and readers and in his sermons and letters he meets them on a very personal and pastoral level.

Newton's letters to Cowper, though loving and kind and often equal to Cowper's in style and composition, nevertheless lack something of this personal depth of fellowship and understanding which is shown in his letters to other friends. This is because Newton was unable to put himself, try as he might, in Cowper's position.

The reason for this goes back to Cowper's illness of 1773 and shows how alike Cowper and Newton really were. From that date onwards Cowper was sporadically visited with times of despondency and doubt regarding his salvation. Newton had never come to terms with Cowper's illness of that time and even twenty-seven years afterwards, he still thought of his friend in terms of one who had lived in full communion with God but was now in utter darkness. As he could not accept the thought of a child of God being left in utter darkness he constantly plagued himself with the thought that Cowper was indeed lost.

We can see in their letters that just as hopes and fears concerning his own salvation alternate in Cowper's letters, so hopes and fears concerning his friend's salvation are reflected in those of Newton. The big difference, however, is that Cowper, at least up to the middle-nineties, had several marvellous experiences of the Lord's presence and was able to testify time and time again to his faith in Christ — whatever happened to him.

Newton himself gave a marvellous testimony to Cowper's faith in 1773 in a sermon preached at St Mary's after Cowper's death. He said, 'I remember one time we were walking together in a very deep snow; the weather was remarkably severe. He desired me to stop and I observed the sweat drop from his face, occasioned by the agony of his mind: he said he knew the Lord was a Sovereign and had a right to do with him what He pleased, and that if he knew that by holding out a finger he could remove what he then felt, he would not do it unless he knew that it were the will of God.' Newton goes on, however, to describe Cowper twenty-seven years afterwards as if he had been constantly in darkness since that time. It became indeed a fixed idea with Newton for twenty-seven long years that his friend knew no happiness at all and that if there were a show of happiness, it was feigned.

Newton tended at times to place far too much importance on the meaning of dreams. He had even written a hymn on the subject for the Olney Church.[54] At the beginning of Cowper's illness in 1773 the poet had told Newton about a dream in which he heard a voice speaking in Latin telling him he would perish. Somehow Newton was so moved by Cowper's vivid account of his dream that he felt it alone was the cause of the poet's later periods of deep melancholy and depression. Although Cowper stressed to Newton in his letters towards the end of his life that he had only twice been mentally ill and that the reason that he was at times in despair was not because of that one dream, but because of similar nightmares which he was perpetually having, Newton stuck to his theory and made it public, adding his own very negative interpretation.[55]

If Newton had kept his feelings to himself on the matter, no harm would have been done, but he told so many friends who visited him that, as a result of this one dream, Cowper was always in black despair that soon Newton's circle, including the Clapham Sect, were talking about Cowper as the poet of the strait-jacket.[56] Thornton, Newton's benefactor, passed on similar thoughts to his American friends, including Benjamin Franklin.

The Evangelical minister Richard Cecil, who knew Cowper only through Newton, went even further in spreading the rumours of a mad poet and says in his biography of Newton that Cowper 'seems to have been at all times disordered in a greater or lesser degree', even before his conversion. He then refers to Cowper's immediate post-conversion years in Olney where 'Providence seems to have appointed Mr Newton ... for the relief of the depressed mind of the poet Cowper'. The period to which Cecil is referring, however, was the very time when Newton was most dependent on Cowper and the poet was at his happiest! Cecil ends his account of Cowper's association with Newton with a reference to 1773 (almost seven years before Newton left Olney) saying, 'Thus Cowper's malady, like a strong current, breaking down the banks which had hitherto sustained the pressure and obliquity of its course, prevailed against the supports he had received, and precipitated him again into his former distress.' Cecil, therefore, using material gained from conversations with Newton, leaves his readers with the impression that Cowper in 1773 reverted back to his pre-conversion mental state. It is then no surprise to find one of the earliest Christian biographers of Cowper[57] building on such faulty information, wishing to entitle his work not *The Life of William Cowper* but rather *The Living Death For Seventy Years of William Cowper*.

Up to 30 October 1784 Newton and Cowper had shown that, whatever their differences, nothing could permanently come between them and they thus remained good friends and allies. Cowper was always reminding himself of the wonderful fellowship he had shared with Newton in the past and still regarded him as the best of pastors. Newton did his uttermost in many ways to show his love and respect for his Olney friend and still valued his advice highly. He managed to visit Orchard Side about twice a year and would then stay for up to three weeks with Cowper. Even when they were together, however, there was a wall of partition between the two and their former intimacy was not renewed. All the same, Newton never ceased to look upon himself as Cowper's nearest and dearest friend. This conviction was about to receive a knock from which Newton only slowly and perhaps never fully recovered.

12.
Cowper's *Task*

As Cowper's manuscript for his new volume grew, he was faced with a choice of action which would prove wrong whatever he decided to do. He had not forgotten Unwin's great disappointment on learning that he had appointed Newton as his editor and go-between when writing *Poems*. He was therefore determined to give Unwin the same token of friendship that he had already given Newton by asking him to take care of his second volume. So in 1784 we find Cowper sending extracts from his new poems to Unwin for comment and appraisal. By October Unwin had received over 5,000 finished lines and was negotiating with Johnson, the publisher. His task was an easy one, as Johnson agreed to publish anything that Cowper wrote without asking to see a line of it first.

Meanwhile Cowper, only too aware of how Newton might react, had not said a word to him about all this. On 30 October 1784, after nearly all transactions with the publisher were complete, Cowper decided to inform Newton about his second volume, which he had decided to call plainly and simply the *Task*. He wrote a long letter to Newton but waited until the very end before telling him briefly that he had placed in Johnson's hands a poem in blank verse, consisting of six books, which he hoped would be in the bookshops by the following spring.

Cowper felt further justified in taking this step as he knew Unwin had still 'little weeds of suspicion', as the poet puts it, that he was not dear to Cowper's heart. A second reason Cowper gave Unwin was that Newton had stopped asking him for help when publishing new works, so he felt he was under no obligation to give Newton any priority. Cowper was perhaps forgetting that Newton had written to him in February of that year requesting a motto in Greek or Latin for a new publication.

Unwin, in his flush of joy and enthusiasm at being chosen as Cowper's editor, rather unwisely told the Thorntons, friends he had in common with Newton, and soon a number of Newton's closest friends knew what he himself still did not know. Joseph Hill and William Bull, two of Cowper's other close friends, were informed by the poet of his new move a week or so after Newton.

Newton is upset

Cowper had to wait several weeks for a reply from Newton. When it came, it expressed in the friendliest of tones his deep mortification at not being taken into Cowper's confidence. Nevertheless Newton demanded to be given a full account of the six books, including excerpts from them, and insisted that he should be sent the proofs from Johnson page by page in order to give his comments.

Although it meant a great deal of hard work, Cowper wrote a summary of the six books for Newton and transcribed a large number of sample verses — a job he disliked doing because of his weak eyes. The poet absolutely refused, however, to have Newton do any editing or checking of the proofs.

Newton's reply did not take long this time and Cowper called it 'fretful and peevish' and immediately sent a 'dry and unsavory' retort back. Newton was most dissatisfied.

He was very grumpy about Cowper's simple title, the *Task*. Cowper had made it clear that this was the task he had been given by God to do, so he thought the title fitting. Newton loved enigmatic, learned titles with lengthy sub-titles and had begged Cowper to supply him with such titles on several occasions. The plain English used by Cowper did not appeal to him. This is rather strange as Newton apparently did not question Cowper's use of the equally simple title *Poems* for his first volume.

Newton also bickered about the sub-headings. In Book II, for instance, Cowper takes up the theme of his ancestor on his mother's side, John Donne. This was the poet who had written the famous 'For whom the bell tolls — it tolls for thee'. With this concept in mind, Cowper called the second book 'Time-Piece' as it dealt with the hour of approaching judgement and the signs of the times. To his surprise, Newton could not see the significance of the heading linked to such a theme.

He also took umbrage at Cowper's calling a snake 'the crested worm' in an idyllic and symbolic scene where a serpent pays homage to a child. In the context it is quite clear to which snake the poet is referring. Cowper pointed out to Newton that the word 'worm' was a common way of referring to the serpent in Eden and was the very name used by Milton in *Paradise Lost*. Fearing that Newton might still not have understood what he meant by 'crested worm', Cowper added, 'No animal of the vermicular or serpentine kind is crested, but the most formidable of all.'[1]

Cowper had mentioned in a second letter to Newton that he had included in his new book a treatise on education dedicated to William Unwin, whom he had assisted from time to time in the upbringing of his children. As Unwin was the governor of a school, the dedication was doubly appropriate. This dedication, however, mortified Newton all the more and he made it plain that he expected Cowper to dedicate his poetry to none other than himself. Newton's next letter was thus another expression of extremely hurt feelings in which he accused Cowper of being like the Medes and Persians who were not prepared to change anything. He urged Cowper at least to consider giving his *Task* a more elaborate sub-title. Cowper wrote back,

> I am neither Mede nor Persian, neither am I the son of any such, but was born at Great Berkhamsted in Hartfordshire; and yet I can neither find a new title for my book, nor please myself with any addition to the old one. I am however, willing to hope that when the Volume shall cast itself at your feet, you will be in some measure reconciled to the name it bears, especially when you find it justified both by the Exordium of the poem and by the conclusion. But enough as you say with great truth, of a subject very unworthy of so much consideration.[2]

Newton was to receive a further snub in this letter. He usually asked Cowper for a confirmation of pieces of local gossip he had heard about from time to time,[3] mostly from a servant he had taken with him from Olney. The poet often refused to supply him with such gossip, only writing about more or less harmless or amusing tales. In this letter he told Newton outright, 'I never spread slander, and therefore very rarely deal in the News of Olney. I could some time have sent you information upon the following disagreeable subject, both because it *is* disagreeable, and because I was willing to wait in hopes that it might prove false, I have 'till now declined it. It seems however that I am warranted to communicate as much of it as decency will permit.' The story was about a disciplinary meeting at the local Baptist Church, but as Cowper felt that he could only relate what 'decency will permit', he did not relate much.

A month later Cowper was still waiting for a reply to this letter but Wilson, his Baptist barber, called on Newton and the two discussed Cowper's new enterprise. Newton sent his regards to Cowper via Wilson, who told him that Newton was still deeply grieved by Cowper's not sending him the manuscript first and dedicating a poem to Unwin rather than himself. The poem dedicated to Unwin had especially upset Newton as it had a high-sounding Latin title, a sub-title and several quotes from the classics accompanying it — the very features Newton had urged Cowper to put at the beginning of the volume instead of the simple title *Task*.

On hearing how hurt Newton was, Cowper decided to write him a friendly conciliating letter, including the two items Newton was always requesting — a poem and a piece of gossip. The poem was an epitaph on Dr Samuel Johnson who had just died, apparently confessing his faith in Christ before going to meet him face to face.

> Here Johnson lies — a sage by all allow'd
> Whom to have bred may well make England proud.
> Whose Prose was eloquence by Wisdom taught,
> The gracefull vehicle of virtuous thought;
> Whose Verse may claim, grave, masculine, and strong,
> Superior praise to the mere Poet's song;
> Who many a noble gift from Heav'n possessed,
> And Faith at last — alone, worth all the rest.
> Oh Man immortal by a double prize,
> On Earth by Fame, by Favor in the skies!

Cowper also sent this epitaph to the *Gentleman's Magazine*, who were only too pleased to print it.

When Cowper had written his first volume of poetry Newton had got in touch with Dr Johnson through mutual friends and asked him to express his opinion of Cowper's work. Cowper had, however, to wait two years before he found out what 'the King of Critics' thought of his poetry. Dr Johnson praised the book but did not review it as Cowper and Newton had hoped.

There has been much speculation as to which friend of Newton's mediated and most biographers feel it must have been Benjamin Latrobe (1725-1786), the Moravian pastor, as Cowper himself suggested his name as a possible go-between. It might equally well have been Boswell, who was intimately acquainted with several of Newton's friends and was a close companion of Dr Johnson. Boswell maintained a keen interest in Cowper as he was subject to depression himself and liked to hear — and spread — stories about other sufferers.

The piece of local gossip which Cowper included in his letter to Newton was about the Rev. Benjamin Page who, after quarrelling with everybody there was to quarrel with, ended his ministry by saying, 'And now let us pray for your wicked Vicar',[4] and left the district for good in more senses than one.

After many highly complimentary remarks and a message from Mrs Unwin to Mrs Newton, Cowper closed his letter, trusting, as we know from a letter to Unwin, that the Lord would enable him to win back his friend's confidence. He told Unwin, 'We shall jumble together again, as people that have an affection for each other at bottom, notwithstanding now and then a slight disagreement, always do.'

It took Newton three months to thaw out but towards the end of April 1985 he wrote rather pompously to Cowper, 'I am perfectly satisfied with the propriety of your proceedings as to the publication.' Cowper did not waste any time telling Unwin the good news, 'We are friends again.'

Unusual features of the *Task*

The *Task* must be one of the most rambling poems ever written. Cowper had developed a *style* which was to be called 'the stream of consciousness' by literary critics and often imitated. The poet compared writing to going for a walk out in the country with a good companion. On the way one notices various features in the landscape, talks about the weather, about politics, about one's work, about one's health, about nature in general and, if the happy wanderer is a Christian, about God and his plan and purpose for mankind. All these items are skilfully linked together with what Cowper calls 'slight connections', which has also become something of a technical term in literary criticism.

The *language* which Cowper uses in the *Task* also introduces a great deal of novelty. Up to Cowper's age it was thought masterly for a poet to adopt a polysyllabic neo-classical language which never calls a spade a spade but uses circumlocutions of a most flowery kind. Schoolmaster Teedon, for example, would never say, 'The garden looks lovely,' but 'The flowery tribe are finely variegated and extremely fragrant.'[5] Cowper was determined to rid literature of this sesquipedalian[6] nonsense and take it back to the simple but beautiful language of the Bible and the oldest language of poetry, Greek. As he told Newton, when giving him a summary of his coming publication, he aimed at 'the plain and simple sublimity of Scripture-language'.

Another new venture in Cowper's poetry was to express feelings of *empathy and sympathy with the world around him*. Up to that time it was considered 'good style' to describe scenes, especially scenes of nature, as if the writer were quite separate and aloof from them. Cowper always had a feeling of being present in his own poems, living and experiencing with his subjects.

Cowper was also new in striving to *make poetry speak the language of prose*. This was a claim Wordsworth made for himself years later but, although Cowper was the first major poet to use this method, the idea actually originated with Isaac Watts (1674-1748), who had laid down rules for poetry eighty years before Cowper and a hundred years before Wordsworth. The lakeland poet read Cowper avidly and declared that he was the only poet worth learning off by heart. In fact Wordsworth learnt so much of Cowper off by heart that his own poetry is often a reflection of Cowper's and he even puts forward Cowper's ideas as his own.

Cowper was a pioneer, too, in *depicting the terrible circumstances of the poor*. Up to this time it was the fashion to romanticize country people and the poor. Every simple, unlettered man was a 'swain' and the simple girl was a 'shepherdess', or even a 'nymph'. The Romantic poets reverted to this after Cowper and they idealized the humble poor as if they had a status to be envied. Cowper, who lived amidst hundreds of almost starving lacemakers, was far too near scenes of poverty to believe such a myth.

In order to implement these reforms Cowper strove to develop a language as free as possible from artificialities and reverted to blank verse as a better channel of expression than rhyme, which tended to make language an artifice and artefact rather than a vehicle of communication. The poet had also learnt from preachers such as Whitefield, whom he greatly admired, to address people in a natural language, even the language of the market-place, instead of forming and shaping an address until it became a scholarly treatise understood by few. Scholars often charge Cowper with being inconsistent in his endeavours to purify the language, claiming he often resorted to archaic forms. Such uses of antiquated speech are, however, confined to Cowper's humorous verse and were added to make his language more quaint and amusing. Thus when Cowper at last decided to lift the veil of anonymity from 'John Gilpin' and have it published with the *Task,* he backdated the language on purpose to heighten the humour in it.

Although there is no artificial structure in the *Task*, Cowper had a definite plan as to what should be included and where it should come in the poem. In his covering letter sent to Unwin with his manuscript he tells his friend,

> In some passages, especially in the second book, you will observe me very Satyrical. Writing on such subjects, I could not be otherwise. I can write nothing without aiming at least at usefullness. It were beneath my years to do it, and still more dishonorable to my religion. I know that a reformation of such abuses as I have censured, is not to be expected from the efforts of a poet; but to contemplate the world, its follies, its vices, its indifference to duty and its strenuous attachment to what is evil, and not to reprehend, were to approve it. From this charge at least I shall be clear, for I have neither tacitly nor expressly flatter'd either its characters or its customs.

He then goes on to say,

What there is of a religious cast in the volume, I have
thrown towards the end of it, for two reasons. First that I
might not revolt the Reader at his entrance, and secondly that
my best impressions might be made last. Were I to write as
many Volumes as Lopez de Vega or Voltaire, not one of them
all would be without this tincture. If the world like it not, so
much the worse for them. I make all the concessions I can that
I may please them, but I will not please them at the expence
of conscience.[7]

Cowper goes on to explain how that what he writes about nature
and the 'delineations of the heart' are all taken from his own
experiences and he has borrowed nothing from other books and
authors.

Introducing his theme

Cowper begins his ramble through the *Task* from the home base of
the very sofa that Lady Austen had told him to write a poem about.
The sofa is described in mock epic tones as being fit for the
pampered and the gouty but Cowper quickly goes on to tell his
readers how he prefers a rural walk to a nap on the couch, and they
are at once taken from the indulging sofa to the hills, valleys and
rivers of the surrounding countryside. Stressing that he intends to
portray reality and not poetic fiction, Cowper calls on Mrs Unwin's
testimony as an eyewitness, saying to her:

Thou know'st my praise of nature most sincere,
And that my raptures are not conjur'd up
To serve occasions of poetic pomp,
But genuine, and art partner of them all.[8]

There follow such exquisite descriptions of nature that one editor
of an Irish literary magazine, who happened to be a Christian,
devoted a whole editorial to them. A few issues later this editor
declared he had to take up the same theme again, and indeed he did
so a third time, praising Cowper as being a better poet than Thomson
and even superior to Milton, and claiming that he transformed the
world of the reader into a veritable Eden.[9]

Cowper goes on to discuss fallen man's pursuit of art as a kind of inborn urge to get back to the beauties of paradise, without realizing that those beauties are all there to be seen in some measure by those enlightened by God. Cowper has now brought his readers to a point where he can take them into deeper truths.

It was becoming the custom of the age to look upon people who were naturally rustic and 'one with nature' as being particularly blessed of God and especially innocent. Those were the days of 'the noble savage' in which poets were urging people to study the highland lassie, the North American Indian and the native of the Friendly Isles in order to find an innocence approaching that of Eden. Mary Shelley's *Frankenstein's Monster* (believe it or not!) and Wordsworth's 'Lucy' were such attempts to urge their readers to go back to the simple country life and thus obtain inner peace. Poets such as Robert Burns, who normally wrote and spoke very good English, chose to write in dialect, not because they treasured it as a language in its own right, but because it created the myth that dialect speakers were nearer the earth and to God than more cultivated speakers.

Cowper had read how Captain Cook had taken Omai from the South Sea Islands and presented him all over Britain where he was exhibited as the noble savage *par excellence*. Cowper explains how there was no 'disinterested good' in Omai, nor was there anything particularly good about the British taking him from his island and parading him around England.

Using a phrase which has since become a fixed expression in the English language, 'God made the country but man made the town,' Cowper closes the first book by admitting that a person can find God more easily in the country, far away from the temptations of the town, but at the same time he gently introduces a suggestion that this also necessitates living a life according to the Scriptures and the will of God.

The 'Time-piece'

Book II, 'The Time-Piece', starts off with a general condemnation of the sinful state of Britain. Cowper castigates a country where people weep when they see a horse mercilessly beaten and chained, but nobody even raises an eyebrow when the same thing is done to a human being, that is, a slave. Explaining that not for all the wealth in the world would he have a slave to till his ground, to carry him or to fan him while he slept, the poet says he would rather be a slave himself than enforce such a burden on others.

He goes on to extol British freedom as a sign of God's good will to its people, and contrasts this with the state of the Roman Catholic countries currently going through a time of natural catastrophes and divine punishment. Lest his readers should be complacent in their freedom as British subjects, however, Cowper warns them:

> If he spar'd not them,
> Tremble and be amaz'd at thine escape,
> Far guiltier England, lest he spare not thee![10]

After eulogizing the work of a poet, Cowper leads the reader on to consider the work of a preacher as being far more important. Using Paul as his pattern of a gospel preacher, he continues:

> Would I describe a preacher, such as Paul,
> Were he on earth, would hear, approve, and own—
> Paul should himself direct me. I would trace
> His master-strokes, and draw from his design.
> I would express him simple, grave, sincere;
> In doctrine uncorrupt; in language plain,
> And plain in manner; decent, solemn, chaste,
> And natural in gesture; much impress'd
> Himself, as conscious of his awful charge,
> And anxious mainly that the flock he feeds
> May feel it too; affectionate in look,
> And tender in address, as well becomes
> A messenger of grace to guilty men.

Realizing that there were worldly men who made a mockery of true preaching such as he described, Cowper warns against going to hear preachers who substitute their own glory for that of Christ. The poet is suddenly extremely scathing in his criticism:

> Behold the picture! — Is it like? — Like whom?
> The things that mount the rostrum with a skip,
> And then skip down again; pronounce a text;

Cry — hem: and, reading what they never wrote
Just fifteen minutes, huddle up their work
And with a well-bred whisper close the scene!
In man or woman, but far most in man
And most of all in man that ministers
And serves the altar, in my soul I loath
An affectation. 'Tis my perfect scorn;
Object of my implacable disgust.
What! — will a man play tricks, will he indulge
A silly fond conceit of his fair form,
And Just proportion, fashionable mien
And pretty face, in presence of his God?
Or will he seek to dazzle me with tropes,
As with the di'mond on his lily hand
And play his brilliant parts before my eyes
When I am hungry for the bread of life?
He mocks his Maker, prostitutes and shames
His noble office, and, instead of truth
Displaying his own beauty, starves his flock![11]

Having scourged the clergy the poet goes on to give a solemn warning against the 'rob'd pedagogues' of Britain's schools and universities who nurture children so badly that they become morally 'crook'd, and twisted and deform'd'. The second book closes with a solemn warning that the plagues of Egypt might soon infest hell-bound Britain.

The 'Garden'

Book III of the *Task*, called 'The Garden', has proved one of the most difficult of Cowper's works to understand. On the surface it reads as if he is merely outlining the idyllic life of someone who builds his own compost heap and grows his own pumpkins. This has led many an undiscerning critic to compare the work to a gardener's catalogue of little poetic merit.

The book, is however, highly typological and eschatological, and readers who have an inkling of Bible language and Bible truths should have little difficulty in spotting the two levels on which this book is written. In the 'Garden' the poet looks to the future and the

return of Christ to a restored Eden before the final consummation.
He thus sees himself thus as God's under-gardener, striving to
prepare both mankind and nature for the Second Coming.

True to Cowper's intention to write only about divine truths
which he himself had really experienced, he gives a detailed outline
of his conversion experience in this book. No statement of Cowper's
has, however, been so misunderstood or so misrepresented as this
triumphant declaration of God's saving grace in Christ. The passage
starts with the words:

> I was a stricken deer, that left the herd
> Long since; with many an arrow deep infixt
> My panting side was charg'd, when I withdrew
> To seek a tranquil death in distant shades.[12]

Here most commentators see Cowper as confessing that he has
lost all trust and hope in human society and has fled to the countryside to lick his wounds in peace. It has thus become a tradition to
look upon Cowper as a lifelong fugitive from human society, and the
title 'the Stricken Deer' is often used to describe his life in Olney and
Weston up to his death. As we have seen, Olney was certainly no
retreat 'far from the madding crowd's ignoble strife', to use Gray's
expressive words. It was actually a mixture of public houses and
poverty and a far from ideal place to live in. Cowper had gone to live
there to sit under the Evangelical preaching of John Newton and not
because it was the back of beyond, or paradise unlimited.

The lines in question have, of course, nothing to do with the
fugitive theory of over-imaginative but spiritually undiscerning
commentators. It must be noted that they are not written in the
present tense, telling the reader how the poet was feeling at the time
of writing. The past tense is used throughout. In order to make this
plain Cowper says it happened 'long since'.

He then goes on to say what it was that happened a long time ago
when he was feeling like a stricken deer:

> There was I found by one who had himself
> Been hurt by th' archers. In his Side he bore,
> And in his hands and feet, the cruel scars.
> With gentle force soliciting the darts,
> He drew them forth, and heal'd, and bade me live.[13]

When the *Gentleman's Magazine* reviewed these lines, the reviewers showed themselves as ignorant of their meaning as scores of later biographers. 'Who was this scarred person who was so helpful to Cowper?' they asked. Their answer baffled Cowper completely, as they came to the conclusion that he was referring to being befriended by the Rev. Morley Unwin at Huntingdon after his stay at St Albans and they made a note in the margin to that effect. Informing Lady Hesketh of this 'howler', Cowper wrote, 'The mistake that has occasioned the mention of Unwin's name in the margin would be ludicrous if it were not, inadvertently indeed, and innocently on their part, profane. I should have thought it impossible that when I spoke of One who had been wounded in the hands and in the side, any reader in a Christian land could have been for a moment at a loss for the person intended.'

In spite of Cowper's amazement at the lack of spiritual insight and scriptural knowledge shown by such a learned journal as the *Gentleman's Magazine,* few modern commentators see anything of Christ's saving work in this passage[14] and even some who do see a reference to Christ merely believe that Cowper is gaining comfort from the fact that Christ also was tormented by sinful men.[15] But rather than the poet merely finding selfish comfort in the fact that he has found a fellow-sufferer, the whole context shows that Cowper is testifying to the saving grace of the Man of Sorrows, who sought him out, gently drew out the darts of sin and suffering, healed him and caused him to live anew.

Cowper goes on next to consider the findings of the scientists of his day who vaunt their human wisdom in examining the works of God. The poet affirms that no amount of peering through a telescope and discovering new worlds will help them discover God. It is in his Word that his mercy shines and he has commanded all to seek him there. Once enlightened by the Word of God, the scientist is far more able to understand creation for,

> The mind indeed, enlighten'd from above,
> Views him in all; ascribes to the grand cause
> The grand effect; acknowledges with joy
> His manner, and with rapture tastes his style.[16]

The poet then recommends the Bible to all as the source of the highest virtue of all, which is truth. Those who earnestly ask God to grant them his light, so that they can understand what real truth is, will find that it is God's joy, his glory and his very nature to impart it freely.

Once Cowper has given his own testimony and urged his readers to seek their own salvation in the Word of God, he returns to his descriptions of nature, seen now through the eyes of a discerning Christian. He outlines how mankind is abusing nature in two ways.

First, nature is used by many merely as a setting for destructive recreation. So-called sportsmen tear across hill and dale, filling it with riot and defiling it with the blood of animals killed for sordid amusement. 'Detested sport', says Cowper, 'that owes its pleasures to another's pain.' He sees countrymen who go in for hunting and angling as self-deluded beings.

Secondly, nature is being abused because man tends to turn his back on God's purpose in nature and 'crowd the roads, impatient for the town'. It is not that Cowper is condemning the town as such, but he believes that if a person rejects God's Word and shuts his eyes to the remains of Eden still discernible on earth in nature and the domestic bliss associated with life in the country, he is entirely shutting himself out from any hope of salvation. What is more, as the towns grow, the countryside shrinks and townish ways take over the thoughts and actions of country people, so that the worldly entertainments of the town and the townsman's outlook on life become the norm for the countryman, too.

Cowper saw the creating of artificial parks as an expression of this townish outlook, for it showed that man had a deep longing to return to some form of paradise from which his sin had banned him, but he clothed this in an artificiality that was a very poor imitation of the real thing. It was symptomatic of this urge, the poet reflected, that a much frequented park in London had laid out its gardens in the form of the signs of the Zodiac.

In contrast to all this Cowper tells of his own idyllic but real experience of nature. He rescued hares from the guns of the hunters and kept them almost as family members, illustrating how they could live in harmony with mankind, as in the paradise on earth foretold by the prophets of old. When he pruned his fruit trees he was acting as God's steward on earth, fulfilling God's command to Adam. In building his hot-bed he was foreshadowing the day when there would be an eternal spring on earth, bringing with it a perpetual time of harvest. By constructing and using his greenhouse Cowper was showing that even in industrial Olney it was possible to unite the produce of all the world in a little glass Paradise Regained, a token of glorious things to come.

The 'Winter Evening'

William Hazlitt (1778-1830), the painter and writer, once wrote, without giving any evidence whatsoever in support of his statement, that Cowper was frightened of a drop of rain.[17] Writer after writer since then has built his opinion of Cowper on this quite erroneous foundation and it has thus become a fixed tradition to regard him as a fair-weather poet. Nothing, however, could be further from the truth. Cowper, always claiming to be different from other poets, maintained that whereas others gained their inspiration from the spring and the sunshine, he saw themes for his verse in all God's seasons and was at his poetic best in winter, with its ice, snow and mud. Thus we find much of the *Task* taken up with winter themes and in the fourth book, 'The Winter Evening' the poet exclaims:

Oh Winter, ruler of th' inverted year,
Thy scatter'd hair with sleet like ashes fill'd,
Thy breath congeal'd upon thy lips, thy cheeks
Fring'd with a beard made white with other snows
Than those of age, thy forehead wrapt in clouds,
A leafless branch thy sceptre, and thy throne
A sliding car, indebted to no wheels,
But urg'd by storms along its slipp'ry way,
I love thee, all unlovely as thou seem'st.
And dreaded as thou art![18]

It is interesting to note that when Wordsworth adopts Cowper's style of describing nature, he transfers Cowper's winter scenes into summer imagery.[19]

In this fourth book, Cowper tells his readers how, after doing the chores of the day, he would settle down in the evening before a bright fire either to read a book, weave nets for the fruit trees, listen to one of the ladies playing the harpsichord or, best of all, enjoy reading the newspaper! Such pen-portraits of the joys of evening, as Cowper experienced them, have adorned many an anthology since.

Cowper by the fireside

His reference to the 'cup that cheers' is one that has remained particularly popular:

> Now stir the fire, and close the shutters fast,
> Let fall the curtains, wheel the sofa round,
> And, while the bubbling and loud-hissing urn
> Throws up a steamy column, and the cups,
> That cheer but not inebriate, wait on each,
> So let us welcome peaceful ev'ning in.[20]

Once settled down with his hot cup of tea, Cowper would open the newspaper and from his 'loophole of retreat' view the world. The fall of stocks, births, deaths and marriages all interested him greatly, and he was especially keen to read any news from abroad. 'Is India free?' he would ask himself, 'or do we grind her still?' Amidst the darkening shadows and the hypnotic glow of the fire Cowper would meditate and muse on the follies of the world. On the particular evening which he describes in the *Task* Cowper's thoughts wander from his boyhood days, when he discovered Milton's *Paradise Lost* and *Paradise Regained* and jumped for joy on reading them, to public houses and 'universal soldiership'. Of the drinking resorts of the common man Cowper says,

> Pass where we may, through city or through town,
> Village, or hamlet, of this merry land,
> Though lean and beggar'd, ev'ry twentieth pace
> Conducts th' unguarded nose to such a whiff
> Of stale debauch, forth-issuing from the styes
> That law has licens'd, as makes temp'rance reel.
> There sit, involv'd and lost in curling clouds
> Of Indian fume, and guzzling deep, the boor,
> The lackey, and the groom: the craftsman there
> Takes a Lethean leave of all his toil;
> Smith, cobbler, joiner, he that plies the shears,
> And he that kneads the dough; all loud alike,
> All learned, and all drunk![21]

Closely linked to the type of man the public house breeds, in Cowper's view, was the conscripted British soldier after his country had first changed and then demobilized him. He was convinced that the practice of 'universal soldiership' robbed the country of some of its best workers at the best time of their lives. After three years of conscription the young man would return with a straighter back and a more fashionable appearance but with an aversion to hard work and the sights and smells of country labour. His mouth is now full of newly learned curses and his belly with beer, so that on his return he breaks not only his mother's heart but also that of his former sweetheart.

When ruminating on the follies and foibles of the world, Cowper's thoughts were never far from the poor and he uses the 'Winter Evening' to describe their plight to his wealthier readers who, as they could afford the guinea for his book,[22] obviously lived in a very different world. The poet makes it quite clear that one must differentiate when talking about the poor.

First of all he defines the *industrious* poor, of whom he says, 'With all their thrift they thrive not.' These poor people comprised the majority of the Olney inhabitants and included most of the believers in the town. Cowper was now receiving substantial sums for their relief from Lord Carrington (Robert Smith 1752-1838), the banker who was also a staunch follower of Pitt and a friend of both Unwin and Newton. It was obviously Cowper's criticism of the attitude towards the poor displayed by Pitt's supporters that had prompted Lord Carrington to appoint the poet as his agent in alleviating their needs in Olney. This fine man, Cowper tells us, denied the poor nothing but his name.

Whatever we may think of the literary value of Cowper's bleak description of the industrious poor in the 'Winter Evening', the poet managed to catch the eye and the ear of many a deep-pocketed benefactor and many a politician, both parties combining to relieve the hardships of the lacemakers. In this sphere alone, Cowper did a transforming work in Olney.

There was a second category of poor people, however, with whom the poet had no sympathy at all. These were the *self-inflicted* poor, who could be found in the dozens of Olney inns, or in hen-houses strangling the necks of hens that did not belong to them, or doing anything base and illegal rather than a spell of honest work. Cowper's heart went out to the wronged wives and battered children, but their sottish husbands and fathers would never see a penny from the poet.

Cowper does not stay long in contemplating the sins of the poor. Realizing that many of his readers would be well-to-do, he does not mince matters when warning them of the temptations and snares particular to their ranks. Nobleman, politician and parson are all told how wealth leads to luxury, and luxury to excess and habitual sloth. A self-indulgent upper class is too concerned with its own selfish aims to worry about those of the lower classes. Cowper is courting criticism when he adds that a much-trodden path into the confidence of those of a higher station in life is by bribing their 'milk-white hands'.

In spite of his campaigns for the poor, Cowper believed that in the divine economy there must be both rulers and ruled and that class divisions were essential to society. He crossed swords with Newton on several occasions on this matter, believing that Newton made himself too accessible to his servants and was too gullible in accepting their opinions. Hence we find Cowper ending his poem on fireside musings with a statement that each person has a special role in society determined by his God-given gifts.

> Some must be great. Great offices will have
> Great talents. And God gives to ev'ry man
> The virtue, temper, understanding, taste
> That lifts him into life; and lets him fall
> Just in the niche he was ordain'd to fill.
> To the deliv'rer of an injur'd land
> He gives a tongue t' enlarge upon, an heart
> To feel, and courage to redress her wrongs;
> To monarchs dignity; to judges sense;
> To artists ingenuity and skill;
> To me an unambitious mind, content
> In the low vale of life, that early felt
> A wish for ease and leisure, and ere long
> Found here that leisure and that ease I wish'd.[23]

It was typical of Cowper that, though very conscious of the fact that he was high-born, he believed his happiness was to be found in the 'low vale' of domestic Olney bliss which he was certain was God's 'niche' for him.

The 'Winter Morning Walk'

In the fifth book, 'The Winter Morning Walk', Cowper is once more out and about before the frosty morning sun has ascended. In depicting the blazing orb rising on a sparkling, long-shadowed landscape, he emphasizes how nature mocks art and no amount of admiring the works of pencil, pen or brush can bear comparison with seeing God's original works in all their glory. The poet goes on to describe the feats of Russian monarchs who found a childish joy in creating artificial palaces of ice, rather than marvelling at the natural ice formations made by God. 'Great princes have great playthings,' is his conclusion.

Cowper then goes on to plead for pacifism, with such a scathing criticism of royalty and their lust for their war-games that it is a wonder that he was not hauled before the judges for libel and provocation to revolution. God's hand can be seen in the fact that Cowper was not a public figure in politics and it was probably this which saved him from such a fate. On the subject of royal playthings, Cowper says,

> But war's a game, which, were their subjects wise,
> Kings would not play at. Nations would do well
> T' extort their truncheons from the puny hands
> Of heroes, whose infirm and baby minds
> Are gratified with mischief; and who spoil,
> Because men suffer it, their toy the world.[24]

In the light of the previous book, in which Cowper so firmly states that there are set classes in society, it would seem odd that Cowper is so critical of kings. There is a biblical reason, however, behind his social philosophy. At Babel, the poet tells us, God, like a shepherd separating his flocks, divided a people united in a common enmity against God and set them in different places and different folds. Jealousy then arose between these peoples and the strongest or wisest were chosen to lead one country against another. Soon these leaders began to think that the world was made in vain if not for them and their foolish subjects supported them in their vanity. From now on in the *Task* Cowper points out to his readers that the only factor that can once more unite mankind is when every knee learns to bow in a joint acknowledgement of Jesus Christ as Lord and King of Kings. If people want liberty from oppression, the poet knows just what kind of liberty they need:

> But there is yet a liberty, unsung
> By poets, and by senators unprais'd,
> Which monarchs cannot grant, nor all the pow'rs
> Of earth and hell confed'rate take away:
> A liberty, which persecution, fraud,
> Oppression, prisons, have no power to bind;
> Which whoso tastes can be enslav'd no more.
> 'Tis liberty of heart, deriv'd from heav'n;
> Bought with His blood who gave it to mankind,
> And seal'd with the same token![25]

The poet goes on to explain how all nature bears the royal stamp of God but the charter sealed and signed by the Creator in his Word, granting liberty to those bought by Christ's vicarious death, transcends all. Then, giving the lie to a host of later critics who accuse Cowper of deifying and eternalizing nature, he argues that, once smitten with the beauty of this world, one might think it eternal but in fact God has 'pronounced it transient, glorious as it is'. It is merely a foretaste of a more glorious creation to come. This world will be swept away, as unworthy of God's eternal honour, but those whom he loves will be saved to shine in another paradise that does not fade away. But Cowper is no universalist. The 'lying hearts' and 'disputers against God', who look to their salvation in the old world, will be confuted and only reap penal woe. The poet emphasizes that 'He is the freeman whom the truth makes free, and all are slaves beside.'

The joys of the redeemed, however, are not merely anticipatory of heaven. No one can appreciate this present world to the same degree as the born-again believer who can look at the entire creation and humbly, but yet with a sense of pride, say, 'My Father made them all!' He alone knows 'who planned and built and still upholds a world so clothed in beauty for rebellious man'. None but he knows what it means to have been blind and now to have received his sight. Herein lies the difference between the nature-worshipper and the Christian. The former praises the landscape, mistaking the effect for the cause. The Christian praises the Author. 'So reads he nature

whom the lamp of truth illuminates', says the poet. Cowper closes
this book with a great crescendo of verse in jubilant praise of the
Divine Word's saving grace:

> Thou art the source and centre of all minds,
> Their only point of rest, eternal Word!
> From thee departing, they are lost, and rove
> At random, without honour, hope, or peace.
> From thee is all that sooths the life of man,
> His high endeavour, and his glad success,
> His strength to suffer, and his will to serve.
> But oh thou bounteous giver of all good
> Thou art of all thy gifts thyself the crown!
> Give what thou canst, without thee we are poor;
> And with thee rich, take what thou wilt away.[26]

The 'Winter Walk at Noon'

Cowper's readers, having followed the poet through the first five
books, now find themselves in the final one, 'The Winter Walk at
Noon', in the realms of deep evangelical doctrine. After depicting
oft-quoted scenes of nature, Cowper discusses human knowledge
and its inferiority to wisdom. 'Knowledge is proud that he has
learned so much,' the poet tells us, whereas 'Wisdom is humble that
he knows no more.'

He then goes on to argue that in the sanctity of nature a person
is in a better position to let the heart reason before the head and to
see in the yearly renovation of a faded world a foretaste of the
restitution of all things outlined in Scripture.

The Puritans, on the whole, held to a very optimistic doctrine of
the end of the world. They taught that they were still living in an
infant world suffering from teething-troubles, yet progressing towards the time when the knowledge of God would cover the earth
as the waters cover the sea.[27] Many believed that this would entail not
only a spiritual renewal, but a visible and material renewal of the
world also.[28] Paradise Lost on earth would be succeeded by Paradise
Regained on earth before the Second Coming of our Lord.

This view had been challenged in the eighteenth century by the
Evangelical writer James Hervey, who argued that, in the book of

nature, winter showed how creation was weakening and dying. In Cowper's day Christians were increasingly leaving the doctrine of salvation out of their gospel and embarking instead on the dubious path of soothsayings and prophecies of doom. By painting hideous pictures of the end of the world, they wished to frighten people out of their sins.

Cowper and Newton, however, shared Jonathan Edwards' vision of a future in which the masses would turn to Christ and live for a time in a world restored from the havoc caused by man's sin. Preaching on Romans 8 and taking up the passage where Paul speaks of the groanings of creation, Newton says,

> Every thing we see confirms our expectation of what God has promised. The whole frame of nature, in its present state of imperfection, so strongly pleads for a future and better dispensation, as necessary to vindicate the wisdom, goodness, and justice of God; and this shall take place when the sons of God shall be manifested, and shall shine forth in the kingdom of their Father. It would be injurious to the honour of God, to suppose that things were at first created in the state they are now in, or that they will always continue so; and therefore the creature, which was originally designed to shew forth the glory of God, is represented as burdened and groaning till those impediments are removed, which prevent it from fully answering its proper end.[29]

Newton makes it clear that he is not speaking allegorically or 'spiritually' about the future of the saints alone, but about 'the whole frame of this lower world', which is to be restored in Christ. He goes on to argue that if the 'secret voice of the whole creation' itself longs for this day, how much more should those who have the light of God's Word! This sermon was preached during Newton's partnership with Cowper and was first published in *Omicron* in 1774, some ten years before Cowper expounded the same doctrine in the *Task*.

So we find Cowper, like Newton elsewhere, arguing in the 'Winter Walk at Noon' that nature only fell because it was dragged down by man but even then it still retained an integral longing to have its burden lifted. He believed that a restitution of creation before the heavenly new creation was a necessary part of God's plan of salvation for his elect. Sin had not only robbed man of his spiritual status but of his stewardship over nature, too. If God's purpose in Eden is to be fulfilled then there must be a full restoration of the Edenic state, with both man and nature again living in an absolute harmony of pre-Fall functions. This is why every instance of the destruction of nature, or of wicked treatment of animals, showed Cowper that men were at work who had no respect for God's plan.

Whilst on the subject of God's purpose in nature, Cowper refers to the Deists, who see no eschatological outworking of the divine will in creation. He contradicts them by recording signs of God's presence in nature and in Scripture, and crowns his argument with his declaration of faith that all is controlled by him 'who wore the platted thorns with bleeding brows'.

After listing further signs of the need for redemption which may be seen in the world, Cowper gets down to his main and final theme:

> The groans of nature in this nether world,
> Which Heav'n has heard for ages, have an end.
> Foretold by prophets, and by poets sung
> Whose fire was kindled at the prophets' Lamp,
> The time of rest, the promis'd sabbath, comes.
> Six thousand years of sorrow have well-nigh
> Fulfill'd their tardy and disastrous course
> Over a sinful world; and what remains
> Of this tempestuous state of human things
> Is merely as the working of a sea
> Before a calm, that rocks itself to rest:
> For He, whose car the winds are, and the clouds
> The dust that waits upon his sultry march,
> When sin hath mov'd him, and his wrath is hot,
> Shall visit earth in mercy; shall descend,
> Propitious, in his chariot pav'd with love;
> And what his storms have blasted and defac'd
> For man's revolt shall with a smile repair.[30]

Cowper then confesses openly why he has chosen the path of being a Christian poet. Such a divine theme has been given him that, arduous as his task may be, not to have attempted it would have been harder still. For the next 250 lines or so the poet of Olney forgets that he suffers from depression, or that he is sometimes afraid that God has removed him from the Lamb's Book of Life, dismisses all thoughts of being far too unclean to be intimate with God and describes 'scenes surpassing fable, and yet true, scenes of accomplish'd bliss!' Gone will be the winter that punished earth because of the Fall. All the seasons will be merged into one universal Edenic spring. Rivers of gladness will water the whole earth, in which there will be no fear of the serpent. In fact, the whole world will cry out, 'Worthy the Lamb, for he was slain for us!' and they will see Salem built by God himself on earth.

With his feelings and thoughts in the future Cowper is still conscious of the scoffers of the present, who are ever demanding, 'Where is the promise of your Lord's approach?' So the poet prays in his poem:

Come then, and, added to thy many crowns,
Receive yet one, the crown of all the earth,
Thou who alone art worthy! It was thine
By ancient covenant, ere nature's birth;
And thou hast made it thine by purchase since,
And overpaid its value with thy blood.
Thy saints proclaim thee king; and in their hearts
Thy title is engraven with a pen
Dipt in the fountain of eternal love.[31]

Cowper now goes on to describe the happy man. He is one whose present life forehadows something of the happy life to come. He is content to dwell on earth, perhaps completely overlooked by the world, until his time comes, knowing his citizenship is in heaven. If he could change his lot, he would not do so because everything is in the faithful hands of the only One whose praise he seeks. As the poet glides from using the third person into the first, it is obvious that he is talking about himself.

Cowper's views on education

The six books of the *Task* were followed by 'Tirocinium' expressing Cowper's radical views on schools. Education in those days left much to be desired. Latin and Greek were the main subjects on the curriculum with a sprinkling of mathematics and usually a dash of very watered-down religious knowledge. Cowper often complained

about the dubious calling of the teacher and felt that young English-
men were being brought up to know more about pagan gods than
they did about Christ.

Cowper wanted to change all that. He wanted pupils to learn who
had made them and to what purpose they were born. He wanted them
to come to a living knowledge of God, rather than merely to
conjugate dead verbs. He thought they should learn to play and learn
by playing. He also believed that girls, as well as boys, should be
given a higher education, recognizing that, whatever their future in
life, a good foundation was the best start for it.

Cowper had himself attended a dame's school, a prep school and
a public school and had known among his teachers and fellow pupils
both the worst of roughs and the best of gentlemen. But on the whole,
he could not recommend any of the types of school which existed in
his day. When William Unwin's children were born, Cowper, who
regarded them as his grandchildren, urged their father not to destroy
their characters by sending them to school but to mould them in the
right way by teaching them himself. This Unwin did with the best
of results. Cowper was always on hand to suggest, for instance, how
to learn geography through jigsaw puzzles and learning games, or
how to manage points of grammar and diction, besides recommending books.

It is commonly supposed that because Cowper persuaded Unwin
to teach his own children, the poet must have been unhappy as a
schoolboy. This was far from being the case as Cowper often
referred with pleasure to his old masters and old school escapades.
It would also be difficult to imagine how anyone who had been so
successful in both academic activities and sports at school could
have been unhappy in attaining such distinctions. The fact that
Cowper's old classmates remained his best friends for many years
shows that his time at Westminster was still a valued part of
Cowper's life long after his schooldays were over.

Although fond memories of Westminster were to remain with
Cowper all his life, after becoming a Christian the poet came to the
conclusion that the whole system of schooling was wrong and that,
even if he had enjoyed school, a better way was possible. This better
way was the subject of the long poem which Cowper added to the
Task, along with 'John Gilpin', which has already been allocated to.

Before we go on to examine the content of the poem, it must be
explained that Cowper, himself the son of a gentleman, had only the

education of gentlemen's sons in mind when writing 'Tirocinium or, A Review of Schools'. *'Tirocinium'* is a word still used in school dictionaries to refer to any form of training or apprenticeship. It is really a military term and comes from the Latin, where it was used to describe the initial training of a soldier. Knowing Cowper's intense dislike of military training, it would seem natural that he used such a word to describe and rectify a wrong course of instruction.

Education for Cowper is the simple exercise of asking pupils questions and receiving answers which in turn motivate them to ask further questions. This would produce pedagogic chaos unless the skilled teacher structured the information learnt and moulded it into a plan of tuition with a fixed aim in view. This aim must be to show God's plan and purpose for his creation and man's place and role in it. To this end, Cowper, looking back on his own pre-schooldays, commended the one-page book from which he had learnt to read and which contained the complete text of the Lord's Prayer. The child should then be taught a spirit of wonder:

> And learn with wonder how this world began,
> Who made, who marr'd, and who has ransom'd man:
> Points which, unless the scriptures made them plain,
> The wisest heads might agitate in vain.[32]

In other words, the best way to teach a child to read is by giving him a full text with a meaningful story that he can understand and appreciate as he stammers out the words. Cowper would be shocked to know that even today, many children are taught to read by pronouncing abstract sounds and syllables without any sense content — something impossible for a large number of pupils and boring and senseless to just as many. Others are taught to read 'odd' words by the 'Look and say' method, but this is hardly better. For Cowper, nothing could be better than the simple stories of the Bible for teaching youngsters to read.[33]

Still keeping to his own experience of his pre-school education at home, Cowper goes on to speak of the delight he found in that wonderful combination of fiction, fantasy and truth, *Pilgrim's Progress*. There you had humour, strong sense and simple style, he adds, as if to make his point clear. But what happens when the child goes to school? Cowper is still speaking from experience. Christian culture is forgotten and the pupil spends the most creative years of his life in a world of mythology and legend where Christian morals are turned upside down. So, Cowper says, if you want your child to become a sot or a dunce, you know what to do: send him to a public school! The poet cannot understand how an English gentleman can spend so many hours a day teaching his favourite horse or his dog to do tricks, not allowing anyone else to interfere with their instruction, and yet can leave the training of his son to a 'menagery '![34]

It was still the custom among the upper classes in the eighteenth century for the eldest son to inherit the estate; the next son would probably become a lawyer and the younger sons would have to enter the church. Few provisions were made for the education of a gentleman's daughter, as it was hoped that she would be married off at an early age to some nobleman, of greater or lesser rank. Thus the public school was full of boys whose fathers dreamed of their becoming famous lawyers, as Cowper's father did, or of their climbing church-ladders and becoming at least a bishop, like Spencer Madan, the poet's cousin and fellow pupil at Westminster.

Forcing boys to learn some Latin and less Greek and then obtaining livings for them through connections with royalty was a 'barbarous prostitution', according to Cowper. He was very hard on the non-believing clergy for good reasons, but the ecclesiastical product of a public school was to him a kind of mass-produced Antichrist. Men with less manners and less vocation than office clerks or humble servants were being thrust on a public who could well do without them. Describing such a bishop appointed through royal influence, Cowper declaims:

> Behold your bishop ! well he plays his part—
> Christian in name, and infidel in heart,
> Ghostly in office, earthly in his plan,
> A slave at court, elsewhere a lady's man!
> Dumb as a senator, and, as a priest
> A piece of mere church-furniture at best
> To live estrang'd from God his total scope
> And his end sure, without one glimpse of hope![35]

Cowper must have been really carried away with his own rhetoric here as he had been to school with several men who had turned out to be fine Evangelical bishops and he had at least one such

Evangelical bishop in the family. He must have realized this as, a few lines further on, he gives names of a few believing bishops, though he stresses that they are exceptions which prove the rule.

After grinding the public schools in the dust for their bad administration, their weak discipline and even weaker morals, Cowper also complains that the schools make strangers of the children, who hardly know their own parents when they go down for the end of term. At Westminster, it was quite common for boys to remain in their lodgings even in the holidays as their parents were away 'taking the waters' or visiting the Court. The poet appeals to the parents' consciences and ask them if they think their children really want to be cut off like this from family life. He then goes on to argue that public school boys by nature prefer to be with their parents and as their fathers, at least, have all had a comparatively good education, they are the very best people to teach their sons.

Cowper then proceeds to give such parents a long list of hints as to how they could bring their children up in the nurture and admonition of the Lord. It must be remembered that he is addressing gentlemen, who usually did not follow a profession but lived a life of leisure. If the father were tied up in business, or did not have the ability to teach his own children, then the poet suggested that he should talk to the local clergyman, who might be glad of the chance to teach a protégé or two. Either do that says Cowper, or become like an ostrich and neglect the young.

> The ostrich, silliest of the feather'd kind,
> And formed of God without a parent's mind,
> Commits her eggs, incautious, to the dust,
> Forgetful that the foot might crush the trust.[36]

Finally Cowper closes the poem by taking up the question of whether he would close all public schools and display a notice on each of them saying, 'This Building to be Let.' The poet is not prepared to go that far, as his alternative method has not yet been tried out enough. He stresses, however, that the schools should either be better managed or encouraged less. The Cowpers had a long tradition of sending their sons to Westminster. After the publication of 'Tirocinium' no further Cowpers were sent there. The poet's own family, at least, had got the message.

With the possible exception of Charles Adam Smith, Cowper

was a lone voice in criticizing the state of the public school in the eighteenth century and he was certainly the only critic to suggest a practicable solution. Though the public schools are better organized and controlled nowadays, they are still a weak alternative to a truly Christian family-centred education. Most of their weaknesses have been taken over by state schools of all types and were Cowper to read through the curriculum for religious knowledge taught in some schools he would be reminded of a poem he wrote in 1784 in defence of Newton, when his friend was accused of cant because he believed the Scriptures. The poet wrote,

> These critics, who to faith no quarter grant,
> But call it mere hypocrisy and cant
> To make a just acknowledgment of praise,
> And thanks to God for governing our ways,
> Approve Confucius more, and Zoroaster,
> Than Christ's own servant, or that servant's Master.

Edward C. Mack, in his *Public Schools and British Opinion 1780-1860*, leans heavily on Cowper for support regarding the earlier period and says, 'Cowper was looked back on, even late in the nineteenth century, as the father of moral criticism, as proved by the necessity that so many defenders [of public schools] have felt of answering his arguments'. Perhaps Cowper may still have a word for us today late in the twentieth century.

The public reaction

Cowper's *Task* hit the public, as one writer in the *Gentleman's Magazine* put it, 'like a blaze of fire'. It immediately became standard reading among all classes of society and went through new editions year after year. Reading the *Task* renewed the public's interest in the *Poems*, which had not sold remarkably well, and many editions of that volume, too were published within the next few years.

The *Critical Review*, a thorough-going Conservative magazine, had been the only paper to be heavily critical of Cowper's former volume. Now they led the praise saying that they had not seen anything with such originality of thought, such strength of argument and such poignancy of satire for a long time. This was in spite of the fact that Cowper had praised liberty and denounced the follies of kings far more in the *Task* than in the *Poems*. The *Gentleman's Magazine* echoed these praises saying that they had seldom seen 'such a combination of *utile* and *dulce*'. *The Monthly Review* admired Cowper's boundless imagination and found him 'always moral, yet never dull'. *The Flapper* called Cowper a 'benefactor of human kind and a minister of Heaven' and wrote that 'In choice of expression Cowper yields to no poet in the English language.'

The literary press, as with one voice, compared Cowper favourably with Shakespeare; they found him superior to Pope and the very best poet since Milton. Soon the magazines and journals were talking about Cowper intimately as 'Mr. C.', knowing that everyone knew that they were talking about William Cowper.

But nobody really knew who Cowper was! It is amusing to study the literary magazines of those days. People were writing in asking for information about the life of the great poet, but the editors knew almost as little as their readers. Even the *Gentleman's Magazine*, to which Cowper had been supplying poems for years, got the few facts wrong that it disclosed about Cowper. 'Corrections' were eventually made, but these proved as erroneous as the first efforts. Never was such a famous poet so unknown to his contemporaries.

On tasting such popularity any other British poet of the day would have basked in the limelight, moved up to London and allowed himself to be entertained at Court in order to enjoy to the full the sweet taste of success. Cowper remained on the banks of the slow winding Ouse. He had enough to do. He was busy from morn till night writing letters, doing language research, refreshing his Greek and studying Homer.

13.
The nightingale and the glow-worm

After the *Task* had been sent off to the publisher's, there was still no end to Cowper's second spring. He continued to spend hours out of doors exploring the surrounding countryside, always taking a note-book with him to jot down his observations in verse.

Once, in early 1785, he made for the neighbouring parish of Lavendon, seeking protection from the wind in the shelter of a long row of poplars there. He had spent many hours in previous years sitting beneath them, meditating and day-dreaming. Now, to the poet's dismay, he found that all the trees had been felled. This led him to compose his famous poem 'The Poplar-Field', which opens with the words:

The poplars are fell'd, farewell to the shade
And the whispering sound of the cool colonnade,
The winds play no longer, and sing in the leaves,
Nor Ouse on his bosom their image receives.

Cowper composed the poem in both Latin and English and the *Gentleman's Magazine* accepted both versions, finding them so good that they printed them twice in different editions. Nichols, the printer, was now kept busy for some time with verses from Cowper, who told friends that 'As fast as Nichols prints off the poems, I send them.'

Cowper was not the only one who wished to reap benefits from his growing reputation and skill as a poet. A number of poems were sent to magazines in Cowper's name which he had not written.

Apparently would-be authors felt that their work had more chance of being published if it bore the name of Cowper.

On another occasion Cowper composed a poem about a rose whose stem had been broken when it was plucked. As William Bull was going to London, Cowper asked him to drop the poem at Nichols' for publication. On his way, Bull showed the poem to a Mrs Cardell, who begged him to let her have the poem for a few days and then she would have her servant deliver the poem to Nichols. Not suspecting anything of a shady nature, Bull gave Mrs Cardell the poem. Weeks later the poem had still not reached Nichols and Cowper gave it up for lost. One day, months later, however, Cowper was shocked to find his poem had been published in the *Gentleman's Magazine* and attributed to Mrs Cardell's pen. Writing to Lady Hesketh about the forgery Cowper said, 'Poor simpleton! She will find now perhaps that the rose had a thorn and that she has prick'd her fingers with it.' This was indeed the case. The editor had added a footnote to the poem, partly in very large letters, stating that Mrs Cardell had forgotten to pay the postage![1]

A widening circle of acquaintances

Meanwhile Cowper was receiving ample testimonies and letters from other sources which brought him great joy and, at times, spiritual comfort. Old friends, such as the Bagots and Lord Dartmouth, sent their congratulations and best wishes on the publication of the *Task,* and Christian leaders in the world of culture, business and church life followed suit, among them John Bacon (1740-1799) and John Foster Barham (1721-1781). Bacon, a famous sculptor and member of the Royal Academy, was also a member of the Eclectic Society recently founded by Newton to encourage Evangelical thinking. The society was founded for ministers only but so high was Bacon's standing amongst Evangelicals that he was allowed to become the society's sole lay-member. Barham was a rich businessman who was also looked upon as a staunch leader of the Moravians.

Another new acquaintance was Samuel Greatheed (d. 1823), a retired army officer, though still comparatively young, who was now studying under William Bull's care for the Independent ministry. Greatheed was to become a founder member of the London

Missionary Society and the first editor of the *Eclectic Review*. He often dined with Cowper and served as an intermediary between the poet and friends scattered throughout England. However, in his eagerness to show that he was Cowper's friend, the retired soldier was at times far too free with the information which he gave to strangers about Cowper's health.

At the time of meeting Greatheed, Cowper described him as 'a well-bred, agreeable young man, and one whose eyes have been open'd, I doubt not, for the benefit of others as well as for his own.'[2] Greatheed preached regularly in Olney and Cowper tells of a conversion through his ministry, adding that he would so like to hear Greatheed preach but the King of Kings had forbidden him to appear before him. One can sense in the poet's words the anguish of soul that he was in when he wrote this and how he longed for the 'prohibition', as he termed his inner conviction, to be lifted.

Cowper's letters from this time abound with references to the local Independents and Baptists and show that he was on the best of footings with them. He was particularly pleased to note the spiritual growth of Raban, the carpenter turned Independent pastor, and Wilson the barber, now an enthusiastic Baptist. In the letter to Newton where he gives news of Greatheed Cowper also tells his friend of the stalwart witness of Wilson, who seemed to be growing in grace every time Cowper mentioned him. Wilson had had the difficult duty of admonishing an adulterous Baptist pastor to turn from his evil ways. The barber's efforts produced no change in the erring pastor but Wilson's advice and witness showed how mature he himself had become as a Christian.

After Scott's departure from Olney in 1785 even more members left the parish church to become Dissenters. 1785 was the year when William Carey started to preach at the Olney Baptist Church, which was now almost a hundred strong and pastored by John Sutcliff, who led the church into great times of blessing. Carey never forgot, however, that it was through the Anglican minister, Thomas Scott, that he had been led to the truth. Writing to Dr Ryland a short time before Scott's death, Carey said, 'Pray, give my best thanks to dear Mr. Scott for his translation of the History, &c., of the Synod of Dort. I would write to him if I could command time. If there be anything of the work of God in my soul, I owe much of it to his preaching when I first set out in the ways of the Lord.'[3]

This was the kind of spirit that Cowper felt was the heart of

Christianity. Brother should be bound with brother in the Lord, whatever his denomination. Mutual respect and Christian love should transcend denominational barriers. Such thoughts led him to write his 'Nightingale and Glow-Worm' (perhaps Anglicans and Dissenters?) in which he affirms that:

> ... jarring sectaries may learn
> Their real int'rest to discern;
> That brother should not war with brother,
> And worry and devour each other.

Other friends that Cowper made at this time were the Throckmortons, or 'Frogs' as he often called them. The Throckmortons were a family of Roman Catholics who held the squireship of Weston. Cowper had known the family as a child and was now drawn to them again out of pity. He knew them to be loyal to the king and that they led a God-fearing life, and he detested the way over-enthusiastic Protestant neighbours made their lives very difficult. Cowper determined to befriend them and found them excellent company. The family members gave Cowper the keys not only to their estate but also to their kitchen gardens, telling him to consider himself free to use them as he wished.

Other new neighbours were Lord Peterborough (commonly known as 'the incautious Lothario'), under whose patronage the Rev. Thomas Jones had his living, and His Lordship's lady-friend, Lady Anne Foley, who had left her husband's company for that of Lord Peterborough. Lady Foley soon became tired of her 'Lothario' and formed a third alliance in 1788. Cowper assured Newton, who was rather doubtful about Cowper's new friends, that he need not fear that he would associate himself with Peterborough.

The poet, a vowed opponent of patronages, had never understood how a stalwart Evangelical such as Thomas Jones could serve such a notorious adulterer. Jones, was in fact making an effort to break from Lord Peterborough's patronage but it was proving most difficult as he had also served as His Lordship's steward and there were many financial matters to be cleared up before he could make himself independent of his master. Peterborough had threatened Jones with a court action should he leave his services. Cowper tells Newton of Jones' effort to break with Peterborough and says, 'His connexion with him [Peterborough] indeed, exposes him at present, to almost inevitable danger of giving offence both to those that are within and to those that are without. It is hardly possible for a minister of the Gospel to be more unsuitably associated.'[4]

Renewed correspondence with Lady Hesketh

Shortly after publishing the *Task* Cowper received a long letter from Lady Harriot Hesketh. He had not heard from her for several years as she had been living abroad for some time, moving from place to place in an effort to find some area of the world which would prove beneficial to her husband's health. Now Sir Thomas was dead and Lady Hesketh had returned to England, eager to renew correspondence with her poet cousin.

There were several reasons for this. One was that Lady Hesketh felt she had neglected her family whilst concentrating on the well-being of her husband; another was that she had spent many years as a child and young adult in Cowper's company and was very fond of him. Although Lady Hesketh never confessed this to her cousin, she had been in love with him over a long period in younger days but had not shown her true feelings as Cowper was at that time engaged to her sister Theadora.

The poet was delighted to hear from his cousin again and many happy memories of childhood and youth flooded back to a mind much in need of positive thoughts. He wrote back at once saying, 'It is no new thing with you to give pleasure, but I will venture to say that you do not often give more than you gave me this morning.' He then reminded his cousin of the joys he had shared with her in the past and gave her a summary of his life since their last meeting.

What he says about Mrs Unwin is very moving. Of her he writes, 'That I am happy in my situation is true. I live and have lived these twenty years with Mrs Unwin, to whose affectionate care of me during the far greater part of that time, it is under Providence owing, that I live at all. But I do not count myself happy in having been for 13 of those years in a state of mind that has made all that care and attention necessary. An Attention and a care, that have injured her health, and which, had she not been uncommonly supported, must have brought her to her grave.'[5] The fact was that Mrs Unwin was now feeling the heavy strain of having looked after Cowper so long. She often had dizzy spells which made her fall easily. She suffered from time to time from pains in her abdomen and sides and was plagued with headaches. Whenever Mrs Unwin was ill, Cowper blamed himself severely for being the cause of it and this in turn made him depressed.

Telling his cousin, however, that there were also brighter sides to his existence, the poet went on to describe how he spent his time: writing three hours in the morning, transcribing in the evening, reading, doing bodily exercise and manual work the rest of the day. He closes his letter with an account of his pet animals, which always played an essential part in his happiness.

A lively exchange of letters now ensued between the two cousins with Mrs Unwin also playing a very active part. Though the two ladies had never met, they found they had much in common. Mrs Unwin sent off fatted fowls to Lady Hesketh and Cowper added a volume of his *Task*, a selection of products from his garden and many an amusing anecdote. Lady Hesketh in her turn sent crates of wine and boxes of oysters, apart from small household items needed by her friends at Orchard Side.

She also contacted other members of the family, such as Earl Cowper, General Cowper, Henry Cowper, who was Clerk Assistant at the House of Lords, Ashley Cowper and his daughter Theodora, besides Bishop Spencer Madan, Martin Madan's brother and Cowper's cousin. (Cowper emphasized in his correspondence with Lady Hesketh that he did not wish her to approach Martin Madan in any way on his behalf.) It was decided that the better-off members of the family should grant their poorer relative £100 per annum with no strings attached. For some time Mrs Unwin had been spending twice as much as Cowper on the upkeep of the house, owing to the poet's lack of funds, although he made a substantial contribution to the domestic needs of the household through his smallholding activities. Now, with the welcome addition of the £100 per annum to his otherwise scanty income, both the poet's pocket and his conscience were relieved.

Cowper's prayer life

Cowper's spiritual well-being was also undergoing a change for the better. He was able to pray freely and see God's answer to prayer. Although he was now very cautious as to what he told Newton about his spiritual life, he informed him, 'My spirits are somewhat better than they were. In the course of the last month I have perceived a very sensible amendment. The hope of better days seems again to dawn upon me, and I have now and then an intimation, though slight and transient, that God has not abandoned me for ever.' [6]

The subject of prayer in connection with Cowper is a baffling one. Time and time again when the poet is depressed, he writes as though he had not prayed for years. For example, he said to William Bull in October 1782,

> Prove to me that I have a right to pray, and I will pray without ceasing, yes and praise too, even in the belly of this Hell, compared with which Jonah's was a palace, a temple of the living God. But let me add there is no Encouragement in the Scripture so comprehensive as to include my Case, nor any consolation so effectual as to reach it. I do not relate it to you, because you could not believe it, you would agree with me if you could. And yet the Sin by which I am excluded from the privileges I once enjoy'd, you would account no Sin, you would even tell me that it was a Duty. This is strange — you will think me mad — but I am not mad most noble Festus, I am only in despair, and those powers of mind which I possess, are only permitted me for my Amusement at some times, and to acuminate and enhance my Misery at others.

When in a depression, Cowper forgot completely the times of fellowship with God he had enjoyed in prayer. As he told Lady Hesketh in May 1786, he could be talking or writing about a subject when without warning his feelings would suddenly either soar or sink and project him into one or other state of mind, shutting him off from all contrary thoughts. In his letters Cowper refers at least a dozen times to his prayers, even though we find interspersed with these other references in which he claims he does not pray, or at least, has no right to pray.

In one letter to Lady Hesketh, for instance, Cowper quotes Watts' lines concerning drops of sacred sorrows which turn into rivers of delight and confesses that his heart is 'light as a bird'. He writes, 'Neither without prayer, nor without confidence in the providential goodness of God, has this work been undertaken or continued. I am not so dim-sighted, sad as my spirit is at times, but that I can plainly discern his Providence going before me in the way.'[7]

A month after writing this letter, we find Cowper still praying, this time for his old schoolfriend Walter Bagot, whose wife had recently died. Bagot, a prosperous landowner-clergyman and brother to a lord and an Evangelical bishop, turned to Cowper in his hour of need saying, 'Oh, my dear friend—Things are much altered with me since I wrote last. My harp is turned into mourning, and my music into the voice of weeping. Her whom you saw and loved, — her whom nobody ever yet saw and knew that did not love; — her have I lost. Pray to God for me, that for Christ's sake he would continue to comfort and support both me and mine under our great affliction.'

Cowper replied comfortingly:

Alas! Alas! My dear, dear friend, may God himself comfort you. I will not be so absurd as to attempt it. By the close of your letter it should seem that in this hour of great trial, he withholds not his consolations from you. I know by experience that they are neither few nor small, and though I feel for you as I never felt for man before, yet do I Sincerely rejoice in this, that whereas there is but one true Comforter in the Universe under afflictions such as yours, you both know him and know where to seek him. I thought you a man the most happily mated that I had ever seen, and had great pleasure in your felicity. Pardon me if now I feel a wish that short as my acquaintance with her was, I had never seen her. I should have mourned with you but not as I do now. Mrs. Unwin sympathizes with you also most Sincerely, and you neither are nor will be soon forgotten in such pray'rs as we can make at Olney. I will not detain you longer now, my poor afflicted friend, than to commit you to the tender mercy of God, and to bid you a Sorrowful Adieu! Ever yours

Wm C.[8]

Comforting as this letter must have been to Walter Bagot, it also throws great light on Cowper's faith thirteen years after the major mental breakdown which most biographers believe ended his trust in his God for ever. Here the poet testifies to his own experiences of the comforting bounties of God and his joy in the fact that such grace is available to all who trust in him. He knows, too, that such comfort can be gained for the saints through the intercession of their brethren. Sparse though references to such prayer may be in Cowper's prose, he reverts to the topic over forty times in his post-1773 poetry.

Oddly enough, it was Cowper's strong conviction concerning the efficacy of prayer that earned him his harshest criticism in the press over his publication of the *Task*. The *Gentleman's Magazine* for April 1786 contained a lengthy letter from a correspondent begging leave to criticize the poet who had been so lately 'liberally applauded' by the magazine. The writer, who signed himself 'Philaretes' (i. e. 'Friend of Virtue'), accused Cowper of being a 'ranter' because the poet criticized 'priests' who 'hide divinity from mortal eyes', and said that they are 'blind and in love with darkness', and deny the deity of Christ.[9] 'Philaretes' is of the opinion that as these clergymen claim to be Christians it would only be charitable to allow them freedom of exegesis, as they have probably studied the Scriptures at least as much as Cowper.

In the poem Cowper goes on to compare these scoffing theologians with an unknown saint who is tucked away in some obscure backwater of society, but whose prayers, nevertheless, engage the notice of God and whose virtues make themselves felt, even though unseen by men, since God takes heed of this man's petitions in governing his world. Such faith in the efficacy of prayer is described by 'Philaretes' as 'spiritual swaggering' and 'worse than praying at the corners of streets', since the Christian presumes that his prayers are responsible for what is in fact simply God's common grace to all mankind.

Cowper, however, knew from experience that 'The effectual fervent prayer of a righteous man availeth much.'[10] He himself had written earlier:

> Pray'r makes the dark'ned cloud withdraw,
> Pray'r climbs the ladder Jacob saw;
> Gives exercise to faith and love,
> Brings ev'ry blessing from above.[11]

The poet speaks of his own illness

One of the many signs that Cowper was at this time feeling far better than he had done for many years was that he was prepared to discuss openly with Lady Hesketh what had happened to him in 1773. Cowper hated to think he was the subject of morbid curiosity and until his letter of 16 January 1786 to Lady Hesketh he had not told a soul about his real feelings at that time. Often certain over-curious or unthinking friends had touched on the matter at an inopportune time and in so doing had occasioned hours and sometimes days of agony for the poet. Lady Hesketh, however, did not plague her cousin with questions about his illness. The result was that he felt he could speak to her about what had happened when he was in a frame of mind suitable for discussing it.

We thus find Cowper giving an account of his 1773 illness to Lady Hesketh with the same openness that he had shown when he described his first attack of mental illness to the Unwins whilst staying with them at Huntingdon. In his letter of 16 January, he thanks his cousin for not pressing him for information about his illness and goes on to write:

> Because you do not ask, and because your reason for not asking consists of a delicacy and tenderness peculiar to yourself, for that very cause I will tell you. A wish so suppressed is more irresistible than many wishes plainly uttered. Know then that in the year 73 the same scene that was acted at St. Albans, opened upon me again at Olney, only covered with a still deeper shade of melancholy, and ordained to be of much longer duration. I was suddenly reduced from my wonted rate of understanding to an almost childish imbecility. I did not indeed lose my senses, but I lost the power to exercise them. I could return a rational answer even to a difficult question, but a question was necessary, or I never spoke at all. This state of mind was accompanied, as I suppose it to be in most instances of the kind, with misapprehension of things and persons that made me a very untractable patient. I believed that every body hated me, and that Mrs. Unwin hated me most of all; was convinced that all my food was poisoned, together with ten thousand megrims of the same

stamp. I would not be more circumstantial than is necessary. Dr. Cotton was consulted. He replied that he could do no more for me than might be done at Olney, but recommended particular vigilance, lest I should attempt my life: — a caution for which there was the greatest occasion. At the same time that I was convinced of Mrs. Unwin's aversion to me, [I] could endure no other companion. The whole management of me consequently devolved upon her, and a terrible task she had; she performed it, however, with a cheerfulness hardly ever equalled on such an occasion; and I have often heard her say, that if ever she praised God in her life it was when she found that she was to have all the labour. She performed it accordingly, but, as I hinted once before, very much to the hurt of her own constitution. It will be thirteen years in little more than a week, since this malady seized me. Methinks I hear you ask, — your affection for me will, I know, make you wish to do so, — Is it removed? I reply, in great measure, but not quite. Occasionally I am much distressed, but that distress becomes continually less frequent, and I think less violent. I find writing, and especially poetry, my best remedy. Perhaps had I understood music, I had never written verse, but had lived upon fiddle-strings instead. It is better however as it is. A poet may, if he pleases, be of a little use in the world, while a musician, the most skilful, can only divert himself and a few others. I have been emerging gradually from this pit. As soon as I became capable of action, I commenced carpenter, made cupboards, boxes, stools. I grew weary of this in about a twelvemonth, and addressed myself to the making of bird-cages. To this employment succeeded that of gardening, which I intermingled with that of drawing, but finding that the latter occupation injured my eyes, I renounced it, and commenced poet. I have given you, my dear, a little history in shorthand; I know that it will touch your feelings, but do not let it interest them too much.

It can be considered one of the guiding miracles of God in the life of Cowper that the poet did not remain a carpenter and maker of birdcages. Whilst working with his saw and plane, Cowper became almost blind in one eye and was thus forced to stop the work. Later his sight was restored and he was able to write poetry to God's glory with the full use of both eyes.

There is a postscript to this letter which Cowper sent a week later. Cowper was keen to tell his cousin what his harrowing experiences had meant to his soul. He thus writes,

> I knew that my last letter would give you pain, but there is no need that it should give you so much. He who hath preserved me hitherto, will still preserve me. All the dangers that I have escaped are so many pillars of remembrance to which I shall hereafter look back with comfort, and be able, as I well hope, to inscribe on every one of them a grateful memorial of God's singular protection of me. Mine has been a life of wonders for many years, and a life of wonders I in my heart believe it will be to the end. Wonders I have seen in the great deeps, and wonders I shall see in the paths of mercy also. This, my dear, is my creed.

It is this creed of Cowper's that has made the man such a shining example, in the same way that Job was. Words similar to Job's mighty declaration of faith, 'Though he slay me, yet will I trust him', were often on his lips — even when he felt that he was in the belly of hell. His testimony moved Nielson Campbell Hanney to write in his work *The Tragedy of Cowper* that Cowper was 'in all matters exterior to himself one of the safest and sanest of men'. He concludes: 'How many men with but a tithe of Cowper's excuse for doing so would have developed into ugliness of personality, and, if blessed with genius, would have devoted it to ignoble ends! Yet he learned the larger obedience by the things which he suffered and kept faith with God and with man.'[12]

In his letter to Lady Hesketh Cowper gives the only hint in his extant writings that he was tempted as a Christian to take his own life in 1773. John Johnson, a younger kinsman of Cowper's, recorded that the poet made a similar statement regarding the year 1773 before being forced to leave his home at Weston in 1795.[13] This statement is appended to Cowper's works by King and Ryskamp unter the very misleading title of 'Cowper's Spiritual Diary' in their belief that Johnson's notes reproduce the poet's very words. A word of caution is, however, necessary here. It is obvious from the known facts that Johnson often completely misunderstood Cowper.

The poet was also notorious for getting his dates wrong, especially when he was depressed, and often confused the events of 1763 with events that followed many years later. For instance, he obviously confused particulars of his 1773 illness with those of his pre-conversion illness of 1763 and predated other events, such as his meeting with the Unwins, to 1763 although he actually first met them some two years later.[14] Furthermore, when trying to remember when Mrs Unwin had been taken seriously ill soon after their removal from Huntingdon to Olney, Cowper dated the illness to 1763, and not to 1767 when it actually occurred. Writing to Samuel Teedon in 1792 of his hope that he would one day find full liberty to trust once more in his redemption, Cowper says that he had had 'fetters clap't on' him twice since 1773. It would appear from the context (as King and Ryskamp also point out) that here again Cowper is confusing 1773 with 1763.

To add to the confusion, the poet wrote to John Newton in December 1792 about 'dreadful 1773', but added that 1786 was 'more dreadful'. Cowper's life throughout 1786 is thoroughly documented and there are no records of a 'more dreadful illness' in that year, though the poet was physically ill for several months during the following year. If Cowper is indeed referring to the years 1773 and 1787 it is very difficult to see what could have been 'more dreadful' in 1787 than 1773. There is thus a strong possibility that Cowper was again confusing the dates and was referring to 1763 and 1773, the only two years in which, according to his own testimony elsewhere, he was mentally ill.

Even if Cowper did contemplate suicide in 1773, this does not mean that he actually attempted to take his own life. The words referring to suicide attributed to him in 'Cowper's Spiritual Diary' — if they are, indeed, his own words — suggest no more than that he had a terrible temptation. Although it was usual for earlier biographers to stress, without giving evidence, that Cowper attempted suicide as a Christian on several occasions, there is a definite trend amongst biographers nowadays to treat all such theories with great caution.[15]

Light and shade in his correspondence with Newton

Cowper's letters to Newton after their row were very cautious and the poet kept them as politically neutral as possible. This was a difficult task as he continued to visit the Olney poor and he felt that the government's attitude to them was highly unchristian. He had been visiting a desolate crippled widow who lived in a derelict mud-walled cottage. She received a shilling a week poor-money from the parish but needed at least two shillings a week to live on. Cowper outlined her case to Newton with a few gentle digs at adverse taxation laws. Newton responded immediately and soon fresh funds were flowing into Olney. This made Cowper feel that things were back to normal with Newton so his letters became more and more cheerful.

Newton was indebted to Cowper for much of his skill in writing humorously. We often find that humorous remarks and clichés originally made by Cowper in his letters are reiterated and built upon by Newton some time later.[16] Where certain evangelical doctrines and customs were concerned, Newton, however, was for maintaining strict seriousness, whereas Cowper could tease his friends about most things, especially if he thought they were being too stiff and starchy. Cowper could never weigh up Newton's humour in this respect and his attempts at humour occasionally met with little understanding on his friend's part.

Such an occasion presented itself in March 1785 when Cowper wrote Newton a teasing letter that obviously did not please his friend. The poet and Mrs Unwin needed a new dining-table. They wanted a table which did not take up too much room and could be folded up and stored away when not in use. Cowper succeeded in procuring a card-table which filled the required rôle, though the pockets, or 'fish-ponds' as Cowper called them, at the corners for the dice, cards etc., often caused cups to be overturned, especially when covered by a tablecloth. Now intent on pulling Newton's leg, Cowper wrote a long letter praising the qualities of the card-table, telling his friend, however, right at the beginning that the table was used for everything but for the activity for which it was designed.

As he emphasizes time and time again in his writings, Cowper thought that card-playing was a complete waste of a Christian's time, so he did not at all anticipate that Newton would fail to respond positively to the teasing. This light-hearted letter seems, however, to have shaken Newton considerably. Newton had on several occasions quoted Cowper in his sermons as an example of a gentleman who had turned his back on the card-table for ever. Now it seemed to him that his friend was being far too light-hearted about a serious subject. He somehow connected this incident with his knowledge that Cowper had recurring doubts of his salvation and thus wrote a very serious, dismal letter to the poet, reminding him of the very things that Cowper's sense of humour was helping him to forget.

Instead of telling Newton to stop harping on that dismal tune Cowper fell again into a depression but wrote gently to his friend:

> I am sensible of the tenderness and affectionate kindness with which you recollect our past intercourse, and express your hopes of my future restoration. I too within the last eight months have had my hopes, though they have been of short duration, cut off like the foam upon the waters. Some previous adjustments indeed are necessary, before a lasting expectation of comfort can have place in me. There are those persuasions in my mind which either entirely forbid the entrance of hope or if it enter, immediately eject it. They are incompatible with any such inmate, and must be turned out themselves, before so desirable a guest can possibly have secure possession. This, you say, will be done. It may be, but it is not done yet, nor has a Single step in the course of God's dealings with me, been taken towards it. If I mend, no creature ever mended so slowly that recover'd at last. I am like a slug or snail that has fallen into a deep well; slug as he is he performs his descent with an alacrity proportion'd to his weight, but he does not crawl up again quite so fast. Mine was a rapid plunge, but my return to day light, if I am indeed returning, is leisurely enough.[17]

Here Cowper is trying to tell Newton that the only way of filling his mind with positive ideas of his salvation is to make sure that the negative ones are removed first. William Unwin had this masterly pastoral touch when writing to Cowper. About the same time as Newton's dismal letter, Unwin had written a cheerful epistle to his friend to which Cowper had replied, 'I thank you for your letter. It made me laugh, and there are not many things capable of being contained within the dimensions of a letter, for which I see cause to be more thankful.'[18] The fact was that when Cowper was able to laugh, his whole outlook became positive. When reminded of dismal subjects, his whole outlook became negative.

This is clearly seen in a comparison of Cowper's 'card-table' letter to Newton with a later one. In the first letter the poet reported in a carefree manner how the spinney where he used to pray with Newton had been cut down and the wood was now being used by the poor of Olney to roast potatoes and boil kettles, adding a couplet:

> Such various services can trees perform,
> Whom once they screened from heat, in time they warm.

Cowper closes his description by saying that he has two wagon-loads of logs from the spinney in his woodloft.

The poet returns to the subject of the spinney after several gloomy letters from Newton which had reminded him of his melancholy convictions. Now he writes,

I told you I believe that the Spinney has been cut down, and though it may seem sufficient to have mention'd such an occurrence once, I cannot help recurring to the melancholy theme. Last night at near 9 o'clock we enter'd it for the first time this summer. We had not walked many yards in it, before we perceived that this pleasant retreat is destined never to be a pleasant retreat again. In one more year the whole will be a thicket. That which was once the serpentine walk is now in a state of transformation and is already become as woody as the rest. Poplars and elms without number are springing in the turf, they are now as high as the knee. Before the summer is ended they will be twice as high, and the growth of another season will make them trees. It will then be impossible for any but a sportsman and his dog to penetrate it. The desolation of the whole scene is such that it sunk our spirits. The ponds are dry. The circular one in front of the hermitage is filled with flags and rushes so that if it contains any water not a drop is visible. The weeping willow at the side of it, the only ornamental plant that has escaped the ax, is dead. The ivy and the moss with which the hermitage was lined, are torn away, and the very mats that cover'd the benches, have been stripp'd off, rent in tatters, and trodden under foot. So farewell Spinney. I have promised myself that I will never enter it again. We have both pray'd in it. You for me, and I for you, but it is desecrated from this time forth, and the voice of pray'r will be heard in it no more. The fate of it in this respect, however deplorable is not peculiar; the spot where Jacob

anointed his pillar, and which is more apposite, the spot once
honour'd with the presence of Him who dwelt in the bush,[19]
have long since suffer'd similar disgrace, and are become
common ground.[20]

By September, Cowper's letters to Newton were becoming more
cheerful again and he was once more his own teasing self. Newton
had been on holiday to Southampton with his niece, Eliza
Cunningham, whom the Newtons had taken on as their own daughter and who had been unwell for some time. The poet tells Newton
that he had enjoyed Southampton with its dancing, cards and high
society, as an unconverted man, but now he could not do so. It is
obvious that Cowper felt that the famous seaside resort for the
pleasure-seeking rich was hardly the place for an Evangelical
minister to take a convalescing Christian young lady.

The poet then goes on to tell Newton of his first antics as a sailor
off the shores of Southampton in the Heskeths' ship, concluding his
tale of claustrophobia in the cabin and general discomfort in stormy
weather with the words: 'I make little doubt but Noah was glad when
he was enlarged from the ark, and we are sure that Jonah was when
he came out of the fish, and so was I to escape from the good sloop
the Hariot.'

In a previous letter Cowper had told Newton that Mr Perry, an
Independent brother well-known to Newton, had just been wrongly
pronounced dead by his doctor. After telling Newton of his adventures at sea, Cowper returned to the subject of Mr Perry saying that
the man whom the doctor had pronounced dead had just walked in
bearing a letter for Newton which he asked Cowper to enclose in his.
The only difference to the man, now fully recovered, Cowper
informed Newton, is that Mr Perry looks more like an angel than
ever. 'Illness sanctified is better than health' was Cowper's final
comment.

Controversy over relationships with Dissenters

This reference to an Independent friend itself included an element
of teasing. Newton had been suffering from severe criticism at the
hands of Independents and Baptists since publishing his *Apology*
and he was beginning to react irrationally against their harsh words.
Instead of keeping to an exposition of his faith based on the Bible,

Newton had started to argue on political lines with Dissenters, striving to show that only Anglicans were true patriots. Cowper had already written a poem lampooning any kind of exaggerated patriotic feeling[21] and he got on very well with a number of Dissenters. Not realizing just how serious Newton was in his criticism, Cowper hardly ever wrote a letter to him without some reference to Independents or Baptists. This must have galled rather than amused Newton as he was soon to condemn all denominations other than Anglicans as being republicans and thus enemies of the king. Newton even went so far as to campaign for the government to put a special control on them.

William Bull was a convinced monarchist and as true an Englishman as any, besides being a man of the Bible. Yet Newton wrote to him, telling him that even orthodox Dissenters were enemies of the government. It is no wonder that Bull wrote to his son on receiving this letter saying, 'Could you think so good a man could be so weak?'[22] Bull hardly ever wrote to his son, who had followed him into the ministry, without advising him to preach nothing but Christ and leave politics completely alone. Nevertheless, even Bull, who was no great friend of republicanism, was accused by the mob of being in league with Thomas Paine and burnt in effigy with a label around its neck saying, 'Tom Paine, Parson Bull, or the Devil'.[23]

Those Evangelicals, such as Romaine, Jones and Scott, who kept up fellowship with Dissenters came under heavy fire. Both Jones and Scott were burnt in effigy and Romaine was accused by his Anglican brethren of being an Antinomian.

It was the heat of controversy in Olney and the surrounding district that finally convinced Scott that he would have to leave and take up his ministry at the Lock Hospital. Cowper, however, felt that Scott, in spite of his weaknesses, would be more useful in Olney than trying to mend the reputation of the Lock after Martin Madan had ruined it so thoroughly. Cowper also thought of the difficulties he himself would have, explaining to a new minister why he could not go to church.

Death of the Newtons' niece

On 6 October 1785 Eliza Cunningham died and Cowper wrote a letter of condolence to John and Mary Newton saying,

To have sent a child to heaven is a great honour & a great blessing; and your feelings on such an occasion may well be such as render you rather an object of congratulation than of condolence. And were it otherwise, yet having yourself, free access to all the sources of genuine consolation, I feel that it would be little better than impertinence in me to suggest any. An escape from a life of suffering to a life of happiness and glory, is such a deliverance as leaves no room for the sorrow of survivors, unless they sorrow for themselves. We cannot indeed lose what we loved without regretting it, but a Christian is in possession of such alleviations of that regret as the world knows nothing of. Their Beloveds when they die, go they know not whither, and if they suppose them as they generally do in a state of happiness, they have yet but an indifferent prospect of joining them in that state hereafter. But it is not so with you. You both know whither your beloved is gone, and you know that you shall follow her, and you know also that in the mean time she is incomparably happier than yourself. So far therefore as she is concerned, nothing has come to pass, but what was most fervently to be wished.[24]

During the days after Eliza's death, Newton wrote an account of her last hours, spent in absolute trust in God, and sent a copy to Cowper who replied:

Your history of your happy Niece, is just what it should be — clear, affectionate and plain: worthy of her, and worthy of yourself. How much more beneficial to the world might such a memorial of an unknown but pious and believing child eventually prove, would the supercilious Learned condescend to read it, than the history of all the Kings and heroes that ever lived! But the world has its objects of admiration, and God has objects of his love. These make a noise and perish, and those weep silently for a short season, and live for ever. I had rather have been your niece or the writer of her story than any Caesar that ever thundered.[25]

Musical performances in church

During 1784 Cowper and Newton had frequently corresponded about the centenary celebrations performed in churches and chapels in honour of the musician Handel.[26] Newton thought of publishing an article against such misuse of sacred buildings and discussed the matter with Cowper. The latter replied in his best satirical style:

My dear friend —

We are much pleased with your designed improvement of the late preposterous celebrity, and have no doubt that in your hands the foolish occasion will turn to good account. A religious service instituted in honor of a Musician, and performed in the house of God, is a subject that calls loudly for the animadversion of an enlighten'd minister, and would be no mean one for a Satyrist, could a poet of that description be found spiritual enough to feel and to resent the profanation. It is reasonable to suppose that in the next year's Almanac we shall find the name of Handel among the red-letter'd worthies, for it would surely puzzle the Pope himself to add any thing to his Canonization. The Bishops however seem to have been rather slack, as indeed they prove themselves to be upon most devotional occasions. I take it for granted that they were hearers, but why were they not performers too? A fiddle would have made a figure in Episcopal hands, and such a spectacle would have added much to the raptures felt by the congregation. But perhaps it was foreseen that being incumber'd with lawn sleeves, they could not conveniently have given the Bow that sweep that is necessary to call out the tone of the instrument. Allowing the force of the objection, they are nevertheless not to be accounted altogether blameless. They might at least have handled the bassoon or the French horn commodiously enough, and by the distension of their cheeks as much as by their performance have given a singular relish to the entertainments of the day.[27]

Cowper, like Newton, was thinking here mainly of the production of Handel's *Messiah* in Westminster Abbey. Newton's article grew into a full-length book as he battled with the problem of an entertainment-mad church. He finally adopted the plan of preaching on the fifty texts misused by Handel in his musical presentation of the *Messiah*, thus making sure that his congregation would associate Christ with the scriptural way of salvation rather than with drums, trumpets and fiddles. Cowper beat Newton to the press, however, with his harangue against church concerts in his *Task* where he says,

> Man praises man. Desert in arts or arms
> Wins public honour; and ten thousand sit
> Patiently present at a sacred song,
> Commemoration-mad; content to hear
> (Oh wonderful effect of music's pow'r!)
> Messiah's eulogy for Handel's sake!
> But less, methinks, than sacrilege might serve—
> (For, was it less, what heathen would have dar'd
> To strip Jove's statue of his oaken wreath,
> And hang it up in honour of a man?)
> Much less might serve, when all that we design
> Is but to gratify an itching ear,
> And give the day to a musician's praise.
> Remember Handel ? Who, that was not born
> Deaf as the dead to harmony, forgets,
> Or can, the more than Homer of his age?
> Yes — we remember him; and, while we praise
> A talent so divine, remember too
> That His most holy book from whom it came
> Was never meant, was never us'd before,
> To buckram out the mem'ry of a man.
> But hush ! — the muse perhaps is too severe;
> And, with a gravity beyond the size
> And measure of th' offence, rebukes a deed
> Less impious than absurd, and owing more
> To want of judgment than to wrong design.[28]

If Cowper thought that putting such concerts on in God's house was a greater sacrilege than any pagan votary would have dared to commit, what would he, or his friend Newton, have thought of the hard rock, heavy metal and rock-a-billy follies that modern evangelicals put on as a substitute for true worship?

By February 1786 Newton had finished his fifty sermons and, as usual, approached Cowper for appropriate mottos from the classical poets. Cowper supplied him with a quote from Virgil's *Ecologues* which translated means, 'Our songs we shall sing the better, when the master himself has arrived,' and one from the Aeneid proclaiming, 'One life shall be given for many.' These two mottos were used by Newton but he added a third by Terence: 'Ah, to handle a matter of such consequence so off-handedly.'

Practical expressions of friendship between cousins

Meanwhile letters were being exchanged at high speed between Cowper and Lady Hesketh. The poet's letters contain simple thoughts and anecdotes which he never expressed to anyone else, such as the fact that he had bought a skipping-rope to help him keep in form, to be used alternatively with his dumb-bells. It is amusing indeed to think of the fifty-five-year-old, now on the plump side, spending an odd moment each day skipping like a happy little girl, or exercising like a prize boxer keen to trim each muscle to its utmost. This is hardly the picture of the inactive hermit many biographers have painted of Cowper!

One of the many healing factors that accompanied Cowper's renewed acquaintance with his cousin was that his nightly fevers and bad dreams disappeared for some time. This left him more cheerful and relaxed during the day.

There was now hardly a room at Orchard Side that did not proudly display some token of Lady Hesketh's kindness. Cowper had been doing the bulk of his writing using an atlas as an underlay, propped up on his wobbly card-table. This moved Lady Hesketh to provide him with a smart transportable writing-desk. No gift could have pleased the poet more, as he told his cousin in his reply: 'Oh that this letter had wings, that it might fly to tell you that my desk, the most elegant, the compactest, the most commodious desk in the world, and of all the desks that ever were or ever shall be, the desk that I love the most, it is safe arrived.' [29] Practical as Lady Hesketh was, she did not forget to present her cousin with enough writing-paper to keep him busy for some time to come. A large solid chair was sent as a companion to the desk.

Many years before, when Cowper's family were threatening to stop their allowances to the poet because he had adopted Dick

Lady Hesketh

Coleman and was keeping a servant — a luxury they thought he could ill afford — the poet received an amount of money from an anonymous friend. Cowper had always thought that this anonymous person was Lady Hesketh, though she would have had no cause to withhold her name. He now began once more to receive gifts and letters from the same anonymous source. As he was now corresponding openly with Lady Hesketh, it was obvious that she was not 'Anonymous', as Cowper called his unknown friend. Thus Cowper wrote to Lady Hesketh in January 1786 informing her that

> Anonymous is come again; — may God bless him, whosoever he be, as I doubt not that he will. A certain person said on a certain occasion, (and he never spoke a word that failed), Whoso giveth you a cup of cold water in my name, shall by no means lose his reward. Therefore anonymous as he chooses to be upon earth, his name, I trust, will hereafter be found written in heaven. But when great princes, or characters much superior to great princes, choose to be incog. it is a sin against decency and good manners to seem to know them. I therefore know nothing of anonymous, but that I love him heartily and with most abundant cause.

It would appear that Cowper had now made a second guess as to who 'Anonymous' was and he had probably guessed correctly. True to his word, however, Cowper never told anyone who he believed his anonymous benefactor was. In fact the person now corresponding with Cowper and assisting him financially was none other than Theadora Cowper, his former fiancée. Theadora had gone through years of acute loneliness and nervous disorder: she had never married, and still retained a deep affection for her cousin William. One comfort to her had been a large collection of poems which he had sent to her and which she had read over and over again and treasured through the many years since their courtship ended.

Perhaps Lady Hesketh's most famous gift to Cowper was the large, lace cap which the poet wears in his portrait by Romney. Much has been written about this cap, which is supposed to show how effeminate Cowper was but, in fact, it was the normal eighteenth-century male headgear for a gentleman when he was not wearing his wig.[30] Before he was given the cap Cowper had worn his own hair bundled in a bag at the nape of his neck, in the French manner, or worn a pigtail, after the British style. He was rather conscious of the fact that his new cap seemed more showy than masculine but always wore it from then on, even when having his picture painted, because it kept his head warm and because it was made by his favourite cousin.

Mrs Unwin had equal cause to praise Lady Hesketh for her generosity. Soon she had new bedding, new carpets, new curtains and new china, and Orchard Side had become a most comfortable place. True to Cowper's character and way of thanking friends, he wrote a long poem entitled 'Benefactions', with one verse for each item received, to thank Lady Hesketh for her gifts. The first verse is about his lace cap:

This cap that so lately appears
With ribbon-bound tassel on high,
Which seems by the crest that it rears
Ambitious of brushing the sky;
This cap to my Harriet I owe;
She gave it, and gave me beside
A ribbon, worn out long ago,
With which in its youth it was tied.

Comfortable as Orchard Side was within, on the outside its walls were crumbling and building experts were saying that they were in danger of collapsing completely. Damp was everywhere and, situated as the house was in the most derelict area of Olney, Cowper's and Mrs Unwin's occupation of it was a perpetual threat to their health.

Cowper's days at Orchard Side were now numbered but before he moved on, its walls were once again to echo the cheerful chatter of a most welcome lady guest. By February 1786 all had been arranged. Lady Hesketh was to visit Orchard Side in the late spring, complete with her entourage.

Cowper would not think of her staying in a hotel and assured her that Orchard Side was quite large enough to accommodate them all. However, when Mrs Unwin heard just how many servants Lady Hesketh was bringing with her, including coach and driver, she realized that Orchard Side was too small and enquired in the neighbourhood for extra lodgings for Lady Hesketh's servants and a shed for the coach. Cowper had not thought of the Vicarage, which had stood almost empty since Scott left for London. The new curate had only taken over a couple of rooms and lived there in very Spartan conditions. A Quaker couple, who had set up business as 'jacks of all trade', suggested the house to Cowper, promising him that that they could furnish the empty rooms at the vicarage for Lady Hesketh and her servants at a fair price.

It was eventually decided that, at the risk of still being cramped, both Cowper's cousin and her servants should stay there. Cowper arranged for the gateway at the back of the Vicarage, which Lady Austen had used, to be reopened, as it was now bricked up and thus Lady Hesketh would have quick access at any time to Orchard Side. The business-minded Quakers had bought up Lord Peterborough's and Lady Anne Foley's furniture when their illicit romance broke up and they left the district. Thus Lady Hesketh would have the very best of furniture though it might come from the worst of sources.

So keen was Cowper to give his cousin the very best that he sent off to London for kitchen utensils and had three tons of the best coal delivered from Bedford. On 17 April he sent his cousin a minutely detailed list of furniture, bedding, drapery, crockery, mops, brooms, brushes, candles, pots and pans. The only items Cowper confessed he had been unable to obtain were books, so he advised his cousin to bring her own.

Newton is concerned about Cowper's friends

Now that Cowper was once again on friendly terms with his family he began to associate through them with a wider circle of friends, both old and new. Lord Dartmouth, for instance, renewed his interest in Cowper through his contacts with Lady Hesketh.

One natural reason for Cowper's joy at this development was that, apart from the curate, he had for many years been the only educated man and the only gentleman in Olney, and he longed for that spiritual and intellectual rapport which could be gained through contact with the best minds in his own class. Newton, in comparison, was in the envious position of living but a stone's throw from a number of his friends and was often the guest of wealthy and educated gentlefolk. Others visited his church regularly.

A second reason was that Cowper was preparing a multi-volumed edition of the works of Homer and thought of financing it

by subscription. He was therefore eager to mobilize all his friends
and relations so that he could gain enough subscribers and go ahead
with his project. William Unwin was especially energetic in this
cause.

As Cowper never left Olney his only contact with the outside
world was through the local Post Office, apart from occasional visits
from friends. Olney gossips picked up the news from the Post Office
and were only too eager to add their own versions to the reasons
behind Cowper's association with some of the most well-known
names in the country, and highly exaggerated rumours were soon
being spread. Nothing of such interest had ever happened before in
the working-class town. These pieces of gossip eventually reached
Newton's ears, most likely through his servants, who occasionally
visited Olney, their home town. Without checking the facts Newton
apparently believed the worst and wrote a very worried letter asking
Cowper why he was associating with such worldly people.[31]

This was a very strange reaction on Newton's part, as Cowper
had kept him well-informed of his actions. Furthermore several of
Cowper's aristocratic correspondents and most of his wealthy ones
were close acquaintances of Newton and some of them, such as the
Smiths and Lord Dartmouth, were amongst his best friends. The
Bagot family were well-known for their Evangelical sympathies, as
were most members of Cowper's wider family. Although Newton
had always been very reserved with Unwin, the latter's Evangelicalism could not be doubted, especially as he had recently been
instrumental in winning back William Wilberforce to a new awareness of his sins and hope in Christ's saving work. Unwin was a close
friend of the Thorntons, the family of wealthy Evangelical merchants, who were also good friends of Newton. Indeed the list of the
400 subscribers to Cowper's *Homer* contains the names of very
many outstanding Evangelicals.

Newton mentioned no names, however, in his general criticism
of Cowper's connections, so it was impossible for the poet to know
which of his friends Newton considered 'worldly'. Apart from the
symptoms of jealousy which Newton invariably showed in relation
to any of Cowper's friends, the only connections Cowper had that
might have given Newton cause to worry were the Throckmortons,
but they were the last people one might have thought worldly and
they regularly entertained Evangelicals at their home. A later letter

from Newton shows that much of his criticism was indeed levelled at Cowper's connections with his Roman Catholic neighbours.

In this it would appear that Newton was making a grave political mistake. He had campaigned in earlier years for liberty for both Dissenters and Roman Catholics, but now he seems to have suspected all of them, without exception, of being involved in seditious political intrigue. Criticisms of the type made by Newton were to move Cowper a few years later to write to the *General Evening Post,* which published in its issue for 21-24 March 1789 an extract referring to the part the Throckmortons had played in organizing celebrations on the king's recovery from a major illness. In this article, the poet, temporarily turned journalist, writes,

> At the seat of John Courtney Throgmorton,[32] Esq; at Weston Underwood, in this county, his Majesty's happy recovery was celebrated on Saturday evening last, with a spirit that did honour to the liberal possessor of that mansion, and highly gratified a joyful neighbourhood. A splendid illumination with the Royal initials and Crown in the centre, together with fire-works of various kinds, afforded a spectacle to the country people, for the sake of which they gladly left a large bonfire, and every thing except a cask of excellent ale, which they emptied in the grove that fronts the dwelling. The Olney band attended, and performed 'God Save the King,' (in which they were joined by the company), together with several other pieces of music, in a manner that well harmonized with the festivity of the occasion.

It is worthy of note that when Grimshawe, who was an Evangelical, published his best-selling complete works of Cowper, one of his reasons for doing so was to unite warring factions in their common admiration of Cowper's works. He therefore portrayed the poet's Calvinism in a way that he believed would be acceptable to Arminians and dedicated his volumes to the Dowager Lady Throckmorton, whom Grimshawe knew and esteemed personally.

Cowper did not react angrily to Newton's accusations although he felt himself innocent of the charges. He was well aware that Newton himself had quite a different approach to other people and lived in a very different world from that of Olney, and he had never criticized his friend directly for often visiting the most fashionable holiday resorts, such as Southampton, Margate and Hastings, where he was the guest of nobility and wealthy merchants. He also never ceased to regard Newton as the pastor *par excellence* and always considered his advice most carefully.

The best explanation of Cowper's relationship to Newton in these matters is to be found in his poem 'The Nightingale and the Glow-Worm', which Cowper obviously wrote autobiographically. The poet had two views of himself which can often appear contradictory. He belittled his own service as a poet and translator, but was fully persuaded that God had called him to this task. Cowper wrote to Newton in July 1791 on hearing that Henry Venn was dying, saying,

> I am sorry that Mr. Venn's labours below are so near to a conclusion. I have seen few men whom I could have loved more, had opportunity been given me to know him better. So at least I have thought as often as I have seen him. But when I saw him last, which is some years since, he appeared then so much broken that I could not have imagined he would last so long. Were I capable of Envying, in the strict sense of the word, a good man, I should envy Him, and Mr. Berridge, and yourself, who have spent, and while they last, will continue to spend your lives in the service of the only Master worth serving. Labouring always for the souls of men, and not to tickle their ears as I do.

Cowper knew that he was not called to be a preacher or an evangelist. Men who were so called were, according to him, those who could rightly claim the 'topmost boughs' in Christian work, just as Homer and Milton had the best claim to be considered nightingales in the realm of poetry.[33] For Cowper, men of God such as Newton, Venn and Berridge were tree-top birds, whereas he saw himself, in the words of 'Table Talk', as no more than a 'grasshopper chirping below' or, as in 'The Nightingale and the Glow-Worm', a mere 'something shining in the dark', that is, as being of no comparative significance but yet someone who had a definite task to perform.

The point Cowper makes in this poem, however, is that 'tree-top' members of the Christian body should respect and love those weaker members who are only able to creep on the ground, and the 'worms' in their turn should not feel envious at not being nightingales, but should humbly do the work they have to do:

> Respecting in each other's case
> The gifts of nature and of grace.

Newton, on the other hand, could never picture Cowper as anything as lowly as a 'worm' and so always demanded of him a witness appropriate to the most holy 'saint'. Newton himself frequented the most fashionable places but he seemed to think that Cowper should not even go on a 'joy-ride' to the next village. Newton recommended reading novels but objected strongly when he heard that Cowper was having Richardson's highly moral works read to him during an illness. Newton mixed with people right across the social and theological scale, but woe to Cowper if he so much as spoke with a Roman Catholic! Newton was always seeking 'outward signs' in his friend, to confirm his view of his spiritual state. When, in Newton's rather individualistic opinion, these 'signs' were not immediately evident, he feared that his friend was either keeping his light under a bushel or departing from the true faith. Neither of these two conclusions was anywhere near the truth in Cowper's case.

Cowper believed strongly that each Christian had his place in God's plan and purpose and he always strove to live a life in keeping with this truth. Some were high-called and some low-called, he believed. The essence of Christian faith was for each person to recognize where God had placed him and what he had to do. Though Cowper regarded himself as more of a cricket or a worm than a nightingale, he believed firmly that he was called and ordained of God to occupy that rôle and was convinced that, small as his own contribution to the work of Christ on earth might be, he was fitted out by divine providence to fulfil this very task. The poet was certain that his calling and work at Olney and later at Weston, however lacking in sensational accomplishments, was completely in the will of God. Cowper even believed that his mental infirmities were also part of this divine plan.

Newton certainly had at this time a less balanced view of a Christian's true calling than Cowper. His belief in a logical and divine connection between the constitutional hierarchy in England

and the Church of England was an opinion highly detrimental to true Christian witness and fellowship. This opinion flourished in the circle to which Newton belonged and was to have dire consequences when the Clapham Sect and Pitt, whom they usually supported, began to look upon support for the Crown as a token of Christian orthodoxy. It was probably Pitt's 'going the whole hog', to use Cowper's expression, and considering reviving legislation to ban Dissenting preaching by 1800[34] that brought the Clapham Sect to their senses and opened their eyes to the fact that true Christian fellowship should override political opinions.[35]

Tragically, at first, the Clapham Sect's opposition to Pitt's move to withdraw preaching licences from the Dissenters was only a matter of self-preservation. On hearing of Pitt's venture Wilberforce went to have supper alone with him and tried to disuade him from his plan, using as an argument that good preachers, such as Robinson of Leicester, Richardson of York, Millner of Hull (he had been dead for almost two years!) and Atkinson of Leeds would soon be in prison. Now not one of these men was a Dissenter, but they were all Evangelicals. In other words, Wilberforce was frightened that once Bible-believing Dissenters were persecuted, the Evangelicals would be next. Cowper pointed out to Newton on more than one occasion that an over-zealous view of the monarchy, or of the Church of England, amounted to idolatry.[36]

Cowper replied candidly and with great restraint to Newton's severe criticism. 'At present,' he told his friend, 'I have no connexions, from which either you, I trust, or any who love me and wish me well, have occasion to conceive alarm. Much kindness indeed I have experienced at the hands of several, some of them near relatives, others not related to me at all, but I do not know that there is among them a single person from whom I am likely to catch contamination. I can say of them all with more truth than Jacob uttered when he called Kid, Venison, The Lord thy God brought them unto me.'[37] The poet goes on to thank Newton for his concern and for the friendship which he always showed to his Olney friend. There is not a word of rebuke in Cowper's letter but he was obviously cut to the quick by Newton's attitude and the matter weighed heavily on his heart.

Newton made matters worse by addressing his reply not to Cowper but to Mrs Unwin and following up this letter by several others to her, thus insulting his friend even further. Gradually

Newton's behaviour started playing tricks on Cowper's melancholy mind and he came to believe that the man in London who wrote such critical, unkind letters could not possibly be the pastor and friend whom he had known so well at Olney in previous years. He began to sink into depths of despair again but the Lord mercifully diverted his mind by the arrival in Olney of Lady Hesketh.

Lady Hesketh's visit and the move to Weston

The poet had been counting the days until Lady Hesketh's visit with eager enthusiasm, promising himself a time of happiness and contentment. When she eventually arrived, however, his nerves were at breaking-point and his cousin was alarmed to find him in a mood very different from that shown in the cheerful letters she had received from him. She had, however, a rare gift of captivating attention and soon she, Mrs Unwin and Cowper were all once more in the best of spirits and really enjoying their time spent together. Cowper was able to tell Newton in his next letter that:

> It was an observation of a sensible man whom I knew well in ancient days, (I mean when I was very young) that people are never in reality happy, when they boast much of being so. I feel myself accordingly well-content to say, without any enlargement on the subject, that an Enquirer after happiness might travel far and not find a happier Trio than meet every day either in our parlour or in the parlour at the vicarage. I will not say, that mine is not occasionally somewhat dashed with the sable hue of those notions concerning myself and my situation that have occupied or rather possessed me so long, but on the other hand I can also affirm that my Cousin's affectionate behavior to us both, the sweetness of her temper and the sprightliness of her conversation relieve me in no small degrees from the pressure of them.[38]

Lady Hesketh felt that a dilapidated house such as Orchard Side was no place for a person who loved beautiful natural surroundings as her cousin did, so she began to persuade him to find a house in a better area. Cowper readily agreed. As the old mansion house at Weston was empty, enquiries were made as to the possibility of renting it on a permanent basis. Squire Throckmorton, the owner, offered Cowper very favourable terms and it was decided in July 1786 to leave Orchard Side after having lived there for eighteen years.

Newton continues to take offence

Cowper wasted no time in writing a detailed letter to Newton informing him of the intended move. Once again Newton did not reply directly but immediately wrote to Mrs Unwin instead, criticizing his friend in the strongest terms. Cowper gave a full account of this 'wormwood' letter when he wrote to William Unwin:

> You have had your troubles, and we, ours. This day three weeks, your mother received a letter from Mr. Newton, which she has not yet answer'd, nor is likely to answer hereafter. It gave us both much concern, but her more than me; I suppose, because my mind being necessarily occupied in my work, I had not so much leisure to browze upon the wormwood that it contained. The purport of it is, a direct accusation of me, and of her an accusation implied, that we have both deviated into forbidden paths, and lead a life unbecoming the Gospel. That many of my friends in London are grieved, and the simple people of Olney, astonish'd. That he never so much doubted of my restoration to Christian privileges as now. In short, that I converse too much with people of the world, and find too much pleasure in doing so. He concludes with putting your Mother in mind, that there is still an intercourse between London and Olney, by which he means to insinuate that we cannot offend against the decorum that we are bound to observe, but the news of it will most certainly be conveyed to him. — We do not at all doubt it. We never knew a lie hatch'd at Olney that waited long for a bearer, and though we do not wonder to find ourselves made the subjects of false accusation in a place ever fruitful in such productions, we do and must wonder a little, that he should listen to them with so much credulity. I say this, because if he had heard only the truth, or had believed no more than the truth, he would not, I think, have found either me censurable or your Mother. And

that *She* should be suspected of irregularities is the more wonderful, (for wonderful it would be at any rate) because she sent him not long before, a letter conceived in such strains of piety and spirituality, as ought to have convinced him that She at least was no wanderer. But what is the fact, and how do we spend our time in reality? What are the deeds for which we have been represented as thus criminal? Our present course of life differs in nothing from that which we have both held these 13 years, except that after great civilities shown us and many advances made on the part of the Throcks, we visit them. That we visit also at Gayhurst.[39] That we have frequently taken airings with my Cousin in her carriage, and that I have sometimes taken a walk with her on a Sunday Evening, and sometimes by myself, which however your Mother has never never done. These are the only novelties in our practise and if by these procedures so inoffensive in themselves, we yet give offence, offence must needs be given. God and our own consciences acquit us, and we acknowledge no other Judges.[40]

As soon as Lady Hesketh arrived in Olney, she began a programme of relief for the Olney poor, providing them with food and clothing and administering comfort to the sick, but it was now Lady Hesketh's turn to come under Newton's suspicion. It is interesting to note that Lady Hesketh was always very critical of Cowper's friends and carefully vetted them regarding their orthodoxy. She was of the opinion that Newton had never behaved as a true pastor should towards Cowper and she even blamed him for making Cowper ill in 1773. Now it was her turn to be considered 'unorthodox' by Newton.

The fact is that Cowper's letter concerning his new-found happiness with the friend of his youth had upset the clergyman greatly. The most surprising point in Newton's letter, however, was his statement that he was applying to William Unwin for further details of the misdemeanours Cowper was supposed to have been guilty of. Newton was in effect, trying to drive a wedge between Mrs Unwin, her son and Lady Hesketh, Cowper's three best friends at the time.

Cowper himself answered Newton's letter to Mrs Unwin on her behalf. First he congratulated Newton on his safe return from yet another holiday jaunt, no doubt wishing to touch his friend's sense of fairness on this matter. Ever since his earliest days as a curate at Olney, Newton had sought relaxation by going on innocent pleasure rides now and then, often being taken in the carriages of rich friends. It was just this kind of harmless occupation which he had labelled sinful in Cowper's case. The poet went on to say:

Your letter to Mrs. Unwin concerning our conduct and the offence taken at it in our neighborhood, gave us both a great deal of concern, and She is still deeply affected by it. Of this you may assure yourself, that if our friends in London have been grieved, they have been misinformed; which is the more probable because the bearers of Intelligence hence to London are not always very scrupulous concerning the truth of their reports; And that if any of our serious neighbours have been astonish'd, they have been so without the smallest real occasion. Poor people are never well employed even when they judge one another, but when they undertake to scan the motives and estimate the behavior of those whom Providence has exalted a little above them, they are utterly out of their province and their depth. They often see us get into Lady Hesketh's carriage, and rather uncharitably suppose that it always carries us into a scene of dissipation, which in fact it never does. We visit indeed at Mr. Throckmorton's and at Gayhurst, rarely however at Gayhurst on account of the greater distance; more frequently though not very frequently at Weston, both because it is nearer, and because our business in the house that is making ready for us, often calls us that way. The rest of our journeys are to Beaujeat turnpike and back again, or perhaps to the Cabinet-maker's at Newport. As Othello says

The very butt and forehead of th' offence
Hath this, no more.

What good we can get, or can do, in these visits, is another question, which they, I am sure, are not at all qualified to solve. Of this we are both sure, that under the guidance of Providence we have formed these connexions, that we should have hurt the Christian cause rather than have served it, by a

prudish abstinence from them, and that St. Paul himself
conducted to them as we have been, would have found it
expedient to have done as we have done. It is always impossible to conjecture to much purpose from the beginnings of a
providence, in what it will terminate. If we have neither
received nor communicated any spiritual good at present,
while conversant with our new acquaintance, at least no harm
has befallen on either side, and it were too hazardous an
assertion even for our censorious neighbors to make, that,
because the cause of the Gospel does not appear to have been
served at present, therefore it never can be in any future
intercourse that we may have with them. In the mean time I
speak a strict truth and as in the sight of God, when I say that
we are neither of us at all more addicted to gadding than
heretofore. We both naturally love seclusion from company,
and never go into it without putting a force upon our disposition; at the same time I will confess and you will easily
conceive, that the melancholy, incident to such close confinement as we have so long endured, finds itself a little relieved
by such amusements as a society so innocent affords. You
may look round the Christian world, and find few I believe of
our station, who have so little intercourse as we, with the
world that is not Christian.

We place all the uneasiness that you have felt for us upon
this subject to the account of that cordial friendship of which
you have long given us proof. But you may be assured that
notwithstanding all rumours to the contrary, we are exactly
what we were when you saw us last. I miserable on account
of God's departure from me which I believe to be final, and
she seeking his return to me in the path of duty and by
continual prayer.[41]

A severe blow

This attitude of Newton to his once best friend was a heavy blow to
Cowper and prepared the way for the end of the poet's 'Second
Spring' and the beginning of a long winter with only very intermit-
tent rays of sunshine. Cowper's health was, however, to receive a
much harder blow than that of the lack of understanding and harsh

criticism of his friend. Newton could not turn to Unwin at once to ask him about gossip and rumours concerning Cowper as he was away on a walking tour with Henry Thornton. Nor was Newton ever able to gain any information from him as Unwin, on returning from his tour to visit Thornton's Winchester home, was suddenly seized with a fever and died on 29 November 1786 after a very brief though painful illness.

14.
The language of Eden

Long before the *Task* was in print Cowper had started on a new poetic project. The first signs of this came in August 1785 when the poet wrote an article for the *Gentleman's Magazine* under one of his many pen-names — this time 'Alethes' — criticizing the current 'best' translation of Homer done by Pope and his team of assistants.

The Cowper family and Pope

Before Cowper came along, Pope was considered the greatest poet of the age. He had become a close acquaintance of the Cowper family when he showed more than a casual interest in the poet's Aunt Judith and had the honesty to say that he found her poetry superior to his own. Nevertheless the Cowpers disliked Pope because of his Catholic views, his artificiality and his attention to form and sound in poetry rather than feeling and truth.

Cowper's father was especially scathing of Pope in a satirical poem attacking Pope's own form and feelings. Pope was a hunchback and his legs were as thin and weak as his head was bald. Nevertheless he was very vain and most conscious of his own importance. He used to try to hide his shape by wearing a great deal of gaudy clothing and at least half a dozen pairs of stockings, pulled on one over the other, to make his shins look more shapely. He loved to have himself painted with a crown of laurels on his head. Dr John Cowper wrote,

The Parallel

Imperial Cæsar's sacred head
Of hair quite barren grown.
He hides a laurel wreath to shade
The baldness of his crown.

So Pope with nature quits the score;
None can his form dispraise;
With wit's bright beams he gilds it o'er,
And hides his crump with bays.

It became clear in 1785 that Cowper wished to dethrone Pope. This was not out of any jealous ambition but because he believed that Pope had degraded poetry by appeasing the popular taste and by striving to make poetry a work of art, a perfection in itself, with no claims to a 'teaching voice'. Poetry, for Pope, was not a means of transforming the age but simply of entertaining the ear.

Cowper first became dissatisfied with Pope as a young Templar after comparing his translation of Homer line by line with the original. Many years later, when Lady Austen was staying in Olney, Cowper again took up Pope's translation to read to Mrs Unwin and their guest as a means of evening entertainment. Knowing much of Homer off by heart in the original Greek, the poet was again struck by the artificiality and pomp of Pope's language in comparison to the simple but expressive style of the Greek poet. He therefore decided to prepare a new translation which brought out the true value of Homer's verse.

The place of the classics

Cowper was to spend more and more time on such translation work as he grew towards old age and it must be asked why he did so. His knowledge of the classical languages, and also of several modern languages, was so good that he could enjoy reading them fluently without resorting to making laborious written translations of them. What purpose did he have in mind? The answer is found in the new attitude to education and learning which was spreading throughout Britain in the eighteenth century.

The Reformation and the Puritans

During the sixteenth and seventeenth centuries there had been a new interest in languages amongst educated people. Thanks to the pioneer work of such scholars as Erasmus of Rotterdam, the classical languages had been rediscovered and were seen as a key to knowledge but also as a key to the Scriptures.

The earlier Puritans had shown their skills in Hebrew, Aramaic and Greek in their translations of the Geneva — commonly known as the Puritan — Bible (1560) and the Authorized Version which succeeded it in 1611. Their work led on to the publishing of the gigantic *Biblia Polyglotta*, with its six folio volumes of Latin, Hebrew, Greek, Syriac, Chaldee, Samaritan, Arabic, Ethiopian and Persian texts.

Evangelical and Pietistic fathers, such as John Owen (1616-1683) of England and Johann Albrecht Bengel (1687-1752) of Germany, expanded this work and brought back Bible-learning from its Roman Catholic exile and presented it in the local vernacular so that every man could read in his own language about the glorious works of God.

The classical languages became so important to the Reformers and Puritans that they became well-versed in Greek and Latin literature, as can be illustrated by the many appeals to these works in their own writings. Samuel Rutherford, for instance, who played such a large part in the Westminster Assembly (1643), could back up his opening argument in his famous *Lex Rex* with quotations from Aristotle and Plato and quoted Cicero at length in his concluding chapter.[1] Calvin studied the classics intensely and his *Institutes* contain many a quotation taken from ancient Greek or Latin authors to illustrate a point and to force home a positive biblical truth. Beza, who worked closely with Calvin, was a professor of Greek. He even used a passage from Plato as the basis for his speech on taking up his appointment as rector of the Genevan Academy, the world centre at the time of Reformed Protestantism.[2] These men could quote classical authors in a theological context without embarrassment as the classics were an accepted part of their culture.

The situation in Cowper's day

Even in Cowper's day most clergymen had received a classical education. Many of them had attended public schools, such as

Westminster, where Greek and Latin were the main subjects, and had gone on to deepen their classical studies at university. It was common for leading Evangelicals to write works on classical authors with almost the same fervour that they wrote theological works.

Martin Madan, one of the pioneers of the Evangelical Revival, translated classical authors in order to make them available to the English reader. He published, for instance, in 1785 *A New and Literal Translation of Juvenal and Persius; with Copious Explanatory Notes, by which these Difficult Satirists are Rendered Easy and Familiar to the Reader*. Cowper stated that this book would appeal, not only be to the *'Illiterati'*, but also to the *'Literati'*; in other words, he saw Madan's work as intended for those with a less classical education, although it was of a high scholarly standard.[3]

James Hervey, another pioneer of the Evangelical Revival, constantly quoted the ancients and published translations from the Greek of Theocritus. Richard Cecil, Newton's friend and biographer, used to say that Homer approached the nearest of all heathen poets to the grandeur of Hebrew poetry.[4] When Cowper wanted to consult a line in Virgil he borrowed the book from Thomas Scott, a fellow Evangelical.[5] Before he obtained his own copy of Homer, he borrowed the book from Thomas Jones, another brother in Christ.

It was still not uncommon in those days for clergymen and other educated people to correspond with their colleagues in Latin, especially when sending letters abroad. It was also still the custom for students to present papers in Latin, and theological students were required to preach and be examined in that language.

Newton, who had no university education, strove hard to master Greek and Latin and gained a basic knowledge of Hebrew. Apparently his Latin became so good that he was able to correspond in Latin with Dutch Christians and was commended by Cowper on that account. Cowper eventually translated the letters from the Dutch brethren into English for publication. It was a thesis that Newton had prepared in Latin that helped him to gain ordination to the ministry of the Church of England.

This interest in the classics was not confined to Anglicans by any means. Dr Doddridge, the prominent Dissenter, quoted extensively from at least a dozen classical and ancient authors chiefly to verify the meaning of a biblical word or to support the historical accuracy of the Bible. Dissenting students were not allowed to attend the universities but formed colleges of their own where the classical languages were an important part of the curriculum. At William Bull's Dissenting Academy, for instance, students learnt to expound God's Word in Latin.

Even the Quaker traders of Cowper's acquaintance showed that they were well versed in the classics. After ordering a bed from a local Quaker, Cowper was delighted to find that it was decorated with 'Phaeton kneeling to Apollo, and imploring his father to grant him the conduct of his chariot for a day'.[6] This classical theme is one which still has a very familiar ring about it even today!

One major use of Latin was on the mission-field. During the latter part of the eighteenth century and the beginning of the nineteenth, Europeans and North Americans who travelled abroad in the cause of God found they could communicate in Latin with educated people all over Europe and the ancient world. In India, in particular, Christian workers found that, whether they were German, Danish, Dutch or British, they could all work together using the same lingua franca. Henry Martyn is renowned for his testimony to Christ in the Latin language, both in Roman Catholic Europe and in the East.[7]

Wesley and the classics

Perhaps the most enthusiastic classicist amongst eighteenth-century Evangelicals was John Wesley, the famous evangelist. He was such an ardent student of Greek that he spent many a day on horseback travelling from one preaching engagement to another, reading and translating from the Greek and writing grammars. A knowledge of classical literature was for him a key to the Scriptures. Even when well over seventy years of age, Wesley avidly studied Xenophon in the original and as late as 1787 we find him trotting along the road reading Blackwell's *Sacred Classics Illustrated and Defended* and saying of the author, 'I think he fully proves his point, that there are no expressions in the New Testament which are not found in the best and purest Greek authors.'[8] When he had the time, Wesley would go to see performances of classical drama in London and said of Terence's *Adelphi* performed at Westminster, '.... an entertainment not unworthy of a Christian. O how do these Heathen shame us! Their very comedies contain both excellent sense, the liveliest pictures of men and manners, and so fine strokes of genuine morality, as are seldom found in the writings of Christians.'[9]

Newton, too, was also much impressed by *Adelphi* and when he published Cowper's autobiography and the poet's story of his brother's conversion, he named the two accounts *Adelphi* after the title of Terence's popular play.

Wesley thought that Homer's *Odyssey* was superior to Milton's *Paradise Regained*, and says of it, 'Was ever man so happy in his descriptions, so exact and consistent in his characters, and so natural in telling a story? He likewise continually inserts the finest strokes of morality; on all occasions recommending the fear of God, with justice, mercy and truth.'[10]

One can hardly imagine an evangelical magazine today introducing a classical text translation competition for their readers, but this is one of the ways in which Wesley made his *Arminian Magazine* popular. Texts were printed from various Greek writers and readers were invited to submit translations for publication!

Cowper's view of Homer

Cowper had a higher opinion of Milton than Wesley but he agreed that a knowledge of the language of the Greek writers was especially important for understanding the New Testament. He also agreed with Wesley in praising the high, almost Christian, moral standard of Homer. 'I verily think that any person of a spiritual turn may read him [Homer] to some advantage,' he told Newton, and went on to say,

> He may suggest reflections that may not be unserviceable even in a sermon, for I know not where we can find more striking exemplars of the pride, the arrogance, and the insignificance of man, at the same time that by ascribing all events to a divine interposition, he inculcates constantly the belief of a Providence, insists much on the duty of Charity towards the Poor and the Stranger, on the respect that is due to superiors and to our Seniors in particular, and on the expediency and necessity of Prayer and piety towards the Gods. A piety mistaken indeed in its object, but exemplary for the punctuality of its performance. Thousands who will not learn from scripture to ask a blessing either on their actions or on their food, may learn it if they please from Homer.[11]

Not surprisingly, then, when it became known that Cowper was to bring out a new translation of Homer, much enthusiasm was shown by Evangelicals. Robert Smith, the follower of Pitt and Member of Parliament for Nottingham who helped the Olney poor through Cowper, was all aflame when he heard of the poet's work on Homer and urged him to publish his proposals in order to gain subscribers. Samuel Greatheed, an Evangelical of the evangelicals, whom Cowper described as 'a man of Letters and of Taste', expressed great admiration for Cowper's translation.[12] Evangelicals all over Britain assisted Cowper in financing the project by payment in advance.

Nineteenth-century misunderstandings

With the close of the eighteenth century evangelicals, on the whole, were to change their minds radically about the importance for a Christian of learning Greek and Latin and it is because of this change in their theories of language, rather than their doctrinal beliefs, that evangelicals lost their interest in Cowper's teaching concerning language during the nineteenth century and the poet gradually faded from the Christian scene as a major contender for evangelical truths.

Even as early as 1817 an anonymous writer in the *Panoplist and Missionary Magazine* expressed 'in the strongest terms' his opinion that Cowper had been wasting his time working on his translation of Homer when he could have been writing 'religious tracts and narratives'. George Cheever, famous for his great work on Bunyan, wrote in his hefty volume *Lectures on the Life, Genius and Insanity of Cowper* in 1856 that Cowper's translating Homer was a 'ludicrous' act and that he believed that the poet's time would have been better spent in composing original verse. Even literary scholars such as Professor Goldwin Smith cannot imagine why Cowper spent so much time on translation. He says in his Cowper biography: 'Why did not Cowper go on writing these charming pieces [i. e. his original verse] which he evidently produced with the greatest facility? Instead of this, he took, under an evil star, to translating Homer.'[13]

The fact is that Cowper did continue producing original verse during his work on Homer when his health allowed it. Much of it is of a highly evangelical nature. This is shown by the many poetic contributions which he sent during this period to *The Times*, the *World*, the *Speaker*, the *Gentleman's Magazine*, the *Northampton Mercury* and the *Morning Herald*, besides at least five anti-slavery ballads which were sung all over the country and sold in their thousands. Indeed it is virtually impossible to trace the full volume of Cowper's productions at this time due to his irritating use of pseudonyms. In particular works that he wrote under the pen-name of Andrew Fridze have not been traced.

Translation as part of a world-view

This radical change in the opinions of evangelicals can only be explained when we see that nineteenth-century believers had lost much of the vision of their eighteenth-century counterparts. The eighteenth century was a time of great optimism concerning the future of the world and progress in international relationships. It was an age of great educational reform and development in worldwide commerce. Believers took this as a sign that God was bringing all mankind together in preparation for the great millennium when all men of all nations would be brothers and peace and harmony would reign over the whole earth. Cowper often expressed this conviction in his letters but his greatest exposition of the theme was certainly in the last book of the *Task*.

Perhaps the most impressive prose rendering of this eschatological view is to be found in Jonathan Edwards' *A History of Redemption from the Fall to the End of Time* published in 1773. The New England author describes the great outpouring of the Spirit before the final triumphant return of Christ to a world transformed and renewed into a second Eden where all barriers of colour and class have been annulled and the sound of men praising God is echoed worldwide. This world will not only be spiritually enlightened but also transformed agriculturally, technologically and educationally.

During the eighteenth century, more and more common people were learning to read the classics of worldwide literature but the demand now was for these works to be available in the mother tongue as this new readership could never afford a classical education. Much interest was therefore shown in translating the so-called dead languages, including Old Norse, and also literary works in modern languages, such as Italian, French and German. Pope and his team of co-workers rendered Homer into very flowery English (1715-1726), Mallet translated the *Eddas* (1755), Bodmer the *Nibelungen Lied* and Percy (1761) edited and translated Chinese, Spanish and Icelandic stories into English. Oriental poetry was also introduced into England via the pen of Sir William James.

The demand for translations became very great on the Continent. Works of the British Puritans were translated into Hungarian and Samuel Richardson's works were translated into French, Dutch and German. Richardson was a close friend of James Hervey and published Hervey's works, thus doing the Evangelical cause a great service. Richardson's works were of a high moral quality and were favourites with Napoleon Bonaparte. Young, Marlowe and Shakespeare were all 'exported' to the Continent at this time.

On the Continent the Dutchman Willem Bilderdijk, whose similarities with Cowper are quite astonishing, and the German Johann George Hamann, who found Christ in England, did their uttermost to point people back to the language of Eden so that they could look forward to an Eden restored. Indeed many Christians of Cowper's generation saw all this translation work as a reversal of the language confusion created at Babel. The nations which had lost their means of communication at Babel were being prepared for the restitution of all things when once again men will be able to join one another from all parts of the world and find verbal unison in praising their Maker. The whole world will be in harmony with God once more.

> All creatures worship man, and all mankind
> One Lord, one Father. Error has no place:
> That creeping pestilence is driven away;
> The breath of heaven has chas'd it. In the heart
> No passion touches a discordant string,
> But all is harmony and love. Disease
> Is not: the pure and uncontam'nate blood
> Holds its due course, nor fears the frost of age.
> One song employs all nations; and all cry,
> 'Worthy the Lamb, for he was slain for us!'
> The dwellers in the vales and on the rocks
> Shout to each other, and the mountain tops
> From distant mountains catch the flying joy;

Till, nation after nation taught the strain,
Earth rolls the rapturous hosanna round.
Behold the measure of the promise fill'd;
See Salem built, the labour of a God!
All kingdoms and all princes of the earth
Flock to that light; the glory of all lands
Flows into her; unbounded is her joy,
And endless her increase.[14]

For Cowper the invention of printing went hand in hand with this reversal. Referring to Newton's popularity in Holland through the printing of *Cardiphonia* in Dutch in 1783, Cowper writes,

> When you wrote those Letters you did not dream that you was designed for an Apostle to the Dutch. Yet so it proves, and such, among many others, are the advantages we derive from the art of printing; an art in which indisputably Man was instructed by the same great Teacher, who taught him to embroider for the service of the sanctuary, and to beat out the Cummin, which amounts almost to as great a blessing as the gift of tongues, diffusing an Author's sentiments upon the noblest subjects through a people.[15]

The rest of this letter is lost but enough has been preserved to show how thrilled Cowper was with the thought of Newton's testimony having an effect on the Dutch resembling that of the Day of Pentecost. Newton's writings became exceedingly popular in the Low Countries and even today many Dutch Christians are familiar with them. Newton's hymns, and those of Cowper, are still well represented in Dutch Reformed hymn-books and the lives of their authors are still included in courses of church history in the leading Dutch universities.

Evangelicals and new developments in education

The Puritans concentrated mostly, with the exception of Italian, on the languages associated with Scripture and related studies. The Evangelicals did not neglect such work but also translated from most of the contemporary European languages. Their literary scope became much broader than that of the mainline Puritans as they were keen to help the common man to read and appreciate good literature. The mid-eighteenth century experienced a revolution in general education sponsored and carried out by the Sunday School Movement.

All over Britain eighteenth-century Evangelicals and Dissenters were founding Sunday Schools for poor children, where the child's body, mind and spirit were cared for. Griffith Jones (1683-1761), who has been called 'the Morning Star of the Evangelical Awakening', founded charity schools as early as 1730, and pioneered a movement in Wales which established no less than 3,000 schools in his lifetime, catering for some 150,000 pupils. Robert Raikes (1735-1811), who was strongly influenced by Evangelicals, set up schools for the poor throughout Britain. Rowland Hill (1744-1833) contributed enormously to the Sunday School Movement and his chapel, (Surrey Chapel, London) ran no less than thirteen affiliated Sunday Schools with a total of 3,000 pupils in attendance. Hill sought Cowper's help when founding his schools and so did Thomas Scott when planning his Sunday School in Olney.

Though it is true that the first concern of the founders was to teach Scripture to their pupils, they realized that this could only be done efficiently when the pupils could read and write and when they were given some general education and social purpose in life. They would then have the necessary rudiments to help them cope with spiritual problems and also enough education to help them obtain work so that they might no longer live a wastrel life.[16] So we find the Eclectic Society, founded by Newton, discussing not whether or not Sunday School pupils should learn arithmetic, but whether they should learn it on a Sunday or in special mid-week instruction classes.[17] The meetings of these Evangelical ministers often included educational matters on the agenda, especially questions of which books ought to be read by the pupils. Newton, of course, always saw to it that Bunyan's *Pilgrim's Progress* was on the curriculum.[18]

There was hardly an Evangelical minister at this time, especially amongst Cowper's friends, who was not going into the highways and byways to find children whom they could clothe, educate and even eventually help to find work. Hannah More, who, because of her friendship with Newton and her high regard for Cowper, must be included in the 'Olney Set', pioneered charity and trade schools, with John Newton and the Clapham Sect acting as her principal advisers.

Hannah More even wrote 'sacred' plays for children's use. This was, however, frowned upon by many Evangelicals, especially as some children reached such proficiency in their roles that they decided to become professional actors.[19] Though great Christian Reformers including John Foxe, famous for his work on the lives of the martyrs, had written morally sound plays, by the end of the eighteenth century Evangelicals, on the whole, rejected play-acting because of the difficulties attached to having Christians playing non-Christian, or even evil, rôles and because plays titivated the appetites of the masses for entertainment rather than edified them.

It was not only the children of the lower classes who were encouraged to read, but their parents, too. The problem now, however, was what to give them to read. Hannah More and John Wesley and other Evangelicals produced a great quantity of 'bowdlerized' and simplified literature besides writing 'easy readers'[20] themselves.

The work of Thomas Bowdler (1754-1825) himself must be mentioned here. Bowdler sought to provide material for general reading to fit the tastes of people affected by the Revival. Thus he could say, 'Those words and expressions are omitted which cannot with propriety be read aloud in a family.'[21] Literary critics always look down their noses at Thomas Bowdler but his *Family Shakespeare* popularized the works of the Bard of Avon more than any other version of the eighteenth and nineteenth centuries. If it had not been for evangelically minded ordinary people, the name of Shakespeare might have been unknown in Britain today.

The Evangelical public meant big business at this time, as witnessed by the many non-Christian publishers who produced works by ardent believers. This is well illustrated by the extremes to which Robert Southey, a vowed opponent of Evangelicalism, went in order to sell his version of Cowper's works, which was published in 1835 in the same year as the Evangelical Rev. T. S. Grimshawe published his. Grimshawe held the copyright to Cowper's works through his relationship by marriage with Cowper's family. Southey, who was Poet Laureate at the time, fearing the competition, told his readers that Grimshawe had produced his edition 'surreptitiously', and threw doubt on his honesty by comparing him to Ignatius of Loyola and those who 'use words with a mental reservation'. Mistakenly thinking that Grimshawe was a member of the Eclectic Society, Southey linked him with John Newton in a most derogatory manner.[22] Grimshawe refused to stoop to Southey's level and argued that his work was not in competition with Southey's edition as both looked at Cowper from different angles. In spite of Southey's slander, and in spite of having the prestige of his being the Poet Laureate to help sell his edition, Southey's work sold less than 6,000 copies in the first year whereas Grimshawe's Evangelical edition had a sale of more than 32,000.

Influential Evangelicals such as William Wilberforce and the Thorntons (John and Henry) were always ready to finance the production of suitable literature for the Sunday and Ragged Schools. John Wesley was second to none in producing simplified literary works (including a novel),[23] translations, abridgements, grammars, dictionaries and histories, to help the less wealthy reading public and to be used as text books in charity schools and training colleges.

It is not generally known that Wesley's *Complete English Dictionary* (1753), which was published two years before Johnson's larger *English Dictionary*, proved a significant rival for Johnson's work over a number of years. It was used especially by readers in the lower classes and was initially designed to help them 'understand the best English authors'.[24] No less a critic than Eric Partridge tells us that it was 'the best small dictionary in English' of that time.[25] It is interesting to note that whereas Johnson leans heavily on nigh-Evangelical literature, such as the works of non-juror William Law (1686-1761), Wesley is concerned with words occurring in more secular literature and prefixes his work with the words: 'The author assures you he thinks this is the best dictionary in the world.' One commentator, G. H. Vallins, even describes Wesley's dictionary as being in places 'a little cold and academic'.[26] Wesley, in particular, lay great stress on a knowledge of classical literature, history and languages and edited many books on these subjects.

The Evangelicals and contemporary secular literature

The eighteenth-century Evangelicals have often been criticized for shutting their eyes to learning and literature and the everyday affairs of the world. They are portrayed as extremely narrow in their culture, shunning anything 'secular' and having a less demanding taste.[27] In fact, the opposite is the case.

Hervey's works are full of favourable references to the writings of Addison, Pope, Thomson, Young and others, whom he must have read diligently. He expressed his honest opinion regarding 'secular' magazines in a letter to his sister dated 12 October 1742: 'I once thought I should make less use of the Spectators than you; but now I believe the reverse of this is true, for we read one or more of those elegant and instructive papers every morning at breakfast: they are served up with our tea, according to their original design. We reckon our repast imperfect without a little of Mr. Addison's or Mr. Steele's company.'

John Newton, who is caricatured in Lord Cecil's biography of Cowper, *The Stricken Deer,* as the most narrow of Evangelicals, advised theological students in his *A Plan of Academical Preparation for the Ministry,* published in 1784, on what to read. He tells his readers that Christian instructors ought to be well versed in the classics and 'well-acquainted with books at large'. They should have a wide knowledge of literature, including 'Belles Lettres', and history, besides theology and should have a 'lively imagination', 'sound judgment' and 'cultivated taste'. This does not sound at all like the narrow image such writers as Cecil give us of this many-sided man of God. Newton was also a keen magazine reader.

Cowper could discuss Fielding, Swift, Lavater, Balzac, Voltaire, Hume, Gibbon (to mention only a few of the many secular authors he read) with his Evangelical friends, such as Newton, Bull, Unwin and Greatheed, because these were men who read widely.

Why Cowper turned to translation

It is only against this background that we can begin to understand why Cowper spent over ten years of his remaining life doing translation work.

He not only wished to give male readers the classics in their own language but also to educate women and girls, who were almost completely shut off from any education of value in those days. This meant that women were always at a disadvantage in male society when languages or literature were being discussed. Cowper did not share the social prejudices of his day regarding women and was determined to do something about it. Cowper aired his views on this subject to Lady Hesketh in 1786, after discussing the views of a particularly enlightened lady on translations from the Greek.

> Whoever the Lady is, she has evidently an admirable pen and a cultivated mind. And while I can please you and Her and others like you, I care not for all the He Critics in the world. I do verily consider some of the Ladies of the present day as being better qualified to judge the Writings of our Sex than the men themselves. Literature has diffused itself among them to a degree unknown in the last generation, their sensibilities are generally quicker than ours, and they have no jealousies or envies, in such a case, to warp their opinion. If a person Reads it is no matter in what language, and if the mind be informed it is no matter whether that mind belong to a man or a woman. The Taste and the judgment will receive the benefit alike in both.[28]

As we have seen, Cowper spent much of his time at school learning to translate. He went line by line through Homer with Dick Sutton at Westminster, as he did later with William Alston at the Temple.[29] It is thus no surprise to find that Cowper's earliest publications were translations.

In 1759 Cowper's translations of the fifth and ninth satires of the first book of Horace were published in the second volume of the *Works of Horace* edited by Duncombe. Cowper regarded Horace as a 'sweet moralist' and thus a poet worthy of translation. He also turned to the works of other ancient Latin writers, such as Virgil and Ovid, for similar reasons. Milton's Italian and Latin works occupied his pen because of the clear Christian teaching in them. Where he found little Christian teaching, such as in the Latin poetry of Vincent Bourne or the French poetry of Madame de la Motte Guyon, he 'Christianized' them. Besides Homer, classical writers like Julianus, Palladas, Callimacus, Miltiades, Isidorus, Marcus, Antipater, Lucillius, Lucianus and Bion remained with Cowper all his life as fitting subjects for translation and poetic comment.

Cowper's interest in modern languages is shown in his early free translation of Houdar de la Motte's *L'Ombre d'Homere* which he accomplished in 1755. Cowper had rarely a good word to say about the French, whom he considered, on the whole, a decadent race. He did confess, however, that their language had many possibilities of expression which English lacked. Perhaps this is why Cowper, in conjunction with his brother, published so much of Voltaire's verse.

The poet also loved to paraphrase biblical texts in poetic form, as his renderings of Psalm 137 and Job chapter 14 show.

Later critics of Cowper's translation work, such as Cheever and Goldwin Smith, mentioned above, failed to appreciate both Cowper's strong sense of calling to translate and the fact that as time proceeded and Cowper became more and more prone to depression, translation work had a beneficial effect on his health. Such critics seem to believe that writing original verse is merely a matter of wanting to or not. Both Cheever and Goldwin Smith think that if only the poet had exercised a little more will-power he could have turned his mind to 'better' things.[30] They fail to see what a positive influence translating from the Greek had on Cowper's search for an ideal language to express Christian sentiments. Nor do such critics accept the fact that in his later years Cowper was at times so plagued with melancholy that he was quite incapable of producing the verse which he would have preferred to write *ad infinitum*. Goldwin Smith actually speaks of Cowper's melancholy as 'fancied ills', which earned Hubert J. Norman's criticism in the *Westminster Review* that the scholar writes like 'an ardent devotee of the cult of Christian Science'.[31]

Cowper found that he often gained relief from his periods of 'pensive and unhappy moods'[32] when exercising all his technical skills in translating. It was as if translation work had become so much second nature to him that he could immerse himself in it and become oblivious to his own personal sorrows and cares. The poet always had a feeling that he must be constantly occupied; he 'abhorred a vacuum'.[33] Thus when not engaged upon original work he found translating the best form of pastime. Even when he was out on his walks he would be constantly turning over, say, a few lines from Homer which he had stored in his marvellous memory. When a satisfactory translation occurred to him he would put his foot on a tree-stump, or a mole-hill, and using his knee or his stiff-brimmed hat as a writing-desk, jot down the lines on a piece of paper he always carried with him for the purpose.[34]

Once, in 1785, Mrs Unwin thought hard work would make Cowper more melancholy and persuaded him to give up translating. Cowper told Lady Hesketh about this and compared his pen to a fiddle, saying, 'I accordingly obeyed, but having lost my fiddle, I became pensive and unhappy, she [Mrs Unwin] therefore restored it to me, convinced of its utility, and from that day to this I have never ceased to scrape... My task that I assign myself is to translate forty lines a day; if they pass off easily I sometimes make them fifty, but never abate any part of the allotted number.'[35]

Newton's attitude to Cowper's translation work was highly ambivalent. At times he supported the work whole-heartedly and at others he was most critical of it. This was all in keeping with Newton's general frame of mind concerning his friend; his attitude had become highly patronizing and he was constantly revising his view of Cowper's standing with the Lord. In January 1787 Cowper decided to have the matter out with Newton as his ever-changing moods were depressing the poet.

At that time Newton was criticizing Cowper for not producing more original verse. It is clear that in doing so he was comparing Cowper with himself. So great were Newton's own powers of concentration and he was such a disciplined writer that he could compose hymns apparently in a never-ending stream, with no sign of stress and strain. He obviously wondered why Cowper, who was so much more gifted poetically than he, could not do the same.

Cowper answered him bluntly:

Why it pleased God that I should be haunted into such a business, of such enormous length and labour, by miseries for which he did not see good to afford me any other remedy, I know not. But so it was. And jejune as the consolation may be, and unsuited to the exigencies of a mind and heart that once were spiritual, yet a thousand times have I been glad of it, for a thousand times it has served at least to divert my attention in some degree from such terrible tempests as I believe have seldom been permitted to beat upon a human mind. Let my friends therefore who wish me some little measure of tranquillity in the performance of the most turbulent voyage that ever Christian mariner made, be contented that having Homer's mountains and forests to windward, I escape under their shelter from the force of many a gust that would almost overset me; especially when they consider that not by choice but by necessity I make *them* my refuge. As to fame and honour and glory that may be acquired by poetical feats of any sort, God knows that if I could lay me down in the grave with Hope at my side in a dungeon all the residue of my days, I would cheerfully waive them all. For the little fame that I have already earned, has never saved me from one terrible night or from one despairing day since I first acquired it. *For* what I am reserved, or *to*[36] what, is a mystery. I would fain hope not merely that I may amuse others, or only to be a Translator of Homer.[37]

Cowper confessed at the time that he felt like a 'dried-up cistern', incapable of original poetic thought. This period did not last long, however, as a year later we find Cowper again publishing a fair amount of original verse (the 'Bills of Mortality' poems, and the anti-slavery ballads). Homer was, however, to stay with Cowper as a prop for the remainder of his life.

Dr John Johnson, Cowper's kinsman and himself an Evangelical minister, defended the matter of Cowper's insistence on the benefits of translation work in his preface to Cowper's translation of the *Iliad*. He writes, 'It has been a constant subject of regret to the admirers of the "Task", that the exercise of such marvellous, original powers, should have been so long suspended by the drudgery of Translation.' He goes on to state: 'I cannot deliver these Volumes to the Public without feeling emotions of gratitude towards Heaven, in recollecting how often this corrected Work has appeared to me an instrument of divine mercy, to mitigate the sufferings of my excellent Relation. Its progress in our private hours was singularly medicinal to his mind.'[38]

Cowper always remained a pragmatist whatever his condition at the time. When he had original verse to write, he wrote it. When his cisterns ran dry he translated with the laconic comment: 'I may very reasonably affirm that it was not God's pleasure that I should proceed in the same track, because he did not enable me to do it.'[39]

Perhaps it was inevitable that generations of scholars after Cowper would regard his translation of Homer as energies ill-spent. Just as the hopes and aspirations of the Evangelical Revival died gradually in the years succeeding his death, so did the interest in the Greek language. Cowper foresaw this and, though he complained that the mother tongue was neglected in education, he was dismayed at the fact that Greek was going out of vogue. Of the ability of future generations of critics to judge his translation of Homer Cowper says,

'Alas! 'tis after all a mortifying consideration that the majority of my judges hereafter, will be no judges of this. *Graecum est, non potest legi*, is a motto that would suit nine in ten of those who will give themselves airs about it, and pretend to like or to dislike.'[40]

Reasons for the choice of Homer

Granted that Cowper felt called to translate and that it was a medicinal balm to him, and when we take into consideration Cowper's history as a translator, it is no surprise to find him turning to Homer for his most important subject. Cowper, who always prided himself on knowing Homer as well as he knew Chevy Chase,[41] felt that the Greek poet had been badly handled by previous translators. The moral nature of his poetry had not been adequately dealt with, nor the simplicity of his language.

In a postscript to his letter to Lady Hesketh dated 15 December 1785, Cowper went into great detail concerning Pope's faults as a translator. He found Pope's verse 'musical and sweet' in places, but quite as often 'lame, feeble and flat'. Homer is 'nervous, plain and natural', but Pope is very flowery and abounds in metaphors totally foreign to Homer's style. Homer writes in an 'easy and familiar' way; Pope is stiff and starchy. Homer calls a spade a spade, whereas Pope changes the language to the 'perfect standard of French goodbreeding'. The Greek poet is an expert at character portrayal, the niceties of which Pope translates clean away. Cowper concludes his letter with the comment: 'In short, my dear, there is hardly any thing in the world so unlike another, as Pope's version of Homer and the original.'

Cowper, ever looking for an ideal language, found that Homer came very close to his scriptural ideal. In fact he could say to Lady Hesketh, 'Except the Bible, there never was in the world a book so remarkable for that species of the sublime that owes its very existence to simplicity, as the works of Homer.'[42]

The poet was even stronger in his praise of Homer's language when writing to Walter Bagot:

The Original surpasses every thing, it is of an immense length, is composed in the best language ever used upon earth, and deserves, indeed demands, all the labour that any

Translator, be he who he may, can possibly bestow on it. Of
this I am sure, and your brother the good Bishop is of the
same mind, that, at present, mere English readers know no
more of Homer in reality than if he had never been translated.
That consideration indeed it was which mainly induced me
to the undertaking; and if after all, either through idleness or
dotage upon what I have already done, I leave it chargeable
with the same incorrectness as my predecessors, or indeed
with any that I may be able to amend, I had better have
amused myself otherwise.[43]

Cowper's aims in translation

When Cowper writes in this vein, it is obvious that he does so as one
conscious of a great task laid on his shoulders, and as one, indeed,
who has a unique calling to do the work.[44] He confessed the
difficulties of this task to his young friend Samuel Rose:

> To exhibit the Majesty of such a Poet in a modern
> language is a task that no man can estimate the difficulty of
> 'till he attempts it. To paraphrase him loosely, to hang him
> with trappings that do not belong to him, all this is compara-
> tively easy. But to represent him with only his own ornaments
> and still to preserve his dignity, is a labour that if I hope in any
> measure to atchieve it, I am sensible can only be atchieved by
> the most assiduous and unremitting attention. Our studies,
> however different in themselves, in respect of the means by
> which they are to be successfully carried on, bear some
> resemblance to each other. A perseverance that nothing can
> discourage, a minuteness of observation that suffers nothing
> to escape, and a determination not to be seduced from the
> straight line that lies before us, are essentials that should be
> common to us both. There are perhaps few arduous undertak-
> ings that are not in fact more arduous than we at first supposed
> them. As we proceed difficulties increase upon us, but our
> hopes gather strength also, and we conquer obstacles which
> could we have seen them, we should never have had the
> boldness to encounter.[45]

Here we see what an enormous sense of mission Cowper had in his work. It is evident that he felt he was stretched to the very limits of his abilities, but was still determined to carry on and complete his task well. We also see how ambitious Cowper was. He was quite open about this to his cousin, Lady Hesketh, to whom he wrote,

My Dear.

If I can produce a Translation of the Old Bard that the Literati shall prefer to Pope's, which I have the assurance to hope that I may, it will do me more honour than any thing that I have performed hitherto. At present they are all agreed that Pope's is a very inadequate representation of him.[46]

Those writers who stress that Cowper felt himself to be — and was — an amateur,[47] might do well to consider that in this passage he is ranking himself above the man who, until he himself came along, was proclaimed the greatest poet of the age. He was sure that the language and style of his own translation would be proclaimed as a major improvement by the critics.[48]

Cowper was one of the earliest and one of the very few writers to outline his ideas on translation in detail and, indeed, to work out guidelines for translation work. These he stated in his preface to the first edition of the *Iliad*.[49]

First he tells the reader that a translation of any ancient poet in rhyme is impossible as, 'No human ingenuity can be equal to the task of closing every couplet with sounds homotonous, expressing the full sense, and only the full sense, of the original.' Cowper therefore recommends blank verse as the ideal verse form for this kind of work.

Secondly, the translator should omit nothing and invent nothing. Fidelity is the very essence of translation work but enough freedom and individuality should be allowed in order to give the work an air of originality. The 'golden rule', which ought to be followed, is, 'Close but not so close as to be servile, free but not so free as to be licentious.'

Cowper considers English to be less musical than Greek but still capable of producing melodious verse in the hands of a good translator-poet. There is 'no subject, however important, however sublime [that] can demand greater force of expression than is within the compass of the English language', he informs the reader.

The poet warns against adopting a high style where it is not needed. The translator should be 'grand and lofty' in the right places and 'allow infallibility to rise and fall with its subject'. In other words, Cowper advises him not to parade his own literary genius and to keep to the varied styles and sentiments of the original and of its characters. The translator should never 'use big words on small matters', except where he is translating the burlesque, as, for example, in the 'Battle of the Frogs and Mice'. Such a method is not for the sober *Iliad*. 'Smooth' lines should be used where the original is smooth and if the original 'limps' where the subject calls for it, the translator should translate in a limping way.

Last but not least, Cowper warns would-be translators not to be monotonous.

A neglected work

Cowper foretold, as already stated, that Greek would lose its influence and soon be a truly dead language even amongst the literati and educated people. Nowadays even where Greek is still taught, there is little room for Homer on the curriculum. Modern didactics determine that the pupil be presented with a whole selection from different authors rather than encouraged to work through either the *Odyssey* or the *Iliad*. The situation is almost as bad regarding translations of Homer. The ancient bard's epics are scarcely read in translations in our schools. It is true that few pupils in Europe go through their school life without hearing of, or reading about, the siege of Troy. 'Ajax', however, is merely a brand-name for various household cleansing agents and the name 'Paris' is limited to the French capital, in the minds of most schoolchildren. The *Odyssey* has fared slightly better. Perhaps the story of Ulysses and his bow is near enough to the Robin Hood legends to appeal to a modern pupil!

Owing to a lack of Greek and cultural connections with the classical world, even amongst literary critics, Cowper's translation of Homer has been greatly neglected. It is the least read, the least commented on, and therefore the least appreciated of all his works. An analysis of its language and style, compared with the original, would be an unprofitable undertaking, and a mere 'labour of love'.

There is obviously little interest shown in English criticism for such a study.

What might — and perhaps ought to — interest not only critics of English literature but also the Christian reader in general is how Cowper's translation work affected and influenced his original verse. This is of especial interest as Cowper spent much of his time from 1784 to the late1790s, first translating and then revising his 'Homer'. He always viewed this work, however, as a stepping-stone to further poetic goals.[50] Although Cowper composed the bulk of his original verse between 1779 and 1784, he did produce a number of very fine poems after this date. It is therefore legitimate to ask, 'Is there any sign that Cowper gained proficiencies in dealing with the language he most admired, which he then used to produce even better original poetry?' We may add the related question: 'Was Cowper's own "critical taper"[51] able to shed new light on his own compositions, after shining for so long on Homer?'

These are extremely difficult questions to answer because of the growing complexity of Cowper's life from the late 1780s until his death.

An enormous task

The first complexity was that Cowper completely underestimated the enormity of the task that lay before him in translating Homer. He was already having problems of conscience about it in the autumn of 1788. Friends were getting alarmed at his apparent obsession with Homer and trying to tempt him away from it for a while. Joseph Hill, who looked after Cowper's financial affairs, was one of these good friends. Cowper replied to his invitation, with the words:

> Nothing can be more picturesque than your description of Wargrove, nor, consequently more beautiful than the subject of it. And I would that I were at liberty for an excursion which I know I should find so perfectly agreeable and to which I have every inducement. But Homer, Homer, Homer, is my eternal answer to all invitations at a distance, and must be so long as I have that great stone to roll before me wherever I go. It will not I hope prove like that of Sisyphus.[52]

A few weeks later we find Cowper jumping at the chance to do, at last, some original work. He had been requested by the Town Clerk of Northampton to provide verses for the Bills of Mortality[53] that the town produced annually. Discussing this with Walter Bagot, he says,

> I am not sorry to be employed by him, considering the task, in respect of the occasion of it, as even more important than Iliad and Odyssey together. To put others in mind of their latter end, is at least as proper an occupation for a man whose own latter end is nearer by almost sixty years than once it was, as to write about Gods and heroes. Let me once get well out of these two long stories, and if I ever meddle with such matters more, call me as Fluellin says, a fool and an ass and a prating coxcomb.[54]

The poet soon found that he had enough work with Homer alone to last him for many more years. He worked so diligently at his translation that he had scarcely time to consider any other kind of occupation. He wrote once more to his old school-friend, Walter Bagot, in 1791, telling him why he was so busy:

> It is a maxim of much weight
> Worth conning o'er and o'er,
> He who has Homer to translate
> Had need do nothing more.[55]

Indeed, Cowper has only two related themes in his letter: Homer and the advantages of blank verse. There is no complaining in the letter. The poet is still in his element, seven years after starting on the *Iliad*. He is, however, so taken up with his work that he has thought for little else. He was neglecting, not only his friends, but himself, and many of his friends thought he was neglecting his talents. Writing to Mrs King a few days later, and apologizing for being so taken up with Homer, he says, 'True it is, that if Mrs. Unwin did not call me from that pursuit, I should forget in the ardour with which I persevere in it, both to eat and drink and to retire to rest. This zeal has increased in me regularly as I have proceeded, and in an exact ratio as a mathematician would say, to the progress I have made towards the point at which I have been aiming.'[56]

Shortly after writing these letters, Cowper was able to send corrected proofs of both the *Iliad* and the *Odyssey* to the printers. His work was published in July 1791.

Frequent interruptions

One of the persistent myths regarding Cowper's work at this time portrays the poet as being completely shut off from the world, slaving away at Homer with no contact with the outside world. Although Cowper complained that he had 'buried himself in Homer's mines' he was far from being lost to the world. Indeed, he had far too much of it in his house. He was now so famous that people were constantly calling on him and disturbing him at his work, so that he was always under the stress and strain of callers. Most seemed to want a peep at the poet at work and many a visitor had embarrassed Cowper by looking over his shoulder when he was in the act of composing verse. He opened his heart to fellow-poet James Hurdis on this subject in the summer of 1791:

> I wish always when I have a new piece in hand, to be as secret as you, and there was a time when I could be so. Then I lived the life of a solitary, was not visited by a single neighbour, because I had none with whom I could associate; nor ever had an inmate. This was when I dwelt at Olney; but since I have removed to Weston the case is different. Here I am visited by all around me, and study in a room exposed to all manner of inroads. It is on the ground floor, the room in which we dine, and in which I am sure to be found by all who seek me. They find me generally at my desk, and with my work, whatever it be, before me, unless perhaps I have conjured it into its hiding-place before they have had time to enter. This however is not always the case, and consequently sooner or later, I cannot fail to be detected. Possibly you, who I suppose have a snug study, would find it impracticable to attend to any thing closely in an apartment exposed as mine, but use has made it familiar to me, and so familiar, that neither servants going and coming disconcert me, nor even if a lady, with an oblique glance of her eye, catches two or three lines of my MSS. do I feel myself inclined to blush, though naturally the shyest of mankind.

The key to the lost language of Eden

Perhaps the most important reason Cowper gave for spending so much time on the classical languages was that they served as a key for him to open the door to the lost language of paradise. Any reader of Cowper's poetry and prose will be struck by the number of occasions the poet mentions and deals with problems of the usage and history of language. Throughout the 1780s and well into the 1790s Cowper researched ardently into the origin and purpose of speech. It is significant to note that most of those critics who do not find Cowper's poetry to their liking, still consider him to be one of the finest of prose writers. Yet the poet's constant prayer was: 'Oh that these lips had language!'[57] and he often found himself unable to express what was in his heart and mind. Often Cowper is portrayed as shy when in fact he was struggling to express his thoughts.

Two of the most famous linguists of the day were Hugh Blair[58] and James Beattie,[59] both of whom had written widely on the origins of languages. Though professing Christians, these men had bowed to the rationalism of the day and to the theories of evolution then beginning to come into vogue. They believed that the first men were speechless beings who gradually, through arbitrary and conventional means, developed a language, starting off with rustic grunts and going on to evolve the complicated languages of modern times. Cowper rejected this theory on many counts.

Firstly, it was contrary to Scripture, and though Blair and Beattie argued that God was involved in the evolutionary process, in reality, God was not needed in their hypothesis.

Secondly, their theory was contrary to scientific knowledge, as the oldest languages known, in particular Greek, were highly inflected and had given rise to a high level of literature which was imitated and simplified, but never bettered, in later history. When advising Unwin's children to study Greek, the poet told them that all languages were barbaric in comparison to that language. Cowper himself tried to invent new literary forms but failed, coming to the conclusion that the ancient Greeks had all the literary genres at their disposal.[60]

Thirdly, Cowper argued that the oldest languages were preserved as highly sophisticated linguistic systems and there was no proof of their ever occurring in more primitive forms. Homer was still considered in Cowper's day to be the greatest poet who had ever lived, yet there was no evidence of any earlier poetry from which his work might have developed.

In April 1784 Cowper wrote a highly amusing letter to William Unwin in which he pointed out the fallacies inherent in any language which came into being according to the principles of evolution. If the theory of linguistic evolution were valid, he argues, incomplete language structures would have developed which would serve no useful purpose until they were completed. Then why would such structures have developed in the first place? This would mean that most of what people say and write is verbal nonsense which will only make sense at some future date. The poet concludes that Adam was created as a fully-fledged human being capable of 'sublime diction and logical combination'.

In his poetry from his earliest efforts after his conversion to his last great poem, 'Yardley Oak', Cowper stressed that the language of Eden was the true, unlearnt, original language of man which Adam used to praise God and for classifying and governing creation in accordance with his office as God's steward on earth. He was firmly convinced that there was such a thing as an ideal original language that was also the true language of poetry. This language was indigenous to and coeval with man in his unfallen state and was void of any artificiality either in content or form. Poetry was a natural, spontaneous communication with God in a language perfectly developed for this purpose, unadulterated by any enhancements or artefacts of the poet. Language, and specifically the language of poetry, was received from God at the moment of creation as part and parcel of human nature and it was used first and foremost to express the gratification of a thankful human, but innocent, heart.

This language, however, was partially lost with the fall of man and later totally confused with the destruction of Babel. Instead of remaining the spontaneous expression of a happy soul in communion and harmony with its Maker and with creation which constitutes true poetry, language degenerated into an artificial verbalization of man's fallen mentality. The more man separates himself from God, the further his language regresses into meaningless artifice. In time, if mankind continues on his foolish way, his language will become so degenerate that he will no longer be capable of expressing eternal truths by it and his wisdom, philosophy and religion will simply function in a vicious circle of logic which bears no relationship to truth or understanding.

Cowper thus taught that language had increasingly degenerated and that if anyone wished to get back to the original language of Eden he had two choices. One way was to accept the Scriptures as the Word of God and see them as the only of God's plan and purpose for man in unfallen language means of verbal communication; the other was to go back to the oldest known languages and study their structure. Cowper chose to do both, believing that in this way he could find the very language that was needed to reunite a soul to God and make him morally and intellectually once more fit for paradise.[61] The two ways to the origin of languages, for Cowper as for most of the Evangelicals of his day, were in fact one and the same, since the New Testament, God's teaching on Paradise Regained, was written in the ancient language of the Greeks.

What the critics said

Cowper's translation of Homer was published in July 1791 and immediately proved a success, bringing in £1,000 in income for the poet in its first year. As usual after publishing a new work, Cowper trembled about what the critics might say. He need not have worried. His main aim had been to prove that the standards set by Pope were wrong and contrary to a right use of language. The *Monthly Review*, a magazine that had often given Evangelicals a verbal thrashing, confessed that it found Cowper's translation superior to that of Pope. The *Gentleman's Magazine*, which published a very detailed review in September 1791, probably written by Nichols, the chief editor, went even further. The reviewer pronounced Cowper's work 'a translation perfect in its kind'.

15.
Life at Weston

When Cowper first learned of William Unwin's death in November 1786, he had no time to think melancholy thoughts. His heart went out to Mrs Unwin and to William Unwin's family. Cowper held the widow, Mrs Anne Unwin, née Shuttleworth, in almost as high regard as he did her husband. Instead of telling Unwin his opinion of his bride in prose when he married, Cowper paid the following tribute to her in verse:

> Sweet Stream! that Winds thro' yonder Glade,
> Apt Emblem of a Virtuous Maid—
> Silent & chaste she Steals along
> Far from the World's Gay, Busy Throng:
> With gentle yet prevailing Force
> Intent upon her destin'd Course:
> Gracefull & Usefull All she does,
> Blessing and Blest where'er she goes:
> Pure-bosom'd as that Wat'ry Glass,
> And Heav'n reflected in her Face.[1]

Cowper persuaded Anne Unwin to visit Weston with her three children so that they might be amongst loved ones. He looked into the matter of the children's education and undertook the legal matters connected with Unwin's death. Unwin had left his money to his children and his property, which was not small, to his wife. As Anne Unwin was also to inherit property which at present belonged to Mrs Mary Unwin, her future was taken care of.

The house at Weston Underwood where Cowper lived

Letters flooded in to Weston bringing condolences from people of all stations in life. Newton added his — writing to Mrs Unwin — but he was still not reconciled to Cowper and his letter shows a total lack of sensibility and taste. Some time earlier he had written to Mrs Unwin, informing her that he had his connections in Olney and Cowper could not do anything without his hearing about it. Now in the very letter which should have brought Mrs Unwin and Cowper comfort, Newton was callous enough to say that he also had his informers at Weston who had already given him cause to reprimand Cowper for his conduct.

John Higgins and his family

It appears that Newton had an acquaintance in Weston called Higgins — whom Cowper did not know — and Higgins had passed Cowper in the street and the poet had failed to greet him. A reprimand for this supposed failure in Christian witness was evidently as important in Newton's eyes as expressing words of comfort to his friends on their losing a son and a close friend.

Cowper was deeply shocked at the letter, especially as he had no idea who Higgins was. However, he did not lose his temper but merely groaned inwardly and replied to Newton, saying first how his heart went out to William Unwin's widow and family and then continuing:

> I do not know Mr. John Higgins even by sight, and if I have at any time pass'd him without showing him the civility due to so respectable a neighbour, it has been owing to no other cause. But he should recollect that it does not rest with me to commence an acquaintance. The resident inhabitants of a place must always make the first advances to a new comer, or they make a visiting intercourse impossible. It can with no propriety originate from me; and I dare say he is well aware of it.[2]

Cowper's remarks as to who should be the first to greet the other became all the more relevant when Cowper sought out John Higgins and found who he really was. Newton had reprimanded his friend for not being the first to greet a young lad of a mere eighteen years whom he did not know. Nevertheless, when they finally met, Cowper took an immediate liking to the boy and asked him and his parents to tea. The poet was delighted to find that young Higgins could recite many of his poems off by heart and was something of an artist. John made a profile drawing of the poet which is the earliest known likeness of him as earlier portraits have been lost. Lady Hesketh was so moved by Cowper's description of Higgins to her that she promptly made the boy a fancy waistcoat.

Though the Higgins family do not seem to have been very affluent when Cowper made their acquaintance, John eventually came into a substantial inheritance through a distant relative. After Cowper's death John proudly wore Cowper's shoe buckles, now in the Olney Museum.

Cowper's greatest joy on meeting the Higgins family was to find that they were sincere believers and when Mrs Mary Higgins died only a few years after being introduced to Cowper the poet wrote for her gravestone:

Laurels may flourish round the conqu'ror's tomb,
But happiest they, who win the world to come:
Believers have a silent field to fight,
And their exploits are veil'd from human sight.
They in some nook, where little known they dwell,
Kneel, pray in faith, and rout the hosts of hell;
Eternal triumphs crown their toils divine,
And all those triumphs, Mary, now are thine.

The poet is much in demand

The new year of 1787 opened in a blaze of popularity for Cowper. Hardly two years after their first publication, his poems were now in their third British edition and two editions had already been issued in North America because of the demand for them there.

Johnson, the publisher, was making a great deal of money but little of it came to Cowper at first as he had given Johnson the copyright to the poems and lost his bargaining position. Hayley maintained that Cowper as good as made Johnson a gift of his first two volumes of poetry. Learning from experience, Cowper had kept the copyright to his Homer but his translation works did not sell as well as his poems. It is estimated that Johnson was in the process of making some £10,000 out of Cowper's original poetry, which was an immense fortune in those days. By 1793 Johnson seems to have had second thoughts on the way he was treating his most successful author and gave Cowper the entire profits of the fifth edition published in January of that year.

Actors such as the famous John Henderson were now earning their livelihood reciting Cowper's works on stage and lectures were given on them up and down the country in village halls and assembly rooms. Charles James Fox and other politicians backed up their arguments in Parliament by quoting Cowper, and his poems were avidly read at the court of George III. Several motions were under way to erect monuments in Cowper's honour and it seemed that every Tom, Dick and Harry were sending their verses, sermons and even plays to him, asking for his approval, or for him to use his influence in their favour.

The following years brought an end to Cowper's days of quiet seclusion. Everyone seemed to take it for granted that Cowper was a man of the world and had an enormous amount of influence. A Welshman by the name of Walter Churchey, a friend of Wesley's, wrote to Cowper asking him to use his influence to have him made Poet Laureate. Churchey insisted that he needed the post quickly as he had a wife and six children to keep. One young lady even approached Cowper to use his influence in obtaining the hand of a a local affluent clergyman in marriage. Now post was pouring in addressed 'To the first of poets and the best of men' and criminals were appealing to the poet to use his influence to save them from the gallows.

Cowper did not ignore any of these pleas and answered the letters conscientiously. He did what he could for the Welshman, corrected his verse for publication and corresponded with him for several years. He began to mediate with the gentleman concerned on behalf of the lady who was interested in marriage but was rather shocked to discover that the young woman had fallen in love with the clergyman's house rather than his person. Cowper even drew up a petition to ask for mercy in the case of a condemned criminal.

Norman Nicholson describes in his biography of Cowper[3] how, after the *Task* was published, Orchard Side became a place of literary pilgrimage. When Cowper moved to Weston, the 'literary pilgrimages' of his devotees increased greatly, possibly because more educated people lived in the vicinity and they presented Cowper as a special attraction to their many visitors.

Cowper could have gladly done without the attention he was receiving. His new study was on the ground floor at the front of the house and any callers could see immediately if he was at home or not. Although Weston was only a small village miles from anywhere, Cowper's visitors travelled great distances to pay him their respects and the poet was never sure of an afternoon's peace.

The strain proves too much

After Unwin's burial and the settling of his affairs, a dismal gloom settled over all that Cowper did. The praise that he was receiving, wrongly as he believed, depressed him further and he had to fight hard against what he called 'nervous fever'. His nights were full of sleepless nightmares and he suffered from giddy pains in the head and acute rheumatism. During periods of respite he was able to send off a letter to Newton in January and several others to friends who had written concerning the death of Unwin or the poet's translation work.

One letter to Lady Hesketh, written on 14 and 15 January, is extremely interesting biographically as it deals with the rumour being spread at that time that Cowper felt himself eternally cut off from God because God himself had proclaimed this in a dream in 1773. The poet mentioned this myth in his letter to Lady Hesketh and said, 'I have not believed that I shall perish because in dreams I have been told it, but because I have had hardly any but terrible dreams for 13 years, I therefore have spent the greatest part of that time most unhappily. They have either tinged my mind with melancholy or filled it with terrour, and the effects have been unavoidable. If we swallow arsenic we must be pois'nd, and he who dreams as I have done, must be troubled. So much for dreams.'

During the following days, weeks and months Cowper was very ill and it was six months before he could write another letter and nine months before he felt really well again. Apart from having a perpetually high temperature and suffering acute discomfort from rheumatism, which made him feel like 'a prisoner bound to his chair', he developed severe eye-trouble and had a head, as he put it, 'like a broken eggshell'. He refused to receive most visitors, locking the door of his study on almost everyone except Mrs Unwin. Nevertheless, during his illness he mentions having guests to dinner and others to tea. It seems that Cowper could never be totally without company.

One welcome exception during this illness was Samuel Rose who visited him once or twice and whose company the poet enjoyed. Rose gave Cowper a book of Burns' poems which the poet read through twice during his illness. When William Bull dropped in and insisted on talking to Cowper, however, the poet tells us, he 'had no great cause to exult in his Success'. Bull was probably not the right companion for Cowper at the time as he too was going through a period of depression and ill-health. Newton offered to come and bring his wife with him to help Mrs Unwin but he also received a firm 'No' from Cowper.

The fact was that Cowper was completely exhausted and over-worked. He felt like 'an ass overladen with sand-bags' and his nerves were very frayed. For years he had started work at six in the morning, not breakfasting until eleven. He had produced two relatively large volumes of poems in record time and had put several years of strenuous work into translating Homer, a task that other translators had only succeeded in doing with a team of co-workers and secretaries. He had composed a large amount of new original poetry after publishing the *Task* and done a great deal of entertaining and letter-writing. On top of this came the trials of losing his best friend, being continually criticized by Newton and moving house. He was also responsible for looking after a very large garden, an orchard and a large field of arable land, as well as a host of animals, which by now included pigs and most likely a cow. Cowper always maintained that gardening was the employment at which he suc-ceeded the best.[4] It was, however, all very tiring and would have worn out a man of far stronger nerves.

The poet tried every available medicine to cure himself and one wonders if many of the patent recipes he tried were not as harmful as the illnesses they were supposed to cure. Cowper's liberal use of laudanum has already been mentioned and he continued to take this dangerous drug. He also regularly used an ointment called 'Elliot's', named after the chemist that made it up, for his eye-troubles. According to Ryskamp and King's research[5] this ointment probably contained compounds of quicksilver such as white mercuric oxide. If Elliot's ointment did contain mercuric oxide — and this was widely used in ointments and make-up at the time — then it is no wonder that Cowper had headaches, fever, trouble with his digestion and nervous system and suffered from acute restlessness, as he describes. These are the very symptoms produced by mercuric poisoning. Many an eighteenth-century lady of fashion painted herself into the grave through generous applications of quicksilver-based cosmetics. The strange thing is that Cowper used Elliot's ointment to relieve his inflamed eyes though mercuric oxide is itself notorious for causing eye inflammation. Other patent medicines Cowper took were salts of tartar and tartar emetic for his stomach, Hoffmann's drops (often five times the prescribed amount) for his nerves, various 'astringents' and 'infusions of bark', of dubious origin and use, and he also resorted to 'phlebotomy', or bloodletting.

Cowper was always prone to what Goldwin Smith calls 'self-revelation'. In other words, he always told his friends in great detail how he was ailing. Some of his letters to Lady Hesketh are so descriptive, especially those dealing with his stomach problems, that the reader's stomach turns with the poet's! Whenever Cowper wrote to new friends, he always gave them a fully detailed account of his 1763 and 1773 illnesses. This was not merely a mild kind of hypochondria but also the poet's method of counteracting rumours. However, he rarely said much about his 1787 illness and it is obvious that he did not suffer in the same way as in previous years.

He was obviously well enough to read from time to time and even tackled books in French and Latin. In fact he spent the later part of his illness reading at a great pace and devouring one volume of travel or history after the other in several different languages. By the time the summer had arrived he had read Burns' poems in broad Scots dialect, John Barclay's political satire, *Argenis*, in Latin, which amused him greatly, Savary's *Travels in Egypt* (in English though it was a French work), *Memoirs du Baron de Trott* and *Memoires d'Henri de Lorraine Duc de Guise* in French, Martin Madan's writings against Joseph Priestly, two volumes of Sir John Fenn's edition of historical letters, *The Letters of Frederic of Bohemia* and a number of religious and political pamphlets. It was as if he were catching up on lost reading time because of his previous literary work.

Even though still ill, Cowper had a healthy sense of humour. Writing to Lady Hesketh in September 1787 about his troubles, the poet ends his letter with the words:

I have a perpetual Din in my head, and though not deaf,
hear nothing aright, neither my own voice nor that of others.
I am under a Tub. From which Tub, accept my best Love
joined with Mrs. Unwin's.

Yours, my Dearest Cousin,

W.C.

Letter-writing

Cowper always maintained that if people were to take him seriously
they had to read his poems rather than his prose. There they would
find the inner testimony of his own soul. Poetry is there to express
eternal truths, whereas prose is there to pass the time of day.
Nowhere is this made more evident than in Cowper's letters to Lady
Hesketh. In them he reaches those heights of expression which
critics so often take over-seriously but which are merely the poet's
way of acommodating to the interests of his reader.

Lady Hesketh had not written for two weeks, which worried
Cowper no end. He thus wrote her a short letter saying, 'I have spent
hours in the night, leaning upon my elbow and wondering what your
silence means.'[6] Two days later Cowper sent off another letter
apologizing for the terseness and the melancholy nature of his last
one as the bad weather had made him sad. There were actually
several letters from Lady Hesketh on the way and soon Cowper had
three to read. The poet was overjoyed and now gave a new description of his 'hours in the night, leaning upon my elbow and wondering what your silence means', saying, 'I heard, saw and felt a
thousand terrible things which had no real existence, and was
haunted by them night and day 'till they at last exorted from me the
doleful Epistle which I have since wish'd had been burn'd before I
sent it. But the cloud has pass'd and as far as you are concern'd, my
heart is once more at rest.'[7] Such language, taken out of context, has
given rise to the opinion that Cowper was mentally ill at this period
but it is really just the language of a gallant gentleman addressing a
lady who was not amiss to hearing such words. In his very next letter
Cowper gave Lady Hesketh an account of his health, which he said
was better than it had been for thirty years!

Cowper was a master at adapting his style and language to suit
the mind and interests of his readers. To Unwin he was almost
always evangelical, cheerful and instructive; to Newton he was

evangelical, political and often miserable; to Bull he wrote very varied letters as Bull was a man of many parts; to John Johnson he was fatherly and like a friendly professor at the same time. Cowper's letters to Hill use business and legal language and his letters to the Lord Chancellor are as stiff and formal as his letters to William Hayley are jocular and friendly. This does not mean that Cowper was guilty of dissimulation but that he really felt all these things in relation to the people he was addressing. It was his way of being all things to all men and of showing how many-sided were his own interests and convictions.

One of the intriguing results of his 1787 illness was Cowper's changed attitude towards Newton. It was not until October that he was able to write to his friend and this letter is perhaps the strangest ever written by Cowper. The poet had long been frustrated and hurt by Newton's dismal, complaining letters. He had compared the sentiments of the letters with the sweet time of fellowship the two men had shared years before and had come to the conclusion that Newton had changed radically. This thought seems to have so affected Cowper that he had begun to believe that the man writing to him from London was an impostor and could not possibly be his old friend John Newton. After his 1787 illness Cowper came to see that he had been the victim of a delusion and accordingly wrote to Newton:

My dear friend

After a long but necessary interruption of our correspondence, I return to it again; in one respect at least better qualified for it than before, I mean, by a belief of your identity, which for 13 years I did not believe. The acquisition of this light, if light it may be called which leaves me as much in the dark as ever on the most interesting subjects, releases me however from the disagreeable suspicion that I am addressing myself to you as the friend whom I loved and valued so highly in my better days, while in fact you are not that friend but a stranger. I can now write to you without seeming to act a part, and without having any need to charge myself with dissimulation. A charge, from which in that state of mind and under such an uncomfortable persuasion, I knew not how to exculpate myself, and which, as you will easily conceive, not seldom made my correspondence with you a burthen. Still indeed it wants and is likely to want that best ingredient which can alone make it truly pleasant either to myself or you, that spirituality which once enliven'd all our intercourse. You will tell me, no doubt, that the knowlege I have gained is an earnest of more, and more valuable information, and that the dispersion of the clouds in part promises in due time their complete dispersion. I should be happy to believe it, but the power to do so is at present far from me. Never was the mind of man benighted to the degree that mine has been; the storms that have assailed me would have overset the Faith of every man that ever had any, and the very remembrance of them, even after they have been long pass'd by, makes Hope impossible.

Mrs. Unwin whose poor bark is still held together, though shatter'd by being toss'd and agitated so long at the side of mine, does not forget yours and Mrs. Newton's kindness on this last occasion. Mrs. Newton's offer to come to her assistance, and your readiness to have render'd us the same service, could you have hoped for any salutary effect of your presence, neither Mrs. Unwin nor myself undervalue nor shall presently forget. But you judged right when you supposed that even your company would have been no relief to me; the company of my Father or my Brother, could they have returned from the dead to visit me, would have been none to me.

We are busied in preparing for the reception of Lady Hesketh whom we expect here shortly. We have beds to put up and furniture for beds to make, workmen and scow'ring and bustle. Mrs. Unwin's time has of course been lately occupied to a degree that made writing, to her, impracticable, and she excused herself the rather, knowing my intentions to take her office. It does not however suit me to write much at a time. This last tempest has left my nerves in a worse condition than it found them, my head especially, though better informed, is more infirm than ever. I will therefore only add our joint love to yourself and Mrs. Newton, and that I am, my dear friend,

Your affectionate

Wm. Cowper[8]

Tributes to Mrs Unwin's devoted care

The poet's reference to Mrs Unwin's 'poor bark' was no exaggeration. She was now sixty-four years of age and had not been in good health for some time owing to dizzy spells which often caused her to fall, headaches, noises in her ears and acute pains in her side. She had looked after Cowper almost day and night for six months and was now completely exhausted. She was never again to recover her full health and was from now on to be a burden to Cowper as he had been to her. Just as Mrs Unwin had always praised God for having the privilege of looking after Cowper, so the poet never flinched in his duty to her and put her health before all his own private interests.

As his landlady grew to suffer more and more from the effects of illness and the early onset of old age, Cowper's heart went out to her all the more and he blamed himself the more for being the cause of her weakness. Writing in 1790 to an Evangelical lady about a portrait of his mother that had been sent to him, the poet said of Mrs Unwin, although she was now little more than an invalid:

> I have lately received, from a female Cousin of mine in Norfolk, whom I have not seen these thirty years, a picture of my own mother. She died when I wanted two days of being six years old, yet I remember her perfectly, find the picture a strong likeness of her, and because her memory has been ever precious to me, have written a poem on the receipt of it. A poem which, one excepted, I had more pleasure in writing than any that I ever wrote. That one was addressed to a lady whom I expect in a few minutes to come down to breakfast, and who has supplied to me the place of my own mother, my own invaluable mother, these six and twenty years. Some sons may be said to have had many fathers, but a plurality of mothers is not common.[9]

Later Cowper told Lady Hesketh that he had indeed had three mothers, as his father had married again after his own mother's death. Cowper said that he did not mention his step-mother in conjunction with his first mother, Ann Cowper, and his third mother, Mrs Unwin, obviously implying that she was not in the same category.

The poem Cowper referred to in the letter quoted above was 'The Winter Nosegay', which he had written to thank Mrs Unwin for her faithful care of him during his 1773 illness.

What nature, alas! has denied
To the delicate growth of our isle,
Art has in a measure supplied,
And winter is deck'd with a smile.
See Mary what beauties I bring
From the shelter of that sunny shed,
Where the flow'rs have the charms of the spring,
Though abroad they are frozen and dead.

'Tis a bow'r of Arcadian sweets,
Where Flora is still in her prime,
A fortress to which she retreats,
From the cruel assaults of the clime.
While earth wears a mantle of snow,
These pinks are as fresh and as gay,
As the fairest and sweetest that blow,
On the beautiful bosom of May.

See how they have safely surviv'd
The frowns of a sky so severe,
Such Mary's true love that has liv'd
Through many a turbulent year.
The charms of the late blowing rose,
Seem grac'd with a livelier hue,
And the winter of sorrow best shows
The truth of a friend, such as you.

An old friendship renewed and new ones formed

From now on there is a great change in Cowper's letters to Newton and they manifest a new spirit. Indeed, a number of the poet's subsequent letters to his rediscovered friend begin with exclamations of great pleasure. We find Cowper writing in September 1788, for example, after a visit from Newton,

My dear friend—

I rejoice that you and yours reach'd London safe, especially when I reflect that you perform'd the journey on a day so fatal, as I understand, to others travelling the same road. I found those comforts, in your visit, which have formerly sweeten'd all our interviews, in part restored. I knew you; knew you for the same shepherd who was sent to lead me out of the wilderness into the pasture where the Chief Shepherd feeds his flock, and felt my sentiments of affectionate friendship for you, the same as ever.

As a gesture of renewed friendship Cowper, who had heard that Newton had approached Johnson again with a request to have his preface added to Cowper's first volume of poems, wrote to the publisher and begged him to include Newton's preface in further editions of his works. It was not, however, until the fifth edition was published in January 1793 that Johnson included the preface.

Cowper was always looking out for opportunities to try out his theories of education and assist young people in their spiritual and literary development. Within the next two years he was to start a firm friendship with three young men who all looked on Cowper ever after as their beloved teacher, spiritual adviser and friend. These were Samuel Rose, John Johnson and James Hurdis. All three made a name for themselves in their various spheres through the training, encouragement and connections that Cowper supplied for them. Rose became a lawyer and literary critic and earned national acclamation for his defence of William Blake, who had been put on trial for treason. Johnson was lured away from studying mathematics by Cowper and introduced to theology, going on to become not only a sound Evangelical minister but also a man of letters. Hurdis sent his poetical works regularly to Cowper for correction and received a good deal of sound gospel advice in return. Through Cowper's rounding up his old friends to vote for him, Hurdis, who was the first poet to produce works after the manner of Cowper, became Professor of Poetry at Oxford.

Samuel Rose

When Cowper wrote his last letter before becoming ill in January 1787, he told Lady Hesketh that a young student named Rose had just called in on his way from Glasgow, where he was studying, to London, bringing with him greetings from several Scots professors and authors. One of these was Henry Mackenzie (1745-1831) who became Cowper's 'friend at a distance' and correspondent. Mackenzie made his reputation through writing *The Man of Feeling* and editing the *Lounger* and the *Mirror*. He was a forerunner of the Romantic poets but stood head and shoulders above the bulk of them in moral integrity.

During Cowper's illness Rose sent Cowper a present of Robert Burns' dialect poems and Rose was the first person to whom Cowper wrote after he recovered. Cowper explained to his new friend that though Burns was perhaps the greatest poet of humble origins who had emerged since Shakespeare, he could not enjoy him thoroughly because of the artificiality of his language. This was quite a hard blow aimed at a young Romantic poet as this school claimed they were doing away with poetic diction and returning to the language of the simple heart. Cowper saw that they were only throwing out one kind of poetic diction so that they might introduce another.

Though he was still only a student, Rose had a very good eye for verse and had already written a number of well-received reviews for the *Monthly Review,* a magazine feared and respected by all British writers. To have a good review of one's works appear in the *Monthly Review* was tantamount to being a 'made' man. It was Rose who took over Unwin's activities as Cowper's go-between in his transactions with Johnson the publisher and he transcribed and commented on much of Cowper's version of Homer. Shortly after Cowper and Rose first met, Rose's father, a classical scholar who ran a school at Chiswick, died and it is clear that the young man, who had treasured his father's instructions dearly, then began to look to Cowper as a new father figure.

After his 1787 illness Cowper slackened his pace somewhat and it is to Rose's pen that we owe an insight into the kind of life the poet now led. Rose wrote to his sister, describing a typical day at Weston:

We rise at whatever hour we choose; breakfast at half after nine, take about an hour to satisfy the *sentiment*, not the *appetite*, for we talk — good heavens! how we talk! and enjoy ourselves most wonderfully. Then we separate — Mr Cowper to Homer, Mr Rose to transcribing what is translated, Lady Hesketh to work and to books alternately. Mrs. Unwin, who in everything but her face[10] is like a kind angel come from heaven to guard the health of our poet, is busy in domestic concerns. At one, our labours finished, the poet and I walk for two hours. I then drink most plentiful draughts of instruction so sweet and goodness so exquisite that one *loves* it for its flavour. At three we return and dress, and the succeeding hour brings dinner upon the table and collects again the smiling countenances of the family to partake of the neat and elegant meal. Conversation continues till tea-time, when an entertaining volume engrosses our thoughts till the last meal is announced. Conversation again, and then rest before twelve to enable us to rise again to the same round of innocent virtuous pleasure.[11]

Cowper was struck by Rose's keen intellect and analytical mind, coupled with a great deal of common sense, and he always addressed him more as a mature colleague than a younger man. Cowper was never embarrassed or irritated by his presence and Rose knew that he could walk in and out of Weston whenever he liked, always sure of a bed, food and deep conversation. The young man took every advantage of this opportunity. The poet was never so directly evangelical when writing to Rose as he was in writing to Johnson and Hurdis but often Cowper approached the matter of religion in a more indirect way. We see an example of this in a letter written 23 June 1788, when the poet comments on the weather and draws lessons from it:

It has pleased God to give us rain, without which this part of our County at least must soon have become a Desert. The meadows have been parched to a January Brown, and we have fodder'd our cattle for some time as in the winter.—

The goodness and power of God are never, I believe, so universally acknowledged as at the end of a long drought. Man is naturally a self-sufficient animal, and in all concerns that seem to lie within the sphere of his own ability, thinks little or not at all of the need he always has of protection and furtherance from above. But he is sensible that the clouds will not assemble at his bidding, and that though clouds assemble, they will not fall in showers because he commands them.

When therefore at last the blessing descends, you shall hear even in the streets the most irreligious and thoughtless with one voice exclaim — Thank God! Confessing themselves indebted to his favour, and willing, at least so far as words go, to give him the glory. I can hardly doubt therefore that the earth is sometimes parched, and the crops endanger'd, in order that the multitude may not want a memento to whom they owe them, nor absolutely forget the power on which all depend for all things.

The letter continues in the same strain and the poet admits that he is sermonizing but obviously he does so with a purpose. Cowper also tells Rose that Anne Unwin and her children have just left after a lengthy stay and that John and Mary Newton are about to replace them, after which Lady Hesketh is to visit them for the winter. Cowper's 'sermonizing' and his reference to Newton may have interested the young man deeply as he planned his next visit to coincide with that of the Newtons. It was a visit in which Cowper and Newton patched up their differences and it is easy to guess what topics were discussed with the young law student. For Cowper it was just like old times, as he told Newton later.

Rose became a most earnest Christian and befriended William Hayley, who wrote a glowing account of the young man's testimony to his faith in Christ and his triumphant witness and brave suffering before dying in his thirty-eighth year.[12]

James Hurdis

In the autumn of 1788 Johnson, the publisher, was sent a poetical work entitled *Adriano: Or the First of June* by a young up-and-coming poet by the name of James Hurdis. Not knowing how to judge the piece Johnson sent it to Cowper for his comments. Cowper was already acquainted with a work called 'The Village Curate' by Hurdis which was almost a plagiarism of Cowper's own style. Apparently he did not realize until some time later that the work he had received for comment was by the same author.

The poet's opinion was that the sentiments 'deserve to be immortal' but the story had many careless hitches in it, which he was sure the author had the ability to rectify. Cowper sent off a list of corrections to Johnson beseeching him to recommend them to the author and adding, 'I am either much mistaken, and have read him through a false medium, or he has few, perhaps no equals in the present day. But, except on favourite occasions he does not put forth half his strength.' This was high praise indeed and very unselfish coming from a poet who was very much aware of his own unrivalled status in contemporary poetry.

When Hurdis heard that no less a poet than William Cowper, whom he much admired, had recommended his work, his joy knew no bounds and Cowper had earned himself a friend for life. The work was corrected quickly and Cowper wasted no time in sending it to influential people as a method of gaining pre-publishing interest in the long poem.

A few years later Hurdis sent Cowper the manuscript of a play he had written on the life of Sir Thomas More with a request for help and comments. Cowper, once a keen theatre-goer, now looked on the theatre as a means of introducing people to the more worldly aspects of life but was cautious about how he put this over to Hurdis. He told the young poet that he felt the work was not suitable for putting on the stage but would certainly be useful as a chamber-piece for evening reading and instruction. Hurdis did not know that Sir Thomas More was an ancestor of Cowper's and the piece on his life had interested the poet greatly. Thus *Sir Thomas More* was edited, corrected and sent off with Cowper's best wishes and Johnson was eventually persuaded to publish it in 1792.

Hurdis was an animal lover and the two poets soon found out that both had spent many happy hours making rabbit-hutches and birdcages and looking after their feathered and furred friends. It was through their common love for animals that Cowper drew Hurdis skilfully into the topic of being a Christian. In one letter dated 13 June 1791 he wrote,

> I am glad to find that your amusements have been so similar to mine; for in this instance too I seemed to have need of somebody to keep me in countenance, especially in my attention and attachment to animals. All the notice that we lords of the creation vouchsafe to bestow on the creatures, is generally to abuse them; it is well, therefore, that here and there a man should be found a little womanish, or perhaps a

little childish in this matter, who will make some amends by kissing and coaxing, and laying them in one's bosom. You remember the little ewe lamb, mentioned by the Prophet Nathan: the Prophet perhaps invented the tale for the sake of its application to David's conscience; but it is more probable, that God inspired him with it for that purpose. If he did, it amounts to a proof, that he does not over-look, but on the contrary, much notices such little partialities and kindnesses to his dumb creatures, as we, because we articulate, are pleased to call them.

Hurdis was still unmarried but evidently was on the lookout for a wife, for he had told Cowper that he went to dances in the hope that these would provide an opportunity to meet 'the right woman'. In the letter referred to above, Cowper, once on the subject of religion, decided to take his new friend further into his Christian confidence on this topic and continued:

> Your Sisters are fitter to judge than I, whether assembly-rooms are the places, of all others, in which the ladies may be studied to most advantage. I am an old fellow, but I had once my dancing days, as you have now, yet I could never find that I learned half so much of a woman's real character by dancing with her, as by conversing with her at home, where I could observe her behaviour at the table, at the fire side, and in all the trying circumstances of domestic life. We are all good when we are pleased, but she is the good woman who wants not a fiddle to sweeten her. If I am wrong, the young ladies will set me right; in the mean time I will not teaze you with graver arguments on the subject, especially as I have a hope, that years, and the study of the Scripture, and His Spirit, whose word it is, will, in due time, bring you to my way of thinking. I am not one of those sages who require that young men should be as old as themselves, before they have had time to be so.

How could anyone possibly be annoyed at being 'preached at' when such a tactful, loving witness to the gospel is at his heavenly work!

John Johnson

One day in January 1790 a 'wild boy', as Cowper describes him, turned up at Weston. His name was John Johnson and he professed to be a relation of Cowper's on his mother's side. The youth had brought Cowper a long poem, which he claimed was from Lord Howard, Duke of Norfolk, another distant relative of Cowper's, with a request that the poet should revise it. His Lordship was to hold anniversary celebrations in his constituency and the poem was to commemorate this event.

The poem, called the 'Tale of the Lute or the Beauties of Audley-End', pleased Cowper in parts but other parts he thought very weak. He noticed that the young man grew thoughtful and silent when he criticized the poem and he began to have doubts about its authorship. He invited young John to stay the night and on the following day they went for a walk in nearby Kilwick Wood. Cowper did no pressing but gave the boy a chance to come out with the truth. During the walk the otherwise honest young man confessed that he himself had written the poem for Lord Howard, who was not quite pleased with it so he had suggested that Johnny from Norfolk, as Cowper came to call him, should consult Cowper about it. The poet was so struck by the boy's embarrassment and remorse at not coming out with the truth from the start that he 'conceived a great affection' for him, as he told Lady Hesketh.

As in the case of Samuel Rose, Cowper put Johnny in touch with Lady Hesketh straight away and she used her influence with her cousin the Bishop of Peterborough, Spencer Madan, (the brother of Martin Madan) so that Johnny made the right contacts. Madan eventually appointed Johnny as one of his chaplains.

Although Samuel Rose looked on Cowper as a father figure, the poet often addressed him as 'Sir' and rarely dropped formal etiquette with him. Johnny from Norfolk, however, was always addressed in the most intimate terms and became like a son to Cowper and Mrs Unwin. He seems to have spent more time with Cowper than he did at home. Indeed he tried to persuade his Norfolk family to come and live at Weston so they could benefit from being constantly in Cowper's company. Several female family members were so taken with the idea that they looked for a house in the vicinity of Weston but nothing suitable was to be found.

Johnny's two aunts, Anne and Harriot Donne, now became

enthusiastic correspondents with their cousin William. Cowper was initially obviously drawn to Johnny because he reminded him of his mother and he also saw in him a younger version of himself. When we examine the portraits of the two men we can see that they do indeed share the very same features. Their hearts were also very much akin. Johnny was extremely shy and this too reminded Cowper of his own youthful failings. He therefore encouraged the boy to mix with others, to rid himself of certain peculiarities of behaviour, to take more pride in his work and not to be so critical of himself. The poet's letters to Johnny are full of encouraging remarks, such as, 'You complained of being stupid, and sent me one of the cleverest letters. I have not complained of being stupid, and have sent you one of the dullest. But it is no matter; I never aim at any thing above the pitch of every-day scribble when I write to those I love.'[13]

Cowper was especially open with Johnny, right from the start, concerning his faith. He told his young cousin to pack up studying mathematics as it would not profit him anywhere outside of Cambridge where he was studying. The older Cowper became, the more he disparaged mathematics on the grounds that it was of dubious scientific use, did not help to enlarge the mind sufficiently and was of no help whatsoever in helping people to reason accurately! Johnny should rather tackle basic jurisprudence, ancient Greek, New Testament Greek and the Church Fathers, besides making himself acquainted with the grace of God, without which nothing can be done.

He also told Johnny to keep up practising on his fiddle, but seemed to have second thoughts about this in a further letter after hearing how fond Johnny was of making music. In July 1790 he told his young relative, 'You do well to perfect yourself on the Violin. Only beware that an amusement so very bewitching as Music, especially when we produce it ourselves, do not steal from you *all* those hours that should be given to study. I can be well content that it should serve you as a refreshment after severer exercises, but not that it should engross you wholly.'[14]

Cowper went into great detail with his kinsman over his proposed course of study and Johnson followed his advice gladly. The following is a further specimen of Cowper's combined academic and spiritual tutorship of his young friend:

You could not apply to a worse than I am to advise you concerning your studies. I was never a regular Student myself but lost the most valuable years of my life in an Attorney's office and in the Temple. I will not therefore give myself airs and affect to know what I know not. The affair is of great importance to you and you should be directed in it by a wiser than I. To speak however in very general terms on the subject, it seems to me that your chief concern is with History, Natural Philosophy, Logic and Divinity. As to Metaphysics I know little about them but the very little that I do know, has not taught me to admire them. Life is too short to afford time even for serious trifles. Pursue what you know to be attainable, make truth your object and your studies will make you a wise man. Let your Divinity, if I may advise, be the Divinity of the glorious Reformation. I mean in contra-distinction to Arminianism and all the isms that were ever broached in this world of error and ignorance. The Divinity of the Reformation is called Calvinism but injuriously; it has been that of the Church of Christ in all ages; it is the Divinity of St. Paul and of St. Paul's Master who met him in his way to Damascus.[15]

With such good advice it is hardly surprising that Johnson developed into an exceedingly gracious, self-denying Christian who so loved his former private tutor that when Cowper became more or less an invalid in his final years, Johnson took him into his own home and cared for him tenderly at great cost to his own purse, health, time and career.

Once he realized that his calling was to become a minister, Johnson wanted to be ordained as soon as possible. Cowper, who could see that he still had not matured enough as a Christian, warned him, 'Woe to those who enter on the ministry of the Gospel, without having previously ask'd at least from God a mind and spirit suited to their occupation.'[16]

As Johnson became aware of his sonship in Christ, he also came to see that his professors at Cambridge were still strangers to God's way of salvation. Several of them, knowing of Johnson's connections with Cowper, had found fault with the poet's religion, as expressed in the *Task*, and tried to talk Johnson out of his faith. He wrote to Cowper asking him what he should do. Should he openly declare opposition, or take a more peaceful approach? Cowper told his young friend,

You will discover in due time that you have no need to hold your peace through fear of any man. In the mean time I commend your silence while religion was the topic. There was no hope that you could convince the disputants, and you might possibly have entangled yourself. But of this I am sure, and rejoice to find you so much of the same mind, that if they do not chuse to be born again, unless God gives them grace to repent of their folly, they shall never see his kingdom.[17]

Cowper attacks the slave-trade

At the beginning of 1788 Lady Hesketh wrote a letter to Cowper that was to start him off on a new literary venture. She suggested that he should ally himself with the new anti-slavery movement and write poetry campaigning for the freedom of slaves.

Cowper had already written against slavery in his *Poems,* where he reminded the British that they too had once been slaves under the yoke of Roman Catholicism but had been freed by the outworking of the gospel. How much more should they then detest the buying and selling of human beings?

Indeed, Cowper had started to attack slavery in his writings some ten years before the matter was seriously taken up by Parliament and he had anti-slavery works published long before either James Ramsey or Thomas Clarkson (who are credited with being the first weighty contenders in the field against slavery) published anything at all on the subject. Clarkson himself, in his *History of the Abolition of the Slave Trade,* refers several times to Cowper, describing him as a 'much admired poet' and a 'great coadjutor' in the cause for the slaves. Quoting some hundred lines from Cowper's anti-slavery verse, Clarkson argues that it was the 'extraordinary circulation of his works' which did so much to attract attention to the evil abuse of fellow humans.[18]

After publishing his first two volumes, Cowper had written nothing more on the slavery problem as it depressed him so much. The subject also raised in his mind theological problems relating to God's sovereignty, as he explained to Newton in February 1788:

It is a subject on which I can ruminate 'till I feel myself lost in mazes of speculation never to be unravell'd. Could I suppose that the cruel hardships under which millions of that

unhappy race have lived and died, were only preparatory to
a deliverance to be wrought for them hereafter, like that of
Israel out of Ægypt, my reasonings would cease, and I should
at once acquiesce in a dispensation, severe indeed for a time,
but leading to invaluable and everlasting mercies. But there
is no room, Scripture affords no warrant for any such
expectations.[19]

Cowper's problem was that up until then he had believed in the
'larger hope' theory. This was the belief that God has his elect not
only amongst those who come under the sound of the gospel, but
also amongst those who have never had the opportunity to hear his
Word, such as those dying in infancy and repentant pagans. As
Cowper could find no backing for this hope in Scripture, he was
compelled to believe that all those who do not personally respond to
Christ cannot be saved. It was 'ruminations' on unsolved problems
of this kind which tended to depress him and in the letter quoted
above we find the poet identifying himself so closely with the tragic
lot of the slaves that he wished he had never been born.

A month later we find Cowper feeling much better and willing
to respond to a request made by the newly formed Society for the
Abolition of the Slave Trade to campaign once more on behalf of the
slaves, this time in song. The request came initially from John
Thornton's daughter, Lady Balgonie,[20] who had approached Newton to try to persuade his friend to re-enter the field. Cowper could
hardly ever refuse a lady a reasonable request so he got to work
again. The result was the ballad 'The Negro's Complaint' which
Cowper, confessing that he was no composer and knew no modern
tunes, set to the old campaigning tune of 'Admiral Hosier's Ghost'.
This song was printed as a broadsheet and appeared in several
newspapers. It was a great success. The ballad is a sober description
of the slave's tragic plight, in which he says,

Forc'd from home and all its pleasures,
Af'ric's coast I left forlorn;
To increase a stranger's treasures,
O'er the raging billows borne;
Men from England bought and sold me,
Paid my price in paltry gold;
But, though theirs they have enroll'd me,
Minds are never to be sold.

Then the slave asks,

> Is there, as ye sometimes tell us,
> Is there one who reigns on high?
> Has he bid you buy and sell us,
> Speaking from his throne the sky?
> Ask him, if your knotted scourges,
> Matches, blood-extorting screws,
> Are the means which duty urges
> Agents of his will to use?

The reply comes:

> Hark! he answers — Wild tornadoes,
> Strewing yonder sea with wrecks;
> Wasting towns, plantations, meadows,
> Are the voice with which he speaks.
> He, foreseeing what vexations
> Afric's sons should undergo,
> Fix'd their tyrants' habitations
> Where his whirlwinds answer — No.

As in almost all Cowper's campaigning poems, there is a sting in the tail for the offender. The slave, treated worse than an animal, challenges the trader with the words:

> Prove that you have human feelings,
> Ere you proudly question ours.

Modern critics of Cowper's poetry tend to shake their heads over Cowper's theology in this song. Fancy believing that God would avenge himself through catastrophes, as if he were a mere nature-bound deity! Cowper, however, is referring to actual catastrophes which had recently affected the slave-trade and to the known fact that there were more white casualties on slavers than on any other kind of ship. It was evidence of the high rate of casualties among the traders that eventually moved the government to stop the slave-trade just as much as any argument concerning compassion for the slaves. Cowper believed that the God of nature brought about change in the hearts of sinful men in his own way.

Others have accepted that 'The Negro's Complaint' was 'an

outstandingly influential anti-slavery song' and 'successful propaganda', but do not consider it 'enduring poetry' or 'art'.[21] Cowper was not, of course, writing for the future in this poem, nor was he hoping to make a name for himself as an artist in words, but seeking to alleviate a present distressing need. Most critics admit that in this he was highly successful.

The 'Negro's Complaint' was quickly followed by 'The Slave-Trader in the Dumps'. In this song Cowper brought all his scathing satire to bear on the topic. The result was a gruesome, blood-curdling picture of the way slaves were tortured and maltreated on board the slave-ships. The following is an excerpt from the poem:

> 'Tis a curious assortment of dainty regales,
> To tickle the Negroes with when the ship sails,
> Fine chains for the neck, and a cat with nine tails.
> Here's padlocks and bolts, and screws for the thumbs.
> That squeeze them so lovingly till the blood comes.
> They sweeten the temper like comfits or plums.
> It would do your heart good to see 'em below,
> Lie flat on their backs all the way as we go.
> Like sprats on a gridiron, scores in a row.

'The Slave-Trader in the Dumps', or 'Sweet Meat has Sour Sauce', as it was also called, did not prove a success as a song. This was either because Cowper could not find a tune to it and merely published the words, or because his satire was not understood by the masses. The poet was already having qualms about writing these ballads, as he began to question their usefulness. 'King Mob' alone was singing the songs and the common people were not in a position to change the country's policy towards the slaves.

Cowper had now found his pace, however, and began to produce one song after another in a matter of days. His third attempt, 'The Morning Dream', which he set to the tune of Tweed-side, did very well and was published in the the *Gentleman's Magazine*. This is hard to believe nowadays as the song, with its almost Augustan language, must have been far more difficult for the masses to appreciate than 'The Slave-Trader in the Dumps'. Cowper realized that it was merely the well-known tune he had chosen that motivated the people to sing the song. He then wrote 'Pity for Poor Africans', after which he composed several others now lost. In 'Pity for Poor

Africans' Cowper once again brings the sting of satire to bear and pours scorn on the arguments of the planters, who say of their slaves:

> I pity them greatly, but I must be mum,
> For how could we do without sugar or rum?
> Especially sugar, so needful we see?
> What? give up our desserts, our coffee and tea!
>
> Besides, if we do, the French, Dutch, and the Danes,
> Will heartily thank us, no doubt, for our pains;
> If we do not buy the poor creatures, they will,
> And tortures and groans will be multiplied still.

Cowper again confessed, this time to his young friend Samuel Rose, that he doubted the success of the venture:

> The subject, as a subject for Song, did not strike me much, but the application was from a quarter that might command me, and the occasion itself, whatever difficulties might attend it, offer'd pleas that were irresistible. It must be an honour to any man to have given a stroke to that chain, however feeble. I fear however that the attempt will fail. The tidings which have lately reached me from London concerning it, are not the most encouraging. While the matter slept or was but slightly adverted to, the English only had their share of shame in common with other nations, on account of it. But since it has been canvass'd and search'd to the bottom, since the public attention has been rivetted to the horrible theme, and we can no longer plead either that we did not know it, or did not think of it, woe be to us if we refuse the poor captives the redress to which they have so clear a right, and prove ourselves in the sight of God and man indifferent to all considerations but those of gain.[22]

Bishop J. C. Ryle, looking back on the great change which took place in the eighteenth century through the work of Evangelicals, said with hindsight, 'The government of the country can lay no claim to the credit of the change. Morality cannot be called into being by penal enactments and statutes. People were never yet made religious by Acts of Parliament.'[23] Cowper shared this view in relation to slavery and became especially critical of the thought current in Britain that the whole human problem could be solved by making laws instead of a general change of heart. Writing to Newton, the poet said, 'Laws will, I suppose, be enacted for the more humane treatment of the Negroes; but who will see as to the execution of them? The Planters will not, and the Negroes cannot. In fact we know that Laws of this tendency have not been wanting enacted even amongst themselves, but there has always been a want of Prosecutors or righteous Judges; deficiencies which will not be easily supplied.'[24]

Cowper's argument, as stated in 'Charity' and 'Expostulations', was that because man had no true picture of himself and no true picture of God he could not perform good works. Only when God's 'enlightening grace' came into a man's life was he able to perform true works of charity. Only that which squares with Scripture and springs from love to God and love to man will stand at the Day of Judgement.

Further requests, however, continued to be made by several influential individuals and organizations begging Cowper to produce more ballads but the poet was compelled, because of his feelings in the matter, to refuse them. Referring to a request from James Phillips, the Quaker bookseller, Cowper told Newton,

> The more I have consider'd it the more I have convinced myself that it is not a promising theme for verse. General censure on the iniquity of the practice will avail nothing, the world has been overwhelm'd with such remarks already, and to particularize all the horrors of it were an employment for the mind both of the poet and his readers of which they would necessarily soon grow weary. For my own part I cannot contemplate the subject very nearly without a degree of abhorance that affects my spirits and sinks them below the pitch requisite for success in verse.[25]

Cowper also came to see that there was a degree of falsity in getting people into an anti-slavery attitude through the entertaining 'fiddle of Verse'[26] when sheer humanity ought to drive them to protest. He suspected that his songs were being sung merely for the sake of their tunes and came to the conclusion that the musical framework to his message was actually harmful to the cause.

Nevertheless, he could not remain silent for long. Slavery continued and in 1792 Cowper decided to take up his pen again, but this time not to music, and wrote the following verses, which were published in the *Northampton Mercury*. Cowper was alluding to the common practice of clarifying wine by pouring blood into it.

To purify their wine some people bleed
A lamb into the barrel, and succeed:
No nostrum, planters say, is half so good
To make fine sugar, as a negro's blood.

Now lambs and negroes both are harmless things,
And thence perhaps this wond'rous virtue springs.
'Tis in the blood of innocence alone—
Good cause why planters never try their own.

Cowper turned to the *Northampton Mercury* because this newspaper had a long anti-slavery tradition and it had grown so swiftly since its early days in the 1720s, when it appeared as a single sheet, that it could now claim to be the most read newspaper in the kingdom.

Of organs and church music

There are many comments made by Cowper regarding church music in this period and none are in any way complimentary — apart from his remarks on the sound of church bells which recalled pleasant memories of past times of blessing.

The people at Olney had decided to have an organ built into their church premises and canvassed Cowper's support. Writing on 1 January 1788 to Lady Hesketh, who was of the opinion that organ music destroyed church worship, Cowper tells her, 'They have begun at Olney a Subscription for an Organ in the Church. Weary no doubt of the unceasing praises bestow'd upon a place well known by the name of Hogs-Norton, they are determined to put in for a share of musical honour.' Cowper is referring here to the once common saying, 'I think you were born at Hogs-Norton, where pigs play upon the organ,' which was used as a reproof to an ill-mannered person. A week later Cowper assured his cousin,

'Depend upon it as a certainty, that I shall never be found a con-
tributor to an organ at Olney: I never mention that vagary of theirs
but with disapprobation.'

In the summer of 1791 the opposition towards Dissenters became acute and, especially in the Midlands, chapels, meeting-
houses and even private houses were burnt to the ground. Tragically
John Newton added his influential voice to this opposition and,
though he himself was opposed to acts of violence, his hearers were
of a different persuasion. The point is, however, that if Newton had
been more diligent in preaching peace rather than strife, so great was
his influence that there might never have been a war against fellow-
believers.

During these times of rioting Cowper wrote a comforting letter
to William Bull and gave vent to his scorn of the new Anglican
substitution of music for true worship. Cowper writes playfully but
with stinging sarcasm against his own church:

> I have blest myself on your account that you are at
> Brighton and not at Birmingham, where it seems they are so
> loyal and so pious that they show no mercy to Dissenters.
> How can you continue in a persuasion so offensive to the wise
> and good? Do you not yet perceive that the Bishops them-
> selves hate you not more than the very Blacksmiths of the
> establishment, and will you not endeavour to get the better of
> your aversion to red-nosed singing-men and Organs? Come
> — Be received into the bosom of mother-church, so shall you
> never want a Jig for your amusement on Sundays, and shall
> save perhaps your academy from a conflagration.[27]

Book reviews

Joseph Johnson, the publisher, was so impressed by the work
Cowper had done on James Hurdis' poetry that he asked the poet to
consider writing reviews on a regular basis for his magazine, *The
Analytical Review*. Cowper readily agreed and in the course of the
next few years reviewed a number of books of varying subject
matter which demanded a detailed knowledge on his part not only
of literature in general, but also of history, science, geology, natural
history of all kinds, geography and theology.

Cowper showed himself to be an astute critic who was not miserly where praise was due. At times, however, he spoke his mind so clearly that authors must have cringed to find that one of the leading literary figures of the day thought so little of their works. Writing in November 1789 about a long poem in six parts called 'An Essay on Sensibility', a subject that appealed greatly to Cowper, he commented:

> There is more good sense in the book than good poetry, though of good poetry also it is not entirely destitute. It bears many marks of a slovenly haste; for, to no other cause can we ascribe the many blemishes with which it is deformed, the author having occasionally given proof of ability. Some of his lines are forcible and well finished; others have a tedious drawl; and his chief fault is the want of compression. We recommend to him to study a classical neatness of versification, without which, though he may be a sensible poet, he will never be an agreeable one. He tells us in his preface that he disclosed his literary secret to no friend before he published it. Had he disclosed it to a judicious friend, it would have appeared with more advantage.

Johnson, who was not an Evangelical by any means, must have been a very tolerant man, as many of Cowper's comments are highly biblical and would have been termed 'enthusiastic' by critics of the eighteenth-century revival.

In April 1790 Cowper wrote a very lengthy review of a work by the North American Joel Barlow in nine books on *The Vision of Columbus*. The reviewer tells us that 'The first book is chiefly occupied in a display of American scenery, without dispute the noblest in the world, drawn with a bold hand, and, in general, with a happy one.' He then goes on to look at the theology expressed in the books. The author sees the world becoming more and more civilized through the outworkings of international trade and co-operation. He maintains that there is a general revelation in the hearts of all men moving them all to believe in God and the need for some form of atonement. He believes that the miracle of Babel will one day be reversed and then all nations will speak one language and share one religion — a form of Christianity — in a time of universal peace. Now this, on face value, might be taken to be very similar to what Cowper himself had taught in his poetry. This similarity is recognized by Cowper but he allows himself a reviewer's freedom to differ and fill in the missing details. He writes,

> We have to observe also, that though the hypothesis by which he accounts for the conversion of all nations to the Christian faith be ingenious, we cannot admit it to be consonant to the strain of scripture, which does not suspend that great event on an universal confluence of all languages into one, but on the conversion of the Jews, whose reingraftment into their own olive-tree, we are expressly told, shall be attended with the fulness of the Gentiles. Neither does the scripture teach us to expect so slow a progress of the dispensations tending to produce this fulfilment of the divine purposes, as Mr. Barlow is willing to suppose. Slow indeed, if the church must wait for it, till in consequence of the intercourse occasioned by commercial voyages, the whole earth shall gradually speak one language. On the contrary, it speaks of lifting up a standard to the nations, and of a nation being born in a day: expressions that imply the utmost suddenness of performance, and such as it may reasonably be supposed would immediately follow on the call of Israel,[28] the circumstances of which call are believed by the best expositors of the sacred text to have been prefigured in the instantaneous and wonderful conversion of the apostle Paul.

Cowper's own remarks on the Jews are brief and scattered. The longest reference to them is in 'Expostulation', where he cites them as a warning to the nations who reject Christ. In this review it is obvious that Cowper has come to believe that God has not cast off Israel and has use for her still in calling the nations to repentance.

One of Cowper's most delightful comments as a reviewer concerns his friend John Newton. On reviewing a book on ornithology written in Latin by a Dutchman, Cowper found that the writer, Nicolai Heerkens, criticized a certain Guenaldus for maintaining that swallows migrate. Heerkens apparently believed that they went into hibernation because there was no evidence to the contrary. Cowper supplied that evidence:

> Now it happens that the writer of this article is acquainted with a person, formerly Captain of a ship in the Guinea-trade,

and a gentleman of the most unsuspected veracity, who has assured him, that once, on his return to England, at a great distance from any land, the rigging of his ship was suddenly almost covered with swallows that settled on it, needing rest. They were in fact so wearied with their long flight, that the sailors took many of them in their hands. The truth of this narration admitted (and true it certainly is) Mr. Heerkens will appear, as we have said, to have denied their migration in a manner much too peremptory. But it happens not unfrequently, that through zeal to correct a supposed error, writers, even of good information, become strenuous advocates for a real one.

There is a story behind these comments by Cowper. During a severe winter (date unknown) Newton informed Cowper that he would be visiting his friend in the following spring. Cowper was so delighted by the news that he composed a poem in anticipation of the visit which he called 'To the Rev. Mr. Newton: An Invitation into the Country'. In this poem he says,

> The swallows in their torpid state
> Compose their useless wing,
> And bees in hives as idly wait
> The call of early spring.
>
> The keenest frost that binds the stream,
> The wildest wind that blows,
> Are neither felt nor fear'd by them,
> Secure of their repose.
>
> But man, all feeling and awake,
> The gloomy scene surveys;
> With present ills his heart must ache,
> And pant for brighter days.
>
> Old winter, halting o'er the mead,
> Bids me and Mary mourn;
> But lovely spring peeps o'er his head,
> And whispers your return.

Then April, with her sister May,
Shall chase him from the bow'rs;
And weave fresh garlands ev'ry day,
To crown the smiling hours.

And, if a tear, that speaks regret
Of happier times, appear,
A glimpse of joy, that we have met,
Shall shine, and dry the tear.

No doubt Newton must have chuckled when he read his friend's strange description of the winter behaviour of swallows and he probably told Cowper about the migrants at sea by way of setting the record straight.[29]

Suicide is a subject on which Cowper comments from time to time, and he always writes as one who considers it a great sin which can never be morally acceptable. As a boy he had been confronted with the topic by his father, who had lost a good friend through suicide, and even at such an early age Cowper had recoiled from the very thought with horror. Hume, the famous philosopher, had written a treatise on suicide, declaring it to be socially and morally acceptable. Cowper came across a detailed review of Hume's work one day in the *Monthly Review* and told William Unwin:

> I have not yet read the last Review, but dipping into it, accidentally fell upon their account of Hume's essays on suicide. I am glad that they have liberality enough to condemn the licentiousness of an Author whom they so much admire. I say liberality — for there is as much Bigotry in the world to that man's errors, as there is in the hearts of some Sectaries to their peculiar modest Tenets. He is the Pope of thousands as blind and as presumptuous as himself. God certainly infatuates those who will not see. It were otherwise impossible that a man naturally shrewd and sensible, and whose understanding had all the advantages of constant exercise and cultivation, could have satisfied himself, or have hoped to satisfy others with such palpable sophistry as has not even the grace of fallacy to recommend it. His silly assertion that because it would be no Sin to divert the course of the Danube, therefore it is none to let out a few ounces of blood from an artery, would justify not Suicide only but Homicide

too... But the life of a man and the water of a River can never come into competition with each other in point of value, unless in the estimation of an unprincipled philosopher.[30]

When reviewing a work entitled *Poetical Essays* by a young student, Cowper became seriously alarmed. The poems were written after the death of the young man's fiancée and he had written in sorrow:

Let us, whom youth, whom health, with joy inspires,
Learn this great lesson from Eliza's fate,
To finish life before that life expires,
Nor wait for seasons that may prove too late.

Cowper comments: 'The line distinguished by italics is a very alarming one, especially considering that it is written by a lover mourning the death of his mistress. His tutor should watch him narrowly, and his bed-maker should every night take care to secure his garters.' The poet is obviously thinking of that evil day in 1763 when he had tried to hang himself by means of a garter, which in the providence of God broke before it was too late.

A new vicar for Olney

In 1787 Moses Browne died. He had been the absentee vicar of Olney for several decades and although an Evangelical had held the appointment merely because of the income it involved. It is true that he had a wife and thirteen children to keep but his greed had caused innumerable difficulties for Newton and Scott, who had done all Browne's work for a fraction of the money he was paid for doing nothing.

Several ministers now applied for the post. Newton still felt that he had responsibilities in Olney and suggested that his friend James Bean should become vicar. Charles Edward De Coetlegan also applied for the post, as did Richard Postlethwaite. Cowper did not know Bean but he knew De Coetlegan and Postlethwaite. De Coetlegen had been Madan's assistant at the Lock Hospital and had stayed on under Scott. He was a prolific writer and editor of the *Theological Miscellany*.

Newton had repeatedly asked Cowper to write articles for De

Coetlegen but the poet had told him, 'I dislike him so much, that had I a drawer full of pieces fit for his purpose, I hardly think I should contribute to his collection.'[31] Cowper does not explain why he had an aversion to the clergyman, apart from saying that his judgement was based on what he had seen of the man and what he had heard. Newton kept up his pressure on Cowper to write for De Coetlegen and the poet finally agreed to write a review, but he was compelled to abandon it as he found the work in question sub-Christian.[32]

Cowper was alarmed at the possibility that De Coetlegen might become a near neighbour, especially as the new curate at Weston, Laurence Canniford, was a man whom he could not tolerate either. Canniford, who had been appointed through William Romaine's influence, had visited Cowper twice, once to help himself to three glasses of wine uninvited and once to sell Cowper some books on old inscriptions which the poet did not want. Cowper seemed to think that the man had not one ounce of spirituality in him though he had been hailed as a second Whitefield. The poet was quick to point out that those who called Canniford a second Whitefield had said just about the same concerning 'Mr. Page of wife-beating memory'.

Cowper's choice accordingly fell on Postlethwaite, an Evangelical friend of the Throckmortons and a man he both knew well and respected. Realizing how stiff the competition was, he decided to draw up a petition on behalf of Postlethwaite and present it to his old school-friend, Lord Dartmouth, who had the patronage of the living. Cowper collected signatures from all the inhabitants of Weston who were of any note and hoped for the best.

What finally happened was communicated to Cowper by William Bull, who also had an interest in Postlethwaite. The young man was not born with a great portion of tact. He was a young rebel who looked on the traditions of the Church of England as being at best mere unbiblical trappings. So when he was interviewed for the vacancy by the Bishop of London, a stickler for form and propriety, he arrived for his appointment still wearing a riding outfit, without cleaning himself up first and — much more important in the eyes of the bishop— without his canonicals. The good bishop was shocked and at once dismissed him in horror, telling his chaplain not to dare admit a man in such attire again. To make the farce even worse, Postlethwaite was so confused by the reception that he clean forgot where he had tied up his horse! All he could remember was that it was near a bridge, and so he and Thomas Scott had to walk along the banks of the Thames checking the bridges. Eventually they found the poor horse tied to the last possible bridge, looking much the worse for having been neglected so long.

Cowper received no thanks for his part in the story; indeed Mr Raban paid him a visit to tell him how he had angered certain people in the district. Mr Bean was eventually appointed to the living and Cowper and he got on so well that they were continually spending time in each other's houses. One of their first topics of conversation was Canniford. When Mr Bean admitted that he found the man a 'terror', Cowper felt quickly drawn to his new friend.

Postlethwaite was eventually taken in hand by Thornton and Lord Dartmouth applied successfully to the Chancellor on his behalf for a post which he found fully to his taste. De Coetlegen had to wait until 1789 before he received another appointment and did not become a vicar until 1794. Finally, to Cowper's great pleasure, Canniford left the district and moved to Ravenstone whose curacy he also served.

All this excitement did not seem to affect Cowper in the least; indeed he said on various occasions between 1788 and 1790 that he felt his youth had returned.

Cowper continues to write verse

In spite of Cowper's work on Homer and the many reviews he wrote, he did not neglect writing original verse. Some of his poetry from this period is the sweetest and most moving that he ever wrote.

It is also couched in a language that has become simpler, clearer and free from the poetic diction and Augustan forms which characterized much of his poetry written before he tackled Homer. In spite of all he had been saying about language up to the late eighties, Cowper had been instinctively modelling himself on poets such as Chaucer and Spenser. Now there was a marked step into a more modern and dynamic form of expression. Instead of projecting his language backwards for quaint effects, he was projecting it forwards for future readers.

Much of Cowper's poetry written in the late 1780s has a fable-like quality. The poet had been studying Rousseau and was shocked to find how grim were his views of a child's education. The

Frenchman, a child of the so-called Enlightenment that brought so much darkness to people's minds, argued that it was wrong to tell children fables featuring talking animals as this was deception of a wicked kind. Cowper thought Rousseau's ideas 'whimsical' and his literary protegé 'Emile' a 'stuck up prig', saying that the Frenchman obviously knew nothing about children. Indeed, the way the philosopher treated his own children was scandalous in the extreme. Cowper wrote in his introduction to a fable on the subject of marriage:

> I shall not ask Jean Jacques Rousseau,
> If birds confabulate or no;
> 'Tis clear that they were always able
> To hold discourse, at least, in fable;
> And ev'n the child who knows no better,
> Than to interpret by the letter,
> A story of a cock and bull,
> Must have a most uncommon scull.

Another fable that Cowper wrote at this time was 'The Needless Alarm', in which he underlines his basically optimistic view of life and shows how the life of an enlightened nature lover recalls the harmony of Eden. Of the fields and woodlands around Weston Cowper wrote,

> The man to solitude accustom'd long
> Perceives in ev'ry thing that lives a tongue;
> Not animals alone, but shrubs and trees,
> Have speech for him, and understood with ease;
> After long drought, when rains abundant fall,
> He hears the herbs and flow'rs rejoicing all;
> Knows what the freshness of their hue implies,
> How glad they catch the largess of the skies;
> But, with precision nicer still, the mind
> He scans of ev'ry locomotive kind;
> Birds of all feather, beasts of ev'ry name,
> That serve mankind, or shun them, wild or tame;
> The looks and gestures of their griefs and fears
> Have, all, articulation in his ears;
> He spells them true by intuition's light,
> And needs no glossary to set him right.

The story centres on a flock of sheep who were frightened into panic by a foraging fox but preserved from a suicidal dash into a pit by the huntsman's horn. The poet then draws the moral :

Beware of desp'rate steps. The darkest day
(Live till to-morrow) will have pass'd away.

One of Cowper's most moving poems is a versification of a story he read in the *Gentleman's Magazine*. A rich nobleman was addicted to gambling and trained a magnificent cock to kill its opponents and thus increase the nobleman's riches. After many triumphs the bird weakened and was at last defeated. The nobleman lost his temper and became so enraged that he started to torture the poor cock in such an inhuman way that onlookers tried to help the poor creature. So great was the nobleman's rage that he burst a blood-vessel and died in the act of slaughtering the bird that had earned him thousands of pounds. Cowper first interviewed those who had known the 'gentleman' and then poured out all his righteous anger in a long poem condemning cock-fighting in general and the nobleman's cruelty in particular.

Another true story, on a far more pleasant note, happened to Cowper himself. Some young ladies had rescued a dog that had been badly burnt and gave it to Cowper. Though it was the ugliest creature alive, owing to having been singed all over and having the end of its tail burnt off, Cowper called it Beau. One day he was walking along the riverside with Beau at his heels. Suddenly he spied some beautiful water lilies and, using his walking stick, tried to pull one towards the bank. As his stick was not long enough, he soon gave up the attempt and continued his walk. Beau, however, could not forget the lilies and when they returned to the spot he jumped into the water, gently took hold of a water lily in his mouth, scrambled back on shore, and laid the lily at Cowper's feet. The poet was so delighted that he wrote 'The Dog and the Water-Lily: No Fable' which is quoted here in part:

It was the time when Ouse display'd
His lilies newly blown;
Their beauties I intent survey'd;
And one I wish'd my own.

With cane extended far I sought
To steer it close to land;
But still the prize, though nearly caught,
Escap'd my eager hand.

Beau marked my unsuccessful pains
With fixt consid'rate face,
And puzzling set his puppy brains
To comprehend the case.

But with a chirrup clear and strong,
Dispersing all his dream
I thence withdrew, and follow'd long
The windings of the stream.

My ramble finish'd, I return'd
Beau trotting far before
The floating wreath again discern'd,
And plunging left the shore.

I saw him with that lily cropp'd
Impatient swim to meet
My quick approach, and soon he dropp'd
The treasure at my feet.

Charm'd with the sight, the world, I cried
Shall hear of this thy deed
My dog shall mortify the pride
Of man's superior breed;

But, chief, myself I will enjoin,
Awake at duty's call,
To show a love as prompt as thine
To Him who gives me all.

Some time afterwards, when they were walking by the same
patch of water lilies, Beau dived in, without any action on the poet's
part, and brought his master another lily. Once again the poet praised
God for the lesson he had learnt.

Lady Hesketh, who was closely in touch with the royal family,
kept her cousin informed of what went on at Court and Cowper

wrote a number of poems to commemorate the actions of the king and queen. One day during the summer of 1788, he received a surprise visit from John Bacon, the sculptor, who had travelled far to see him. Bacon had been commissioned to design a clock-case for the king and wished Cowper to compose a Latin motto for it. Cowper provided the sculptor with two from which Bacon chose one. The clock-case can still be seen in Buckingham Palace.

Soon it seemed a settled matter that as the position of Poet Laureate was vacant, Cowper should fill it. Naturally Lady Hesketh had brought all her influence into play in support of the motion. Cowper, however, declined politely, explaining that appearances at Court would be fatal for him.

The poet wrote a number of children's hymns during this period, both for Mr Bean, the new vicar of Olney, and Rowland Hill, the highly successful minister of Surrey Chapel, London.

He also wrote several poems which were appended to the Yearly Bill of Mortality published by the town clerk of Northampton. These poems became so popular that they were sold as broadsheets at threepence a poem. Among them is the lovely didactic poem beginning:

He lives who lives to God alone,
And all are dead beside;
For other source than God is none
Whence life can be supplied.

Some of these poems are outstandingly evangelical and were obviously meant to shake the living to the very roots in their contemplation of death. Asking why it is that man fears death so much, Cowper says,

Whence has the world her magic pow'r?
Why deem we death a foe?
Recoil from weary life's best hour,
And covet longer woe?

The cause is Conscience — Conscience oft
Her tale of guilt renews:
Her voice is terrible though soft,
And dread of death ensues.

Then, anxious to be longer spar'd,
Man mourns his fleeting breath:
All evils then seem light, compar'd
With the approach of death.

'Tis judgment shakes him; there's the fear,
That prompts the wish to stay:
He has incurr'd a long arrear,
And must despair to pay.

Pay ! — Follow *Christ*, and all is paid:
His death your peace ensures:
Think on the grave where he was laid,
And calm descend to yours.

The commentary on Milton proposed

Cowper had now become successful as a prose writer, a poet, a
hymn-writer, a reviewer, a translator and a literary critic. He had as
yet, however, not published anything as a commentator or editor. In
1790 Joseph Johnson decided to produce the crowning work of his
career. It was to be a *Milton Gallery* after the style of the famous
Boydell's *Shakespeare Gallery*. Johnson planned a magnificent
work, profusely illustrated, including a scholarly commentary on
John Milton's works and translations of his Latin and Italian poems.
For his painter Johnson turned to the Swiss artist Henri Fuseli, who
had painted the illustrations for Boydell's *Shakespeare Gallery*, and
for his commentator, editor and translator he chose William
Cowper. It was a work that, in God's providence, Cowper was tailor-
made to perform and would give the poet an unlimited opportunity
to witness to his Master in the homes of the entire reading public

As the decade drew to a close, Cowper could look back on a
period of great toil but also of great success in the work he had been
given to do.

16.
The two Williams

Cowper never fully recovered from the death of his good friend William Unwin and the loneliness he experienced during the next few years was deepened by the loss of one after another of his closest friends and acquaintances. It seemed that the poet had hardly finished writing one epitaph when he was called upon to write another.

Ashley Cowper, the poet's favourite uncle, died in 1788 and his cousin Martin Madan died in May 1790. Madan had become such a puzzle to Cowper that he had deliberately shunned him ever since he had published his books on polygamy. Cowper told Lady Hesketh about his mixed feelings concerning their cousin when he learnt of his death:

> Your news of Martin's death reach'd me in one of my melancholy moods and I reflected on it and felt it accordingly. What he was in reality God only knows. That he once seem'd to have grace is certain, and that no man had a mind more evangelically enlighten'd is equally so. The Giver of Grace and light, and He only, knows how to make allowance for the unavoidable effects of situation in life, constitution, errors in judgment, and those occurrences which give an unavoidable warp to the conduct. If by his providence he places one of his own people under the influence of any or all these possible causes of declension in spirituality of heart and mind, He will consider it, and to him, as you observe, the delinquent must be left; He has saved, I doubt not, thousands

who in man's account have perish'd, and has left many to perish whom their survivors have been ready to canonize. Of Martin therefore in his present state I will hope the best, judging and condemning not Him, but his abominable and foolish book which for the sake of his connexions I wish that he had never written. The book indeed is pretty much forgotten, but it will never be forgotten that Polygamy has been defended and recommended in a Christian land and by a Minister of the Gospel, and that his name was Madan.[1]

Madan's wife passed away a year later. She had been made a laughing-stock by the 'polygamous parson', as her husband was dubbed, and had suffered terribly as a result of his publications. She had, however, stood bravely by his side in all his controversies. The Madans' daughter, Sarah, however, was outraged at her father's conduct and in turn shocked her parents by leaving the Evangelical fold and becoming a Roman Catholic.

The next to die was Mrs Scott, who went to be with her Lord in September 1790 after a short and sudden illness. Whilst dwelling on the subject of her death, Cowper thought of Thomas Scott's grief at being left alone and imagined what his own sorrow would be like should he be bereft of the 'one comfort' remaining in his life, Mrs Unwin.

The death toll amongst Cowper's circle continued and in the same month in which Mrs Scott died Cowper was commissioned by Bacon to write the official epitaph for John Howard, the prison reformer. Two months later another social reformer, John Thornton, died, and although he had not always understood Cowper, he had on many occasions given the poet reasons to praise God for his generosity.

When it was obvious that Thornton was dying, his daughter, Lady Balgonie, approached Cowper through William Bull to write an epitaph for her father. Though suffering from a violent cold and busy putting the final touches to his translation of Homer, he quickly composed a poem expressing his thoughts on the life of the famous benefactor. It starts off rather laboriously in praise of Thornton, in the traditional style of the age, but gradually becomes more pointedly evangelical and at the same time more poetic. After showing that Thornton's real treasures were in heaven, the poet goes on to say,

And tho' God made thee of a nature prone
To distribution boundless of thy own
And still, by motives of religious force,
Impell'd thee more to that heroic course;
Yet was thy liberality discreet;
Nice in its choice, and of a temp'rate heat;
And, though in act unwearied, secret still,
As, in some solitude, the summer rill
Refreshes, where it winds, the faded green,
And cheers the drooping flow'rs — unheard, unseen.
Such was thy Charity; no sudden start,
After long sleep of passion in the heart,
But steadfast principle and in its kind
Of close alliance with th' eternal mind;
Trac'd easily to its true source above,
To Him, whose works bespeak his nature, Love.
Thy bounties all were Christian, and I make
This record of thee for the Gospel's sake;
That the incredulous themselves may see
Its use and pow'r exemplified in thee.

Death of Mary Newton

Next it was Mrs Mary Newton's turn to end her pilgrimage. She had been especially dear to Cowper's heart ever since his early days at Olney. Mrs Newton's sufferings before her death were a great trial not only to herself but to her husband, as during her final illness she had grave doubts as to her salvation. These dark thoughts eventually subsided and Mary Newton was enabled to look forward peacefully to dying in the Lord.

This news caused Cowper to write to Newton saying,

> Your letter affected us with both joy and sorrow. With sorrow and sympathy respecting poor Mrs. Newton, whose feeble and dying state suggests a wish for her release rather than for her continuance, and joy on your account, who are enabled to bear with so much resignation and cheerful acquiescence in the will of God, the prospect of a loss which even they who knew you best, apprehended might prove too much

for you. As to Mrs. Newton's interest in the best things, none, intimately acquainted with her as we have been, could doubt it. She doubted it indeed herself, but, though it is not our duty to doubt any more than it is our privilege, I have always considered the self-condemning spirit to which such doubts are principally owing, as one of the most favorable symptoms of a nature spiritually renewed, and have many a time heard you make the same observation.[2]

Belief in the validity of such a self-condemning spirit was so much a part of Cowper's theology that he could not imagine a true Christian life without it. In this matter Cowper was consistently Quietistic — as was William Bull — and this is one of the many keys to understanding the causes of the two men's deep melancholy.

Mary Newton died ten days later, on 15 December 1790, and Cowper was too moved to write Newton a lengthy letter of condolence but took up the subject briefly in several letters, only to turn quickly, through grief, to other topics.

However, Mary Newton's death was not the only reason that made correspondence with Newton difficult at this time. The old mariner had once more begun to write to Cowper in a jealous way, entreating him to send whatever he wrote in the way of poetry to him first, rather than to other friends.

It was not until the following summer that Cowper was able to open his heart concerning Mary. Newton must have been feeling very weak, low and lonely and had written a letter to Cowper exhibiting that strange mixture of feelings that he was apt to display in letters at such times. He pleaded for signs of friendship from Weston and condemned himself for not having been a better husband to Mary. On a completely different note, though in the same letter, he sternly reprimanded Cowper for the work he was doing on Homer. The poet took up Newton's thoughts concerning his wife with a letter full of brotherly love and common sense saying:

You do justice to me and Mrs. Unwin when you assure yourself that to hear of your health will give us pleasure. I know not, in truth, whose health and well-being could give us more. The years that we have seen together will never be out of our remembrance, and so long as we remember them we must remember you with affection. In the pulpit and out of the pulpit you have labour'd in every possible way to serve us, and we must have a short memory indeed for the kindness of a friend, could we by any means become forgetful of yours. It would grieve me more than it does to hear you complain of the effects of time, were not I also myself the subject of them. While he is wearing out you and other dear friends of mine, he spares not me, for which I ought to account myself obliged to him, since I should otherwise be in danger of surviving all that I have ever loved, the most melancholy lot that can befall a mortal. God knows what will be my doom hereafter, but precious as life necessarily seems to a mind doubtful of its future happiness, I love not the world, I trust, so much as to wish a place in it when all my Beloveds shall have left it.

You speak of your late loss in a manner that affected me much, and when I read that part of your letter I mourn'd with you and for you; But surely, I said to myself, no man had ever less reason to charge his conduct to a wife with any thing blameworthy. Thoughts of that complexion, however, are no doubt extremely natural on the occasion of such a loss, and a man seems not to have valued sufficiently, when he possesses it no longer, what, while he possess'd it, he valued more than life. I am mistaken too, or you can recollect a time when you had fears, and such as became a Christian, of loving too much, and it is likely that you have even pray'd to be preserved from doing so. I suggest this to you as a plea against those self-accusations which I am satisfied that you do not deserve, and as an effectual answer to them all You may do well too to consider that had the Deceased been the Survivor, she would have charged herself in the same manner, and I am sure you will acknowledge without any sufficient reason. The truth is that you both loved at least as much as you ought, and, I dare say, had not a friend in the world who did not frequently observe it. To love just enough and not a bit too much, is not for creatures who can do nothing well. If we fail in duties less arduous, how should we succeed in this, the most arduous of all?[3]

In the same letter Cowper gives Newton a detailed analysis as to why he felt a Christian scholar should engage his time with Homer.

A month later Henry Venn, author of the Christian best seller *The Complete Duty of Man*, died and Cowper wrote to Newton saying how he had never met anyone more lovable than Venn and how he would have liked to have seen more of him. Venn respected Cowper highly, calling him 'that astonishing instance of grace', and wrote of the great kindness he had received at the poet's hands when visiting Olney. Cowper confessed to Newton that in contrast to people like Venn who laboured so diligently for God, he merely 'tickled people's ears'.[4]

Mrs Unwin suffers a stroke

Cowper, who so diligently longed for true friends, became more and more melancholy as he heard of the decease of those who had added sparkle and warmth to his life and grew more and more afraid that he would lose Mrs Unwin. His housekeeper, friend and substitute mother had had a severe fall in December 1788 which seems to have been caused by a stroke. She never recovered her full walking strength after that experience and developed a very large tumour on her side which caused her constant pain.

Exactly three years later, in December 1791, Cowper was writing at his desk and Mrs Unwin was sitting at the fireside when suddenly the poet heard her call out, 'Oh Mr. Cowper, don't let me fall!' Cowper dashed across to save her and managed to prevent her from falling out of her chair. This time there was no doubt that Mrs Unwin had undergone a stroke. She was paralysed all down one side, saw everything turned up-side-down and lost her power of speech. Cowper told Rose, 'She has been my faithful and affectionate nurse for many years, and consequently has a claim on all my attentions. She has them, and will have them as long as she wants them, which will probably be, at the best, for a considerable time to come.'[5]

When the accident happened Lady Hesketh was ill in bed at Weston with a severe attack of rheumatism but she got up to help Mrs Unwin and in the process caught a bad chill and became much worse. The poet, who for so long had looked upon the two ladies as his nurses, now had to look after them both all through Christmas and well into the New Year.

The nightingale in winter

In spite of all these melancholy experiences, we still find Cowper basically optimistic and trusting that God would one day remove for ever the gloom that so easily beset him.

On New Year's Day, 1792, for instance, he was out walking in the surrounding countryside when he made a surprising discovery. He told John Johnson about the incident and said, 'You talk of Primroses, that you pulled on Candlemas Day; but what think you of me, who heard a Nightingale on New Year's day? Perhaps I am the only man in England, who can boast of such good fortune: good indeed; for if it was at all an omen, it could not be an unfavourable one.'[6] By the 'good omen' Cowper meant, of course, that God would again reveal himself and banish the winter of his sufferings.

Ever looking forward to the eternal spring of the millennium in which every tear would be wiped away, Cowper wrote down his experience in verse, producing a poem which was often to be imitated, but never bettered, by the Romantic poets:

To the Nightingale
Which the Author Heard Sing on New-Year's Day, 1792

Whence is it, that amaz'd I hear
From yonder wither'd spray,
This foremost morn of all the year,
The melody of May?

And why, since thousands would be proud
Of such a favour shewn,
Am I selected from the crowd,
To witness it alone?

Sing'st thou, sweet Philomel, to me,
For that I also long
Have practis'd in the groves like thee,
Though not like thee in song?

Or sing'st thou rather under force
Of some divine command,

Commission'd to presage a course
Of happier days at hand?

Thrice welcome then! for many a long
And joyless year have I,
As thou to-day, put forth my song
Beneath a wintry sky.

But thee no wintry skies can harm,
Who only need'st to sing,
To make ev'n January charm,
And ev'ry season Spring.

The poet is accused of supporting the slave-trade

Before the normal season of spring arrived in 1792, Cowper was
horrified to find himself the subject of rumours he would never have
deemed possible. The many myths that have since gathered like flies
about Cowper's person were already beginning to be spread around
amongst Evangelicals and social reformers of note. Stories kept
coming to the poet's ear to the effect that he, who had written so
much against the slave-trade, had become an ardent contender on its
behalf.

Some of these stories were obviously based on misunderstandings of a political and social nature. For instance, the Rev. Joseph
Jekyll Rye, vicar of Dallington and Oadley and one of the influential
men Cowper had approached to help Hurdis obtain his appointment
as professor, wrote to Cowper to inform him that he was widely
suspected of supporting the slave-trade and that the prime minister
himself had been notified of this.

It seems that, unknown to Cowper, a political lobby had been
organized which campaigned for a ban on imports of sugar to
England. If no sugar were bought, none would be produced and thus
the necessity of keeping slaves in the West Indies would be abolished. These well-meaning but rather short-sighted friends of the
Negroes did not stop to think of the fate of the slaves should the sugar
trade go into a slump. Slave-drivers thought nothing of throwing a
whole cargo of slaves into the sea if they thought they could not sell
them at a profit, or if they were not allowed to land them for one

reason or another. There was nothing to suggest that, once their slaves became a burden and an embarrassment to them, the planters would not adopt the same inhuman methods. Cowper had warned against the folly of thinking a sinful people could be reformed by political activity, both in his poetry and in letters to influential people, but many Christians of the day were putting their hope in laws.

Be this as it may, someone had reported that Cowper took sugar in his tea, and this was taken to mean that he must be in favour of the slave-trade and against the anti-sugar campaigners. 'Proof' of this rumour was found in the 'fact' that a petition had been drawn up in Olney against the slave-trade and Cowper had allegedly refused to sign it.

Whilst these misunderstandings concerning Cowper's views on slavery were growing, nobody, it seems, thought of asking the poet himself for his explanation until several months had past and anger against him had snowballed at a preposterous rate. Instead of seeking an explanation at its source, the sanctions lobby looked elsewhere for reasons why Cowper had changed course so drastically.

A reason was soon found, and widely believed. It was left to Frederick Smith, the Quaker, to inform Cowper of what was supposedly 'common knowledge'. Smith told Cowper it was firmly held that he had been reading the history of Africa and 'had found that formerly the Species increased so fast that they were under the necessity of destroying or eating one another lest the country should be overstocked with Inhabitants, and on this ground thou objected to move in a petition to Parliament saying that the present mode of the Slave Trade was prefereable thereto'.[7]

These evil reports came to Cowper's ears at the same time as news reached him that yet another woman had been publishing his works under her own name. He wrote to Lady Throckmorton saying, 'I may say with Milton that I am fallen *on evil tongues and evil days*, being not only plunder'd of that which belongs to me, but being charged with that which does not.'[8] Cowper replied to Frederick Smith:

Dear Sir,
    I hold myself truly obliged to you for giving me an opportunity to contradict a report as false as it is injurious to me. I live in the neighbourhood of an ingenious people, and

who seem daily to exercise their ingenuity in the fabrication of some falsehood or other. I have not very often been the subject of their Aspersions myself, but by this which they have now treated me with, they make me ample amends for all past omissions.

I have not these many years read a history of Africa, and when I read that history last I found no such assertion; neither is it probable that any writer on that subject should have been silly enough to make it. Having never in my life met with it till I found it in your letter, it is of course impossible that I can ever have made the speech or entertained the vile opinion imputed to me. In fact I abhor the slave trade to such a degree, that even if the abolition of it were sure to leave them under a necessity of devouring each other, which is absurd to suppose, I had much rather that they should, than that we should devour them.

The only reason why I did not sign the petition was, that not living in the Parish of Olney, it was not brought to me.[9]

Cowper had heard about the Olney petition from schoolmaster Teedon who had told him that the Olney ministers, Bean (Anglican), Sutcliff (Baptist) and Hillyard (Congregationalist) were collecting signatures. Cowper had shown interest in the project but was told that it concerned the parish of Olney only and not those living in Weston. Even so, Cowper sent a guinea via Teedon to help cover overheads.

In his reply to Joseph Rye, Cowper took up the matter of what Rye had felt duty-bound to tell Pitt concerning the poet's practice of taking sugar with his tea:

I am truly sorry that you should have suffered any apprehensions, such as your Letter indicates, to molest you for a moment. I believe you to be as honest a man as lives, and consequently do not believe it possible that you could in your Letter to Mr. Pitt; or any otherwise, wilfully misrepresent me. In fact you did not; my opinions on the subject in question, were, when I had the pleasure of seeing you, such as in that Letter you stated them to be, and such they still continue.

If any man concludes because I allow myself the use of

sugar and rum, that therefore I am a friend to the Slave Trade, he concludes rashly, and does me great wrong; for the man lives not, who abhors it more than I do. My reasons for my own practice, are satisfactory to myself, and they whose practice is contrary, are, I suppose satisfied with theirs. So far is good. Let every man act according to his own judgment and conscience, but if we condemn another for not seeing with our eyes, we are unreasonable, and if we reproach him on that account, we are uncharitable, which is a still greater evil.[10]

Cowper was never a man to remain silent when a defence was called for and he soon knew what action he had to take. He would write a letter to the *Northampton Mercury,* which was read by most of those who were opposed to the slave-trade, and once more air his views in public. As William Wilberforce himself was coming under heavy criticism at this time, the poet decided to kill two birds with one stone and clear both himself and the Evangelical politician from the slanderous aspersions. So, on 16 April 1792, after writing to Rye, Cowper sat down, composed a sonnet and another letter and posted them off to the *Northampton Mercury*, which published them on the twenty-first of that month. The poet wrote,

To the Printers

Sirs,
    Having lately learned that it is pretty generally reported both in your county and this, that my present opinion concerning the Slave Trade differs totally from that which I have heretofore given to the public, and that I am no longer an Enemy, but a Friend to that horrid traffic, I entreat you to take an early opportunity to insert in your paper the following lines, written no longer since than this very morning, expressly for the two purposes of doing just honour to the gentleman with whose name they are inscribed, and of vindicating myself from an aspersion so injurious.
    I am etc.

Wm. Cowper
Weston Underwood, April 16, 1792

Sonnet

Addressed to William Wilberforce Esq.

I praise thee, *Wilberforce!* and with disdain
Hear thee by cruel men and impious call'd
Fanatic, for thy zeal to loose th'enthralled
From exile, public sale, and slav'ry's chain.
Friend of the poor, the scourg'd, the fetter-gall'd,
Fear not lest labour such as thine be vain.

Thou hast achiev'd a part, hast won the ear
Of Britain's Senate to thy glorious cause,
Hope smiles, joy springs, and though cold caution draws
Delay between, the better hour is near
That shall remunerate all thy pains severe
By peace to Afric, fenced with British laws.
Then let them scoff — two prizes thou hast won—
Freedom for Captives, and thy God's — *Well done.*

Cowper was more than successful in his action. Only four days
later a further sonnet appeared in the *Mercury*'s pages, this time
written by someone called S. M'Clellan and addressed to William
Cowper Esq., in which Cowper was praised in similar terms to those
he had used in praise of Wilberforce and in the final line he was
proudly proclaimed 'patron' of the anti-slavery campaign. From
then on the silly rumours concerning Cowper and the slave-trade
died out.

A closer relationship with Teedon

Many of Cowper's letters from this period reveal that the poet was
enduring great spiritual suffering. He felt cut off from God more
often and at times he shrank with fear and dread at the thought that
God held him in contempt and abhorrence. It was now that the
character of Samuel Teedon, the Olney schoolmaster, whom so
many biographers call 'mad' or at least 'half-mad', emerges more
and more in Cowper's letters as a man sent by God to comfort the
friend whom he revered so much.

For some time Cowper had been changing his views about Teedon. At first he had been amused by his quaintness and later was often annoyed by his pedantic nature. Gradually, however, Cowper began to see within the unpolished shell a kernel which displayed kindness, thankfulness and faithfulness. Teedon also knew how to pray and prayer was the one spiritual exercise that Cowper always found difficult.

It is a dismal fact that it is this prayerful nature of Teedon that has been taken as evidence by many biographers that the schoolmaster eventually gained some kind of evil power over Cowper and they have misunderstood these Christian prayers as a kind of soothsaying. Often the Teedon-Cowper correspondence, which survives mostly in the form of short notes, contains enigmatic expressions which are highly difficult to understand. This has caused many a commentator to think, either that they reveal signs of madness on the part of both correspondents, or that Cowper was being duped by a charlatan. The editors of the new Oxford University Press edition of Cowper's works have done a marvellous job in clearing up a number of these enigmas and shown that such letters would have been quite understandable to Christians of the time. In one letter to Teedon, for instance, Cowper writes,

> This morning I rose in rather a more cheerful frame of mind than usual, having had two notices of a more comfortable cast than the generality of mine.
> I waked saying—
> I shall perish.
> which was immediately answer'd by a vision of a wine glass and these words—
> 'a whole glass.'
> In allusion no doubt to the famous story of Mrs. Honeywood.
> Soon after, I heard these—
> 'I see in this case just occasion of Pity.'[11]

Here the editors point out that Cowper is referring to a well-known story recorded by Thomas Fuller in his *History of the Worthies of England*. A certain Mrs Honeywood suffered from periods of acute depression and, though minister after minister attended her, she could find no comfort. Once in agony of soul she took a glass in her hand and said to her comforters, 'I am as surely damn'd as this glass is broken,' and threw it with great force to the ground. As if by a miracle the glass rebounded from the ground and remained whole. Eventually Mrs Honeywood regained her faith. Thus what at first glance seems to some to be the incomprehensible product of a wandering mind is really a strong declaration of faith on Cowper's part that God would work the seemingly impossible and 'keep his glass whole'.

Teedon began a long correspondence with Cowper on the subject of prayer. He encouraged the poet to pray without ceasing and showed him how to bridge the times when he could not pray freely by using the prayers for certain occasions in the *Book of Common Prayer*. Cowper took these prayers and altered them to suit his particular case. Though we read in many of his letters to Teedon that Cowper found no comfort through prayer, there are as many or more letters which show that he recognized that God answered Teedon's prayers and that prayer helped Cowper himself to find an approachable God.

Typical of these letters is one Cowper wrote to Teedon concerning a visit from Newton in early June 1792 in which Cowper tells Teedon,

> Your prayer that Mr. Newton's coming might be blest to me, was answer'd before it was made. He was here on Saturday Morning and I received him with more spiritual affection than I have felt these 5 years; received him with a lively reconciliation of the comforts which God, in years past, had dispens'd to me under his ministry.
>
> Your pray'rs also for Mrs Unwin are, I hope, in a way to be answer'd. Her strength returns daily, and though her complete recovery must be a work of time, there is reason from present appearances to hope That time will come.

When Newton visited Cowper again, however, and heard about his connections with Teedon, he reacted negatively to the news and at once sought out the schoolmaster and quarrelled with him. Teedon entered in his diary that he had been visited by Newton, who 'behaved ill'. Newton preached at Olney on the first two Sundays in July and also at a Tuesday and Thursday meeting. Teedon tells us demonstratively that on Sunday, 8 July, two days after his row with Newton, 'None but myself heard Mr. Newton who preached from

James I C. v 26 Matt c v 14 in the eve, Heb. 6 c. v 12,' showing that he did not bear a grudge against the man.[12] Three days later Teedon wrote in his diary that Cowper had told him that his note and prayers of the day before had refreshed him, indicating that Cowper still cherished the prayer fellowship with him.

Whatever may be said in criticism of Teedon, it must be admitted that he was a great source of strength to the poet on many occasions, and it must also be said to his credit that he never displayed that extreme and seemingly unnatural jealousy that most of Cowper's friends showed to one another.

Milton leads to friendship with Hayley

The second comfort given Cowper at this time was his work on Milton. The poet often maintained that when his hands were empty, his head followed suit. Now his hands were full once more and he settled down to translating Milton's Latin and Italian verse before going on to his major commentary on *Paradise Lost.*

It was his work on Milton that was to bring the poet his third great source of comfort and introduce him to a most extraordinary friend who not only showed the poet that deep respect and love which many others had already shown him, but sacrificed his own time and energies to serve him almost as devotedly as Mrs Unwin herself. This man was William Hayley (1745-1825), whose place Cowper had taken as Britain's leading poet.

The way the two men became friends is one of the most interesting stories in the history of literature. Whilst Johnson was busy planning his *Milton Gallery*, the rival publishers Boydell and Nichol were planning a major biographical work on the life of Milton. For this task they chose the poet William Hayley. Hayley was educated at Eton and Cambridge and studied law at the Middle Temple before taking up a career as a poet and patron of the arts. A man of means, he had inherited a vast house in a square mile of gardens at Eartham on the south coast and gathered around himself a large coterie of authors, poets, painters, architects and social reformers, which included Romney, Blake, Charlotte Smith, Gibbon, Anne Seward, Flaxman, Warton and Howard.

Hayley became famous by writing such works as *The Triumphs of Temper* in 1781 and achieved equal notoriety by publishing *A*

Philosophical, Historical, and Moral Essay on Old Maids in 1785. In both works Hayley gave a great deal of advice to unmarried and unmarriageable women. Hayley, according to his biographer Morchard Bishop, was seen by many as a 'bigotted' Whig and a 'fierce' Christian.

His extraordinary kindness and faithfulness to his friends was second to none, but both he and his wife Eliza suffered from nervous disorders and ill health which usually developed when they were together. Consequently Hayley and his wife lived separated from each other for the greater part of the year and they shared their joint responsibilities by letter. Thomas Alphonso Hayley, the Hayleys' son, was of a sweet and blameless character, but, in order to discredit his father, Johnson and other friends of Cowper's spread the rumour that he was illegitimate. Johnson thought he had discovered the 'real' mother but was quite wrong in his assumption.

Writing to John Johnson some time later, Hayley summed up his attitude to life in a song of his own composition:

> Of all the gifts the heavens dispence,
> Or nature can impart,
> Be ours that charm to every sense,
> True gaity of heart!
>
> Ever a cheerful hope maintain,
> Be fortune kind or coy!
> For hope alleviates every pain,
> And heightens every joy.

One day in early February 1792, Hayley was sitting in his study reading the newspaper when he discovered an article referring to his work on the life of Milton. The writer informed his readers that Cowper, too, was writing a life of Milton, so the two major poets were now keen rivals and were trying to outdo each other. Hayley was shocked, but when he looked into the matter was pleased to discover that Cowper was editing Milton's poems and not writing a biography. Nevertheless he decided to write to his fellow-poet saying that he in no way considered himself Cowper's rival and that he was an admirer of his verse. He therefore sent Cowper the following letter accompanied by a sonnet:

Dear Sir,

I have often been tempted by affectionate admiration of your poetry, to trouble you with a letter; but I have repeatedly checked myself in recollecting that the vanity of believing ourselves distantly related in spirit to a man of genius, is but a sorry apology for intruding on his time.

Though I resisted my desire of professing myself your friend, that I might not disturb you with intrusive familiarity, I cannot resist a desire equally affectionate, of disclaiming an idea which I am told is imputed to me, of considering myself, on a recent occasion, as an antagonist to you. Allow me therefore, to say, I was solicited to write a Life of Milton, for Boydell and Nicol, before I had the least idea that you and Mr. Fuseli were concerned in a project similar to theirs. When I first heard of your intention, I was apprehensive, that we might undesignedly thwart each other; but on seeing your proposals, I am agreeably persuaded, that our respective labours will be far from clashing...

To you, my dear Sir, I have a grateful attachment, for the infinite delight which your writings have afforded me; and if, in the course of your work, I have any opportunity to serve or oblige you, I shall seize it with that friendly spirit which has impelled me at present to assure you both in prose and rhyme, that I am,

Your very cordial admirer,

W. Hayley.[13]

Cowper! Delight of all, who Justly prize
The splendid Magic of a strain divine,
That sweetly tempts th' enlighten'd Soul to rise,
As sun-beams lure an Eagle to the skies!
Poet! to whom I feel my heart incline
As to a Friend, endear'd by virtuous ties!
Ne'er shall my name in Pride's contentious line
Of hostile Emulation cope with thine;
No — let us meet, with kind fraternal aim,
Where Milton's shrine invites a votive throng!
With Thee I share a passion for his fame,

His Zeal for Truth, his scorn of venal blame;
But Thou hast rarer gifts: to Thee belong
His Harp of highest tone, his Sanctity of song.

Here we have a marvellous testimony to Hayley's true humility. Although Cowper's *Task* had dethroned Hayley as England's leading poet, the man was prepared not only to recognize Cowper as his master but to see in him a second Milton.

Hayley did not dare to send this important letter via the normal postal service but as a friend was journeying to London, he asked him to take the letter to Johnson's the publishers and ask them to forward it on to Cowper in their dispatches to the poet. The friend took the letter to London and it was promptly put on the mantelpiece at Johnson's — and forgotten. Hayley spent several long weeks of torture believing that Cowper had received his letter but did not think it worth a reply. He became convinced that this was the case as a friend of his, who thought he knew Cowper, had told him that the poet would in no way accept a letter written in such a spirit. That 'friend' was wrong. After nearly six weeks Johnson suddenly remembered the letter and had it sent to Cowper. The poet read it with great delight, but on seeing the date was filled with remorse and wrote off immediately to Hayley saying,

My Dear Sir—
    Your Letter gives me the sincerest pleasure, and at the same time, the late arrival of it, the greatest uneasiness. What must you think of a man who could leave so valuable a favour almost six weeks unacknowledged? A Liberality like that of the amiable writer was certainly such as entitled him to other treatment, and even you, candid and generous as you are, must at least have begun by this time to suspect me of the most stupid insensibility. But let the blame be imputed to the blameworthy, and let the innocent go free. Your pacquet dated the 7th. of last month, reached me not till six o'clock this evening. Thanks to my Bookseller who neglected to send it sooner, and by his unreasonable delay has put my nerves and spirits to a trial, not the first of the kind that they have sustained from Him, but certainly the severest.
    When I saw the Newspaper to which you allude, and in which we seem'd to be match'd like two racehorses against each other, my first sensations were not unpleasant, for I felt

myself not a little flatter'd by the supposed competition between us. But sensations of a very different kind succeeded, and such as were nearly akin to the most dispiriting despondence. I never thought myself very well qualified for my present enterprize, for though I have all my life been at times occupied in reading and admiring Milton, I had not once look'd into him with the eyes of a Commentator; nor did I, nor had I any reason to judge myself in any measure equal to yourself either in point of Learning or other ability for such an employment. Guess then how I must feel myself relieved by the information you give me that we are to act each in a distinct province, and that I shall have no disgrace to fear on this occasion save from myself only. — He who knows the hearts of all, knows that in thus speaking and in thus describing my feelings in this instance, I have spoken nothing but truth.

I rejoice that you are employed to do justice to the character of a man, perhaps the chief of all who have ever done honour to our country, and whose very name I reverence. Here we shall not clash or interfere with each other, for a Life of Milton is no part of my bargain. In short we will cope with each other in nothing but that affection which you avow for me, unworthy of it as I am, and which your character and writings and especially your kind letter have begotten in my heart for you.

A thousand thanks to you for your Subscription, though the honour of your name is all the benefit that I shall derive from it, who am, on this occasion, Bookseller's Labourer, and nothing more. As many also for your Sonnet, of which you speak more modestly than justly, and which I will not call a Compliment because I will not wrong your sincerity, or even seem to do it. May I always so write and so act as to continue in your good opinion, and send me now and then a line to tell me that I still possess it. Believe me, my Dear Sir, duly sensible of your kindness, as in truth I am, and your much obliged and

affectionate humble Servant

Wm Cowper.

Every remark of yours on Milton will be highly valued by me.[14]

Hayley was almost beside himself for joy on receiving Cowper's reply and wrote back at once. He told Cowper that if they were to continue being friends it would be best if they told each other their life stories and he started off straight away with his own.

Hayley's story might well have been taken from a page in Cowper's own life history. He tells his friend that he was once an amusing companion but had suffered from years of ill health and miseries and had endured calamities that even Cowper, with all his imagination, could never have thought possible.

As to his 'genius', he told Cowper, 'I declare by the Almighty Giver of it, I esteem your poetical Powers far above those, that I ever thought myself possess'd of in my vainer days — when I had certainly an uncommon quickness and facility in composition — of late years I have reckon'd my Fancy almost as much crippled as my limbs.'[15] Hayley ended by inviting his new friend to stay with him at Eartham.

In a way, nothing could have been more calculated to cheer Cowper up. He was in his 'There is no one in the world who must suffer as I' moods and here was a brother poet almost boasting of the very same symptoms! Cowper explained that he could not make the long journey to Eartham but suggested that Hayley should come and be nursed (Cowper's own word) at Weston.

Soon the two friends were corresponding happily together and Cowper told Hayley, 'God grant that this friendship of ours may be a comfort to us all the rest of our days in a world where true friendships are rarities, and especially where, suddenly form'd, they are apt soon to terminate. But, as I said before, I feel a disposition of heart towards you, that I never felt for one whom I had never seen, and that shall prove itself, I trust, in the event a propitious omen.'[16] Eventually Hayley was persuaded to visit Cowper with his research books on Milton and his unfinished manuscript as the two had decided to assist each other in their various projects. Cowper invited Samuel Greatheed, too, to form a trio of students of Milton.

The first months of 1792 were painful ones for Cowper who found, because of a complaint which he told Hayley rhymed with 'smiles', that he could hardly sit down except with great discomfort. He wrote to Rose and told him that he had an illness called by the term used for 'those things on which they sometimes lay the foundation of bridges'.[17]

Defence of Warren Hastings

Whilst Cowper was impatiently awaiting Hayley's visit, another matter was also troubling him. He had always been highly critical of the corruption shown by the East India Company and the way it treated the Indians. This evil state of affairs had at last come to the notice of the British Government and names were being named and reputations lost as offenders were being rooted out. Cowper was frightened that rather than the truly guilty being punished, scapegoats were being found in their stead.

At Westminster Cowper had, to use his own words, 'enjoyed sweet company with' a boy called Warren Hastings who was to become Governor-General of India. It appeared that Hastings had been chosen as the scapegoat which would save the face of the East India Company. Always one to defend the underdog, Cowper wrote,

> *To Warren Hastings Esqr.*
> *By an old Schoolfellow of his at Westminster*

> Hastings! I knew thee young, and of a mind,
> While young, humane, conversible and kind,
> Nor can I well believe thee, gentle *then*,
> *Now* grown a villain and the *worst* of men,
> But rather some suspect, who have oppress'd
> And worried thee, as not themselves the *Best*.

Cowper sent the poem off to Lady Hesketh to have it inserted in one of the London papers, but apparently his cousin thought the poem was too politically loaded and refrained from carrying out his request. The poem was first published by Hayley after Cowper's death.

A welcome visit and a shattering blow

On Tuesday, 15 May, Hayley arrived at Weston and was greeted like a long-lost brother. Each poet had suffered attacks of nerves wondering what kind of reception he would get from the other. They need not have worried. They took to each other immediately, were quickly the very best of friends and looked forward to a long period of hard work and fun together. Sadly, this was not to be.

A week later, Cowper and Hayley were coming back from a stroll when Greatheed rushed out to meet them in great excitement. Mrs Unwin had had another terrible stroke and was apparently at death's door. Cowper dashed into the study where Mrs Unwin had been talking with Greatheed and found his dear friend completely paralysed down one side and unable to open her eyes or speak.

At first it looked as though Cowper himself would collapse but he held himself together, though he cried out in grief, 'There is a wall of separation between me and my God.' Hayley acted quickly, took hold of Cowper, looked him straight in the face and said, 'So there is, my friend, but I can inform you I am the most resolute mortal on earth for pulling down old walls, and by the living God I will not leave a stone standing in the wall you speak of.' Cowper examined Hayley's features carefully for some moments, gradually growing calmer as he did so, and suddenly grasped his friend's hand and said simply, 'I believe you.' Hayley's biographer Morchard Bishop tells us that in this way 'The crisis was past, and it was Hayley's inspired imbecility that had averted it.' Cowper accepted the words as inspired, but he certainly did not think them imbecilic. Writing to Lady Hesketh about Hayley's help, he wrote, 'It has happen'd well, that of all men living the man most qualified to assist and comfort me, is here, though 'till within these few days I never saw him, and a few weeks since had no expectation that I ever should. You have already guessed that I mean Hayley. Hayley the most benevolent and amiable of his kind, and who loves me as if he had known me from my cradle.'[18]

Hayley at once turned himself from a poet into a nurse. He contacted Dr Austin at St Bartholomew's in London and asked him to come and attend Mrs Unwin. He combed the neighbourhood and at last found an electrical machine at the home of a former businessman, Mr Socket. In the workings of providence, when Socket had recently been declared bankrupt his creditors had taken everything except the electrical machine, not knowing what it was. Kindhearted Hayley not only hired the machine, but also took Mr Socket's fifteen-year-old son into his care to relieve his father's purse. Finding the young man well-educated Hayley eventually gave him the job of tutor to his own son.

An electrical machine was thought to be a cure-all in those days and Hayley set to work giving Mrs Unwin electrical shocks whilst young Socket turned away at the handle producing enough current. It seemed to help, and as soon as Mrs Unwin regained a little of her strength she would have no one but Hayley to apply it, complaining that others hurt her.

Eventually Hayley had to go back to Eartham but not before urging Cowper to bring Mrs Unwin there. He also first visited Lady Hesketh and informed her in detail of all that was happening at Weston so that she could use her influence and even make a visit to help her cousin's friend.

Cowper followed up a melancholy letter to Teedon, written whilst the shock was still on him, with more cheerful words, saying, 'I have a short moment to thank you for your prayers, and tell you that they are so far answer'd as that she continues to recover strength. Continue to pray for us both.'

Although Lady Hesketh had first recommended Hayley's works to Cowper before they got to know him personally, she was rather dubious about Hayley's Christian testimony and became jealous of the attention Cowper was showing him. Sensing this, Cowper wrote to her telling her to expect Hayley and continuing,

> Our good Samaritan Hayley has been all in all to us on this very afflictive occasion. Love him I charge you dearly for my sake, and as much as you needs must for his own. Where could I have found a man, except himself, who could have made himself so necessary to me in so short a time that I absolutely know not how to live without him? He is both the best poet, as you know, that the kingdom could have afforded me, and considering that he is not such by profession, one of the best physicians. He glows with benevolence to all men, but burns for my service with a zeal for which you will adore him.[19]

This affection was not one-sided. Hayley's letters to his other friends are aglow with praise for Cowper, calling him 'one of the most interesting creatures in the world' and praising his 'rare genius'. In Cowper, he declares, he has found the ideal friend.

Cowper's other friends were not slow to point out Hayley's defects to the poet but Cowper would have none of it and looked upon Hayley as a messenger from God and a brother in Christ. The

Rev. Walter Bagot was quite incensed that Cowper should associate with the author of a book which purported to put 'Old Maids' in their place. Bagot was burdened with five unmarried sisters — a fact which Cowper felt should have inclined him to be grateful for the advice given by Hayley — but Bagot saw Hayley's work as an insult to the fair sex and broke with Cowper over the matter. When Cowper told Hayley that in gaining one friend, he had lost another, Hayley immediately concluded that he was referring to Newton. Cowper assured him that Newton had not reacted in this way but he did not disclose Bagot's name. To be on the safe side, Cowper read Hayley's book on 'Old Maids' and found it praiseworthy.

Hayley's contact with Cowper definitely stabilized him in the faith. He acquired a deeper interest in spiritual things and composed some fine hymns after getting to know Cowper. Whatever his orthodoxy, so great was the selfless love and attention that Hayley showed to Cowper in the coming years that his name has become permanently associated with the poet along with those of John Newton, Mary Unwin, William Unwin, Lady Hesketh and John Johnson.

The visit to Eartham

It is interesting to note that at this time Hayley seemed to have little idea of Cowper's proneness to depression and his letters relating to matters at Weston are far more concerned with alleviating Mrs Unwin's burdens than those of Cowper. Hayley soon realized that Mrs Unwin could not receive all the care and attention she needed at Weston and he invited his new friend to bring Mrs Unwin to his home at Eartham for the winter, where she would benefit from the fresh air and sunshine of the south coast and treatment from doctor friends.

At any other time this would have been a preposterous suggestion to make as Cowper had hardly stirred from the district for thirty years and the prospects of a three-day journey of several hundred miles would have given the poet a horrid fright at the best of times. However, Cowper was prepared to do anything within reason that would help Mrs Unwin and so he consulted Teedon on the matter. The schoolmaster made it a subject of prayer and found several encouraging words in the Bible. These he passed on to Cowper, who took them as a sign that he should accept Hayley's offer. This caused something of a stir amongst several other friends of Cowper's who had made the poet similar offers which had been declined.

On Wednesday, 1 August 1792, Cowper set out for Eartham, accompanied by Mrs Unwin, Johnny of Norfolk and two servants. The poet had written to several friends and relations, arranging that they should meet him on the way and book rooms for the nights spent on the journey. The first night's stop was at Barnet, where Cowper was greeted by Samuel Rose, who had arranged for rooms in a local inn. Cowper found the place terribly noisy and was sure that Mrs Unwin would not be able to rest properly there. He was, however, pleasantly surprised to find that she spent a peaceful night.

On the following day, accompanied by Rose who had walked from London, the party journeyed through the centre of the capital, crossing Westminster Bridge, reminiscent of so many of Cowper's childhood escapades when he played truant from school. They then journeyed on to Kingston, where they were met by General Cowper. The poet merely guessed who his cousin was, as the two men had not seen each other since Cowper's lawyer days. The second night was spent in a very quiet inn at Ripley and the not-too-weary travellers reached Eartham the following night.

Cowper's description of the wild Sussex hills seen by moonlight remind of scenes from the gothic novels of his day. The poet had never visited a hilly district in his life and he describes insignificant hills as if they were the highest Swiss Alps.

By the time the party reached Eartham Cowper already thought that Mrs Unwin was looking better. Cowper's first letters from Eartham describe the splendid house overlooking the sea as a veritable Eden. Writing to Lady Hesketh, he praised both Hayley's generosity and the beautiful countryside, declaring that he had never felt better. There was also a marked improvement in Mrs Unwin.

Johnny, too, was in his element. He marvelled at the paintings of famous people on the walls of Hayley's mansion and stared with awe at the poet's library, which was thirty feet long, twenty-four feet wide and fourteen foot high. He was thrilled at meeting the great painter Romney and even more delighted to hear that Romney wished to paint Cowper's portrait.

Johnny was also enraptured by the character of Charlotte Smith, the authoress, who had been mercilessly thrown out, together with her eight children, by her affluent husband and left without a penny apart from what she could earn from writing. She, too, like so many other people in need, found a sheltering roof over her head at Hayley's. Mrs Smith and Cowper understood each other at once and the authoress begged Cowper to look over her work. Her next publication was duly dedicated to him.

To make the party complete Hurdis, the poet who was so indebted to Cowper for previous help, arrived and stayed some days at Eartham.

What seems at first sight a delightful group of poets, painters and authors, with a gushing young Johnny almost spellbound at such a gathering of celebrities, must really have presented a most tragic picture. Romney suffered from acute melancholy and possibly a bad conscience (he had deserted his wife) and brought his worries to Eartham. Charlotte Smith, a wronged woman, did not know what the future had in store for her and her very large family. Cowper was full of worry over his work on Milton and Mrs Unwin's health. Mrs Unwin herself was still suffering the effects of a severe stroke. Hurdis had come, at Cowper's request, to be comforted over the death of his favourite sister and Hayley, the cripple, was burdened down with his own — mostly self-afflicted — marital problems. On hearing of one another's woes, the group actually had a good cry together. The surprising thing was that all these melancholics were exceedingly happy in one another's company. Even Mrs Unwin, who was given electric shocks daily by Hayley, felt that being at Eartham was doing her a world of good and it was not long before she could walk outside with assistance and began to speak more clearly.

The only odd man out was Johnny, who usually had not a care in the world but was now growing suspicious of his new host. Before these suspicions arose, however, Johnny wrote to his sister Cath in August to tell her, 'As for our dearest Cousin, he is ten times younger than ever I saw him — and laughs from morning till night. He is quite blooming and active...'[20]

Here at Eartham the poet was freer than at Weston to continue his work on Milton as there were so many others who were eager to look after Mrs Unwin. Hayley's twelve-year-old son, in particular, became especially attached to her and often took her for walks in her wheelchair. Cowper had therefore, with Hayley's assistance, turned once more to his commentaries on *Paradise Lost* and his translations of Milton.

Whilst at Eartham, however, Cowper learned from Samuel Rose that Johnson, the publisher, was having doubts about the future of his *Milton Gallery*. He still wished to publish what Cowper had already more or less completed (i. e. material for the first volume only), but instead of proceeding with the rest of the work he was thinking of bringing out a rival biography to the one which Hayley was preparing for Boydell and Nichol. A lady, Cowper was told, would supply the biography. Cowper told Rose that he had no doubt that there were ladies who would be able to write a good biography of Milton, but they would never be able to write one as good as Hayley's. He had seen and talked over Hayley's work with him and knew it to be beyond rivalry.

Cowper was now in a very awkward position. Johnson told him in a letter that he wanted his volumes on Milton to rival those published by Boydell and Nichol, even though he knew that Cowper was working closely with Hayley. This meant that Cowper found himself torn between his allegiance to Johnson and his friendship with Hayley, and that he would now be considered Hayley's rival. The poet made it quite clear that his loyalty lay with Hayley and that he would write to Johnson and warn him of the folly of what he proposed. Whether it was as a result of Cowper's advice, or because he could not reach an agreement with his illustrator, or because of the financial straits prevalent in the country owing to the trouble in France, Johnson ultimately abandoned the project, but it was not until a year or so later that Cowper learnt that his own contributions had also been dropped.

Meanwhile Cowper was working hard with Hayley on Milton and also translating Andreini's *Adam,* a lengthy work that many scholars believed had inspired Milton to write *Paradise Lost. Adam* is the story of the first man, the first sin and the banishment from Eden. It was written to express 'the inexpressible goodness' of God and to show how he is 'perpetually and grievously offended' by mankind. At the end of the poem Adam acknowledges the depth of his sin and yet is given a hope of future salvation from God which moves him to say,

Greater than my offence I now acknowledge
Your mercy, O my God!
Since you, become the sovereign friend of man,
To him, though ruin'd, now extend your hand!

The work ends with the angels outlining the future of the elect, culminating in their ultimate deliverance through the redeeming work of the Son of God.

Ye progeny of Adam,
Whose race we shall behold adorn the world,
Ye shall not pray in vain
To your high Lord, the fountain of all mercy.
Be leaves of that pure branch,
On which the Word Incarnate shall be grafted!
Thunder, infuriate Hell,
Be stormy! yet his leaf shall never fall:
To him a joyous offspring
Is promised by the Lord of heaven's great vineyard,
Stricken, transfixt, enkindled in a blaze,
And burning with eternal love for man.

Johnny complains of Hayley

Johnny watched this literary co-operation with growing suspicion as he had not expected his beloved friend and hero, Cowper, to treat Hayley as a literary equal or to accept so much of Hayley's advice in his work. When Johnny was given the task of transcribing the text so that it could be sent off to the publisher's, he complained to his sister that 'Some of the *bold* and *forcible* language of our dear Bard [was] crossed out, and supplanted by some *flimsy tinsel* lines of his Brother Poet, and in more instances than one Hayley has absolutely translated a whole Poem — although those that he has done are very short to be sure, consisting only of six or seven lines at most, but then there is scarcely a page but he has *murdered* in *my* opinion.'

Johnny went on to say that to combine Hayley's and Cowper's styles in the same work was as bad as 'mixing French with Old English' and he assured his sister that he would put his foot down and not have Hayley tamper with Cowper's work.[21] Cowper, however, respected Hayley's opinion highly and was quite prepared to accept his friend's advice. There is little evidence to be found in *Adam* of the mixture Johnny alleges; in fact it is the language of the *Task* which shines through the work with no mean light. Furthermore, Cowper carefully edited Hayley's biography and added a number of translations of his own, so the 'murdering' was mutual.

This was not the only point which upset Johnny, however. There had obviously been talk at Eartham about what would happen if Mrs Unwin should die. According to Johnny, Hayley did not expect her to last through the winter and he had suggested that Cowper should come and spend the rest of his days with him. Such a turn of affairs would be most harmful to Cowper, in Johnny's opinion, as Hayley would have too great an influence on the poet and he himself would have less access to him. It is obvious, reading between the lines, that Johnny was worried that Cowper would be so taken up with Hayley that he would have no time for his young Norfolk friend and kinsman. It is also obvious that Johnny was beginning to adopt the same patronizing attitude towards Cowper that Newton sometimes manifested and that Lady Hesketh was to develop to a high degree.

Johnny need not have worried that Cowper intended to settle at Eartham as, now that Mrs Unwin appeared, to him at least, so much better, he was eager to get back to his own study at Weston, where he hoped to start on more original compositions rather than translations. The poet had no intention whatsoever of giving up Weston and, indeed, when he did eventually leave the Lodge, it was Johnny himself, aided and abetted by Lady Hesketh, who literally dragged him away from the home he had come to love and which had given him stability of mind and purpose.

Cowper decided to leave Eartham on 17 September but to take a more leisurely journey home so that he could spend at least a night at General Cowper's home in Ham. The poet's letters at this time show that he had hardly ever been happier and he was enjoying himself no end. Johnson's letters, on the other hand, are full of complaints. He is certain that Cowper does not like the way the rooms are heated; he is sure that Cowper must dislike the food; he believes that the poet must suffer from Hayley's practice of keeping the blinds drawn instead of letting in the noonday sun; he criticizes the skinflint way he is looked after; he hints that Hayley is not the man he appears to be; indeed, his description of Eartham is the very opposite to Cowper's.

In all fairness to Johnny, he honestly believed he was acting in the poet's interest in being so negative in his attitude to Hayley, but there is obviously more than a hint of jealousy in Johnny's criticism. This was all rather hard on Hayley, who had invited Johnny to stay with him merely so that he could share the pleasure of Cowper's company with his host. Indeed, Johnson was biting the hand that fed him in a most disagreeable way. This development in Johnson's character is important to note as he gradually forced his ideas of what were good for Cowper onto the poet and at times went to extremes that could in no way have been in Cowper's interest.

Meanwhile Cowper was writing to Teedon to tell him that, whereas he usually turned to his praying friend when things were going wrong, at present he had to tell him that he had nothing to complain about.

Return to Weston

Cowper left Hayley's haven with very mixed feelings. He had enjoyed himself perhaps more than he had done for the last twenty years and was now as firmly Hayley's friend as he had ever been. He had also come to love Hayley's son who had been so very kind to Mrs Unwin. Little Thomas Alphonso, who had inherited his father's crippled figure as well as his talents, accompanied Cowper part of the way and had to return home on foot in the pouring rain. Once out of sight of Eartham, the tears gushed from Cowper's eyes. The Hayleys' eyes were wet, too.

Cowper was full of new ideas and longed to start writing again in the peace and quiet of his own study. No sooner had he left Eartham, however, than he started to miss his friends and comforted himself by writing to them only a few hours after leaving. Then a heavy depression set in which left Cowper only after he had reached Ham, where he spent a very pleasant time with General Cowper finding out how the various members of the family were getting on. The conversation came round to Thurlow whom the general accused of being a hard-hearted man who had brought many an insult on the Cowper family, especially in the case of Ashley Cowper. The poet's heart went out to his old friend and he assured his cousin that Thurlow was the kindest of men. Cowper was careful to ensure that Johnny took full part in the conversation and introduced him to his kinsman as a sound Evangelical who was shortly to be ordained for the ministry of the gospel.

After leaving the general's, the party stopped at Rose's in London and had a dish of chocolate before journeying with him to

St Albans, where Rose's mother lived. The way home to Weston presented no difficulties though Mrs Unwin was always in danger of falling off her seat and Johnny had eaten some beef at Barnet which had disagreed with him and he had to stop on the way to rid himself of it.

Once back at Weston, Cowper had to forget all his dreams of tranquillity and peace. Chaos reigned at first until everything was made shipshape again after an absence of over six weeks. When Cowper had settled down, we find him writing invitations to all and sundry and it was not long before the house was bursting with visitors again. The result was that due to 'perpetual and unavoidable interruptions' the poet could not find the time or the energy to write.

He had written several letters on a most cheerful note to Teedon but he was once more overtaxing his strength and on 3 October 1792, only a few weeks after returning from a very rejuvenating long holiday, we find him writing to Teedon, 'I feel myself in short the most unpitied, the most unprotected, and the most unacknowledg'd Outcast of the human race.' It was to become a constant complaint of Cowper's that the more company he had, the more lonely he became. This was to a great extent his own doing, as Cowper was always extremely hospitable but could never find a true balance between having company and being overwhelmed by the crowd. During the next two years Cowper was to fill his house to bursting-point, not only with guests such as Hayley, Lady Hesketh, Johnny, Newton and his other good friends, but with many a waif and stray and, at times their whole families. Yet in the midst of all this, the poet felt lonelier and lonelier as the months went by and he was never again to know that peace of mind and relaxation which he had enjoyed so much at Hayley's Eden.

Commentary on Milton's *Paradise Lost*

Another, greater Eden, now began to occupy the poet's time once again. This was his commentary on *Paradise Lost*. Cowper was still working on it, though with difficulty because of his commitments as Mrs Unwin's nurse. The poet was never to see his work finished and it was not until after his death that Hayley gathered up what he could find of Cowper's work on Milton and published it in a most luxurious volume. Though Hayley did not find all that his friend had written, what he published shows what a fine grasp of evangelical theology Cowper still possessed.

At the outset of his work on Milton Cowper makes it clear that it is Milton's strong belief in the Bible and the efficacy of its language in expressing divine truths that makes his verse so expressive and poetic. Critics have censured Cowper for writing a religious commentary on Milton rather than a literary one. In so doing, they have shown that they do not come up to Cowper's literary ideal. According to Cowper, it was Milton's usage of biblical truths and biblical language which made him the literary genius he was.

Although Cowper believed Milton to be the most biblical of poets, he did not allow his respect for the Puritan to hinder him from criticizing passages in *Paradise Lost* which he considered unbiblical. One of several such cases is when Milton, in Book II, line 916ff., describes how God created the world, using 'dark materials' in his work of creation. Cowper comments:

> This is a poetic account indeed, but rather a mechanical one of the creation, and such as while it supposes the Deity to have needed means with which to work, falls far below the scriptural idea that he created all things out of nothing. The first verse in the Bible tells us with a most magnificent simplicity that 'In the beginning God created the heaven and the earth' and is perfectly silent as to any material with which he formed them. To suppose indeed the existence of matter antecedent to the creation, is to suppose it eternal, and is, for that reason, as unphilosophical as it is unscriptural, and the very word *creation* implies existence given to something which never before existed.

Another example is to be found in Cowper's comments on Book III, line 210 ff, referring to a willing Agent who is prepared to die for his elect. Cowper fears that Milton has not made it clear enough who it is that is to accomplish this salvation and quotes Romans 3:25-26: 'Whom God hath set forth to be a propitiation ... that he may be just and the justifier of him which believeth in Jesus.' He goes on to say, 'The reader, however, since all are not conversant enough with Scripture to know it, is to be admonished that the ensuing reference of this arduous enterprise to the Angels, is a mere poetic fiction. Christ is always mentioned there, as the only *possible substitute*, because he alone was *worthy*.'

On the whole, however, Cowper sees in *Paradise Lost* the essence of the gospel which he sums up at the end of his commentary. There is perhaps no better summary of the gospel in print even today. Cowper writes,

Man, in the beginning, is placed in a probationary state and made the arbiter of his own destiny. By his own fault he forfeits happiness both for himself and for his descendents. But Mercy interposes for his restoration. That Mercy is represented as perfectly free, as vouchsafed to the most unworthy; to creatures so entirely dead in sin, as to be destitute even of a sense of their need of it, and consequently too stupid ever to ask it. They are also as poor as they are unfeeling, and were it possible that they could affect themselves with a just sense and apprehension of their lapsed condition, have no compensation to offer to their offended Maker, nothing with which they can satisfy the demands of his justice, in short, no atonement. In this ruinous state of their affairs, and when all hope of reconciliation seems lost for ever, the Son of God voluntarily undertakes for them; undertakes to become the Son of Man also, and to suffer in Man's stead the penalty annext to his transgression. In consequence of this self-substitution Christ becomes the Federal head of his church, and the sole Author of salvation to his people. As Adam's sin was imputed to his posterity, so the faultless obedience of the second Adam is imputed to all, who, in the great concern of Justification, shall renounce their own obedience as imperfect, and therefore incompetent.

The sentence is thus reversed as to all Believers, 'Death is swallowed up in Victory', the Saviour presents the redeemed before the throne of the Eternal Father, in whose countenance no longer any symptom of displeasure appears against them, but their joy and peace are thenceforth perfect. The General Resurrection takes place, the Saints are made assessors with Christ in the judgment both of Men and Angels, the new heaven and earth, the destined habitation of the Just, succeed, the Son of God, his whole undertaking accomplished, surrenders the Kingdom to his Father, and God becomes All in All.[22]

The poet ends his commentary by saying that there are many scoffers who claim that these views are merely the invention of contemporary Evangelicals but Milton's testimony from the previous century show that they have been held by Christians of all ages.

Critics have claimed that Cowper's summary of the Christian faith is merely 'poetic fiction'. This is clearly not the case, as shown by his letter to Johnny Johnson shortly after the latter had made a bold profession of faith and claimed an assurance that he should enter the ministry. The poet writes on 11 April 1793,

> What you say of your determined purpose, with God's help, to take up the cross and despise the shame, gives us both great pleasure. In our pedigree is found one at least who did it before you. Do you the like and you will meet him in heaven as sure as the Scripture is the word of God. The quarrel that the world has with evangelical men and doctrines, they would have with a host of angels in the human form, for it is the quarrel of owls with sunshine, of ignorance with divine illumination.

Hayley intervenes on Cowper's behalf

Cowper's interest in the poor with whom he liked to surround himself was meanwhile taking a heavy toll on his purse. Buying ingredients and making up medicines for distribution to the poor, caring for 'swarms' (Lady Hesketh's word) in the kitchen and giving a guinea to anyone he met who appeared to be in need were all costly enterprises and Cowper had a steady income of no more than £150 a year. There was no more money coming from the Thorntons and it seems that the Smith family had also stopped supplying the poet with funds for the poor of Olney and Weston.

Johnson, the publisher, had also been a great disappointment to the poet, who felt that he had been downgraded to his bookseller's labourer. Johnson apparently maintained that the income on Cowper's works before the fifth edition hardly covered costs. This must have been an immense exaggeration as Cowper's poems were selling very well indeed.

One day Hayley asked Cowper to be frank and tell him just how much money he had in hand. He was shocked to find that Cowper's income was well below his expenses and that he had been a burden on Mrs Unwin to the tune of many hundreds of pounds. Resolute Hayley decided to do something about this. He thought that England had benefited so much from his friend's uplifting verse that it would be an easy matter to persuade the government to give Cowper a sinecure post or provide him with a pension such as Dr Johnson had been awarded for his literary contributions to the culture of the country.

Hayley knew Lord Chancellor Thurlow and he also knew that the latter had once been Cowper's best friend, so he decided to start there. Thurlow, however, was in no mood to see Hayley as he was bowed down by his own troubles. Pitt was campaigning against him and had told the king that either Thurlow had to go or he would resign himself.

Hayley put the pressure on and the Lord Chancellor eventually invited him to a breakfast at which Lord Kenyon, the Chief Justice, was also present. As William Cowper's grandfather had been Chief Justice and his grandfather's brother had once been Lord Chancellor, Hayley must have felt that he would obtain a fair hearing. So he came straight to the point and argued that it would be a simple matter for the king, who had just recovered from an illness, to give thanks to God for his recovery by conferring a pension on Cowper, who had at times suffered from a similar complaint. This was rather tactless of Hayley, as the king had recovered from a stroke of insanity and had no wish to have this generally proclaimed. Thurlow appeared to be interested and Hayley sent Cowper a jubilant note.

Pitt had his way for a time, however, and Thurlow was forced to step down, and although Hayley kept reminding him about Cowper, he either did not or could not undertake anything. Disappointed in Thurlow, Hayley decided to tackle the prime minister himself. He thus wrote a carefully worded letter but, as in the case of his first letter to Cowper, he dared not entrust such an important epistle to the post and gave it instead to a friend in the government who promised to let Pitt have it at a convenient time. Once again the letter remained unanswered for many weeks and it eventually proved that the person entrusted with the letter had never delivered it. When Hayley discovered this, he asked for the letter to be returned and then sent it off by the normal post. Still no reply came.

Hayley turned once more to Thurlow, who told him to go and see

Lord Spencer, who was an admirer of Cowper's and a near neighbour. Instead of addressing Lord Spencer directly, Hayley asked his
friend Gibbon, author of the famous *Rise and Fall of the Roman
Empire* and a former schoolfriend of Cowper's, to mediate for him
but Gibbon refused point-blank.

'My Mary!'

Meanwhile at Weston Mrs Unwin's improvement had shown itself
to be of a very short duration. As usual, Cowper blamed himself for
her weakness and his care for his faithful friend and his sorrow for
causing her so much ill led him to compose a most moving poem.
In it he expresses his deepest feelings about the woman who was
now a physical and mental wreck, her mind, even if still active,
unable to express itself properly and her once beautiful face disfig-
ured rigidly by paralysis. Cowper's tears turned to words as he
wrote,

> *To Mary*
>
> The twentieth year is well-nigh past,
> Since first our sky was overcast;
> Ah would that this might be the last!
>   My Mary!
>
> Thy spirits have a fainter flow,
> I see thee daily weaker grow—
> Twas my distress that brought thee low,
>   My Mary!
>
> Thy needles, once a shining store,
> For my sake restless heretofore,
> Now rust disus'd, and shine no more,
>   My Mary!
>
> For though thou gladly wouldst fulfil
> The same kind office for me still,
> Thy sight now seconds not thy will,
>   My Mary!

But well thou play'd'st the housewife's part,
And all thy threads with magic art
Have wound themselves about this heart,
    My Mary!

Thy indistinct expressions seem
Like language utter'd in a dream;
Yet me they charm, whate'er the theme,
    My Mary!

Thy silver locks, once auburn bright,
Are still more lovely in my sight
Than golden beams of orient light,
    My Mary!

For could I view nor them nor thee,
What sight worth seeing could I see
The sun would rise in vain for me
    My Mary!

Partakers of thy sad decline,
Thy hands their little force resign;
Yet, gently prest, press gently mine,
    My Mary!

And then I feel that still I hold
A richer store ten thousandfold
Than misers fancy in their gold,
    My Mary!

Such feebleness of limbs thou prov'st,
That now at every step thou mov'st
Upheld by two; yet still thou lov'st,
    My Mary!

And still to love, though prest with ill,
In wintry age to feel no chill,
With me is to be lovely still,
    My Mary!

But ah! by constant heed I know,
How oft the sadness that I show   .
Transforms thy smiles to looks of woe,
    My Mary!

And should my future lot be cast
With much resemblance of the past,
Thy worn-out heart will break at last,
    My Mary!

Hayley continues his quest

At the same time as Cowper was composing the above lines Hayley
was turning his attention back to Pitt and in November 1793 begged
the prime minister to grant him an interview. This time Pitt reacted
promptly and gave Hayley the required audience at eleven o'clock
on Friday, 29 November.

Hayley had a bad attack of nerves and could hardly prepare
himself for the ordeal. He hired a large carriage so that he could drive
up to the prime minister's in style and told his lackey, Joseph, not to
sit beside him but to climb onto the back so as not to make a bad
impression. On the way to Downing Street Hayley went into a fit of
nervous laughter at the show he was putting on and his biographer
tells us that he arrived at Pitt's door in hysterics.

The prime minister, who was now also war minister, received
Hayley as an old friend, told him how much he loved Cowper's
poetry and agreed that a pension for him would be a good thing.
Hayley burst into tears and asked if he could tell Cowper at once that
he was to receive a pension. Pitt told Hayley not to rush things and
he would hear shortly what he proposed to do. Unfortunately, Pitt
was not as good as his word and forgot all about the matter.

In January 1794 Gibbon died and Hayley wrote a letter of
condolence to Lord Spencer, Gibbon's most intimate friend. In the
same letter he broached the subject of Cowper's pension. His
Lordship replied positively saying that the times were hard but he
would see what he could do. He appeared to do nothing.

Meanwhile, Cowper, left without Hayley's company and becoming less and less master of his own house because of plotting
relatives, was in a deep depression. The snubs Hayley was receiving

in high places and the state of his friend's health exasperated him so much that he lost his temper and, throwing aside all caution, wrote a stern letter to the prime minister at the end of February, giving him a piece of his mind and even blaming him for helping to bring on Cowper's latest depression through failing to act on his behalf. He also wrote a poem in which he severely criticized the prime minister and sent it to a mutual friend, knowing full well that Pitt would be shown it. Pitt ignored the letter and the poem would have served only to antagonize him.

A week after writing to Pitt, however, Hayley heard from Lord Spencer that he had indeed been working on Cowper's behalf and that he believed something could be done for the poet.

Trouble at Weston

Meanwhile trouble was brewing at Weston at an alarming rate. At the beginning of April, Hayley received a letter from Samuel Greatheed urging him to return to Weston as the only hope left to restore Cowper 'to himself, to his friends, to the public, and to God'. Wondering whatever could be wrong, Hayley left the final activities concerning Cowper's pension to Samuel Rose and set out for Weston only to find Cowper in the darkest despair. Lady Hesketh and Johnson were there and the poet was refusing to co-operate with them in any way and even accusing them of wanting to put an end to his life.

A few days after Hayley's arrival, on 22 April 1794, a royal warrant was issued:

> *George R.* — Whereas we are graciously pleased to grant and allow unto Samuel Rose Esq and to his executors or administrators, an annuity, or yearly pension of £300, in trust for William Cowper Esq, the same to commence from the 5th day of July 1794, *Our Will and Pleasure is,* that by virtue of our Generall letters of Privy Seal, bearing date the 5th day of November 1760, you do issue and pay or cause to be issued and paid, out of any our Treasure or Revenue in the receipt of the Exchequer applicable to the uses of our civil government, unto the said Samuel Rose Esq and to his executors or

administrators, the said annuity or yearly sum of £300, In Trust [for] and for the use of the above mentioned William Cowper, without account, to commence from the fifth day of July 1794, and to be paid Quarterly or otherwise as the same shall become due, and to continue during our pleasure. And for &c. 1st July 1794 in the 34th year of our reign. By his majesty's Command.

W. Pitt   J. T. Townshend   J. Smyth.

Commisioners' Treasury.

It had taken Hayley almost two years of intense intervention to reach this favourable outcome but now Cowper was in such a distressed state that he was hardly able to appreciate what had happened. In order to see how this acute deterioration in Cowper's spirits developed we must now look at what had been happening at Weston during Hayley's enforced absence.

17.
The path of sorrow

Writing once to a Christian lady who was battling bravely under great persecution in France, Cowper reminded her that though there might be occasional joys and triumphs in the Christian life she must be prepared to find that:

> The path of sorrow and that path alone
> Leads to the land where sorrow is unknown,
> No trav'ler ever reach'd that bless'd abode,
> Who found not thorns and briars in his road.[1]

The last six years or so of Cowper's life provide ample evidence that sometimes God's saints must wander through the valley of the shadow of death with little present comfort to help them on their journey to their blessed abode. Cowper found his own path blocked time and time again by 'thorns and briars' and like Bunyan's Pilgrim before his conversion, Cowper, after his conversion, carried a great burden of sorrow on his back.

It is exceedingly difficult to trace accurately Cowper's journey through the last years of his life. Either the poet wrote few letters during this period, or few of them have been preserved. These last few years are indeed heavily documented, but only by the pens of others who did not see the world through Cowper's eyes or share his views about what was good for him.

Cowper's final problems started whilst Hayley was devoting all his energies to obtaining a government sinecure post or a pension for him, and after the poet's happy and contented stay at Eartham which marked the fulfilment of a lifelong desire to have a friend in whom he could trust totally and lastingly.

The search for a real friend

Cowper's view of a friend may best be expressed in the words of Proverbs 18:24: 'A man that hath friends must shew himself friendly: and there is a friend that sticketh closer than a brother.' He detested the kind of 'friendship' he described when he wrote,

> The man, who hails you Tom or Jack,
> And proves by thumping on the back
> His sense of your great merit,
> Is such a friend, that one had need
> Be very much his friend indeed,
> To pardon, or to bear it.

Cowper had a higher view of friendship than merely being chums with a man or than having a romantic relationship with a woman. To him:

> True friendship has in short a grace
> More than terrestrial in its face,
> That proves it Heav'n-descended:
> Man's love of woman not so pure,
> Nor when sincerest, so secure,
> To last till life is ended.

Friendship, he believed, should be nothing less than a touch of heaven and a foretaste of that joy to come when all earthly sorrows are over and the saints share full harmony one with another in heaven.

It is interesting to note that Cowper's poem 'Friendship', from which these lines were taken, was never published in Cowper's lifetime although it was offered to Johnson in several versions.[2] Perhaps Johnson thought the poem too 'other-worldly'. Hayley published it after Cowper's death in all its variant forms.

Cowper's life was one long search for friends who would never fail him. His first great friend, Sir William Russell, died tragically shortly before Cowper had to part with his first and perhaps only romantic love, Theadora. The ups and downs of the relationship with Theadora, where angry scenes alternated with heart-felt reconciliations, served only to fray Cowper's weak nerves and their courtship was totally lacking in the truly stable friendship of the kind Cowper so much desired. Nevertheless, all his life Cowper was troubled by the thought, 'Was it right to have parted with Theadora?' and there is some evidence to suggest that 'the known duty' that Cowper always said he had failed to perform was related to her.[3]

Newton provided an ideal friendship for a number of years but his almost effeminate jealousy often angered or disappointed Cowper. Neither Lady Austen nor Lady Hesketh could ever become to Cowper anything more than engaging, devoted sisters whom he loved to have around but with whom he could not share the depths of his soul. The poet always kept his distance with Teedon in spite of the great help he received from him. This was because of Cowper's ingrained conviction that only those on the same rung of the social ladder could really be true friends. Johnny Johnson could never have attained to the position of Cowper's best friend as he was so much younger and very immature and, besides, Cowper had looked upon him as a son from their very first encounter.

Neither was the kind of friendship Cowper sought to be found in Mrs Unwin. From the start she was Cowper's ideal Christian mother and he loved her dearly. It was, however, the love of a child for an older, wiser and more stable person and could never turn into anything like the 'just reciprocation' that Cowper sought in his ideal friendship. What could he offer the woman who had given him her motherhood? Only his sonship.

William Unwin had proved the ideal friend with whom a 'just reciprocation' was indeed possible, but he died, leaving a great void in Cowper's heart which made him search the countenance of every man he met in the hope of finding a fitting counterpart. Cowper at one time thought that James Hurdis showed signs of becoming a second Unwin but soon found that he lacked that vitality and stability of character that had characterized his dead friend.

In Hayley Cowper at last found 'an Israelite indeed, in whom there was no guile', even after he had been told tales of weaknesses in his new friend's character. Cowper believed, moreover, that Hayley possessed one virtue that was lacking in all his other friends: he was not 'subject to the jealous mood'. This made him a friend whose judgement could be trusted, and Cowper was increasingly finding himself in need of such a friend.

Lady Hesketh's distrust of Hayley

Lady Hesketh and Johnny Johnson, however, saw Hayley in a very different light, and one which cast long shadows of jealousy. Many letters of these two devoted relatives of Cowper are extant and they give us a deep insight into the intrigues and plottings which went on between them to keep out of Cowper's sight not only Hayley but also anybody else who had any stronger claims on the poet's love and protection.

Whilst Hayley was busy trying to obtain a pension for Cowper, Lady Hesketh was deep in correspondence with Johnny on the subject of his supposed failings. A lady-friend had hinted that Hayley, though not an 'Infidel', was lacking in 'Rational Piety' and included in his Christianity such a large measure of enthusiasm and superstition that he could not possibly be the right kind of company for Cowper. This information, which Lady Hesketh confided to Johnson in a letter written on 15 November 1792, merely confirmed her opinion of Hayley who, she believed, was sure to 'disturb and derange' Cowper totally. She was therefore very surprised to hear that her cousin, after being friends with Hayley for some time, was still in 'good spirits' and was 'well in health'. She assured Johnny, however, that she expected Cowper's future to lie in his and Rose's hands alone.[4] The implication in the letter is obvious: Cowper's future is to lie in the hands of the two young men providing they do what Lady Hesketh tells them and that they have nothing to do with Hayley.

Cowper puts pen to paper once more

Whilst Lady Hesketh was corresponding with Johnny and complaining about the harmful effect Hayley was supposed to be having on her cousin, Cowper himself was busy writing to his fellow poet and telling him that he was longing to receive a promised portrait of his friend as the very sight of it would be a comfort to him. Even though Cowper's eyes were giving him trouble and he was suffering from bad toothache, he had not lost his sense of humour. He told Hayley in November 1792 that 'Divines have observed, that as our first father Adam sin'd with his teeth, so they are the part of us that first decays, and in which we sooner suffer excruciating pain than in any other.'

At the same time the poet was busy demolishing yet another two myths, harmless enough, which were being circulated in the best newspapers. The *Gentleman's Magazine* had announced that Lady Hesketh was the original authoress of the John Gilpin story and that Cowper had merely put this into verse form. He was also supposed to be translating Lucan. Both stories were completely untrue. Cowper was actually working on a number of original poems, including a sonnet of thanks to Romney and the epic poems, 'The Four Ages of Man' and 'Yardley Oak'.

Lady Hesketh was ill at this time and had little contact with Cowper until well into the new year and it was well for his peace of mind that he had not yet discovered his cousin's plans for his future.

Cowper had started his 'thank you' sonnet for Romney whilst at Eartham but was unable to finish it until a good month after returning to Weston. He had got on well with his fellow melancholic and had allowed Romney to do a crayon portrait of him, a request the poet had refused others on the grounds that the subject was 'worthless'. Cowper hated the thought of a portrait of himself being exhibited as if it were some idol for veneration. When, for instance, Johnson expressed a wish to have a portrait of Cowper adorn the next edition of his verse, the poet refused permission. Romney had found Cowper a good subject for painting as he was impressed by the look of genius in his face. In tribute to the painter, Cowper wrote,

Romney! expert infallibly to trace,
On chart or canvas, not the form alone,
And 'semblance, but, however faintly shown,
The mind's impression too on ev'ry face,
With strokes that time ought never to erase
Thou hast so pencil'd mine, that though I own
The subject worthless, I have never known
The artist shining with superior grace,
But this I mark that symptoms none of woe
In thy incomparable work appear.
Well! I am satisfied it should be so,

Since, on maturer thought, the cause is clear
For in my looks what sorrow could'st thou see
When I was Hayley's guest, and sat to thee?

Typical of Cowper's later verse is his 'The Four Ages', which contains themes hailed by literary critics as paving the way for the Romantic movement. Here we have the inner thoughts of a man who is speaking as if he were universal man. The poet is in 'conference with his heart', listening to its words, hearing and acquiescing. The voice which appeals to Cowper, however, is not the disembodied voice of inspiration which the Romantics talk about, but the voice of his own conscience. As in his earlier verse, he warns mankind against searching for hidden knowledge when all he needs to know in this life is at his feet and at his service. Cowper ends this fragment true to his role as mentor:

Myst'ries are food for angels; they digest
With ease, and find them nutriment; but man,
While yet he dwells below, must stoop to glean
His manna from the ground, or starve, and die.[5]

As in all of Cowper's longer poems written for publication, the subject of paradise is to be found in these fragments of unfinished verse. The poet echoes the words of the psalmist, 'What is man, that thou art mindful of him?' and poses the question concerning man which the schoolmen have failed to answer:

Knows he his origin? — can he ascend
By reminiscence to his earliest date?[6]

Cowper leaves the question unanswered here, as he never finished the poem. He told Hayley in December 1993 that he was looking forward to working on it that winter, but such was the impact of the new problems that came upon him through the agency of Lady Hesketh that he never found the peace of mind to continue writing it. He had obviously intended the 'Four Ages' to be a major contribution to a third volume of poems which he planned to publish.

Cowper did, however, give at least a partial answer to the question he had raised here in another poem from this period, the

'Yardley Oak'. This lengthy fragment is, on the surface, the story of a thousand-year-old tree near Weston but, going deeper, it also tells the story of the origin and destiny of man. The poem shows how Cowper's later original verse has been enriched by his linguistic studies whilst translating Homer. In fact, lines 56 to 60 are 'borrowed', as Cowper puts it, from the *Iliad*.[7]

Hugh I'Anson Fausset tells us in his *William Cowper* that the hollow oak at Yardley Chase 'was to evoke perhaps the deepest harmonies which Cowper wrung from nature'.[8] These 'deepest harmonies' for Cowper, writing at the end of his poetic career, are in fact still the same as the harmonies he had sought all his life. They are the harmonies of Eden. It is thus typical of Cowper, the Poet of Paradise, that he ends this last epic work with a portrayal of the Garden of Eden and a description of man as one who was created perfect and at once able to communicate freely with his Creator and take up his tasks as God's steward on earth.

> One man alone, the father of us all,
> Drew not his life from woman; never gaz'd,
> With mute unconsciousness of what he saw,
> On all around him; learn'd not by degrees,
> Nor owed articulation to his ear;
> But moulded by his Maker into man
> At once, upstood intelligent, survey'd
> All creatures, with precision understood
> Their purport, uses, properties, assigned
> To each his name significant, and filled
> With love and wisdom, render'd back to Heav'n
> In praise harmonious the first air he drew.[9]

There is a marvellously novel personification of history in the final lines of this portrayal. Explaining that Adam was a man who needed no tuition, Cowper says,

> ... No tutor charg'd his hand
> With the thought-tracing quill, or task'd his mind
> With problems; history, not wanted yet,
> Lean'd on her elbow, watching Time, whose course,
> Eventful, should supply her with a theme.[10]

There the poem ends. But it is here that Cowper saw his task as beginning. History was furnished with her eventful theme, according to Cowper, with the fall of man and the fading of Eden. Cowper always saw himself as the tutor who was to take up the divine theme, 'The Renovation of a Faded World,'[11] and with his 'thought-tracing quill', point man the way to Paradise Regained.

A return to Homer

Although still full of plans for the future, Cowper nevertheless realized he was growing older and no longer had the same energies as in former years. He was also troubled now and then with the thought that instead of preparing himself for so long to produce great poetry, he had actually been wasting his time on baubles in doing translation work. Yet he could not leave Homer alone and set to work on a new edition which would both keep his mind fom sinking into gloom and help him to pay his way. This conviction that he was doing his second best was conveyed to Johnson in a 'thank you' poem.

In the summer of 1793, Johnny Johnson, wishing to surprise his kinsman, had a classical bust placed on a pedestal in the poet's garden. Cowper took the object to be a bust of Homer and wrote to Johnny in verse, pouring out his own heart:

> *To John Johnson, Esqre. on his presenting me with an antique Bust of*
>
> *Homer*
>
> Kinsman belov'd, and as a son, by me!
> When I behold this fruit of thy regard,
> The sculptured form of my old favourite bard,
> I reverence feel for him, and love for thee.
> Joy too, and grief — Much joy that there should be
> Wise men and learn'd, who grudge not to reward
> With some applause my bold attempt and hard,
>
> Which others scorn. Critics by courtesy.
> The grief is this, that sunk in Homer's mine

I lose my precious years, now soon to fail,
Handling his gold, which, howsoe'er it shine,
Proves dross, when balanced in the Christian scale.
Be wiser thou — Like our forefather Donne,
Seek heavenly wealth, and work for God alone.

Feelings ascribed to nature

Whilst working again on Homer, Cowper had many an interesting exchange of views with Thomas Alphonso Hayley. The young boy was a keen student of Greek and diligently compared Cowper's translation with the original, offering the poet his own views when he felt that he had a helpful contribution to make. In one of his letters he professed to be shocked that Cowper had lowered his high standard of language by using the word 'reel' to describe the movement of a mountain, as if the mountain were drunk. Surely Cowper was letting his imagination and language run away with him! Cowper justifies his use of the word by referring to biblical imagery saying:

> Where the word 'reel' suggests to you the idea of a drunken mountain it performs the service to which I destined it. It is a bold metaphor; but justified by one of the sublimest passages in Scripture, compared with the sublimity of which even that of Homer suffers humiliation. It is God himself who speaking, I think, by the prophet Isaiah, says, 'The earth shall reel to and fro like a drunkard.'[12] With equal boldness in the same Scripture, the poetry of which was never equalled, mountains are said to skip, to break out into singing, and the fields to clap their hands. I intend, therefore, that my Olympus shall be still typsy.[13]

This view of God's whole creation as a living entity, capable of groaning and travailing under the load of sin imposed on it by the fall of man, was later to be built upon by the Romantics with their insistence on an active, living nature. When describing nature Cowper does not merely depict facts observed, nor just the thoughts, feelings and empathy of the observer. He sees nature as expressing feelings itself. Where Wordsworth can describe waves — and even daffodils — as dancing with glee, Cowper can write, describing a snowy winter scene:

> … Earth *receives Gladly* the thickening mantle, and the green
> And tender blade, that *fear'd* the chilling blast,
> *Escapes unhurt* beneath so warm a veil.[14]

Even words in these lines which have not been emphasized, such as 'chilling' and 'warm', really refer to nature's feelings, as they are written entirely from the point of view of the earth and the grass, and not from that of the human observer. Unlike Cowper, however, the Romantics tended to see nature as a living entity, separate from God's working in and through it, and thought of it as capable of self-control in a pantheistic sense.

A period of cheerful activity

In spite of his awareness that his poetic energies were on the decline, the spring, summer and early autumn of 1793 provided Cowper with the most productive, and in many ways happiest, period that he had experienced since the death of Unwin. This is to be seen chiefly in Cowper's poetry written in this year, which extolled Christian love and true friendship, but many of his letters, especially those to Hayley, are merry and optimistic. He was still haunted by attacks of depression and lack of assurance but the heavens never remained overcast for long and the poet, in spite of his morbid bent, often found signs that God had not forsaken him. Thus he could write to Samuel Greatheed:

My Dear Sir—
     I thank you heartily for the next best thing to your company, your very friendly and obliging letter, as well as for the kind enquiries it contains; and am truly sorry, as is my poor Invalide, that we have been deprived so long of the pleasure of seeing you by the sufferings you have endured from so painful an illness. May He heal you to whom your prayers are so warmly and frequently offer'd to obtain health for me.

Mrs. Unwin, I desire to thank God for it, continues as well as she was, notwithstanding the uncomfortable season which too often deprives her of the air and exercise she wants. She has lately by advice of Mrs. Rose's mother enter'd on a course of Tar-water, from which she seems already to derive some benefit; sleeps more, and is less subject to a marble-coldness in the extremities.

I am myself much as usual, except that for two or three days past, having been much agitated with terrours in the night, I have been more afflicted with melancholy and dejection than is common even with me. — Accept mine and Mrs. Unwin's thankful acknowledgments for your unremitted supplications in our behalf. I build some hope upon them, that God has not entirely and altogether forsaken me, as I should otherwise conclude that he has, finding little or nothing in my own experience year after year, to warrant a more favorable conclusion. But the Spirit knows the mind of God, and if the Spirit inclines your heart to prayer for me, it must be because he has a design in my favour, and purposes to grant the petitions he inspires.[15]

Cowper's belief in Reformed doctrine is still not shaken in the least during this period, as is evident from remrks he made when he was sent the manuscript of Charlotte Smith's latest work, *The Emigrants,* to edit. This work deals with the problems arising during the French Revolution. Cowper tells Hayley that Mrs Smith ought to indicate that many of the problems of the French are due to 'the superstition that plunges them in their present miseries'. The poet is here referring to Roman Catholicism. He goes on to write,

Nothing occurs to me that could be advantageously added unless perhaps a retrospect to similar sufferings of our own countrymen, whether in the days of Queen Elizabeth or in those of Charles 2d. under Laud I cannot remember, but 2000 were ejected for non-conformity to the Church-ritual, ministers of the Gospel, men of the most exemplary lives, and many of them men of learning. Some of these sought refuge in America, and others who carried on their ministry where they could, were persecuted from one place to another, and at last

died in prison. The whole recital may be seen in Neale's
History of the Puritans, and soon read.

Were the poem my own, I should in the course of it take
occasion of seasonable and righteous invective against the
National Convention. An assembly in which has been
discover'd the least respect for God, his word and ordinances
that ever was shewn by any. Who have disclaim'd all reverence for religion, true and false together, and while they boast
their zeal for liberty, have by want of tenderness for the
consciences of others, obliged these unhappy men to renounce their country.[16]

By the summer of 1793 Cowper was going through a significant
change, both physically and mentally. He realized that he was no
longer as creative as he had been, and he saw that the time was
approaching when he would have to stop working so hard and use
the time to prepare himself more for the life to come. So he busied
himself in his garden and about the home, attempting to make both
as comfortable as possible for two 'old-age pensioners'. He built a
little cabin in his garden which he called 'The Hermitage' and fitted
it out as a place where they could rest on sunny days. He wrote of
it:

This cabin, Mary, in my sight appears,
Built as it has been in our waning years,
A rest afforded to our weary feet,
Preliminary to — the last retreat.

A tiny moss-covered hut in a nearby shrubbery became a
favourite retreat of the poet's and he set up an inscription in it
containing the words:

Here, free from riot's hated noise,
Be mine, ye calmer, purer joys,
A book or friend bestows;
Far from the storms that shake the great,
Contentment's gale shall fan my seat,
And sweeten my repose.

The inscription was soon stolen, probably by a souvenir hunter

pleased to own one of Cowper's original poems. The poet replaced
it with a passage similar to one from his *Task*:

> No noise is here, or none that hinders thought;
> Stillness, accompanied with sounds like these,
> Charms more than silence. Meditation here
> May think down hours to moments. Here the heart
> May give a useful lesson to the head,
> And learning wiser grow without his books.[17]

It seemed that Cowper was becoming resigned to his lot. He
knew that Mrs Unwin would not get better but he still cherished her
company for what she had been and what she still represented for
him. Though he was now rarely finding themes to write about, he
could still thank God in verse for every sign of support and
faithfulness Mrs Unwin had shown him. In 1793, wishing to express
his gratitude to Mrs Unwin before the creative gift of poetry left him,
he wrote,

> Mary! I want a lyre with other strings;
> Such aid from Heaven as some have feign'd they drew!
> An eloquence scarce given to mortals, new,
> And undebas'd by praise of meaner things!
> That, ere through age or woe I shed my wings
> I may record thy worth with honour due,
> In verse as musical as thou art true.
> Verse, that immortalizes whom it sings!
> But thou hast little need: there is a book.
> By seraphs writ with beams of heav'nly light,
> On which the eyes of God not rarely look;
> A chronicle of actions just and bright!
> There all thy deeds, my faithful Mary, shine.
> And since thou own'st that praise, I spare thee mine.

When Hayley visited Cowper in November 1793, he found him
busy at work on new projects. However, he still found time to check
through Hayley's biography of Milton and Hayley checked through
his new edition of Homer. As soon as Cowper was finished with
Hayley's biography, the latter dashed off to George Nichol to have
it published, only to meet with the greatest disappointment of his

life. Nichol, who was also the king's bookseller, was shocked at the highly democratic tone of the work and refused to publish it unless it were radically altered. Hayley trusted in Cowper's positive judgement on his work and refused to comply. He thought it would be unfair to Milton and to his friend Cowper to 'dishonourably garble' the biography.

Eventually Hayley hit on an ingenious idea which led to the best possible compromise in the circumstances, even if it was of rather dubious morality. He agreed to alter the work providing Nichol supplied him free of charge with five hundred copies of the lavishly done illustrations for the book. Nichol agreed and Hayley then proceeded to have five hundred copies of his original version of the biography printed elsewhere, using the illustrations he had bargained from Nichol. In this way Hayley rescued a good work from oblivion at the same time as he saved his pride, but he was for ever after suspected of double-dealing.

A deepening shadow

Whilst Hayley was at Weston during November 1793, he noticed that there was something worrying Cowper which he was keeping to himself. Hayley supposed at the time it was merely Cowper's consideration for Mrs Unwin who, Hayley believed, was now entering her second childhood. Mrs Unwin was indeed at the centre of Cowper's concern but not in the way that Hayley suspected.

This anxiety was to increase throughout the following months and would put an end once and for all to Cowper's plans for his later years of domestic bliss and work on a further volume of poems. It was this development that moved Samuel Greatheed, in April 1794, on his own initiative, to send the urgent letter to Hayley mentioned at the end of the last chapter, begging him to return with all haste to Weston and to revive the depressed spirits of a poet lost in anguish and despair.

Lady Hesketh's interference

The cause of all this anguish was to be found in the behaviour and aspirations of Lady Hesketh and Johnny Johnson, who were making plans for Cowper which were directly opposed to the poet's own and which would prove disastrous for his welfare.

In the autumn of 1793 Lady Hesketh had begun to be most troublesome and had written letters to Cowper which caused him great alarm. Her Ladyship was intent on taking matters at Weston into her own hands and planned to take over the running of the house, no matter what Mrs Unwin or Cowper felt about it. Cowper needed a woman in the house, Lady Hesketh maintained, and as she had written Mrs Unwin off entirely, she believed herself to be the needed woman.

First Lady Hesketh decided to cut down on Cowper's servants. One servant per 'person' became her maxim. She seemed to forget that she, herself, was always surrounded by a bevy of servants and even when she visited Cowper or travelled elsewhere she took with her at least two manservants, a butler, a coachman, a cook and several ladies in waiting.

Then she intended to rid the house of all 'the idle people' in it. Now not only Cowper but also Mrs Unwin had always been careful to entertain strangers and when a young girl, a near relative, found herself homeless, Mrs Unwin adopted her, just as Cowper had adopted Richard Coleman so many years before. By 1793 this girl, Hannah Wilson, was a bright-eyed, pretty girl in her late teens. Lady Hesketh, ignoring Mrs Unwin's feelings completely, decided that Hannah should be the first to go. She wrote a letter to Cowper saying she was planning to visit Weston but could not as long as Hannah was there, hinting that when she arrived she did not want to see the girl still at Weston. Lady Hesketh gave as an excuse that the 'fire of Hannah's bright eyes' might seduce her young manservant. The good lady did not think, in order to keep peace with Mrs Unwin, of dispensing with her own male lackey in favour of a female one! She also insinuated that Hannah should have been treated as a servant by Mrs Unwin and not as a relative, and that the girl had been spoilt and was now too big for her shoes. Her spiteful attitude towards Hannah even went as far as cancelling an order the girl had made for a hat, on the grounds that the young lady was not fit to wear such a dignified article of clothing.

When she wrote to inform Johnny of her plans for Hannah, Lady Hesketh also spoke disparagingly of Mrs Unwin and it was not long before she was planning to remove her, too. Lady Hesketh had never understood Cowper's relationship with Mrs Unwin and had always considered her as more of a servant than Cowper's guardian. She had always been compelled to treat Mrs Unwin as an equal, however, as the latter came from a very good family, was extremely well read and had a tongue with which she was quite capable of defending herself. Now that Mrs Unwin was old and ill and unable to stand up for herself Lady Hesketh thought that Cowper was wasting his time looking after her. She did not understand the moral and spiritual debt the poet owed his old housekeeper and friend.

Hayley, on the other hand, was well aware of what Cowper owed Mrs Unwin and quite understood the poet's attachment to her. Referring to Cowper's illness back in 1773 he wrote,

> In 1773, he sunk into such severe paroxysms of religious despondency that he required an attendant of the most gentle, vigilant, and inflexible spirit. Such an attendant he found in that faithful guardian, whom he had professed to love as a mother, and who watched over him; during this long fit of depressive malady, extended through several years, with that perfect mixture of tenderness and fortitude, which constitutes the inestimable influence of maternal protection. I wish to pass rapidly over this calamitous period, and shall only observe, that nothing could surpass the sufferings of the patient, or excel the care of the nurse. For that meritorious care she received from Heaven the most delightful of rewards, in seeing, the pure all-powerful mind, to whose restoration she had contributed so much, not only gradually restored to the common enjoyments of life, but successively endowed with new and marvellous funds of diversified talents, and courageous application.[18]

Lady Hesketh spent the winter and much of the following year at Weston and during this time she did her best, by fair means and foul, to get Mrs Unwin to leave Weston and go to live with her daughter in Yorkshire. She did not seem to care where Hannah went, just as long as she went.

When Mrs Unwin refused to tolerate such ideas Lady Hesketh threatened to force Cowper to leave Weston on his own and was shocked (so she herself says) to hear Mrs Unwin say that even if the angel Gabriel himself were to try to separate Cowper from her, she would not agree. By this time Lady Hesketh was showing open enmity against the invalid woman and writing about her as if she thought she was a wicked witch. She now referred to her not by her proper name but as 'the enchantress' or 'the Old Lady', and she began to tease and taunt her mercilessly.

Mrs Unwin had difficulty holding herself erect as a result of her strokes but she made great efforts to keep her head high in spite of great pain. Lady Hesketh accused Mrs Unwin of faking her infirmities, saying that she could not be as ill as she pretended to be if she could hold her chin so high. This was, of course, a preposterous insult to the poor invalid and it was obvious that Lady Hesketh merely wanted to hurt her.

Another instance of Lady Hesketh's and Johnny Johnson's lack of feeling towards Mrs Unwin is shown by an incident concerning Mrs Unwin's teapot. She owned a beautiful old solid silver teapot with her family's crest on it. One day Johnny and Lady Hesketh said they would have it repaired. The teapot came back looking totally different and bearing the Cowper family crest. This upset Mrs Unwin badly and Lady Hesketh used the incident as another pretext to have a row with her. Cowper had to sit between the two quarrelling ladies and urge them to be at peace with each other.

Next Lady Hesketh decided to work on Johnny and persuade him to give up the appointment as a curate he had just taken up after his ordination, buy a house in Norfolk and then remove Cowper from Weston.

The effects on Cowper's health

During all this time Lady Hesketh was apparently completely unaware of what she was doing to her cousin in plotting to separate him from the very person who had destroyed her own health in looking after him. She was prepared to take any steps to better the poet's situation apart from asking him for his own opinion.

The thought of leaving Weston made Cowper tremble with fear and several times he lost his temper with Lady Hesketh. This is the first time that we ever read of him going into a rage. Yet Lady Hesketh took all these signs of anger and anguish on his part as further indications that she was right to take Cowper away from Weston. Once Cowper saw that his anger had no effect on his cousin, he merely left the room whenever she started being awkward. Lady Hesketh, who had taken his outbursts of temper as signs that he was demented, now thought that he was getting better.

Johnny was overjoyed to think that he would soon have Cowper under his care, but the poet was tired of being seen by him only as a subject to be pitied, without a will of his own, and he told Lady Hesketh that he did not want to see Johnny at Weston as long as he remained in such a state.

It is not surprising, in the light of all this, that Cowper complained to Teedon in January 1794, 'Never man was worried as I am, and unless God interpose marvellously for my deliverance, I must perish.' In a postcript, however, he added, 'Since I wrote the above I have had the Lord's presence largely for a few minutes.' This was, as far as we know, the last statement of hope that ever issued either from Cowper's pen or from his lips. He was about to enter a period of gloom with scarce any intermission and was to become the victim of the completely misguided machinations of his relatives. From this time on, Cowper no longer referred to Lady Hesketh with affection as 'Dear Cozzy-Wozzy-' or even 'Dearest Coz'. Similarly John Johnson was never again addressed by the poet as 'My dearest Johnny boy', nor even as 'Johnny', but merely as 'Mr Johnson', or plain 'Johnson'.

It was while Lady Hesketh was making these energetic attempts to force her will on Cowper that the poet sunk into deep depression in 1794 and appeared to regard his relations as his enemies, not even wanting to accept food from their hands. As we have seen in the last chapter, Hayley came to the rescue at Greatheed's bidding and Lady Hesketh and Johnson had to experience the mortification of seeing how much trust Cowper had in his fellow poet, in contrast to his attitude towards them.

Hayley had left his sickbed to attend to Cowper and was in a high fever himself. Furthermore, in his efforts to find financial backing for Cowper he had greatly neglected his own interests and was now in such extreme financial difficulties that he had to borrow the money for the journey to Weston from a friend. It was no doubt these facts, quite as much as her jealousy, that prompted Lady Hesketh to tell Hayley during this visit that he was as mad as her cousin.

Nevertheless, with the arrival of Hayley Cowper soon regained his appetite and he improved still further when Thomas Alphonso joined them. Hayley stayed with Cowper for a little over four weeks but then his own health broke down so completely that he had to leave Weston and take Thomas, who was far from strong himself, with him. Cowper was heartbroken at being parted from his friends. Alone once more with the relations who were causing him so much pain, the poet sunk into black despair.

The threat of impending departure

Whilst Cowper was frantically praying for a miracle to keep him with Mrs Unwin at Weston and to be left in peace, Lady Hesketh and Johnson were putting the finishing touches to their plan to remove their kinsman from the home he had come to love so much.

Johnson even went so far as to tell his sister Catharine that 'If anything short of a miracle can restore the Spirits of the most aimiable of men, as well as the greatest of Poets, it must be the step we are going to take.'[19] Incredible as it may seem, all Cowper's protests at what was happening to him were interpreted by Johnson as proof that he really wished to leave Weston. If Cowper ignored the topic, this was taken as his silent approval and when he complained in anguish that once he left the district, he would fall right into the hands of his 'tormentors', even this was taken as confirmation that deep down in his heart he really did want to get away from Weston. Never was there, to use a phrase of Hemingway's, such a 'fateful misunderstanding'.

Lady Hesketh and Johnson planned Cowper's removal well in advance, but failed to think out properly what would happen to him once he left Weston. Even a mere matter of days before their departure, their destination was still a matter of speculation. As a result Cowper was eventually dragged from house to house over a period of many months before Johnson decided they had found a permanent home for the poet in a 'rambling, dreary Lodge upon the hill at Dunham'. This is Johnson's own description of the home he had sought out for Cowper — and he knew that the poet did not like hills.

One change in plans had to be made, however. The two conspirators had now given up hope of separating Mrs Unwin from Cowper as she refused either to be parted from her 'son' or to give Lady Hesketh and Johnson the satisfaction of dying. Both Cowper and Mrs Unwin also insisted on carrying out their responsibilities

towards Hannah Wilson. As the whole point of the scheme seemed
to be to separate Mrs Unwin and Hannah from Cowper, one wonders
why Lady Hesketh and Johnson went ahead with their plans.
Johnson could have lived at Weston as happily as anywhere else. He
had enough personal income to live on and, though he had given up
his post as a curate, his influential relatives could soon have found
him a church near Weston or some sinecure post.

28 July 1795 was chosen as the departure date and Cowper
looked upon it as a day of doom. He felt that God had deserted him
and cast him out of paradise. According to Johnson, Cowper kept a
diary of his panic-stricken thoughts up to the day before his
departure. On 26 July he wrote, 'Awoke this morning and lay awake
4 hours Oh in what agonizing terrours! I have, I can have no faith in
this Norfolk journey, but am sure that either I shall never begin it,
or shall never reach the place. Could ye spare me, what mercy should
I account it.' The next day, the eve of their departure from Weston,
Cowper's words are even more harrowing:

> To morrow to the intolerable torments prepared for me.
> See now, O God, if this be a doom, if this a condition such as
> a creature of thine could have deserved to be exposed to. I
> know that thou thyself wast not without thy fears that I should
> incur it. But thou would'st set me on the slippery brink of this
> horrible pit in a state of infatuation little short of idiotism, and
> would'st in effect say to me — Die this moment or fall into
> it, and if you fall into it, be it your portion for ever. Such was
> not the mercy I expected from Thee, nor that horror and
> overwhelming misery should be the only means of deliver-
> ance left me in a moment so important! Farewell to the
> remembrance of Thee for ever. I must now suffer thy wrath,
> but forget that I ever heard thy name. Oh horrible! and Still
> more horrible, that I write these last lines with a hand that is
> not permitted to tremble![20]

Farewell to Weston

The last thing Cowper did at Weston was to leave a pathetic
reminder of his having lived there on one of the window shutters.
First he wrote,

> Farewell, dear scenes, for ever closed to me,
> Oh, for what sorrows must I now exchange ye!

Then he added words which can hardly be equalled as an expression of agony of soul:

> Me miserable! how could I escape
> Infinite wrath and infinite despair!
> Whom Death, Earth, Heaven, and Hell consigned to ruin,
> Whose friend was God, but God swore not to aid me!

On the day of departure Johnson, who described himself as 'abundantly delighted' and 'enchanted' that Cowper was now under his care, hired two coaches to transport Cowper, Mrs Unwin, Hannah Wilson and the Roberts, Cowper's ever-faithful servants, to North Tuddenham, a two-days' journey away. There Cowper was to be the guest of Catharine Johnson and her friend Miss Perowne for several weeks.

At the start of the journey it was obvious that Cowper was expecting something terrible to happen when they reached Olney, but Johnson pulled down the blinds and diverted his thoughts with conversation. Soon Cowper became fairly cheerful and muttered to himself that he was in a delightful dream. During the first evening stop on the Great North Road, Cowper and Johnson went for a moonlight walk in the nearby churchyard and the poet conversed at great length with his kinsman about the poet Thomson. Johnson felt it was like old times. This was the last cheerful conversation, according to Johnson, he was ever to have with Cowper even though the poet was to live with him for another five years.

Once at North Tuddenham Johnson took Cowper to see his cousin Anne Bodham at Mattishall, the next village. The poet was hardly in the house before he was presented with a painful reminder that he was no longer at Weston and his home had been broken up. There on the wall was his own portrait, painted at Weston by Abbott. Cowper clasped his hands together and with a heartbreaking sigh wished that he was once again enjoying those relatively blessed days at Weston.

It is still a matter of conjecture what happened to much of Cowper's belongings and furniture after his forced departure from Weston. Tracing the history of items in the Olney Museum shows that many of Cowper's personal belongings were spread abroad soon after he left Weston. Certainly some plundering, especially of the poet's unpublished works, furniture and garden fittings, must have taken place. Cowper's faithful servant Sam was able to rescue several important manuscripts but many others 'disappeared' mysteriously and are lost or, at least, still awaiting rediscovery. Cowper's much-loved sundial was immediately removed from his garden after he left Weston and placed in the garden at Throckmorton Hall. The 'Frogs' also set up Cowper's bust of Homer in the 'Wilderness' where Cowper had loved to walk. Their butler came into posession of Cowper's fly table and articles of the poet's bedding were spread far and wide around Weston.

Move to Mundesley

Whilst staying at North Tuddenham, Johnson looked out for a place of permanent residence and found a house to let in Mundesley, twenty miles from Norwich on the Norfolk coast not far from Cromer.

As soon as Cowper settled in at Mundesley, Johnson took him to see all the sights around and on one of these trips the two men hired a room at a lodging-house and had a meal prepared. Johnson screwed up his nose at what was put before them. It was 'very ordinary food', consisting of 'very old' beans and bacon and apple pie, 'the worst I ever saw'. To Johnson's amazement, Cowper tucked in with a hearty appetite as if there were nothing more delicious in this world. Although this surprised Johnson, it need not surprise readers who are familiar with Cowper's mind and writings at the time. For a long time the poet had hardly eaten more than a scrap of food given to him by Lady Hesketh or Johnson as he was afraid that they were trying to poison him. Now that he had the chance of eating a meal prepared by others, no matter how humble, his natural appetite was allowed full sway.

The beach at Mundesley was flanked by high cliffs, and Cowper, always afraid of heights, was terrified at the view down from the cliff-top. As he saw the cliffs being eroded mercifully by the sea he thought of his own life ebbing away far from the place he had come to love as his home. He told Lady Hesketh: 'At two miles' distance on the coast is a solitary pillar of rock, that the crumbling cliff has left at the high water-mark. I have visited it twice, and have found it an emblem of myself. Torn from my natural connexions, I stand alone and expect the storm that shall displace me.'

Cowper is obviously rubbing home the point that Lady Hesketh is to blame for his situation. He closes his letter by wishing that he could end it 'affectionately yours', but explains that every feeling that would warrant such a display of affection has long since, as Lady Hesketh well knows, left his bosom. If the poet had been as blunt as this with his cousin earlier, he might have spared himself years of lethargy and anxiety.

Cowper was still unable to be equally frank with Johnson who, he realized, was acting according to the lights he had in looking after his kinsman. William Blake, the poet and artist, who was later to befriend Johnson, said of him that he was 'known by all his Friends as the most innocent forgetter of his own interests'.[21] This is undoubtedly true but Johnson was not always good at judging what other people's best interests were.

Once, when Johnson was away, Cowper took the opportunity to write to his old friend and neighbour the Rev. John Buchanan at Weston. He wanted to know what was going on at Weston, 'my beloved Weston, since I left it, hopeless of ever seeing it again'. Surprisingly Cowper hints to Buchanan that if Johnson had been at home, he would not have allowed the poet to write in order to satisfy his curiosity concerning the place he loved. The sum total of the letter to his old friend is that Cowper is bored but his boredom is alleviated by the long walks of over fifteen miles he takes and the beautiful views out at sea. The last line to Buchanan is sad and pathetic. 'Tell me if my poor birds are living,' says the poet. 'I never see the herbs I used to give them without a recollection of them, and sometimes am ready to gather them, forgetting that I am not at home.'

It is indeed a pity that Johnson was not present to read Cowper's letter and to repent of the sorrow he had brought on his lonely kinsman. In mentioning his birds Cowper had put his finger on the crux of his dilemma. His motto had always been:

An idler is a watch that wants both hands,
As useless if it goes as when it stands.[22]

The poet regarded practical work, and especially gardening and animal husbandry, as the primeval duty of man since the Fall. To Cowper the sin of idleness in not doing one's duty as God's under-gardener and steward on earth was as great as that of committing lewdness or breaking the Sabbath.[23] Furthermore, keeping himself occupied with physical work had always been a means Cowper had used to ban melancholy. When the poet was so very ill in 1773, for instance, he gradually recovered his mental health through his close contact with his animals. Newton noticed one day that when feeding his chickens, Cowper was so amused by their droll behaviour that he began to chuckle. It was then that Newton first realized that his friend was on the mend. Later, taming his hares had helped Cowper to keep his own feelings under control.

Now, removed from his pets, his hens, his ducks, geese, pigs and cows (Cowper had bought two whilst at Weston) the poet felt like a watch without hands. Johnson was aware of this and was con-stantly giving him 'therapeutic' work to do. It was, however, a poor substitute for the healthy meaningful outdoor work Cowper had done hitherto. Typical of Johnson's methods to pass the time was when he gave Cowper the task of signing his name in all the four hundred books he had rescued from Weston.

Johnson, full of the kindest intentions, now began to patronize Cowper to a high degree, telling him when he was expected to take up a revision of his Homer and when he ought to write and to whom. Lady Hesketh began to call Johnson Cowper's 'General'. Earlier biographers have claimed that when Cowper said that he had been told to write, he was referring to imaginary demons who were dictating to him what he should do.[24] This was a ridiculous assertion, as the 'demons' were no more and no less than Johnson, who was striving to ban Cowper's burdens and fears and occupy his mind productively. Johnson was, however, denying Cowper his own will more and more and the poet found it was 'cruel' to have to write to order.

Once Johnson went on a journey to Weston, of all places; why, Cowper did not know. As he was leaving he told Cowper that if he wrote at all it must be to Newton. Summoning up all that was left to him of his self-determination, Cowper told Johnson that he would not. Instead he wrote to Lady Hesketh and told her, quoting Isaiah, 'I shall never see Weston more. I have been tossed like a ball into a far country, from which there is no rebound for me ... to have passed the little time that remained to me there, was the desire of my heart.

My heart's desire, however, has been always frustrated in every thing that it has settled on, and by means that have made my disappointments inevitable.'[25] Lady Hesketh took this letter as an insult after all she had done for her cousin to get him away from Weston. She never bothered to visit Cowper once after forcing him to leave the home he loved.

Move to Dunham Lodge

In October 1795 Johnson took his guests to live for a few weeks at his home in East Dereham, a small but busy market town in Norfolk. Cowper was comparatively happy there and obviously expected that they would now settle down in East Dereham and stop moving around. Lady Hesketh, however, was convinced that East Dereham would be too noisy for Cowper and insisted on their moving to Dunham Lodge, which was remote and quiet.

From Johnson's letters we also learn that he honestly beieved East Dereham was the last place Cowper really wanted to live in. This was because Johnson never seemed to take Cowper's words at their face value but always read into them what he thought Cowper really meant. For instance, when Cowper entered Johnson's home in East Dereham, thinking it was to be his permanent abode, he said to Johnson, 'I thank you for this.' Johnson gives his interpretation of these few words: 'I thought, at the time he spoke it — he meant something of this sort "I thank you for letting me pass the *night here*, instead of with the *Tormentors*."'[26] Later Johnson realized that Cowper meant what he had said and nothing more. As Johnson is the main source of information concerning what went on in Cowper's mind during the last years of his life, it is evident from the many obvious cases where Cowper *said* things which Johnson *interpreted* in a highly imaginative way, that the latter is not always a reliable factual source.

Further trials at East Dereham

Though Cowper did some little work on Homer at Dunham Lodge, he felt more and more miserable as time went on. Eventually, realizing that Cowper liked the Lodge as little as he did himself, but still not heeding the poet's pleas in favour of East Dereham, Johnson removed his entire household back to Mundesley. They were hardly seven weeks there when Cowper eventually put his foot down and persuaded Johnson to take them all to East Dereham.

Johnson, Cowper, Mrs Unwin and Miss Perowne now settled down in Johnson's own house but further trials accompanied the poet. Even at East Dereham Lady Hesketh's controlling hand influenced all that took place. Cowper had become inseparable from his manservant, Samuel Roberts, who had been with him ever since his days at St Albans. Sam had been converted through Cowper's witness and had remained true to Christ and faithful to Cowper. This servant and friend Lady Hesketh now decided was superfluous at East Dereham and dismissed him and his wife Anne from Cowper's service. They went to live with Sam's mother at Weston.

A few weeks after moving to East Dereham, Cowper lost another faithful friend of eleven years standing. Beau, the subject of several of Cowper's poems, was found dead on the parlour carpet. One of the poet's last more cheerful poems, written in July 1793, had been an affectionate description of an occasion when Beau killed a fledgling:

On a Spaniel Called Beau Killing a Young Bird

A Spaniel, Beau, that fares like you,
Well-fed, and at his ease,
Should wiser be, than to pursue
Each trifle that he sees.

But you have kill'd a tiny bird,
Which flew not till to-day,
Against my orders, whom you heard
Forbidding you the prey.

Nor did you kill, that you might eat,
And ease a doggish pain,
For him, though chas'd with furious heat,
You left where he was slain.

Nor was he of the thievish sort,
Or one whom blood allures,
But innocent was all his sport,
Whom you have torn for yours.

My dog! what remedy remains,
Since, teach you all I can,
I see you, after all my pains,
So much resemble man!

Beau's Reply

Sir I when I flew to seize the bird,
In spite of your command.
A louder voice than yours I heard,
And harder to withstand:

You cried — Forbear! — but in my breast
A mightier cried — Proceed!
'Twas nature, Sir, whose strong behest
Impell'd me to the deed.

Yet much as nature I respect,
I ventur'd once to break
(As you perhaps may recollect)
Her precept, for your sake;

And when your linnet, on a day,
Passing his prison-door,
Had flutter'd all his strength away,
And panting press'd the floor,

Well knowing him a sacred thing,
Not destin'd to my tooth,
I only kiss'd his ruffled wing,
And lick'd the feathers smooth.

Let my obedience then excuse
My disobedience now,
Nor some reproof yourself refuse
From your aggriev'd Bow-wow!

If killing birds be such a crime,
(Which I can hardly see)
What think you, Sir, of killing Time
With verse address'd to me?

Even over the death of Beau Johnson revealed how different his thoughts and opinions were to those of Cowper. The poet belonged to a class of Christians, including his contemporaries William Bull, John Newton, John Ryland and Augustus Toplady, who saw animals as recipients of some form of everlasting grace linked with the restitution of all things at the coming of Christ.[27] An animal was a creation of God with a definite eschatological purpose and woe be to the man who trod negligently on a snail or even a worm! Not realizing this, Johnson had Beau stuffed and put in a glass case in his home where the dog's master could see him daily.

The taxidermist, however, made a number of blunders. Forgetting to measure Beau before preparing the animal for stuffing, he stretched the skin so much that the resulting 'Beau resurrected' had quite different proportions to Beau in his former life. The thoroughbred spaniel looked as though he had had a sausage-dog in his not-too-distant ancestry. Johnson arranged for the stuffed dog to have a water lily in its mouth. The resulting plant concocted by the taxidermist had a water lily head perched on a long stiff stem adorned with convolvulus leaves. The taxidermist was obviously as bad at botany as he was at stuffing animals — and Cowper, the keen botanist and one-time master of beloved Beau had to look at the monstrosity for the rest of his life!

Death of Mrs Unwin

Cowper could not pause long to mourn the loss of his four-legged friend as a greater loss was at hand. Mrs Unwin took a turn for the worse after being taken to East Dereham and by December she was obviously terminally ill. She died on 17 December and Johnson wondered how he could break the news to Cowper. He opened a book and began reading to the poet, obviously wishing to compose Cowper's mind before he had to face the shock. After a few moments, he put the book down and told Cowper what had happened. Johnson did not allow Cowper to see Mrs Unwin until her body had been prepared for burial and it was growing dark, thinking, oddly enough, that Cowper would be able to stand the sight better in the twilight. After looking intently at his dear old friend, Cowper clasped his hands together, looked up to heaven in agony of soul and cried out, according to Johnson, 'Oh God — was it for this?'

Mrs Unwin was buried by torchlight at 7.30 p.m. on 23 December. Cowper was neither invited to nor told of the burial which was timed so late in the day because of one of Johnson's whims. The Powleys had come down from Yorkshire three days after Mrs Unwin's death, hoping to find her still alive. They were the only people, apart from Johnson and Miss Perowne, who took part in the burial.

Mrs Unwin was hardly laid to rest when Lady Hesketh wrote to Johnson one of the most callous letters she had ever written. She still had apparently no idea of the Christian love, respect, affection and gratitude the poet had felt for his invalid housekeeper and friend, and wrote that Mrs Unwin had been 'totally useless in all respects' to her cousin and a 'dead weight' on his shoulders. Her death, according to Lady Hesketh, was a 'Release to everyone'.

Lady Hesketh had obviously not learnt from the last poem Cowper had written before her fateful visit in the autumn of 1793 which was to more or less end his poetic career. It was written after the first signs had been given that Lady Hesketh was intent on driving out the 'swarms' which 'infested' Cowper's kitchen. The poet had read an article in the *Buckinghamshire Herald* about two chaffinches which had built their nest in the tackling of a ship whilst it was docked at Greenock. One bird was away looking for food and the other bird was left sitting on their four eggs when suddenly the ship sailed out of the dock for the high seas. When the foraging bird came back, his mate was gone but he flew all around the docks until he found the right ship and the two were reunited for the entire journey. Cowper used this story to outline what true friendship was and how it carried true friends through all the trials and troubles of life. He makes it quite clear in the poem that the foraging bird would have been much better off if he had left his mate to face the stormy seas alone but his love and responsibilities prevented him from doing so. Perhaps Cowper had got wind of what Lady Hesketh planned to do with Mrs Unwin and thus wrote the poem to show that there was no such thing as being 'totally useless' or 'a dead weight' in true friendship.

William Hayley shared Cowper's higher opinion of Mrs Unwin. His views of Mrs Unwin's relationship to Cowper were kinder and more Christian and showed far more understanding than Lady Hesketh's. He summed up her true relationship to Cowper in his epigraph for her gravestone:

> Trusting in God, with all her heart and mind,
> This woman proved magnanimously kind;
> Endured affliction's desolating hail,
> And watch'd a Poet thro' misfortune's vale:
> Her spotless dust angelic guards defend,
> It is the dust of Unwin, Cowper's friend!
> That single title in itself is fame,
> For all, who read his verse, revere her name.

Mrs Unwin had well deserved such a telling epitaph.

Johnson says little about Cowper in the first six months of 1797 apart from the facts that he was growing fatter and had developed a double-chin. The poet had started to sleep in the early afternoons on a couch in a room adjoining Johnson's study. Johnson had a large stand-mirror placed at the correct angle in the doorway between the two rooms so that when Cowper awoke, he would not feel deserted but see Johnson working away at his desk.

Teedon had been trying for some time to contact Cowper but Johnson, at Lady Hesketh's bidding, had warded off all attempts by the schoolmaster to approach either Cowper or Lady Hesketh herself. Lady Hesketh was no doubt worried that Teedon might scrounge on her for his Olney work. A year later Teedon died but Lady Hesketh told Johnson to keep the news from Cowper and arranged for the financial support Cowper gave Teedon annually to be given to the schoolmaster's dependents who continued to help with the school.

Meanwhile, Lady Hesketh had a new idea. She wrote to Johnson in June 1797 telling him that he should give up the post he now held as curate to several churches in East Dereham and, through the influence of her cousin, the Bishop of Peterborough, obtain a living in Lincolnshire. In that county Cowper could then be entrusted to the care of the king's medical adviser, Dr Francis Willis, who was notorious for his harsh treatment of the mentally ill and his use of strait-jackets and gags. Her idea was that Cowper should live in Willis's asylum and Johnson could visit him there from time to time. Johnson is to be commended for refusing to enter into this new scheme of Lady Hesketh's. Besides, Cowper was now busy at work on yet another edition of his Homer and showing that, apart from his longing to be back at Weston and his sense of doom, he was still a rational being on all other counts and fully capable of academic work.

Hayley's 'vision'

Perhaps Johnson discussed Lady Hesketh's new proposals with Cowper, as something happened in the middle of June to send the poet into one of his worst depressions. Johnson was sensible enough to recognize that Hayley was the only person able to cheer the poet up when he himself failed to do so and so he told Cowper to write to his much neglected-friend. Cowper wrote only two sentences which Hayley described to his son as 'a few of the most gloomy and pathetic lines that ever flowed from the pen of depression': 'Ignorant of everything but my own instant and impending Misery, I know neither what I do when I write nor can do otherwise than write because I am bidden to do so. Perfect Despair the most perfect that ever possess'd any Mind has had Possession of mine you know how long, and knowing that, will not need to be told who writes.'[28]

Hayley pondered over this letter for two days, sitting with his elbows on his knees and his face in his hands, trying to work out what he could do for his friend. His mind wandered and he went off into a fit of day-dreaming. It was then that the idea came. He saw with his inward eye the throne of God with his own mother and Cowper's praying before it. An angel came to him and told him that Cowper would recover and that soon Members of Parliament, judges, bishops, the prime minister and even the king would be writing to him and he should take this as a sign indicating that heaven had granted him a 'celestial Emancipation from Despair'. Finally the heavenly messenger told Hayley to write quickly to Cowper and tell him the good news.

Very early the next morning, Hayley saddled his horse and rode over to Chichester to consult a doctor friend on whether this kind of information would help a person who suffered form depression. So keen was he on his errand that he did not realize that other people were still in bed when he arrived and his doctor friend appeared in the parlour, rubbing the sleep out of his eyes, wearing his nightshirt. Never one to be made embarrassed by causing such inconvenience, Hayley approached the good doctor, took hold of his pulse and told him with mock gravity that he should not allow himself to be dragged out of a warm bed so soon. He then told him of the poet's letter and his thoughts concerning his solution to Cowper's problems. The doctor, who appears to have known Cowper, thought the idea was just the right thing to lift him out of his dejection. Hayley then went home to write a letter to Cowper informing him of his 'ecstatic vision'. He also decided to write one to Johnson, too, to keep on the right side of Cowper's relations whom he knew to be very reluctant allies.

Hayley had to wait almost three weeks before Johnson replied and went through a thousand anxieties in the meantime. Johnson seemed to be favourably impressed with the idea and said that Cowper had read the letter in silence, which Johnson took to mean that the poet was cheered by the news. Hayley was now doubly rewarded as he felt he had pleased both Cowper and Johnson. The latter sent Hayley's letter to Lady Hesketh and asked her for her comments. Lady Hesketh thought that Hayley's idea was basically good. She put her finger, however, at once on the weak spot. What would happen now if Cowper received no letters? She thus wrote to Hayley, putting this question to him, suggesting that there was no possibility of a flow of letters such as he had described.

Hayley was not the man to have such a 'vision' and not be given the wherewithal to back it up. He duly got down to work. William Wilberforce was the first to be approached and that godly man was soon sending off a two-paged letter to the poet, enclosing a book he had recently written. Hayley got in touch with Thurlow, who told friends that one mad poet was soliciting on behalf of another but promised, nevertheless, to induce prominent people to write to Cowper. Thurlow even sent a draft of a letter to Lord Kenyon outlining what he thought would be suitable words. Lady Hesketh felt that Thurlow himself should not write as the 'vision' would best be fulfilled by letter-writers who were more or less strangers to Cowper. Next Hayley contacted a bevy of bishops. The Bishop of London, Dr Beilby Porteous, wrote a long letter to Cowper encouraging him to trust in the truths of his own lines,

> That he, who died below, and reigns above,
> Inspires the Song, and that his name is Love!

telling him that he must possess that love as much as any man alive. 'Not an atom of it,' was Cowper's reply.

Cowper, of course, had seen through the ruse and objected strongly to it and said he felt he was being derided. Johnson cried out, 'Say not so, of the good Beilby, Bishop of London!' to which Cowper replied, 'I should say so of an Archangel, were it possible for an Archangel to send me such a Letter, in such Circumstances.'

Sometimes letters came at the most appropriate moment. Johnson was reading the Bishop of Llandaff's book *Apology for Christianity* to Cowper when a three-paged letter from that very person arrived. Soon Cowper had received a good number of letters from prominent Christians, the last being from the writer Hannah More, who also sent Cowper two of her volumes. It all left Cowper cold, although Johnson still stuck to his theory that when Cowper did not comment, it meant his approval, and the poet had only actually protested at the Bishop of London's letter.

The ruse might have worked if they had stuck to Hayley's 'vision'. Lady Hesketh and Johnson, however, lacked the ability to carry such a thing through with the efficiency of someone like Hayley and blundered badly over it, overdoing things immensely. Lady Hesketh, as remote-controller and stage manager, began to tell Johnson and his helpers by letter how to organize little scenes built around the letters to Cowper and how they should always arrange for the conversation to centre around them when the poet was present. The willing helpers learnt their parts and performed little one-act plays about the letters in true amateur dramatic spirit. Johnson would suddenly say, as if the idea had just come to him, 'Miss Perowne. Don't you recollect something about a Letter's coming to Mr C. in the summer from Mr Hayley, containing a wonderful vision which He had lately had?' Miss Perowne then took up her cue and replied, 'I certainly do remember it and have often thought of it since.' Then Sam Dent, who had been given Samuel Roberts' job, would perform his part, after which Miss Perowne would get up and innocently say, as if she were in a Jane Austen novel, 'By the by I will go and look for Mr H's letter.' Cowper — the only non-actor on stage — would say, 'No pray don't!', but the play had to go on. It was no wonder that Cowper thought he was being taken for a ride. Not to be outdone by Hayley, Lady Hesketh announced some time later that she had had a similar dream to Hayley's but by this time Cowper was not willing to be duped at all.

When Hayley heard that his 'vision' had not been successful, he wrote to Lady Hesketh saying that he was thinking of buying a smaller house at Felpham, the small town near Eartham, and he would like to give Cowper his mansion. He then added, most likely with his tongue in his cheek, that Lady Hesketh could move in to Eartham with Cowper so that she could nurse him. Lady Hesketh was shaken by the 'astonishing idea' and politely refused the offer.

As a token of appreciation for Hayley's efforts on Cowper's part, however, she presented him with a silver writing set.

Dreams and voices in the night

All this time Cowper was spending nights of extraordinary terror. He often dreamt that he was called by an evil-looking personage to take a glimpse behind some thick curtaining where the poet saw an executioner getting the block ready to support the neck of the next victim. Then Cowper would see himself being lead to the block to be slaughtered.

Johnson was fascinated by these dreams and recorded them one by one in a book, which he had bound specially for the purpose and entitled *Pro and Contra,* and tried to interpret them. He became preoccupied in seeking unnatural causes in them and soon he himself was hearing noises just like Cowper and becoming convinced that strange powers were on the loose in his house. Johnson got far more excited about these things than Cowper but all of this was hardly any comfort to the poet. Johnson would go to his 'patient' in the mornings, whilst the horror of his nightmares was still upon him, and ask him to describe his nightly torments. The best thing that can happen to such dreams is that they disappear when the sufferer awakes. Discussing and 'analysing' Cowper's nightmares during the daytime made them more real to him and they stuck in his memory all the more. Thus Cowper was haunted by his terrors for the rest of the day.

This was not, however, Johnson's greatest folly in misguidedly doing his best to help Cowper. The poet always referred to voices that condemned him in the night. These voices, as far as can be ascertained, were understood by the poet as impressions on the mind rather than acoustic manifestations. Nevertheless, Johnson thought he had found a cure. He got workmen to make a hidden hole in the wall between his bedroom and Cowper's and affixed a long tin tube to it. Then at various times in the night Johnson would rouse Cowper from his nightmares by booming 'comforting words' through the hole in the wall like a disembodied Pyramus talking to Thisbe. It is not known how Cowper reacted to this farce, though it probably added to his misery. During his last few years of life, the poet regarded any word of hope as an attempt to mock him, and here were his best friends haunting him throughout the night with ghostly voices uttered down an echoing speaking-tube!

The 'Castaway'

The one theme that occurred again and again in Cowper's letters after he was forced away from Weston was that he was not free and that 'There can be no peace where there is no freedom.' Linked to this was the conviction that he was lost because he had been transplanted from his true home. Cowper interpreted this both physically and spiritually.

In early 1799 Johnson read a newspaper story to Cowper about a number of icebergs which had broken loose from a sea of ice and floated many hundreds of miles into warmer, for them alien, waters. The poet felt that the story was an apt illustration of what had happened to him. This caused Cowper to write two original poems on the topic, both in Latin and English. The first he called 'On the Ice Islands' and the second, 'The Castaway', was written immediately following it as if they were one poem. 'On the Ice Islands' is a poetic description of the movement of the icebergs until their destruction from 'the darts of Phœbus, and a softer air'. These, the poet tells us, should be a warning to all to keep to their natural abode:

> Lest ye regret, too late, your native coast,
> In no congenial gulf for ever lost.

'The Castaway' is a more tragic piece and might well have been written as a personal interpretation of what 'The Ice-Islands' signified to Cowper. The poem tells the true story of a sailor who was washed overboard in stormy seas and, though all his friends were near at hand, they could not get him back into the boat and eventually were forced to leave him to perish. After describing the sailor's tragedy of being 'deserted, and his friends so nigh', Cowper turns to his own case and writes,

> But misery still delights to trace
> Its 'semblance in another case.

No voice divine the storm allay'd,
No light propitious shone;
When, snatch'd from all effectual aid,
We perish'd, each alone:
But I beneath a rougher sea,
And whelm'd in deeper gulphs than he.

Cowper's last original work, 'The Castaway', has provided many a biographer with a platform on which to build his theory of Cowper's life and poetic ability. Although this poem was Cowper's sole poetic testimony to absolute despair since his conversion, and although it was written at a time of life when he was at his worst health-wise, it is still taken by many modern writers, such as King and Newey, to be the truest and clearest testimony to Cowper's lack of faith and abundance of ability and it is seen as the key whereby critics are able to open the secrets of all his poetry. The very uniqueness of the 'Castaway' ought to make commentators cautious about drawing too many conclusions from it. The mood and convictions expressed in this poem are not typical of Cowper's works, nor were they a permanent part of his mental make-up. It is ridiculous to use the 'Castaway' as the touchstone and key to the interpretation of all Cowper's other works, as it is obvious that the poet is referring in the poem to his post-Weston period and to the intense gloom it brought with it.

Cowper had a yo-yo-like nature which ever swung him from 'downs' to 'ups'. The bulk of his optimistic, believing verse provides ample evidence that his heart and head throughout his comparatively long life were chiefly influenced by the 'ups'. He suffered longer spells of depression in the last year of his life than at any time before and during this period Cowper was at his least creative. Yet this 'lesser creation' of Cowper's is projected back onto Cowper's entire life and used as the key to its interpretation.

The poetic ability manifested in the 'Castaway' has been denied by none. The poem is generally seen to be, in the words of William N. Free, 'one of Cowper's greatest and most Romantic poems'. Its thematic similarities with Romantic works such as 'The Rime of the Ancient Mariner', with which it is often compared, are, however, mainly superficial. Cowper, true to himself, compares himself spiritually with an event that actually took place. Coleridge's poem is all sheer fantasy. The 'Ancient Mariner' is couched in a thickly laid on poetic diction which Cowper would have reserved only for his most humorous or satirical poetry. Apart from perhaps the phrase 'the whelming brine', Cowper's language is the true language of seafaring men and of his contemporaries. Coleridge's poem is fraught with superstition, whereas Cowper's poem reflects sheer resignation to fate.

The fact that Cowper's poem, like Coleridge's, reveals so much inner reflection, indicates that the poet has taken a great step from his Neo-Classical days and is to be seen as the pioneer of the Romantic movement. This factor is strengthened by the acutely personal testimony in the poem, which is supposed to be typically 'Romantic', though Coleridge's work only reflects indirectly on the author. Indeed Bernard Martin, in his Newton biography, *An Ancient Mariner,* more than suggests that Coleridge had John Newton's escapades on the ill-fated *Greyhound* in mind when writing 'The Rime of the Ancyent Marinere',[29] as his famous Romantic poem was originally called. Comparing feature with feature would suggest that 'The Castaway' is far more Romantic in theme and structure than Coleridge's work, which is heavy in poetic diction and concepts borrowed from ancient pagan poetry.

According to Cowper's own theory of poetry, however, the 'Castaway' is not poetry at all, as its language is not that of Eden and does not suffice to act as a means of communication that unites the longing soul with God. When the 'Castaway' is compared with the *Task*, it pales and withers into insignificance.

Cowper's last days

In the autumn of 1799 Johnson decided to move to yet another house in East Dereham. This time he first consulted Cowper as the house was in the busiest part of the town, but Cowper said at once that he liked it. They moved in on 11 December and as soon as Cowper entered the house, he took possession of it by curling himself up on a couch and falling fast asleep.

For a few weeks the poet seemed in comparatively good health and he worked on a new revision of his *Iliad* and translated several other short classical works into English and Gay's *Fables* into Latin. By the end of January, however, Cowper's legs began to swell rapidly and it was soon clear that he had developed dropsy. Realizing that Cowper was in very bad shape, Johnson sent a letter to Hayley, begging him to come and help, but Hayley's own son, Thomas Alphonso, who was still not out of his teens, was on his deathbed and Hayley could not come.

Cowper died on Friday, 25 April 1800. He was suffering from no particularly fatal disease, according to the doctor's report. He merely died because he was completely worn out.

There is a hopeful story attached to Cowper's death. When Johnson went into the poet's room at five minutes to five on that Friday afternoon, he saw that Cowper was dead. Yet the poet's face had changed dramatically. Gone was the look of terror and anxiety that had so caused his brow to fold and his eyes to appear swollen and frightened. He wore, according to Johnson's words, a relaxed smile — a look of holy surprise.

We shall give John Newton the last word. When the old mariner heard of Cowper's death, though bowed down with infirmities, rapidly going blind and deaf and with his memory in ruins, he quickly penned a few verses expressing his longing to be gone from this earth and to be once again with his companion of so many years. After describing his friendship with Cowper he went on to say, looking 'far beyond Jordan':

My friend, my friend! and have we met again,
Far from the home of woe, the home of men;
And hast thou taken thy glad harp once more,
Twined with far lovelier wreaths than e'er before;
And is thy strain more joyous and more loud,
While circle round thee heaven's attentive crowd?

Oh! let thy memory wake! I told thee so;
I told thee thus would end thy heaviest woe;
I told thee that thy God would bring thee here,
And God's own hand would wipe away thy tear
While I should claim a mansion by thy side,
I told thee so — for our Emmanuel died.

Postscript

When Cowper died, Hayley was struggling with the realization that his own son, Thomas Alphonso, was fast approaching the end of his earthly pilgrimage even though he was still not twenty years of age. Within a week of Cowper's death he, too, was dead and Hayley had lost the two people whom he loved most in the world. His third best friend, Romney, was seriously ill and was shortly to follow Cowper and Thomas Alphonso. Hayley now fell into a fit of despondency so deep that his friends began to fear that he would end his life as Cowper had done.

Anna Seward, the 'Swan of Lichfield', who had shown great jealousy of Hayley's admiration for Cowper,[1] wrote critically of the latter in her publications and told Thomas Park, a joint friend of the three, in a private letter that Hayley would never break down under the weight of sorrow as even when his son died, he could ease his pain by composing verse. Miss Seward was obviously insinuating that Hayley's sadness was not really genuine and in this she was quite wrong. She was correct, however, in assuming that Hayley could forget himself in writing in praise of others.

After a short period of mourning Hayley went into a whirlwind of action, planning a major work, *The Christian Navigator,* preparing a biography of his son and campaigning for a monument to be erected to Cowper's memory. Hayley planned to have on his own tomb the simple inscription, 'The Friend of Cowper',[2] yet he believed that Cowper had deserved a tomb fit for a king and set about planning an edifice that would have been the envy of many a monarch. Lady Hesketh, however, clashed with him on this matter.

She argued that a great monument was all very well for some get-rich-quick soap-boiler who had nothing else to be remembered by, but her cousin would be remembered for his work rather than the size of his tombstone. The good lady was right in this but this time Hayley would not kowtow to her as he felt it was not his own honour that was at stake but Cowper's. He thus set his own poetic abilities to work and also enlisted the help of the sculptor Flaxman and poet-engraver Blake.

Work begins on a biography

Soon Hayley was to start on an undertaking which was to bring him back into public acclaim and line his pockets with at least £11,000, an unbelievable sum in those days. Greatheed had started on a biography of Cowper but, because of very personal and obviously highly dramatized and misleading details he had spread concerning Cowper's life, he had aroused the animosity of Lady Hesketh and in so doing lost all claims to be Cowper's 'official' biographer, with access to documents that Johnson quickly put under copyright.[3]

Newton had never been in Lady Hesketh's good books as she attributed to him much of the blame for causing Cowper's 1773 illness. There was also the matter of Newton's funeral sermon, which had been, to say the least, highly indiscreet, and which stood in the way of any co-operation between him and Lady Hesketh; and any biography, she insisted, could only be published with her blessing. Newton had attempted to write a biography but got no further than writing sixteen pages of undiluted praise and floundered when he came to the unsolvable problem of the poet's melancholy.

Realizing what a tremendous obstacle Lady Hesketh could be, but at the same time what a powerful ally she would make, Hayley trod cautiously and cunningly. In July 1800 he wrote to Johnson, suggesting that the latter should write a biography of his kinsman. Johnson was now, however, happily settled down in pastoral work and was also occupied with planning a new edition of Cowper's *Homer* and editing the poet's letters for publication. He thus, as Hayley had hoped, quickly declined the offer.

Next Hayley wrote to Lady Hesketh, telling her that hers was the only heart, memory and hand capable of accomplishing such a task. Lady Hesketh was completely bowled over by such a suggestion and the animosity and jealousy she had felt towards Hayley crumbled and all but disappeared. She wrote back, offering, in her own words, a 'pacific letter' and 'an olive branch', claiming that Hayley was the very man for the job and not herself. However, she gave the would-be biographer very strict orders about what was to be written and what not.

Hayley quickly finished the biography of his son that he was working on and by the autumn of 1800 he was hard at work on a *Life* of Cowper. This entailed a great deal of research and travelling, as Lady Austen, possibly Theadora, Greatheed, Newton, Hill, Thurlow, Bagot and many other old friends of Cowper's had to be consulted.

Lady Hesketh was highly displeased to find that Hayley had chosen Greatheed as his right-hand man in obtaining information. She wrote a warning letter to Hayley in which she said, 'Oh dear — can you Sir really suppose that I feel no enmity against the Man who has destroy'd my peace of mind for ever! — who has injured a whole family in its tenderest point! — has cruelly and inhumanly revealed Secrets disclosed to Him, under the sacred seal of Friendship! And broke ev'ry tye that binds man to man.' 'There was good reason for Lady Hesketh's warning but Hayley was satisfied he could handle Greatheed, and, indeed, became good friends with him.

Hayley the gentleman and Greatheed the gallant ex-officer looked to Lady Austen to provide them with a good deal of information and they soon found themselves quite hypnotized by her charm. The resulting stories they obtained from her concerning Cowper make excellent entertaining reading but directly contradict other well-established facts. Such experiences with his 'sources' made it highly difficult for Hayley to sift the wheat from the chaff as Cowper had appealed to a wide range of people, most of whom placed different interpretations on the poet's actions and words.

William Blake was a tower of strength to Hayley and worked on the illustrations for the biography and also as Hayley's amanuensis. Blake was very happy to do the work as he had once said that he saw the divine countenance in man nowhere as clearly as in Milton and Cowper. Blake had had very little education and asked Hayley to teach him Greek. Both men combined their love for Cowper with their interest in the Greek language and, after a day's hard work, they would spend their evenings going through Cowper's translation of the *Odyssey* and comparing it with the original.

Hayley was able to complete the biography within a year but it was to grow and grow as the demand for further information concerning Cowper forced Hayley to prepare one edition after another.

The memorial to Cowper

Soon, too, plans for Cowper's tomb were complete and Lady Hesketh was gradually won over. Hayley was the happiest man in Britain. He had a large sarcophagus sunk into the floor of the north transept of Dereham parish church, bearing a brass plaque with the poet's name on it. Above the tomb, on the adjacent wall, he placed a large sill adorned with a huge marble Bible standing upright and, leaning on it, a smaller volume with 'The Task' written on its spine. A large quill, delicately worked in marble, was draped over the two books. Underneath this monument he placed the words:

In Memory

of William Cowper, Esq.

Born Hertfordshire, 1731
Buried in this Church, 1800

Ye, who with warmth the public triumph feel
Of talents, dignified by sacred zeal,
Here, to devotion's bard devoutly just,
Pay your fond tribute due to Cowper's dust!
England, exulting in his spotless fame,
Ranks with her dearest sons his fav'rite name
Sense, fancy, wit suffice not all to raise
So clear a title to affection's praise;
His highest honours to the heart belong;
His virtues form'd the magic of his song.

Two large plaques were then mounted into the wall bearing verses by Hayley paying tribute to the service rendered to God in caring for Cowper by Mary Unwin and the woman who had tenderly looked after the poet in the last few years of his life, Margaret Perowne.

Enormous as this monument to Cowper's memory was, lovers of his poetry were not satisfied with Hayley's work and demanded a more fitting memorial. Plans were made to surmount Hayley's work with a gigantic window depicting scenes from Cowper's life and poetry. It was not until almost 100 years later, in 1905, that this project was finally put into practice, giving Cowper's earthly remains a resting-place which kings and emperors might envy. The stained-glass window was planned by people who knew their Bibles quite as well as they knew Cowper's works. The two central lights show a full-length portrait of the poet in his study in company with his tame hares. The two side-lights depict four scenes from the poet's work illustrating the truths of the gospel. The whole beautifully coloured window is crowned with the words from Romans 3:25 which were instrumental in Cowper's conversion: 'Whom God hath set forth to be a propitiation through faith in his blood, to declare his righteousness for the remission of sins that are past, through the forbearance of God.'

Though many lovers of Cowper felt that the poet had been given a fitting edifice, once again Cowper's own wishes had been thwarted by those nearest to him. The poet, who had always stressed that he wished for a simple burial and would not allow his portrait to appear in his books, would have been appalled at this gigantic full-length portrait of him adorning an enormous window taking up an entire chapel in an ancient parish church as if he were some mediæval 'saint'.

As soon as St Nicholas' Church was fitted out with his memorial to Cowper's work, the never-tiring Hayley started plans for a cenotaph to be set up in London which was to include in the inscription the following lines:

> Hail him, ye prophets! and, ye saints, embrace
> A genuine son of your celestial race!
> Love your benign instructor, age! and youth!
> Charm'd by his fancy, tutor'd by his truth;
> And bless the bard, whose monitory verse,
> Which youth delights to learn, and age rehearse,
> May raise, by wings to just devotion given,
> Myriads to hail him as a guide to Heaven![5]

Cowper memorial window, East Dereham Parish Church

Although this project had a much wider following than the monument at East Dereham and was written about in the very best newspapers, it came to nothing.

Hayley's biography of Cowper

Though it was obvious that Hayley had harboured no thought that he might make a financial profit out of his Cowper biography, he was nevertheless overjoyed to find that he had produced a veritable best seller. Cowper, though dead, had not yet reached the height of his popularity but his name was rapidly becoming a household word. People were clamouring to know more about the author of the *Task* and his poetic message and more about the 'divine chit-chat', as his letters came to be called. Edition after edition of his works was called for and soon Johnson the publisher could hardly keep up with the demand for further editions of Cowper's poems, while Hayley's two-volumed biography had grown to four volumes.

Hayley's biography leaves much to be desired and the details it gives of Cowper's life can be found in a far more complete form in later works. Where Hayley's work is invaluable, however, is in his descriptions of Cowper's character as he knew him. Newton's sixteen-page character sketch of the poet was limited to the twelve years or so of their friendship in Olney. Hayley's pen describes Cowper's character in his last ten years of earthly pilgrimage. The biographer is aware that his readers may think he is exaggerating at times but emphasizes that this is not the case and that his description of Cowper's faith and character is true and just.

First of all, Hayley tells us that Cowper was, of all the people he had ever met, the one who approached the nearest to moral perfection. Hayley describes the sixty-two-year-old Cowper, as he first met him, as a strong and sturdy man of middle stature with light brown hair and bluish-grey eyes who had a ruddy complexion and was always dressed neatly but not in a finical way. The physical characteristic that fascinated Hayley the most, however, was Cowper's voice. He had been trained by his father in early infancy to recite and declame and he could make use of every pitch and tone of his voice to put homely truths across to his hearers. It was a voice you could listen to for hours without tiring.

Secondly, Hayley was attracted by the way Cowper's language
was completely interwoven with that of the Bible. He claims that
few ministers of the gospel had ever searched the Scriptures more
diligently than Cowper and that 'a spirit of evangelical kindness and
purity pervaded the whole tenor of his language, and all the conduct
of his life'.

Cowper's popularity and influence

Hayley's pen-portrait of Cowper helped enormously to create a
demand for Cowper's poetry, and the sale of Cowper's works during
the latter part of the eighteenth century and the first half of the
nineteenth century was enormous by any standards. In England
alone ninety-three editions of Cowper's works were published
between 1786 and 1837, not counting many reprints of Cowper's
hymns and poems that appeared in the secular newspapers and in the
many Christian magazines coming into vogue at the time. No less
than thirty lengthy biographies were written in the century following Cowper's death, and reviews on these works, as well as of the
various editions of Cowper's poems, helped spread Cowper's fame
throughout the English-speaking world. Perhaps no other poet was
ever praised in verse by fellow-poets, good and bad, as Cowper was,
and the many glowing comments in poetry by writers such as
Fanshawe, Beck and Browning would fill a fair-sized volume on
their own.

Popular as Cowper was in England, there is a good case for
arguing that he was even more popular in the United States and it is
certain that he was the favourite poet of the majority in that land for
a longer period than he was in England. There were almost as many
editions of Cowper's works printed in North America as in England
during the same period, though the population there was far less.
Publishers in thirteen leading North American towns were kept busy
for many years producing rival versions. American school-children
were taught rhymes to help them remember the names and works of
English poets. It is no accident that the rhyme dealing with Cowper
had his name coupled with the epithet 'super' to show both how it
was pronounced and how it was honoured. For a hundred years after
Cowper's death, any first-class American poet was compared with
Cowper and if the comparison was favourable, as in the case of

Whittier, then the poet in question was hailed as 'the Cowper of the West'!

All this American devotion to Cowper caused Professor Lodwick Hartley[6] of North Carolina University to estimate that the average literate American family towards the end of the colonial period owned the works of three authors apart from the Bible: these were Milton, Bunyan and Cowper. Norma Russel (Lady Dalrymple-Campneys), who compiled an enormous list of all publications by Cowper's hand up to 1837,[7] estimates that the early New Zealand settlers left Britain with an average of two books in their packs, the Bible and Cowper.

In the light of the enormous popularity of Cowper's Christian verse, it will come as no surprise to discover that well-established church historians believe that the poet was perhaps even more influential than great preachers of the eighteenth century such as Edwards, Rowland, Whitefield and Newton in spreading the message of the Evangelical Awakening. Balleine, in his *History of the Evangelical Party in the Church of England,* tells us of Cowper's poem the *Task*:

> This poem carried its message into quarters which the movement had not yet touched. Men who would have scorned the preaching of Grimshaw or the pages of Venn could not help reading the masterpiece of the first poet of the day, and the world of culture awoke to the fact that Evangelicalism was not a vulgar delusion of the masses, but a philosophy of life, which could appeal effectively to educated men.[8]

Balleine was obviously an Evangelical himself and thus might be thought to be too biassed in his assessment of Cowper's influence. We may therefore look to the writings of a non-evangelical, indeed a high-churchman, John H. Overton, who tells us in his definitive work on the eighteenth century that even Whitefield, with 'all his burning eloquence', and Wesley with 'all his indomitable activity', did not contribute as much to the Evangelical Revival as William Cowper. The historian continues:

> Poems do not make converts in the sense that sermons do; nevertheless, it is doing no injustice to the preaching power of the Evangelical school to assert that Cowper's poetry left

a deeper mark upon the Church than any sermons did. Through this means Evangelical theology in its most attractive form gained access into quarters into which no Evangelical preachers could ever have penetrated. The bitterest enemy of Evangelicalism who read Cowper's poems could not deny that here was at least one man, a scholar and a gentleman, with a refined and cultural mind and a brilliant wit, who was not only favourably disposed to the obnoxious doctrines, but held them to be the very life and soul of Christianity.[9]

Cowper as a poet — a final assessment

All that is left now for the author to do is to draw whatever conclusions are legitimate from Cowper's biography and highlight some features of Cowper's contribution to the spread of the gospel through the medium of poetry.

Perhaps first a word about classifying Cowper. He concentrated on themes quite out of the scope of other poets and differed radically from them in his theory of language and its purpose. It is hardly meaningful, for instance, to link Cowper with the Romantics because they, too, wrote about nature. Their view of nature is further away from Cowper's view than it is from that of the the Augustans. Labels such as Neo-Classical, Classical Romantic, Post-Augustan, Pre-Romantic, and even Romantic have been given Cowper. If Cowper must be classified, on the grounds that classification has some purpose in viewing a poet against the background of a particular cultural development, then it would fit the facts best to call Cowper simply 'the Evangelical poet' or 'the poet of Evangelicalism'. Evangelicalism was certainly a great cultural movement, as prominent in its day as ever Neo-Classicism was. It formed a style of language which brought education and learning down to the realms of the lower classes, down to the multitudes. This was done without straining the English language or emptying it of any of its qualities. Without 'Evangelicalism' there would have been no Romanticism.

Cowper's poetic theory is rooted in his acceptance of the biblical doctrine of creation. He thus saw poetry as the original and ideal form of language. This does not mean that Cowper fixed permanently on a particular linguistic model, say, the English of the

Authorized Version, or on a particular verse form, for instance, the sonnet. His model was always what he thought could express the truth succinctly and directly at the time of writing. This gave Cowper the advantage — and the ability — to change his language to suit the fashion of his immediate contemporaries, sometimes in spite of his own personal taste. He even strove to so purify poetry that what he wrote would be understandable in years to come. He did this by striving to eliminate all artificialities and embellishments and to concentrate his subject matter on that which every man, in all ages, experiences: nature and nature's God.

Cowper thus left the Neo-Classical manner of describing nature from the point of view of a detached observer, and depicted nature as being the very environment in which man lived, moved and had his being. This was because, to Cowper, nature showed God's immanent presence in the world and was proof to those who had been enlightened by the Word of God that simply to be alive within nature was to be in God's care and keeping. Thus, in God's plan to restore all things, nature is never complete without man, nor man without nature.

Cowper's poetry was one great anticipation of a future, based on God's promises made in the past in his Word. Its subject was the destiny of man. In a way, Cowper was striving to create a poetry that was timeless. He also sought a language which could teach man to communicate directly with nature as did Adam, and thereby take up the office he held in Eden as God's steward and lord over the fauna and flora. This is why Cowper always looked for that element in language which was akin to the natural music, harmonies and sounds of nature.

The fact that Cowper turned to blank verse shows the urge he felt to free himself of the traditional shackles of poetic convention. He was, however, too conscious of the usefulness of certain traditional rhyming forms and measures to reject good instruments of expression, merely because they were old. Thus, he saw, for instance, that the sonnet and the ballad had a continual use and he sought to put them to this use.

Central to Cowper's thinking was the use of poetry to reconcile man with God. For him, Christ's atonement was definitely an 'at-one-ment' with God, and not only with God, but also with creation. As man had pulled creation down at the Fall, so creation would be restored along with man. Conversion, for Cowper, was a complete act of reconciliation but also a sign of greater things to come. Cowper was a poet most fitted to teach such a reconciliation. He had alternatively a strong sense of God's presence with him, but at times experienced equally strong feelings of being utterly rejected by God. When Cowper had a sense of the presence of God, his one wish was to communicate this to his fellow men. When he felt himself rejected, he attributed this to his own sin and disobedience and wrote to warn the world to flee such things and look to God.[10] Newton could thus say at Cowper's burial service that his friend could comfort others, even when he found no comfort himself.[11]

Cowper had a very balanced character in spite of his periods of depression. Though he believed the Bible with all his heart, he read widely in sound 'secular' literature and loved a joke. He was even mildly vulgar at times. He was as interested in financial matters as any other man. He was a man every man and woman could look up to, except hypocrites and prudes. He was exceedingly kind to animals. He was a man of feeling who could identify himself with other men and their needs. There is something timeless about such a character who can be both godly and yet so very human, without a trace of hypocrisy. This perhaps explains why there is apparently no end to the amount of biographies being written about the poet and there is still a stream of articles about his verse coming from literary journals and magazines over two hundred years after his first works were published.

Cowper's poetry revealed new tendencies in its social application. He was the poet of the rejected. He campaigned in poetry for the poor of Olney. He wrote about the lives of outcasts such as gypsies. He did not idealize them, as the Romantics did, but described them in their dirt and in their squalor. His lines on Crazy Kate, a demented woman who had experienced a great tragedy, show how he was moved by such a person's plight. Cowper protested loudly against the colonization of a people against their will as in the case of India. He was one of the foremost campaigners against slavery and cruelty to animals.

Cowper was something of a reformer in his view of art. Art as an imitator of nature was no art to him. Nature, for Cowper, was art itself and the true artist was the one who saw culture as the transforming of nature, inclusive of man, into the future purposes of God. The language which described and fostered this art was also, in and of itself, true art, as it was part of the natural creative outworkings of God in his world. It was language used for its original and highest purpose.

All these characteristics of Cowper's poetic theory illustrate Cowper's principal calling in life. This was to be a monitor pointing the way to paradise regained. All his linguistic and poetic endeavours, all his teaching concerning sin and salvation; all his efforts at political and social reform, as also his doctrine that nature is the handmaid of grace — all point forward in Cowper's poetry to the eternal spring. Then the preparatory task of the Christian poet will be at an end. All men will once again be poets and the knowledge of the Lord will cover the earth as the waters cover the sea.[12]

Biographical sketches

Lady Anna Austen, née Richardson (1738?-1802) was married to Robert Austen (1708-1772) in 1755, five years before he became a baronet. She lived with her husband in France for many years but after his early death she decided to settle down in the village of Clifton near Olney. Most biographers write of Lady Austen as a beautiful, vivacious, flirtatious, woman of the world, full of thoughts of high life, romantic escapades and social aspirations. If this were the case, why should she have retired at the early age of forty to the very backwaters of society? The truth of the matter is that Lady Austen was an active Evangelical and was drawn to the Clifton-Olney area because of Thomas Scott's ministry at Olney and the fact that her sister was married to Thomas Jones, the curate at Clifton, a man well known for his Evangelical stance.

There has been much speculation regarding a possible romance between Cowper and Lady Austen. There is no doubt that the poet was drawn to her because of her wit, love for poetry, vivacity and Christian enthusiasm. William Hayley and Samuel Greatheed visited her shortly after Cowper's death and indicate that Lady Austen would have been only too pleased to have become Cowper's wife. Cowper, however, saw in Lady Austen a Christian sister who served as the muse for several of his works including the *Task*. When she became too demanding of his time and affections, Cowper told her soberly that she should not think of him as more than a brother and friend.

Speculations shown by King and Ryskamp, claiming that Mrs Unwin forced Cowper to part with Lady Austen, and those by Kenneth Povey, arguing that Cowper 'banished' Lady Austen from Olney, are too fanciful to be taken seriously. The first theory is based on the idea that a drab, matronly, unread figure such as Mary Unwin was bowled over by the beautiful, witty, well-read personality of Lady Austen. The second theory is based on the idea that Cowper and Lady Austen ended their friendship in a great quarrel and the poet showed Lady Austen the door, never to be entered by her again.

Both theories belong to the realm of fanciful gossip. Mary Unwin was far from the drab, tied-to-the-kitchen-sink woman of many a commentator. She was born into a middle-class family of some property and her letters written before her conversion show that she had loved to appear at balls and in the company of the belles and beaux of the day. Even Lady Hesketh, who became greatly jealous of the influence Mrs Unwin held over Cowper, had to admit that she was very intelligent and well-read. As to beauty, if contemporary portraits are anything to go by, Mrs Unwin would certainly have taken first prize in any competition with Lady Austen. Mary Unwin never aspired to being more than Cowper's housekeeper and 'adoptive mother' and there is no proof of her ever interfering in who Cowper ought or ought not to fall in love with.

As to the 'banishment' theory, Lady Austen lived for some time in the neighbourhood after both she and Cowper decided not to let their friendship go any deeper and Cowper assisted her legally after the supposed 'banishment' to obtain property which was rightfully hers. During the years after their parting both friends continued to speak highly of each other.

Walter Bagot ('Watt') (1731-1806) was a landowner-clergyman, son of a baronet and close relation of Lord Dartmouth. Cowper, Bagot and Lord Dartmouth were very good friends at Westminster and Bagot had joined Cowper there in youthful poetry-writing.

The earliest extant Cowper letter was written to Walter Bagot on 12 March 1749. Cowper described Bagot to Lady Hesketh in 1785 as 'a good and amiable man' and said after taking up correspondence with him again after a break of some time, 'I felt much affection for him, and the more because it was plain that after so long a time he still retained his for me.' 'Watty' was of a strong Evangelical character though he lived almost as a recluse at times, spending most of the day reading theological and classical works instead of attending to his pastoral duties (the livings of Blithfield and Leigh which he held belonged to his family). He was very influential in persuading relatives and friends to subscribe to Cowper's *Works*.

Bagot broke with Cowper during 1792-1793 because of the poet's friendship with William Hayley, of whom Bagot did not approve. Hayley had written a book on the pitfalls and wrongs of leading a spinster's life and 'Watty' had five sisters in this situation. Though Hayley never showed any animosity to Bagot, Newton did, and it was the fact that Bagot's 'chariot' (among others) was seen parked near Cowper's house that made Newton think that Cowper was leading a 'dissipated' life.

Cowper's letter to Bagot after hearing of the loss of his wife in 1786 is one of the most moving Cowper ever wrote.

William Bull (1738-1814) was born at Irthlingborough, Northamptonshire and was such a great character in the history of the eighteenth-century
church that it is a wonder that his memory has not been better preserved by
subsequent generations of Christians. Bull was brought up by his grandfather and early in life he felt a calling to the Dissenting ministry. He
studied at the Daventry Dissenting Academy and on completion of his
studies became minister of Newport Pagnell Independent Church, which
he pastored at the time of his meeting Cowper.

Bull was a very learned man and judged by Cowper to be one of the
most brilliant judges of literature in the country. He was deeply interested
in education and founded an Academy for Dissenting Ministers. True to his
practice of looking well beyond the borders of denominationalism, he
asked John Newton to draw up the rules for the college and gave him a say
in its curricula. Another 'outsider' Bull brought in was John Thornton, the
rich Evangelical merchant who helped finance the college and eventually
took over its management.

So influential was Bull in his ministry and so free from confessional
bigotry that Anglicans, Baptists and Independents alike opened their
pulpits to him. Thus Bull was as much at home preaching for the large
congregations of Rowland Hill and John Berridge as he was preaching in
the tiny Dissenting chapels across the country. Bull lived at a time when the
Dissenting churches were rapidly identifying themselves with the fate of
the American colonists who were seeking.independence and were thus
widely accused of being followers of Paine and enemies of the
government. Although Bull refused to mix politics with the pulpit, and
warned his clergyman son of such dangers, he was burnt in effigy by
ignorant and over-zealous royalists who believed he must be a leading
Paineite because of his high position amongst Dissenters.

Bull supplied Newton's pulpit at Olney from time to time and had often
asked his Anglican friend to introduce him to Cowper, telling him he was
mortified to know that so 'wonderful a monument to the Power of Divine
Grace' was near at hand and Newton would not introduce him. It was not
until Newton left for London, however, that he agreed and arranged for
Bull to go and visit Cowper. Bull and Cowper got on like the proverbial
house on fire and Cowper wrote glowing reports of Bull to his relations and
friends. To William Unwin he said,

> You are not acquainted with the Revd. Mr. Bull of Newport.
> Perhaps it is as well for you that you are not. You would regret still
> more than you do, that there are so many Miles interposed between
> us. He spends part of the day with us to-morrow. A Dissenter, but
> a liberal one; a man of Letters and of Genius, master of a fine
> imagination, or rather not master of it; an imagination, which when
> he finds himself in the company he loves and can confide in, runs
> away with him into such fields of speculation as amuse and enliven

every other imagination that has the happiness to be of the party. At other times he has a tender and delicate sort of melancholy in his disposition, not less agreeable in its way. No men are better qualified for companions in such a world as this, than men of such a temperament. Every scene of life has two sides, a dark and a bright one, and the mind that has an equal mixture of melancholy and vivacity, is best of all qualified for the contemplation of either. It can be lively without levity, and pensive without dejection. Such a man is Mr. Bull. But he smokes tobacco — nothing is perfect — *nihil est ab omni parte beatum.*[1]

It is typical of Cowper that as soon as he made a new friendship, he wished to share it with others. It is also typical of Cowper that he looked for the same balance of melancholy and cheerfulness in others that he ever kept as a guideline for his own conduct. It is because critics have spent too much time analysing and, indeed, psycho-analysing Cowper's melancholy that they have forgotten the gay spark of life which was so often part of him. Cowper is showing in his pen-portrait of Bull how balanced the two sides of a true man can be.

Ashley Cowper (1701-1788), Cowper's favourite uncle and the father of Harriot and Theadora. Ashley was a small plump man who always wore a wide-brimmed white hat with a pink lining. This moved Cowper to say that if anyone met his uncle they would mistake him for a mushroom, pick him up and carry him off in a basket. Ashley's size and shape did not prevent him from becoming an extremely influential man in state matters and politics and he held sinecure posts that brought him in many thousands of pounds a year.

It was at Ashley's home in Southampton Row that Cowper spent some of the happiest years of his life and it was there that the poet learnt to take church-going seriously. William fell in love with Ashley's daughter, Theadora, and the fact that Ashley so encouraged his nephew to gain an influential post in the House of Lords was probably linked with a desire to have his daughter married to a man of means. Ashley encouraged William to write poetry and served as a critic for much of William's verse. This fact led William to say, 'No man has a better Taste than my Uncle, and my opinion of it is such that I should certainly renounce the pen for ever, were I to hear that he wish'd me to do so.'[2]

Ashley was susceptible to severe bouts of melancholy and depression and would withdraw himself for weeks from society to nurse his woes. He wrote a treatise on suicide which was probably the one William, whilst still a child, discussed with his father.

Maria Frances Cecilia Cowper, née Madan (1726-1797), commonly known as 'Mrs Cowper', was Cowper's cousin and Martin Madan's sister. Before her conversion she was a gifted actress and had performed in Racine's *Athalie* in French. From 1766 to 1781 Cowper corresponded regularly with his cousin who shared his deep faith in the gospel. These letters show Cowper at his evangelical best and he writes in a language so scriptural that it is difficult to know when he is quoting the Bible verbatim and when he is expressing his own thoughts. Cowper's modern critics have difficulty tracing the source of his language, always looking to other poets for signs of influence. Thus when Cowper quotes Isaiah, one commentator is sure that Cowper is being influenced by Churchill and when he quotes Revelation another believes he must be quoting Milton. If modern scholars, who are apparently ignorant of the Scriptures, would analyse Cowper's works in the light of the Bible, they would discover a totally new Cowper.

After the autumn of 1781 it appears that correspondence between the two cousins stopped for almost nine years. This date coincides with the publication of Martin Madan's books on bigamy which Cowper combatted so fiercely in his poems. There are other signs, too, to suggest that feelings were aroused against Cowper amongst the Cowpers and Madans because of the poet's outspokenness. In January 1790, Mrs Cowper began to ask Newton about William's welfare and eventually the two cousins were writing to each other again.

Like most of the Cowpers and Madans, Maria Cowper wrote poetry and in 1792 she sent a manuscript volume of poems to Cowper to be edited and commented on. Cowper revised the whole volume and Mrs Cowper had it published as *Original Poems, on Various Occasions, by a Lady*. Cowper's name was placed on the title-page as reviser.

William Hayley (1747-1825) was educated at Eton and Trinity College, Cambridge, though he left university without taking a degree. He was subsequently successful in studying law at the Middle Temple. Hayley was married to Eliza Ball in 1869 but after twenty years of living together the couple decided to live in separate households. Eliza was very highly strung and mentally unbalanced for long periods at a time. She seemed to believe that separation from her husband was for the good of both and, though living apart, the couple continued to be on the best of terms.

Hayley is best known as a patron of artists, writers, historians, poets, social reformers and Evangelical protégés such as George Romney, Edward Gibbon, Charlotte Smith, William Blake and John Howard. Hayley was a man of letters in his own right and had refused the post of Poet Laureate. He was moved to approach Cowper when the newspapers proclaimed that Cowper was Hayley's rival in preparing a volume of Milton's works. Actually Hayley was preparing a biography and Cowper was editing Milton and translating his Latin and Italian works, so no rivalry was involved. Hayley was subsequently invited to Weston and Cowper to Hayley's seat at Eartham in Sussex and the two cemented an unbreakable friendship.

It was inevitable that Hayley would reap the jealousy of Cowper's other friends and both Lady Hesketh and John Johnson used every means in their power to present Hayley in a bad light before Cowper, although Hayley had shown both of them remarkable kindness and understanding. When their own treatment of Cowper miserably failed, however, Hesketh and Johnson turned to Hayley for help and it was Hayley who succeeded in obtaining a royal pension for Cowper. Even Hayley, however, was not quite free from jealousy and in his biography of Cowper he stressed that he was Cowper's best friend and not Newton.

It is interesting to note that Hayley took in hand the education of the untaught William Blake and introduced him to the classical languages by reading Milton with him and comparing Cowper's translation of Homer with the original. Blake said that he saw more of the 'countenance divine' in the face of Milton and Cowper than in any other creature and it is clear that Blake's earlier evangelical poetry and especially his 'green' verse are influenced by Cowper.

Hayley went to great sacrifice and personal expenditure to support Cowper during the last decade of his friend's life. He was justly rewarded after Cowper's death as his biography of Cowper brought him in a considerable fortune.

Lady Harriot Hesketh (1733-1807), Cowper's first cousin and the daughter of Ashley Cowper, was in love with Cowper as a young woman but kept her affections to herself as she believed her sister, Theadora, would eventually marry him. Harriot married Sir Thomas Hesketh of Rufford Hall, Lancashire in 1761 and toured Europe with him in search of a climate that would be advantageous to his poor health. Sir Thomas died in 1778 leaving Cowper £100.

Lady Hesketh's attention returned to Cowper after he had published the *Task* and she became one of the poet's most fervent correspondents and visitors, heaping on her cousin and his housekeeper many gifts in the form of clothing, furniture and domestic appliances. Cowper's famous indoor cap, which he wore in lieu of a wig, was made for him by Lady Hesketh. It is obvious that at a time when Newton was becoming increasingly taxing and critical of Cowper, Lady Hesketh brought a real ray of sunshine and friendliness into his life.

However, as Mrs Unwin grew older and weaker, Lady Hesketh determined to take her household into her care and did everything in her power to have Mrs Unwin removed from Cowper's home. It was really in hope of getting rid of Mrs Unwin, who refused to leave Weston, that Lady

Hesketh planned to force Cowper to move from there. After his removal from Weston Cowper blamed Lady Hesketh for turning him into a tree without roots and her intense care for her cousin waned so considerably that shortly before his death, though Cowper was active and sane enough to prepare a new edition of his Homer and write original poetry, Lady Hesketh planned to have him forcibly admitted to a lunatic asylum in Lincolnshire notorious for its cruel treatment, including the use of strait-jackets.

Joseph Hill (1733-1811) was one of the few close friends of Cowper's who did not turn their backs on him after his period of insanity and conversion. Hill came of a wealthy legal family and was closely connected with a number of Cowper's relations, especially his uncle, Ashley. Cowper introduced Hill to Thurlow, who recognized his gifts and took him into his services, eventually appointing him as Secretary of Lunatics in 1778. Hill became Cowper's financial adviser after his conversion and looked after the poet's financial affairs up to his death. It is quite obvious that he supplied Cowper generously with money when the poet had no funds to his name. Hill, though never, as far as we know, professing Christ, was very open to Cowper's evangelical doctrines and many of the poet's letters to his friend are out and out evangelistic and would have greatly offended a less liberal person or a lesser friend.

James Hurdis (1763-1801) was educated at St Mary Hall and Magdalen College, Oxford before entering the Church of England ministry. Hurdis was a poet and had already published a volume entitled *The Village Curate* before becoming acquainted with Cowper. The volume is a direct and deliberate imitation of Cowper's verse for which Hurdis was full of admiration. Cowper first heard of Hurdis when he was sent his work *Adriano* by Joseph Johnson in 1788 for appraisal and comment. Cowper gave the book a very good and long review which Johnson published and which must have helped Hurdis immensely to gain the public's ear. After learning of Cowper's work on his book, Hurdis wrote to his fellow-poet, thus commencing a correspondence and friendship which lasted many years.

Cowper felt that he had found a new William Unwin in James Hurdis. The young poet, however, did not enjoy the same faith as Unwin and was far more delicate in his constitution and temperament. It was through Cowper that Hurdis was introduced to poet-patron William Hayley and when a seat for a professorship in poetry became vacant at Oxford, Cowper wrote to all the vote-holders he knew to persuade them to cast their votes in Hurdis' favour. Hurdis obtained the post.

John Johnson (1769-1833) a near kinsman of Cowper's on the Donne side, was educated at Bungay Grammar School, Essex and Gonville and Gaius College, Cambridge. He first met Cowper in January 1790 when he brought him a poem to criticize, claiming it was written by someone else although he had really written it himself. Cowper soon discovered the bluff yet came to feel a deep and lasting affection for the young deceiver whom he called 'the wild boy'. Cowper quickly realized that Johnson had the gifts to become a worthy minister of the gospel rather than waste his time on the mathematical studies he was pursuing. Johnson followed Cowper's advice to become a minister and was ordained a deacon in July 1793.

Johnson was obsessed by Cowper's character at first and well-nigh mesmerized by every word proceeding from his friend's mouth. Throughout the 1790s he would snap up every little saying of Cowper's, no matter how insignificant, write it down and analyse it carefully for any secret and even supernatural message that might lie within it. Gradually, aided and abetted by Lady Hesketh, he came to the conclusion that he ought to take care of the ageing Cowper under his own roof, far from the poet's beloved home at Weston. Having no settled home of his own, Johnson dragged Cowper from house to house, all the time discussing the poet's dreams with him and psycho-analysing Cowper's oral and physical reactions. It is obvious from Johnson's own testimony that his interpretations of what Cowper meant were often very wide of the mark. Johnson even, in a wild desire to help Cowper regain the cheerfulness lost when he lost his home and came under Johnson's care, practised psycho-therapy on his 'patient' by making him listen throughout his sleepless nights to haunting words spoken down a tube with an outlet hidden in the poet's room.

It is a tragic reminder of how scholars still insist on perpetuating the myth that Cowper was a mad poet that King and Ryskamp have ended their 'standard work' on Cowper by quoting four pages of harrowing disjointed moanings which they have found in Johnson's hand and which they believe reflect Cowper's state of mind. Other quite sane and edifying 'jottings' (such as his comments on Dr Samuel Johnson) which were written at the same time, or even later, in Cowper's own hand have been ignored completely.

Joseph Johnson (1738-1809) was born at Everton, near Liverpool, and was successful in establishing himself as a publisher and bookseller in the capital in 1772. Johnson was of a very liberal persuasion and sought to publish books which were new and indeed revolutionary in their contents. He thus published any works which did not toe the established line, including those of Thomas Paine, Joseph Priestly, Mary Wollstonecraft and Erasmus Darwin. Johnson saw early the dynamic contents of John Newton's works and also was pleased to publish the *Olney Hymns*. Newton first introduced Cowper to Johnson in conjunction with his 'Anti-Thelyphthora', after which the publisher was prepared to take on anything Cowper wrote without seeing a line. This was with the exception of Cowper's long poem 'Friendship' which was apparently too idealistic even for Johnson.

Johnson encouraged Cowper to write as much as possible and showed an early interest in his letters as well as his poems. He also persuaded the poet to do even hack work and write reviews. He was, however, an astute businessman and drove such a hard bargain with Cowper that the poet virtually made him a present of his first volume. Cowper was more business-minded when it came to publishing his second volume and he accused Johnson of disgraceful avarice. The £1,000 he received for his *Task*, however, was but a very small fraction of what Johnson made.

Martin Madan (1725-1790) was educated at Westminster and Christ Church, Oxford before going on the study law at the Inner Temple in 1747. He was called to the Bar in 1748 but became an itinerant preacher two years later after being converted through John Wesley's ministry. He eventually became an ordained minister in the Church of England but allied himself with the Countess of Huntingdon and pastored a work of hers at the Lock Hospital for vagrant women. It was here that Madan developed his musical abilities and sought to fetch the prostitutes off the streets and to Christ by providing musical concerts and choir-led community singing. Madan became so obsessed with the fate of those under his care that he developed a case-law theology whereby married men who committed adultery should be compelled to take on the prostitutes, sluts or in some cases genuinely wronged women to be their lawfully bigamous wives. Madan wrote a lengthy multi-volumed work with a brilliant display of Hebrew knowledge to popularize his theory and this obtained a surprisingly large backing in the circles which he frequented. It is interesting to note that it was Martin Madan and his followers who pointed the finger of suspicion at William Huntington and like-minded upright Christians and accused them of being 'Antinomians' because they were not prepared to follow the precepts of the law that allowed men such as David, the beloved of God, to take more than one wife.

Martin Madan was Cowper's first cousin and had helped lead him to Christ. Cowper was persuaded by Newton to take up his pen against his own cousin and in writing against Madan's bigamous heresy, Cowper became an author of note.

John Newton (1725-1807), son of a Jesuit merchant sea captain, brought up in the strictest Roman Catholic manner, and a Dissenting mother who looked to the Bible and Isaac Watts' writings for her teaching. John's mother died when he was six years of age and only five years later the young boy was sent to sea by his father after a bare minimum of education. Newton's life after this period up to his becoming curate of Olney parish church in 1764 is one of the most colourful and adventurous on record. Though still only a child, Newton was convinced that he should one day marry his cousin Mary Catlett and he remained true to his promises to her throughout wild years of being press-ganged, shipwrecked and marooned. He planned mutiny, murder and suicide before being forced into slavery and eventually becoming a slave-master himself. These were years, however, in which Newton was constantly aware of being in the presence of God, who broke into the seaman's life with the full grace of forgiveness after a tremendous ordeal at sea in 1747.

Newton, who met Cowper in 1764, immediately felt a deep fellowship with him and invited him and his housekeeper, Mrs Unwin, to join him in Olney. The two friends then spent twelve years together in which they were rarely separated for more than a night's sleep at a time. For the first six years of this friendship Newton almost idolized his friend and strove to imitate him in all respects. Gradually, however, as Cowper's health waned, Newton became Cowper's chief comforter and, at times, even nurse, until his own health was ruined in the attempt. Parallel with his own intense care of Cowper, Newton became increasingly unpopular with his church and was compelled to leave Olney in 1780 when he accepted the living of St Mary's Woolnoth, London. After Newton's departure the two friends kept up a steady correspondence marred at times by differences in theology, politics and methods of Christian witness.

There is perhaps no figure, short of Cowper himself, who has been less understood by observers of eighteenth-century life. Literary critics have invariably judged Newton to be a strong but simple-minded fanatic who used his harsh Calvinistic principles as a lash to whip his hearers into heaven. Invariably they see Cowper as being the main victim of this lash. On the other hand, evangelical writers have seen Newton as a man of iron with superior health, with scarcely a failing, who was always successful as a minister and was the main prop in Cowper's life of illness, madness and suicide attempts. Both these views are false. Even as a child Newton was very tender and delicate and preferred to play with 'Mama' rather than with the robust neighbouring children. His health was never better, to use his own description, than 'mediocre' and he was guilty at times of long periods of child-like sulking and was very easily upset when he felt his friends — whom he tended to idolize — were letting him down.

There were two main faults in Newton's ministry, according to Thomas Scott, who, on a human level, owed his salvation to Newton. Firstly, Newton had an over-proportionate love for gossip which finally ruined his ministry at Olney. When Newton preached exegetically, he was a master, but he preferred to take the problems of his parishioners with him into the pulpit and discuss topically their Christian relevance. When doing this Newton was not afraid of naming names and his parishioners were often shocked to find themselves subjects of their minister's sermons. Scott tells us in his *Letters and Papers* that Newton 'could not preach a plain and practical sermon, without exciting inquiries throughout the town, "What has been the matter? Who has been telling Sir something that led to this subject?"'[3]

The second failing according to Scott was that Newton could not hold his position in relation to his parishioners and lost almost all his influence and authority by talking down to them and refraining from admonishing them and showing them where they were going wrong. Scott even calls Newton an 'Eli' for spoiling his spiritual sons and daughters. This was because Newton believed that 'It was enough to preach the truth; for, that being established, error would fall of itself.' Scott complained that when he took over Newton's church at Olney the town was swarming with Antinomians as a result of Newton's lax ministry and he had to build up a new congregation as most of those who sat under Newton had left the church.[4]

It was this love of unchallenged gossip from dubious sources and over-identification with those under his charge that caused Newton to believe almost everything he heard from backstairs servants about Cowper and his friends and make him at times jealous and hyper-critical of the poet's life and Christian walk. It is the sad truth that most of the negative and often quite untrue rumours spread concerning Cowper's health and Christian standing originated from Newton's tongue and pen. These were spread at a time when, according to William Bull, Newton's memory was in ruins and, according to John Johnson, he was in his second childhood. Thus, though Cowper had given Newton, at his request, a written description of his pre-conversion experiences in the strictest confidence, Newton allowed all and sundry — including a woman suffering from insanity — to copy and reproduce this document in whatever form they thought fit. This original document is now lost and the over 400 variant readings of the numerous copies are the only source of evidence for Cowper's alleged suicide attempts.

Mary Newton (1729-1790), née Catlett, wife of John Newton, was a close friend both of Cowper and of Mrs Unwin. She was married to Newton on 12 February 1750 after a courtship of many years during which she saw very little of her sea-faring fiancé. Even after conversion and marriage, her husband embarked on three successive voyages to Africa as a slave-trader, not realizing how guilty his conduct was before the Lord. These voyages were, however, stopped when Newton one day went into a severe fit which robbed him of all his senses and caused his doctors to forbid him any further occupation at sea. This, humanly speaking, inexplicable illness so shook Mary that she became extremely ill herself and it was not until months after her husband's recovery that Mary became well. From then on Mary's health was of a very delicate nature, coupled with long bouts of depression and doubts of her standing in Christ.

Though Mary Newton was extremely fond of her husband she remained independent in thought concerning Newton's relationships with his friends. She scolded her husband (though only when writing letters to him, as she confessed she would not have dared to do this to his face) for his dealings with Dissenters in his earlier Olney years. This was because Newton would invite a great many Dissenting ministers to share his table whereas Anglicans were conspicuous only by their absence. Mary was particularly puzzled when Newton broke off his allegiance to Cowper for a while to covet the friendship of William Bull. 'Bull has become your Pope,' was Mrs Newton's candid comment.

Cowper always took great care to send Mary Newton cheerful and humorous letters and it is to her that he sent most of his poetry dealing with mundane things such as the price of fish and the state of coconuts gone sour. Whenever any form of estrangement came between him and Newton, Cowper would be sure to write to Mrs Newton saying that both he and her husband were still the best of friends and that nothing had come between them that could permanently spoil their friendship.

Cowper stood particularly near to Mrs Newton when Evangelicals within the Countess of Huntingdon Connexion began to propagate the bizarre theory that God had planned bigamy as a cure for those men who had committed adultery. These do-gooders pointed a finger at Newton, believing that any slave-driver must be an adulterer and demanded that Newton took on extra wives — this without any Christian feeling whatsoever for the only rightful Mrs Newton.

Mary Newton had a long, painful illness before her death in which she was denied all comfort from God and all assurance of his saving grace. Suddenly, only a matter of days before her homecall, she entered at last into the enjoyment of assurance of salvation that she so much coveted and she entered into glory in deep fellowship with her Maker.

Matthew Powley (1740-1806) originally came from Westmorland and was educated at Queen's College, Oxford, where he was threatened with expulsion for his Reformed thinking. He was a constant visitor to Olney in Newton's early days there and married Susanna Unwin (1746-1835) in 1774. Powley eventually became curate of Slackthwaite (1767) and vicar of Dewsbury (1777) and held both posts until his death.

Powley was a keen Evangelical and stood very close to the Countess of Huntingdon Connexion, in whose chapels he often preached. His wife was rather suspicious of Cowper, as she felt her mother was constantly making financial sacrifices on his behalf. Powley, however, was very fond of Cowper and asked him for advice on numerous occasions, particularly when dealing with the Wesleyans and their perfectionist heresy. When Fletcher applied for permission to preach in Powley's church, the clergyman refused on the grounds that anyone preaching that he was perfect could not be good enough for an Evangelical pulpit.

Samuel Rose (1767-1804) was educated at Glasgow University and Lincoln's Inn and called to the Bar in 1796. Rose visited Cowper in 1787, bringing him the respects of his Scottish professors who had read Cowper's first two volumes of poems. In his spare time, Rose earned money by writing for the *Monthly Review* and editing Goldsmith's works. As a law student he compiled two volumes of law reports for publication.

Although Cowper was suffering from acute rheumatism and pains in the head when he met Rose, the poet found in the youth a perfect 'Emile' and invited him to come and go at Weston at his leisure, an invitation Rose was quick to accept. Rose's descriptions of his life at Weston with Cowper, Lady Hesketh and Mrs Unwin are idyllic and verge on the sublime. Cowper did not neglect Rose's spiritual instruction and when Newton visited Weston, Cowper made sure that Rose also was present. Cowper introduced Rose to Hayley who made him a trustee of Cowper's pension.

It was through Hayley that Rose met William Blake. One day the engraver-poet found a drunken soldier in his garden and without further ado removed him from his property. The soldier, however, protested that he had confiscated the garden in the name of the king, which meant that Blake's repulsion of him was tantamount to treason. Blake hired Rose to take up his case and though Rose was successful, the case cost him his life. Rose had always been in very delicate heath and as a result of walking backwards and forwards to the court in the worst of weathers, he caught a severe cold which developed complications and finally killed him.

Thomas Scott (1747-1821), son of a grazier, was born at Braycroft in Lincolnshire, the tenth of thirteen children. After five years at boarding school Scott was apprenticed to a surgeon but was sacked within two months and then had to work as a labourer for his father, studying in his spare time with a view to becoming a clergyman. At this time Scott saw in the ministry a means of a better income, less working hours and a chance to be able to read, write and study in leisure. Though many applicants who had five times Scott's education were turned down the young twenty-five-year-old was ordained as a deacon on 20 September 1772.

Eventually Scott settled down as a curate in Weston Underwood and came under the influence of John Newton, whose witness to truths yet unknown to Scott impressed the young curate greatly. Scott began to reconsider his standing before God when two of his parishioners lay dying. He was too unconcerned with their plight himself to call on them, so Newton visited them, a kind deed which brought tears of shame to Scott's unenlightened eyes. For the next few years Scott heard Newton preach and corresponded with him until he was gradually led to a saving knowledge of Christ.

There was still a great deal of worldliness in Scott, however, which caused him to covet Newton's church at Olney and at the same time retain the two curacies he already held, with a view to the extra income which this would bring him. When it became evident to Newton that he would have to leave Olney, he urged his congregation to accept Scott as his successor. This they refused to do at first because they would not be dictated to by Newton and did not want a minister who would be continually dividing his attention between three churches a good way from one another. This latter reservation was shared by Cowper, who found Scott too avaricious by far and refused point-blank to go and hear him preach. Eventually, after the disastrous ministry of the Rev. Benjamin Page (who, Cowper said, refused to turn over a new leaf), Scott became the minister of the Olney Church at a time when it had lost its congregation. He was very unhappy there and soon moved to London where, of all places, he took over the ministry of the Lock Chapel, a place notorious for breeding 'bigamous parsons'.

Cowper's reservations concerning Scott left him only very slowly. Playing on Scott's continual interest in surgery, the poet said that Newton had used the poultice in preaching but Scott used the scalpel. Nevertheless Scott felt drawn to Cowper and often consulted him on problems of the ministry. This obviously flattered and moved Cowper who slowly came to like Scott and treat him as a young student who had not yet put off his childishness but would become a good scholar some day. It was Cowper who took hold of Scott's autobiography *The Force of Truth*, edited and revised it and gave it the shape that caused it to be read over the years as a standard display of what conversion can do to a man who by nature is irredeemable.

Scott went on to see better days and was of great use to the church of Christ through his commentaries and writings. But this profitable period is outside the scope of Cowper's biography.

Samuel Teedon (d. 1798), the Olney schoolmaster, is seen by many commentators as 'Cowper's fool', or at least as a charlatan pretending to religious foolishness. By others he is looked upon as a kind of soothsayer whose nigh-magical incantations impressed Cowper greatly, thus making Cowper the 'fool'. He is also seen as a scrounging rogue.

There was nothing, however, 'foolish' about Teedon, who had enjoyed a thorough education. It is easy for critics to declassify Teedon's religious fervour for want of such fervour in themselves but there is nothing in either Teedon's or Cowper's many letters to suggest that Teedon's Evangelical religion was not most sincere.

It is quite true that Teedon was an immitigable scrounger but it could be argued that he had no other choice. He was determined to make a go of a school whose pupils were almost all living below the poverty line and where little money was forthcoming from their parents. Teedon's policy was that it was the duty of those Olney citizens who could contribute to the financing of the school to do so as this was for the good of the entire town. Cowper knew that Teedon always begged for a purpose and was impressed by the spirit of gratitude that he always showed when receiving money even though he felt it was the donors' duty to give.

Cowper was rather put off by Teedon's very formal civility, pedantic nature and his somewhat incomprehensible way of mixing plain English with as many Latinisms as possible. The poet soon found out, however, that Teedon was a praying man and respected and admired him for this virtue. Teedon's letters to Cowper were a source of strength to the poet, especially when he began to realize that Lady Hesketh and John Johnson were not quite the friends he had thought them to be. Teedon continued to write to Cowper after the latter was removed from Weston but Johnson, following Lady Hesketh's orders, did not allow Cowper to read his letters. Even Teedon's death was kept secret from the poet.

Lord Chancellor Thurlow (1731-1806), First Baron Thurlow, was the eldest son of a clergyman. He was educated at King's School, Canterbury, then Gonville and Gaius College, Cambridge from which he was sent down for not attending chapel and for disorderly behaviour. Although Cowper wrote him an urgent letter after his own conversion, pleading the cause of the gospel, Thurlow remained unconcerned with spiritual matters and, whenever form and custom demanded that he entered a church (the Test Act was still in power), he would do so with his hat placed firmly on his head.

After university success was denied him Thurlow tried his hand at law, joining Cowper as a fellow-clerk at Chapman's, the solicitor's. He then spent much of his time with Cowper and his cousins 'giggling and making giggle' at Southampton Row. It was during this period of their friendship that Cowper saw that Thurlow had the makings of a Lord Chancellor and told him so to his face, adding, 'I am a nobody and will remain a nobody.'

According to contemporary reports Thurlow was a very brutal man and, knowing Cowper's hatred of bullying, commentators are agreed that Thurlow was the last kind of person Cowper would befriend. Yet the poet saw in Thurlow a man of astute learning and great kindness. He was the kind of man who would — and often did — give his last penny to alleviate the burdens of some poor and starving soul. Writing to the Rev. Thomas Carwardine in 1792, Cowper defended his one-time friend, who had been severely criticized, by saying,

> I know well the chancellor's benevolence of heart, and how much he is misunderstood by the world. When he was young he would do the kindest things, and at an expense to himself which at that time he could ill afford, and he would do them too in the most secret manner. I know not what is become of her now, but in those days there was a certain Miss Christian, the daughter, if I mistake not, of a Norfolk clergyman, who had been a friend of Thurlow's father. The girl was left penniless, and he established her in Tavistock Street as a milliner, disbursing three hundred pounds to furnish a shop for her. I went with him to the house, and having seen her, am ready to swear that his motives were not, nor could be, of the amorous kind, for she was ugly to a wonder. No creature I believe knew anything of this *truly Christian* intrigue but myself only. When I think on these things, and hear them spoken of as I sometimes do
>
> ... *væ meum*
> *Fervens difficile bile tumet jecur.*[5]

Nevertheless Thurlow cut Cowper when he became 'religious' and did not take up correspondence with him again until he had become well known as an interpreter of Homer. Cowper was very hurt at being thus neglected by his former best friend, as also by George Colman of the 'Nonsense Club', and poured out his thoughts on the matter in his poem 'Valediction':

> Farewell, false hearts! whose best affections fail
> Like shallow brooks which summer suns exhale,
> Forgetful of the man whom once ye chose,
> Cold in his cause, and careless of his woes,
> I bid you both a long and last adieu,
> Cold in my turn and unconcern'd like you.

Cowper's display of unconcern over Thurlow's neglect was mere 'poetic licence', however, and the poet showed a keen interest in Thurlow's rocketing career through his correspondence with Joseph Hill, Thurlow's secretary. When Thurlow became Lord Chancellor Cowper penned his 'I told you so' in the words:

Round Thurlow's head in early youth,
And in his sportive days,
Fair science pour'd the light of truth,
And genius shed his rays.

See! with united wonder cried
Th'experienc'd and the sage,
Ambition in a boy supplied
With all the skill of age!

Discernment, eloquence, and grace,
Proclaim him born to sway
The balance in the highest place,
And bear the palm away.

The praise bestow'd was just and wise;
He sprang impetuous forth,
Secure of conquest where the prize
Attends superior worth.

So the best courser on the plain
Ere yet he starts is known,
And does but at the goal obtain
What all had deem'd his own.

Thurlow was able to be of use to Cowper in the poet's declining years when, pushed and pulled by William Hayley, he became active in campaigning for a royal pension for his former best friend.

Mary Unwin (1724-1796) was the daughter of an Ely draper and the wife of the Rev. Morley Unwin (1703-1767). Shortly after leaving St Albans for Huntingdon, Cowper met her son William Unwin (see below) at church and invited him to tea. Cowper was invited to lunch at the Unwins the following week and was immediately filially attracted to the newly converted Mary Unwin who became from then on Cowper's 'adoptive mother' and took him in as a paying guest. After Morley Unwin's tragic death, Cowper, in accordance with the Rev. Unwin's last wishes, remained with the family. As there was little Christian witness in Huntingdon, however, and tongues began to wag about Mrs Unwin's changed life (she had been something of a society woman before conversion), the Unwins and Cowper accepted John Newton's invitation to join him in Olney.

At Huntingdon Mrs Unwin had to suffer the gossip of the unconverted but at Olney it was the converted of all walks of life, including John Thornton, Newton's patron, who made Mrs Unwin's life miserable. She was accused of having ulterior, and even amorous motives for her kindness to her much younger lodger. It was partly because of these unfounded rumours and partly because he was working long hours in the services he performed for Newton that Cowper's health broke down in 1773. Mrs Unwin strove industriously to look after her ailing lodger with the same love and care that she had shown previously in nursing a complete stranger, a homeless woman, to health and strength. Even here, however, Thornton continued to speak unkindly about Mrs Unwin, wrongly accusing her of giving more care to Cowper than she would have done if he were a woman. Newton came magnanimously to Mrs Unwin's assistance and allowed Cowper to stay at the Vicarage for over a year until he was restored physically and greatly healed mentally.

Although Mrs Unwin bravely thanked the Lord for the privilege of looking after Cowper amidst evil gossip, the strain gradually told on her. Her great beauty was spoilt by several strokes and she aged prematurely, becoming increasingly more paralysed as the years sped on. Cowper's poems 'To Mary' and 'Sonnet to Mrs Unwin' testify strongly to the Christian love Cowper felt for his housekeeper-friend and to his remorse for the trouble he had caused her, admitting to her that ''Twas my distress that brought thee low, My Mary!'

Cowper had hoped to make up for the worries he had caused Mrs Unwin in their youth by providing her with security and comfort in old age. He thus built bowers in the garden where they could sit in the evening sun and erected greenhouses so that Mary could always have the fresh flowers she loved so much. Lady Hesketh, however, put an end to all this and caused Mrs Unwin to suffer more in old age than at any other time in her life. Mrs Unwin died after a life full of care, convinced that apart from Cowper there was no love to be had from other close 'friends'. John Johnson had her buried in torchlight in the middle of the night due to one of his very odd whims. William Hayley, who had been kept at bay by Lady Hesketh and Johnson, knew Mary Unwin's worth, however, and wrote an epitaph explaining how

Trusting in God, with all her heart and mind,
This woman proved magnanimously kind,

and invited all to 'revere her name'. Mrs Mary Unwin has long deserved a biographer who is prepared to give her all due reverence.

William Unwin

William Cawthorn Unwin (1744-1786), Mrs Mary Unwin's only son, was educated at Charterhouse and Christ's College, Cambridge, where he gained high distinctions in the classical languages. Unwin felt strongly called to the ministry and his evangelical sermons so influenced the thoughts of his ecclesiastical superiors that after a very short curacy they appointed him rector of Stock with Ramsden Bellhouse in Essex, where he remained until his death.

The newly converted William Unwin became the first of Cowper's Christian friends after his own conversion and this friendship never wavered but grew stronger throughout the years. Unwin saw in Cowper a fatherly figure and a man who had so tasted of life that he could give good advice on all occasions. Thus there is hardly a problem ranging from Sabbath-keeping to face-painting about which Unwin did not turn to Cowper for information and guidance. When Unwin's sons were born he looked naturally to Cowper for assistance concerning their education and Cowper wrote a long poem, 'Tirocinium', a treatise on education, which he dedicated to Unwin.

Having great friends such as William Unwin and John Newton was not easy for Cowper as most of his friends seemed to want to claim him for their very own. When Cowper published his first volume of poems he asked Newton, as his literary mentor, to look after the necessary proceedings with the publishers and told Unwin little of his plans. When this fact came out into the open Unwin was mortified to find that Cowper had chosen Newton in favour of himself. When Cowper was about to publish his second volume, he therefore asked Unwin to serve as his editor and go-between — an act which cut Newton to the quick.

When Unwin died Newton told Bull that his life had not been one which could have made an interesting subject for a biography but William Unwin will be remembered by evangelicals as the man chosen to lead William Wilberforce back to God when the up-and-coming politician had begun to forget the vows he had made his heavenly Master as a child.

Bibliography

Editions, collections and selections

Baird, John D. and Ryskamp, Charles, eds. *The Poems of William Cowper,* Oxford, vol. i, 1980.

Benham, William, ed. *The Poetical Works of William Cowper,* Globe Edition, London, 1879.

Bruce, John. *The Poetical Works of William Cowper — With Notes and a Memoir,* Aldine Edition, London (undated copy).

Fausset, Hugh I'Anson, ed. *Cowper's Poems,* Everyman, London, 1966.

Grimshawe, T. S., ed. *The Works of William Cowper—His Life and Letters — by William Hayley Esq.—Now First Completed By the Introduction of Cowper's Private Correspondence,* London, 1835, 8 vols.

Hayley, William, ed. *Cowper's Milton,* J. Johnson, London, 1808.

King, James and Ryskamp, Charles, eds. *Letters and Prose Writings of William Cowper,* Oxford, 4 vols, 1979-1984.

Milford, Humphrey S., ed. *The Poetical Works of William Cowper,* Oxford, 1905.

Newton, John and Cowper, William. *Olney Hymns — in Three Books,* 1st edition, 1779. Bicentenary facsimile edition published by the trustees of the Cowper and Newton Museum, Olney, Bucks, England.

Russel, Norma. *Bibliography of Cowper to 1837,* Oxford Bibliographical Society, 1963.

Southey, Robert, ed. *The Works of William Cowper, Esq. — Composing His Poems, Correspondence, and Translations — With A Life of the Author,* London, 1835, 14 vols.

Spiller, Brian, ed. *Cowper: Poetry and Prose,* London, 1968.

Stebbing, H., ed. *The Poetical Works of William Cowper,* London, 1843.

Willmott, Robert Aris, ed. *The Poetical Works of William Cowper,* Routledge's British Poets, London, 1866.

Biographies

Bishop, Morchard. *The Life, Works and Friendships of William Hayley,* London, Gollanz, 1951.

Bull, Josiah. *John Newton: An Autobiography and Narrative,* The Religious Tract Society, London, 1868. (Contains Cowper's commentary on John's Gospel.)

Cecil, Lord David. *The Stricken Deer — The Life of Cowper,* London, 1944.

Cheever, George Barrell. *Lectures on the Life, Genius and Insanity of Cowper,* New York, 1856.

Edwards, Brian H. *Through Many Dangers — The Story of John Newton,* Evangelical Press, 1975 edition.

Fausset, Hugh I'Anson. *William Cowper,* New York, 1968.

Free, William N. *William Cowper,* New York, 1970.

Hartley, Lodwick C. *William Cowper: Humanitarian,* North Caroliana University Press, 1938.

King, James. *William Cowper,* Duke University Press, 1986.

Martin, Bernard. *An Ancient Mariner: A Biography of John Newton,* Wyvern Books, London, 1960.

Nicholson, Norman. *William Cowper,* London, 1951.

Quinlan, Maurice J. *William Cowper: A Critical Life,* University of Minnesota Press, 1953.

Sargeaunt, Rogers and others. *Cowper in London, Papers Read before the Cowper Society,* London. Everett & Co., 1907.

Stokes, Henry Paine. *Cowper Memorials,* Oliver Ratcliff at the Cowper Press, 1904.

Symington, Andrew J. *The Poet of Home Life: Centenary Memorials of William Cowper,* 'Home Words' Office, London, 1900.

Thomas, Gilbert. *William Cowper and the Eighteenth Century,* London, Allen & Unwin, 1948.

Taylor, Thomas. *The Life of William Cowper,* R. B. Seeley and W. Burnside, 1835, 4th ed.

Wright, Thomas. *The Life of William Cowper,* London, 1892.

Works of criticism and appreciation
either dealing specifically with Cowper
or dealing with him in detail amongst others

Golden, Morris. *In Search of Stability: The Poetry of William Cowper,* New York, 1960.

Hartley, Lodwick. *William Cowper: The Continuing Revelation,* North Carolina University Press, 1960.

Newey, Vincent. *Cowper's Poetry: A Critical Study and Reassessment,* Liverpool University Press, 1982.

Roy, James A. *Cowper and His Poetry,* Norwood Editions, 1977.

Spacks, Patricia Meyer. *The Poetry of Vision,* Harvard University Press, 1967.

Historical and critical works dealing with the eighteenth century, including Cowper and his background

Abbey, Charles John and Overton, John Henry. *The English Church in the Eighteenth Century,* London, 1886, (2 vols).

Baugh, Albert C. *A Literary History of England,* London, 1948.

Balleine, George Reginald. *A History of the Evangelical Party in the Church of England,* London, 1951.

Barnes and Noble. *An Outline History of English Literature,* vol. 2, New York, 1961.

Benson, Louis F. *The English Hymn: Its Development and Use in Worship,* Hodder & Stoughton, 1915.

Birrell, Augustine. *Res Judicatae,* London, 1892.

Brooke, Stopford Augustus. *Theology in the English Poets,* Everyman's Library (Introduction dated 1874).

Cairns, William Thomas. *The Religion of Dr Johnson and Other Essays,* Oxford University Press, 1946.

Clifford, J. L. *Eighteenth Century English Literature,* New York, 1959.

Crofts, J. E. V. *Eighteenth Century Literature: An Oxford Miscellany,* 1909.

Clarkson, Thomas. *The History of the Abolition of the Slave Trade,* London, 1808.

Day, M. S. *English Literature, 1660-1837 (2),* New York, 1963.

Elton, Oliver. *A Survey of English Literature (1780-1830),* 2 vols, London, 1933.

Fairchild, Hoxie N. *Religious Trends in English Poetry,* 5 vols, New York, 1939-1962.

Feingold, Richard. *Nature and Society: Later Eighteenth-Century Uses of the Pastoral and Georgic,* 1978.

Gill, Frederick Cyril. *The Romantic Movement and Methodism,* 1966.

Graham, Walter. *English Literary Periodicals,* New York, 1930.

Heim, William J. *Critical Survey of Poetry,* ed. Magill, Frank, Salem Press, 1982, pp. 610-19.

Lecky, William Edward. *A History of England in the Eighteenth Century,* 7 vols, London, 1899.

May, George Lacey. *Some Eighteenth-Century Churchmen,* London Society for the Promotion of Christian Knowledge, 1920.

Nowak, Maximillian, E. *Eighteenth-Century English Literature,* Macmillan History of Literature, 1983.

Reynolds, Myra. *The Treatment of Nature in English Poetry between Pope and Wordsworth,* Chicago, 1909.

Roberts, William. ed. *Memoirs of the Life and Correspondence of Mrs Hannah More,* New York, 1838.

Saintsbury, George. *A History of English Prosody,* vols 2-3, New York, 1923.

Saintsbury, George. *A History of Nineteenth-Century Literature,* 1780-1895, Macmillan, New York, 1927.

Sargeaunt, John. *Annals of Westminster School,* London, Methuen, 1898.

Schöffler Herbert. *Protestantismus und Literatur: Neue Wege zur englischen Literatur des 18. Jahrhunderts,* Göttongen, 1958.

Shepherd, Thomas B. *Methodism and the Literature of the Eighteenth Century,* London, 1966.

Sherwood, Gilbert and Piper. *The Rural Walks of Cowper,* Paternoster Row, London, undated.

Tyerman, Luke. *The Oxford Methodists,* New York, 1873.

Wilde, H. O. *Der Gottesgedanke in der englischen Literatur: Das Problem der Entwicklung von Puritanischer zu Romantischer Literatur,* Breslau, 1930.

Dissertations

Ella, George Melvyn. *Paradise and Poetry: An In-Depth Study of William Cowper's Poetic Mind*, The Cowper and Newton Museum, Olney, 1989.

Hannay, Neilson Campbell. *The Religious Element in the Life and Character of William Cowper*, Harvard University, 1919.

Hantsche, Arthur. *William Cowper, sein Naturgefühl und seine Naturdichtung*, Leipzig University, 1901.

Hoffmann, Willy. *William Cowpers Belesenheit und literarische Kritik*, Berlin, 1908.

Huang, Roderick Tsui En. *William Cowper: Nature Poet*, Oxford University Press, 1957. (As dissertation, *William Cowper's Conception and Description of Nature*, Northwestern University, 1955.)

Lanham, Luise. *The Poetry of William Cowper in its Relation to the English Evangelical Movement*, University of North Carolina, 1936.

Lawton, Edith. *The Criticism of William Cowper*, Boston University, 1941.

Mack, Edward Clarence. *Public Schools and British Opinion 1780-1860*, Columbia University Press, 1938, reprint Connecticut, 1973.

Possehl, Willi. *William Cowpers Stellung zur Religion*, Rostock, 1907.

Quinlan, Maurice James. *Victorian Prelude*, Columbia University Press, 1941.

Ryskamp, Charles. *William Cowper of the Inner Temple*, New York, Cambridge University Press, 1959.

Schmidt, Kuno. *Das Verhalten der Romantiker zur Public School*, Bonn, 1935.

Thein, Adelaide Eve. *The Religion of William Cowper: An Attempt to Distinguish between His Obsession and His Creed*, University of Michigan, 1940. Dissertation Abstracts V. i., 1943, pp. 24-5.

Tietje, Gustav. *Die poetische Personifikation unpersönliche Substantiva bei Cowper und Coleridge*, Kiel, 1914.

Journal, magazine and newspaper articles

Anon. 'An Account of the Life and Death of William Cowper,' *Gospel Magazine and Theological Review*, V, 1800, pp.428-37.

Baird, John D. 'Cowper's Despair: An Allusion to Terence,' *Notes and Queries*, February 1978, p.61.

Beyer, A. 'Studien zu William Cowpers Task,' *Archiv für das Studium der neueren Sprachen und Literatur*, Braunschweig, 1888, pp.115-40.

Blunden, Edmund. 'William Cowper: Harmonist of the Countryside,' *The Times*, 13 November 1931, pp.15-16.

Bolton, Sir William. 'The Poet Cowper and his Surroundings,' *Transactions of the Royal Society of Literature of the United Kingdom*, 2nd ser. XXII, 1901, reprint 1970.

Boyd, David. 'Satire and Pastoral in "The Task",' *Papers on Language and Literature*, 10, 1974, pp.363-77.

Bradford, Gamaliel. 'Diversions of a Lost Soul,' *Atlantic Monthly*, v. 134, 1924, pp.361-70.

Bridgman, Richard. 'Weak Tocks: Coming to a Bad End in English Poetry of the Later Eighteenth Century,' *Modern Philology*, February 1983, pp.264-79.

Brown, Marshall. 'The Pre-Romantic Discovery of Consciousness,' *Studies in Romanticism*, 17, 1978, pp.387-412.

Brown, Marshall. 'The Urbane Sublime,' *English Literary History*, 45, (1978), pp.236-54.

Cavit, T. E. 'A Plea for Cowper,' *Gentleman's Magazine*, vol. 296, 1904, pp.607-16.

Chapman, Edward Mortimer. 'One Hundred Years After,' *Outlook*, LXIV, 1900, pp.918-21.

Collyer, Adelaide. 'Unpublished MSS of the Poet Cowper,' *Universal Review*, 25 June 1890, pp.279-93.

'Correspondent, A. 'Cowper's Last Years,' *Times Literary Supplement,* 5 October, 12, 1951 and 12 October, 13, 1951.

Danchin, Pierre. 'William Cowper's Poetic Purpose: as seen in his Letters,' *English Studies,* 46, 1965, pp.135-244.

Dawson, P. M. S. 'Cowper and the Russian Ice Palace,' *Review of English Studies,* 31, 1980, pp.440-43.

Dawson, P. M. S. 'Cowper's Equivocations,' *Essays in Criticism,* 33, January, no.1, 1983, pp.19-35.

Dowden, Edward. 'Cowper and William Haley,' *Atlantic Monthly,* 100, 1907, pp.74-87.

Eaves, T. C. Duncan and Kimpel, Ben D. 'Cowper's "An Ode on Reading Mr Richardson's 'History of Sir Charles Grandison'"', *Papers in Language and Literature,* Winter 1966, vol. 2, pp.74-5.

Ella, George Melvyn. 'Cowper the Campaigner,' *Evangelical Times,* October 1984, pp.4-5.

Ella, George Melvyn. 'The Olney Hymns and Their Relevance for Today,' *Bible League Quarterly,* April-June 1986, pp.420-25.

Ella, George Melvyn. 'William Cowper: "A Burning Bush which was not Consumed,"' *Banner of Truth,* Issue 256, January 1985, pp.4-11.

Ella, George Melvyn. 'John Newton's Friendship with William Cowper' *Banner of Truth* , Issue 269, February 1986, pp.10-19.

Ertl, Heimo. '"The manner wherein God has dwelt with my soul": Methodistische "Lives" im 18. Jahrhundert,' *Anglia,* Band 104, Heft 1/2, 1986, pp.63-93.

Fairchild, Hoxie Neale. 'Additional Notes on John Johnson's Diary,' *Modern Language Association of America,* xliii, 1928, pp.571-2.

Förster, Max. 'Cowpers Ballade John Gilpin,' *Englische Studien,* LXIV, 1929, pp.380-416, LXV, 1930, pp.26-48.

Frazer, J. G. 'William Cowper,' *Nineteenth Century,* Jan-June, LXXXVII, 1926, pp.103-4.

Frye, Northrop. 'Towards Defining an Age of Sensibility,' *English Literary History*, 23, 1956, pp.144-52.

Gilbert, Dorothy Lloyd and Pope, Russell. 'The Cowper Translations of Mme Guyon's Poems,' *Modern Language Association of America*, LLIV, 1939, pp.1077-98.

Golden, Morris. 'Churchill's Literary Influence on Cowper,' *Journal of English and Germanic Philology*, LVIII, 1959, pp. 655-65.

Gregory, Hoosag K. 'The Prisoner and his Crimes, Summary Comments on a Longer Study of the Mind of William Cowper,' (Ph.D.), *Literature and Psychology*, VI, 1956, pp.53-9.

Gregory, Hoosag K. 'Cowper's Love of Subhuman Nature: A Psychological Approach,' *Philological Quarterly*, XLVI, 1, January 1967, pp.42-57.

Grew, Sydney and Eva Mary. 'Cowper: His Acceptance and Rejection of Music,' *Music and Letters*, 13, 1932, pp.31-41.

Griffin, Dusty. 'Cowper, Milton and the Recovery of Paradise,' *Essays in Criticism*, 31, 1981, pp.15-26.

Hannay, Neilson Campbell. 'The Tragedy of Cowper,' *The Saturday Review of Literature*, 28 November 1931, pp.225, 328.

Hartley, Lodwick. '"The Stricken Deer" and His Contemporary Reputation,' *Studies in Philology*, XXXVI, 1939, pp.637-50.

Hartley, Lodwick. 'The Worm and the Thorn: A Study of Cowper's Olney Hymns,' *The Journal of Religion*, XXIX, 1948-49, pp.226-9.

Hartley, Lodwick. 'Cowper and the Evangelicals,' *Modern Language Association of America*, 65, 1950, pp.719-31.

Hartley, Lodwick. 'Cowper and Mme Guyon: Additional Notes,' *Modern Language Association of America Publications*, 56, 1941, pp.585-7.

Holmes, Eugene D. 'The Question of Cowper's Indebtedness to Churchill,' *Modern Language Notes*, XII, 1898, pp.165-70.

Houghton, Sidney M. 'Olney Hymns,' *Bible League Quarterly*, October-December, 1979, pp.276-9.

Hunt, Carew R. N. 'John Newton and William Cowper,' *The Nineteenth Century,* August 1941, pp.92-8.

Johansen, John Henry. 'The Olney Hymns,' *The Papers of the Hymn Society,* XX, 1956, The Hymn Society of America, pp.1-25.

Jones, Myrddin. 'Wordsworth and Cowper: The Eye Made Quiet,' *Essays in Criticism,* 21, 1971, pp.236-47.

Jones, Powell W. 'The Captive Linnet: A Footnote on Eighteenth Century Sentiment,' *Philological Quarterly,* XXXIII, III, July 1954, pp.330-37.

Judson, Alexander C. 'Henry Vaughan as a Nature Poet,' *Modern Language of America Publications,* 42, 1927, Part I, pp.146-56.

King, James. 'Cowper's Adelphi Restored: The Excisions to Cowper's Narrative,' *Review of English Studies,* 30, 1979, pp.291-305.

Knight, George Litch. 'William Cowper as a Hymn Writer,' *The Hymn,* I, 1950, pp.5-12, 20.

Kroiter, Harry P. 'The Influence of Popular Science on William Cowper,' *Modern Philology,* May 1964, pp. 281-7.

Kroiter, Harry P., Cowper. 'Deism and the Divinization of Nature,' *Journal of the History of Ideas,* 21, 1960, pp.511-26.

'L'. *The Flapper,* Dublin, XXX, 14 May, pp.117-20, XXIV, 28 May, pp.133-6, XXXVIII, 11 June, pp.149-52. Later published as the work of Alexander Knox in *Eighteenth-Century Essays,* Scott Elledge, ed, Ithaca, 1966.

Law, Alice. 'Cowper and Wordsworth,' *Fortnightly Review,* LXXI, February 1902, pp.363-4.

Lynd, Robert. 'William Cowper,' *The London Mercury,* II, 1920, pp. 55-64.

Mandel, Barrett John. 'Artistry and Psychology in William Cowper's Memoir,' *Texas Studies in Literature and Language,* XII, 1970, pp. 431-42.

Martin, Bernard. 'Fresh Light on William Cowper,' *Modern Language Quarterly,* XIII, September 1952, pp.253-5.

Martin, L. C. 'Vaughan and Cowper,' *Modern Language Review*, XXII, 1927, pp.79-84.

Morris, John N. 'The Uses of Madness: William Cowper's Memoir,' *The American Scholar*, 34, 1964-65, pp.112-26.

Moyer, Reed. 'The Letters of Gray, Walpole and Cowper,' *The Sewanee Review*, 13, 1905, pp.367-71.

Murdoch, Brian. 'Poetry, Satire and Slave Ships: Some Parallels to Heine's "Sklavenschiff",' *Forum for Modern Language Study*, 15, 1979, pp.323-35.

Murray, Iain. 'William Cowper and his Affliction,' *Banner of Truth*, Issue 96, September 1971, pp.12-32.

Musser, Joseph F. 'William Cowper's Syntax as an Indication of His Relationship to the Augustans and Romantics,' *Style*, vol. xi, Summer, 1977, No. 3, pp.284-302.

Musser, Joseph F. 'William Cowper's Rhetoric: The Picturesque and the Personal,' *Studies in English Literature*, 19, 1779, pp.515-31.

Myers, Robert Manson. 'Fifty Sermons on Handel's Messiah,' *Harvard Theological Review*, XXXIX, October 1946, pp.217-41.

Newey, Vincent. 'Cowper and the Description of Nature,' *The Critical Forum, Essays in Criticism*, vol. XXIII, April 1973, pp.102-8.

Norman, Hubert J. 'The Melancholy of Cowper,' *Westminster Review*, CLXXV, 1911, pp 638-47.

Pollard, Arthur. 'Five Poets on Religion: Cowper and Blake,' *Church Quarterly Review*, October, CLX. 1957-58.

Porter, Lawrence E. 'Hervey: A Bicentenary Appreciation,' *Evangelical Quarterly*, 31, 1959, pp. 4-20.

Povey, Kenneth, 'Cowper and Lady Austen,' *Review of English Studies*, X, 1934, pp.417-27.

Povey, Kenneth. 'The Banishment of Lady Austin,' *Review of English Studies*, XV, 1939, pp.392-400.

Povey, Kenneth. 'The Text of Cowper's Letters,' *Modern Language Review*, 22, 1927, 22-27.

Povey, Kenneth. 'Some Notes on Cowper's Letters and Poems,' *Review of English Studies*, vol. 5, 1929, No. 18, April, pp.167-72.

Povey, Kenneth. 'Notes for a Bibliography of Cowper's Letters,' *Review of English Studies*, vol. 7, 1931, No. 26, April, pp.182-7.

Povey, Kenneth. 'Further Notes for a Bibliography of Cowper's Letters,' *Review of English Studies*, vol. 8, 1932, No. 31, July, pp. 316-19.

Povey, Kenneth. 'Notes on Cowper's Letters III,' *Review of English Studies*, vol. 10, 1934, No. 37, January, pp.76-8.

Povey, Kenneth. 'Notes on Cowper's Letters IV,' *Review of English Studies*, vol. 12, 1936, No. 47, July, pp.333-5.

Price, Warwick James. 'Cowper's "Task": A Literary Milestone,' *Sewanee Review*, 24, 1916, pp.155-64.

Quinlan, Maurice J. 'William Cowper and the Unpardonable Sin,' *Journal of Religion*, XXIII, 1943, pp.110-16.

Quinlan, Maurice J. 'William Cowper and the French Revolution,' *JEGP*, 50, 1951, pp.483-90.

Quinlan, Maurice J. 'An Intermediary between Cowper and Johnson,' *Review of English Studies*, vol. 24, 1948, No. 94, April, pp. 141-7.

Quinlan, Maurice J. 'Cowper's Imagery,' *Journal of English and Germanic Philology*, XLVII, 1948, pp.276-85.

Quinlan, Maurice J., ed. 'Memoir of William Cowper,' *Proceedings of the American Philosophical Society*, vol. 97, No. 4, September 1953, pp.359-82.

Ridley, H. M. 'Great Friendships: William Cowper and Mrs Unwin,' *Canadian Magazine*, LIX, 1922, pp.438-42.

Revard, P. Stella. 'Visions and Revisions: A Study of Paradise Lost II and Paradise Regained,' *Papers in Language and Literature*, 10, 1974, pp.353-62.

Ringler, Richard N. 'The Genesis of Cowper's "Yardley Oak",' *English Language Notes,* vol. 5, 1967-68, pp.27-32.

Rogers, Deborah D. 'Cowper's "Ode on Reading Richardson's History of Sir Charles Grandison" Again,' *Papers in Language and Literature,* 18, 1982, pp.416-20.

Shafer, Robert. 'William Cowper,' *Bookman,* LXXIV, 1931, pp.287-97.

Sherbo, Arthur. 'Cowper's Connoisseur Essays,' *Modern Language Notes,* 70, 1955, pp.340-42.

Sherburn, George. 'Poets, Critics and Daily Life,' *Sewanee Review,* 1953, pp.346-7.

Spiller, Robert E. 'A New Biographical Source for William Cowper,' *Modern Language Association of America Publications,* 42, 1927, Part 2, pp. 946-62.

Tarver, J. C. 'Cowper's Ouse,' *Macmillan's Magazine,* 82, 1900, pp.135-44.

Thein, Adelaide E. 'The Religion of John Newton,' *Philological Quarterly,* XXI, 2 April 1942, pp.146-70.

Todd, William B. 'Cowper's Commentary on the Life of Johnson,' *Times Literary Supplement,* 15 March 1957.

Whiting, Mary Bedford. 'A Burning Bush: New Light on the Relations Between Cowper and Newton,' *The Hibbert Journal,* XXIV, 1926, pp.303-13.

Reviews

Anon. 'Cowper's Adelphi,' *Gentleman's Magazine,* April 1802, pp.335-6.

Anon. 'Hayley's Cowper,' *Gentleman's Magazine,* May 1803, pp.433-41.

Anon. 'Hayley's Life of Cowper,' *Edinburgh Review,* vols 1-2, April 1803, pp.64-87, vol. 3, July 1804, pp.273-84.

Anon. 'Cowper's Memoir', 'Johnson's edition of Cowper's poems', 'Greatheed's Memoir', *Electic Review,* October 1816, pp.313-43.

Anon. 'Review of Cowper's Memoir,' *Panoplist and Missionary Magazine,* vol. XIII, 1817, pp.65-77.

Anon. 'Johnson's Edition of Cowper's Letters,' *Quarterly Review,* October-January 1823-24, pp.185-99.

Anon. 'Recent Lives of Cowper, (Southey and Grimshawe),' *Edinburgh Review,* July 1836, pp.177-95.

Anon. 'Reviews on Wright's Life of Cowper, Hartley's William Cowper: Humanitarian, Fausset's William Cowper and Cecil's Stricken Deer,' *The Eighteenth Century,* pp.157, 197, 280-81, 306.

Anon. 'Fausset's The Poems of William Cowper, Power and Gentleness,' *Times Literary Supplement,* 19 November1931, pp.901-2.

Bloom, Edward. A. 'Ryskamp's "William Cowper of the Inner Temple, Esquire, "' *MLR,* 1960, pp.395-6.

Clifford, James L. 'Quinlan's William Cowper, A Critical Life, Reflections on the Sward,' *Saturday Review of Literature,* 4 April 1953, p.32.

Collyer, Adelaide. 'Unpublished MSS. of the Poet Cowper', *Universal Review,* 25 June 1890, pp.271-93.

Cowie, Alexander. 'Hartley's William Cowper: Humanitarian, Land-Locked Poet,' *Saturday Review,* June 18 1938, p.18.

Dalrymple-Champneys, Norma. 'Ryskamp's and King's edition,' *Notes and Queries,* February 1981, pp.82-84, December 1982, pp.557-8.

Dalrymple-Champneys, Norma. 'Baird's and Ryskamp's edition,' *Notes and Queries,* February 1982, pp.83-4.

Dewar, M. W. 'Paradise and Poetry,' *English Churchman,* p.6, 26 January & 2 February 1990.

Ella, George Melvyn. 'William Cowper: A Review Article,' *Banner of Truth,* Issue 274, July 1986, pp.16-22, 24.

Francis C. John, 'The Cowper Centenary,' *Notes and Queries,* 21 April 1900, pp.301-9.

Gregory K. Hoosag. 'Ryskamp's William Cowper of the Inner Temple, Esquire,' *Journal of English and German Philology,* 59, 1960, pp.158-61.

Hanney, Neilson C. 'Quinlan's William Cowper: A Critical Life,' *Journal of English and German Philology,* 53, 1954, pp.125-6.

Hartley, Lodwick. 'Master of Prose,' *Saturday Review of Literature,* 5 January 1952, pp.12-13.

Harvardiensis, 'Southey's Edition of Cowper,' *Notes and Queries,* 8 August 1857, pp.101-2. See Maitland, S. R.

Haslip, Joan. 'Cecil's Stricken Deer,' *The London Mercury,* April, XXI, pp.565-7.

Haney, John Lewis, ed. *Early Reviews of English Poets,* Philadelphia, 1904, (Reprint, New York, 1970).

Legg, John. 'Paradise and Poetry,' *Evangelical Times,* p.17, April 1990.

Maclean, George. 'Paradise and Poetry,' *Banner of Truth,* issue 323-4, August-September 1990, p.62.

Maitland, S. R. 'Southey's Cowper,' *Notes and Queries,* 22 August 1857, pp.152-3.

Martin, T. D. 'Paradise and Poetry: A Review Article and Reflection upon Cowper's Work,' pp.321-7, *Bible League Quarterly,* April-June 1990.

Osgood, Charles. 'Cecil's The Stricken Deer, Tragic Greatness,' *Saturday Review of Literature,* 10 May 1930, p.1026 ff.

Southron, Jane Spence. 'Hartley's William Cowper: Humanitarian, A Portrait of An Early Liberal,' *The New York Times Book Review,* 25 December 1938, p.6.

Tomkins, A. D. R. 'Hartley's William Cowper: The Continuing Revaluation,' *Notes and Queries,* January 1962, pp. 35-7.

Miscellaneous

Baker, Frank. 'James Hervey, Methodist Prose Poet,' *London Quarterly and Holborn Review*, pp. 62-8 (copy undated).

Bentley, G. E. 'Blake, Hayley and Lady Hesketh,' *Review of English Studies*, New Series, vol. VII, 1956, pp.264-86.

Bull, Josiah. *Memorials of the Rev. William Bull*, London, 1864.

Bull, Josiah. *Letters by the Rev. John Newton*, RTS, 1869.

Cecil, Richard, ed. *The Works of The Rev. John Newton*, 6 vols, London, 1824, Banner of Truth Trust reprint, 1985.

Dallimore, Arnold. *George Whitefield: The Life and Times of the Great Evangelist of the Eighteenth-Century Revival*, 2 vols, Banner of Truth Trust, 1980.

Dwight, Sereno E., ed. *The Works of Jonathan Edwards*, 2 vols, 1834, facsimile, Banner of Truth Trust, 1979.

Furneaux, Robin, *William Wilberforce*, Hamish Hamilton, 1974.

Hervey, James. *The Works of The Rev. James Hervey, A.M. (With 'Life')*, Edinburgh, 1837. (Quotes are taken from this edition.)

Johnson, Catharine Bodham, ed. *Letters of Lady Hesketh to the Rev. John Johnson, LL.D.*, London, 1901.

Jones, Mary Gladys. *The Charity School Movement: A Study of Eighteenth-Century Puritanism in Action*, Cambridge 1964.

Lloyd-Jones, D. M. *The Puritans: Their Origins and Successors*, Banner of Truth Trust, 1987.

Madan, Martin. *Thelyphthora or a Treatise on Female Ruin etc.*, Dodsley in Pall-Mall, 1781.

Midgley, Graham, ed. *John Bunyan: The Poems*, Oxford, 1980.

Murray, Iain. *The Puritan Hope*, Banner of Truth Trust, 1975.

Newe, John. *A Concordance to The Poetical Works of William Cowper*,

London, 1887 (Does not include the bulk of Cowper's translation work or many of his minor poems.)

Offer, George, ed. *The Whole Works of John Bunyan,* London, 3 vols, 1862.

Ollard, S. L. *The Six Students of St. Edmund Hall: Expelled from the University of Oxford in 1768,* A. R. Mowbray, 1911.

Pollock, John. *Wilberforce,* Lion, 1982.

Pennington, David and Thomas, eds. *Puritans and Revolutionaries: Essays in Seventeenth-Century History Presented to Christopher Hill,* Oxford, 1978.

Scott, Thomas. *Letters and Papers,* ed. John Scott A. M., Seeley and Sons, London, 1824.

Shedd, W. G. T. *Calvinism Pure & Mixed: A Defence of the Westminster Standards,* New York, 1893, Banner of Truth Trust. reprint 1986.

Vallins, G. H. *The Wesleys and The English Language,* London, 1957.

Wright, Thomas. *The Town of Cowper,* London, 1886.

Wright, Thomas, ed. *The Diary of Samuel Teedon,* 1902.

References

Introduction

1. See especially chapter 3, 'The Evangelical Phase'.

2. Norman Nicholson, *William Cowper,* London, 1951 p.75.

3. Hugh I'Anson Fausset, *Cowper's Poems,* Everyman, Dent, 1966, Introduction, p.vii. See also Fausset's *William Cowper,* New York, 1970.

4. James King and Charles Ryskamp, eds, *Letters and Prose Writings of William Cowper,* 5 vols, 1979-1986.

5. A possible exception here is Cowper's own account of his early life, published under the name of *Adelphi* (supplied by Newton) by King and Ryskamp. This seems to be very much a 'restored' text and the last word has certainly not been spoken as to its complete authenticity.

6. It is a moot point whether or not Cowper was mentally ill during his third major illness of 1787. The evidence points rather to physical exhaustion and physical illnesses.

7. George Barrell Cheever, *Lectures on the Life, Genius and Insanity of Cowper,* New York, 1856.

8. Newton died before his version was published but meanwhile he allowed others to publish copies from the original in his possession.

9. See, for instance, John White's *The Masks of Melancholy,* IVP, first British edition, pp.141 ff. in which White quotes a lengthy account (based more or less on Newton's publication) of a supposed suicide attempt by Cowper *after* conversion. In a later edition White, who is discussing 'Christian' suicide, admits very, very briefly that he got his facts wrong in his first edition and the attempts were made before Cowper's conversion. Nevertheless he still quotes the story, as an example of the way even a Christian can be moved to take his own life.

10. Cecil, *Stricken Deer,* ch. 3.

11. *London Mercury,* II, 1920.

12. *Blackwoods,* August 1912.

13. See review of Fausset's biography of Cowper in the *Eighteenth Century Magazine,* vol. xix, 1938.

14. Note, for instance, the opening pages of Bernard Martin's otherwise excellent *The Ancient Mariner.* Martin depicts Newton as a small boy longing to play football

with the village ragamuffins. In actual fact he told them that he preferred to play with 'Mama'.

15. 'Charity', lines 9-14.

Chapter 1 — The early years

1. See H. P. Stokes, *Cowper Memorials,* Cowper Press, 1904, p.142 and other biographies.
2. *Ibid.,* p.142.
3. *Ibid.,* p.148.
4. *Ibid.,* p.147.
5. See, for instance, letter to John Newton, 29 March 1784.
6. 'On the receipt of my mother's picture.'
7. See, for instance, Cowper's *Memoir (Adelphi),* in King & Ryskamp, *Letters and Prose Writings of Cowper,* vol. I, p.6.
8. See 'Tirocinium', an educational treatise in poetic form.
9. 'On the receipt of my mother's picture.'
10. *Ibid.*
11. 'Tirocinium', lines 131-40.
12. *Adelphi,* King & Ryskamp, *Letters and Prose Writings of Cowper,* vol. 1, p.5. All earlier autobiographic information is also taken from *Adelphi.*
13. *Ibid.,* p.5.
14. Letter to John Buchanan, 5 September 1795.
15. Letter to William Unwin, 23 May 1781.
16. Special maundy money was granted to the school for this purpose.
17. Cowper wrote to his pupil and friend Samuel Rose in August 1792, 'Green and buff are colours in which I am oftener seen than in any others.'
18. Other sources say 'she' was brought in a sedan chair.
19. King & Ryskamp, *Letters and Prose Writings of Cowper,* vol. 1, p.7.
20. *Ibid,* p.8.
21. 'Table Talk', lines 506-10.
22. *Task,* IV, lines 709-17.

Chapter 2 — Apprentice to the law

1. Letter to John Duncombe, 16 June 1757.
2. Letter to Samuel Rose, 9 October 1787.
3. Letter to Mrs Madan, 15 October 1767.
4. See letter to Lady Hesketh, 17 April 1786.
5. 'Progress of Error,' lines 307-10.
6. *Adelphi,* King & Ryskamp, *Letters and Prose Writings of Cowper,* vol. 1, p.8.
7. *Olney Hymns,* Book III, Hymn LXIII.
8. See letter to John Duncombe, 21 November 1758
9. See *Adelphi,* King & Ryskamp, *Letters and Prose Writings of Cowper,* vol. 1, from which all subsequent references to Cowper's pre-conversion life are taken if not stated otherwise.
10. This and all succeeding poems written to Theadora are taken from Baird and Ryskamp, *The Poems of William Cowper,* vol. i, Oxford, 1980.
11. From a poem written in 1755 starting, 'All-worshipp'd gold! thou mighty mystery!'
12. From 'The Symptoms of Love'.

13. From 'Bid Adieu, my Sad Heart, Bid Adieu to thy Peace'.
14. From 'Written in a Quarrel'.
15. From 'This Evening, Delia, You and I'.
16. From 'Hope, like the Short-Liv'd Ray that Gleams Awhile', written perhaps 1757.
17. i. e., stockings
18. Letter to John Newton, 4 December 1781.
19. King & Ryskamp, *Letters and Prose Writings of Cowper*, vol. 1, p.11
20. *Task*, V, lines 861-6.
21. *Task*, VI, lines 238-40.

Chapter 3 — Crisis and conversion

1. Letter to Lady Hesketh, 31 July 1762.
2. Letter to Clotworthy Rowley, 2 September 1762.
3. *Adelphi*, King & Ryskamp, *Letters and Prose Writings of Cowper*, vol. 1, p.17.
4. Letter to Lady Hesketh, 9 August 1763.
5. J. C. Ryle, *Christian Leaders of the 18th Century*, Banner of Truth Trust, 1978, p.288.
6. The book was published anonymously in 1658 and was probably the work of Archbishop Sterne. King and Ryskamp suggest Richard Allestree as its author.
7. To be fair it must be said that some eighteenth-century Evangelical writers, such as Dr Doddridge, spoke highly of Tillotson.
8. Cowper is combining several verses of Scripture including Psalm 42:7; Job 16:14 and Job 7:14
9. Cowper's account of his illness and conversion can be read in *Adelphi* which is prefaced to King and Ryskamp's collection of his works.
10. Isaiah 33:15-16.

Chapter 4 — New and lasting friendships

1. 'Conversation,' lines 679-702.
2. Cowper is referring to a character in *Letters Writ by a Turkish Spy* which made popular reading in the seventeenth and eighteenth centuries.
3. Letter to Joseph Hill, 24 June 1765.
4. Letter to Joseph Hill, 12 November 1766.
5. Letter of Lady Hesketh to John Johnson, 27 September 1793.
6. Letter to Joseph Hill, 3 July 1765.
7. Luke 8:35.
8. Letter to Martin Madan, 24 June 1765.
9. Letter of Lady Hesketh to John Johnson, 6 June 1797, *Letters of Lady Hesketh to the Rev. John Johnson, LLD,* Jarrold and Sons, London.
10. Letter to Lady Hesketh, 18 October 1765.
11. Letter to Lady Hesketh, 4 July 1765.
12. Letter to Lady Hesketh, 1 July 1765.
13. Letter to Lady Hesketh, 4 July 1765.
14. Quoted from K. C. Balderston, *Thraliana*, Clarendon Press, 1951, p.444.
15. Taken from 'Extracts from Mrs. Thrale's Collection of Letters' found in Arthur Compton-Rickett, *A History of English Literature*, 1933, p.244.
16. Letter to Lady Hesketh, 16 January 1786.

17. See *Adelphi*, King & Ryskamp, *Letters and Prose Writings of Cowper*, vol. 1.
18. Letter to Mrs Cowper, 18 October 1765.
19. Martin Madan, *Psalms and Hymns*. There were numerous editions of this book from 1760 onwards.
20. Letter to Mrs Cowper, 20 October 1766.
21. See, for instance, 'The Garden' in Book III of the *Task*.
22. Letter to Mrs Madan, 10 July 1767.
23. Letter to Mrs Cowper, 13 July 1767.
24. 'Truth,' lines 357-60.

Chapter 5 — The mariner's tale
1. I have relied chiefly on Newton's own account of his life as related to the Rev. T. Haweis, available in numerous editions under the title *The Life of the Rev. John Newton* (otherwise known as his *Authentic Narrative*) and Newton's *Autobiography* edited by Josiah Bull. Further details concerning Newton's life can be found in his *Works* (which are far from 'complete') published recently by the Banner of Truth Trust. There is still a large amount of unpublished manuscript material by Newton's hand.
2. Letter to Lady Hesketh, 4 July 1765.
3. Newton is paraphrasing and 'Christianizing' words of Propertius.
4. An exegesis of John chapter 1.

Chapter 6 — Life at Olney
1. Thomas Wright, *The Loved Haunts of Cowper*, London 1894, p.23. Alsatia is a very industrialized area of France.
2. Cowper's word for a newsagent's.
3. Cowper tried to talk Wilson out of taking this step and was successful for a time. What eventually turned the scales was the unchristian testimony of Newton's successor, the Rev. B. Page.
4. Abraham Booth (1734-1806) was to become the pastor of a Calvinistic Baptist Church at Little Prescot Street, Goodman's Fields some seven months later.
5. Samuel Burford was pastor of a Calvinistic Baptist Church at Currier's Hall, Cripplegate.
6. Letter to Mrs Madan, 18 June 1768.
7. There is a difference of opinion as to *who* said the words. *That* they were said has never been in doubt.
8. Letter to Mrs Madan, 26 September 1767.
9. Letter to Joseph Hill, 21 January 1769.
10. Letter to Joseph Hill, 29 January 1769.
11. Letter to Mrs Madan, 18 June 1768.
12. All subsequent references to John Cowper are taken from his brother's account of his conversion, placed after his account of his own conversion under the title *Adelphi* to be found in the first volume of King & Ryskamp's collection.
13. Letter to Mrs Unwin, 11-12 March 1770.
14. See Josiah Bull, *The Autobiography and Narrative of John Newton*, 1868 (afterwards referred to as Newton's *Autobiography*), p.172.
15. *Ibid.*, p.189ff.
16. Letter of John Newton to Cowper, 2 March 1771, *Ibid.*, p.174.

17. 'A Review of Ecclesiastical History', Newton's *Works,* vol. iii. p.288, Banner of Truth, 1985.

18. 'Hope', lines 556-93.

19. See Josiah Bull's collection of Newton's letters, *Letters by the Rev. John Newton,* RTS, 1869, pp.151-66.

20. The background to this story has been obtained chiefly from Newton's *Autobiography* and letters quoted by Bernard Martin in his *Ancient Mariner.* For a full but by no means conclusive discussion of the farce concerning Cowper's alleged lack of sexuality see Charles Ryskamp, *William Cowper of the Inner Temple Esq.,* Cambridge University Press, 1959.

21. See Newton's *Autobiography,* p.197.

22. *Ibid.,* p.200.

Chapter 7 — The child of God walking in darkness

1. Newton's *Autobiography,* p.201.

2. From 'Epitaph to a Hare'.

3. Letter to John Newton, 24 September 1780.

4. Jonathan Edwards, *A Narrative of Surprising Conversions,* Banner of Truth Trust, vol. i., p.343 ff.

5. Thus Cowper starts his longest poem, *Task,* with the words, 'I sing the Sofa'.

6. William Wordsworth, Preface to *Lyrical Ballads,* 1800.

7. Taken from Martin's *Ancient Mariner,* p.176. It was usual in the eighteenth century to start a sentence with a small letter after a full stop. Cowper followed this practice at times.

8. See Newton's *Autobiography,* p.214. See also *The Autobiography of William Jay,* Banner of Truth Trust, 1974, p.290 (chapter on 'Ryland').

9. Letter of Newton to Lord Dartmouth,17 February 1776, Newton's *Autobiography,* p.219.

10. Letter to Mary Newton, 4 March 1780.

11. Bull lived at Newport Pagnell, only a few miles from Olney.

12. Letter to William Unwin, 8 June 1783.

Chapter 8 — Cowper's library

1. See, for instance, *The Story of Squire Cowper,* Occasional Paper No. 4, July 1980.

2. *Task,* Book IV, lines 704-17.

3. Letter to Mrs Cowper, 14 March 1767.

4. Letter to Lady Hesketh, 16 February 1788.

5. Letter to Lady Hesketh, 31 March 1788.

6. The 'trifle' was:

> In vain to live from age to age
> We modern bards endeavour,
> But write in Patty's book One page—
> You gain your point for ever.

7. William Roberts, ed. *Memoirs of the Life and Correspondence of Mrs Hannah More,* New York, 1838, pp.144-5.

8. *The Thoughts of the Evangelical Leaders, Notes of the Discussions of the Eclectic Society, London During the Years 1798-1814,* Banner of Truth Trust reprint, 1978.

9. Letter to John Newton, 5 November 1785.
10. Letter to John Newton, 19 February 1788.
11. Letter to John Newton, 8 April 1781.

Chapter 9 — Walking into public notice
1. Letter to William Unwin, 28 March 1780.
2. Letter to William Unwin, 24 June 1781.
3. Letter to William Unwin, 1 May 1779.
4. Newton's address in London.
5. Letter to Newton, 31 July 1780.
6. When the riddle was published in the *Gentleman's Magazine* after Cowper's death, a reader solved it with the answer 'a kiss'.
7. It might be thought exaggerated to refer to a 'coffee-house' in such a negative way but such houses were of very low repute in Cowper's day. Even in his most rakish period, Cowper confessed there was only one coffee-house in the whole of London that one could frequent without the risk of finding oneself in the most ribald and vulgar company.
8. Up to this time hymn-singing in Anglican church services was almost unknown and most churches were without organs and other musical instruments.
9. Wesley's *Journal*, 22 October 1768.
10. *Ibid.*, 9 August 1778.
11. *Ibid.*, 22 October 1768.
12. During the Calvinist-Arminian controversy at the end of the eighteenth century, many Calvinists argued that Occiduus, meaning 'west', was a reference to the Wesleys, (i.e. 'West-leys'). Hayley thought that the reason why Cowper's first volume did not sell well for the first three years or so was that believers thought he was attacking Wesley. Internal evidence in Cowper's works points to either Martin Madan, the West End pastor, or his brother Spencer as the 'culprit'. Occiduus also means 'near death' and 'perishing'.
13. 'The Progress of Error', lines 124-68.
14. Roberts, *Memoirs of Hannah More,* p.170. (Miss More had just published *Manners of the Great.*)
15. Madan's emphasis.
16. Letter to John Newton, 19 November 1780.
17. Sternhold was one of the authors of the metric psalms sung in the Anglican service. Many later hymn-writers regarded his work as mere doggerel — Cowper disagreed with them.
18. Newton's *Autobiography*, p.250.
19. Letter to John Newton, 6 February 1780.
20. Mrs Unwin's son-in-law, the Rev. Matthew Powley, was also very helpful in influencing Riland for the good.
21. Letter to Mary Newton, 5 June 1780. In his published version Cowper replaced the first verse with the lines:

> Reas'ning at every step he treads,
> Man yet mistakes his way,
> While meaner things, whom instinct leads,
> Are rarely known to stray,

and made a few other minor alterations.

22. 'Anti-Thelyphthora,' lines 58-67.

23. George Offer, *The Whole Works of John Bunyan*, 1867, vol. III, p.87.

24. Newton's *Autobiography*, p.252.

25. Horace's *Satires*, I. ii. 54, 'This is how to make friends and keep them friends.' Source given in King & Ryskamp, *Letters and Prose Writings of Cowper*, vol. i, p.361. Letter to John Newton, 5 July 1780.

26. Horace, *Epistles*, II. i. 258-9: 'My modesty does not allow me to attempt a task which is beyond my strength to bear.'

27. Letter to John Newton, 18 February 1781.

28. Letter to John Newton, 27 November 1781.

29. Letter to John Newton, 25 February 1781.

30. Letter to William Unwin, 11 May 1781.

31. Cowper pronounced 'haste' with a short vowel to rhyme with 'last', also with a short vowel. Although Olney is now well within the area of Britain where vowels are pronounced long, older inhabitants of Olney still pronounce their vowels short, often reminding one of a Yorkshireman's speech. Cowper went to great pains to adopt the local pronunciation.

32. Letter to William Unwin, 24 June 1781. Cowper is referring in his final sentence to a baby's teething-ring.

33. Letter to John Newton, 12 July 1781.

34. Letter to John Newton, 25 August 1781.

35. Letter to John Newton, 22 October 1781.

36. Letter to William Unwin, 6 October 1781.

37. 'The Progress of Error,' lines 444-7.

Chapter 10 — The *Poems*

1. Vincent Newey, *Cowper's Poetry*, Liverpool University Press, 1982, p.147.

2. 'A Poetic Epistle to Lady Austen,' lines 20-22.

3. 'Retirement,' line 708.

4. Letter to William Unwin, 4 August 1783.

5. *Task*, VI, lines 751-58.

6. Letter to Lady Hesketh, 15 May 1786.

7. 'Poetic Epistle to Lady Austen', lines 3-8, 9-14.

8. Letter to William Unwin, 18 June 1780.

9. See, for instance, letter to Joseph Hill, 9 May 1781.

10. Letter to Mrs Cowper, 19 October 1781.

11. See, for instance, Cowper's letter to Lady Hesketh in December 1785 where he outlines in detail his purpose in composing his two volumes.

12. 'Table Talk,' lines 584-93.

13. 'Conversation', lines 881-6.

14. *Ibid.*, lines 887-90.

15. *Ibid.*, lines 751-3.

16. Newton's *Works*, vol. 1, 'A Plan of a Compendius Christian Library,' p.236.

17. 'Table Talk,' lines 716-25.

18. *Ibid.*, lines 726-33.

19. *Ibid.*, lines 734-9.

20. 'Charity', lines 5-14.

21. Macaulay, *Critical and Historical Essays*, 5 vols, Tauchnitz Edition, Leipzig, 1850, vol. 1, pp.331-3.

22. *Ibid.*, p.332.
23. *Ibid.*, p.215.
24. 'Progress of Error,' lines 1-12.
25. *Ibid.*, lines 460-69.
26. 'Charity', lines 623-26.
27. 'Progress of Error', lines 307-26.
28. *Ibid.*, lines 606-24.
29. 'Truth,' lines 58-70.
30. Letter to Joseph Johnson, 6 August 1781.
31. 'Charity', lines 557-60.
32. 'Truth', lines 317-36.
33. 'Charity', lines 83-96.
34. *Ibid.*, lines 123-36.
35. 'Hope', lines 447-64.
36. 'Charity,' lines 137-40.
37. *Ibid.*, lines 180-83.
38. *Ibid.*, lines 200-217.
39. An exception for Cowper was in lands where no population had been suppressed and no tyranny practised. Such an exception, in his opinion, was to be found in the American colonies. See letter to John Newton, 13 January 1782. The future of the American colonies was often a topic for discussion between the two friends.
40. 'Expostulation', lines 364-75.
41. *Hymns Ancient and Modern Revised,* Hymn 578, v. 2.
42. 'Expostulation', lines 85-94.
43. *Ibid.*, lines 95-122.
44. *Ibid.*, lines 376-85.
45. *Ibid.*, lines 414-27.
46. *Ibid.*, 636-53.
47. 'Table Talk', lines 260-67.
48. 'Truth', lines 337-8.
49. 'Charity,' lines 339-48.
50. *Ibid.*, lines 349-364.
51. 'Anti-Thelyphthora', lines 40-45.
52. *Ibid.*, lines 46-51.
53. 'Conversation', lines 165-8.
54. *Ibid.*, lines 311-24.
55. *Ibid.*, lines 245-60.
56. *Ibid.*, lines 283-94.
57. *Ibid.*, lines 235-40.
58. *Ibid.*, lines 505-46.
59. 'Truth', lines 238-43.
60. 'Hope', lines 39-54.
61. 'Truth', 257-78.
62. 'Hope', lines 133-48.
63. 'Retirement', lines 79-98.
64. 'Hope', lines 742-53.
65. 'Retirement', lines 346-64.
66. 'Truth', lines 573-86.

67. Letter to William Unwin, 23 May 1781.
68. i. e. those who practise baptism by immersion.
69. 'Charity', lines 608-11.
70. See Nicholson, *William Cowper*, pp.106-7. This poem is, for Nicholson, an example of what he calls Cowper's 'primitivism'.
71. See Wordsworth on Cowper in his preface to *Lyrical Ballads*.
72. Vincent Newey, in *Cowper's Poetry*, pp.282-4, does quote the final verse but cannot see the 'wood' of Cowper's faith for the 'trees' of his own method of analysis.
73. See 'Hope', lines 754-9.

Chapter 11 — Second spring
1. See the chapter 'Second Spring' in Quinlan's work, *William Cowper: A Critical Life*, Greenwood Press, 1953 and also the chapter of that name in Hugh I'Anson Fausset's biography, *William Cowper*.
2. Letter to Lady Hesketh, 12 October 1785.
3. Letter to Thurlow, 25 February 1782.
4. Letter to Joseph Hill, 12 April 1783.
5. See Boswell's lengthy note on the incident in his *Life of Johnson*, John Murray, New Edition, 1876, p.499.
6. See Goldwin Smith's *Cowper*, p.127.
7. Letter to John Johnson, 18 January 1791.
8. See 'Conversation', lines 245-60.
9. From 'The Nativity'.
10. See 'The Distressed Travellers':
    I sing of a journey to Clifton
    We would have perform'd if we could,
    Without cart or barrow to lift on
    Poor Mary and me thro' the mud...
11. See S. L. Ollard, M.A., *The Six Students of St. Edmund Hall. Expelled from the University of Oxford in 1768*, Mowbray, 1911.
12. See letter to John Newton, 7 July 1781.
13. Letter to William Unwin, 29 July 1781.
14. He had married a woman who had brought an illegitimate daughter into the marriage and, as the couple seemed incapable of looking after the child, she was taken in care by Mrs Unwin and brought up as her daughter.
15. Letter to Wiliam Unwin, 9 February 1782.
16. Letter to William Unwin, 24 February1782.
17. Actually the tale was not new to Cowper who had told it — or a very similar one — to Mary Newton in 1780. A letter in Newton's hand was discovered in 1952 referring to Cowper's story in which the clergyman says, 'We more than smiled at your account about F. Freeman's horse, the faster he ran, the more the panniers clatter'd, the more they clatter'd the faster he ran.' See Bernard Martin, 'Fresh light on William Cowper, *MLQ*, XII, 1952, pp.253-5.
18. Letter to William Unwin, 20 November 1784.
19. See Cowper's sermon outline in letter to William Unwin, dated 27 November 1784. In typical manner Cowper adds, 'If you can make use of it — It may be said of Me Who being dead, yet preacheth.'

20. See Dr Doddridge's beautiful account of Col. James Gardiner's conversion entitled *Some Remarkable Passages in the Life of the Hon. Col. James Gardiner*, Bungay, 1808.

21. Letter to William Unwin, 28-29 July 1785.

22. Letter to William Unwin, 30 April 1785.

23. Letter of John Newton, 2 September 1780.

24. Letter to John Newton, 10 August 1780.

25. Cowper is referring to the incident related in Acts 16 where a young woman had a spirit of divination and called Paul and Silas 'servants of the most high God'. Nevertheless Paul commanded the spirit to leave her.

26. Letter to John Newton, 7 November 1781.

27. See the discussion on the dangers of Calvinism and Arminianism in *Thoughts of the Evangelical Leaders*, p.505 f.

28. Letter to John Newton, 21 December 1781.

29. See Cowper's letter to Powley dated 24 June 1782 in which he encloses an excerpt from Newton.

30. Dr Martyn Lloyd-Jones used to stress that the best way to comfort people who are beset with a particular fear is to bring them relief by helping them to talk and think about other things.

31. Letter to John and Mary Newton, 14 March 1782.

32. Letter of Newton to Thornton, 4 August 1773, Newton's *Autobiography*, pp.195-6.

33. The fact that Milton in the previous century praised melancholy in his verse shows how dangerous it is to generalize in this way.

34. See the opening words of James Hervey's 'Meditations among the Tombs', Robert Blair's 'The Grave' (Blair, like Cowper, could combine the melancholy and humorous in a highly entertaining way) and Edward Young's 'Night Thoughts'. Young, in his 'Night Thoughts', echoes the very symptoms of Cowper's melancholy, showing clearly that Cowper was by no means the 'odd man out' in reflecting the feelings he did.

35. Letter to Mrs King, 4 August 1791.

36. Scott, who was the last of the three to experience the fever, responded to it by having an attack of asthma. Thus three men of God reacted to the same virus in three completely different ways according to their personal habits and natures.

37. Thomas De Quincey describes his own symptoms when taking opium in his book *The Confessions of an English Opium-Eater*. At times De Quincey's descriptions are almost identical with those of Cowper.

38. An area in southern Italy which was visited by violent earthquakes in early 1783.

39. Letter to John Newton, 8 September 1783.

40. Probably Forster's *A Voyage Round the World* (1777).

41. Certain Evangelicals at the time were maintaining that 'The cause of Pitt is the cause of God.'

42. Letter to William Unwin, 3 July 1784.

43. Hannah Wilson, whom Mrs Unwin had taken in care.

44. Cowper's servant's child.

45. Perhaps Smith's most balanced, most satirical and most influential attack was against the Society for the Suppression of Vice (formerly the Proclamation Society) in the *Edinburgh Review* in January 1809.

46. Perhaps the only time Cowper did not agree with Hayley was when they discussed Cook. Cowper felt that Cook was wrong to behave as if he were some semi-divine emissary, even allowing himself to be worshipped. Hayley, who had met and talked with Cook, protested that he was quite the opposite in character.

47. *Letters by the Rev. John Newton,* p.163.

48. *Ibid.*

49. *A Plan of Academical Preparation for the Ministry,* published 1784.

50. Letter of John Newton, 19 November 1800. From Newton, *Letters and Conversational Remarks,* London, 1809.

51. See Cowper's letter to Newton dated 22 May 1784, in which Cowper deplores such antagonism shown to his friend.

52. The Banner of Truth Trust's edition of Newton's *Works.*

53. Letter to John Newton, 11 April 1784.

54. 'On Dreaming,' *Olney Hymns,* Book II, Hymns XCVIII.

55. See Newton's account of Cowper in his funeral sermon on Exodus 3:2-3. See Mary B. Whiting, 'A Burning Bush: New Light on the Relations Between Cowper and Newton', *The Hibbert Journal,* XXIV, 1926, pp.303-13.

56. See Geoffrey Scott and F. A. Pottle, eds, *Private Papers of James Boswell from Malahide Castle,* (19344) XVIII.

57. Rev. George Gilfillian.

Chapter 12 — Cowper's *Task*

1. Letter to John Newton, 11 December 1784.

2. Letter to John Newton, 24 December 1784.

3. In a letter to a clerical society discussing why faithful ministers 'decline in apparent usefulness', Thomas Scott says that it was Newton's love of gossip which ruined his ministry in Olney, causing him to lose 'almost all his authority and influence'. *Letters and Papers of the Late Rev. Thomas Scott,* ed. John Scott A.M., Seeley and Son, pp.314-17.

4. Moses Browne.

5. See Cowper's letter to Joseph Hill, 29 June 1785.

6. Humorous term in literary criticism for such polysyllabic words.

7. Letter to William Unwin, 10 October 1784.

8. *Task,* II, lines 150-53.

9. Alexander Knox in *The Flapper,* Dublin, xxx, xxxiv, xxxviii, 1796.

10. *Task,* II, lines 158-60.

11. *Ibid.,* lines 385-429.

12. *Task,* III, lines 108-11.

13. *Ibid.,* lines 112-16.

14. See G. Ella, *Paradise and Poetry,* Cowper and Newton Museum, pp.226 ff. for a more detailed study of this passage.

15. See, for instance, Morris Golden, *In Search of Stability,* p.42.

16. *Task,* III, lines 225-8.

17. See 'Hazlitt on Cowper' in *Cowper: Poetry and Prose With Essays by Hazlitt and Bagehot,* ed. Humphrey S. Milford, Clarendon Press, 1953. Hazlitt also states that Cowper 'shakes hands with nature with a pair of fashionable gloves on', which suggests he had never read Cowper's lines on building a compost heap.

18. *Task,* IV, lines 120-29.

19. See G. Ella, *Paradise and Poetry*, pp.213-31 for a lengthier discussion.

20. *Task*, IV, lines 36-41.

21. *Ibid.*, lines 466-79.

22. Cowper had a 'guinea' edition made for the wealthy and an unbound, cheap edition for the poor.

23. *Task*, IV, lines 788-801.

24. *Task*, V, lines 187-92.

25. *Ibid.*, lines 538-47.

26. *Ibid.*, lines 896-907.

27. See Iain Murray's admirable book *The Puritan Hope*, Banner of Truth Trust, 1971.

28. See the writings of John Bunyan and especially Jonathan Edwards on the subject.

29. Newton, *Works*, vol. 1, pp.331-2.

30. *Task*, VI lines 729-47.

31. *Ibid.*, lines 855-63.

32. 'Tirocinium', lines 127-30.

33. Schools all over Europe are gradually turning their backs on phonetic-based reading and are once again adopting the 'story method' by which units of sense are learnt rather than mere units of sounds. Cowper would be very pleased!

34. Cowper's own word for the public school.

35. 'Tirocinium', lines 420-27.

36. *Ibid.*, lines 789-92.

Chapter 13 — The nightingale and the glow-worm

1. Letter to Lady Hesketh, 8-9 January 1787. 'The Rose' appeared in the June 1785 issue of the *Gentleman's Magazine*.

2. Letter to John Newton, 4 June 1785.

3. Quoted from J. B. Meyers, *William Carey*, London, 1887, p.18.

4. Letter to John Newton, 27 August 1785.

5. Letter to Lady Hesketh, 12 October 1785.

6. Letter to John Newton, 3 December 1785.

7. Letter to Lady Hesketh, 23 January 1786.

8. Letter to Walter Bagot, 27 February 1786.

9. *Task*, VI, lines 871 ff.

10. James 5:16.

11. 'Exhortation to Prayer,' *Olney Hymns*, Book II, Hymn LX.

12. *The Saturday Review of Literature*, 28 November 1931, p.328.

13. See King & Ryskamp, *Letters and Prose Writings of Cowper*, vol. iv, 'Cowper's Spiritual Diary'. The section contains nothing approaching a 'spiritual diary' but a number of disjointed jottings of a harrowing nature which Johnson claimed came originally from Cowper. It is surprising that more positive 'jottings' of Cowper from this period — such as his comments on Samuel Johnson — which are extant in Cowper's own hand, have not been published by the editors.

14. See letter to William Hayley dated 6 April 1792 in which Cowper writes of his 1763 illness.

15. Note, for instance, King's *William Cowper*, p.178, in which the author points out that the earliest 'evidence' supposing that Cowper tried to commit suicide was

a newspaper article dated 1890, i. e., written over 100 years after the alleged event. See Collyer, Adelaide, 'Unpublished MSS of the poet Cowper,' *Universal Review*, 25 June 1890, pp. 279-93.

16. See Bernard Martin, 'Fresh Light on William Cowper', *Modern Language Quarterly*, p.253 ff, XIII, 1952 for a typical example.

17. Letter to John Newton, c.15 April 1785.

18. Letter to William Unwin, 20 March 1785.

19. See Mark 12:26 and Deuteronomy 33:16.

20. Letter to John Newton, 9 July 1785.

21. 'The Modern Patriot', 1780.

22. *Memorials of the Rev. William Bull*, p.221.

23. *Ibid.*, p. 244.

24. Letter to John and Mary Newton, 16 October 1785.

25. Letter to John Newton, 5 November 1785.

26. The organizers of the celebrations chose the wrong year! Handel was born in 1685.

27. Letter to John Newton, 21 June 1784.

28. *Task*, VI, lines 694-719.

29. Letter to Lady Hesketh, 7-8 December 1785.

30. See, for instance, portraits of Cowper's North American contemporary Samuel Hopkins (1721-1803), who wore an almost identical cap.

31. It was Thomas Scott's frank opinion that Newton's love of hearing and spreading gossip drove many of his parishioners in Olney to leave his church and flock to the Dissenters. Newton had the unwise habit of mentioning, whilst preaching, gossip he had picked up about certain people so that his hearers who felt themselves referred to would be trying to puzzle out who had told tales instead of receiving a blessing from the spoken word. See *Letters and Papers of the Late Rev. Thomas Scott*, ed. John Scott A.M., London, 1824, pp.315 f.

32. Cowper spelt the name in various ways but probably slipped into using the 'g' rather than the 'ck' because he nicknamed the family 'the Frogs'.

33. See 'Table Talk', lines 576-7.

34. See Robin Furneaux, *William Wilberforce*, London, 1974, p.198.

35. Even in later years, however, according to Wilberforce's diary and the testimony of his sons, Robert Haldane, the great Scots evangelist, was seen by Wilberforce as an unlikely candidate for the missionfield because of his political views, even though Haldane repeatedly emphasized that he kept politics out of his ministry. See Alexander Haldane's book, *The Lives of Robert & James Haldane*, Banner of Truth Trust, reprint of the 1853 edition, for a discussion of Wilberforce's attitude to Haldane. Not wishing to throw doubt on Wilberforce's evangelicalism, the author goes as far as to suggest that Wilberforce's diary entries concerning Haldane must have been altered by later biographers.

36. See, for instance, letter to John Newton dated 22 July 1791.

37. Letter to John Newton, 20 May 1786.

38. Letter to John Newton, 22 June 1786.

39. Five miles from Olney. Home of the Wright family with whom Cowper had very little in common. He had frequently walked there because of the beautiful scenery but now he was feeling his age somewhat, he was glad of a lift there in a carriage.

40. Letter to William Unwin, 24 September 1786.
41. Letter to John Newton, 30 September 1786.

Chapter 14 — The language of Eden
1. See Samuel Rutherford, *Lex, Rex, or the Law and the Prince; a Dispute for the Just Prerogative of King and People*, 1644, Sprinkle Publications Reprint, Harrisonburg, 1980, pp.1, 3, 233, 234.
2. See Herbert Schöffler, *Protestantismus und Literatur*, Göttingen, 1958, p.5. Schöffler's main argument is really that the Puritans were against the teachings of the ancients, but his numerous quotes from Puritan works only show how familiar they were with the writings of Greek and Latin philosophers and statesmen.
3. See letter to Martin Madan, 8 June 1789.
4. *Remains of the Rev. Richard Cecil, M.A.*, 'Remarks on Authors,' London, 1816, p.177.
5. See letter to William Unwin, 12 July 1784.
6. Letter to Lady Hesketh, 28-29 May 1786.
7. See John Sargent's great book *The Life and Letters of Henry Martyn*, Banner of Truth, 1985 (first published 1819).
8. Wesley, *Journals*, vol. 4, entry for 2 April.
9. *Ibid.*, 14 December 1768.
10. *Ibid.*, 5 September 1769.
11. Letter to John Newton, 24 June 1791.
12. See letter to Lady Hesketh, 1 February 1788.
13. Goldwin Smith, *English Men of Letters*, p.91.
14. *Task*, VI, lines 783-804. Cowper refers to the animals worshipping man as God's regent and steward on earth as he believed that the conditions which prevailed in Eden would be restored in Paradise Regained.
15. Letter to John Newton, 29 June 1783.
16. See letters to John Newton, 5 November 1785 and 16 November 1791. See also *Thoughts of the Evangelical Leaders*, especially entries for 22 January 1798, 17 September 1798, 21 June 1802, 16 June 1806, 20 April 1807 and 7 June 1813. See also entries under 'Sunday schools' in Quinlan's *Victorian Prelude*.
17. See *Thoughts of the Evangelical Leaders*, p. 525.
18. *Ibid.*, p.260.
19. *Ibid*,. p.158.
20. *Ibid.*, p. 14. Here More's *Village Politics by Will Chip* is praised. The Rev. J. Venn, writing on the work of the society as 'a medium of circulation, and for the communication of knowledge in the most ready way', says, 'Already had the powerful pen of Hannah More been most successfully employed in this important service, and her incomparable little tract "Village Politics by Will Chip", had, with astonishing rapidity, reached every corner of the kingdom: many hundred thousand were circulated in London alone: many thousands were sent by Government to Scotland and Ireland; and men of the soundest judgment went so far as to affirm, that it had most essentially contributed, under Providence, to prevent a revolution.'
21. Thomas Bowdler, *Family Shakespeare*, quoted from Herbert Schöffler's *Protestantismus und Literatur*, p.175.
22. See Southey's 'Preface', vol. I of his *Cowper's Works*.
23. Wesley abridged and adapted Henry Brookes' novel, *The Fool of Quality*. See

T. B. Shepherd's *Methodism and the Literature of the Eighteenth Century*, 1966, for details of the Wesleys' enormous contri-bution to the spreading of better quality literature.

24. See *The Wesleys and the English Language*, Four Essays by G. H. Vallins, Epworth Press, 1957, *John Wesley's Dictionary*, p.26 (Wesley's 'To the Reader').

25. *Ibid.*, p.30.

26. *Ibid.*, p.32.

27. See, for instance, Lord David Cecil's caricature of the Evangelicals' culture in *The Stricken Deer*, ch. III, 'The Evangelical Phase'. Cecil's historical fantasies are not atypical. Quinlan in his *Victorian Prelude* gives a more balanced account of the Evangelicals' attitude to literature and secular learning. See also Lecky, Overton and Balleine on the subject.

28. Letter to Lady Hesketh, 22 May 1786.

29. Sir Richard Sutton (1733-1802) became Under-Secretary of State and later Lord of the Treasury. William Alston (1728-1799) became a lawyer. Cowper also read through Pope's translation with Alston during their Temple days.

30. See Cheever, *Lectures on Life, Genius and Insanity of Cowper*, pp. 218-19 and Goldwin Smith, *William Cowper*, p.41. Goldwin Smith seems to believe that Cowper was merely a hypochondriac (see p.126).

31. See Norman, *Westminster Review*, p.644. Norman also refers to Cheever's 'illogical' statements concerning Cowper, p. 643.

32. Letter to Lady Hesketh, 15-17 December 1785.

33. See letter to John Newton, 3 December 1785.

34. See letter to Mrs King, 14 June 1790.

35. Letter to Lady Hesketh, 15-17 December 1785.

36. Cowper's emphasis.

37. Letter to John Newton, 13 January 1787.

38. Quotes taken from Johnson's 'Preface' in Southey's edition of *Cowper's Works*, vol. XI, p.xxvi ff.

39. Letter to John Newton, 13 January 1787.

40. See letter to Walter Bagot, 19 March 1788. The Latin quote is a variant of 'It's all Greek to me,' and means, 'It is Greek and thus cannot be read.'

41. See letter to Lady Hesketh, 10 January 1786.

42. Letter to Lady Hesketh, 15-17 December 1785.

43. Letter to Walter Bagot, 5 January 1788.

44. See letter to John Newton, 18 February 1786: 'I have not entered on this work, unconnected as it must needs appear with the interests of the cause of God, without the direction of his providence, nor altogether unassisted by him in the performance of it.'

45. Letter to Samuel Rose, 13 December 1787.

46. Letter to Lady Hesketh, 17 November 1785.

47. See Lodwick Hartley, *William Cowper: The Continuing Revelation*, Chapel Hill, 1960, p.54.

48. See letter to Mrs King, 5 October 1790.

49. See Southey, *Cowper's Works*, vol. XI, p.vii ff.

50. See, for instance, letter to Walter Bagot, 30 October 1788 and letter to John Newton, 24 June 1791.

51. See letter to Walter Bagot, 5 January 1788: 'My first 13 Books have been

Criticised in London; have been by me accommodated to those Criticisms, returned to London in their improved state, and sent back to Weston with an Imprimantur. This would satisfy some poets, less anxious than myself about what they expose in public; but it has not satisfied me. I am now revising them again by the light of my own critical taper, and make more alterations than at first.'

52. Letter to Joseph Hill, 25 October 1788.

53. See Cowper's interesting and amusing account of how he came to write these poems in his letter to Lady Hesketh, 27 November 1787.

54. Letter to Walter Bagot, 30 October 1788.

55. Letter to Walter Bagot, 26 February 1791.

56. Letter to Mrs King, 2 March 1791.

57. See 'On the Receipt of my Mother's Picture'.

58. The Rev. Hugh Blair (1718-1800) was author of the famous two-volumed *Lectures on Rhetoric and Belles Lettres* and Regius Professor of Rhetotic in the University of Edinburgh.

59. Dr James Beattie (1735-1803) published numerous books on moral philosophy, language and poetry. He was a poet of note and translator himself.

60. See, for instance, Cowper's letter to Hayley, 27 June 1792. Modern literary evolutionists do not accept this reasoning, saying that science fiction is a new literary genre unknown to the ancients. Cultic sects such as the New Agers often claim that science fiction is a post-Christian evolution and channel of revelation. This is quite false. The *Vera Historia* of Lucian of Samosata (A. D. 150) portrays an interplanetary James Bond figure who visits the moon and the sun and gets involved in inter-galactic warfare. There are many passages in the Bible, including Ezekiel chapter 1, which, speaking in purely literary terms, use this genre.

61. See the final section of 'Conversation', 'Yardley Oak', lines 167-78, *Task,* VI, lines 348-63, 'Table Talk', lines 584-93 and Cowper's comments on Blair and Beattie in King and Ryskamp.

Chapter 15 — Life at Weston

1. Sent to Willam Unwin, 8 June 1780.

2. Letter to John Newton, 16 December 1786.

3. Nicholson, *William Cowper,* p.152.

4. See letter to Mrs King, 11 October 1788.

5. See King & Ryskamp, *Letters and Prose Writings of Cowper,* vol. iii, p.158 and footnote.

6. Letter to Lady Hesketh, 18 January 1788.

7. Letter to Lady Hesketh, 16 February 1788.

8. Letter to John Newton, 2 October 1787.

9. Letter to Mrs. King, 12 March 1790.

10. The result of a stroke.

11. Quoted from Cecil, *The Stricken Deer,* p.235 f. I have been unable to trace this letter.

12. See Hayley's short biography of Rose in vol. iii, pp.424-43 of his 1812 edition of Cowper's biography.

13. Letter to John Johnson, 18 December 1790.

14. Letter to John Johnson, 8 July 1790.

15. Letter to John Johnson, 7 June 1790.

16. Letter to John Johnson, 20 May 1792.
17. Letter to John Johnson, 5 November 1792.
18. T. Clarkson, *The History of the Abolition of the Slave Trade*, pp.108-9, 188-91.
19. Letter to John Newton, 19 February 1788.
20. Née Jane Thornton (1757-1818), daughter of the wealthy merchant who was Newton's patron.
21. See, for instance, Newey, *Cowper's Poetry*, p.237.
22. Letter to Samuel Rose, 29 March 1788.
23. Ryle, *Christian Leaders of the 18th Century*, p.22.
24. Letter to John Newton, 19 April 1788.
25. Letter to John Newton, 5 June 1788.
26. See letter to Walter Bagot, 17 June 1788 for the expression 'fiddle of Verse'.
27. Letter to Willam Bull, 27 July 1791. Cowper wrote to Newton on 22 July giving him a flea in the ear, saying, 'What a horrid zeal for the church, and what a horrid Loyalty to Government have manifested themselves there! How little do they dream that they could not have dishonour'd their Idol the Establishment more, and that the Great Bishop of souls himself with abhorrence rejects their service!' A further break in correspondence between the two men ensued after this letter.
28. Cowper is referring to Isaiah's call to God's people 'unto the end of the world' in Isaiah 62 and also to Isaiah 66:8, which speaks of Zion giving sudden birth to her children.
29. It could be that Cowper was merely following the poetic tradition of Virgil when he referred to swallows hibernating as, after writing the above review, he wrote to Joseph Hill again about swallows which had slept all winter, in an obviously Virgilic context. See letter to Joseph Hill, 6 March 1791.
30. Letter to William Unwin, 12 July 1784.
31. Letter to John Newton probably written in early 1784. See King & Ryskamp, *Letters and Prose Writings of Cowper*, vol. ii, p.209 f.
32. This was probably a review of the works of Caraccioli, the French mystic writer, who, according to Cowper, was not prepared to admit that 'Man is known to be nothing and Jesus all in all.' See letter to John Newton dated 8 March 1784 and the unfinished review in King & Ryskamp, *Letters and Prose Writings of Cowper*, vol. v, p.179 ff.

Chapter 16 — The two Williams
1. Letter to Lady Hesketh, 11 May 1790.
2. Letter to John Newton, 5 December 1790. The letter is only partly preserved.
3. Letter to John Newton, 24 June 1791.
4. See letter to Newton dated 22 July 1791 and Venn's letter to Mrs Riland dated 7 March 1769, in *The Life and A Selection from the Letters of the Late Rev. Henry Venn*, ed. Rev. Henry Venn (Jr), London, 1835.
5. Letter to Samuel Rose, 21 December 1791.
6. Letter to John Johnson, 11 March 1792.
7. Taken from King & Ryskamp, *Letters and Prose Writings of Cowper*, vol. iv, p.xxxi.
8. Letter to Lady Throckmorton, 16 April 1792.
9. Letter to Frederick Smith, 20 March 1792.
10. Letter to Joseph Rye, 16 April 1792.
11. Letter to Samuel Teedon, 1 January 1793.

12. This is a very enigmatic statement. It seems to indicate that Newton preached in an almost empty church but might merely mean that Teedon was the only member of his family who went to church on that Sunday.

13. Blake's *Hayley*, p.144.

14. Letter to William Hayley, 17 March 1792.

15. Quotes from Hayley's letters are taken from Morchard Bishop's, *The Life, Works and Friendships of William Hayley*, London, Gollanz, 1951.

16. Letter to Willam Hayley, 6 April 1792.

17. Piles.

18. Letter to Lady Hesketh, 24 May 1792.

19. Letter to Lady Hesketh, 26 May 1792.

20. See *Letters of Lady Hesketh to the Rev. John Johnson, LLD*, p.20.

21. *Ibid.*, p.22.

22. Cowper's comments can be found in King & Ryskamp, *Letters and Prose Writings of Cowper*, vol. v, p.143 ff.

Chapter 17 — The path of sorrow

1. 'Epistle to a Lady in France: A Person of Piety and Much Afflicted', lines 9-12.

2. Of course, Cowper's remarks on friendship in 'Retirement' were published in his first volume of poems.

3. See Cowper's Latin poems *'Tales er nostri viguissent, Jesus, Amores'* and *'Heu quam remotus vescor ab omnibus'*. The poems use highly symbolic language. Cowper could be expressing regret at being cut off from Theadora (as Ryskamp & King take it); they could equally well refer to the poet's feeling of being cut off from Christ.

4. See Lady Hesketh's letter to Johnny Johnson dated 27 September 1793.

5. 'The Four Ages', lines 35-8.

6. *Ibid.*, lines 22-3.

7. See *Iliad* 6, line 176.

8. See Fausset's *William Cowper*, p. 273.

9. 'Yardley Oak,' lines 167-78.

10. *Ibid.*, lines 180-84.

11. *Task*, VI, line 124.

12. Isaiah 24:20.

13. Letter to Thomas Hayley, 14 March 1793.

14. *Task*, IV, lines 329-32.

15. Letter to Samuel Greatheed, 3 February 1793.

16. Letter to William Hayley, 1 April 1793.

17. Compare with *Task*, VI, lines 83ff.

18. Hayley's *Cowper*, vol. i, p.205.

19. See Johnson's letter to his sister Cathy, dated 10 July 1795.

20. See King & Ryskamp, *Letters and Prose Writings of Cowper*, vol. iv, p.467ff.

21. See Bishop, *Life, Works and Friendships of William Hayley*, p.275.

22. 'Retirement', lines 681-2. Cowper takes up this theme more than thirty times in his poetry.

23. See, for instance, *Task*, IV, the story of the 'universal soldier', lines 613-58.

24. See, for instance, Edward Dowden, 'Cowper and William Hayley (From Unpublished Sources)' *Atlantic Monthly*, 100, 1907.

25. Letter to Lady Hesketh, 26 September 1795.

26. Johnson's emphasis. See Johnson's account entitled *Cowper's Last Years*. Diary extracts 28 July 1795 to 3 February 1800, *Times Literary Supplement*, 5 October 1951, p.12.

27. See Thomas Wright's *Life of Augustus Toplady*, p.212ff., for an account of these friends' views concerning animals and heaven.

28. Letter to William Hayley, 19 June 1797.

29. Bernard Martin, *An Ancient Mariner*, 'Conclusion,' p.236 ff.

Postscript

1. Seward claimed that Cowper 'demonised the deity'.

2. His actual epitaph read, 'The Friend & Biographer of Cowper'.

3. When Lady Hesketh received a copy of Greatheed's MS, she told Hayley that Greatheed had 'Insulted the Ashes of that friend of whom he is *unworthy* to *speak*, and planted *Daggers* in the hearts of ev'ry Individual of his afflicted family... No Honest man, who was *Himself in his Senses* cou'd have acted as Mr. G. has done!' Letter of Lady Hesketh to Hayley, 3 October 1800 (Quoted from copies in the Olney Museum).

4. Quoted from Bishop, *Life, Works and Friendships of William Hayley*, p.268.

5. For the full inscription see Hayley's *Cowper*, vol. iv, p.174.

6. Lodwick Hartley, *William Cowper*, Durham N.C., 1960, p.8.

7. See Norma Russel, *A Bibliography of William Cowper to 1837*, for a detailed survey of earlier publications.

8. Balleine, *History of the Evangelical Party in the Church of England*, p.75.

9. Quoted from the one-volume edition of Abbey and Overton, *The English Church in the Eighteenth Century*, London, 1887, p.383.

10. See letter to Samuel Rose, 23 July 1789.

11. See Mary Whiting's article 'A Burning Bush' in the *Hibbert Journal*, for a detailed review of Newton's sermon with many quotes.

12. Isaiah 11:9

Biographical sketches

1. Letter to William Unwin, 8 June 1783.

2. Letter to Lady Hesketh, 23-24 December 1785.

3. Scott, *Letters and Papers*, p. 315ff.

4. *Ibid.*

5. Horace, *Odes*, I. xiii, 4: 'My liver becomes tumultuous with bile that seethes.'

Index

Abbreviations: C = William Cowper. Other abbreviations refer to the subject of the entry in which they occur.

Dates given only for persons influential in the life of Cowper or in the more important events of his day.